Endre Sík
THE HISTORY OF BLACK AFRICA
VOLUME IV

ENDRE SÍK

THE HISTORY
OF BLACK AFRICA

VOLUME IV

AKADÉMIAI KIADÓ · BUDAPEST 1974

Translated by
SÁNDOR SIMON

CONTENTS

after the Kabaka's return. — The 1955 reforms. — Elections in 1958. — The report of the Wild committee. — New parties. — Consultations about the constitution in April–May 1960. — The position of the British government. — The Lukiko's decision of September 1960 and the memorandum of October 5. — A provocative statement by Governor Crawford. — The Lukiko's declaration of independence and its decision on secession. — Miners' strike in February 1961. — Elections in March 1961. — The Munster report. — The London conference in September–October 1961. — The elections in April and change of government in May 1962. — The London conference in June 1962. — Independent Uganda. — Bibliography.

and after the uprising. Inter-party agreement. Birth of the independent Republic of the Sudan. — Bibliography.

LIST OF PLATES

CHAPTER XV

BRITISH EAST AFRICA

The policy of British imperialism in the East African colonial possessions was essentially the same as everywhere in the British colonies. The aim was twofold: to spare no effort to keep the territories in colonial subjection and to put down the African struggle for independence, but the tactics varied in the four different territories. The cause of this lay in the difference of the problems due to the specific geographical and historical backgrounds.

Characteristic of Kenya were the relatively large number of European settlers, the alienation of great expanses of land from Africans, the confinement of most African tribes to reserves, and the struggles fought over many decades by the larger tribes (mainly the Kikuyu) against the colonialists. In Uganda the British imperialists amalgamated tribal monarchies under a single colonial regime, and promoted in them the transition from tribal communities to feudal societies. In Tanganyika the policy of the British imperialists was largely determined by the relatively small number of European settlers and the fact that after World War I this territory, as a former German colony, had become a British mandated territory, to be transformed into a trust territory under British administration after World War II. In Zanzibar the British colonialists had to allow for the particular sections of the population (Africans, Arabs and Indians) and the existence of an Arab sultanate as well as the strategic importance of the colony.

In Kenya the British colonialists favoured the settlers, supported their aspirations for total control of the territorial government, and applied repressive measures and police terror to keep the Africans from taking any counteraction.

In Uganda the object of the British imperialists was to cut down the last bits of autonomy of the four African feudal states (Buganda, Bunyoro, Toro and Ankole) united under the colonial regime, to strengthen and centralize the colonial administration.

In Tanganyika they propagated the so-called "partnership" principle to secure their positions. This principle meant participation in government by the Africans constituting more than 98 per cent of the population on an equal basis with the Europeans making up 1/4 per cent and the Asians (Indians and Arabs) amounting to hardly 1 per cent.

With regard to Zanzibar the British planned to annul self-government under the guise of an "African state" and to divest the Sultan of all his powers for good.

The means of achieving these aims included provocations and terror in Kenya (the Mau Mau affair, KENYATTA's imprisonment, etc.), the use of force in Uganda (the depoirtation of the Kabaka), the propagation of the partnership principle in Tanganyka.

However, the British failed in these schemes everywhere. In spite — and partly as a result — of their policy, the independence aspirations soared and the freedom movements gained ground. In Kenya neither provocations nor terror could bring the desired result. In Uganda the deportation of the Kabaka still promoted African unity and strengthened the independence movement. In Tanganyika the partnership idea proved a failure. The Africans everywhere demanded independence, and nothing could force them to give up this demand. The British imperialists, under pressure from liberal opinion at home and world public opinion, were compelled to withdraw step by step and renew the time-tested methods in all four territories: pitting the African tribes against one another, adopting sham administrative reforms, and planting their own men in African organizations.

The Plans of Federation

Already in the inter-war years the policy of the British colonialists was aiming to unite the East African territories in federation (see Vol. II, p. 199). During the war they took a number of practical measures to co-ordinate the economies of those territories with a view to the better utilization of their natural resources for the purpose of the conduct of war.[1] Immediately after the war, in the autumn of 1945, the Colonial Secretary of the Labour government, CREECH JONES, issued a White Paper ("Colonial Paper No. 191") in which he announced the formation of an "East Africa High Commission" composed of the three Governors to handle the common affairs of the three East African colonies (Kenya, Uganda, Tanganyika), assisted by a Central Legislative Assembly with an executive organization consisting of five colonial officials. Participating in the Legislative Assembly, in addition to official members, would be representatives of the three racial groups (Europeans, Africans, Indians) in equal numbers. The White Paper specified the powers of the Central Legislative Assembly, stipulating that only the official members should have the right to initiate legislation, and the decisions should come into force only with the assent of the High Commission, after which the territorial legislatures could not alter them.

After his tour of East Africa in 1946 CREECH JONES, being pressed by the Kenya settlers, issued another White Paper ("Colonial Paper No. 210") in 1947, changing the initial provisions.

1. The document provided that the Central Legislative Assembly should be composed of 23 members: 7 officials of the High Commission as ex-officio members, 1 appointed Arab member and 5 members from each of the three territories; one of these was to be an official appointed by the Governor, three would be unofficials representing the three racial groups, and one member to be elected by his territorial legislature. This meant in practice that 16 of the 23 members were Europeans.

2. The purview of the High Commission might be extended only with the approval of all three territorial legislatures.

3. The work of the High Commission should be reviewed and discussed every four years, and its maintenance would require separate legislative approval from all three territories.

[1] See vol. III, p. 80.

4. The measures adopted by the central executive organization could be carried out only with the consent of all three Governors.

The settlers accepted the revised proposals, but the Africans and Indians in all three territories rejected them on the ground that, owing to European over-representation in the territorial legislatures, both the High Commission and the Central Legislative Assembly would be controlled by Europeans. This notwithstanding, CREECH JONES announced on July 28, 1947, that the proposals would be implemented. He repudiated the objections of Africans and Indians and argued hypocritically that the proposals ensured equality of racial representation. On January 1, 1948, the High Commission was established by the "East Africa (High Commission) Order in Council".

Although it was stressed in the White Paper that the proposals did not mean to be aimed at the political association of the territories, Africans and Indians viewed the setting up of the High Commission with dislike for the same reason as they opposed the plan of federation. As the Central Legislative Assembly and the executive organization of the High Commission functioned in Nairobi, there was no doubt but that both would come under the influence of the racist Kenya settlers and their government, and that consequently Uganda and Tanganyika would also be brought under their control.

Events of the next few years demonstrated that the British government was not satisfied with setting up the High Commission, but that it regarded this as a step toward the realization of its federation plans.

The Africans, recognizing the economic advantages of having the High Commission, soon reconciled themselves to its existence. When in 1951 the three territorial legislatures first had to decide upon the maintenance of the High Commission, none were against it. But on November 14, 1951, Governor Sir PHILIP MITCHELL of Kenya sent the British Colonial Secretary a lengthy memorandum describing the economic and social problems of the East African territories, and proposed that a special commission be appointed to study those problems and formulate recommendations for their solution.

Accordingly the British government in January 1953 appointed an East Africa Royal Commission (composed of seven economic and financial experts) to inquire into the problems.

Neither the MITCHELL memorandum nor the government instructions to the commission said a word of any political problem, namely the problem of federation. But the economic problems which it was the task of the commission to examine (land question, agricultural and industrial development, labour, living standard, etc.) were so much rooted in the colonial policies pursued in those territories that the proposals to be made for their solution, no matter what the authors wanted or what they knew, had to imply a political stand.

And as regards the British government, although it had set no political tasks, it certainly expected the commission, its economic conclusions and recommendations, to provide new arguments in favour of its scheme of federation. Nothing proved this better than Colonial Secretary LYTTELTON's ominous statement on June 30, 1953, concerning the chances of federation. His remarks provoked so violent indignation in Uganda that he was compelled to withdraw his words, and the British government issued another statement to calm public opinion.

It was partly due to the Uganda events that the British government did not make public the federation scheme until two years later, until after the presentation of the commission's report.

The Africans had already shed their aversion to the High Commission and were co-operating with it, but they continued opposing the federation plans, while waiting for the report of the East Africa Royal Commission.

The report of the East Africa Royal Commission 1953–1955 was made public in June 1955.[1]

The commission did a thorough job. After a careful study of the problems it made frankly objective proposals for what should be done (from the capitalist point of view) to ensure the economic development of the three territories. This objectivity meant disregard for the interests of Africans, their traditional conditions and thinking, just as for the colonial policies of the imperialists. A good number of recommendations were unacceptable to the Africans (complete disregard for traditional tribal customs and relationships, suppression of tribal landed property, proletarization of the peasantry, etc.), and several proposals (liquidation of the reserves, elimination of racial restrictions in the economic sphere, etc.), as well as the failure to mention the necessity of political federation, went against the adopted policies of the British government.

So not only the Africans gave the commission's report a hostile reception, but the local colonial authorities (the Governors and the High Commission) as well as the British government made severely critical comments[2] on a number of proposals put forward in the report.

Since the report was not suitable for promoting the issue of federation, the British government put aside the scheme for the time being, and contented itself with making the best of the existing machinery, the High Commission and its organs accepted also by Africans, to establish a closer association of the three territories.

While the British colonialists were pressing for the federation plan so hateful in the eyes of the Africans, leaders of the African independence movements under the influence of the idea of Pan-Africanism were striving to unite the East African territories to their own liking.

It became obvious that federation could not hold up the independence movement, because the Africans, regardless of tribal and party affiliations, were resolutely against the imperialist plan of federation, since they saw in it the extension of the racist regime of the Kenya settlers to the other three territories. On the other hand, the settlers, except those of Kenya, were also mostly opposed to federation because it would have meant domination by Kenya. Though all Kenya settlers wanted federation, yet they had their own conception of it which was not in keeping with the British official line.

The idea of a federation of the East African countries was not foreign to the Africans fighting for independence either. What they emphatically rejected was only a kind of federation planned by the imperialists to consolidate their own colonial rule.

Pan-African Freedom Movement for East and Central Africa

The proposal was first made in 1957 for the African members of the Legislative Councils of Kenya, Uganda and Tanganyika to meet to discuss their common prob-

---

[1] Cmd. 9475. London, 1955.

[2] Great Britain Colonial Office: Despatches from the Governors of Kenya, Uganda and Tanganyika and from the Administrator, East Africa High Commission, Commenting on the East Africa Royal Commission 1953–1955 Report. Cmd. 9801. London, 1956.

lems. The meeting did not come off, but hardly had a year gone by when the idea was materialized in a different form.

In March 1958 African political leaders of Kenya, Uganda and Tanganyika attended as observers the First Conference of Independent African States in Accra, where it was decided to summon a conference of all African peoples. There the political leaders of East Africa decided to establish the Pan-African Freedom Movement for East and Central Africa (P.A.F.M.E.C.A.) as a regional group of the conference of all African peoples.

In September 1958 leading African politicians of Kenya, Uganda, Tanganyika, Zanzibar and Nyasaland, headed by JULIUS NYERERE and TOM MBOYA, met in Mwanza (Tanganyika) and appointed a committee to co-ordinate the struggle against colonialism in the countries of East and Central Africa. The purposes of the organization were summarized as follows:

"To foster the spirit of Pan-Africanism in order to rid all the East and Central African territories of imperialism, white supremacy, economic exploitation, and social degradation by stepping up nationalist activities to achieve self-government and establish parliamentary democracy.

"To co-ordinate nationalist programmes, tactics, projects, and efforts for the speedy liberation of the said territories.

"To assist in the establishment and organization of united nationalist movements of African territories through political education, periodic conferences, and the encouragement of inter-territorial African contacts in all fields.

"To establish a joint East and Central African Freedom Fund.

"To pursue non-violence in African nationalist struggles for freedom and prosperity."

The conference took a stand against racialism on the part of Europeans and Africans alike.

The setting up of a federation of East African countries was not discussed at the conference.

The next conference of P.A.F.M.E.C.A. was scheduled to meet at Kampala in August 1959, but since the Uganda administration did not grant permission, it was held at Moshi in Tanganyika in September 1959. The conference concentrated all attention on the problems of the freedom movements of the countries of East and Central Africa: it condemned the state of emergency declared in Nyasaland and Uganda, called upon the African group of the Kenya Legislative Council to form a united front, etc. The question of Central African Federation was still not under discussion.

A few months after the Moshi conference, however, a leading personality of P.A.F.M.E.C.A., JULIUS NYERERE, at the Addis Ababa Conference of Independent African States (July 1960), spoke in favour of uniting the four territories in a Central African Federation, and declared that as soon as Kenya, Uganda and Zanzibar would, like Tanganyika, win self-government, federation would be immediately realizable, and that, for this purpose, Tanganyika would be willing even to postpone her accession to independence. He said: "We must confront the Colonial Office with a demand not for the freedom of Tanganyika, and then for Kenya, and then for Uganda, and then for Zanzibar, but with a demand for the freedom of East Africa as one political unit."

NYERERE succeeded in having his viewpoint accepted by his party, the Tanganyika African National Union (T.A.N.U.). The Kenyan leaders MBOYA and GICHURU, with whom he discussed the question, gave their enthusiastic support, and their party, the Kenya African National Union (K.A.N.U.), also gave its approval to the idea of federation.

But the Ugandan leaders, regardless of party affiliations, held the view that federation would be a topical issue only after the interested countries had won independence. The leader of the Uganda National Congress (U.N.C.), MILTON OBOTE, said: "It is futile to try to think outside Uganda before solving internal problems. In the long run the idea is attractive."

In the meantime African aversion to the East Africa High Commission had entirely disappeared. For example, K.A.N.U. President GICHURU told the *East African Standard* in July 1960: "The East Africa High Commission might well form the nucleus of a federation and it would be unwise to break it down and lose the services of its experts."

K.A.N.U. and T.A.N.U. leaders consistently advocated the idea of federation. At a mass meeting in Dar es Salaam in July, for example, NYERERE stated that if the individual East African territories should be left alone, they would inevitably become puppets of more highly developed countries which would then dictate to them.

P.A.F.M.E.C.A. in 1960 managed to hold a meeting at Mbale in Uganda. President MBOYA told in his opening address that the situation was ripe for them to agree on the establishment of a Central African Federation and to work out its plan. The conference passed a resolution on this subject. It pledged support to the LUMUMBA government of the Congo, but spoke in reproving terms about the Lukiko decision on Buganda's secession from Uganda.

In January 1961 the K.A.N.U. leaders in agreement with NYERERE called a new P.A.F.M.E.C.A. conference in Nairobi to discuss the question of federation. The Kenya African Democratic Union (K.A.D.U.) did not take part because it disagreed with P.A.F.M.E.C.A. which insisted that Africans in every country must work for unity in their struggle for freedom and that tribal considerations must be excluded from politics.

The conference stated that the political and economic federation of the East African territories was an essential prerequisite of the unity of their peoples and their social progress, but it should be created by governments elected and controlled by the people. Therefore the forthcoming elections in Kenya, Uganda and Zanzibar should be followed by the formation of African-controlled governments under African prime ministers, and these governments should hold a summit meeting to discuss all necessary steps. At the conference NYERERE expounded that federation should be realized when all four territories had internal self-government. He repeated what he had said at Addis Ababa in July 1960, namely that he was ready to postpone the independence of his country by a few months if this step could promote the simultaneous independence of the four territories.

But the circumstances turned out differently. Elections did not lead to the formation of a responsible government in any one of the three countries. (In Kenya the government was formed by K.A.D.U., in Uganda by the Democratic Party which obtained the majority, and in Zanzibar a coalition of three parties came to power.) With such governments, of course, the summit meetings proposed by NYERERE could not take place, let alone that these governments were very much preoccupied with internal political problems of their countries.

Considering that the East Africa High Commission and the Central Legislative Assembly set up in 1948 did not suit any longer the changes that had occurred in the three territories during the past decade, the British government in 1960 appointed a commission under JEREMY RAISMAN to recommend reforms in the composition and powers of those bodies and measures to strengthen and promote economic co-ordination in the three territories.

The commission worked out its proposals, with which the territorial governments agreed. The British government in July called a conference in London of the official and political leaders of Kenya, Uganda and Tanganyika to discuss the steps to be taken on the basis of the commission's report, with special regard to the forthcoming independence of Tanganyika.

The participants reached an agreement as was stated in the official communiqué: "Delegates agreed that it would be in the interests of all the territories to ensure that whatever constitutional changes might take place in the future in East Africa, common services at present provided by the East Africa High Commission should continue to be provided on an East African basis. They further agreed that the arrangements made must be fully compatible with the sovereignty of Tanganyika when Tanganyika became independent."

They agreed also that the East Africa High Commission of the three Governors would be replaced by an East African Common Services Organization constituted by an elected leading minister from each of the three territories. Furthermore, they set up four triumvirates of ministers from each territory, one for the affairs of communications, one for finance, one for commerce and industry, and one for social and research services. The Central Legislative Assembly was reorganized so as to include ex officio the members of the East African Common Services Organization and the four triumvirates as well as nine representatives from each of the three territories (not necessarily members of the legislatures). The new Central Legislative Assembly would have the same powers as the former one, except for defence and internal security.

Under the agreement the Governors of Kenya and Uganda reserved the right to withhold assent from any decision or measure taken by the triumvirates or the new Assembly, in case they found it to be in conflict with treaty obligations of the United Kingdom.

Finally it was agreed that the services of the Organization could be provided to Zanzibar on the basis of agreement with the governments of the three countries.

The London agreements, made public in a White Paper, were considered and approved by all three territorial legislatures. The entry into force of these agreements put an end to the uncertainty until then prevailing in leading political circles (especially in Kenya) with regard to inter-territorial economic co-ordination. In the Kenya Legislative Council, for example, concern at some practical issues left unsolved was expressed not only by the white Minister for Finance (MACKENZIE) and some members of K.A.D.U., but even JULIUS KIANO from K.A.N.U. who took part in the work of the High Commission as Minister of Commerce expressed concern over economic difficulties. But K.A.N.U. as a whole and the majority of K.A.D.U. members invariably insisted on the necessity of federation. For example, ROBERT MATANO, a K.A.D.U. member, said at the meeting of the Legislative Council: "We all agree we need federation. There is no argument there."

The second half of 1961 brought a turn in the history of P.A.F.M.E.C.A. The organization was initially formed as a union of freedom fighters of the countries of East and Central Africa to intensify the independence struggle against imperialism. The papers of the first conference at Mwanza in 1958 still made no mention of federation. In the meanwhile, however, when the accession to independence of a number of African countries had brought closer the prospect of independence for the East African countries, too, political leaders in East Africa made use of their existing joint organization also to promote their efforts aimed at building an East African Federation. And now that the London agreements did not deal with the question of federation — which meant that the question might not be taken up officially until independence — P.A.F.M.E.C.A. found this task all the more important.

By the end of 1961 the composition of P.A.F.M.E.C.A. had changed essentially: it was gradually joined by independence movements of countries outside East and Central Africa. This broadening of the basis of the organization manifested itself especially at the independence celebrations of Tanganyika in December 1961. NYERERE's invitation to the festivities was accepted, in addition to representatives of the freedom fighters of East and Central African countries, also by delegates from freedom fighters of South Africa, the British Protectorates in southern Africa and the Portuguese colonies, as well as representatives from two independent states, Ethiopia and Somalia. They all applied for admission to P.A.F.M.E.C.A., which thus was changed to an organization supported also by three independent states (Tanganyika, Ethiopia, Somalia). The main objective of this organization was to give every necessary assistance to all African independence movements, and it was at the same time a third regional organization of African unity in addition to the Casablanca and Monrovia groups.

The next conference of P.A.F.M.E.C.A., held at Addis Ababa in February 1962, was attended by delegates not only from East and Central Africa but also from southern African countries under racist oppression (the Republic of South Africa, South West Africa, the British Protectorates, Angola and Mozambique). Accordingly the organization then changed its name to P.A.F.M.E.C.S.A. (Pan-African Freedom Movement for East, Central and South Africa). KENNETH KAUNDA of Northern Rhodesia was elected president to replace TOM MBOYA.

These events led to changes in the activities of the organization as well. The original purpose of the organization was to secure independence by non-violent means. But now that P.A.F.M.E.C.S.A. included in its programme the provision of assistance to independence struggles in countries such as South Africa, Southern Rhodesia and the Portuguese colonies, where as a result of the police terror of the racist regimes the freedom movement of the oppressed people could not avoid violence and the use of armed force, the organization could no longer abide by the principle of non-violence. The situation was made still more difficult by the fact that sovereign states also co-operated with the organization. Therefore its resolutions and appeals could express views only with regard to concrete issues beside the admissibility of violence. At the Addis Ababa conference of February 1962, for example, P.A.F.M.E.C.S.A. in its resolution on the question of Central Africa appealed to the affiliated organizations and governments "to support by all means at their disposal any action which our brothers in Central Africa should undertake to effect the dissolution of the Central African Federation". Similar resolutions were also adopted on assistance to the armed struggle for independence waged in South Africa and other colonial territories.

The objective of the organization regarding federation also changed. Until then the aim had been to unite only the four former British East African colonies after independence, now the aim was to establish a broader federation with the participation of Ethiopia and Somalia, to be joined later by the countries of Central and Southern Africa. The conference appealed to Ethiopia and Somalia to contact the East African Common Services Organization with the view of their joining it and the already existing East African common market. (This was done, and both states sent their observers to the meetings of the Central Legislative Assembly in 1962.)

The organization in 1962 concentrated its attention mainly on the burning problems of Northern Rhodesia, and in this connection it held in May a restricted meeting at Mbeya, in the south of Tanganyika.

The first meeting of the Central Legislative Assembly took place in Nairobi at about the same time. KENYATTA, who presided over the meeting, voiced the necessity of establishing closer political links. He said notably: "There already exists in East Africa a common market, and all of us have experienced the value of this economic link between Tanganyika, Uganda and Kenya. We shall have to consider in due course whether this economic liaison should not be strengthened by a closer political association in East Africa and, if so, when. The Common Services Organization certainly provides a basic framework on which the structure of closer political association could be built."

Another K.A.N.U. member (MWAI KIBAKI) explained in detail the further practical steps that might be taken to strengthen economic co-operation.

With the establishment of the Organization of African Unity in 1961, P.A.F.M. E.C.S.A., just like the regional groups of independent states, lost its reason for existence. Its tasks, including the establishment of closer economic and political links between independent African states, as well as support to the struggle of peoples fighting for freedom and independence, were taken over by the Organization of African Unity comprising independent states and liberation movements alike. In accordance with an agreement between the O.A.U. and NYERERE and KAUNDA, P.A.F.M.E.C.S.A. decided its dissolution on September 24, 1963, and the handling of assistance to independence movements was taken over by the O.A.U.'s Liberation Bureau in Dar es Salaam (the so-called Committee of Nine, composed of representatives of Algeria, the United Arab Republic, Ethiopia, Guinea, Congo-Kinshasa, Nigeria, Senegal, Tanganyika and Uganda).

After 1956, under the influence of the revolutionary changes in some African countries (Sudan, Ghana, etc.), the independence movements underwent rapid development in the East African territories, too. The drastic or hypocritical methods used by the colonialists raised obstacles to this development but could not prevent it. The growing pressure of world opinion, and especially the accession to independence of a number of former colonies in Africa and their appearance in the United Nations during 1960 and 1961, compelled British imperialism to retreat. It had to acquiesce first in the independence of the trust territory of Tanganyika, but tried hard to drag out the liberation of the other three colonies.

Uganda had to wait more than a year (until October 1962) while Kenya and Zanzibar waited more than two and a half years (until December 1963) to win independence.

BIBLIOGRAPHY

C. T. BRADY, *Commerce and Conflict in East Africa*, Salem, Mass., 1950.
J. K. MATHESON and W. E. BOVILL (ed.), *East African Agriculture*, London, 1950.
Lord HAILEY, *Native Administration in the British African Territories*, London, 1950.
ROLAND OLIVIER, *The Missionary Factor in East Africa*, London, 1952.
J. KIANO, *East Africa: The Tug of War Continues, Africa Is Here*, New York, 1952.
East African Future. Fabian Colonial Bureau, Controversy Series No. 9. London, 1952.
Opportunity in Kenya. Fabian Colonial Bureau, Research Series No. 162. London, 1953.
Ю. ПОТЕХИН, Британская Восточная Африка под гнетом английского империализма
    [British East Africa under the Yoke of English Imperialism]. From a collection of articles published by the Soviet Union Academy of Sciences. Moscow, 1953.

LYNDON P. HARRIES, *Islam in East Africa*, London, 1954.

Africa Bureau: Future of East Africa. A summary of the report of the Royal Commission with an index to the report. London, 1955.

Africa Bureau: Reflections on the Report of the Royal Commission on East Africa, London, 1955.

The Economy of East Africa: A Study of Trends, Nairobi, 1955.

M. MACMILLAN, *Introducing East Africa*, 2nd ed., London, 1955.

JOHN A. NOON, "Political Developments in East Africa", in CALVIN W. STILLMAN (ed.), *Africa and the Modern World*, Chicago, 1955.

PHILIP MASON, *A New Deal in East Africa: The Basic Arguments and Certain Implications of the Report of the Royal Commission on East Africa*, London, 1955.

W. H. WHITELEY, "The Changing Position of Swahili in East Africa". *Africa*, Vol. 26, No. 4 (October 1956), pp. 343–353.

R. E. WRAITH, *East African Citizen*, London, 1959.

D. S. ROTHCHILD, "East African Federalism", in *Toward Unity in Africa*, Washington, 1960.

J. E. GOLDTHORPE and F. B. WILSON, *Tribal Maps of East Africa and Zanzibar*. East African Institute of Social Research, East African Studies No. 13. Kampala, 1960.

P. S. WRIGHT, "Political and National Movements in East Africa", in BISHESHWAR PRASAD, *Contemporary Africa*, Bombay, 1960.

L. W. HOLLINGSWORTH, *The Asians of East Africa*, New York, 1960.

WILLIAM J. BARBER, *The Economy of British East Africa*, London, 1961.

PAUL FOSTER, *White to Move?* London, 1961.

CRENFORD PRATT, "East Africa: The Pattern of Political Development", in M. MACLURE and D. ANGLIN (ed.), *Africa: The Political Pattern*, Toronto, 1961, pp. 110–124.

A. KIRBY, "East Africa in Transition", in *The Africa of 1961*, London, 1961.

LUGO TAGUABA, "East Africa : The Last Phase to Political Independence", *Freedomways*, 1962, No. 4.

F. B. WELBOURN, *East African Rebels: A Study of Some Independent Churches*, London, 1962.

Г. УСОВ, «Национальная буржуазия и освободительное движение в Восточной Африке» [National Bourgeoisie and Liberation Movement in East Africa], *Мировая экономика и международные отношения*, 1962, No. 4.

H. J. SPIRO, *Politics in Africa*, Englewood Cliffs, N. J., 1962; ch. VII: "East Africa: Tribalism and Violence", pp. 97–114.

E. W. RUSSELL and D. A. HAWKINS (ed.), *The Natural Resources of East Africa*, Nairobi, 1963.

R. OLIVER and G. MATHEW, *History of East Africa*, London, 1963.

T. SZENTES, *Kelet-Afrika a szabadság útján* [East Africa on the Road to Freedom], Budapest, 1963.

A. J. HUGHES, *East Africa: The Search for Unity*, Baltimore, 1963.

R. COX, *Pan-Africanism in Practice: An East African Study*, New York, 1964.

HISTORICAL WORKS

L. W. HOLLINGSWORTH, *A Short History of the East Coast of Africa*, London, 1949; new edition, 1951.

R. REUSCH, *History of East Africa*, Stuttgart, 1954.

ZOE MARSH, *East Africa through Contemporary Records*, Cambridge, 1961.

KENNETH INGHAM, *A History of East Africa*, London, 1962; 3rd ed., 1965.

V. HARLOW and E. N. CHILVER (ed.), *History of East Africa*, Vol. II, New York, 1965.

M. S. M. KIWANUKA, *Mutesa of Uganda*. East African Literature Bureau, 1969.

OFFICIAL PUBLICATIONS

Inter-territorial Organization in East Africa. Col. 191. H.M.S.O., London, 1945.

St. J. ORDE-BROWN, *Labour Conditions in East Africa* (Report), London, 1946.

Inter-territorial Organization in East Africa: Revised Proposals. Col. 210. H.M.S.O., London, 1947.

A. G. C. DEUBER, *British East Africa: Economic and Commercial Conditions in British East Africa (Kenya, Uganda, Tanganyika and Zanzibar) during the immediate post-war period*. H.M.S.O., London, 1948.

Great Britain Colonial Office: An Economic Survey of the Colonial Territories, 1951.

The East African Territories, London, 1954.

H. Dow (chairman), *Report of the East Africa Royal Commission 1953–55*, London, 1955.

Great Britain Colonial Office: Despatches from the Governors of Kenya, Uganda and Tanganyika and from the Administrator, East Africa High Commission, Commenting on the East Africa Royal Commission 1953–55 Report. Cmd. 9801. London, 1956.

The Future of East Africa High Commission Services. Report of the London Discussions, June 1961. H.M.S.O., London 1962.

CHAPTER XVI

KENYA

Britain's Post-war Policy in Kenya

From the end of the 19th century onwards the history of Kenya colony was a striking and telling example of the colonial policy of British imperialism. The vociferous British champions of civilization ruined and plunged into poverty the African peoples by alienating their most fertile land and introducing heavy taxation.

After World War II the importance of Kenya for the British imperialists was increasing. Having lost a whole series of strategic bases in the Near and Middle East (India, Egypt, Palestine), they found Kenya most fitted to be developed into a strategic base. To attain this aim they had to build roads and airfields, to develop agriculture and industry, and these projects needed — in addition to capital — the assistance of the settlers who aspired to independence and the more intense utilization of the cheap (and in part free) labour of African millions.

Accordingly the post-war policy of Britain was directed towards increased economic development of the colonies, by breaking the resistance of Africans and silencing their demands, by forcing them to serve meekly the united interests of monopoly capitalists and settlers.

Accordingly, immediately after war's end, still in the autumn of 1945, on the insistence of the settlers a Development and Reconstruction Authority was established, a ten-year plan of the economic development of Kenya was adopted, and, for the co-ordination of different construction and other investments, a permanent Planning Commission was set up, composed of officials of the colonial administration and a single unofficial member, ALFRED VINCENT, leader of the settler group in the Legislative Council. The Colonial Office stressed in its propaganda for the ten-year plan that African interests should be taken into account as far as possible. The emptiness of this phrase is demonstrated by the facts that (1) the British government contributed all in all £3 million to the planned investments amounting to £17,586,000, stipulating that the rest should be covered from taxes and loans, that is to say, for the most part by collecting further taxes from the Africans; (2) the Africans did not take part in the formulation and adoption of the plan (nor were they consulted), and were represented neither in the Planning Commission nor in the Development and Reconstruction Authority.

Under such circumstances it is no wonder that for lack of money the realization of the plans was going slower than expected. A considerable part of the available means was used for the construction of strategic roads, harbours and other military installations, for which purpose the colonial administration, for want of labour, imported 2,000 Italian ex-soldiers. It is characteristic that in 1948 the not too important sum originally allotted for African education was still further reduced "for lack of financial means".

Characteristic of the government's indulgence towards the settlers and of its complete disregard of the African demands is the fact that the British government accepted the settlers' anti-African plans of federation and changed the composition of the Legislative and the Executive Council to favour the settlers.

In the post-war years, when the independence struggle of the colonial peoples was advancing irresistibly all over the world, the great colonial powers (Britain and France), in order to preserve their positions, were compelled to think about introducing new, more democratic looking methods (neocolonialism!). The Kenya settlers who, to secure their privileged position, were long dreaming of creating an East African Union under the rule of Kenya, now, making use of the threat posed to the British colonial empire by the colonial peoples' aspirations for independence, demanded more insistently the realization of their federal schemes.[1]

Although the British government did not agree with the settlers striving for independence from Britain, yet in a federation of colonies it also saw a guarantee of retaining those territories, and therefore, as we have seen before, in spite of unanimous African protest, it set up the East Africa High Commission, the Central Legislative Assembly and its executive organization as a central government.

Until 1952 the Legislative Council of Kenya had had neither African nor European elected members. The Council was composed of official members and a few appointed European settlers, who were obliged to give their votes in favour of the government on all major issues. As far back as 1944 a "reliable" African was admitted as appointed member (the Kikuyu ELIUD MATHU), followed by another in 1947 (the Luo J. B. OHANGA), with the right of consultation, but this composition of the Council could not promote African interests.

In 1952, seven years after the end of war, the British colonialists at last brought themselves to initiate a "democratic" reform in the composition of the Kenya Legislative Council. The reform really contained some democratic elements — in favour of the anti-African minority of European settlers — but effected no essential change in the underprivileged position of the Africans. The 1952 reform reduced the number of the official Council members to 10 (including the Governor and his deputy) and provided 21 seats for 14 European, 6 Asian (Indian) and 1 Arab elected members in addition to 6 Africans appointed by the Governor, but the Africans and the elected members had no power of decision in the Council because the 10 official and 18 appointed unofficial members secured a majority to the government even if all elected members and the Africans voted together. (On principle the Governor was empowered to appoint even Africans among the 18 unofficials, but in practice

---

[1] The far-reaching federal schemes of the settlers were formulated by their leader, ALFRED VINCENT, in these terms: "As a first step, Kenya, Uganda and Tanganyika would federate to form an East African Union; Nyasaland, Northern Rhodesia and Southern Rhodesia to form a Central African Union; the four West African colonies to form a West African Union. The next step would be a federation of these three new Unions with the Union of South Africa. Finally and *pari passu*, with the progress of Western Union in Europe, would come federation with French, Belgian and Portuguese territories to form a United States of Africa with a unified defence policy."

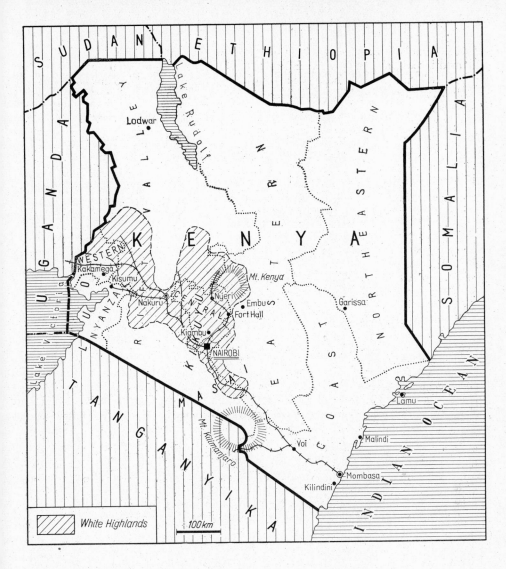

The map shows Kenya with surrounding countries SUDAN, ETHIOPIA, SOMALIA, UGANDA, TANGANYIKA, and the INDIAN OCEAN. Cities and features labelled include Lodwar, Lake Rudolf, Kakamega, Kisumu, Nakuru, Njeri, Mt. Kenya, Embu, Fort Hall, Kiambu, NAIROBI, Garissa, Lamu, Malindi, Mombasa, Kilindini, Voi, Mt. Kilimanjaro, Lake Victoria. Regions: WESTERN, RIFT VALLEY, NYANZA, CENTRAL, KIKUYU, MASAI, EASTERN, COAST, NORTHEASTERN. Legend: hatched area = White Highlands; scale 100 km.

all of them were settlers and were obliged to vote in favour of the government on major issues after all.)

So the "democratic reform" of the British government drew not a single elected representative of the five million Africans into the work of the highest legislative organ of their country.

The British colonialists enforced the same kind of "democratism" also when they revised the composition of the Executive Council in the first years following the war. The majority of the Executive Council invariably consisted of colonial officials, but after the war the Governor added to them a few unofficial members nominated from among the European settlers and appointed an African member in 1951. The 1952 reform left the Executive Council unchanged in this composition.

The Labour government, which after the war took over this policy in Kenya, remained in power until November 1951. During the six years in power the Labour party, which calls itself a socialist party of the working class, demonstrated beyond question that its policy differed from the Conservative policy only in words, not in essence, and that the dispossessed Africans could expect of it nothing but fanciful liberal phrases.

The Kenya chiefs' delegation attending the victory celebrations in London under the leadership of ELIUD MATHU, the only African member of the Legislative Council, availed itself of the opportunity to inform Labour Colonial Secretary HALL of the grievances of Africans and the racist schemes of the settlers. HALL assured the Africans that the Labour government had no intention to back the settlers' aspirations. A few months later, however, he was succeeded by A. CREECH JONES, who in the summer of 1946 visited Kenya, talked with Governor MITCHELL and the settler leaders; he assured the settlers that his government had "not the slightest intention of allowing the white settlements to be liquidated, today, to-morrow or at any other time". And he told the Africans that "better conditions can only come to you through hard work and obedience to the Government officials".[1]

It is characteristic of the double-dealing of the Labourites that in 1947 CREECH JONES stated in his message to the Governors of British colonies the following: "The whole-hearted co-operation of the Governments and people of the colonies is essential if colonial production is to play its part in the rehabilitation of a world ravaged by war, in the restoration of economic stability in the United Kingdom, and in the development of the colonies themselves."

No wonder therefore that, after such statements by a member of the Labour cabinet, Governor MITCHELL rudely inveighed against the Africans on the grounds that they dared to demand political and economic equality, while he encouraged the settlers by saying: "It is an historical fact that the lands we have turned into farms and towns were vacant lands when we came here . . . This land we have made is ours by right — by right of achievement."

The launching of the ten-year plan for the promotion of monopoly interests, the establishment of the Planning Commission and the Development and Reconstruction Authority in this connection, the concessions made to the anti-African policy of the rightist settlers (federal plans to suit the settlers, White Paper No. 191 which disregarded the African interests, and White Paper No. 210 which was still more outrageous), and at the same time the introduction, instead of the reforms demanded by Africans, of insignificant reforms which did not affect the conditions of the Africans in the least — all were measures stamped by the Labour government in power.

But the hypocritical African policy of the Labour Party, this policy of promoting in practice the dirty business of colonizers in spite of its outward propaganda, is best demonstrated by the fact that it was under the Labour government in power, namely with its connivance and approval, that the most heinous crime in the history of British colonialism was committed (and this in the middle of the 20th century!)

---

[1] The same CREECH JONES, as an opposition member, said this in 1943: "My party have always opposed the White Highlands policy and the eviction from the land of the Africans . . . We would not countenance it, even at the present time".

by evicting 30,000 Kikuyu peasants from their lands and reducing them to the fate of shelterless beggars.[1]

The Situation of the People in Kenya after the War.
The Kenya African Union

As appears from a United Nations study published in 1953, the average annual income of an African worker in Kenya was £27, while an Asian or any other non-European earned £286 and the European made £660 a year. The per capita yearly income was £5 18s. in the African sector and £205 14s. in the non-African sector. In other terms, the Africans constituting 97.1 per cent of the population received 49.1 per cent of all personal income, while 50.9 per cent went to the non-Africans totalling only 2.9 per cent of the population.[2]

Forty-eight per cent of the agricultural labourers in 1953 were paid less than 25s. a month (30 workdays), and 26 per cent received less than 20s. There were squatters who were paid less than 15s. a month. The yearly pay of the Africans in government service and other employment was under £50 a year, while the lowest-ranking European employee was paid £600 per year.

After the banning in 1940 of the Kikuyu Central Association (K.C.A.) theAfricans had no major political party in Kenya. In 1945 ELIUD MATHU, the single African member of the Legislative Council, organized the Kenya African Study Union, which was then joined by HARRY THUKU among others. This organization was a year later transformed into a political party, the Kenya African Union (K.A.U.), and it elected THUKU its chairman. Since, however, he maintained his leadership of the Kikuyu Provincial Association he had founded in 1934, which enjoyed the support of the chiefs and collaborated with the government, he was forced to resign as K.A.U. chairman a few months later, and his post was taken over by JAMES GICHURU.

The party set itself the aim of mobilizing all Kenya tribes to launch a common fight against oppression and for the independence of the country.

In December 1946 the Kenya African Union and the East African Indian Congress submitted a joint memorandum to the British Prime Minister, expressing the hope that "His Majesty's Government will not destroy faith in the honesty of Labour. Surrender to the clamour of an intolerant minority would be a denial that the democratic approach influences the British Government, even when guided by the Labour Party ... The Colonial Office has accepted the views of the white community of Kenya which forms the minority of the Kenya population, and disregarded African opinion, which supported White Paper 191."

In the autumn of 1946, after an absence of 15 years, JOMO KENYATTA returned home. In 1947 he took over the K.A.U. chairmanship from GICHURU.

---

[1] The lands in question had at the time been given to the peasants in place of the better lands taken away from them and given to the settlers. Expropriation now was without compensation on the groun that the Africans failed to comply with the rules of soil conservation. Many of them attempted to resist. The courts passed judgement in this case on April 5, 1948, sentencing 47 men and 26 women to imprisonment, a number of men were fined or sent to prison for two months. Thousands of people lingered in misery without land, shelter and jobs for many years.

[2] *Special Study on Social Conditions in Non-Self-Governing Territories,* United Nations, New York, 1953.

Under his direction the party called upon the Africans to take an active part in the political struggle, and warned them at the same time to refrain from any violence. The party grew rapidly and spread all over the country. And KENYATTA, who was touring the country and spoke to the people at mass meetings (his audience often exceeded 25,000), gained unprecedented popularity. It was due to his great popularity that the party was joined, in addition to Kikuyu, also by large numbers from other tribes, mainly Luo and Wakamba. KENYATTA's generally recognized authority was also the guarantee that the party was able to preserve its unity all the time, in spite of frequent internal dissension between the radical and the moderate wing of the party.

K.A.U. was the only political organization of the Africans which represented the interests of all tribes of the country, and which, setting aside tribal and local considerations, always kept in view the general interests of the country. There were smaller parties and organizations, of a local or sectarian character, whose purposes and tactics were different from those of K.A.U. but their majority also recognized the prestige of KENYATTA and his party, and sympathized with their struggle for the great political objectives. K.A.U. endeavoured to win them over to itself, but condemned their tribalist attitudes and terrorist methods, and tried to persuade them to abandon such policies and join in the political struggle waged by peaceful means.[1]

K.A.U. kept in touch with a number of non-political organizations, such as the trade unions (K.A.U. backed the African Workers' Federation, took part in its strikes and persuaded the workers to raise also political demands),[2] African churches (among them the African Orthodox Church and the African Independent Pentecostal Church), schools and cultural societies (in 1947 KENYATTA undertook to head the Githunguri Training College and was active in the work of the Kikuyu Independent Schools Association and the Kikuyu Karinga Education Association).

The 1947 Memorandum of the Kenya African Union

On June 1, 1947, K.A.U. held at Nairobi a national conference of representatives of all major Kenya tribes (Kikuyu, Luo, Masai, Akamba, Kavirondo, etc.). The conference worked out and put in writing the Union's declaration of aims stating:

"1. That the political objective of the Africans in Kenya must be self-government by Africans for Africans, and in that African State the right of all racial minorities would be safeguarded.

"2. That more African seats should be provided immediately in the Kenya Legislative Council, and condemned the inequality of racial representation in the Inter-Territorial East African Central Assembly.

"3. That more land be made available both in the Crown Lands and in the highlands for settlement of Africans.

---

[1] Such organizations were, for example, the *Dini ya Msambwa* sect in the north of Nyanza and the *Dini ya Jesu Kristo* sect in Central Province, which resorted to terror against white colonial rule and organized uprisings and killings.

[2] Thus it supported the 1947 strike of the African Workers' Federation in Mombasa, then the strike of the workers of the Uplands Bacon factory a few miles away from Nairobi in September 1947, as well as the Nairobi workers' political demonstration in the same month. The police opened fire on the strikers and demonstrators and killed several Africans.

"4. That compulsory and free education for Africans, as is given to the children of other races, is overdue.

"5. That the Kipandi[1] with all its humiliating rules and regulations be abolished immediately.

"6. That the deplorable wages, housing and other conditions of African labourers be substantially improved and that the principle of 'equal pay for equal work' be recognized."[2]

These demands were laid down in a memorandum addressed to the British government. In a few months' time the party managed to collect a million signatures to the memorandum, which was then taken by MBIYU KOINANGE and ACHIENG OBEKO to London, where they intended to present it to the Colonial Secretary of the Labour government. In the meantime, however, as a result of the change of government in London, the Colonial Office had been taken over by OLIVER LYTTELTON of the Conservative Party. The new Colonial Secretary having refused to receive the African delegates, these went to Paris, where they submitted their memorandum to the UN Economic and Social Council in session there, which distributed the document among the members.

Back in London the delegates, with the support of the Congress of Peoples Against Imperialism and a number of socialist and liberal M.P.s, held public meetings throughout England to explain their petition to be presented to the British Parliament and signed by several leading figures of British progressive opinion.

In London KOINANGE said among other things that the Kenyans were "no longer prepared to be diverted by minor political or economic reforms. Although Africans look to world opinion and especially to the British people for support, they realize that fundamentally they must rely on themselves for the achievement of full equality. In spite of all forms of oppression and persecution, the political consciousness of the people of Kenya has been growing rapidly. The Kenya African Union has become the national democratic movement which gives expression to their aspirations."

The growing popularity in England of the African action made the Kenya settlers increasingly nervous. Almost simultaneously with the African move the European elected members of the Legislative Council stated their views in a memorandum. They requested that the British government should not make room in Kenya for "African nationalism on the line of West Africa", and that "any statements which suggested that such a thing was possible . . . should be considered as seditious", and they said they would "take matters into their own hands". They exerted growing pressure upon the Governor to have K.A.U. banned and KENYATTA arrested. Since, however, KENYATTA and K.A.U. had always consistently abided by the legal forms and means, the Governor could not bring himself to take the proposed step, but in September 1952 he sent two of his ministers to London to ask for the Colonial Secretary's opinion. In the meantime the Kenya settlers and the reactionary press in Britain, as well as Tory M.P.s who had economic and other interests in common with the settlers, conducted a vigorous provocative campaign of slander against K.A.U. and its leaders.

To get the British government to ban the party and arrest its leaders, the reactionary forces needed some excuse. They used as a pretext the fact that some extreme

---

[1] The pass system binding upon Africans.
[2] G. PADMORE, *Africa: Britain's Third Empire*, London, 1949, pp. 231–232.

elements of the desperate African population in Kenya (in the same way as, and not more frequently than, in Tanganyika or Uganda, for example) resorted to acts of violence (killing, looting, and arson). They spread rumours that these acts were committed by an alleged secret organization, which they called "Mau Mau". At the same time they accused KENYATTA and his party (who consistently called upon the Africans to refrain from violence in the political struggle) of directing this secret movement, and claimed that this movement was in fact the underground organization of K.A.U.

The settlers understood that the Conservative take-over in Britain made it possible for them, by stemming the political advance of the Africans and scaring the British government, to carry out their long-cherished dream, to take the colonial administration into their own hands.

By raising the slogan of "fighting the Mau Mau movement" the settlers and their reactionary friends in London prevailed upon the British government to introduce a terror regime and to start a veritable colonial war against the Africans, provoking thereby just what they pretended to fight against: the massive violent response of Africans.

The K.A.U. Memorandum of 1950

By 1950 the K.A.U. organizations had covered the whole territory of the country and its members numbered more than a hundred thousand. The party was going to address to the British Parliament a new memorandum containing the demands of five million Africans:

They demanded that the number of African members of the Legislative Council be raised from four to twelve, and that the African members be elected, not nominated. They protested against the settlers' demand that Europeans should have parity in the legislature with all other races combined. They did not demand universal suffrage for Africans but wanted "a common roll for all races on a basis suitable to the circumstances of the colony", and no fewer African seats in the Executive Council than any other race group possessed, as well as adequate representation on all local and municipal boards.

They demanded that racial discrimination be prohibited by law, and that higher posts in the civil service be made accessible to Africans, and they requested more aid for the school and agricultural education of Africans.

They demanded also the lifting of the restrictions on freedom of assembly and movement, and emphasized that the restrictions imposed by the colonial authorities and chiefs only led to the proliferation of secret societies.

This action of the Africans prompted the European settlers, who were afraid of losing their privileges, to make a countermove. The "Kenya European Electors' Association" in March 1948 submitted to the government a proposal holding the K.A.U. leaders, especially KENYATTA, responsible for the African strikes, political movements and anti-government activities, and demanded their deportation.

The Labour government did not accede to this demand because it feared that KENYATTA's arrest would only add to his popularity. On the other hand, all it did to meet the African demands during the five years in power was that it raised the number of nominated African members of the Legislative Council from two to four and abolished the Kipandi in 1949.

British Provocations.
The Repressive Legislation of 1952

The British government and its colonial agencies, instead of examining and remedying the complaints of the Africans, resorted to the means of terror and provocation.

In September 1952 the British Attorney-General of Kenya was to London to talk over the necessary steps with the Colonial Office. After returning to Kenya, on September 25 he introduced to the Legislative Council a number of emergency bills, the chief provisions of which were:

"(1) Control of the African press and organization.

"(2) Restriction of the movement of Africans suspected of belonging to the Mau Mau Society.

"(3) Licensing of printing presses, unless specially exempted, and powers to seize and destroy newspapers printed on unlicensed presses.

"(4) Registration of organizations with ten or more members, except co-operatives, trade unions and Freemasons. Societies not registered or exempted were automatically declared unlawful. Societies with international affiliations could be prosecuted.

"(5) Confessions made to police officers may be used as evidence against Africans and evidence can be taken on affidavit.

"(6) A British provincial commissioner who is satisfied that any African is a member of Mau Mau may order his arrest and deportation to a restricted area. Disobedience of such an order is punishable by a fine of a hundred pounds or twelve months imprisonment."[1]

Afterwards came a number of similar acts of terror legislation. One such act held the Africans jointly responsible if any African village failed to surrender persons accused of being associated with Mau Mau. Another act empowered the Exco member for security affairs, if he deemed it necessary in the interest of law and order, to evict the African population of any district, and even to destroy the livestocks and other personal property of the evicted people.

The Trial and Conviction of Kenyatta

On October 22, 1952, the colonial authorities arrested Jomo Kenyatta, President of the Kenya African Union, and five other members of the K.A.U. Executive Committee. They were indicted of having organized and directed the Mau Mau movement under the guise of the Union. They were brought to trial not for political offences but for common crimes. The trial was held at Kapenguria, a small village in the Northern Frontier District, and lasted from November 24, 1952, till April 8, 1953.

As it was common knowledge that Kenyatta, both in his name and on behalf of K.A.U., condemned the terror acts, he was charged that he did so only in public while secretly fostering the Mau Mau movement, and that he could have stopped it if he had wanted to.

The chief crime imputed to Mau Mau, and for which Kenyatta was taken to court, was that they were killing Europeans and intended to exterminate all white settlers. The truth is, however, that before Kenyatta was arrested only one single white person had fallen victim to the disturbances.

[1] G. Padmore, *Pan-Africanism or Communism?* London, 1956, pp. 248–249.

Before the court KENYATTA said among other things:

"'... We are not guilty and we do not accept your findings ... We do not feel that we have received justice or the hearing we would have liked ... We feel that this case, from our point of view, has been so arranged in order to strangle the Kenya African Union, the only African political organization which fights for the rights of the African people. But what we have objection to and shall continue to object to is discriminations in the government in this country. We shall not accept that, whether we are in jail or out of it ... This world has been made for human beings to live happily, to enjoy the good things and the produce of the country equally ...'"

Then he turned to the magistrate and went on to say: "You being a European, it is only natural that you should feel that we have something against Europeans. I feel that you should not have stressed so much that we have been entirely motivated by hatred for Europeans. Our activities have been against injustice to the African people and if you think that by asking for African rights we have turned out to be what you say is Mau Mau, we are very sorry you have been misled. What we have done and shall continue to do is to demand rights for the African people as human beings, that they shall enjoy the same facilities as other people. We look forward to the day when peace shall come to this land and that the truth shall be known that we, African leaders, have stood for peace.

"None of us would condone mutilation of human beings. We are human and have families of our own, and none of us would condone such activities as you think we are guilty of. I am asking for no mercy at all on behalf of my colleagues. We are asking that justice be done, and that injustices that exist may be righted."[1]

Among the accused of the KENYATTA trial there were many Luo and Wakamba.[2]

The court found them all guilty and sentenced each accused to seven years' hard labour. The convicted Africans appealed first to the Kenya High Court, which in January 1954 rejected the appeal, and then to the Privy Council in London, which in May 1954 confirmed the sentence passed by the Kenya court.

The Closing of the Kikuyu Schools and Colleges

In November 1952, when Colonial Secretary LYTTELTON was in Nairobi, the Kenya African Union requested him to provide greater opportunities for the school education and vocational training of Africans. In reply to the request a few days later the Kikuyu Independent Schools were closed down, their teachers arrested and confined to internment camps as "Mau Mau agitators".

Banning of the Kenya African Union

Two months after KENYATTA's conviction Governor Sir EVELYN BARING declared the Kenya African Union unlawful. The decision was made public in a broadcast statement by the "Chief Native Commissioner", who gave as a reason that the Union was a cover organization for Mau Mau terrorists, and many Union members

---

[1] PADMORE (1956), pp. 263–264.
[2] In June 1954 the authorities arrested 170 Wakamba on the charge of participation in the Mau Mau movement. According to official reports, the Wakamba members of the movement totalled 3,000.

were in contact with Mau Mau. But the Chief Commissioner gave himself away by inadvertently referring to the real cause of the banning decision in these terms:

"We would not have wished to stop political associations with sincere aspirations for the legitimate development of African interests and progress, but the Kenya Government can never again allow such an association as the Kenya African Union. Moreover, the Government cannot permit the formation of any African political societies on the same lines as the Union while there is still such trouble in the country. We will, however, give assistance and recognition to those local associations which have been reasonable and sincere in the interests of their own peoples."[1]

From what the Chief Commissioner said it was clear why the Union had to go out of existence: the British government could not tolerate in a colony a political organization which worked towards the unity of all African tribes living in the territory and mobilized them for the common struggle. The colonialists favoured those tribal organizations leaning to separatism which were under the direction of chiefs and other agents appointed and paid by the colonial authorities. The authorities might then easily set them against one another and thus prevent the Africans from combining politically against colonial exploitation and for independence.

At the news of KENYATTA's arrest JAMES GRIFFITHS (the former Labour Colonial Secretary), speaking in parliament on behalf of the Labour Party, expressed the hope that the arrest of KENYATTA would not turn "the most important organization of the Africans", the Kenya African Union, against the Kenya administration and reminded the government of the danger of breaking with the Union: "If it is proscribed and banned, who is to lead and advise the African? It is of the utmost importance that there should be, at this time more than any other, a responsible political organisation to which Africans can look for leadership." But the government paid no heed to this warning.

Counter-action of the African Population

In response to the terror measures of the government the provisional leadership of the Kenya African Union on November 28, 1952, issued the following manifesto:

"In the name of the people of Kenya we demand:

"(1) The abolition by law of all racial discrimination as being repugnant to morality and civilized standards and contrary to the principles of the United Nations.

"(2) That the paramount need of the Africans for land be satisfied. Meanwhile, there must be no further immigration of Europeans and Asians, except on a temporary basis for the purpose of providing personnel for essential services and industries.

"(3) The extension of educational facilities, including technical facilities by

"(a) establishing institutions of full university status in East Africa in the shortest possible time;

"(b) arranging for a greatly increased number of African students to proceed overseas for higher studies, and the provision of a Fund from which students wishing to go abroad can obtain loans;

---

[1] PADMORE, *op cit.*, p. 253.

"(c) multiplying the number of primary and secondary schools so that in the shortest possible time all African boys and girls shall have at least had the benefits of compulsory education.

"(4) The immediate introduction of the system of election, not nomination, for all African unofficial members of the Legislative Council.

"(5) A Common Roll for all three races.

"(6) The reservation of an equal number of seats for Africans and non-Africans on the unofficial side of the Council.

"(7) A franchise for Africans based initially on literacy and/or property qualifications and including women.

"(8) The nomination of equal numbers of Africans and non-Africans on the official side of the Council.

"(9) The direct election, not nomination, of all African members of the proposed Constitutional Committee for Kenya, and that the number of African, Asian and European members of the Committee be equal — failing which, Her Majesty's Government in Britain should be requested to set up an impartial Committee of British constitutional experts.

"(10) The election of Africans to all County, District, and Municipal Councils and Boards: and the establishment of County, District Locational and Municipal Councils and Boards on an electoral basis in the African Land Units. An immediate increase in the membership of African Councillors in the Nairobi Municipal Council representing not less than the membership enjoyed by the European community. The same to apply to the Municipal Boards of Mombasa, Nakuru, Eldoret and Kisumu.

"(11) The trade unions be allowed to function freely, that registration be optional and not compulsory, and combination of trade unions be permitted.

"(12) Full opportunity for Africans to demonstrate their loyalty to Kenya by serving in commissioned ranks in the Defence Forces and in the senior posts in the Civil Service.

"(13) Assistance in the economic development of African farms, in the form of loans on easy terms and the provision of agricultural schools where appropriate courses can be administered to African farmers.

"(14) The payment of uniform prices to all producers of primary produce of which the purchase and sale is controlled, and the abrogation of all restrictive practices in the growth of certain crops.

"(15) Equal pay for equal qualifications and work.

"(16) The immediate increase in the minimum wage by thirty-three and one third per cent to offset the high cost of living, and the provision of adequate housing accommodation for the thousands of homeless and bedless African workers in Nairobi and Mombasa.

"(17) The right of freedom of assembly and speech, without interference by the police or the administration, and the repeal of the relevant sections of the Police Ordinance, in accordance with the terms of the United Nations Charter.

"(18) The terms of reference of the Royal Commission be widened to include a survey of lands in Kenya.

"(19) The earliest possible repeal of all recent repressive legislation including the Bill for the Registration of Societies.

"(20) The release or immediate trial of all persons arrested since October 20th.

"(21) Facilities to enable the independent African Press to start functioning again.

"(22) The removal of all restrictions on the legitimate activities of the Kenya African Union.

"(23) The immediate implementation of the Universal Declaration of Human Rights."[1]

A few days later, on November 4, when Colonial Secretary LYTTELTON was on a visit in Nairobi, the Union handed him a memorandum signed by F. W. ODEBE and J. A. Z. MURUMBI. The note stated that, as a consequence of the banning of public meetings and the stringent measures applied against the press, the Africans had no way of explaining their position, and depicted the situation and problems of the Africans in an objective tone:

"We are of the opinion that much of the present trouble is due to the fact that Africans are not adequately associated with the machinery of government to make them feel that they are a real part or partners in the Government of the country. This has the twofold effect of denying to the Government the benefit of considered representative African opinion in the making of Government policy; and, on the other hand, of creating the impression in the minds of the people that the Government, because of its composition, does not work in the interests of Africans. During the last 30 years, while the requests of the European community have been readily conceded, the representations of the African community have been consistently ignored. This has led the ordinary African to believe that only if he has a Government of his own can he benefit, and not otherwise. He refuses to believe that his interests can be safeguarded by the European community . . .

"The Government of the country is being steadily transferred to local Europeans, thereby creating a *fait accompli* as in some other parts of the African continent. This has brought about a deep sense of frustration and bitterness in the mind of the African, who finds his efforts at constitutional progress thwarted and of no avail.

"We believe that another main cause of the present unrest is the intense land hunger prevalent among Africans — more particularly among those residing in the Central Province. The land question has been debated for years, but it has never been so serious as it is today. It forms the core of the agitation, the burning point in African minds. We see the so-called squatters evicted from the highlands, which have been reserved for European settlement, and made to cultivate land in the already over-populated and greatly eroded Reserves. At the same time they see thousands and thousands of acres of land lying idle — in wait for some European to make up his mind to settle in Kenya. The Africans also observe with growing resentment the frequent attempts being made at public expense to induce them to do so while they themselves are desperately in need of land.

"We earnestly request an immediate cessation of immigration to settle on land, as such immigration can only aggravate the position further. We realise that restricted immigration is both necessary and in the interests of the African in the field of technical and industrial development, but even in this category unrestricted immigration would do much damage and be misunderstood unless an Immigration Board, on which not less than half the members represented on the Board were Africans, were established, whose decision would be final, subject to the Governor's approval.

"The present unsatisfactory position in the Reserves is partly due to overcrowding and partly due to the fact that Africans were positively hindered from learning progressive methods of agriculture. Attempts made by Mr. John Ainsworth, one-time Provincial Commissioner of Nyanza, to introduce legislation providing for im_

[1] *Op. cit.*, pp. 250–252.

proved agricultural technique, encountered strong opposition from the settlers on the grounds that a policy aimed at making the Reserves remunerative and self-sufficient would deprive them of cheap labour."[1]

Further on the memorandum stated the fact of rising costs of living making it very difficult for the African worker "to make both ends meet, even at a very low level of subsistence". The Africans often had "to resort to crime as a means of supplementing their low wages in order to exist". The Kenya African Union had "no desire to justify crime which may have been provoked by want and poverty", but only called attention to the well-established fact. Though the African spent, according to a report of the Government Labour Department, 72 per cent of his expenditure on food, the report admitted, characteristically enough, that "there is no question but that malnutrition exists among the majority of tribes, and improved diet is essential for improved output of work; the present low output is a major problem, but this is often due to the lack of physical ability to carry out a full day's work. In many cases the diet provided by employers is inferior even to that in the Reserves, particularly in the case of the pastoral tribes".[2]

The memorandum stated in conclusion:

"We hold the view that there is nothing so essential to the healthy progress of this country as the development of political institutions and parties fully representative of the people, knowing their views, giving vent to their grievances, and in turn guiding them to accept conclusions and decisions arrived at by reason and discussion between conflicting viewpoints. It is, therefore, very important for political organisations to be at liberty to hold public meetings in order to gauge the feelings of their members and supporters, and to offer guidance and assistance to them, especially when it is so much needed as in the present times of stress. The banning of all public meetings during the last few months has further aggravated the sense of frustration arising from loss of free expression; this, if examples provided by the history of other countries are any guide, tends to exacerbate the radical elements and encourage them to indulge in violence over which their leaders have little control in the absence of the means of public speech and a free Press which constitute their sole channel of contact with the broad masses. For these reasons we earnestly hope that the Government will permit the free expression of opinion and remove all restrictions on the holding of public meetings. It is also hoped that the ban imposed on 52 African newspapers and broadsheets will be lifted as soon as possible. We also view with grave concern the Societies Bill, which is now a permanent feature of the Statute Book. Even in completely normal times a Society can be declared illegal under the Bill by the Registrar simply refusing to register it without an appeal to any Court of Law.

"There is no doubt that serious crime has been perpetrated by adherents of subversive organisations. It is also probably true to say that many well-known criminal elements have joined their ranks for the extra protection afforded ... We all join whole-heartedly in condemning this crime, and will do our best to stamp it out. We wish, however, to point out that any action on the part of Government which has the effect of greatly hindering non-violent, constitutional political activity ... might result in furthering the cause of subversive organisations. We strongly feel that the effort of the Government to wipe out subversive activities will be greatly

[1] R. K. PANKHURST, Kenya: The History of Two Nations, London, 1953, pp. 90–91.
[2] Op. cit., pp. 91–92.

34

accelerated by the Kenya African Union representing the basic demands of the African peoples of Kenya.

"Finally, we feel obliged to draw your attention to the fact that the African people fail to understand why most of their leaders have been taken away from them during this critical hour, when their calming influence would have had a most salutary effect. We earnestly request the Government to do their best to clarify the position and thereby relieve the anxieties and misconceptions which exist in the minds of Africans in Kenya."[1]

Although the memorandum, as we can see, gave evidence of a great measure of moderation and readiness for co-operation, the Colonial Secretary ignored it completely.

A year later, in September 1953, JOSEPH MURUMBI (who had been Secretary of the K.A.U. until its banning in July 1953) went to London to present concrete peace proposals to the Colonial Secretary. The proposals, which, if accepted, might have been suitable for putting an end to the abnormal situation prevailing in Kenya, were the following:

(1) Release on bail of the political leaders, on the basis of their co-operation in restoring peace and discussion with the Colonial Office regarding essential reforms.

(2) A Round Table Conference of Representatives of all races in Kenya with a view to acceptance of a programme of political, social and economic reforms.

(3) The development of land in the African Reserves to the fullest capacity.

(4) Making available to Africans land in the Highlands not yet sold to Europeans.

(5) Community Projects, Co-operative Farming and Rural Industries should be introduced in the Reserves and technical and financial help welcomed from the United Nations, British, American, Indian and other sources.

(6) The principle of parity should be adopted in representation in the Executive and Legislative Councils of Kenya.

(7) Political democracy should also be applied to local government.

(8) The progressive elimination of the colour bar.

(9) The encouragement of the co-operation of educated and politically minded Africans in all schemes of political, economic and social developments.[2]

Although MURUMBI's proposals received support from a number of Labour M.P.s, trade-union and co-operative functionaries, the Colonial Secretary disregarded them completely like the memorandum of the Congress a year before.

Provocative Statements by the English Settlers in Kenya

One of the most rabid leading politicians in the Kenya English society at the time was Colonel GROGAN, who, as doyen of the settler community, had an influence also upon the colonial administration.[3] At the first meeting of the Kenya British Empire

---

[1] *Op. cit.*, pp. 92–93.

[2] PADMORE, *op. cit.*, pp. 258–259.

[3] This perverse prophet of colonial exploitation and racism propagated already in his book published in 1902 that Africans must be forced to work: "I have small sympathy with the capitalist regime . . . But it is the regime in which we live as yet, and till it top-heavy crumbles to the ground the native too must fall in line. We have stolen his land. Now we must steal his limbs . . . Compulsory labour is the corollary of our occupation of the country." Cf. EDWARD S. GROGAN and ARTHUR H. SHARP, *From Cape to Cairo*, London, 1902, pp. 365, 367—368, 377–378.

Party, a political organization of the extreme right-wing settlers, GROGAN incited to pogrom against the Kikuyu. The only answer to Mau Mau was, he said, "to teach the whole Kikuyu tribe a lesson by providing a 'psychic shock'." He proposed that the government arrest one hundred Mau Mau suspects and hang twenty-five of them in public before the eyes of the other seventy-five, who should then be sent home to spread the news. And if this should not be enough to terrorize the Africans, all Kikuyus should be expelled from their holdings, which then should be confiscated and sold to white settlers.

A Kenya missionary, Bishop WALTER CARY, in his book *Crisis in Kenya* published in 1952, declared that the Kikuyu were a "dishonoured tribe", "murderers and inefficient farmers" not to be tolerated in the vicinity of the white settlers. He added that the European colonists would never accept "Kikuyu occupation" but would either achieve independence from England in the wake of the Americans or join South Africa.[1]

The "liberal" leader of the European elected members of the Kenya Legislative Council, MICHAEL BLUNDELL, in a statement to Reuter's, took a stand in favour of extending the Kenya regime to Uganda and Tanganyika, for the establishment of a British East African Federation, and for its union with the Central African Federation. The Kikuyu, he said, "would in future have to put up with a long period of severe discipline to prove to them that the government must be obeyed. I think we shall have to control their government, their assemblies, their schools and their press". Finally he proposed that the immigration policies be revised, that the number of European settlers be increased by adding "the right type" of colonists, because, in his view, the settlers in the past had "indulged in too much conciliation" towards the Africans.

Anglo-American Liberal Opinion

Commenting on the repressive measures of the government, the London *Observer* wrote this: "It is seriously questionable whether the Government's policy of fighting terror with terror is not responsible for exacerbating the situation . . . Such methods are likely to perpetuate bitterness and to leave no alternative to wholesale killing."

The *Manchester Guardian* published a letter from a so-called "terrorist", DEDAM KIMATHI, who said that there was no such thing as Mau Mau, there existed only poor Africans and poverty could be remedied, but not by bombs and other weapons: "The policy of the Kenya Government of driving people away without good grounds, and of confining them to their reserves, has resulted in a thousandfold increase in Mau Mau in the forests. Young men, women, and even old persons, are in the forests because they are afraid of being killed, of badly beaten, or confined, as they are by the policy of the Kenya Government . . . If colour prejudice is to remain in Kenya, who will stop subversive action, for the African has eyes, ears and brains?"

The *Daily Telegraph* published photographs showing portable gallows the like of which had first been used by the Italian fascists in the war against Ethiopia.

Here are a few lines from a report of *The New York Times* correspondent in Nairobi: " . . . it is hardly denied here that a certain number of persons have been killed in

[1] He had preached in the same tone in the inter-war years, emphasizing that forced labour was needed to secure African "co-operation" because "where Negroes are, white man will not do manual work. And the Negroes will not disappear as have savages of other lands".

one way or another who almost certainly were not Mau Mau . . . There is a tendency to shoot down any women heading towards the forest."

A British soldier serving in Kenya wrote to the same paper: "Prisoners are often brutally treated, many are shot and none are fed. Apparently the government makes no provision for feeding prisoners."

A *Peace News* reporter, REGINALD REYNOLDS, stated that the Kenya Police Reserve was responsible for more terror than Mau Mau: "Patrols of K.P.R. men go and come. They regard as an enemy any Kikuyu known to be a supporter of the Kenya African Union — now banned after the failure to kill it by arresting its leaders.

"For an African even to be educated is to be suspect. 'Why,' asked one Kikuyu pointedly, 'is it nearly always the educated Africans who fail to halt when challenged by a patrol and are shot dead ? . . .'

"There are lawyers who have details of many unpleasant cases — alleged murders and beatings . . . but nobody imagines they represent more than a small fraction of the total . . .

" . . . If only one-tenth of the allegations should turn out to be true the case against the Government would be a heavy one . . ."[1]

Two Labour M.P.s, FENNER BROCKWAY and LESLIE HALE, went to visit Kenya. Although they deeply condemned the Mau Mau terror, the settlers gave them a hostile welcome, and the authorities received them with suspicion. Their visit was unsuccessful because they could not freely meet Africans. It happened even that an African was arrested when he was seen talking to BROCKWAY. Others, with whom the visitors had appointments, disappeared before the appointed hour. When visiting the province the M.P.s were escorted by police and soldiers, and could talk with Africans only in their presence, and with chiefs only with the permission and participation of the District Officer. Thus it was this officer who informed the M.P.s of the conditions of the Africans and the Mau Mau case, and the chief concerned only nodded yes. On their return to London the two M.P.s stated: "We disagree profoundly with Mr. Oliver Lyttelton when he says that social and economic griev- ances are not the cause of Mau Mau. Mau Mau is an ugly and brutal form of extreme nationalism. It is based on frustration. These frustations arise from among other things the humiliation of the colour bar; the destruction of the old tribal system; land hunger; wages which do not in thousands of cases satisfy physical hunger; appalling housing conditions, and the fantastic rise in the price of posho (maize flour), the staple food."[2]

British Terror in Kenya

A group of Kikuyu women wrote a petition which three British women M.P.s forwarded to Queen ELIZABETH. The petitioners complained about the atrocities committed by the colonial authorities, the police and British troops. Here is an excerpt from the petition:

"We are not ashamed to let Your Majesty know the troubles inflicted on us by both the ordinary police and the military police, together with the District Com- missioners.

---

[1] PANKHURST, *op. cit.*, pp. 108, 109, 102, 103.
[2] *Op. cit.*, p. 94.

"Women and children sleep outside in the bush for fear of the police who, we are told, are here to protect us during this state of unrest.

"Our husbands have been arrested and detained under the Emergency Regulations and only women have been left to look after their homes, children and holdings.

"The police, while patrolling the Native Reserves, constantly commit rape on us, even though some of us are pregnant or have just given birth. Communal slave-labour has been introduced by the Kenya Government, and women are mercilessly collected from their homes to go and work in police camps. There the police commit untold atrocities, such as raping and beating for no reason . . .

"Collective punishment has been imposed upon us. In many cases our property and stock have been confiscated and our children are left in a state of famine and without support, while our husbands are in detention camps miles and miles away from us . . ."[1]

In his afore-cited book R. PANKHURST mentioned a written statement by another group of Africans. In it we read among other things:

"The atrocities being committed by the Security Forces, i.e. military forces, Kenya Police Reserve, and Home Guards, in the Central and Rift Valley Provinces of Kenya are so bad that it is clear that their intention is to finish the Kikuyu tribe. In spite of that the Colonial Office and Kenya Government have concealed these atrocities and have persistently denied these occurrences . . .

"The District Officers in the two mentioned provinces started to arrest as many Kikuyu as possible . . . When such people are detained in the camps they are brutally beaten, one by one, and broken arms, ribs and skulls are the lot of such victims. After such beatings the men are given an oath swearing as follows: 'May this oath kill me, if I ever claim for land; if I ever say that all the lands of Kenya do not belong to Europeans; if I ever see anyone, be he my father, mother, brother or sister, or my neighbour talking about land or politics, and I do not report him to the Government.'

"Such a person is then branded (with a hot steel) on the shoulder. People given such an oath are many — and they have been told to curse and disbelieve the leadership of Mbiyu and Kenyatta.

"Secondly, in these provinces, people are arrested by District Officers and are forced by torture to admit that they have taken Mau Mau oaths (the alleged confessions) and forced to mention some other people's names. After such tortures, such men mention anyone who is immediately arrested and shot either on the spot or taken to the bush and shot there and left to rot away.

"As regards detainees, it is intended to force them to admit that they were oath administrators as well as members of Mau Mau, so that most of them can be convicted . . .

"Raping of women by Askaris is still going on. Money, articles from African shops, and money from the women who have been detained and/or killed are daily being taken by force from Africans."[2]

A most general complaint of Africans was that arrested men, while allegedly being conveyed to a detention camp, were ordered out of the lorry and told to go, but after walking a few steps they were shot in the back.

In exaggerating the terror acts of Africans and making mass arrests the colonialists were guided by economic considerations, too. In Kenya they had introduced more

[1] *Op. cit.*, pp. 104–105.
[2] *Op. cit.*, pp. 105–106.

than half a century before, and had been applying ever since, different forms of forced labour, including the practice of hiring African detainees for work.[1] The Mau Mau affair now came in handy for forcing thousands of Africans to do gratuitous labour. Barely a few days after the introduction of the state of emergency, in October 1952, Governor BARING announced in the Legislative Council that as soon as the required number of detainees would be available the prison authority would convey more Africans to the various detentions camps for the purpose of forced labour "to the economic advantage of the Colony". He soon translated words into deeds: thousands of Africans were dispatched to construct huge airfields. One such airfield was built on the seabord near Lamu, and another eight miles from Nairobi (Embakasi). The latter ("the first hand-made airfield of the world") covers an area of two square miles with four runways, and its construction required of African workers, equipped with only spades and hammers and directed by armed guards, to move a million tons of earth and half a million tons of rock.

On September 1, 1954, upon his return home from a visit to London, TOM MBOYA gave a news conference. In his statement to the press he drew the attention of the authorities to the conditions of the families of the men held for "screening" as Mau Mau suspects. Such families were in most cases removed from their homes and sent back to the reserves, where they had no way of supporting themselves. "The children were found", he said, "wandering into the markets, looking for food, and sleeping in empty houses."[2]

A Provocative Statement by Governor Baring

On October 20, 1953, Governor BARING made the following statement in the Legislative Council: "It is felt that some striking action should be taken against the few villainous leaders of the Mau Mau movement. For this reason a Bill will shortly be introduced providing for the forfeiture of land held in the Kikuyu land unit by two classes of persons. First, those convicted of certain serious offences connecting the offenders with the direction of the Mau Mau movement and, secondly, any still at large who might be declared subject to the provisions of the Bill — that is in practice the best known gang leaders now opposing the forces of law and order."[3]

At the same time he announced "other security measures", namely an expansion of the armed forces stationed in the territory, and the intensification of the military operations against Mau Mau. Characteristically, the following day General ERSKINE, Commander of the British forces in Kenya, said that he saw no military answer to Kenya's troubles. The problem was, he said, "purely political — how Europeans, Africans and Asians can live in harmony on a long-term basis. If the people of Kenya

---

[1] The African was obliged to work for nothing 90 days a year. For failure to do so he got 6 months in jail or was fined $14 to $70. The British compelled 750,000 to 1,000,000 men, women and children to leave their homes and settle in other places to do work in forest clearance, on road and other constructions. In addition to the 29 existing jails they established a number of detention camps which hired Africans out for work. There were 32 such camps with 8,431 detainees in 1930, and 47 camps with 18,247 inmates in 1951. The prison authorities' income from the hiring of African labour was £14,851 in 1938 and £74,118 in 1951. Besides, the detainees had to do paid work, for a few pennies, on road construction and other public works.

[2] PADMORE, *op. cit.*, p. 258.

[3] *Op. cit.*, p. 256.

could address themselves to this problem and find a solution they would have achieved far more than I could do with security forces".[1]

The Dirty War of British Imperialism in Kenya

The Kenya settlers identified themselves with the extreme anti-African mentality of the South African racialists. In the slightest easing of the conditions of Africans they saw undue "appeasement", a threat to their own interests, and their constant pressure upon the colonial administration resulted in the passage of the 1952 anti-African laws.

The British administration adopted this terror legislation under the pressure of settlerdom, but the settlers were still not satisfied, they wanted more: a direct attack on the Africans, meaning to deprive them of every opportunity of political organization. Their demand was heeded, the British administration banned the Kenya African Union. The settlers grew bolder. They found the time had come to get the British government to fulfil their old dream of turning Kenya into "white man's country" on the model of the Union of South Africa. And the settler-dominated colonial administration, on the pretext of the state of emergency declared to protect law and order, got a veritable terror campaign launched against the Africans. This action soon grew into large-scale formal military operations, a veritable colonial war. In these military actions conducted against unorganized Kikuyu masses which were unarmed or equipped at most with primitive weapons, the British authorities deployed, besides the local police force and the Kenya regiment of white settlers, more than 30,000 British troops and about 50,000 Kikuyu fighters enlisted under duress in the "King's African Rifles" and the "Kikuyu Home Guards". These were regarded as traitors by the majority of the Kikuyu. By forcing them to take up arms against their own tribesmen, the government provoked the bloodiest events of the disturbances going on for years: the so-called "Lari bloodshed"; to revenge for the treason the Kikuyu in March 1954 massacred several hundred such traitors in the Lari district.

British company commanders started a veritable man-hunt after the Kikuyu: they awarded the soldiers who killed the largest number of Africans in a single action.

The colonial authorities, to break any communication between town leaders and the rural masses, arrested 50,000 Kikuyu in Nairobi and deported them (this was called "Operation Anvil").

The dirty war on the Kikuyu cost Britain £1 million every month in 1954.

The British colonialists and their advocates hypocritically asserted that serious punishments were imposed upon soldiers and officers who used violence and committed excesses against African captives. A true admirer of British colonialism, the American writer JOHN GUNTHER, made this enthusiastic comment on such a case: "One British officer was sentenced to five years in jail for torturing suspects. It is a substantial tribute to English character that in the midst of a crisis which tore everybody's nerves to bits, the few Britons who lost their heads and behaved badly were promptly punished by British courts."

This generalization was proved wrong by evidence collected by R. PANKHURST.

A British court martial in Nairobi tried the case of Captain G. S. L. GRIFFITHS on November 24–27, 1952. It was proved at the trial that the captain had killed

[1] *Op. cit.*, p. 257.

and ordered to kill countless Africans detained on the suspicion of terrorism, and that he had offered his men money rewards for every African killed, that he instructed them to kill anybody whose skin was black. Despite this, the captain was acquitted.[1]

On December 16, 1952, the Governor made a statement promising that the policemen guilty of atrocities would be severely punished. Barely two weeks later a police inspector was committed to trial for having killed eight Africans on his own. The court qualified the act as "justifiable homicide" and acquitted the defendant.

False Witnesses and Falsifiers of History

In describing the Mau Mau affairs as a provocation by the British imperialists, we do not deny the acts of violence committed by the oppressed African masses in the early fifties. We do not claim that those events were invented by the British, but we do claim — because it is the truth — that the facts were falsified and over-dramatized. Just like the case of the ritual murders in Basutoland. Just as there, here also thousands of innocent people were killed and tens of thousands were imprisoned. Both the mass movements stirred by the despair of suffering Africans and the independence movement advocating non-violence were blamed for aims which they did not promote and methods which they did not employ. The British imperialists did that in order to be able to make other African peoples and world public opinion believe that their deeds of horror and rule of terror were legitimate reprisals.

The principal falsifier, of course, was the British government itself. Signal evidence of this was, first of all, the KENYATTA trial, which can convince anybody of the British government's bad faith and of KENYATTA's innocence.[2]

For nearly ten years the British government found it better to keep silent on the Mau Mau affair. Until 1960 hardly anything had been made public in official documents. A large number of books, pamphlets and articles on the Mau Mau affair appeared from the pen of "private individuals" — mostly British settlers in Kenya. Some of these persons were themselves active participants in the heinous acts committed by the police and the colonial authorities. (For example, L. S. B. LEAKEY, the son of a missionary, who had grown up among the Kikuyus, spoke their language well, rated as an expert on Kikuyu tribal customs and laws, served as an intelligence officer in World War II, and was an official interpreter at the trial of KENYATTA in 1952; WILLIAM W. BALDWIN, an American adventurer in the pay of the Kenya police; Police Superintendent IAN HENDERSON, a British settler in Kenya, who acted as *agent provocateur* and was a star witness for the prosecution in the KENYATTA trial,[3] and many others.) Other such authors were settlers who concerned themselves with their own material interests and privileged positions, regarded the Africans as inferior beings, and thought it fit to back the anti-African policy of the government and help to hush up the atrocities perpetrated by the colonial authorities. (For example, Kenya settler C. T. STONEHAM, who originally was a hunter and stayed in the Union of South Africa for years following World War I, after returning to Kenya set up business and became famous for his cruel treatment of the Kikuyu

[1] For details, see PANKHURST, *op. cit.*, pp. 106–109.
[2] See M. SLATER, *The Trial of Jomo Kenyatta*, London, 1955.
[3] SLATER, *op. cit.*, pp. 93–96.

porters; missionary Bishop WALTER CARY; farmer J. F. LIPSCOMB, etc., etc.) Their works are typical instances of false testimony and falsification of history.[1]

It was only years later, in 1960, that the British government decided to release an official paper on the Mau Mau affair. The Colonial Secretary in May 1960 presented to Parliament his report entitled *Historic Survey of the Origins and Growth of Mau Mau*. The report was prepared between October 1957 and August 1959 by a colonial official, F. D. CORFIELD, who for over thirty years (since 1925) had filled various diplomatic and military functions in the service of the British government. The assignment he received on October 17, 1957, was

"To examine and report to H.E. the Governor on —

"*(a)* the origin and growth of *Mau Mau*, including the circumstances which permitted the movement to develop so rapidly without the full knowledge of the Government;

"*(b)* any deficiencies which made themselves apparent in the Government machine."[2]

It was not by chance that the government had not resolved to start an investigation until 1957 and that the report had not been made public until 1960. As early as December 1953, and again in December 1955, Captain BRIGGS, a settler politician, had proposed in the Legislative Council the conduct of such an inquiry. On both occasions the colonial administration refused on the ground that it was not time yet to conduct such an inquiry because the state of emergency was still effective. This position of the administration was understandable, since the proposal of the right-wing settlers was directed against the government. Not that the settlers kept the African interests in view and wanted to shed light upon the misdeeds of the government and the authorities. On the contrary: they charged the government and the authorities with having failed to act against the rebelling Africans on time and energetically enough.

Why the government changed its mind in 1957 is also understandable. The reason was twofold: (1) On many occasions in 1956, and again in June 1957, the settlers urged an investigation in the Legislative Council, and world events (aggression on Egypt, independence of the Sudan and Ghana) impelled the British government to calm down the oppositionism of the settlers; (2) under the impact of the same events the British government saw it necessary that the institution of an inquiry should appease world public opinion angry about the "dirty war" waged in Kenya.

The British government got the inquiry started in October 1957 but was still hesitating for the time being over the publication of the report. On November 11, 1958, the Chief Secretary of the colonial government, questioned by Captain BRIGGS in the Legislative Council, stated that the government could not promise to let the report be discussed in public, "because although it is the intention of the Government

[1] Cf. L. S. B. LEAKEY, *Mau Mau and the Kikuyu*, London, 1952; PATRICK MONKHOUSE. "The Mau Mau in Kenya", *Manchester Guardian*, 12, 17, 18, 20 and 24 November 1952; C. T. STONEHAM, *Mau Mau*, London, 1953; W. CARY, *Crisis in Kenya*, London, 1953; ANNETTE ROSENTIEL, "An Anthropological Approach to the Mau Mau Problem", *Political Science Quaterly*, Vol. 68, No. 3 (September 1953), pp. 419–432; J. C. CAROTHERS, *The Psychology of Mau Mau*, Nairobi, 1954; L. S. B. LEAKEY, *Defeating Mau Mau*, London, 1954; C. T. STONEHAM, *Out of Barbarism*, London, 1955; J. F. LIPSCOMB, *White Africans*, London, 1955; W. BALDWIN, *Mau Mau Man Hunt*, New York, 1957; I. HENDERSON, *Man Hunt in Kenya*, New York, 1958.

[2] *Historic Survey of the Origins and Growth of Mau Mau*, p. 1.

that the Report should be in a form which could properly be published it may not necessarily be in the public interest to do so."[1]

A year later, on November 19, 1959 (when the report had been before the government for three months), the Chief Secretary, in reply to a question by BRIGGS, said that "as soon as the Government had had time to consider the Report it would be published".[2]

In 1960 further independent states emerged in Africa (Cameroun, Togo), and a number of others were on the eve of independence. The British government did not hesitate any longer: it published the report — after omitting or redrafting parts of it.[3]

The report served a twofold purpose: to calm down the settlers and to appease world public opinion (primarily in the newly independent African states). The means to this end was one and the same: slandering the Africans, falsifying the facts, exaggerating the terror acts committed by Africans, and covering up the bloody atrocities perpetrated by the government, the authorities, the police and troops. But although the government — and upon its instructions the author — did everything possible to present the facts in a favourable light,[4] this masterpiece of a falsification of history provides the scholars capable of reading between the lines with ample material to prove that what took place in Kenya during the 1950's was, on the one hand, a desperate and as yet misdirected independence struggle waged by the oppressed and exploited African tribes and, on the other hand, a large-scale manoeuvre of provocation and a bloody colonial war of aggression carried on by the British colonialists.

The Causes and the Essence of Mau Mau

The essence of the Mau Mau affair and the real causes of the continued terrorism of the Kikuyu were truthfully, pertinently and briefly summed up by G. PADMORE as follows:

"There is no doubt that the die-hard European settlers, aided and abetted by certain British officials and their influential friends in Britain, are the people really responsible for the present state of unrest in Kenya. The very term *Mau Mau* was invented by the settlers' Press to discredit the popular African leaders and justify

---

[1] *Op. cit.*, p. 291.

[2] *Ibid.*

[3] Cf. CORFIELD's preface to the report.

[4] Characteristic of the "conscientiousness" and "objectivity" of the author of the report is that, by his own account, he relied mostly on information received from a colonial official of the name of RYLAND and on the above-mentioned works typifying the falsifications of history, among them mainly the two books by L. S. B. LEAKEY. (Cf. pp. 5–6 of the report.) As regards the second task of the inquiry (that concerning the government machine), it is a striking fact that the author devoted to this matter only two of the sixteen chapters of his report, namely 20 pages out of 321 (Chapters XII–XIII, pp. 235–254). Even there he was trying hard to find excuses for the violations of law by the authorities instead of exposing their provocations and acts of terrorism. However, his endeavour misfired, since by trying to excuse the misdeeds of the authorities he himself acknowledged those facts. Only one instance of the lot: To the author's submission, under English law nobody can be convicted on the ground of the testimonies of his accomplices without appropriate evidence in support, yet, in the author's opinion, the Kenya authorities could not observe this rule because, "As it was estimated that at least 80 per cent of the Kikuyu had taken the Mau Mau oath . . . and they were all therefore potential accomplices in any Mau Mau crime, the strict application of this rule increased immeasureably the difficulty of the police in obtaining convictions."

the white man's legalized terror against a once peaceful and long-suffering people. Long before the world outside Kenya ever heard of Mau Mau, the Africans were beginning and praying the British Government for help and deliverance from the white settlers' rule. They did so through what restricted constitutional means were open to them . . ."[1]

"Although the name has never been satisfactorily defined, as no such word as 'Mau Mau' exists in the Kikuyu language, its socio-economic causes are easier to explain. Mau Mau is not an organized political movement with a regular membership, officers and constitution like the Kenya African Union. It is a spontaneous revolt of a declassed section of the African rural population, uprooted from its tribal lands and driven into urban slum without any hope of gainful employment, due to the absence of an Industrial Revolution able to absorb them as proletarians. All the pseudo-anthropological assertions about Mau Mau being a 'religion', is sheer nonsense. Mau Mau hymn singing and oath taking are merely psychological devices borrowed by desperate young men from freemasonry and missionary sources to bind their adherents to their cause. In trying to elevate Mau Mau into a 'religion' and ascribing obscene practices to them, the whites hope to shift all responsibility for what has happened upon the Africans and explain it all as a sudden reversion to savagery, which demands their continued presence in Kenya to bring the Africans back on the path of civilization."[2]

"Under the guise of establishing the Queen's peace, the Kikuyu fighters for land and bread are being exterminated in order to provide *lebensraum* for a few thousand British colonists."[3]

"European settlers, like the French *colons* in North Africa, are the real opponents of inter-racial co-operation and partnership. They are the ones who deserve our condemnation, not the Arabs and Africans."[4]

J. GUNTHER sums up the fundamental reasons for Mau Mau as follows:

"1. Feeling among the Kikuyus (right or wrong) that they had been defrauded of their land.

"2. The squatter system, and overcrowding on the reserves. Forty per cent of agricultural Kikuyus are landless.

"3. Detribalization, and the miserable uprooted lives led by the new urban proletariat in Nairobi close to the reserves.

"4. Religious factors [?] . . .

"5. The growth of an African educated class, which gave leadership to the disgruntled masses.

"6. Above all, the injustices of color bar."[5]

In another place GUNTHER describes the African grievances as follows: "When we were in Nairobi Africans could not:

"1. Buy a drink of hard liquor.

"2. Go out at night without a pass.

"3. Carry arms.

"4. Assemble publicly or privately, even in groups of three or four, or listen to their leaders.

"5. Buy land in the White Highlands.

[1] PADMORE (1956), p. 242.
[2] *Op. cit.*, p. 247.
[3] *Op. cit.*, p. 255.
[4] *Op. cit.*, p. 265.
[5] JOHN GUNTHER, *Inside Africa*, New York, 1953, pp. 372-373.

"6. Grow coffee or sisal, except under certain restrictions. (The Africans say that the British imposed this ban to keep coffee and sisal prices up.)

"7. Go to 'white' restaurants, night clubs, movies, and the like, or use a European public toilet.

"8. Put on their own dances . . ., or give playlets traditional to tribal life.

"9. Vote.

"Grievances over education, low wages and intolerably bad housing conditions existed of course long before the Mau Mau emergency, but have become intensified. One sore point has been that Africans in the civil service get only three-fifths of the pay of whites for the same work."[1]

Lyttelton's Constitution of 1954

In 1954 Colonial Secretary LYTTELTON introduced a constitutional reform. This reform did not affect the composition of the legislature, but replaced the Executive Council by a Council of Ministers which had, in addition to the Governor and the Deputy Governor, six official and eight unofficial members: three elected Europeans, two elected Asians and one appointed African, plus two nominated European members. The Africans demanded at least two ministerial places, but the settlers protested and the African demand was rejected. Thereupon ELIUD MATHU, the senior African member of the Legislative Council and the only African on the Executive Council, resigned. (Finally another African, J. B. OHANGA, was persuaded to accept a ministerial place.)

Part of the settlers found even this minor concession too much, and this "reform" led to a split among the Europeans. Those who accepted the reform founded the United Country Party, led by MICHAEL BLUNDELL, for long years the leader and spokesman of the European Electors' Union. Those who were opposed to the reform, because they openly advocated "white supremacy" and were against African participation in government, aligned themselves in the Federal Independence Party. As regards the two new parties, PADMORE made this pertinent remark:

"The latter party is unashamedly for 'white supremacy' and more honest than Mr. Blundell and his followers. For the United Country Party, while it ostensibly supports multi-racial co-operation, limits its membership to Europeans only. 'The Party may open its membership to Africans and other non-Europeans when the multi-racial nation has been achieved,' declared Blundell. This astounding piece of political humbug is a testament to the paradox in which racial arrogance has caught up the white settlers of Kenya. Even their so-called liberal leader, Blundell, is unable to extricate himself from the *Herrenvolk* doctrine which he has himself helped to create."[2]

The "Reforms" Proposed by the British Government in 1955–56

Considering the mounting discontent of the Africans, the British government found it necessary to make some concession to subdue the unrest. Since 1953, when African political organizations were banned, Africans were forced to organize under-

---

[1] *Op. cit.*, p. 376. The author concludes his remarks in the following terms: "No solution is possible for Kenya's troubles without African participation. The dream, held by some Britons, of making it a white supremacy state in perpetuity, is gone forever."

[2] PADMORE, *op. cit.*, p. 261.

ground. In June 1955 the colonial government eased the ban, permitting African parties to operate at the district level, except in the Central Province, where a nominated Council of Loyalists was permitted to function. In the same year a one-member commission (WALTER COUTTS) was appointed to work out an appropriate election system under which African members of the legislature should be elected, not appointed. COUTTS drafted a plural voting system in which suffrage was subject to a number of qualifications (property, education, etc.), and the elector had one, two or three votes according as he had one or more qualifications. The government accepted this proposal in the hope that under this system the elected African members would come from among the well-to-do and educated upper class of Africans who might be expected to be moderate and loyal to the government. But while COUTTS proposed that the system should be applied for the election of all members (Europeans included) of the Legislative Council, that is he designed the proposed reform as a democratic measure, the government applied it to Africans alone. Of course, the Africans regarded it as another device of serious racial discrimination, because the European suffrage was not subject to any qualification whatever.

The most extreme elements of the settlers joined neither of the two parties, but rallied in a separate group led by Captain BRIGGS.

In the 1956 legislative elections six members of BLUNDELL's party and eight members of BRIGG's right-wing group were elected.

In the elections two candidates from the recently formed Capricorn Society also stood for election. Since, however, they demanded the elimination of racial discrimination, they were defeated because none of the three settler groups voted for them.

In October 1956 the government complied with the 1954 demand of the Africans for another ministerial place, and at the beginning of 1957 it raised the African membership of the Legislative Council from six to eight.

The British government hoped that the 1954 constitutional reform and the lifting of the ban on political organizations would help to calm down the disgruntled Africans. As we shall see below, this hope was in vain. In permitting local parties to operate the British government applied the traditional tactical principle of "divide and rule" to weaken the Africans. In the absence of national parties, the local organizations were guided practically only by tribal and local interests. Small local parties were mushrooming, which, being organizations licensed and controlled by the government, could not lead a real political struggle for the African rights, while a large scope was given to the arbitrary rule of local leaders — mostly chiefs and government-supporting "loyalists" — who, being free from control by higher authorities and receiving no programme or instructions from above, directed their organizations in accordance with their own interests and considerations. However, the most politically conscious tribe, the Kikuyu, whose national party had been banned in 1953, did not cease to wage their underground struggle. Notably they formed the *Kiama kia Muingi* (People's Party), which made efforts to organize a passive resistance campaign.

The election of the eight African legislators took place in March 1957. Those Africans, mostly Kikuyu, who could not verify that they had been loyal at the time of the government actions against Mau Mau, were not allowed to register to vote. For lack of national parties and a uniform programme, the electoral campaign was characterized by tribal quarrels and rivalries between chiefs, and was concerned with problems and demands of local interest with no regard to national affairs. In spite of this the government expected in vain that the plurality of vote would

help to send "moderate" Africans to the Legislative Council: all candidates campaigned against the 1954 constitution and the Coutts electoral system, and the
newly elected members were those professing the most radical views.

The Lennox-Boyd Constitution

In 1957 Lennox-Boyd, the new Colonial Secretary, went to Kenya and discussed
further constitutional reforms with representatives of the settlers and Africans. His
mission was a failure because the Africans refused to talk about reform unless their
demand for appropriate parliamentary representation was fulfilled, while the settlers
disagreed with any increase in African representation. In default of agreement,
the Colonial Secretary ordered the new constitution to be introduced.

Under this reform the number of elected African members was raised from 8 to
14, that of Europeans also to 14, and that of Asians to 8; besides, the Legislative
Council, in which representatives of all three racial groups had seats, should elect
an additional 12 members: 4 Europeans, 4 Africans and 4 Asians ("specially elected
members" or "crossbench members"). The reform set up a so-called Council of State
composed of members to be appointed by the Governor to consider racially discriminatory Legislation and to report to the Colonial Secretary.

Lennox-Boyd said that British control over Kenya would be maintained and
the racial proportion of the seats in the Legislative Council should remain for at
least ten years.

The settlers were strongly in favour of this "constitution" because it secured the
European majority in the legislature, although it meant a bit of progress for Africans,
but the Africans in general categorically opposed it. They demanded the abandonment of the Council of State and of "crossbench members", the raising of the number
of African elected members from 14 to 23, that is an African majority against the
14 European and 8 Asian elected members. They demanded also that the composition
of the Council of Ministers be changed accordingly and Kenya eventually become a
democratic state with universal franchise, and that a constitutional conference be
convened immediately on the basis of consultation with all groups of the population.

The additional six African members under the new constitution were elected in
1958. On this occasion Eliud Mathu was defeated by Julius Kiano who also was
a Kikuyu. The election of the "crossbench members" took place in April of the same
year.

The elected settler representatives and some of the nominated European members
offered the Africans and Asians mutual support for their respective candidates,
but both the Africans and the Asians refused.

The African-elected Africans and some of the Asian members were against the
election of "special" members. The African members declared that any African who
stood for a "special seat" was "a traitor to the African cause", and called upon the
African population to boycott such candidates politically, economically and socially.
Despite this there were Africans who broke the boycott: the first to take part in
the election to "special seats" was Musa Amalemba, a Muluya, followed by seven
others, four of whom were elected. (Amalemba even accepted a portfolio, thus violating the boycott of the Executive Council.)

The 1958 elections clearly demonstrated that the Africans were right to reject
the British lies about the "inter-racial character of the elections", because the election
results were decided by an artificially created European majority.

Characteristically, the only European who had the confidence of Africans, ex-Minister of Finance ERNEST VASEY, when standing for a special seat, was defeated by the Europeans and could enter the legislature only as a nominated member.

After the elections the African elected members maintained their opposition to the constitution and refused to take part in the government, but the "crossbench members" accepted various governmental posts, and they formed an association of their own as opposed to the Elected Members' Organization. At the first meeting of the newly elected Legislative Council the Governor in his inaugural address announced that the British government had rejected the African demands. The African elected members became so enraged that they walked out in protest against the Governor's person and the composition of the Legislative Council. Afterwards they remained absent from the deliberations until April 1959, when the Colonial Secretary made known that the constitutional conference would be convened in January 1960.

New Parties (C.E.M.O., K.N.P., K.I.M.)

All the African elected members of the Legislative Council, often with the participation of Arabs and Asians and one European (S. V. COOKE), worked together in the Constituency Elected Members' Organization (C.E.M.O.). They continued boycotting the Council of Ministers and demanded that a constitutional conference should work out new reforms (democratic government, African majorities in the Legislative and Executive Councils, progress towards independence). Later they started a boycott of the Legislative Council, too, and conducted a countrywide propaganda campaign for the release of KENYATTA who, having served his prison sentence, was still kept in detention.

Discussions took place within C.E.M.O. about the establishment of a united nation-wide political party, but the plan failed for various reasons: mutual suspicion between the scattered, politically backward rural tribes and the more progressive urbanized tribes (Kikuyu, Luo), and constant rivalry between their leaders. What C.E.M.O. as a whole failed to achieve was accomplished by many of its African members together with all Indians and Arabs and one European (COOKE): in May 1959 they formed the Kenya National Party (K.N.P.).

The primary purpose of the party was to unite all race groups in the struggle for democracy and independence, and it voiced moderate demands accordingly. It demanded independence by as late as 1968, "a democratic Kenya nation" and a common electoral roll, with African majorities in the legislature and the Council of Ministers, a parliament with a Lower House and an Upper House, the continuance of some nominated seats and seats reserved for minority groups in the Legislative Council and the Council of Ministers. The Chairman of the party was MULIRO,[1]

---

[1] MASINDE MULIRO, son of a Muluya peasant, was born in the Elgon district in 1922. He was educated in Uganda and at Cape Town University where he took courses in philosophy, pedagogics and history. In 1954 he returned to Kenya and taught first in a Kikuyu girls' school and then in a teacher's training school. In 1957 he was elected Legco member for Northern Nyanza. In May 1959 he was a member of the interparty delegation which urged the British Colonial Secretary to convene a constitutional conference.

a Muluya; its Vice-Chairman the only European member, COOKE, its Secretary NGALA,[1] and its Treasurer ARVIND JAMIDAR, an Indian.

The K.N.P. programme was too radical for the Europeans and too moderate for the vast majority of Africans. The followers of a more consistent African policy soon broke with the K.N.P., and they formed, with the participation of MBOYA, ODINGA and KIANO, the Kenya Independence Movement (K.I.M.) under the chairmanship of TOM MBOYA. K.I.M. demanded general elections, the suppression of all nominated and "specially elected" seats, the reduction of the number of seats reserved for minority groups, and immediate responsible government by the party that won the general elections. It demanded furthermore the opening of the White Highlands to Africans and the possibility for Africans to settle in the area as well as a stop to European immigration. It demanded compulsory eight-year school education for African children and the integration of European and African schools. It declared in its statement of policy: "African freedom will be achieved only through African nationalism. We refuse to sacrifice our nationalism for vague and deceptive non-racialism or multi-racialism, designed to deflect the African from his rightful goal — that Kenya must be free and independent."

In 1959 the Kenya government lifted the ban on nationwide political parties so that it allowed such parties to function as long as they were "multi-racial" in composition, that is, they had to admit European and Asian members as well. (This was not obligatory for the exclusive European and Asian parties.) The K.N.P. was allowed as a "multi-racial" party, but the K.I.M. application was rejected in September 1959. Thereafter the K.I.M. members pursued their activities within the People's Convention Party, which MBOYA had founded in Nairobi at the beginning of 1959, and which was officially recognized as a district organization.

The K.N.P. was under strong attack from K.I.M. and the African majority for its opportunism and multi-racialism, and its application for membership in P.A.F.M.E.C.A. was rejected at K.I.M. instigation. This fact and the differences arising within the party (mainly in respect of the land question) between Africans and Asians, as well as the realization that a united African front would be necessary at the forthcoming constitutional conference in London, led the K.N.P. leaders to adopt a more radical position and to enter into contact with K.I.M. This was done in November 1959: the K.N.P. joined K.I.M. and the two parties formed the African Elected Members' Organization to present a united front at the London conference. The K.N.P. maintained its separate organization and in December it ousted its non-African members.

Among the Indians living in Kenya (Hindus and Sikhs as well as Muslims) there were adherents of more radical and more moderate policies, but they agreed almost unanimously on the fundamental African demands, and their basic organization, the Kenya Indian Congress,, supported the Kenya Independence Movement in almost every point.

---

[1] RONALD GIDEON NGALA, a carpenter's son from the Giriama tribe, was born in Mombasa in 1922. He went to Kikuyu primary and secondary schools and took his teacher's degree at Makerere College in Uganda. He taught from 1946 to 1952 and was principal in Kenya schools (Kifili, Mbale, Mombasa) from 1952 to 1956. In 1956 he went to London for a course in pedagogics, then returned to Kenya to become school inspector in the Mombasa district. At the same time he was engaged in politics: In 1953 he became a member of the Mombasa African Advisory Body; in 1954 he was nominated to the Municipal Council of Mombasa; in 1957 he was elected a member of the Coast Regional Assembly. He was one of the delegation which in 1957 went to London to ask the British government to introduce a new constitution.

In May 1959 BLUNDELL, by arrangement with the government, formed the New Kenya Party (N.K.P.) with the support of half the European elected members, most of the unofficial nominated members and all the specially elected members. But since the party, despite the liberal speeches of BLUNDELL, did not support the major African demands (a common electoral roll, the opening of the White Highlands to non-Europeans), none of the African and Asian elected members joined the party; on the other hand, BLUNDELL's vocal liberalism and his overdone loyalty to the British government's policy were a warning to a part of the settlers: the party's policy statement adopted in June, for example, was signed only with reservations by ten of the European elected members.

In August 1959 BRIGG's right-wing group and the extreme rightist Progressive Local Government Party[1] merged to form the United Party. This new party published a statement proposing the abolition of the Legislative Council which, in its opinion, was entirely irrelevant since the government had an absolute majority in it, and suggested instead the establishment of regional assemblies, extension of the powers of the local authorities, and a central inter-racial consultative assembly to discuss the legislative measures with the government. The statement stressed that British colonial rule in Kenya would last a long time, and so an African majority government was out of the question in the foreseeable future. Finally it took a stand for "separate development" of the Africans. With this extreme anti-African policy BRIGGS succeeded in inducing a considerable part of the N.K.P. membership to join the United Party.

The settlers had still another liberal party, the Kenya Party formed by the Capricorn Society. This party embraced also some demands of the Africans (a separate constitutional chapter on "personal rights", African representation at par with the aggregate of European and Asian members, 24 to 12 + 12, and a common electoral roll), but at the same time: (1) its programme still accepted reserved seats for Europeans and Asians, (2) it contemplated responsible government for Kenya only by 1966, and (3) it admitted only European members. For a time a leading role in the party was played by ex-Minister of Finance ERNEST VASEY, who had the confidence of Africans, but in November 1959 he accepted the post of Minister of Finance in Tanganyika and left the country. After his departure the activity of the party considerably declined.

The Kenya Conference in January–February 1960

The British government had made careful preparations for the constitutional conference convened in January 1960. In December 1959 Colonial Secretary MACLEOl visited Kenya and talked with African political leaders. The latter, irrespective of party affiliations, demanded the unconditional release of KENYATTA and independence for Kenya in 1960. MACLEOD assured them that the British government's firm intention was to lead the country to independence, and that the ways and means of the solution would be worked out at the coming constitutional conference with the participation of the Kenya parties. His effort to influence the mood of Africans is characterized by the following event. During MACLEOD's stay in Nairobi Africans

---

[1] The former Federal Independence Party under a new name.

and Indians clashed in street battles, as a result of which one Indian died and more than thirty suffered injuries. The Colonial Secretary said in this connection: "Any kind of violence is regrettable. In this case, however, it is clear that the disturbances were not premeditated or organized."

In the first half of January, obviously upon instructions from above, several measures were taken to impress the African delegates preparing for the conference. On January 7, police inspector PASCOE of Nakura was sentenced to six months in jail for having detained an African, before this went to trial, in the station house from May to November. On January 12 the Governor issued an order terminating the state of emergency declared on account of the Mau Mau affair seven years before. The restrictions on the freedom of movement of members of the Kikuyu, Embu and Meru tribes and the repressive pass laws were repealed. Also the licensing of printing presses and the special powers of the authorities to seize "unlicensed publications" were revoked. Governor RENISON told the press in this connection: "We have now been given a real possibility of turning our thoughts from past tragedies towards future problems. This is the best possible prelude to our constitutional conference. I hope this conference will prelude our combined realistic efforts enabling us to shape a Kenya nation, in which there will be room for all peoples of Kenya."

The conference was convened for January 18. Participating in the conference held at Lancaster House were a joint delegation of Africans led by NGALA, and MBOYA, two delegations of European settlers (the New Kenya Party headed by BLUNDELL, and BRIGG's extremist United Party), as well as representatives of the Asian-Arab bloc. The Africans requested that KENYATTA be released immediately and permitted to participate, but their request was rejected.

Right at the outset the conference came up against difficulties. The delegations were entitled to make use of the services of advisers. The Africans' adviser was an American Negro lawyer, THURGOOD MARSHALL, and they intended to invite as second adviser PETER MBIYU KOINANGE, the eminent exiled fighter of the Kenya Independence Movement. The British government refused to consent on the ground that KOINANGE had been KENYATTA's close associate in the Kenya African Union and had been exiled for having been implicated in the events of the early fifties (Mau Mau!). The African delegates threatened to leave the conference if they were not allowed to invite KOINANGE. It was no use, and the meeting was opened, but with no Africans participating, and so the conference could not get under way. MACLEOD finally proposed a compromise solution: KOINANGE should be furnished with an admission pass to Lancaster House but not to the conference chamber, and his presence would be officially ignored. The Africans agreed.

After two weeks of wrangling the deliberations started at last. On February 1 MACLEOD in his opening address declared that the government's aim was to draw up a constitution which would make it possible for the Africans to obtain the majority both in the legislature and in the government, and the final goal was independence for Kenya under African majority rule (he added: "I hope within the Commonwealth") by ensuring that all racial groups of the population might live in Kenya participating in public life. Then he outlined the preconditions of this double goal: Kenya could become independent provided that Africans as well as other communities in Kenya took a share in the government of the country, and the government was responsible to a legislature reflecting the various opinions expressed by the people in general elections held on the basis of "one man, one vote"; finally all ethnic groups should have the opportunity to participate in the administrative apparatus in the spirit of mutual understanding, and for this end the interests of minorities should be protected by constitutional safeguards.

He emphasized that the task of the conference was only to plan the first step in the constitutional development of Kenya, but the right of decision was reserved for the British government.

The right-wing United Party, which stubbornly clung to the colonial regime and the white settlers' rule and would not even hear of African majority, indignantly rejected the principles put forth by the government. It refused to discuss on this basis and walked out of the conference chamber. (However, it again attended the plenary meetings a few days later.) The other delegations started discussing, for the time being, in committees and unofficial gatherings.

Three committees were formed. One dealt with the problem of extending the suffrage and with the composition of the legislative body, the second with the composition and powers of the government to be formed, and the third with the constitutional safeguards of the individual and minority rights.

The Africans, who wanted Kenya to win independence still in 1960, demanded the introduction of universal suffrage on the basis of "one man, one vote" and a cabinet with a majority of African ministers responsible to the legislature; they were ready to reserve a limited number of seats in the legislature for the racial minorities.

The New Kenya Party agreed to the gradual extension of the suffrage and the principle of African majority, but insisted on the institution of "specially elected members" of the Legislative Council. Part of the Asians backed the African demands, but their majority stood halfway between the Africans and the New Kenya Party.

Talks in committees and in private went on for weeks. The delegations agreed on several points, but they still disagreed on a series of important issues ("specially elected members", composition of the government, details of the safeguards of minority rights).

It appeared that the conference would close without results when MACLEOD, on February 12, to break the deadlock, made certain proposals, based on the growing mutual understanding of the various groups, for principles to govern the elections to the Legislative Council and the composition of the government. In fact, he only summed up the points on which there was agreement and on which there was not, and declared that the new constitution would be drawn up in the course of the year with due consideration to all agreements and disagreements; it would considerably extend the franchise (every African able to read and write, or holding an office, or having a yearly income of £ 70 at least, would be entitled to vote in the elections to be held early in 1961) and ensure African majority in the Legislative Council, while maintaining representation for the European and Asian minorities out of proportion to their members. Africans would get a few portfolios in the government, but the Council of Ministers would be presided over by the Governor, and the majority would consist of appointed officials and settlers.

The Colonial Secretary's speech and proposals satisfied neither the Africans nor the New Kenya Party. The Africans found the concessions too little. BLUNDELL and his party found them excessive. The Africans just as BLUNDELL were ready, while stressing their reservations, to accept MACLEOD's proposals as a step forward to their goals, but first they hesitated to accept because they feared that their compromising stand would cause them to lose many of their followers. Form this point of view it would have been more advantageous for both parties if the conference had closed without success, and if the compromise constitution had been imposed upon them by order, than that their followers blamed them for the shortcomings of the constitution.

After two days' reflection and further talks, they nevertheless decided to accept MACLEOD's proposals, with some reservations, as the next stage towards independence. When they announced their decision in the plenary meeting of February 15, it seemed there was nothing to prevent the conference from ending in an agreement. Only the BRIGGS group rejected the proposals categorically, but they did not threaten to boycott them.

In the last minute, however, another obstacle was raised to a peaceful conclusion. Disagreement arose again in respect to individual and minority rights. The Africans insisted that cultivated lands might be alienated only against adequate compensation. The settlers, on the other hand, who had occupied the best and most fertile lands of the country (White Highlands), wanted safeguards against any sort of compulsory expropriation. Both settler delegations agreed, because African access to power, in the absence of constitutional safeguards, would inevitably threaten compulsory purchase and compensation. But the delegates of the Africans suffering from land hunger could by no means agree to guaranteeing the integrity of the estates owned by Europeans. However, MACLEOD, who hinted only in general at "land titles" in connection with individual rights, making no distinction between African and European owners, found the way out of this hopeless situation, too. He asked the delegations to "take note" of his ideas of the future of landed property pending an agreed solution of the question.

From the 1960 Conference to the 1961 Elections. K.A.N.U. and K.A.D.U.

As soon as the conference was closed, Governor RENISON stated in London that, considering the good results, he would withdraw the ban on Kenya political parties and study the possibility of lifting the restriction on the freedom of movement of the popular leader, Chief KOINANGE.

On his return to Nairobi MBOYA was received by an enthusiastic crowd of twenty thousand people. He then held a mass meeting in the Nairobi stadium to render account of the London conference. He emphasized the future constitutional provisions intended to favour the Africans. He pointed out that the Europeans and Asians who in the future wished to obtain seats in the new legislative body would have to secure the backing of Africans, too. When he concluded his account he called upon the audience to disperse, but the enthused crowd did not move. The police had to use tear gas and truncheons to scatter the people. A policeman and a demonstrator were injured.

The head of the United Party, BRIGGS, declared on his return home that his party would use "every constitutional means" to defeat the London agreement which, in his view, would lead to an African dictatorship "as in the Sudan and Ghana". He added that his party intended to align against the London agreement all those Africans, Arabs and Asians who disapprove it, and therefore the party would in the future admit non-Europeans among its members. Further on he warned the white settlers not to haste to sell their estates, because there was hope of altering the situation.

The unity the African leaders had shown at the Lancaster House conference was short-lived. The struggle for leadership started. MULIRO wanted to develop his Kenya National Party into a nationwide organization, while MBOYA wanted to form a party of his own, and the radical wing, KIANO and ODINGA, planned a broad-based popular movement without MBOYA. Owing to the disunity of the rivals NGALA managed to assume leadership.

The Africans' entry into the government was dragged out, because MBOYA and MULIRO insisted that they would not co-operate with the government until KENYATTA was freed. After much discussion among the African leaders and with the Governor, they at last reached a compromise. MBOYA and MULIRO stayed out but their lieutenants, KIANO, NGALA and MIUMI, accepted portfolios, and a fourth African, TOWETT, became an assistant minister.

At long last the majority of the African elected members, together with a number of politicians outside the Legislative Council, issued in March a declaration proposing the formation of the Uhuru [Freedom] Party of Kenya "to bring unity of purpose and action, so necessary in a national struggle of any country for freedom and independence".

In the same months they held the constituent meeting at Kiambu with the participation of delegates from thirty political organizations. The party was formed there, but its name was changed to the Kenya African National Union (K.A.N.U.). They unanimously wanted KENYATTA, who was still in detention, to become party president. Since, however, the colonial administration refused to register the new organization as a nationwide party unless they abandoned this scheme, they were compelled to yield. Consequently GICHURU was elected President, ODINGA Vice-President, MBOYA General Secretary and NGALA Treasurer.

This did not yet mean unity either. MULIRO still endorsed the K.N.P. and associated with local leaders in Kalenjin country. He attended their mass meeting in Kapkatet, where they formed the Kalenjin Political Alliance (K.P.A.), which pretended to represent the people of rural Kenya. The Alliance was joined by the "District Associations" set up under MOI in 1959 in Baringo, Kericho, Nandi and Elgeyo, and by the recently formed Masai United Front. In a statement issued at Eldoret on May 21, 1960, the K.P.A. leaders announced that they would not join K.A.N.U. and they invited the smaller tribes to join the Alliance and to develop it into a national party.

NGALA felt a little slighted in K.A.N.U. and did not accept the post of Treasurer. His Coast African People's Union merged with MULIRO's K.P.A., which was willing to surrender the leadership to him. Together, at a joint meeting in June held at Ngong in Masailand, they established the Kenya African Democratic Union (K.A.D.U.). NGALA was elected President of the new party, MULIRO became Deputy President, and MOI filled the post of Secretary.

The parties constituting K.A.D.U. maintained their separate existences. Unlike K.A.N.U. with its strict discipline and centralized leadership, which in principle was against any kind of tribal and personal rivalry, K.A.D.U. was an alliance of various tribal organizations. Personal differences existed also among K.A.N.U. leaders, but those were only differences on principle.[1] The conflict between K.A.N.U. and K.A.D.U. was essentially not a consequence of differences between the tribes affiliated with the latter,[2] nor of personal rivalry among its leaders (as is represented by many bourgeois authors),[3] but it sprang from the difference of their policies.

[1] The two main antagonists, MBOYA and ODINGA, were members of the same tribe (Luo), but the latter belonged to the radical wing and the former to the more moderate group within the party. On August 15, 1960, while in Peking, ODINGA talked about U.S. imperialism threatening all Africa. He said: "Imperialism — collective imperialism — engineered by Washington has tried to crush the independence of the Congo in its infancy. As you know, that conspiracy has failed. It is not only the Congo which is threatened by U.S. imperialism but the whole of Africa. Kenya is greatly threatened by U.S. imperialism."

[2] Though a large number of K.A.N.U. members came from the two great Bantu tribes (Kikuyu and Luo), yet all other Bantu tribes supported the K.A.N.U. policy, while K.A.D.U. was joined by those smaller, mostly pastoral, tribes, other than Bantu, which NGALA had

[3] Cf., e.g. A. J. HUGHES, *East Africa: The Search for Unity*, London, 1963, p. 133.

While K.A.N.U. waged a consistent and intransigent principled fight for independence the K.A.D.U. leaders, aware that the vast majority of the Africans followed the K.A.N.U. policy, strove to obtain the support of the "liberal" wing of the settlers (the New Kenya Party) and pursued an opportunist and moderate policy. While K.A.N.U. consistently stressed the need for unity and equality of all Africans, and demanded a strong, united central government, the K.A.D.U. leaders, taking advantage of the differences and past grievances of the smaller tribes, demanded only minority rights and the division of the country into autonomous tribal districts.

Reaction from the European and Indian Settlers

The London conference created a new situation for the white settlers. It was impossible for them not to see that their privileged position was hopeless. Up to that time also they had viewed with concern the changes occurring all over Africa (independence for the Sudan, Ghana and Guinea; events in the Congo, Uganda, Tanganyika and other countries), but they had believed that, with the aid of their British protectors, they could so much consolidate their political and economic positions that the African masses ruined and oppressed by bloody police terror were scared into helplessness. Now they had to realize that their hopes were collapsing. The London conference convinced them that the British government could be expected to delay only, but not to prevent, the coming to power of the African majority. The settlers' reaction to the new situation was not uniform. Many regarded the future of settlerdom as hopeless, but even those who were not so pessimistic felt for the time being only a great uncertainty, and therefore they decided to leave the country.

They withdrew as much capital as they could from the country,[1] and ever more landowners offered their estates for sale. There began a flow of repatriating settlers to the mother country. New investments in agriculture and industry were reduced to a minimum, and only the most indispensable purchases were made, the labour force in plantations, industrial units and in commerce was cut. As a consequence the market stagnated, unemployment was rising, public revenues diminished, the budget deficit went up, and the administration was compelled to stop all public works. An economic crisis threatened. At the same time the dwindling of job opportunities brought with it an increase in the output of African agricultural production, namely commodity production.

The old aggressiveness of the white settlers in Kenya vanished, the use of force and armed resistance was not even talked of. It happened a single time that a European member of the Legislative Council proposed the organization of settler troops for the event of a repetition in Kenya of the Congo disorders. In reply to this proposal MBOYA said: "It's stupid and unnecessary because what has happened in the Congo cannot happen here. We are better organized because we have passed through

---

managed to mislead with his demagoguery. Only part of a single major Bantu tribe (the Abaluya) supported K.A.D.U., and they were attracted by the personal influence of MULIRO and AMALEMBA. But the tribes affiliated to K.A.N.U. and K.A.D.U. were divided not by tribal but by political differences.

[1] The amount of capital withdrawn between March and November 1960 was estimated at $ 28 million. Large sums were transferred not only to England, but to Switzerland, India and Pakistan.

the mill and our political experience over a long period of years will help us tremendously." The settlers, whose policy had not even thus far been uniform, now split into three groups:

1. CAVENDISH-BENTINCK resigned as Speaker of the Legislative Council, declaring that he was displeased with the trend of events, and formed the Kenya Coalition. The new party opposed the government policy and fought against the constitutional reform and the African aspirations for independence, while clinging to the settler privileges. Close allies of the Coalition were the Convention of Associations and BRIGGS's United Party.

2. BLUNDELL and his "liberal" New Kenya Party were also alarmed at the events turning against the settlers' privileged position. They also saw with anxiety the steady advance of Africans, but they applied a more flexible, double-faced policy. They thought that, with the support of the right-wing "moderate" African elements (K.A.D.U.) and in co-operation with them, they would succeed in dividing the Africans and thus slowing down the developments, that is, blocking the African achievements. BLUNDLEL said that "with imagination and an adjustment in their outlook, the European community can continue to make a major contribution in the economic field and in influencing African political thought through their reserved seats". To the right-wing settlers, who after his return accused him of indulgence towards the African demands, he said that no radical reforms had been accepted, that British control would remain in the Council of Ministers with no African Chief Minister, and that this result was due to the efforts of the New Kenya Party.

3. The Kenya National Farmers' Union (K.N.F.U.) and its leaders, PETER MARRIAN and Lord DELAMERE, were in touch with the Coalition but kept off politics, claiming that their Union was a purely economic organization.

Each of the three groups sent a delegation to London to negotiate with the British government. CAVENDISH-BENTINCK flooded the ministries with the complaints and demands of the settlers. He accused the British government of betraying the Europeans whom it had encouraged to settle in Kenya with brilliant promises. He demanded the slowing down of constitutional progress, greater representation for the settlers in the Legislative Council, separate school education for the European children, indemnity for the white settlers who suffered material losses owing to the reforms, and assurances for the future of white civil servants.

All he achieved with his action was that Kenya's already weak credit on the London money market was sinking further. BLUNDELL, to rehabilitate Kenya's weakening credit, turned against CAVENDISH-BENTINCK, strongly criticized his position and tried to paint the situation and the future of settlerdom in brighter colours.

The K.N.F.U. leaders, MARRIAN and DELAMERE, went to London at the same time as the Coalition delegation, but they did not join in the political campaign. They were interested only in the farmers' economic problems. They called at ministries and banks, trying to procure loans and credits to buy the estates of the farmers who wanted to sell. (They believed that, once the possibility existed, part of the farmers would put off their plans.)

At last, setting aside the differences between BLUNDELL and CAVENDISH-BENTINCK, the three delegations went together to see the Foreign Secretary to press for support to the scheme of purchasing the settlers' estates.

As it turned out, however, this was unnecessary. The three delegations were still in London when the Kenya Minister of Agriculture tabled a relevant bill in the Legislative Council.

The Indians of Kenya also grew panicky with the outcome of the London conference. A local African government seemed to their majority (shopkeepers, handicraftsmen, civil servants) more frightening than colonial rule. They feared that Africans would gradually oust them from industry, commerce and the civil service. Their concern was all the greater since, in case of losing their means of subsistence, unlike the English settlers who were free to return to the metropolitan country, the Indians had no place to go: India with her starving millions could hardly have secured their livelihood. Having dreamed of the advent of democracy for several decades and having fought for it, they were now alarmed at its approach. The Kenya Indian Congress hesitated for a long time, but at last its progressive leaders realized that the only right way for them was to support the radical demand for African independence. A considerable section of the membership left the Congress and formed the Kenya Freedom Party, which soon afterwards joined K.A.N.U. as its Asian wing. Most of the Muslim Indians (notably the Ismailis headed by AGA KHAN) also supported the K.A.N.U. line.

The Land Scheme

Between the London conference and the elections of February 1961 the most important step taken by the Kenyan government was the presentation in July of a land reform bill by Minister of Agriculture BRUCE McKENZIE. The Colonial Office and the Kenyan government set themselves two aims with this scheme: 1. to enable the European landowners to sell their estates at reasonable prices if they decided to leave the country after independence under an African government, and 2. to enable the thousands of landless Africans to buy land with public support, by obtaining loans and long-term credits. In this way they tried to remove one of the main causes of African mass discontent, to damp the independence aspirations of the radical masses.

To promote the success of the scheme, the government appropriated six million pounds over three years for the purchase of the land offered for sale by European settlers, and promised to provide further bank loans for buying up lands and for helping the new owners to settle down and to equip and develop their holdings. The law envisaged two kinds of peasant farm: larger estates (50 acres) for experienced agriculturists and smaller holdings (a few acres) for those who had never before carried on farming. For this latter category the law contemplated distributing 60,000 acres of land every year among 4,500 African families.

But the feasibility of the scheme had two prerequisites: 1. the inviolability of the farmers' land title (for this end, the African leaders who would in the future constitute the majority in government should undertake to guarantee this title); 2. the willingness of foreign banks to advance the loans necessary to carry out the scheme (for this end, order and stability should be ensured in the country).

The first requisite was soon fulfilled by the African leaders (cf. pp. 60, 70), but the surest guarantee of order and stability, the release of KENYATTA, was delayed.

African Actions

In January 1960 the Governor had terminated the state of emergency declared on the pretext of Mau Mau years before. Thousands of Africans were released from the jails and camps where they had been held, convicted or unconvicted, on account of complicity in the Mau Mau movement. Necessary and useful as this belated positive step was from the point of view of bringing life in the country back to normal, it also aggravated to a great extent the already difficult economic and political situation of the country. The Africans set at liberty, Kikuyu in the first place, could hardly get jobs in the changed conditions. Most of them had no land; and those who had any in the past had since been dispossessed of it in punishment. Job opportunities were scarce because of the recession, therefore most of the released Africans only added to the number of unemployed and they settled in the vicinity of their own tribes. Intertribal differences broke out among the penniless, landless and jobless Mau Mau veterans who had suffered many years' imprisonment, on the one hand, and the well-to-do, prosperous landed tribesmen, on the other. To the minds of the former, the latter enjoyed those better incomes and conditions of work and living for which they had fought many years and even suffered in jail, and now their reward was joblessness and poverty.

These desperate have-nots often committed robbery and other acts of violence. The colonial police and authorities tendentiously represented these poverty-induced common offences as symptoms of a Mau Mau revival. How much of what they had "found out" and based their opinion upon was true and how much of it was pure fiction would be difficult to establish. Here are a few occurrences.

In March it was officially reported that in a place 170 kilometres from Nairobi three Africans had murdered an Indian woman and her two children and mutilated the bodies "Mau Mau fashion". The Governor issued an appeal to the population to help the police in search of the murderers.

On April 5 the Nairobi police made it known that Africans, probably with the intention of robbery, had attacked a missionary and a mission sister and wounded them seriously with hunting knives.

The state of emergency terminated in January of the year before was again declared in several areas of the country in July.[1] The official communiqué stated that there was "a growing incidence of subversive activity reminiscent of Mau Mau" in Nairobi, in the Central Province and Rift Valley, and therefore restriction orders were issued under the public security ordinance of 1960. The communiqué stated further that the idea of Kenyan independence was already generally accepted, the only problem was how to attain it "most effectively and securely", but "those habits of thought and action which were characteristic of the Mau Mau organization threaten Kenya's orderly progression toward independence".

A few days later the police arrested 60 Africans on the charge of "Mau Mau activity", organization of secret societies and participation in Mau Mau oath-taking rituals. But in default of concrete evidence the suspects were charged neither with conspiracy for murder nor with forming a central organization (the past charges against Mau Mau).

On September 21 the Kikuyu KOLONELIO GATHUNG was sentenced to seven years' imprisonment for "activities in the Mau Mau terrorist movement".

A week later, on September 28, Kikuyu Chief MWANGI MUMO got nine years in prison for having arranged for the administration of oaths "in the Mau Mau terrorist organization".

---

[1] By the terms of the "reservations" of the January ordinance the Governor was empowered to impose a curfew and, if necessary, put restrictions on the movement of any person, to limit the traffic of vehicles, to close down shops, etc., but the reservations did not provide for his authorization to make arrests.

*

Governor RENISON said that after Kenya's accession to independence Britain would no longer be in a position to observe her agreement under which the Masai tribe had been assigned an area of 60,000 square miles. NGALA jumped to the occasion to win the Masai support for his party. On his advice the Masai invited an Irish lawyer, OBEIRNE, to defend their title, and upon NGALA's initiative over 300 Masai leaders (many of whom came from remote places) assembled on July 24 in Nairobi to discuss their problem with the Irish attorney. OBEIRNE recommended them to appeal to the British government and request it to guarantee their land title for the time after independence. NGALA incited the Masai to rally in a political organization to avoid being swept away by their arch-enemy, the Kikuyu.[1]

The Masai leaders' meeting lasted seven hours, but no decision was made. They saw it necessary to have further consultations to decide whether to make a request to the British government or to present a petition to The Hague International Court of Justice, asking it to compel the British government to respect the agreement concluded with the Masai regardless of its future decision concerning the rest of Kenya.

The Masai needed neither a lawyer nor a court, because the Kikuyu had no intention to occupy their lands. But NGALA got what he wanted: he succeeded in winning the Masai over to the K.A.D.U. policy, to keep alive their hostility towards K.A.N.U. and the Kikuyu, and thus in increasing the differences between them and the Bantu tribes supporting K.A.N.U. Armed conflicts with the Wakamba tribe occurred in September. Seven people died in a conflict which took place at Sultan Hamud along the railway line to Dar as Salaam, 112 kilometres from Nairobi. The next week, about 35 kilometres from Nairobi, Wakamba tribesmen rushed upon Masai, who counter-attacked with spears and arrows. Three of the 60 Wakamba attackers were killed, thirty were arrested.

K.A.N.U. held its first pre-election mass meeting outdoors with the participation of 3,000 people at Ngong near Nairobi on November 5. The speakers were GICHURU and MBOYA. The meeting was attended also by nearly two hundred Masai, who stood weaponless at a far side of the place. When a speaker charged that the backward tribes obstructed the struggle for independence, the Masai grew angry and took out their weapons hidden somewhere nearby and fell upon the crowd. As a consequence of this incident, a Kikuyu died and five were seriously wounded. The police, which, in the view of MBOYA and other K.A.N.U. leaders, intervened too late, repelled the attackers with truncheons and tear-gas bombs. The K.A.N.U. youth members in retaliation broke into the Nairobi office of K.A.D.U. and smashed the furnishings before the police could drive them out. For fear of further disturbances the police banned the K.A.N.U. meeting scheduled for next day in Nairobi. MBOYA declared that K.A.N.U. would in the future take care of the protection of its own meetings and said: "We are not prepared to turn the other cheek to the Kenya African Democratic Union."

Under the impact of the September events the colonial administration got an official inquiry started into the problem of "intertribal conflicts". The commission

---

[1] Characteristically, NGALA made this remark in his speech at the meeting: "It is no use looking to America as they have in the Congo. By his agreement with an American businessman, Lumumba had sold the Congo's freedom to America for 50 years."

of inquiry (headed by a one-time British magistrate, WILLIAM LINDSAY, with two young African lawyers assisting) was set up in October. The inquiry was ineffective because the commission, leaving out of account the political aspect of the problem, after hearing policemen, colonial officials and European farmers as witnesses, found that the underlying causes of the intertribal differences were cattle thefts and quarrels over water distribution.

The government, especially K.A.N.U. Minister of Commerce and Industry KIANO, tried to calm the population, African, European and Asian alike. He said in a statement: "We have to make it clear to both African and European farmers as well as Indian traders that in this country they may look into the future with confidence."

With this end in view KIANO drew up plans to improve the economic situation of the country. He saw the main task in the increasing of production and the establishment of processing plants of the textile, leather, and food industries. He also intended to draw the greatest possible number of Africans into retail trade and handicrafts. He allocated a fund for the granting of credit to Africans who wished to start business, and organized courses of 9 to 12 months in commerce and trade.

The rightist majority of the European settlers, however, was not satisfied with KIANO's measures and assurances. On October 7 CAVENDISH-BENTINCK called together representatives of the settlers' organizations and European members of the Legislative Council in Nairobi to discuss the situation. BLUNDELL was also present. CAVENDISH-BENTINCK bitterly attacked Britain's colonial policy and accused BLUNDELL of supporting the British policy of appeasement towards Africans and British efforts to split the settlers' front. He called upon the settlers to vote for the Kenya Coalition candidates in the forthcoming elections. Some white M.P.s also requested that those who were unwilling to live under African rule should get an opportunity to sell their estates at reasonable prices and to leave the country without material losses.

BLUNDELL tried to soothe the Legco members but it was to no avail. At last 38 of the 42 settlers present decided to support the Coalition candidates.

African politicians and more sensible elements of settlerdom also made efforts to ease the tension. Early in November MBOYA accepted an invitation from European landowners and visited the area which was so far regarded as an exclusive place for wealthy European farmers and planters (White Highlands). The settlers entertained him in their exclusive "North Kinangop Club", where no African had ever been allowed to set foot. MBOYA made a speech there, trying to reassure the settlers that African rule would endanger neither their land nor their money.

At about the same time, on November 2, Governor RENISON, speaking of the coming elections, made the following statement: "I myself am facing these changes with greater sureness now that responsible leaders are showing that they realize land an teach their followers two facts about minorities in Kenya: that it is not the way of the world that minorities should seek to perpetuate domination when others are ready to take responsibility, and that it is equally important to a country's stability and reputation and progress that minorities should not be dominated or put in fear."

GICHURU, upon his return from London where he had talked with Colonial Secretary MACLEOD, declared: "I hope the Europeans will be sensible and not elect people who will antagonize the Africans."

In connection with the forhcoming elections K.A.N.U. issued a statement on November 19, demanding independence at once and the immediate release of KENYATTA. It reassured the European settlers that they had nothing to fear from an

African government, but reminded them to deal with the problems of Kenya individually, not in groups. And it pointed out to the British colonialists that, when K.A.N.U. would come to power, they would have to dismantle the military bases built to defy the will of Africans, because such installations were a threat to the independence and neutrality of the country. In the meantime K.A.N.U. and the African masses continued campaigning for the release of KENYATTA.

On October 25, the eighth anniversary of the arrest of JOMO KENYATTA, thousands of Africans demonstrated in Nairobi for the release of their leader. As a token of protest on that day they refrained from smoking, drinking spirits and using public transport facilities.

On October 30 GICHURU spoke of his London talks with MACLEOD and said that he believed KENYATTA would soon be set free.

On December 12 K.A.N.U. declared that after the elections to be held in February 1961 the party would neither accept ministerial seats nor take part in the work of the Legislative Council until KENYATTA was released.

At the end of January 1961 the Kenya Federation of Labour invited the unionized workers to start a three-month general strike coupled with a hunger strike to obtain the termination of KENYATTA's detention. In his statement explaining the Federation's strike call MBOYA stressed that, though the strike was a peaceful move, demonstrations would be held in many parts of the country.

The United States and West Germany "Show Interest"

During that year the United States in rivalry with Great Britain increased its activity to prepare the ground for its political and economic penetration of Kenya. The U.S.-controlled World Bank in May 1960 granted the Kenyan government a loan of $5.6 million to finance the development of farming and stock-breeding and to build the road network necessary for the marketing of their produce.

Political leaders of Kenya planned to send a large number of Kenyan students to colleges in the United States, and their main concern was to get the necessary financial means. During the presidential election campaign in the United States, in August 1960, the State Department of the Republican administration offered them an aid of $100,000 for this end. Thereupon MBOYA declared in Nairobi on August 21 that they would accept neither the money offered by the Republicans nor the still greater sum offered by the Democrats campaigning for JOHN F. KENNEDY. He said they would gladly accept any financial assistance from private persons, foundations and organizations, but they did not wish to be obliged to American political parties or government agencies.[1]

In November 1960 an American Roman Catholic Bishop, FULTON J. SHEEN, arrived in Nairobi and made a week-long tour of Northern Province. Officially the aim of his visit was to call on Catholic missions and to ordain a new African bishop. It is characteristic that on his way back to New York the American bishop stopped for several days in Johannesburg, South Africa.

[1] How inconsistent MBOYA was in this respect can be seen among other things from the fact that hardly a year later he sent to the United States his "personal representative" in the person of a wealthy Pakistani graduated in America, ABDUL GHAFUR SHEIK, who requested and obtained money from private firms like Shell Oil Company for the purpose of sending Kenyan students to the United States and for the rehabilitation of young Kenyan criminals. He also recruited young Americans to go to Kenya as members of the "Peace Corps" making propaganda for the United States.

The American feelers were soon followed in Kenya by West German rivals. In January 1961 a West German delegation arrived in Nairobi "to study the possibilities of assistance to Kenya".

Elections in February 1961

The elections promised at the London conference early in 1960 were held in February 1961.

The international situation made the colonialists realize that it was impossible to prolong the disfranchisement of the African majority of Kenya. They felt compelled to grant franchise to broad masses of Africans, but they took care to prevent the election results from expressing the will of the African majority.

1. The elections took place in three stages, and this left its mark on the results. Of the 65 members 53 were elected on the common roll, but 20 seats out of the 53 were reserved for the non-African minorities (10 for Europeans, 8 for Asians and 2 for Arabs). Those running for the reserved seats first had to obtain a majority of the vote in the primary of the respective racial group. The remaining 12 members (4 Africans, 4 Europeans, 3 Asians and 1 Arab) were elected as "National Members" by the constituency representatives.

2. The right to vote in the general election was subject to literacy and other qualifications (holding of a public office, over £ 75 income a year, or 40 years of age). This meant that all adult European males could vote, but only a fraction of the Africans were qualified.

3. The constituencies were delimited by the colonial authorities, who saw to it that the urban areas and the regions inhabited by Kikuyu, Luo and other radical-spirited tribes were under-represented and the scarcely populated pastoral districts were over-represented in the legislature.

The election results were greatly influenced by the inorganization of the political parties and the personal rivalries between political leaders. The parties, first of all K.A.N.U., had two or more candidates in several constituencies: an unofficial candidate stood for election against the official candidate of the party, or the party even let two official candidates present themselves. Consequently the votes of the party were divided, and so the opponent was elected in many constituencies where the official candidate of the party might have relied upon a certain majority.

K.A.N.U. and K.A.D.U. were campaigning from largely identical platforms. The manifestoes of both parties demanded independence and unity, categorically rejecting the idea of regionalism, and included in their electoral slogans the demands for independence, industrialization, the modernization of African agriculture, the Africanization of the civil service and, first of all, the release of KENYATTA and other political leaders in prison or under restrictions. Both parties promised to guarantee private property and referred only vaguely to partial expropriation of European land, making no mention of the issue of indemnity. Shortly thereafter, however, prompted by consultations with the settlers' New Kenya Party, K.A.D.U. issued a policy statement in which, at variance with its former manifesto, it advocated regionalism and guarantees of European-owned landed property. On the other hand, K.A.N.U., while demanding the freeing of KENYATTA, pledged during the campaign that it would not participate in the government until KENYATTA was released.

The vast majority of the Africans, including the two largest tribes (Kikuyu and Luo) and smaller ones like the Masai and Kalenjin, supported K.A.N.U. Only the Somali tribes in Northern Province refused to stand by the two African parties.

Namely they wished their territory to secede from Kenya and be joined to the independent Somali Republic, and therefore decided to boycott the Kenya elections. (The only "independent" Somali candidate who ran for election was elected unopposed.)

The Indians had no separate election platform, their majority supported K.A.N.U., the rest stood behind K.A.D.U. The Arabs living in the ten-mile Coastal Strip, on lease from the Sultan of Zanzibar, opposed the African parties which wanted to belong to Kenya, and so they demanded autonomy and campaigned under this slogan in the election.

The manifestoes of the settler parties (BLUNDELL's New Kenya Party and CAVENDISH-BENTINCK's Kenya Coalition) also differed little in their policies, since they concentrated on the white electorate. With the progress of the campaign, however, the differences between the two parties became accentuated. The reactionary Coalition, in accordance with the racist principles of its leaders, was against the independence aspirations and democratic demands of Africans, notably KENYATTA's release. On the other hand, BLUNDELL and his party voiced more and more liberal-sounding demands during the campaign. They still did not support the African independence efforts, and opposed even any radical constitutional reform in the near future, but they emphasized the need for co-operation with African leaders and were ready to promote the immediate release of KENYATTA. In view of the impending elections the Coalition leaders also made an attempt to approach the African parties, but they met with flat refusal on both sides.

As a result of the elections, 19 seats were won by K.A.N.U. and 15 by K.A.D.U., while 3 seats went to the Kenya Indian Congress, 2 to the Kenya Freedom Party, 7 to the New Kenya Party (BLUNDELL) and 3 to the Kenya Coalition (CAVENDISH-BENTINCK). The remaining 16 seats were obtained by "independent" candidates (Europeans, Indians, Arabs and one Somali).

Thus the Africans had a formal majority in the Legislative Council (all the more so since some of the "independents" also supported the policy of K.A.N.U. or K.A.D.U.), and K.A.N.U. won a fine victory over K.A.D.U. (This was seen only to a small extent from the number of seats obtained, and was due to the aforementioned inequitable delimitation of the constituencies. The fact is that the 143,079 votes cast for K.A.D.U. were opposed by K.A.N.U.'s 590,661 votes, that is more than 80 per cent of the electorate.)[1]

That the election was a shameless parody of democracy, and that the African majority was only a deceptive illusion, is characterized also by the fact that the White Paper of February 25, 1960, concerning the elections authorized the British Governor, in case he found that the elected majority was no sufficient guarantee of support for the government's policy, to appoint further members to the Legislative Council (!).

The Blunders of Mennen Williams

Immediately after the Kenya elections an illuminating incident occurred, which revealed the double-dealing policy and the true face of the Anglo-American neocolonialists.

---

[1] In spite of the fact that in the third round of elections K.A.D.U. made an election pact with the settlers' N.K.P.

Mennen Williams, the U.S. Assistant Secretary for African Affairs, in February 1961 toured thirteen African countries to make propaganda for his government's neocolonialist policy. On February 20, when delivering a speech in Kenya, he brought himself to say that the U.S. policy in Africa proceeded from the principle "Africa for the Africans". His utterance provoked stormy indignation among the English settlers of Kenya and in the imperialist press of Britain. The American diplomat then quickly backtracked, explaining that he understood the term African to apply "to all people of Africa regardless of their race or color." The Department of State of the United States backed up Williams and identified itself with his explanation. The State Department spokesman, Lincoln White, on February 24 expressed his regret that the critics of Williams had not taken notice of this explanation.

On the same day Mennen Williams visited also Uganda, where he again made a slip of the tongue in a speech at Kampala. He declared that the United States wished to see a strong and firm African government in every African country, otherwise a vacuum would arise where "another kind of tyranny" could enter. When he was asked what he meant by "another kind of tyranny" he replied: "Well, perhaps worse than they suffered before. But I withdraw that phrase. I don't mean that the British are tyrannical." Then he said that in the opinion of the United States the Africans should work out their own destiny without external political intervention, but this should not mean that the United States thought that all political influences from outside must cease immediately. He added: "The British Government must obviously be involved here. I think they are making an honest effort to meet the exigencies of African problems."

This confused statement and the fact that the same day, after flying to Tanganyika, he declared that he wanted to meet "the colony's Governor-General", roused another wave of indignation not only in England, but in the National Committee of the Republican Party in the United States. The party's official organ, *Battle Line*, vehemently attacked Williams who "has managed to anger just about all sides involved in African affairs by blundering along with all grace and tact of a wounded wild boar".

To save the U.S. government's battered prestige, President Kennedy himself found it necessary to intervene. At a televised news conference early in March he wholly identified himself with Williams's phrase "Africa for the Africans", meaning all those who regard themselves as Africans, irrespective of their race or colour. Finally he assured Williams of his endorsement and expressed his satisfaction with the diplomat's African tour.

Forming of the Government. Opening of Parliament. The Kenyatta Crisis

The February elections were followed by a few months of government crisis.

Governor Renison said that Kenyatta would not be released immediately. Mboya presently announced that his party demanded not only the freeing of Kenyatta but also his appointment as Chief Minister. Kiano, the Minister of Commerce and Industry, resigned after the Governor's announcement.

The Governor had repeated talks with K.A.N.U. and K.A.D.U. leaders in an effort to persuade them to join the government, but without avail. Finally he proposed that they go together to see Kenyatta at Lodwar. Ngala and Muliro agreed, but Mboya and Gichuru, the President of the party, declared: "Nothing short of Kenyatta's release will satisfy the Africans."

On March 8 Ngala and Muliro flew to Lodwar to see Kenyatta and talked with him. After their return they said that Kenyatta did not approve of the action of the K.A.N.U. leaders, declared his willingness to lead the movement if the people of Kenya so desired, and called upon the African political leaders to form a united front in all matters of concern to the country.

The K.A.N.U. leaders remained adamant. On March 12 Gichuru sent an identical cable to every one of the British Commonwealth Prime Ministers sitting in London, requested their intercession for Kenyatta's release and stressed the significance of such a step for the peace and unity of Kenya.

After the election of the "National Members" on March 16 the 65-member Legislative Council with an African majority was complete, and the opening meeting was scheduled to take place on April 6, but Governor Renison refused to convene it because no government had been formed as yet. In fact the forming of the government dragged on since the African politicians made their participation subject to the immediate release of Kenyatta, but the British government was unwilling to comply.

The day before the election of the "National Members", March 15, Ngala had still affirmed that his party would recall its ministers because of the refusal to free Kenyatta. The two parties held consultations, as a result of which five K.A.N.U. and six K.A.D.U. members went to visit Kenyatta at Lodwar. Back in Nairobi the two parties announced that they would not enter the government but would form the opposition in the Legislative Council. Gichuru read out the joint statement based on long hours' talks with Kenyatta and formulated with his help. The statement contained four points:

(1) Unity is of prime importance for the Kenya independence movement. (2) K.A.N.U. and K.A.D.U. agree to co-operate for the attainment of two principal aims: complete independence for Kenya in 1961 and Kenyatta's unconditional and immediate release. (3) The differences between the two parties being rooted in personal rivalry and conflicts of personal interests, they call upon all Africans in Kenya to refrain from any destructive activity harmful to the movement. (4) An inter-party consultative committee of leaders is set up to facilitate co-operation.

Governor Renison declared that he would not lift the restriction on Kenyatta's freedom of movement until the government was in operation and until he was satisfied that the government functioned properly and that Kenyatta's release would not endanger public order. British Colonial Secretary Macleod on a surprise visit to Nairobi spent two hours in talks with African leaders on April 3, but since he endorsed the Governor's inflexible position, nothing could be done. He concluded by remarking that in case the political deadlock continued, it would endanger public order, too, so further efforts should be made to come out of the impasse.

On April 4 Kenyatta was moved with his family from Lodwar, a place 500 kilometres from Nairobi where he had been detained since April 1959, to Maralal at a distance of only 300 kilometres.

Macleod, on his return from Africa on April 7, was asked by newsmen at London airport what his idea was of a Kenyan government if Kenyatta was to remain in detention. He replied that the solution was up to the local parties (that is to say, the Governor and the African leaders) to decide. He added that Kenyatta would be released as soon as the Governor was satisfied that this step would not andanger law and order.

On the same day the Minister of Works of the Kenyan government, Ibrahim Nathoo, resigned. He was the third minister in a week to leave the government because of the delay of Kenyatta's release.

The Colonial Secretary and the Governor permitted KENYATTA to give a press conference at Maralal. On April 11, taking the occasion, KENYATTA spent three hours answering the questions from the assembled journalists and then gave a televised interview. This was his first public appearance since his conviction in April 1953. According to *The Times* correspondent he revealed himself as a highly capable politician who was taller by a head than other leaders of African independence movements and who would not rest until he achieved independence for his country.

First of all, KENYATTA stated that the African countries had to rid themselves of the rule of colonialism and imperialism by constitutional means. He demanded independence for Kenya at once. To the question when he thought Kenya should be granted independence he replied: "Today. Look at Sudan, look at Tanganyika, look at Somalia. Just next door. I do not think these countries are any more advanced than Kenya, yet they have their independence." And he added that the Africans in Kenya were "quite capable of running their government".

He thought it necessary for Kenya to have a democratic parliamentary system, but he believed that MACLEOD's constitutional reform and particularly a Legislative Council whose decisions were open to the Governor's veto were outmoded.

Regarding the anxiety of the white settlers and certain minority tribes he said: "In an independent Kenya all citizens will be respected and will be equal in the eyes of the law."

He declared that the sentence passed on him nine years before was unjust, because he had never approved of the atrocities committed by Mau Mau, that he approved only non-violence in the constitutional struggle. The CORFIELD report published a year before, which presented him as organizer of the Mau Mau movement, he said, was "a pack of lies" worth to be thrown into the fire. As to Mau Mau he remarked by the way: whether it had helped or harmed the independence movement would be decided by history. In this connection, commenting on Governor RENISON's remark calling him "a leader of darkness and death", he stressed: "That is not true. My leadership has not been to darkness and death but to light and prosperity." He called the Governor, who was reluctant to meet him, "stubborn and obstinate", a "badly advised" man.

When asked whether he felt aggrieved by the government for the restrictions imposed on him, he replied with this biblical sentence: "Father, forgive them, for they know not what they do."

In the next few months, too, the Africans regarded it as their main task to obtain KANYATTA's release. Demonstrations for this end were staged one after another. On March 13, for example, in the streets of Thomsons Falls a crowd of a thousand marched in procession led by three Kikuyu women singing and shouting slogans. The peaceful demonstrators were dispersed by police who arrested the three leaders.

April 15 was declared "Kenyatta Day" and a general strike was called in Nairobi for the day. On April 14 in the Commons Labour M.P. STONEHOUSE, with reference to the recent release of HASTINGS BANDA, demanded the freeing of KENYATTA and other political prisoners. Colonial Secretary MACLEOD replied that a revision of the case was under way, but the government would not release him because it had been and was still the policy of the government not to release anybody who might be a threat to public security. The next day the celebration of "Kenyatta Day" in Nairobi took place without disorder and incident. Many African workers, including domestic servants except hotel employees, took part in the strike.

On April 23, back from the Monrovia conference, MBOYA was welcomed at Nairobi airport. He said that he had declared at Monrovia: unless KENYATTA was set free in three months' time, they would launch a passive resistance campaign and call upon the African ministers to step down. In the crowd assembled to receive him a brawl broke out between MBOYA's followers and his political opponents. The police intervened and arrested ten persons, a woman among them.

In the middle of April MBOYA was to the United States. On April 16 in Washington he gave a televised interview, and the next day in New York he gave a news conference at the Carnegie Endowment International Center. In the television interview he said among other things:

"People perhaps misunderstand what we are fighting for. We are not merely fighting to remove and replace the present European settler regime of colonialism. We are fighting for something much bigger.

"We are fighting for the fulfilment of something. That something is, firstly, the removal of colonialism as a handicap, of European settlerism and of racism, but with a hope that once this is removed we can then settle down to fighting for the real thing — against disease, against poverty, agains ignorance, and once again for the re-establishment of confidence among our people, of self-respect, of self-fulfilment.

"This, to my mind, is going to be the bigger struggle, and it is here that we will be able to judge whether our struggle had been successful or not . . .

"Independence and self-government is merely a means to enable us to achieve the end, and the end is the self-improvement of our people, the higher standard of living, pride in themselves, a rediscovery of their lost dignity."

At the news conference, speaking of the question of South Africa, he gave expression to the indignation of the African peoples over Britain and Canada continuing to conduct profitable business with the racist regime of South Africa even after its secession from the British Commonwealth. He reminded Britain and Canada that, unless they changed their attitudes, the African and Asian states might reconsider whether they would stay within the Commonwealth. At the same time he bitterly attacked the United States for its refusal to join the African delegations in voting sanctions against the government of South Africa because of its apartheid policy.

As to the problems of Kenya, he said that, although his party had won a majority in the legislature of the colony at the February elections, he would not enter the government until Britain fulfilled their two principal demands, until KENYATTA, the future Prime Minister of Kenya, was released and until a new constitution was introduced which guaranteed internal self-government and complete independence in the current year of 1961.

Before his departure from America, on April 20, he and KENNETH KAUNDA visited in Washington President KENNEDY, whom they requested to use his influence with the British government to promote the independence of their countries, for this was the only way of preventing their peoples from resorting to violence in order to achieve their aim. MBOYA also asked the President to intercede for the release of KENYATTA.

Hardly a month had gone by after the K.A.N.U. and K.A.D.U. leaders' visit to KENYATTA and their joint statement issued on that occasion, when K.A.D.U. leader NGALA, following consultations in London with MACLEOD, on April 19 started talks with Governor RENISON about the forming of the new government. Three days later the Governor and the K.A.D.U. parliamentary group, headed by NGALA, appeared at Government House and made a solemn joint statement announcing that they were agreed on K.A.D.U.'s participation in the government, and that the Governor had decided to begin at once the building of a dwelling house for KENYATTA and his family in Kiambu where they would be permitted to return "in due course". NGALA made an appeal to all African elected members of the Legislative Council to support the new government.

The new government was formed with four high officials of the colonial administration and eight elected ministers: four Africans (NGALA, MULIRO and TOWETT from K.A.D.U. and BERNARD MATE from K.A.N.U., who accepted the government post after breaking with the policy of his party), three Europeans (WILFRED HAVELOCK, who had so far been also Minister of Local Government; MICHAEL BLUNDELL as Minister of Agriculture, and PETER MARRIAN as Minister of Tourism; the latter resigned later to join the K.A.N.U. parliamentary group and was succeeded by the "independent" HOWARD-WILLIAMS), and one Asian. This secured a two-thirds majority for the Europeans in the government.[1]

Neither MBOYA nor GICHURU nor the European liberal leaders (DEREK ERSKINE and BRUCE McKENZIE) entered the government, but the K.A.D.U. leaders, who had thus far endeavoured to outbid the K.A.N.U. executives in insisting on the refusal to accept ministerial places until KENYATTA was freed, now changed their minds when MACLEOD agreed that NGALA as member of the government should be styled "Leader of Government Business", and promised to permit KENYATTA to return to his birthplace in Kiambu and to build a home for him there.

GICHURU announced on behalf of K.A.N.U. that those members who supported NGALA would be expelled from the party. The party's Vice-President, ODINGA, denounced NGALA as an accomplice in the colonialist plot.

On May 3 GICHURU declared that his party would do its utmost to bring about the fall of the new government, and it would do so by constitutional means.

With the formation of the government the objection of the Governor to the opening of the Legislative Council was removed.

The real reason for delaying the opening of parliament was that the Governor did not find the majority secured. Since he could no longer delay it, he made use of his right laid down in the White Paper of February 1960 and appointed to the Council another 11 members upon whom he could safely rely.

The opening meeting was held on May 11. Governor RENISON, when arriving at the parliament building, was received by a crowd of nearly five thousand people booing at him. After oath-taking, majority leader NGALA made a motion "to help create conditions to facilitate the release of Jomo Kenyatta". Thereafter K.A.N.U. President GICHURU proposed the immediate release of KENYATTA and the lifting of the ban on political meetings, and MBOYA presented a motion of no confidence.

Unrest in the Tribes and among the Settlers. K.A.N.U. Activities and the Headaches of the K.A.D.U. Government

K.A.D.U.'s opportunism resolved the problem of establishing a government. The solution fulfilled the expectations of the British government. By supporting K.A.D.U. and NGALA and helping them to power they hoped to counteract K.A.N.U.'s

---

[1] Before the elections, when a government with a K.A.N.U. majority was expected to emerge, the New Kenya Party and the Kenya Indian Congress promised to support the future government. This was obviously why nearly all the elected N.K.P. members polled the votes of the K.A.N.U. electorate. This notwithstanding, the party supported the K.A.D.U. government, in which BLUNDELL and two other members of his party as well as one of the Indian Congress (ARVIND JAMIDAR) accepted portfolios. BLUNDELL's two associates (DEREK ERSKINE and former Minister of Agriculture BRUCE McKENZIE) and the other four Indian members remained loyal to K.A.N.U. and joined its opposition group.

consistent anticolonialist policy and to harm as they could the prestige and mass influence of KENYATTA, the most "dangerous" of the freedom fighters. They understood that his release could not be delayed for long, so they tried to create a *fait accompli* still before his return to political life.

Most of the Africans — primarily the two great tribes, the Kikuyu and the Luo — trusted the K.A.N.U. policy, but the broad masses could not yet shake off the fetters of the old tribal mentality and the oppressive memories of more than a half century of colonial domination. In the Europeans they saw enemies who had stolen their land and killed thousands of their brothers. Mutual distrust and fear prevailed among the tribes. The rural tribes did not trust the urbanized ones and their politicians, they were afraid of their advance to power.

The K.A.N.U. leaders tried to put these tribes at ease. "Danger would come," MBOYA said, "not from traditions or tribalism, but from a struggle for power between the parties. Inevitably this would produce violence and instability."

Among the Africans, the Kikuyu included, there were still many who lived in the atmosphere of the past and did not yet understand the change of time.

On March 16 the colonial authorities released KUNGU KARUMBA, who had been convicted of Mau Mau activity at the same time as KENYATTA. Being a Kikuyu member, KARUMBA returned to his tribe's reserve and said he would spend a half year there and would then plunge into politics again, but that he would join neither K.A.N.U. nor K.A.D.U., because he recognized only the K.A.U. (banned years before) as representative of the interests of the people of Kenya.

The conditions were made worse by elemental disasters. A large section of the African population, mainly pastoral tribes, were threatened by famine owing to drought and worm invasion. Caterpillars had caused damage to Kenya every year, but the ravages were especially enormous in 1961.[1] To this was added the complete absence of rain. The fodder shortage had caused 180,000 cattle to perish by mid-June. The government took urgent steps to increase the maize imports and to carry them by military lorries to the rural areas, but in many places the aid came too late.

The poverty-stricken Africans suffering from land hunger, unemployment and elemental disasters often took to using violence and attacking European families.

Still in February the police in the village of Nguthera in Central Province, acting on a complaint from white farmers, investigated cases of theft and illegal use of pasture land. The Kikuyu villagers attacked the police. In a strife between them a police inspector and three Africans were injured. The police asked for reinforcement, and over thirty Africans were arrested.

Two weeks later, on March 11, at Dandora near Nairobi twenty Africans carrying knives and sticks broke into the home of a settler family and attacked the occupants. Two seriously wounded men had to be taken to hospital. In the vicinity of Nairobi this was the third attack in a week against settler families.

On May 5 six Africans (Kikuyu) invaded a solitary farm near Molo owned by the Osborn couple living there with three children. They searched and looted the buildings and seized arms and ammunition, and manhandled the couple so brutally that the wife died and the gravely injured husband had to be taken to hospital in serious condition. (The three children were asleep and escaped unharmed.)

To justify their police regime the colonial authorities already in 1960 claimed that the offences committed by Africans were "reminiscent of Mau Mau". In 1961,

---

[1] Trains between Mombasa and Nairobi were four or five hours late because the tracks were overswarmed with worms and the wheels were spinning in place.

after the elections, they went still futher. The Defence Minister of the colonial administration, ANTHONY SWANN, banned a secret African organization called the "Kenya Land Freedom Army", which was alleged to have been formed by former Mau Mau terrorists mostly from the Kikuyu tribe. The banning order referred to a membership of "between 500 and 2,000", of whom a hundred had been arrested.

The charge against the secret organization was that its members had taken the oath not to co-operate with the government and the whites and, if so ordered, to steal arms, ammunition and money, to commit murders, and to occupy the lands of Kikuyus loyal to the government.

The provocative nature of this ban is demonstrated by the fact that, as pointed out in the banning order itself, the organization was not a direct but a potential threat to security, since its members committed acts of violence individually, not in groups. And, characteristically enough, the minister stated that the leader of the secret society was a Mau Mau terrorist by the name of KARIUKU CHOTARA, who had pleaded guilty of the killing of eighteen people and was now in prison; that the organization had been founded by Mau Mau terrorists who were associated with CHOTARA and had been imprisoned with him, but they had been released the year before; that the organization had been discovered when the police searching MUTURI KAIRUKU's home for stolen goods, had found there a list of 150 members of the "Land Freedom Army" Nairobi branch and a document which was evidence that a "militant and aggressive action" was brewing.

The European settlers were seized with panic. They feared that the Africans, once in power, would strip them not only of their privileges but of their estates as well. For this reason they tried hard to sell their lands at good prices, but mostly to no avail.

The implementation of the land scheme of April 1960 went on verly slowly. Of 3.600 European farmers only 800 offered their estates for sale. The arable land on sale amounted to over 1,125,000 acres. But the government agency in charge was in no hurry. In the first nine months it was occupied with planning and organizing, and so all in all a few thousand acres were bought up in a year, until April 1961. True, the Africans did not show much interest in land purchases. The vast majority of the politically backward, illiterate Africans thought that it was no use buying land for money, because after the Africans' access to power all European estates would be expropriated without compensation and allotted to landless Africans. This is the explanation of why only a few hundred Africans were prepared to buy land in a whole year.

MBOYA and GICHURU attempted to put the settlers at ease. GICHURU said: "Europeans and Asians who wish to continue to live here and who will accept an African majority have nothing to fear. We hope they will co-operate fully with the Africans in the life of Kenya . . . Land titles will be honoured and land reform will be for the benefit of the whole country."

The settlers did not trust these assurances and regarded the recent African atrocities as "a revival of Mau Mau". On May 7 at Njoro near Nakuru two hundred white farmers held a meeting where they decided to send a deputation to London, requesting the British government to take urgent practical steps for the protection of their personal and material security and to indemnify the Osborn family.

At the beginning of June the European settlers presented to the British Parliament a petition with 3,800 signatures asking the government to take action to guarantee their land titles. They related that African leaders questioned the settlers' land titles and threatened expropriation of European-owned lands after independence, that therefore it was difficult for the white settlers to sell their estates, and this could be helped only if the British government saw to it that expropriation was only against adequate compensation.

The administration was alarmed also at occasional disturbances among the tribes of the Northern Frontier District. In the middle of April, the police in Northern Province had to unarm a Turkana band of 300 men equipped with modern (Belgian and Swiss) firearms, who had for days been waging a bloody battle with the Dodoth tribe beyond the Uganda frontier.

The administration was invariably preoccupied with the problem of federation of the four East African territories (Kenya, Uganda, Tanganyika, Zanzibar). On this issue all Kenyan parties were agreed.

In June the Legislative Council stated that federation was desirable politically and economically alike. Accordingly the government on August 3 set up a commission of Legco members to examine the related questions. The commission, headed by NGALA, was composed of seven members of the government party, that is K.A.D.U., and seven of the opposition K.A.N.U.

The forming of the government did not yet solve the crisis, since the real cause — KENYATTA's detention — had not been removed. Events showed that without the solution of this question no normal political life was possible in Kenya. As was pertinently remarked by an English liberal journalist: "In a sense . . . it appears that Kenya is Mr. Kenyatta's prisoner rather than the other way round."[1]

KENYATTA remained the most urgent problem of the country. The African masses waited with mounting excitement for the release of KENYATTA, whom most of them expected to solve all their problems, to alleviate their situation, to achieve their freedom and independence.

On June 15 K.A.N.U. and K.A.D.U. leaders together went to visit KENYATTA, and after returning to Nairobi they announced their decision to continue fighting in common to win independence for Kenya still in 1961. This happened hardly 24 hours after the Legislative Council, in which NGALA's government party had the majority, voted for a Bill demanding only internal self-government by the end of 1961. The K.A.N.U. members did not take part in the vote.

At KENYATTA's advice the K.A.D.U. members remained in the government, and K.A.N.U. continued as the opposition.

On June 19 a delegation of the Kenya Indian Congress called on KENYATTA at Maralal. KENYATTA assured them that after independence the African leaders would take care of the personal and material security of all Kenya citizens, either African or European or Asian; that the "white" officials had nothing to fear, they could safely stay in the country, and if they were ready to co-operate with the government, they might retain their actual posts.

On July 10, a Sunday, K.A.N.U. followers organized in Nairobi a big demonstration in which about 30,000 people took part. The Deputy Speaker of the Legislative Council put the question whether they would be disposed to peaceful co-operation with the Europeans, and they answered in chorus: "Yes!"

In his speech at the meeting MBOYA demanded that independence be proclaimed still in 1961, and that elections be held before the proclamation of independence, after delimiting the constituencies, on equal terms for all qualified voters. Finally,

[1] *The New York Herald Tribune*, June 30, 1961.

he demanded KENYATTA's immediate release, and this demand met with an enthusiastic applause.

On August 1 MACLEOD told the British Parliament that KENYATTA would soon be freed. He said among other things:

"The Governor of Kenya has informed me he has decided, if there is no deterioration in the security position, that Jomo Kenyatta should be moved to Kiambu about the middle of August and his restriction order revoked a few days after. This decision has the full support of the British government. I believe that this decision, difficult though it is, is in the best interests of all the peoples of Kenya, and that it should be taken now."

The minister's announcement to the House of Commons was received with satisfaction by the Labour Party and with concern by the right wing of the Conservative Party. Tory M.P. MAYDON said that KENYATTA's release "will cause grave concern among Africans and Europeans in Kenya and other territories in Africa and among a great many people in this country."

Secretary MACLEOD told Parliament that his decision was based upon Governor RENISON's report which said: "I am confident that, with my government behind me, I can accept and contain any extra security risk which now remains on Jomo Kenyatta's release. It is arguable that the economy is likely to be more damaged by the uncertainty caused by his continued restriction." The Governor stated also that since moving to Maralal "Kenyatta has given every indication that he is now in no way irreconcilable to the maintenance of law and order and to the association of all the peoples of Kenya with its progress to independence".

The Release of Kenyatta

In Kenya the Governor announced that KENYATTA would be moved to the Gatundu Reserve near Nairobi and remain in security detention for a while, until the excitement over his return subsided. The construction of the house built for him was financed by K.A.N.U., while K.A.D.U. bought him a luxury car; the furnishings were gifts from some settler leaders and a Kenya Indian society.

The African masses waited for the return of KENYATTA with great excitement. Demonstrations for independence were held by large crowds cheering him. Police were several times dispatched against demonstrators. On August 13 in the morning, for example, 500 people proceeded towards the centre of Nairobi and shouted "independence" and "freedom". The crowd was dispersed with tear gas.

Still on August 11 KENYATTA made an appeal (this was also broadcast) to the people of Kenya, reminding them to keep calm "in the interests of the unity and peace of our entire people", stressing the hope that after his release he would soon be in a position to visit all places and hold public meetings.

He was moved to Gatundu on August 14. Although the time of his arrival was kept secret to avoid any demonstration, he was received there by 3,000 rejoicing people. He was welcomed by NGALA, the K.A.D.U. leader, on behalf of the government and by GICHURU, MBOYA and MULIRO in the name of K.A.N.U. In his address of welcome NGALA said: "This is the greatest day of Africa. From here on we march to a new destiny." KENYATTA said in his reply: "I plan to unify my people — the Africans and citizens of Kenya."

On August 20 KENYATTA declared that the future independent Kenya would need a democracy not after the British fashion but "adjusted to African life" and would pursue a policy of neutrality. The same day, a Sunday, about twenty-five thousand people proceeded to Gatundu (using cars, lorries and buses) to see him, but the police kept them away.

On August 21, in the morning the British District Commissioner handed KENYATTA the written order freeing him from restrictions and permitting him to move freely in Kenya and speak at public meetings. On this occasion KENYATTA received back the silver-headed walking stick and a ruby ring which had been taken from him at the time of his arrest in 1952. A few minutes later KENYATTA stepped over the fence enclosing his house and greeted the crowd of about a hundred people gathered there in the morning chill.

On August 22 KENYATTA visited the Kikuyu population of the reserve and received the leaders of both K.A.N.U. and K.A.D.U., who told him about their agreement of last week (see below).

On the same day he received a visit from RENISON, the British Governor of Kenya. The meeting took place at the District Commissioner's Office in Kiambu. According to the official communiqué they discussed the future of Kenya. KENYATTA stated that the talks were productive and would promote the forthcoming negotiations in Nairobi about the constitution and the land issue. As to KENYATTA's participation in the Legislative Council they did not come to terms.

The agreement between the two parties was made public on August 24. They agreed to form a provisional coalition government and to demand the granting of independence to Kenya by February 1962 and the convocation of a Kenya constitutional conference for September to put an end to the racial distribution of parliamentary seats; to request the British government to repeal the ordinance under which KENYATTA as an ex-convict could not be elected to the Legislative Council. The two parties were agreed also that the treaty between Britain and the Sultan of Zanzibar regarding the Coastal Strip should be cancelled and the territory should be recognized as part of Kenya.

August 25 was the day of KENYATTA's first public act. A rejoicing crowd of 3,000 assembled around the parliament building. The demonstrators enthusiastically greeted KENYATTA who, in the company of other political leaders, appeared on the balcony and spoke to the people. In his speech he emphasized that the inter-party agreement was proof that the fear of a future African government was groundless, since the parties laid down in a resolution that the future government of Kenya would respect the human rights, including the land titles.

The Situation of the Country and the Struggle of K.A.N.U. after Kenyatta's Release

In the first few weeks following the release of KENYATTA it seemed that the two parties would co-operate under his guidance, and some K.A.D.U. leaders even believed the two parties would unite under KENYATTA as president.

K.A.N.U. and K.A.D.U. held a series of joint public meetings, at which KENYATTA spoke, throughout the country. On September 10 at a meeting in the Nairobi stadium KENYATTA declared: ". . . all Kenya land for Africans and if Kenya did not get freedom at once, we are going to take it . . . God gave us this country and we are keeping it . . . Foreigners can go, and we will shut the doors to new ones."

This apparent unity of the two parties did not prove to be lasting. It became clear that the majority of the Africans endorsed the radical policy of K.A.N.U. and that the leaders of this party would soon have to take up posts in the government. This meant that some K.A.D.U. ministers would have to resign. K.A.D.U. leaders who had joined the campaign for KENYATTA's release only under the pressure of public opinion — TOWETT and other leaders of the Kalenjin Alliance — now spoke up more loudly against the K.A.N.U. policy. Even those who had stood most firmly by KENYATTA and had contributed to the success of the campaign — NGALA and MULIRO — now vociferated against the policy of K.A.N.U. and KENYATTA.

Under such circumstances KENYATTA, realizing that it was impossible to unite the two parties, accepted the post of K.A.N.U. President.

In November the Governor talked with the parliamentary groups of the two parties about the chance of forming a coalition government. K.A.N.U. stated that though it represented the majority of the population, it respected the previous agreement that K.A.N.U. and K.A.D.U. should have equal shares in the government. The K.A.D.U. parliamentary group, however, in which Europeans played the leading part, insisted that the principle of equality should apply only to the Africans: the government should consist of four Africans from K.A.N.U., four Africans from K.A.D.U. and four Europeans associated with K.A.D.U. The Kenya Coalition and Deputy Governor ERIC GRIFFITH-JONES made compromise proposals for a slight K.A.D.U. majority. K.A.N.U. would have been ready to accept even this solution, but the Governor, who saw support for the policy of the colonial administration assured only by a K.A.D.U. majority, rejected the compromise. Thus nothing came of a coalition government, and K.A.N.U. remained the party in opposition and was excluded from the government.

Kenyatta's Struggle for Independence

Early in November KENYATTA went to London and talked with Colonial Secretary REGINALD MAUDLING. He declared that he saw no reason for continuing the Nairobi talks. He handed MAUDLING a memorandum requesting an earliest possible constitutional conference to be held in London, followed by general elections and the granting of independence to Kenya on February 1, 1962.

The Colonial Secretary assured him that the British government was willing to grant independence to Kenya if the African parties, K.A.N.U. and K.A.D.U., agreed between them, but he promised a constitutional conference only for the spring of 1962 because he first wished to visit Kenya to see for himself.

During the few days of his stay in London KENYATTA was several times insulted by an English reactionary right-wing organization. Demonstrators threw at him eggs and bloody chicken entrails, and called him a mass murderer.

After his return to Nairobi, on November 19, KENYATTA stated: "Kenya wants independence immediately, but this is being delayed by British imperialists."

On November 22 the European settlers' United Kenya Club gave a lunch in KENYATTA's honour at a fine Nairobi hotel, where two hundred people attended: Europeans, Africans and Asians in fairly equal numbers. In his toast KENYATTA stressed: "You Europeans and Asians must learn, and learn very quickly, how to respect Africans and to feel how you can work with Africans on an equal basis. If you can do that, you will have no difficulty with us."

On November 23 MAUDLING told the House of Commons about the repeal of the ordinance preventing KENYATTA's entry into the Legislative Council.

Towards the end of November MAUDLING went to Kenya and talked with the leaders of the parties about the future constitution, allegedly with a view to helping to bridge the existing differences. His real aim, however, was to exploit these differences, to prolong the division of Africans and thus to raise obstacles to the radical anti-imperialist programme of the majority party. Partly he succeeded in this. K.A.D.U. President NGALA, with reference to the need for guarantees of the rights of minority tribes, demanded a federal government for independent Kenya, and leaders of the Somali tribes wanted the Somali-inhabited regions, nearly a quarter of all Kenya territory, to secede from Kenya and be joined to the Somali Republic. But K.A.N.U., which enjoyed the support of the vast majority of the population, categorically opposed any such and similar separatist endeavour and demanded the establishment of a strong, independent central government.

Before his departure MAUDLING called a press conference, where he declared that in case the London negotiations early next year would work out an agreement on the constitution, nothing would prevent the granting of independence.

On January 12, 1962, KENYATTA was unanimously elected to the legislature in the Fort Hall constituency, and from the next day he attended the meetings of the Legislative Council. At a mass rally of his party on January 21 KENYATTA said that from that time on Europeans also would have to address Africans as "bwana",[1] and if they refused, they should leave the country.

KENYATTA's return to public life in the latter half of 1961 electrified the political atmosphere. But new elemental disasters added to the critical situation of the country's economy and to the discontent of broad masses of the African population.

The people of Kenya had hardly recovered from the ravages caused by the drought and worm invasion at the beginning of the year, when new, more terrible calamities descended on them. On October 13 the government talked about 180,000 people suffering from famine, whose provision required tens of thousands of pounds of food every month. Soon afterwards began the rainy season which, after the prolonged drought, now brought unparalleled rainfalls. Huge areas were submerged, hundreds of villages were inundated, and a considerable part of the crop, which was already very poor owing to the drought, was destroyed, hundreds of thousands of the livestock perished in the floods, many roads and bridges got damaged, hundreds of Africans died, tens of thousands remained without shelter, and hundreds of thousands were doomed to starvation. On November 15 Governor RENISON, with reference to the "grave emergency", appealed to the British government for help.

Help did not fail to come. With the assistance of the Army, the Navy and the Royal Air Force, and of various ministries, the British government dispatched to Kenya considerable supplies of food which, however, proved far from enough for the more than 400,000 starving Africans of the flood-stricken areas. Besides, with its usual duplicity, London took advantage of the grave situation to reinforce its weakening positions in the agitated colony. The provision of assistance was made a pretext for raising the strength of the British armed forces stationed in Kenya. Part of the rescue teams remained in the country to distribute the aid. In this connection MBOYA stated at a party meeting in Nakuru that the Africans did not desire the presence of British troops, they could distribute the foods all by themselves.

The United States government, uninvited to do so, joined in the rendering of assistance. It cannot be said to have overdone it by sending a few tons of its surplus corn to the starving flood victims of East Africa (Kenya, Uganda, Tanganyika). True, it did not get paid for the shipments, but it made ample profits on the side: under the guise of aid shipments a U.S. air base was established in Nairobi, and the

---

[1] An equivalent of "mister".

corn sacks served propaganda purposes with the inscription: "Gift from the United States of America".

The growing discontent of the African masses impelled the government to accelerate its land scheme. In September the British and Kenyan governments agreed to allot lands to an additional 12,000 African families in the areas where up to that time only European settlers owned estates. (The previous arrangement covered 8,000 families.) The two schemes envisaged the distribution of 350,000 acres of former European-owned land among the Africans in two years. The implementation of the two plans called for £14 million ($40 million). The British government undertook to finance the new arrangement and began negotiations for the financing of the previous scheme with the International Bank for Reconstruction and Development and the Colonial Development Corporation.

By the end of November the Kenyan government managed to obtain for this purpose a credit of $8.4 million from the World Bank, and in January 1962 it received a loan of £3 million ($8.6 million) from the West German government, as McKENZIE said, with the proviso that two-thirds would be invested in agriculture and one-third in commercial business.

The parties feverishly prepared for the constitutional conference. Disputes on principle did not cease between K.A.N.U. and K.A.D.U. Aware of the weak points of his party's political line, NGALA saw it necessary to take with him to the conference a constitutional expert to help in the formulation of the position of K.A.D.U.: early in January he enlisted the services of the Swiss lawyer Dr. ZELLWEGER as counsellor.

The openly anti-African right wing of the settlers suffered a painful loss before the conference: their most powerful and most active representative, the leader of the United Party, LLEWELYN BRIGGS, died in November 1961.

The London Conference of 1962

The constitutional conference in London opened on February 14 and lasted seven weeks, closing on April 6. The deliberations were attended by 82 delegates under the chairmanship of Colonial Secretary MAUDLING.

In his opening address MAUDLING emphasized that the only purpose of the conference was to draw up a constitution for a future independent Kenya, but for the time being independence was premature. Political differences between the African parties during the conference were nevertheless overshadowing the conflicts between the Africans and the British government. KENYATTA's majority party, K.A.N.U., which represented the interests of the two largest tribes, the Kikuyu and the Luo, wanted a united central government. On the other side, NGALA's minority party, K.A.D.U., which had the smaller tribes behind it, was in favour of a weak federal government and demanded broad regional autonomy to protect the rights and interests of the minority tribes against the central government. That Kenya should become an independent state under an African government was no longer contested by the British government either, the only point of contention was the date for independence.

KENYATTA and his party displayed a good deal of common sense and were ready for compromises for the sake of agreement. In spite of this, discussions went on for weeks, without success because of the obstinacy of the K.A.D.U. leaders. The conference seemed to end with failure after nearly two months' futile verbal sparring, when at last it was possible to find halfway solutions which each of the parties could regard as partial enforcement of its own standpoint. Accordingly, independent Kenya would get a bicameral legislature: a lower house to be constituted through national elections and composed of members elected in evenly delimited constituencies on the basis of universal adult suffrage, and an upper house consisting of representatives of the six regions. The way of appointing the members of the upper house was to be determined later.

The legislature was to choose a strong central government responsible solely to parliament. In the six regions the local tribes should elect and control their own regional assemblies whose powers covered local government, education and public health, and the implementation of the land scheme (to the exclusion of the "Scheduled Areas", the former White Highlands). Constitutional amendments should be within the competence of the upper house.

K.A.N.U. and K.A.D.U. were to form a provisional coalition government; on the principles laid down in London, they should work out the final constitution by the end of July, and hold parliamentary elections by its terms. The leader of the party winning in the election would have to agree with the British government for a timetable of independence.

A special clause of the constitutional proposals ensured the rights of the minorities (including Europeans, Asians and Muslims). Most of the white settlers already acquiesced in the idea of an African majority government. The related agreement was even signed by their representative from the Kenya Coalition. Representatives from the Somali and Masai tribes did not sign because their demands were ignored. (The Somalis demanded the secession of their district to Somalia, and the Masai wanted back a part of the fertile former "European lands".) The Masai delegate, JOHN KEEN, who was an organizing secretary of K.A.N.U., left the conference three days before the signing took place, because MAUDLING refused to meet their demand.

A whole series of problems were set aside or postponed by half-way measures and decisions. In the land issue, for example, it was decided that the long-established reserves would remain under tribal control, but their problems should be submitted to the regional assemblies. On the other hand, any decision concerning the best lands formerly owned by Europeans (the White Highlands) would fall under the jurisdiction of a Central Land Board. Similarly it was laid down that "the central government would be responsible for the armed forces and the ultimate sanction of law and order, but the day to day responsiblity for law and order would rest with the regional assembly".

No decision was made on the future of the Northern Frontier District, whose Somali inhabitants wanted to join independent Somalia. The future of the Coastal Strip under the sovereignty of the Sultan of Zanzibar was also shelved. (The Commissioner appointed to study the question, Sir JAMES ROBERTSON, proposed in December 1961 that the area be integrated with Kenya after independence, which should then pay compensation to the Sultan for the surrender of his sovereignty. During the conference the Sultan declared his readiness to waive his sovereign rights in case the rights and traditions of his subjects living there were constitutionally safeguarded. Therefore the issue was postponed until the adoption of the constitution.)

Likewise no decision was made on one of the most important issues, the date for accession to independence. Still before the conference KENYATTA stated: "We believe the British government will fix the date of our independence for this year, because we are convinced that its delaying is desirable neither to Britain nor to us." But he was bitterly disappointed in his expectation. He had to rest satisfied with a verbal promise of the British government to grant independence after a "triat period" (! ?) following the introduction of the new constitution.

Revision of the regional and constituency boundaries was also put off for the next year.

The coalition government was formed immediately as agreed. KENYATTA obtained the portfolios of Constitutional Affairs and Economic Development, and MBOYA became Minister of Labour.

Under the agreement each of the two African parties should have had seven governmental places. But Colonial Secretary MAUDLING told KENYATTA that the British government objected to OGINGA ODINGA assuming the post of Finance Minister because ODINGA, the Vice-President of K.A.N.U., had been a leader of the Kenya national independence struggle.

This outrageous breach of agreement roused profound discontent in the K.A.N.U. delegation. Under strong British pressure, however, KENYATTA had to agree to ODINGA being left out of the government, which, by the way, included not only African members. The Council of Ministers was presided over by the Governor, and two important portfolios, Defence and Justice, were left in the hands of colonial officials.

When KENYATTA returned from the conference on April 8, he was welcomed in Nairobi by a jubilant crowd of about twenty thousand. Speaking to the people on this occasion, he expressed the conviction that the just formed coalition government would not last long, because K.A.N.U. would win in the next elections and take over power.

Struggle for Independence between the 1962 London Conference and the Elections in May 1963

A full year went by before the general elections which had to precede accession to independence. The elections could not be called until the controversies over the constitution had been settled by reconciling somehow the differences between K.A.N.U. and K.A.D.U. And the date of independence could not be appointed without the holding of elections.

Internal tensions were growing. The dragging out of the granting of independence still increased the exasperation of the African masses caused by land hunger and unemployment. To all this were added the tribal differences all over the country. General poverty and discontent often prompted people to criminal acts, and tribal differences resulted in grave conflicts in many places.

The crimes the Africans committed in despair worried the coalition government, and notably K.A.N.U. According to official records Africans robbed Europeans in 18 cases during the first three months of the year. There was nothing to indicate that the assaults were of a political character or committed by organized gangs. On the contrary, it was evident that the occurrences were all desperate actions by destitute people against well-to-do persons. But among the British colonial officials and the European settlers there were always some who liked to impute any African misdeed to the (actual or presumed) criminal activity of the subversive Land Freedom Army and tried to undermine thereby the prestige and reputation of K.A.N.U.

In the spring of 1962 the government had much trouble with the tribal unrest which persisted for months in the regions bordering on Uganda, the Sudan, and Ethiopia. At the end of February the Kenya government, acting upon complaints from Uganda, started a police action, in co-operation with the Uganda and Sudan authorities, to disarm the Turkana tribe living in an area of 13,000 square miles in the Northern Frontier District. The Turkana in the past year had many times raided the Dodoth tribe in Ugandan territory to steal cattle and ivory. According to official reports of the Uganda government about 300 people on both sides fell victim to more than 150 incursions, and the attackers had driven off more than 4,000 cattle. During the two-week police action 123 firearms and lots of ammunition were confiscated from the Turkana tribe, and eight Turkana tribesmen were killed. A month later 40 members of the Dodoth tribe from Uganda made an inroad into Turkana country, killing 11 and wounding 6 people (women and children among them). They stole 200 cattle, but they were caught by the Kenya police before getting to the Uganda frontier. In the ensuing exchange of fire three robbers were killed and two wounded.

During summer the government's position was made difficult by organized strikes of extreme left-wing trade-union leaders who were against MBOYA. Labour Minister MBOYA declared that if the unions irresponsibly misused the right to strike, the government would be compelled to consider curtailing this right. MBOYA's firm stand was supported also by KENYATTA. In August the Labour Ministers of Kenya, Uganda and Tanganyika met at Kampala, Uganda, and issued a joint communiqué, appealing to the trade-union leaders to take into account the national interests and refrain from irresponsibly resorting to strikes.

The K.A.N.U. ministers grasped every opportunity to propagate the political and cultural programme of the party. In May 1962, for example, in a speech at the annual conference of the International Press Institute in Paris, MBOYA criticized the African press for its majority being controlled by foreign capitalists and backing the policy of the colonialists instead of the independence struggle of the Africans. He declared that the Africans in every country needed a national press of their own, which should serve the interests of their respective country, not foreign interests. Even though this national press would not be perfect for the time being, he added, it was nevertheless more desirable than the unscrupulous scribbling of some foreign newspapermen.

KENYATTA's popularity was growing throughout the country. The K.A.N.U. executive and a conference of delegates from the party membership gave him broad personal powers to direct the party.

Early in June mayoral elections were held in Nairobi. For the first time in the city's history Africans were elected unopposed as Mayor and Deputy Mayor.

The K.A.N.U. and K.A.D.U. leaders decided to hold a seven-day joint meeting in August in Nairobi and invite leading politicians of the country to attend and join in preparing constructive proposals for the further development of Kenya after independence.

In July British Colonial Secretary MAUDLING made a five-day visit to Kenya. His double purpose was: 1. to try to reconcile the views of the coalition partners (K.A.N.U. and K.A.D.U.) and draw up a compromise constitution acceptable to both; 2. to announce the British government's decision to make it possible, by granting Kenya £15 million in loans and aid, to buy about one-third of the land owned by European settlers (1 million hectares) and to distribute it among Africans.[1]

---

[1] The scheme provided for the purchase and allotment of only small and medium estates. The large areas of coffee, tea and sisal plantations and the large stock-raising farms were excepted from the scheme. The hypocritical explanation offered was that if these farms were dismembered only half the African labourers employed in them could be given land, the other half would add to the number of jobless Africans and thus aggravate the problem of land hunger further.

The visit achieved nothing. The compromise proposals satisfied the leaders neither of K.A.N.U. nor of K.A.D.U. MAUDLING claimed that the fixing of the time-table of independence was premature, and that elections could not be held before 1963. He stressed that the election of the Legislative Council must be preceded by elections to the regional assemblies. He stated further that after the general elections another constitutional conference should be held.

Each party found that the concessions made to the other were excessive. K.A.N.U. demanded a democratic electoral system, speedier Africanization of the government apparatus, and wanted a strong, unified central government. K.A.D.U., on the other hand, insisted on the federal scheme and demanded complete tribal autonomy for the regions. (One day NGALA left but next day, having changed his mind, he returned. However, he still held to his position.)

Neither the settlers nor the Africans were satisfied with the British government's decisions regarding the land issue. All of them were of the opinion that the British government should have "taken over" much more land. In addition, the Africans held the view that the five-year term of the scheme was too long.

After MAUDLING's visit the Kenyan government, which was worried by the discontent of Africans and settlers, still at the end of July sent to London its competent minister, MCKENZIE and three other members of the government, to request London to shorten the proposed term and to extend the land reform to the settler estates in the Coastal Strip and in the west of Rift Valley, between the Nandi and Kipsigi tribes.

In August a delegation headed by MBOYA went to London and spent ten days in talks about financial aid to Kenya. They managed to obtain Foreign Secretary SANDYS' promise to grant Kenya aid and loans to the tune of £7 million. The Colonial Development Corporation also promised a loan of £ 1.5 million. The delegation later had similar talks in Bonn and Washington.

The West German government voted a loan of £2.5 million by making its use subject to its special approval. It allowed, for example, that in the next two years half a million pounds be spent on road construction — on condition that during the same period the Kenyan government would allot £250,000 to the same end. In the United States the Kenya delegation succeeded in obtaining a loan of £3 million from the World Bank.[1]

In August MBOYA went to Israel, too, to negotiate with the Israeli Federation of Labour about an agreement on assistance to Kenya in the establishment of co-operative shops and a large building enterprise.

At the end of July the fifty-year-old Kenya Indian Congress decided to stop pursuing political activities. S. G. AMIN, the party president, declared that the meddling of Europeans and Asians in the political quarrels of Africans could only do harm.

But the conference planned for August to create the unity of K.A.N.U. and K.A.D.U. did not come about. The differences between K.A.N.U., which demanded a united strong central government, and K.A.D.U., which strove to transform the country into a federation of autonomous republics, proved to prevail over the efforts at unity. Referring to pressure of business, KENYATTA refused to take part, and

---

[1] The United States showed rather great interest in the Kenya opportunities. Assistant Secretary for African Affairs MENNEN WILLIAMS in May 1962 again went to Kenya. He attended the opening meeting of the Legislative Council session. He talked in private with KENYATTA, whom he invited on behalf of his government to make a visit to America. In August 1962 Kenya received the American statistician LAMONT HUXTABLE as a UN technical assistance adviser for a year's stay.

NGALA said the conference was a "K.A.N.U. trick" and appealed to the K.A.D.U. followers to boycott it, while he flew to Somalia for the proposed duration of the conference.

In the latter half of the year the government was again given much trouble by the recurring conflicts between the tribes of the Northern Frontier District. In the first days of September 300 soldiers and police were flown to the Ethiopian border, because the Merille tribe of Ethiopia launched night raids upon two Turkana villages, killing all the inhabitants (who in spring had been disarmed by the police) and carrying off all their livestock. The pursuing squad overtook the Merille robbers retreating to the frontier, killed two and captured three, while the rest escaped, but the cattle were driven back. The British government sent a note of protest to the Ethiopian government.

The Turkana did not stop making raids on the Ugandan tribes beyond the frontier (Dodoth, Karamajong, Suk, Jie), who responded with similar actions. This veritable tribal warfare went on for months. The most active on the Uganda side, together with the Dodoth, was the 172,000-strong Karamajong tribe. As to the latter we read in an official report:

"The Karamajongs seem to raid their neighbours if and when they please and the country is in a state of continual warfare, which seems to become increasingly serious and more widespread all the time."

The same report put the number of Turkana and Uganda tribal raids at "nearly 700", in the course of which 404 people were killed on the two sides, the looted cattle numbered 81,394, of which 20,054 were returned to their owners with the help of the armed forces.

After long negotiations the Turkana and Karamajong chiefs "concluded peace" on September 18: they agreed to stop the raids on both sides.

But the peace was short-lived. A month later the Turkana made a night raid into the region of Agopo Pass, killing two people and driving off 300 cattle of the Dodoth. Not waiting for the troops to arrive, the Dodoth retaliated: they killed 42 Turkanas and recovered most of the stolen cattle. The chiefs on both sides claimed the affair was an arbitrary action by irresponsible young fighters, and peace was restored for the time being. The troops were withdrawn.

In the last months of the year the persecution of the Kikuyu started again on the pretext of Mau Mau revival. On October 5 the police arrested 26 Kikuyus on the charge of membership in the Land Freedom Army, which the authorities regarded as the successor to Mau Mau. A few days later, on October 12, in the village of Molo 190 kilometres from Nairobi, a sentence of seven years' imprisonment was meted out to the 73-year-old head of the local K.A.N.U. branch, KINYANJUI MUTEGI, who had allegedly admitted having been a founder of the secret organization called the Land Freedom Army which followed in the traditions of Mau Mau, and having directed the gangs of the Rift Valley organization. Another member of the Molo branch of K.A.N.U., DAVID GICHOLE, as an alleged "officer" of the Land Freedom Army, got five years in prison. An additional 14 persons, also alleged to be members of the secret organization, were sentenced to prison for different terms. At the same time the Nairobi police disclosed that 19 more Kikuyus had been arrested on the suspicion of belonging to that organization. According to the police report the Land Freedom Army wanted to oust the white population of Kenya.

"Friends" of K.A.N.U. spread various rumours about the purposes of the secret organization. They frightened the settlers with the lie that the Africans had formed this organization in order to seize power by force of arms. And they scared the tribes backing K.A.D.U. by telling them that the Kikuyu had established the secret organization to wage armed struggle with a view to grabbing the best jobs and the best lands for their own tribe after independence.

Relaxation

On October 21 KENYATTA announced that K.A.N.U. was ready to admit Europeans and Asians among its members: "From today those Europeans and Asians who want to co-operate with us, who agree that Africans should govern this country, have the door open to them."

In November the British government appointed to the post of Governor of Kenya a reputed liberalist, MALCOLM MACDONALD, son of the late Labour Prime Minister RAMSAY MACDONALD. The new Governor, a couple of hours after his arrival in Nairobi on January 4, not waiting to be installed in office, gave a press conference where he said he wished to co-operate with the Africans and would help them to realize their independence aspirations; the elections would be put through "as rapidly as possible", whereupon Kenya would become self-governing with a Prime Minister as head of government, and the British government "would lose no time" doing everything necessary for the sake of Kenya's complete independence.

McKENZIE again went to London to urge the British government to speed up the land reform. Upon returning from London at the end of January he could report on the success of his mission: the British government decided to fulfil the land scheme in three years instead of five.

The mood of a great number of settlers also changed. The President of the Kenya National Farmers' Union, Lord DELAMERE, who had once been the most vociferous champion of the settlers' privileges, in his New Year's address to the Union's membership stated that in spite of the existing difficulties the white settlers still had a future in Kenya, and that those who had left the country for fear of African rule had acted rashly. "There are so many great problems here, but I believe they are all solvable", he said. He told his audience that many of those who had sold their estates or had offered them for sale to the government now wanted to buy new lands in other parts of the country, and a growing number of those who had left were returning to Kenya. In DELAMERE's view, for the economy of Kenya to prosper, they needed the guarantee of law and order and "a spirit of tolerance between farmers of all races".

The Africans were increasingly alarmed at the British government's delay in appointing the date of independence. In a speech on November 14 KENYATTA requested the British government to fix the date of election for the spring of 1963 and independence by the end of 1963 at the latest; or else his party would withdraw from the coalition government; he demanded at the same time that Britain dismantle immediately her military bases in Kenya. KENYATTA gave expression to this demand in his cable to the Saudi Arabian delegation to the United Nations after its disclosing that Britain was stockpiling nuclear weapons at her Kawaha base in Kenya.

In November 1962 an East African university was opened in Nairobi for peoples of the four British East African territories, and in January 1963 Kenya's 28 primary schools accessible so far only to children of European settlers opened their doors to African and Asian children, too.[1]

[1] Seven secondary schools of the settlers admitted Africans and Asians from January 1960 onwards, but very few African children could make use of this possibility: only those who had

In February 1963 British Foreign Secretary SANDYS made a three-week tour of Kenya. Like MAUDLING six months earlier, he made this visit in an effort to smoothe the differences between the two African parties and to persuade them into a compromise on the still controversial points of the constitution, about which experts in London and Nairobi had been consulting for months without success.

He could not settle the main difference between K.A.N.U. and K.A.D.U. (strong central government or federation), but he made the two parties agree to the constitutional provision granting self-government to Kenya and putting an African majority government headed by an African Prime Minister in charge of the administration. On the last day of his stay in Kenya, March 8, SANDYS announced that the elections would take place between May 16 and 28. He said also that the Sultan of Zanzibar had consented that Kenya should continue to administer as part of the country the Coastal Strip he had let on lease to Britain for many decades, and that the British government had decided to grant local autonomy also to the Somali-inhabited seventh region of Kenya.

The direct reason for this decision of the British government was the growing tension between the governments of Somalia and Great Britain. From the first day of her independence Somalia had demanded that Kenya's Somali-populated region (with 250,000 inhabitants and about one-third of the national territory) be joined to the independent Somali Republic. The demand was supported by the majority of the Somali population of the territory, and demonstrations occurred day after day, often coupled with rioting, which would be put down energetically by the police. On such an occasion, towards the end of February, rioters clashed with the police, and a number of Somalis were killed. At the news of the incident violent mass demonstrations broke out in Mogadishu, and Somalia recalled her diplomatic representative from London, whereupon the British Ministry of War ordered the British troops in Nairobi to be put on the alert. It was presumably this tension that the British government intended to relax by granting autonomy to the Somalis of Kenya.

Back in London DANDYS on March 12 announced to the Commons the government's decision and gave as a reason that without the consent of the Kenyan government Britain could not settle the territorial claim of Somalia, all the less since both K.A.N.U. and K.A.D.U., as well as the majority of the Kenya population, categorically rejected the Somali claim. By creating an autonomous region they left the question open and waited for it to be settled by the future government of independent Kenya. He added that this handling of the issue was agreeable to K.A.N.U. and K.A.D.U., and the decision, he hoped, would be accepted as a "gesture of good will" also by the Somali government.

But SANDYS was mistaken on this point. The British decision roused general indignation in the Mogadishu parliament. Members demanded the severance of diplomatic relations with Great Britain. In the Somali-inhabited northern parts of Kenya desperate demonstrations followed one another. The demonstrators demanded the annexation of the region to Somalia, inveighed against Britain, and tore down the Union Jack. About a hundred people began throwing stones upon the British Dis-

a perfect command of English, since teaching was in this language; and those whose parents could afford to pay the high tuition fees and other school expenses (meals and school uniform). In the first year hardly more than two or three African and four or five Asian children went to those schools. (The school of the most obstinate white farmers in Molo admitted one African and one Asian only after long procrastination.) The popuation of the three racial groups was as follows: over 8 million Africans, 180,000 Asians, and 66,000 Europeans.

trict Commissioner's house at Marsabit. The Commissioner, five policemen and a civilian were injured. The police dispatched to disperse the crowd killed ten Somalis (a ten-year-old boy among them).

On March 15, 1963, the Kenya police reported the successful completion of the action started to liquidate the Land Freedom Army. From August of the preceding year, according to the report, 10,568 persons had admitted that they had been members of the organization, and during the arrests the police had seized 392 firearms and lots of ammunition. How many of those arrested had been convicted of activity in the organization was left unmentioned in the report. Since the authorities had found no evidence of the previous charges either (the organization's alleged purpose was to exterminate or to expel the white settlers, or to seize power), the report asserted that the secret aim of the organization had been to occupy by force of arms the settler estates in Rift Valley and the White Highlands after independence. This accusation was obviously intended to justify the mass arrests and the severe sentences, to demonstrate its truth to K.A.N.U., whose leader, KENYATTA, was definitely opposed to any forcible land seizure intended after independence.

While certain forces tried to incite other tribes against the Kikuyu, that is essentially against K.A.N.U., by referring to "the danger of reviving Mau Mau traditions", there were many signs of the growing consciousness and cohesion of Africans. At the time when the above-mentioned police report was published, the British military command reported a "mutiny" of African students of the military academy which was training N.C.O.s for the future Kenya armed forces: 150 young Africans from various tribes went on strike because of the dismissal of a few of their colleagues and refused to go on duty over a couple of days. The strike was conducted in an orderly manner, without any violence or disturbance.

After SANDYS left Kenya, an increasingly vigorous election campaign got under way, whose atmosphere was determined by the sharpening conflicts between the two parties and the differences of the tribes backing them as well as by the growing bitterness of the starving African masses.

The election contest of the two parties was especially violent in the western parts of the country, where K.A.N.U. made efforts to win the K.A.D.U.-influenced tribes over to its own policy. To disturb the K.A.N.U. meetings, K.A.D.U. followers often resorted to violence.

A still greater concern of the K.A.N.U. leaders was the struggle between factions inside the party. In February a party functionary, NGEI, the political leader of the Kamba tribe numbering 800,000 people, with a great part of his tribesmen left K.A.N.U. and formed the African People's Party.[1] NGEI charged that K.A.N.U. leaders, notably MBOYA and ODINGA, pursued factionalism against each other, and both served the interests of foreign powers: MBOYA favoured the United States, and ODINGA supported the policy of the Eastern countries. But NGEI's political programme was no different from that of K.A.N.U.

Another substantial loss suffered by K.A.N.U. was that many of MBOYA's Luo followers deserted him and joined a group which rallied in a united Luo front and opposed the K.A.N.U. policy of unity.

A greater threat than these desertions was posed to K.A.N.U. by the internal factionalism between MBOYA's and ODINGA's followers. This antagonism went so far that they put up candidates against each other in many places. (In ODINGA's constituency, at Bondo near Kisumu, MBOYA's father-in-law, WALTER ODEDE,

---

[1] Soon after the May elections NGEI and his followers again joined K.A.N.U.

was nominated as a candidate opposed to ODINGA.) Having drawn the lesson from the 1961 elections, KENYATTA had to warn members of his party that those who stood for election in opposition to official candidates would be expelled from the party even in case they won the election.

NGALA tried to exploit the internal struggle of K.A.N.U. He attempted to persuade NGEI and his followers to join K.A.D.U., but to no avail. In his party propaganda he used the radical views of ODINGA and other K.A.N.U., left-wingers as an argument to obtain the favour of the Europeans and Asians in fear of reforms, to win them over to K.A.D.U., and he achieved some success in this effort.

At the end of April K.A.N.U. outlined the party programme for the time of self-government and after independence. Accordingly the party wanted to build up a system of "African socialism" in Kenya, guaranteeing freedom of speech and of the press as well as the free operation of trade unions.

The Election of May 1963. The Kenyatta Government

In the days preceding the elections clashes occurred in several places between followers of the warring parties. A K.A.N.U. election meeting was due to take place in NGEI's native town, where his African People's Party had its headquarters, at Kandungo situated east of Nairobi. KENYATTA himself prepared to go there and make a speech. A group of NGEI's adherents from the Kamba tribe, armed with poisoned arrows, lay in ambush on the road leading to Kandungo about 30 miles from Nairobi, with the intent to kill KENYATTA who was to come by car. Owing to ill health KENYATTA cancelled the trip, but the police discovered the group lying in ambush and unarmed them.

The place where the K.A.N.U. meeting was held in Kandungo was surrounded by a tough crowd of 500 Kamba tribesmen in arms. The demonstrators threw about stones and used knives and spears in resisting the police who dispersed them with truncheons and tear-gas bombs. The casualties amounted to 18 gravely wounded Africans and one injured police inspector.

The same day (it was a Sunday) followers of the two parties clashed at Tala and Kitala, two villages about 50 kilometres from Nairobi. The police here separated the brawlers by shooting in the air, but the riot produced more than a dozen wounded men.

The elections were held from May 18 to 28. The African electorate numbered 2,668,569 (out of a population of 8,300,000). The contest for the seats in parliament was practically between the two great African parties, K.A.N.U. and K.A.D.U. Standing for election were also candidates of the NGEI-led African People's Party in league with K.A.D.U. and of two minor parties (the Baluba People's Union and the Coast People's Party). Since the vast majority of Africans were illiterate, the ballots were marked with symbols ("lamp", "rhinoceros", etc.) chosen by the candidate concerned. The voter had to name the symbol to the election officer, who then ticked off the name of the candidate.

The elections proper did not pass without incidents either. In the township of Isiolo in the Northern Frontier District, for example, a crowd of a thousand Somalis assembled on May 24 to frighten away the voters. The police first used tear gas to scatter the people. Since this was to no avail, they used their weapons, unleashing a veritable battle. The number of casualties was not recorded.

The elections were designed to return 119 members to the House of Representatives and 41 to the Senate. But since the Somali population of the Northern Frontier

District, who demanded secession to Somalia, boycotted the elections, only 112 seats in the lower house and 38 in the Senate could be filled, and only six of the seven regional assemblies were elected.

KENYATTA's party won a firm majority. KENYATTA was elected unopposed.

K.A.N.U. and the independents associated with it obtained 71 of the 112 seats in the House of Representatives and 20 of the 38 seats in the Senate, and thus controlled three of the six regional assemblies. There was only a single candidate (among 725) proposed by the European settlers, but against the African candidate he polled not even ten per cent of the vote.

In Nakuru, the centre of the White Highlands, which had thus far been regarded as the mainstay of K.A.D.U., all three seats were won by K.A.N.U. candidates. The same happened in another town of the area, Kericho, and in Voi in the Coastal Strip. Among the major cities K.A.D.U. won only in Mombasa.

At the close of the vote the streets of Nairobi were swarmed by thousands of young Africans who demonstrated enthusiastically and cheered KENYATTA as "father of the nation".

After the announcement of the election returns KENYATTA made the following statement: "On this great day in the history of our nation, I pledge that the K.A.N.U. government which is about to take office will be guided in its task by the principles of democratic African socialism. We shall build a country where every citizen may develop his talents to the full, restricted only by the larger aim we have of building a fair society. The right of all their property will be fully protected ... Our government intends to do away with the terrible poverty of so many of our people ... We do not expect to do all this from foreign charity. We are not going to compromise our independence by begging for assistance."

MBOYA said the election results were "natural" and logical, and added: "Despite the help from British and other elements, the tribalists and racialists have failed. But we do not intend to indulge in recriminations ... This is not going to be a government for K.A.N.U. supporters only."

In conformity with the results of the elections, KENYATTA on May 28 was appointed first Prime Minister of Kenya. Governor MACDONALD issued an official statement announcing that on June 1 Kenya would be granted internal self-government with KENYATTA as Prime Minister, and the new constitution would come into force.

On May 30 Governor MACDONALD unexpectedly made another statement. He announced that, by virtue of the constitution of self-government, the powers reserved for the Governor (external relations, defence and internal security) were conferred upon KENYATTA.

KENYATTA formed his government on May 30. He kept the portfolios of external affairs, defence and internal security. The government had another twelve members, including ODINGA as Minister of Home Affairs, GICHURU as Minister of Finance and Economic Planning, KIANO as Minister of Commerce and Industry, and KOINANGE as Minister of State for Pan-African Affairs.

The Policies of the Kenyatta Government

On June 1, 1963, KENYATTA as the first Prime Minister of Kenya took the oath of office before Governor MACDONALD. The ceremony was held outdoors, in the presence of an enthusiastic crowd of 15,000. The Governor announced the entry into force of the constitution granting Kenya complete internal self-government.

The celebration was not disturbed by any incident, but some hours later oppositionist elements provoked clashes with K.A.N.U. followers who supported the government. The police dispersed the trouble-makers with tear gas, and four people with injuries were taken to hospital.

At the end of June SANDYS, on behalf of the British government, agreed in London with three representatives of the Kenyan government that independence would be granted to Kenya by the end of the year, and prior to that a new conference would be called to London to remove the differences between the parties and to draw up the final text of the constitution.

In preparation for the forthcoming constitutional conference Governor MACDO-NALD in mid-July started talks in Nairobi with leaders of the two parties, KENYATTA and MBOYA on the one hand, NGALA and NGEI on the other. Far from removing the differences, the talks still more intensified them. The opposition did not acquiesce in its election defeat: NGALA and other leaders of the opposition stuck by the idea that power should be shared between a central government and the regional, tribal governments. On the the other side, KENYATTA and MBOYA, having learned from the Congo example, found it inadmissible to invest the regional authorities with functions other than those of local administration. Quite the contrary, they held the view that concentration of all powers in the hands of a united, strong central government was indispensable. Before the constitutional conference NGALA, who stubbornly insisted on the principle of regionalism, tried to influence the British government by threatening to use force to divide the country into regions inhabited by smaller tribes (Kalenjin country, Masailand, Coastal Strip) to become separate independent states. Since the K.A.N.U. leaders also abided by their position in favour of a strong central government, NGALA on August 23 broke the negotiation with the Governor and declared that he would not discuss the K.A.N.U.-proposed revision at the London conference either.

The last constitutional conference before independence opened in London on September 25. The conference under the chairmanship of SANDYS was attended by ten delegates from the government of Kenya, five from the opposition, and three from the European settlers. The K.A.N.U. delegation was headed by KENYATTA and the K.A.D.U. delegation by NGALA. The most important issue to be decided was whether the regional governments should remain as K.A.D.U. desired or whether the country should have a strong central government as demanded by KENYATTA and his party.

At the opening meeting KENYATTA stressed that the powers of the regional and tribal organs must be reduced and the powers and authority of the central government strengthened. He declared that if the British government prevented the constitution from being revised to this effect, he would not accept the actual constitution as binding upon him.

On October 7 municipal elections were held in Nakuru, which NGALA had intended as the capital of an independent state to be separated from Kenya. K.A.N.U. won 17 seats out of 18, and one seat was obtained by an independent candidate. K.A.D.U. was utterly defeated. (The same had happened at the Nairobi municipal elections at the end of September; K.A.N.U. won 27 seats out of 30, independents gained three, and K.A.D.U. none.)

The same day the K.A.N.U. leaders sent the British Colonial Secretary a cable reminding him that in case the London government could not arrive at an agreement with the Kenya delegation, Kenya would draw up her constitution by herself and submit it to a referendum. The British government did not respond.

Two days later K.A.D.U., at an executive meeting with party Chairman DANIEL MOI presiding, passed a resolution to separate about a quarter of the Kenya territory under the jurisdiction of the K.A.N.U. government, and to form an independent republic comprising the fertile Rift Valley, Western Province, the North East Region and the rural Coast (with the seaport Mombasa), with Nakuru as capital and NGALA as President of the Republic. On October 10 NGALA displayed the map of the planned new state at a press conference, and announced his party's claim officially in a ninety-minute conversation with SANDYS.

In a broadcast message to his party KENYATTA warned the population to remain calm, pointing out that the separatist plan was nothing else than a blackmailing manoeuvre to force the Kenyan and British governments to make certain concessions, but that all this was not to be taken seriously. In his speech at the conference on October 11 he said: "The Kenyan government is strong, firm and popular, it will not allow itself to be provoked by the bragging claptrap of leaders who have lost touch with reality."

How right KENYATTA was could be seen already the next day, when the K.A.D.U. leaders withdrew the plan of secession and explained the party resolution by claiming that it was a false interpretation by a Nairobi paper.

The British government still did not bring itself to make a final decision.

Hearing about the foot-dragging at the London conference, the K.A.N.U. ministers and M.P.s in Nairobi sent KENYATTA a cable on October 15, requesting the Kenya delegation to return to Nairobi before the 20th, and demanding that independence be proclaimed on that date, the eleventh anniversary of KENYATTA's arrest, and asking KENYATTA to take the oath of President of the independent state.

KENYATTA and MBOYA had a last, decisive talk with SANDYS, but still to no avail, and they made known their decision that, to comply with the will of their people, they would leave the conference, return home, and proclaim independence without the consent of the British government.

But this was not to pass. Conscious of the actual situation in Kenya, the British government finally understood that it was impossible further to ignore the demands of K.A.N.U., which were also the will of the people of Kenya. On October 16 SANDYS handed KENYATTA the definitive text of the constitution which reflected the K.A.N.U. position on all essential points of dispute. Namely: it invested the central government with full powers in security matters (armed forces, police) and in the guidance and control of state administration, and it made the revision of the constitution (including changes in the purview of regional authorities) subject to a three-quarters majority in both houses of parliament or to a two-thirds majority in a referendum.[1]

The conference was closed on October 19, after adopting the new constitution and setting December 12 as independence days.

A few hours before the signing of the agreement the K.A.D.U. delegation walked out of the conference, and NGALA reiterated his separatist threat before representatives of the press.

KENYATTA declared: "We have got what we came for. Independence has been confirmed. Whatever changes are made to the constitution are not made just for K.A.N.U. but for the good of the whole country."

The closing of the conference coincided with a change of government in Britain. The adoption of the constitution of Kenya was the last act of the MACMILLAN govern-

---

[1] The preceding version prescribed a 90 per cent majority of the Senate.

ment. The agreement was sanctioned by the government of the new Prime Minister, Sir ALEC DOUGLAS-HOME.

Having come out on top, KENYATTA and his delegation flew back to Nairobi on October 20. From the airport they drove direct to the new stadium where a mass meeting was held. Thousands of rejoicing Kenyans welcomed them on both sides of the road.

In his speech at the meeting KENYATTA told about the hard struggle they had had to wage in London in order to achieve their aim: from December 12 Kenya would be an independent state with a strong central government and a flexible, workable constitution. He emphasized that in independent Kenya there would be place for everybody, regardless of tribal or racial origin. He called upon his political antagonists to make peace with the government and co-operate with K.A.N.U. in eliminating poverty, ignorance and diseases, and in raising the living standard of the population.

Problems of the Kenyatta Government

From the granting of "complete self-government" to the proclamation of independence six months went by. During this period the KENYATTA government had to cope with lots of problems and difficulties.

The main preoccupations of the government were the serious situation of the African population, the problems of economic development and the shaping of foreign policies.

With the termination of the terror that had prevailed in the early fifties, and with the British imperialist switch-over to the policy of neocolonialism, the political and social situation of the Africans improved a great deal, but there was no change for the better in their economic situation and living conditions. The increasing land hunger, the succession of elemental disasters (drought, floods, worm invasion and cattle plague, smallpox epidemic), mass unemployment and, added to all this, the still operative laws of racial differentiation and restrictions still meant destitution and suffering to millions of Africans.

At the moment of taking office, KENYATTA and his government felt the heavy burden of the sad colonial past. They had to tackle lots of tasks to liquidate it. And not only the tasks were hard, but the government met with incomprehension and prejudices even on the part of the masses, whom they tried to raise politically, economically and culturally. More than half a century of colonial oppression and the racist policies of the colonialists, far from helping to overcome the traditional tribalism and racial prejudice of the African masses, rather hindered the efforts of those few who had already shaken off the fetters of century-old backwardness and tribal narrow-mindedness and considered it their sacred duty to promote the advance of their backward brothers. The majority of the population of Kenya, primarily the two largest tribes (Kikuyu and Luo), trusted KENYATTA and the soundness of K.A.N.U.'s policy, they were convinced that it was the only passable road towards their goal, independence, towards the improvement of their lot. But a number of smaller and backward tribes, even part of the Kikuyu and Luo, found that the land scheme was progressing too slowly and that KENYATTA and K.A.N.U. were too indulgent towards Europeans and Asians. Many of the older generations, who had for years been fighting hard against the oppressors, and many of the younger people, who had inherited the memories and traditions of their fathers' struggles, could not understand the change of time, could not see that the cause of independence and freedom required of them, not opposition and destruction, but discipline and constructive work, co-operation among all peoples of the country. Referring to past struggles and suffering, to the actual difficult situation and the problems of the masses, they demanded the speeding up of the reforms, extreme radical measures against Europeans and Asians, expropriation of European lands without compensation and their distribution among the Africans, as well as nationalization of European-owned enterprises. The most extreme of these malcontents assembled in secret organizations swearing to wage armed fight against Europeans, and established a "Young Guard" to perform acts of terrorism.

But KENYATTA and the K.A.N.U. government firmly abided by their sensible, moderate policy. KENYATTA himself called attention to the dangers of the activity of such extreme elements. In his speech at Kalou in the middle of August he labelled those organizations harmful to the cause of independence and called upon the authorities to take energetic action against them. And the government quietly proceeded with the gradual implementation of its realistic programme.

The government regarded as one of its main tasks to improve the situation of the African masses, and therefore it was busy creating the prerequisites of putting an end to land hunger and unemployment. It worked out a land reform, establishing a public fund to buy up the estates of Europeans who prepared to leave the country. It declared that every African claimant would be given land under the plan, but arbitrary land seizure would not be tolerated.

Still before independence the government began allotting the purchased land to African claimants, who were granted long-term credits enabling them to buy farms and implements and start cultivation.

Among the first to receive a new farm was the widow of an executed guerrilla leader: she obtained 14 acres of land. KENYATTA made a tour of the Highlands, where he warned the Africans not to occupy land arbitrarily. For the time being 2,500 African families were resettled in their ancestral country.

KENYATTA paid much attention to economic questions, as K.A.N.U. had laid down in its statement of policy that political liberties and equality were not enough; the people were entitled to be liberated from economic exploitation and social unequality; the party had decided to lead the country on the road of socialist economy.

On the plane of agriculture the K.A.N.U. government saw the way of socialization in the organization of co-operatives and the increase of production. Furthermore, starting from the view that it was an economic folly to continue importing finished goods produced abroad from Kenya's raw materials, the government stood up in favour of industrial development. This principle provided three main features of the economic policies of the government:

1. The government considered the abandonment of the economic policy of monoculture to be in the national interest.

2. Considering that economic growth was largely dependent on foreign investment, the government saw it necessary to continue to guarantee to capitalists the freedom of business and the export of profits, on condition only that investment projects must be in harmony with Kenya's interests, national policies and economic needs.

3. For this end the government thought it necessary to introduce extensive and effective state control of the whole economy, or if it was in the national interest, to nationalize certain sectors of industry, or some of their units, against compensation.

In the spirit of the K.A.N.U. programme the government set itself the task of eliminating all forms of racial differentiation and restriction. Accordingly its task was: (1) to change the state of racial inequality in the public service, commerce and other fields; (2) to ensure the enforcement of the principle of "equal pay for equal work", regardless of racial or tribal origin;[1] (3) to do away with racial segregation in health and educational institutions.[2]

At the same time KENYATTA and his government repeatedly and categorically stated that they regarded the European settlers not as enemies but as equal citizens of the country.

It was necessary to stress this because in some places where almost all the settlers had sold their estates and departed, it occurred more than once that Africans occupied the farm of one or another settler left alone to himself, and they drove off his livestock and damaged his equipment.

At a popular meeting in Nakuru on August 12 KENYATTA declared that his government needed the work and skill of Europeans who were willing to co-operate. He pointed out that the European farmers engaged in cultivating their land were always welcome to Kenya and should not fear for the security of their farms. The time had come, he said, to let bygones be bygones and to have more confidence in each other. He especially impressed the Europeans by his admission that his government had also committed mistakes, for which he apologized, as he also did not bear grudge against the Europeans for their mistakes and for his long imprisonment.

On the approach of independence many of the Europeans living in Kenya — primarily farmers and city businessmen, traders and professionals — came to understand that they might safely continue their activities in Kenya under an African government. Among the farmers there were still some who prepared to leave the country, they only waited for a good bargain to sell their estates, but the majority of the farmers, in general Europeans, decided to hold on. Of the 55,000 Europeans an estimated 35,000 intended to remain in the hope that law and order would be ensured also after independence.

The foreign policy of the government was guided by a double aim; to safeguard the complete independence and sovereignty of the country, and to strive to bring about the unity of African peoples. To this end, the government adopted a policy of neutrality and non-alignment: not to join any military bloc, not to allow any foreign state (Britain included) the maintenance of military bases in Kenya, to try to establish good relations, economic and cultural ties with all countries, irrespective of their social system, and with the governments of all states, regardless of their ideologies (except the racist governments of South Africa, Southern Rhodesia and Portugal).

The government stuck by this policy of non-alignment in every respect. While the K.A.D.U. leaders were unable to formulate a uniform view regarding the future

[1] According to the British government's *East African Yearbook 1963* the monthly wages of skilled workers in 1960 was from £ 200 for Europeans, £15 to £75 for Asians, and £10 to £30 for Africans. That is, the African received six to seven times less than his European fellow workers for the job which he performed with the same qualification as the others. The difference between wages of the race groups was in fact much more considerable, since few Africans were in a position to obtain the necessary skills. According to the same publication' in the nine largest cities of Kenya the average monthly pay of unskilled labour in 1962 was 104 shillings, in the next largest four cities it was only 87 shillings.

[2] Until then there had been separate hospitals and schools for Europeans, Asians, Arabs and Africans. Few of the African children could go to school, and relatively few of those who finished primary school gained access to secondary and still fewer to higher school.

of the British military bases,[1] the K.A.N.U. government stated officially that, in harmony with its policy of non-alignment, it would not allow foreign military bases to be maintained in Kenya territory.

The same principle of non-alignment dictated the policy of the KENYATTA government in its relations with the socialist great powers. While some K.A.N.U. leading politicians who had been to China, ODINGA and JOHN KALI, came to no small extent under the ideological influence of the Chinese leaders, KENYATTA always took care not to commit himself to any one of the contending socialist states, but to cultivate friendship and good co-operation with them. When, for instance, Prime Minister CHOU EN-LAI of China sent him a message informing him of his intention of convening a world conference for the total prohibition of nuclear weapons, KENYATTA gave a prudent non-committal answer: his government shared the desire of the Chinese government to see that the world was freed as soon as possible from the threat of nuclear warfare and Kenya supported any effort in this direction, but the prevention of the production and proliferation of nuclear weapons would take much time, so the Kenyan government welcomed every step leading towards the reduction of the existing danger.

At the same time he sent a delegation headed by two members of his government, Minister of Commerce KIANO and Minister of Agriculture McKENZIE, to the Soviet Union and other East European socialist countries to carry on talks about intensifying the commercial contacts.

When the delegation returned to Nairobi from its visit to the Soviet Union and six socialist countries of East Europe on November 4, MacKENZIE declared that they had found that Kenya could build advantageous commercial ties with the socialist countries, securing the import of goods of great importance for the economy of Kenya, thus agricultural and industrial machinery, bicycles, etc., which had so far been purchased in South Africa, and creating markets for certain products of Kenya, such as coffee, mineral soda, etc.

The greatest result of their trip, however, was the agreement under which states of the Eastern bloc undertook to send expert delegations to Kenya. The question of technical aid was also taken up, and they obtained fellowship awards in technology.

In the months preceding accession to independence the Kenyan government manifested more clearly than ever before its hostility to the South African government and the Portuguese colonialists. On October 1, Minister of Justice MBOYA while in London said that he saw only one way of communicating with South Africa and Portugal — the way of force. If the world wanted the peoples of southern Africa to avoid using force against the terror rule of the Pretoria government, it had to be prepared to use force from outside by itself. MBOYA requested Great Britain to stop supplying arms to Portugal and South Africa. On November 13 Minister of Commerce KIANO announced that as Kenya would win independence on December 12, the government would, in accordance with the recently passed resolution of the Addis Ababa conference of African states, immediately lay embargo on all imports from South Africa and the Portuguese colonies.

The second aim (promotion of the idea of African unity) prompted KENYATTA to take an active part in the work of the Organization of African Unity, to support

---

[1] In two days the K.A.D.U. leaders issued three different statements on this matter: the first said the foreign bases were incompatible with national sovereignty; the second held that they should remain until the danger of Somali secession was over; and the third proposed that the question be decided by the future government of independent Kenya.

the independence struggle of the African peoples still in colonial subjection, and to take measures with a view to creating closer political and economic relations between the countries of East Africa. Two days after his taking office, on June 3, he discussed these questions with President Sékou Touré of Guinea passing through Nairobi, a few days later with Julius Nyerere of Tanganyika and Milton Obote of Uganda, who went to Nairobi to consult with Kenyatta about the proposals for a federation of the countries of East Africa.

But they failed in their effort to establish a federation of the four East African countries still in 1963. Kenyatta and Nyerere were of the opinion that the East African Union should be formed at the earliest possible date, but the summit conference of the heads of state or government of the four countries, intended to decide the issue in the middle of September, did not meet because Obote had excused himself on account of ill health. Besides, Obote thought the matter was not urgent, at first he had to overcome the opposition of those who feared that the future of the Kingdom of Buganda would be jeopardized by federation. The fact was that Uganda was to win independence in October, and it was expected that the Kabaka of Buganda, Mutesa, would be elected President of the newly independent state. And it could be predicted that in case of his election Mutesa would oppose the federation of Uganda with the other three East African countries.

Kenyatta's government was worried by the recurring disturbances in the Northern Frontier District and by the regional issues (the Somali aspiration for secession and the problem of the Coastal Strip).

In June and July a number of tribal incidents occurred on the Sudan border of Kenya. Merille tribesmen coming from Ethiopia attacked the Turkana tribes of Kenya and killed 39 people early in June and again 23 in July.

At the end of July the British Colonial Secretary received a delegation of the Somali-populated Northern Province of Kenya. The delegation told the minister that if the British government should not allow the territory to join neighbouring Somalia before December 12, Kenya independence day, the Somali population of the area would have to use force. The British government was faced with a dilemma. Compliance with the Somali demand would have created a conflict with the government of Kenya on the eve of independence, and its refusal would have made it necessary to send troops from Nairobi to the Northern Province to put down the Somali revolt. Governor MacDonald thought that he could solve the problem by inviting the government of the Somali Republic to send its representative to Nairobi to discuss the question. It was even proposed that the question of the right of self-determination of the Somalis of Kenya should be brought to the United Nations or the Organization of African Unity. Since MacDonald's initiative failed, the British Foreign Secretary made a proposal to the government of Somalia for a meeting of their representatives in Rome on August 25 to discuss the question concerning Northern Province. The government of Somalia accepted the invitation, but the delicate issue could not be settled.

What could be settled, on the other hand, was another border dispute with Ethiopia. At the end of September Kenyan Minister Murumbi in charge of the Prime Minister's Office had talks in Addis Ababa, where he succeeded in smoothing out the differences between the two countries in connection with the boundary problems. The two countries agreed to disarm the tribes living in the borderland, and to convene a high-level conference of governmental representatives of four countries (Ethiopia, Kenya, Uganda, Sudan) for the definitive settlement of all boundary questions.

While the delegation of Kenya was talking in London about accession to independence, the government managed through diplomatic channels to arrive at a favourable agreement with the government of Zanzibar about the future of the Coastal Strip. Zanzibar surrendered its sovereignty over the area and relinquished its right to the rent received until then without demanding any kind of compensation. In return it stipulated only that the Zanzibari citizens of the area should enjoy freedom of speech and religion on an equal footing with the Kenyans. KENYATTA willingly accepted this condition and described the agreement as a big triumph of "justice, comprehension and neighbourliness".

On the other side, the border incidents with Somalia and Ethiopia continued in spite of repeated attempts by the Kenyan government to settle the problem by way of negotiation. The deputy chief of the Eastern Province of Kenya, AHMED FARAH, sent word to the government on Nocvember 20 that the outbreak of war with Somalia was to be feared as soon as Kenya had acceded to independence on December 12. He stated that to his knowledge Somalia was preparing to attack the country, supplying arms to the Somalis of Kenya, and the secessionists planned to display the Somali flag in the Northern Province on December 12. FARAH said the recent negotiation between KENYATTA and the Somali Foreign Minister was "idle and futile talk". His communication proved to be well founded. During the week following his message armed Somali bands crossing the boundary raided eight times the police stations in the district of El Wak. On December 8 ten armed Somalis attacked the police station at Gurar.

In spite of the arrangement entered into between the two governments at the end of September, the intrusions across the Ethiopian border did not stop. Armed bands of Ethiopian tribes invaded the district of Marsabit, killed 22 members of the Galuba tribe, wounded two others, and drove away 10,000 cattle. Policemen on camels pursued the robbers and recovered about four thousand cattle.

On November 13 the Kenya parliament, upon a motion by KENYATTA, decided that Kenya after independence would join the British Commonwealth.

Accession to Independence

On the occasion of the proclamation of independence the KENYATTA government issued an amnesty order. On December 6 KENYATTA met former guerrilla leaders and on behalf of the government invited them to attend the independence celebrations. At the same time he appealed through them to all former Mau Mau warriors and other guerrilla fighters who were still hiding in the woods to come out. He assured them that, if they surrendered their weapons until the 16th, they would not be harmed and would receive food and clothing.

Those hiding in the woods started to come forward on December 7, and the next day a good number of them were already walking free in the streets of Nairobi.

On December 9, five thousand political prisoners were released, among them 1,500 members of the Land Freedom Army. Twenty-four military leaders of the organization, who had been detained without trial in remote regions, were also set free.

The government issued a statement, calling upon the European settlers to continue tilling their farms and assured the landless Africans that during 1964 further lands would be expropriated and allotted to them.

KENYATTA's negotiations and statements were intended to prepare the quiet transfer of power. In connection with the fears that the boycott of trade with South

Africa would do serious harm to the economy of Kenya, Minister of Commerce and Industry KIANO declared that on his tour of East Europe he had achieved considerable results in providing new markets for the Kenyan products.

Early in December preparations for the independence celebrations of the 12th were in full swing.

Already on December 10 KENYATTA appointed the first five envoys of Kenya to represent the newly independent state in Washington (and New York at the UN), Moscow, Peking, Cairo and Paris.

The day before independence British Prime Minister DOUGLAS-HOME announced that the Commonwealth governments unanimously decided to admit Kenya to membership.

On December 12, 1963, in the Freedom Stadium built for this very occasion, Prince PHILIP as special representative of Queen ELIZABETH II, in the presence of delegates from 78 countries and 40,000 jubilant Africans, solemnly proclaimed the independence of Kenya and handed power over to KENYATTA. Thereafter he swore in former Governor MACDONALD as British High Commissioner who would henceforth represent the United Kingdom in independent Kenya, and then administered the oath to KENYATTA as Prime Minister of the newly independent state.

Afterwards KENYATTA made a speech: "This is the greatest day in the history of Kenya and the happiest day in my life. Relations between Kenya and Great Britain have not been severed; quite the contrary, they have become closer now that our two countries will co-operate in the Commonwealth, this singular union of free and independent states."

After this introduction he called upon all citizens of the country, regardless of race, sex and religion, to work together for the raising of the living standard of the people. At the same time he emphasized that independent Kenya, as a member of the large family of the nations of the world, would have to serve the cause of the peace of mankind.

Following his speech tens of thousands of the Africans who had assembled in the stadium and at the hill-side all around celebrated, singing and dancing, for over three hours the advent of the independence won at the price of long suffering and struggle. In the first night of independence a team of alpinists hoisted the flag of Kenya at the glacier-covered peak of the mountain rising over Nairobi.

In the main square of Nairobi, at the place of the toppled bronze statue of Lord DELAMERE, the one-time English settler leader who had stolen the land of Africans, a fountain was built whose spirting jets of water symbolizing the rise of the people of Kenya heralded a new, happier era for Kenya.

On December 13 KENYATTA officially applied for membership in the United Nations Organization.

BIBLIOGRAPHY

N. HUMPHREY, E. H. LAMBERT and P. WYN HARRIS, *The Kikuyu Lands*, Nairobi, 1945.
S. and K. AARONOVITCH, *Crisis in Kenya*, London, 1947.
Kenya Controversy. Fabian Colonial Bureau, Controversy Series No. 4. London, 1947.
Sir PHILIP MITCHELL, *The Agrarian Problem in Kenya*, Nairobi, 1947.
H. E. LAMBERT, "The System of Land Tenure in the Kikuyu Land Unit. Part I: History of the Tribal Occupation of the Land (Communication No. 22)", in *School of African Studies*, Capetown, 1950.
N. FARSON, *Last Chance in Africa*, London, 1950.

MARY PARKER, "Race Relations and Political Development in Kenya", *African Affairs'* Vol. 50, No. 198 (January 1951), pp. 41–52.

R. K. PANKHURST, *Kenya: The History of Two Nations*, London, 1953.

FENNER BROCKWAY, *Why Mau Mau? An Analysis and a Remedy*, London, 1953.

COLIN WILLS, *Who Killed Kenya?* London, 1953.

Opportunity in Kenya. Fabian Colonial Bureau, Research Series No. 162. London, 1953.

PHILIP E. MITCHELL, *African Afterthoughts*, London, 1954.

D. H. RAWCLIFFE, *The Struggle for Kenya*, London, 1954.

CHRISTOPHER WILSON, *Kenya's Warning*, Nairobi, 1954.

M. KOINANGE, *The People of Kenya Speak for Themselves*, Detroit, 1955.

MARTIN L. KILSON, "Kikuyu: A Study of Relationship between Land and Kikuyu Political Movements", *Journal of Negro History*, April 1955.

M. SLATER, *The Trial of Jomo Kenyatta*, London, 1955.

Lord ALTRICHAN, *Kenya's Opportunity: Memories, Hopes and Ideas*, London, 1955.

ELSPETH HUXLEY and MARGERY PERHAM, *Race and Politics in Kenya*, London, 1955.

E. CAREY FRANCIS, "Kenya's Problems as Seen by a Schoolmaster in Kikuyu Country", *African Affairs*, Vol. 54, No. 216 (July 1955), pp. 186–195.

E. FLETCHER, "Kenya's Concentration Camps: An Eyewitness Account", *Peace News*, London, May 4, 1956.

MARTIN L. KILSON, "Behind the Mau Mau Rebellion", Dissent 3/1956, pp. 264–275.

E. A. VASEY, "Economic and Political Trends in Kenya", *African Affairs*, April 1956.

TOM MBOYA, *The Kenya Question: An African Answer*, London, 1956.

H. E. LAMBERT, *Kikuyu Social and Political Institutions*, London, 1956.

L. S. B. LEAKEY, "The Economics of Kikuyu Tribal Life", *East African Economic Review*, Vol. 3, No. 1 (July 1956), pp. 165–180.

GEORGE BENNETT, "The Development of Political Organizations in Kenya", *Political Studies*, Vol. 5, No. 2 (June 1957), pp. 113–130.

Gangrene. With an Introduction by PETER BENENSON. London, 1959.

TOM MBOYA, *Kenya Faces the Future*, New York, 1959.

Further Documents relating to the deaths of eleven Mau Mau detainees at Hola Camp in Kenya. H.M.S.O., London, 1959.

Kenya: No Solution Possible without Jomo Kenyatta's Leadership (1960).

Historical Survey of the Origins and Growth of Mau Mau, London, 1960.

JOMO KENYATTA, *Kenya: The Land of Conflict*, London, n. d.

G. BENNETT and CARL G. ROSBERG, *The Kenyatta Election: Kenya 1960–1961.*

G. DELF, *Jomo Kenyatta: Towards Truth about "The Light of Kenya"*, London, 1961.

"Why Kenya Must Be Free Now!" *The New Kenya*, May–June 1961.

S. WOOD, *Kenya: Tensions of Progress*, London, 1962.

Report of the Kenya Constitutional Conference 1962. H.M.S.O., London, 1962.

FRED MAJDALANY, *State of Emergency: The Full Story of Mau Mau*, London, 1962.

JOSIAH MWANGE KARIUKI, *"Mau Mau" Detainee*, Oxford, 1963.

Kenya Independence Conference 1963, London, 1963 (Cmd. 2156).

GEORGE BENNETT, *Kenya: A Political History—The Colonial Period*, Oxford, 1963.

TOM MBOYA, *Freedom and After*, Boston, 1963.

TOM MBOYA, "The Party System and Democracy in Africa", *Foreign Affairs*, July 1963, pp. 650–658.

JOMO KENYATTA, *Harambee!* The Prime Minister of Kenya's speeches 1963–1964. New York 1964..

CARL G. ROSBERG Jr. and JOHN NOTTINGHAM, *The Myth of Mau Mau: Nationalism in Kenya*, New York–London, 1968.

DONALD L. BARNETT, *Mau Mau from Within*, London, 1967.

M. P. K. SORRENSON, *Land Reform in the Kikuyu Country*, Oxford, 1968.

CHAPTER XVII

UGANDA

Uganda was in several respects different from the other three British East African colonies.

In this territory the British imperialists made a colonial entity of four large (Buganda, Ankole, Toro and Bunyoro) and a number of smaller tribal states, in which already before the era of colonialism a peculiar system of tribal feudalism had emerged with tribal chiefs as feudal landlords and the African peasantry as serfs.

The staple products of the country, cotton and coffee, were grown for the most part by small peasant holdings in a system of traditional tribal rule. This prompted the colonizers to secure the capitalist exploitation of this colony by further developing the existing embryonic feudal system of tribes, and not by alienating the land of Africans and establishing European farming settlements, which would have resulted in the proletarization of the African peasants. It was due to this circumstance that the number of Europeans among the nearly five million inhabitants of Uganda in 1948 was less than one tenth of a per cent (3,448 out of 4,917,555) and also in 1959 was less than one and a half per thousand (10,866 out of 6,435, 155).

In the first half of the 20th century this policy of the British colonialists was a success. After World War II, however, the experiences of half a century, and the changes in world politics owing to the war, led them to introduce a new policy in Uganda, too.

1. The recurrence of world economic crises (notably the fluctuation of the world market price of cotton and coffee) made them understand the danger involved in monoculture. In order to introduce in Uganda the cultivation of new products, however, it was necessary to increase the crop yield of the land and to adopt more advanced agricultural methods. This they tried to attain by drafting and implementing economic development plans, on the one hand, and by developing European plantation farming, on the other. As early as mid-1946 they invited to Uganda a "development specialist" in the person of E. B. WORTHINGEN, who framed, and a year later submitted, a ten-year plan of economic development for Uganda. And in July 1947 the Governor appointed a "Development Commissioner" (DOUGLAS HARRIS) to supervise the implementation of the plan. At the same time, on the basis of the designs and proposals of C. R. WESTLAKE, an engineer who had also been invited in 1946, the British administration decided the construction of a huge dam and hydroelectric power plant near Jinja on the upper reaches of the Nile. (The 150,000-kilowatt power station was completed by 1954, the building costs came to about $22 million as against the estimated $4,803,700.) As to the settlers, their number grew almost threefold in ten years.

2. In the post-war period, when independence aspirations were spreading rapidly all over Africa, the main preoccupation of the colonialists was to create favourable conditions for any emergency in order to retain their economic positions and political influence in the colonies as long as they were in power there. In this effort they found themselves opposed in Uganda by two main factors: the narrow-mindedness and stubborn clinging of tribal leaders (feudal rulers and chiefs) to their traditional rights and privileges, and the nationalism of African politicians, mostly young intellectuals, who had risen above tribal seclusion and were aspiring after independence and democratic development. The aim of British colonial policy was, by making use of the opposition of those two elements, to play off one against the other. This explains why British policy in Uganda was wavering for two decades: now, as the conservative protector of the historically established order and traditions, it courted

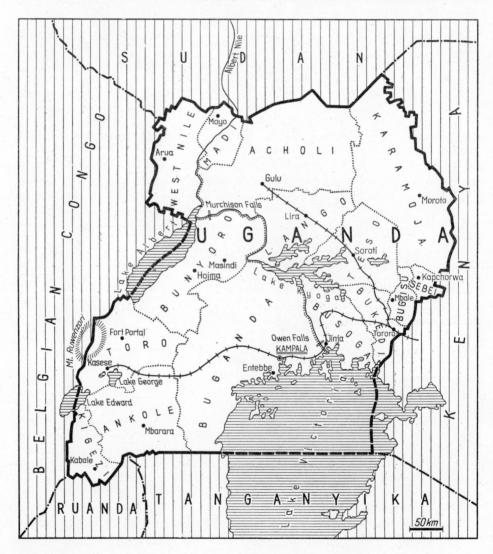

the Kabaka and other tribal rulers, trying to persuade them to hold back the progressive politicians; and now, as the apostle of progress and democracy, it endeavoured to mobilize the latter for the struggle against the conservative traditional leaders, to win them over to the promotion of the neocolonialist policies.

3. The peculiar position of Uganda was instrumental in the fact that after the war the British government renewed its abortive attempts to unite the East African colonies in a federation. Considering the purely agrarian character of the country, the nearly complete lack of large estates, and the insignificant number of European settlers, the British colonialists thought they could maintain their economic and political domination of more developed Kenya, in the framework of the East African Federation to be established. The fact is that the leading part in the administration of Kenya was played by a relatively numerous European settler population, and up to the end of the fifties the British government had believed the Europeans would manage to remain on top in Kenya and to maintain their domination also within the Federation.

After the war hard times came upon the peoples of Uganda. The peasantry had to bear a double burden of oppression and exploitation. To improve their lot and to obtain freedom they had to fight against two forces: the traditional feudal rulers and colonial oppression. Their struggle encountered a number of difficulties. The fight against feudalism was checked by the circumstance that the landlords were at the same time tribal chiefs, and in most people the spirit and tradition of tribalism were still so alive that they gave in only very slowly to more enlightened thinking, and also by the fact that in a way the feudal rulers also fought against the colonialists, for independence, and on this point their interests coincided. But the anti-imperialist struggle for independence was ultimately not weakened, but rather intensified, by the policy of the colonialists, whose aggressive manoeuvres (deportation of the Kabaka, persecution of the politicians favouring independence) compelled the different strata of the African population, despite their tribal and class differences, to progress towards a front of national unity.

"Reforms" between 1945 and 1949

As the first reform in October 1945 three African members were added to the Legislative Council, but they were not elected representatives of Africans: one was a minister nominated by the Kabaka, another the Katikiro of one of the three western tribal kingdoms (Bunyoro, Ankole, Toro), and the third the Secretary-General of different western districts (Busoga, Bugisu, Bukedi, Teso), in turn. This reform did nothing to make the Council more democratic. The three Africans, even if they had been elected by the people, would have been helpless against the large majority of European officials and unofficials; these were known to be trusted men and reliable supporters of the British government, and their participation in the Legislative Council meant nothing to the Africans, who regarded this organ as a mouthpiece and tool of the British government. But the British found the presence of even these three loyal Africans dangerous, and in 1946 they appointed two extra European unofficials to the Council, and increased also the number of officials accordingly to maintain the government's majority.

At the same time a change was made also in the Executive Council, which until then had been composed of only British colonial officials. The "democratic" reform consisted in including, besides the officials, *one* unofficial member: the longest serving member of the Legislative Council, who then happened to be an Indian.

Just as meaningless was the "democratic" reform of the Lukiko promised years before and introduced in 1945, providing for the election of 31 Africans to the 89-member Lukiko. As far as democracy was concerned, the reform was a step backward rather than forward. Until 1945 the Lukiko included three ministers of the Kabaka, twenty Saza chiefs and 66 members nominated by the Kabaka. Under the reform only six of the sixty-six remained, but 31 elected members and 28 chiefs (14 Gombola and 14 Miruka) were added to their number. This reform thus changed the mouthpiece of the Kabaka into one of the chiefs, who then wielded a large majority not only against the Kabaka but against the elected Africans as well (48 to 31). Besides, the 31 "elected" members were not democratic popular representatives either, because they were not elected directly but by several indirect stages.

In 1946 the number of elected members was raised from 31 to 36, but this did not change a bit in the situation.

In this way the British government attained what it wanted: (1) it curtailed the powers of the Kabaka, (2) it paralyzed the progressive elements by leaving them to be at the mercy of chiefs who were more reactionary than the Kabaka, and (3) it obtained more loyal support from chiefs by fulfilling their old desire.

In addition to the central organs of administration, also the organs of local government were reformed. On February 25, 1947, the Colonial Secretary instructed the Protectorate government to set up responsible local organs. But the colonial government complied with its instruction only nearly two years later, in 1949, when it issued the African Local Government Ordinance. It was laid down that certain matters, which had until then been handled by the central colonial government, should be referred to the Buganda government or the respective African organs of local administration. But the ordinance had had no practical value, because these African organs continued to be directed and controlled by officials of the central colonial government.

Of equally no practical value was another regulation issued in 1949, the Crown Lands (Amendment) Ordinance, which confirmed African security of land tenure.

That the British government did not at all intend these reforms to democratize the colonial regime of Uganda is clearly seen from two acts passed by the Legislative Council on August 9, 1948: an amendment to the existing press law, and a new restriction on freedom of assembly. The former authorized the government, in case a newspaper published an article, report, letter or advertisement which in the Governor's judgement contained a false or distorted statement of facts, to oblige the paper in question to publish, on a specified date and in the same position as the original article, a correcting statement prepared by the government. Failing which the proprietor or the editor of the paper, or both, were made liable to fine or imprisonment, or both. Following the entry into force of the new law several editors were imprisoned.

The other piece of legislation provided that the Governor was empowered, if he saw it necessary in the interest of order and tranquillity, to proclaim any area a "gazetted area" where the gathering of more than 250 persons was subject to prior police permission. For evasion of this provision (which applied to religious processions, too) penalties were to be imposed on organizers and participants alike.

A pertinent evaluation of these regulations is given by GEORGE PADMORE in his book published early in 1949:

"The restrictions which these regulations place upon the nationalist movement, farmers' organizations, the African Press, and even trade union activities are obvious. They completely counteract any constitutional advance, and can quite readily be invoked to create any atmosphere of terror. They constitute strong arm measures introduced by a short-sighted Governor having the blessing of the Colonial Office. These attempts to muzzle the Press and kill the budding nationalist movement in Uganda will only increase resentment among the supporters of the Bataka Movement and reinforce their suspicions of British intentions. The Baganda refer to their country as 'the land of black martyrs', and recent events and strong arm measures will maintain their strong belief that today, as in the past, the soil of Uganda must be soaked in blood to bring a little social justice and political democracy to the common people."[1]

PADMORE's prophetic words were proved true by events still in the latter half of the year.

Riots in 1949

The British Colonial Office's White Paper No. 210[2] provoked unrest in all of Uganda, especially in Buganda. The Africans, first of all the Baganda, interpreted the establishment of an inter-territorial government and parliament as a means for the British colonialists to extend to Uganda their regime introduced in Kenya and Tanganyika.[3]

Amidst the fear of the threat hanging over the future of the small peasant farmers of Uganda the Bataka Party managed to move broad masses of the politically and economically aggrieved peasantry to take action in defence of their interests.

Early in March 1949, the day before the opening of the forthcoming session of the Lukiko, a leader of the Bataka Party sent the Kabaka a telegram requesting him to increase the number of elected members to 60 and to expel from the Lukiko certain ministers and Saza chiefs who did not enjoy the confidence of the people, or else the Lukiko would not meet in session. The sender of the telegram was promptly arrested and sentenced to two years' imprisonment.

The following day the Bataka staged a mass demonstration around the Lukiko building and declared that if their demands should not be fulfilled, they would prevent the Lukiko from meeting. The Kabaka managed to send the people away by promising that he would consider their demands.

Thereafter, during March and April, debates and meetings followed one another. The Bataka Party and the Farmers' Union called mass meetings to discuss the peasants' grievances and criticized various measures of the colonial administration while their representatives had several times conversations with the Kabaka, but with no success.

On April 25, 1949, a crowd of thousands of people assembled around the Kabaka's residence. The Kabaka received a ten-member delegation who presented a five-point demand of the people: (1) democratization of the government, enabling the people

---

[1] G. PADMORE, *Africa: Britain's Third Empire*, London, 1949, p. 240.

[2] *Inter-Territorial Organization in East Africa: Revised Proposals*. H.M.S.O., London, 1949.

[3] And for good reason, since the White Paper stated among the tasks of the proposed East African High Commission: "Exercising the usual powers of the Colonial Government in respect of them ... to hold land ... enact legislation applying to East Africa as a whole with the advice and consent of the Central Assembly."

to elect their chiefs by themselves; (2) raising of the number of elected members of the Lukiko to sixty; (3) dismissal of the Kabaka's ministers; (4) a right for the peasants to gin their own cotton; (5) freedom for the peasants to market their produce on their own account.

The Kabaka promised to reply to the demands through the Katikiro (Prime Minister). But when the Katikiro came forth with the reply in the afternoon, the mob was in a hostile mood and refused to hear him. So the Kabaka's message was communicated by means of loudspeakers. It said that the Kabaka would consider their economic demands but was unwilling to dismiss the chiefs. The people were not satisfied, but they scattered when told to go home.

The next day, however, again tens of thousands came together before the Kabaka's house. Police were called out and started to arrest the ringleaders. The crowd resisted, whereupon the police attacked with truncheons to disperse the demonstrators. But the people continued to resist, and this was the beginning of mass disorders which then went on for days in many places. Houses of a number of chiefs and government officials of high rank were burned down or ravaged, shops were ransacked, etc. The Governor declared the state of emergency, banned the Bataka Party and the Farmers' Union, and ordered their leaders to be arrested; furthermore, he set up special detachments of Europeans and Asians to subdue the riots and called troops to Kampala from Kenya. The number of arrested rioters was 1,724.

It is characteristic of the attitude of HATHORN HALL, the British Governor of Uganda, that, not waiting for the result of the inquiry into the disorders, already on April 27, in a message to the population of Uganda, he branded the disturbances as the doing of rabble-rousing "Communist agents": "A comparatively few evil and self-seeking men have brought great trouble and disgrace upon Buganda. Acting on Communist inspiration from their so-called representatives in Britain, they are seeking to oppose by violence, intimidation, arson and murderous assault all constituted authority of the Protectorate Government and of the King's forces of law and order. In so doing they are following the usual pattern of Communist penetration, with which people in Europe and the Far East are already familiar. Their attempt was prefaced by a long campaign of foul lies and slander aimed at deceiving the people and shaking their confidence in His Highness' Government and the Government of the Protectorate. This too follows the usual Communist pattern."

The KINGDON commission appointed to inquire into the origins of the disturbances presented its report in February 1950. The report was a typical document drawn up to justify the action of the colonialists, describing the riots as prearranged political uprising to overthrow the Kabaka's government.

On the other hand, the truth was that the riots were not directed against the Kabaka, they manifested the people's resentment against some ministers and chiefs, their objection to the heavy burdens imposed by the British colonial regime. This is clearly shown by the appeal of the Bataka Party inviting the people of Buganda to take part in the demonstration in front of the Kabaka's residence. We read in this leaflet: "All the people, natives of Buganda, men and women, old and young come, come. Come to the centre, Mengo, where the world will present before His Highness the complaints of the people. The same complaints about which they have cried to him several times. Come so that we may inform the Kabaka of the things that are undermining him and our country, Buganda."

The report claimed that the complaints voiced by the demonstrators were wholly unfounded, that no essential reform was needed either in the structure of the Buganda government or in Buganda's relationship with the Protectorate of Uganda. It contained a few minor recommendations (for example, the hearing of advisers before appointing officials to the government apparatus and nominating members to the Lukiko), but at the same time it sharply criticized even the DUNDAS reforms as premature and proposed a return to the former state of affairs: "It is plain that the mass of the people themselves were not ready for the change and would welcome a return to pre-1944 conditions."

In its commentary to the KINGDON report the British administration of Uganda expressed its agreement with the findings of the commission and stated that the conduct of the British colonial authorities and troops during the disturbances had been "admirable". Further, the Buganda government was recommended "to consider new techniques for the handling of emergencies and the need for more efficient policing".

Reforms between 1950 and 1953

The composition of the Legislative Council was again changed in 1950. According to this, the Council had sixteen official and the same number of unofficial members (eight Africans, four Europeans and four Asians). The European and Asian members were still nominated by the Governor. The selection of six out of the eight Africans was made as follows: the Lukiko of Buganda and the provincial councils of the Northern, Eastern and Western Provinces each submitted a list of nomination, from which the Governor chose two names for the Northern and Eastern Provinces and one for the Western Province and Buganda each, and submitted them through the Colonial Office for confirmation by the King of England. One of the remaining two African members was nominated by the Kabaka, and the second by the other three tribal kingdoms (Bunyoro, Ankole, Toro), in turn. The list of the nominees, after approval by the Governor, was also submitted to the Colonial Office, that is, to the King, for definitive confirmation. Since, however, the Lukiko, which held that participation in the Legislative Council was incompatible with the 1900 Agreement, refused to nominate members, the second member for Buganda was also nominated by the Kabaka.

Despite the fact that the reform permitted as many unofficial African members as Europeans and Asians altogether, the majority of the Africans still refused to recognize the justification of a Legislative Council for Buganda, because the 1900 Agreement provided for no intermediate forum between the Lukiko and the British Governor except the Kabaka.

Changes in the Legislative Council were accompanied by the introduction of changes in the composition of the Lukiko: the number of elected members was raised from 36 to 40, and the Miruka chiefs were dropped (they were closely associated with the Bataka Party, which demanded the raising of the elected membership of the Lukiko to sixty). The mandate of the elected members was for three years, just like the office of the Kabaka's ministers, and eligibility was extended to women, who nevertheless were not qualified to vote.

The majority of the Africans, although far from satisfied with the reforms, still accepted them as small steps forward. But the tribal rulers were particularly upset because of the reforms. At their conference of 1952 they passed a resolution demanding that the Legislative Council, before adopting a bill, should ask for the opinion of the tribal rulers; that the tribal kingdoms should be named "countries", and their governments should be styled not "local government" but the governments of

Bunyoro, etc.; that the government should be empowered to buy shares of the companies and co-operatives making investments in their territory; that the governments might send more young people to study on scholarship overseas, etc.

After the 1949 disturbances the colonial government set about carrying out the reforms announced by the Local Government Ordinance. In the Protectorate 1951 Report the Governor formulated the purpose of the reforms as follows: "They are designed to ensure the closest co-operation between chiefs and people, to provide the people as a whole with some experience of local government on democratic lines, to promote the growth of executive responsibility and, in the case of the Agreement districts (Bunyoro, Ankole, Toro), to supplement the traditional personal relations between ruler and ruled with more democratic institutions."

The high-sounding phrases about the government's "democratic" intentions concealed its actual designs which guided the government in the introduction of the reforms. The reform of local government served to promote three aims:

1. To weaken the position of the rulers of the three smaller tribal kingdoms, to paralyze their aspirations for greater autonomy on the model of Buganda, to suppress their separatist efforts;

2. to weaken the position of the chiefs and their role in local government;

3. to grant the Africans apparently democratic rights, active participation in local government, while leaving intact the powers of the central colonial government.

London was guided by these intentions when in 1952, after ANDREW COHEN, the new Governor of Uganda, took office, it appointed C. A. G. WALLIS to conduct an inquiry into the state of local government, and the same considerations were reflected in the recommendations of his report submitted in 1953.[1]

The main recommendations of the WALLIS report were the following:

Uganda should remain an undivided state, not to be constituted as a federation of free African states.

Local government should be controlled jointly by the organs of local administration and the central government.

European officials and specialists of the central government should integrate their activities with the work of the local organs.

The chiefs should cease to be rulers and legislators of their tribes and become executives of the local authorities representing the popular will.

For the local authorities to know better the opinions and concerns of the local population they represented, their jurisdiction should be limited to smaller areas than that of the country and district councils established under the 1949 ordinance.

The WALLIS report provoked vehement debates among the Africans, both in and outside the Legislative Council. It was received with general uneasiness in Bunyoro, Ankole and Toro, because the people thought that it posed a threat to their rights established by old agreements.[2]

During the debate in the Legislative Council the demand was raised that, in case the WALLIS recommendations should become law, the reorganization of local government should not be immediately binding everywhere. In view of the fears of the Africans the government stated in its comments on the WALLIS report that the changes would not be forced upon the districts, that these would be free to decide

[1] C. A. G. WALLIS, *Report of an Inquiry into African Local Government in the Protectorate of Uganda*, Entebbe, 1953.

[2] The WALLIS recommendations did not apply to Buganda, where direction and control of local government were exercised by tribal authorities (the Kabaka and the Lukiko), not by the colonial administration.

whether to carry them out and, if so, to what extent.[1] But since the Africans still had doubts, the debate went on for over a year and was closed only with the adoption of the District Administration (District Councils) Bill on January 13, 1955.

After the 1949 riots, in the early fifties, the British colonialists devoted more attention to economic problems than to political and administrative questions. They often pointed out in their statements that the related government measures were intended to promote the economic and social well-being of the African population. In reality, however, the greater part of those measures served, entirely or in the first place, the interests of capitalist companies and European merchants profiteering on the products of Uganda. Even those steps which were taken seemingly in the interest of the African population meant very little or nothing at all to the Africans. Part of the Africans, especially well-to-do farmers and traders, could be made to believe that it all promoted also African interests. Their large majority, however, were alarmed at the economic measures and planned reforms of the colonialists, for they saw in them a justification of their old fear that sooner or later the British colonialists would transform also Uganda into a "white man's country" of the Kenya type.

An ordinance of February 1952 created the Uganda Development Corporation with a registered capital of £5 million, on the understanding that the funds might be increased subsequently with the approval of the Governor and the Legislative Council. It was made a task of the corporation to "promote, guide and assist in the financing, management or establishment of schemes for the better organization and modernization and a more efficient carrying out of any undertaking and the conduct of research into the industrial and mineral potentialities of the Protectorate".

The ordinance referred in general only to the economic development of the "Protectorate", but the corporation's entire activity demonstrated that its actual purpose was to promote the profitable investments of European big capitalists. The government had a 75 per cent share in the corporation, and it appointed rich businessmen to the board of directors; the government-appointed president of the corporation, J. T. SIMPSON, announced in August 1952 that the enterprise was joined by three large, internationally known, joint-stock companies, which would start to extract the mineral resources (pyrochlore, magnetite, etc.) in the area of Sukulu in East Uganda. In November of the same year Governor COHEN announced that the corporation would found a government-subsidized company for the development of the iron and steel industry and would concern itself also with both mining and agricultural development.

Towards the end of 1953 this corporation (jointly with the Colonial Development Corporation) concluded a £6.5 million contract with Messrs. Fobisher Limited for financing the putting into operation of the Kilembe copper mines.

The colonial administration itself was also busy organizing commercial companies of monopoly interests. That is how it established under its own control and auspices the Uganda Fish Marketing Corporation for the purchase and sale of the entire haul of the fisheries on Lake George and Lake Edward. The government stood behind the Toro cement works, too.

In July 1950 an ordinance provided for the creation of a Credit and Savings Bank, purportedly with a view to enabling Africans to obtain loans for the development of their farming and trading activities and for constructions and co-operative enter-

---

[1] *Government Memorandum on the Report by Mr. C. A. G. Wallis of an Inquiry into African Local Government in the Uganda Protectorate*, Entebbe, 1953, p. 6.

prises. But the bank gave loans only on mortgage or on the deposit of securities or bonds. Mortgage loans were granted only to those who owned land, and few Africans could raise other kinds of security. Consequently hardly any African made use of this opportunity, so the government in October 1953 organized an African Loans Fund Control Committee with local agencies in the provinces. These investigated the living conditions, financial standing and reliability of the applicants, and it was upon their recommendation that the Committee approved the loan, which then the Bank paid out in cash. Thus the granting of loans was actually a new means to turn as many wealthy Africans as possible into loyal supporters of the colonialists.

The Africans showed little interest in the big economic schemes and enterprises of the government. They were interested in what the government would do to solve their burning economic problems, the land issue, the development of farmers' co-operatives, aid to the cotton- and coffee-growing African peasants, namely the removal of the restrictions on their marketing activities.

As for the land issue, the Governor in 1950 made a statement in the spirit of the land ordinance of the preceding year, assuring the Africans that Uganda would not become a country of European settlerdom. He declared that the outlying lands were controlled by the Protectorate government and reserved for the African population, and that such land could be alienated only after hearing the opinion of the local authorities and only for purposes of the economic and social welfare of the population. This statement of principle sounded well, but what was in the interest of public welfare was decided in practice by the colonial administration; and for the Africans to be able to buy the lands reserved for them, they would have needed, besides the right to do so, appropriate financial means, which most of them did not possess, and which were not provided to them either by law or by well-sounding statements.

The Co-operative Societies Ordinance of 1946 and the Companies Ordinance were supposed to promote the establishment of marketing co-operatives and trading companies of Africans. The colonialists noted with satisfaction the rapid propagation of farmers' co-operatives. The truth is that progress in this respect started very slowly (the first co-operative was formed in 1947, and in 1948 there were all in all eight registered co-operative societies in the country), but the number of co-operatives grew fast from 1950 onwards, and it reached 800 by 1953. This rapid growth, however, was of questionable value in view of two circumstances:

1. The government's 1952 report on the co-operative movement stated that "members of these associations were extremely loose, only the mere selling or handing over for the purpose of sale of a bag of cotton to the Union was, we believe, considered by the leaders sufficient to call such person a member".[1]

2. Of greater importance than these small co-operatives having loose memberships was another organization of African peasants formed and officially registered already in 1947, the Uganda African Farmers' Union, which grew rapidly so that in two years it united thousands of African farmers and mobilized them for an active struggle for their demands, but which together with the Bataka Party had been banned by the colonial administration in 1949. Since the ban was not lifted later either, the Union could function only illegally.

One of the main grievances of the cotton-growing African farmers was that they could not have cotton gins of their own, and thus before selling their produce they

[1] *Commission of Inquiry into the Progress of the Co-operative Movement in Mengo, Masaga and Busoga Districts*, Entebbe, 1952, pp. 2–3.

had to apply for the help of European or Indian ginners, who then ruthlessly exploited this situation. Therefore the Africans had for long been demanding the right to buy or acquire ginhouses in their own name, but it was in vain.

Labour Colonial Secretary GRIFFITHS told a press conference in Entebbe on May 11, 1951, that the government planned to nationalize the cotton ginneries. This announcement alarmed the African peasants. To reassure them, the government in September 1951 made public its intention of purchasing 35 unprofitable ginneries out of the 193 existing in the country and offering them for sale to co-operatives of Africans on the condition that one-third of the purchase price should be paid in cash and the rest should be repaid as government loan with interest in instalments over thirty years.

At first the Africans were glad to hear about this, but they again took alarm when it became known that, in the absence of voluntary buyers, the African co-operatives would be obliged to buy the unprofitable ginneries. And the Africans were not pacified either when LENNOX-BOYD, during his visit to Uganda in January 1952, said on behalf of the Conservative government that Africans must not be confined to the cultivation of cotton, but they must be enabled to gin their crops in their own ginneries. The African cotton growers became still more alarmed when they heard about the latest plan of the government to keep in its possession part of the expropriated gins and only to let them by lease to co-operatives which could not afford the required down payment. This plan was opposed by only those who wished to have ginneries of their own or those who already had one. To these the ginneries taken on lease meant disadvantage in the keen competition with those who only paid for the use of gins and did not have to invest in the business.

Finally the 1953 Acquisition of Ginneries Ordinance accorded the right to African co-operatives and made it somewhat easier for them to acquire ginneries. How unsatisfying this arrangement was could be seen from the fact that three years after the promulgation of the ordinance, in 1956, only eight of the 131 ginneries in operation in Uganda were owned by African co-operatives.

With a view to increasing the participation of Africans in the growing, preparation and sale of coffee, the 1953 Coffee Industry Ordinance provided for the creation of a Coffee Industry Board. It was made a task of the Board to supervise the production of coffee and to organize its distribution and marketing. The Board was entirely in the hands of the colonial administration and followed its intentions, yet this arrangement had the positive result that by concentrating control over coffee production, it did away with the difference which had existed between the ways of selling coffee crops by Europeans and Africans.

The Uganda National Congress

The first important political party of Uganda, the Uganda National Congress, was formed under the leadership of IGNATIO MUSAZI in 1952. The party set itself the aim of uniting all tribes of Uganda, achieving self-government and control of economic affairs by Africans. Its manifesto declared, for example:

"Uganda is essentially an African country and must always remain so. It follows naturally from this that its fate must, and will, be determined by the majority of the people of Uganda, Africans. But this does not mean that the citizens of Uganda from other races, provided they take on Uganda citizenship, will be denied their rights."

Europeans and Africans alike were invited to the inaugural rally of the party, and one of the principal speakers of the meeting was a leader of the European community, C. C. BIRD. Despite this the party found little support among non-Africans, and although most of its leaders came from the Baganda, it won very few followers among them.

In Buganda the Lukiko and the chiefs opposed the new party because they thought it would jeopardize their privileges, and the ordinary people disliked it because they wanted to remain loyal to the banned Bataka Party. To acquire support for the party, its leaders seized upon local issues in some places. In Toro they campaigned against the creation of the Queen Elizabeth National Park. In Bugisu they backed the Coffee Union in its dispute with the government, and in Busoga they supported the local chiefs' demands regarding the land issue.

Joint Statement by the Kabaka and Governor Cohen

Governor COHEN, who took office in January 1952, was instructed by the British government to introduce a democratic-looking system in Uganda while curtailing the powers ensured by the 1900 Agreement to the tribal authorities of Buganda (the Lukiko and the chiefs), and not to let the rights taken from the tribal authorities pass into the hands of elected organs of the people (as would have been required in a truly democratic system), but to strengthen the positions of the colonial regime. The idea was that if this could be done in the strongest of the tribal kingdoms of Uganda, there would be nothing to prevent it in the smaller tribal states, so that Uganda, where the colonialists had so far enforced only direct rule through the tribal authorities, would become a unitary British colony under the absolute rule of the Protectorate government, while the introduction of pseudo-democratic parliamentary representation and administration would create the impression that the people had already obtained self-government, making it possible to delay the granting of independence for a long time to come.

After long negotiations Governor COHEN succeeded in reaching an agreement with the Kabaka, under which in March 1953 they issued a joint statement on the constitutional reforms to be introduced in Buganda. The reform provided for two essential changes: (1) Sixty out of the eighty-nine seats in the Lukiko would be occupied by elected representatives of the people instead of chiefs or other Africans nominated by the Kabaka, who in turn would undertake to hear the opinion of the competent committee of the Lukiko before appointing his ministers. (2) A number of functions of local importance (education and health, soil improvement and animal hygiene, etc.) would be taken from the organs of colonial administration and referred to the Buganda tribal government, and the European and African officials in charge of those affairs would also be placed under the jurisdiction of the Buganda government.

The above reforms were results of discussions with the Kabaka and his ministers. After the publication of the joint statement the Governor, without having consulted the Kabaka and his ministers, or either the Lukiko or the Legislative Council, introduced certain "reforms" to change the composition of the Legislative Council and the Executive Council, but with little regard for the African interests.

The number of the unofficial members (so-called "representatives") of the Legislative Council was raised from 16 to 26, and six unofficial members were brought into the Executive Council which had thus far been composed of officials only. But half of the members of both Councils were British officials, and half of the unofficials were "representatives", and again half of the "representatives" and only two of the six unofficial members of the Executive Council were Africans, the latter two having been chosen from among the obedient supporters of the British government. To the unofficials of the Legislative Council were added ten appointed, so-called "crossbench" members (who, whenever the government found it necessary, were obliged to cast their vote in favour of the government).

The Baganda felt suspicious about these new political measures taken without asking for their opinion. The only point which they accepted willingly was the increase in the number of elected members of the Lukiko.

Deportation of the Kabaka

On June 30, 1953, Colonial Secretary LYTTELTON told the British Parliament that the British East African colonies (Kenya, Uganda, Tanganyika, and Zanzibar) would unite in a closer association, possibly federation. This announcement roused a general outcry in Uganda. In the absence of the Kabaka (who just happened to be in London attending the coronation of Queen ELIZABETH II), his ministers wrote Governor COHEN a letter which read among other things: "The statement of the Secretary of State for the Colonies is bound not only to shake the foundations of trust among our people but will also deadly damage the good relations which hitherto exist between the Baganda and the British."

The Governor forwarded this letter to the Colonial Office, and in his reply to the Buganda ministers he tried to calm them. At the July 6 meeting of the Legislative Council, which also protested against the Colonial Secretary's speech, Governor COHEN, to soothe public opinion but not to contradict his superior at the same time, made the following hypocritical statement, obviously upon instructions from the Colonial Secretary himself:

"I have been authorized by the Secretary of State to say that fears which there may have been in this matter are groundless. What may ultimately happen in the future no one can foresee at the present time. As regards the present intentions of Her Majesty's Government I have been authorized to say that the Secretary of State's speech did not indicate any change of policy . . . that the future development will take local public opinion fully into account and that the assurance previously given . . . that the establishment of the East African High Commission and Assembly is not to be regarded as involving the political fusion or federation of the East African territories still holds good."

The Legislative Council was satisfied with this statement and terminated the debate over the issue. The Governor's explanation pacified the Toro tribal government, too.

This declaration, however, far from satisfying the Kabaka and his government (his ministers and the Lukiko), still hardened them to resistance. They really took it for what it was worth: a step backward from the more concrete previous promises, with which the British government had assured them that it did not intend to establish a federation. It was evident that by "public opinion" which it promised to "take into account" London meant the hearing of the Legislative Council, in which the majority was wielded by supporters of the colonial government, not by representatives of African opinion, and whose "hearing" raised obstacles neither to a federation of the British East African colonies nor to the establishment of the East African High Commission, although African public opinion was most definitely against those plans. After that statement it was understandable that the Kabaka should no longer take seriously the 1953 agreement on the future development of Uganda as a unitary state.

Back from London the Kabaka entered into new talks with the Governor, categorically protesting both against the speech of the Secretary of State for the Colonies and against the double-dealing explanation offered by the Governor. He presented two new demands on behalf of Buganda: first, that the affairs of Buganda should be transferred from the Colonial to the Foreign Office; and second, that a day should be set for the independence of Buganda.

The Kabaka was not alone with this standpoint. He was joined first of all by the rulers of other three major tribal states of Uganda (Toro, Bunyoro, Ankole), who in their joint letter of August 10 to the Governor protested against the Colonial Secretary's statement and the Governor's conduct, and demanded "entire effective revision of the relationships which now exist between Her Majesty's Government and our respective states". The Kabaka's view and demands were also supported by African political parties which otherwise would differ in their opinions, among them not only the progressive Uganda National Congress and the illegal Bataka groups, but also such conservative organizations as the All-Ugandan Party.[1] The Uganda National Congress at its meeting on September 19 adopted a resolution against the idea of federation, took a stand in favour of independence, and demanded the transfer of the affairs of Uganda from the Colonial Office to the Foreign Office. The resolution emphasized: "We know for certain that our brothers in the neighbouring countries such as Toro, Ankole, Teso, Lango and all brothers in Uganda agree with us and are also determined in the same way."

In the early days of October the Lukiko also passed a resolution condemning the plan of federation, and it made its position known to the Kabaka in a letter, requesting him not to send members to the Legislative Council. It gave as a reason that when it would come to pass, the federation proposal would be imposed upon the Council, and this would be an insult to Buganda which had its own recognized legitimate parliament, the Lukiko, and that to send representatives to the Legislative Council would be a blow to the country's prestige. Thereupon the Kabaka replied in his letter of October 13 that he understood the opinion of the Lukiko and would inform the Governor accordingly when the nomination of new members would be discussed, and then he would let the Lukiko know the result of his talks with the Governor.

Since the talks brought no result, the Governor declared that "the Kabaka and the Buganda Government must publicly accept the Secretary of State's final decision even though their thoughts were different . . ." The Kabaka then replied that he felt compelled to tell the truth to his people, and if he had to choose whether to be loyal to the British government or to his own people, he would choose the latter. Thereupon the Governor flew to London for instruction and returned with an ultimatum of three points requiring the Kabaka to undertake:

"1. That he would accept the decisions of Her Majesty's Government and that he would not make statements opposing these decisions; that he would not by word or deed encourage other persons to oppose them; and that he would inform the Great Lukiko publicly at its meeting that these decisions must be accepted.

[1] While all parties stood by the Kabaka's demands unanimously, they did not interpret them in the same way: the Uganda National Congress thought the demands should be applied to Buganda alone, and the All-Ugandan Party would have them applied to the whole of Uganda.

"2. That he would positively co-operate in the future progress of Buganda as an integral part of the Uganda Protectorate, and reaffirm the statement contained in Paragraph 16 of the Memorandum on the Constitutional Development and reform in Buganda issued last March; and that he would give a particular undertaking to submit names of Baganda members for appointment to the Legislative Council, and that he would inform the Great Lukiko publicly at its next meeting that he would submit these names.

"3. That he would co-operate loyally with Her Majesty's Government and the Protectorate Government in the organization and administration of Buganda in accordance with the 1900 Agreement."

The Kabaka refused to accede to these demands, and then the Governor on November 30 let him know that the British government withdrew its recognition from him. The Kabaka was immediately deported to London.

On December 2 Minister of State for Colonial Affairs HENRY HOPKINSON announced to the House of Commons that the return of the Kabaka was out of the question. Thereupon, on December 5, the Kabaka sent a cable from London to his ministers, instructing them to swear an oath to the Regent and expressing the hope that the Lukiko would continue its normal work and the people would keep calm and not put up resistance to the colonial authorities.

The vast majority of the Baganda really contained themselves, and the Lukiko voiced its regret that the Kabaka, owing to his absence, would not be able to extend his hearty welcome to Queen ELIZABETH who prepared to visit Uganda to inaugurate the Owen Falls power plant.

In December the Lukiko sent representatives to London to press for the return of the Kabaka. They said that the Kabaka, when he had refused to comply with the Governor's demands, had given expression to the views of his ministers and legislature, and if he had not done so he would have lost the support of his people, that he was in no position to make his ministers and the Lukiko follow the policy of the British government. LYTTELTON declared that his government's decision was final, the Lukiko should elect a new Kabaka but he stressed that Uganda would be an African state with appropriate guarantees for the minorities. The Baganda agreed and said they were willing to accept for Buganda a federal status within Uganda instead of self-government, and assured the British government that on this basis the Kabaka, if allowed to return home, would be ready to give the undertaking required from him. But LYTTELTON gave the non-committal reply that the British government could not afford to reverse the decision of deportation provoked by the Kabaka's obstinacy.

In the meantime the other traditional tribal rulers (the "kings" of Ankole, Bunyoro and Toro) also appealed to the Colonial Secretary to allow the Kabaka to return.

Report of the Hancock Commission

On February 23, 1954, the British government announced to parliament that a commission under Professor KEITH HANCOCK would be appointed to work out recommendations for the reorganization of the Buganda government and the status of Buganda within the Uganda Protectorate. It stressed that it intended to develop Uganda into a self-governing state in which the government would be in the hands of an African majority, that the constitution would guarantee also the rights of the minorities living in Uganda, "but this will not detract from the primarily African character of the country".

The state of emergency declared on November 30, 1953, was terminated on April 1, 1954, but both the British government and officials of the Protectorate government maintained that the deportation of the Kabaka was irrevocable. Towards the end of April the Uganda National Congress made an appeal to the Baganda people to boycott all non-African shops and amusement places for three months in protest against the deportation order, and in June the boycott was prolonged indefinitely. The government responded by reintroducing the state of emergency, and the Governor declared that he would not negotiate until the boycott was ended. He said also that the government for the time being had no intention to impose a new Kabaka upon the Baganda.

The Lukiko and the Baganda, who since the Kabaka's deportation had been concerned only about his return, first were suspicious of the HANCOCK appointment, for they saw in it a diversionary move of the government. Later, however, in the hope that the commission might be instrumental in the recall of the Kabaka, the Lukiko at its meeting of March nominated its representatives to the commission.

The commission got down to work at the end of June and, having formulated its recommendations in the course of July, it discussed them with Governor COHEN between July 30 and September 15. The discussions resulted in the definitive proposals which also the Governor signed.

The proposals were for a change in the relationship between the British colonial administration and the traditional tribal government, restricted the absolute rule of the Kabaka and gave more rights to his ministers and the Lukiko.

But the authority of the British colonial administration was left intact. The commission confirmed the provision of the memorandum of March 1953 that local affairs should be transferred from the colonial administration to the Buganda organs; it proposed the establishment of a Civil Service Board, revoking at the same time the Kabaka's right of control over the civil service.

The Kabaka retained the right to appoint the Prime Minister (Katikiro) from among the nominees of the Lukiko, but the Governor still had the right of veto. The other ministers should be chosen by the Katikiro after consultation with the Governor and subject to his approval. And the ministers should be responsible to the Lukiko, not to the Kabaka.

To avoid conflicts between the British administration and the Buganda government, the commission proposed the creation of a permanent consultative body and recommended the two governments to hold, if necessary, joint meetings on the ministerial level. In case this arrangement would not help to reconcile the views of the two governments, the Governor should be empowered to give the ministers "formal advice". It was proposed that the appointment and removal of chiefs should be within the competence of an Appointments Board composed of Baganda, but its decisions should be subject to the approval of both governments. Guidance and control of the ministers and chiefs thus ceased to be exercised by officials of the Protectorate government, and the ministers of Buganda were given the right to decide within their scope of authority. The British Resident's role was confined to consultative and advisory functions. In this way the differences or conflicts arising between the Buganda and the British government would not affect the person of the Kabaka, who — as was expressed in the commission's report — "would become the symbol of the unity of the people of Buganda and of the continuity between their past, present and future".

The commission proposed that the Kabaka make a solemn declaration expressing his agreement with the provisions of the new constitution, and if he did so and abided by it, the British government should not refuse to recognize him.

Finally the commission recommended the Lukiko to reverse its decision not to send Baganda representatives to the Legislative Council.

The African members of the commission hoped that the measures envisaged in the recommendations would make it easier for the British government to permit the Kabaka to return.

The Return of the Kabaka

In September 1954 three members of the Lukiko brought an action to the High Court at Kampala to decide that four newly elected Lukiko members could not take their seats under the terms of the Uganda Agreement of 1900 until their appointment was confirmed by the Kabaka, whom the British government had deported in violation of the Agreement. The legal representative of the petitioners (the liberal lawyer DIPLOCK) argued that the only wrong the Kabaka had done was his observance of the duty to consult his people's representatives and his having told frankly that he was not satisfied with the statement of the Colonial Secretary. The High Court considered the petition and decided that the deportation of the Kabaka was illegal.

This decision strengthened the unity of the people of Uganda and their persistence in clamouring for the return of the Kabaka, and at the same time aroused the sympathy of British public opinion for the Kabaka. On the other hand, the British government, whose prestige had suffered from the court decision and its repercussions, was compelled to relax its severity.

On November 15, 1954, a simultaneous statement was made by the Colonial Secretary to the House of Commons and by the Governor to the Lukiko in Kampala, promising far-reaching reforms in the spirit of the HANCOCK recommendations. They declared their acceptance of the commission's proposals on the understanding that if the Lukiko should endorse them unchanged, it might decide in nine months from endorsement whether to elect a new Kabaka or to insist on the return of MUTESA.

The Colonial Secretary's statement was received favourably in the British Parliament, but in Kampala the mere mention of the election of a new Kabaka roused so vehement indignation that the Governor could not finish his speech and had to leave the Lukiko meeting.

The Lukiko discussed the matter for weeks. The Baganda objected to three aspects of the case: that the British government first had spoken with the Governor about the HANCOCK recommendations and submitted them to the Lukiko only later as an ultimatum barring any change, and they were angered mainly by the time-limit of nine months. At last, on the grounds that the constitutional proposals could not be discussed in the absence of the Kabaka, the Lukiko rejected the HANCOCK report as a whole, and set up a commission to work out new proposals. After consultations with DIPLOCK the new commission decided to propose acceptance of the HANCOCK recommendations with some changes. The British government did not take a stand forthwith but found it better to wait for the Lukiko's formal decision. At its meeting of May 6, 1955, the Lukiko approved the report of the commission and appointed a drafting committee to draw up the final document, whereupon the Colonial Office next day formed its own committee to talk with the Lukiko committee.

Agreement was made difficult primarily by three circumstances. The Lukiko set up another committee and sent it to London to request the immediate return of the Kabaka. The Uganda National Congress also sent a delegation to London. It demanded independence at once and threatened that if the negotiations failed the people would proclaim complete independence. The third difficulty was caused by a statement made by the government in April, announcing its intention of introducing a ministerial government of seven members including an Asian. The Lukiko found this wholly unacceptable and categorically rejected it at the same time as it decided to appoint the drafting committee.

But both sides were interested in the success of negotiations, because a failure would have resulted in a growing mass influence of the radical National Congress, and this was contrary to the intentions of both the British government and the Buganda tribal government. Therefore both sides were willing to yield and thus they arrived at an agreement. The Baganda declared their readiness to take part in the Uganda Legislative Council, dropped their objection to the appointment of an Indian minister, and accepted the position of the British government that the Kabaka might return only after the definitive endorsement of the agreement by the Lukiko. And the British government reduced to six weeks the formerly fixed nine-month time-limit and, upon the insistence of the delegates, made a firm promise in the preamble to the agreement that the East African Federation would not be established as long as "local public opinion on this issue remains as it is at the present time", unless it would change considerably, and "should the occasion ever arise in the future to ascertain public opinion in terms of the aforesaid assurance, the Protectorate Government will at that time consult fully with the Buganda Government and the other authorities throughout the country as to the best method of ascertaining public opinion".

Soon after this agreement the Kabaka returned to Uganda.

The Formation of Parties after the Kabaka's Return

The Uganda National Congress viewed the deportation of the Kabaka as an imperialist attack on the rights of Africans, and therefore, in spite of its democratic orientation, it took an active part in the campaign for the Kabaka's return. It sent a delegation to London, overwhelmed the Protectorate government with petitions, and organized a boycott of European shopkeepers in protest against the Kabaka's deportation. This conduct enhanced the party's influence in Buganda. In London the Secretary of State for the Colonies talked only with the Lukiko delegates, not with the emissaries of the party, whose petitions went unheeded, and even its boycott failed. Though this failure again reduced the popularity of the party, after the return of the Kabaka it still managed to win four of the five seats reserved for Buganda in the Legislative Council. The party continued to devote its main attention to the provinces outside Buganda, where it succeeded in winning support among the radical-minded youth, one of whom was MILTON OBOTE.[1]

[1] APOLLO MILTON OBOTE was born in 1926 in Lango District in Northern Uganda. He was educated in Protestant mission schools of Lango and Jinja, and graduated from Makerere College in Kampala. Thereafter he was employed by building enterprises at Jinja in Uganda and at Kabete in Kenya. Here he entered the service of Standard Oil and, until his return to Uganda (1957), he served his political apprenticeship with K.A.U. in Kenya.

Meanwhile two African parties of religious background were formed in the country. In 1955 young people educated at the Budo Protestant College founded the Progressive Party under the leadership of ERIDADI MULIRA, and in 1956 the Catholic community, at the initiative of their bishops, formed the Catholic Democratic Party.

The 1955 Reforms

After the return of the Kabaka the reforms promised by the government were introduced. Accordingly the Executive Council was composed of 11 members, including six colonial officials and five unofficials (3 Africans, 1 European and 1 Asian) plus two African parliamentary secretaries. Of the three African members only one was full minister, two were only assistants to Europeans of ministerial rank. The 60-member Legislative Council included 30 Africans, of whom only 18 were elected (indirectly), five ex-officio members of the Executive Council, and seven government representatives. The other half of the Legislative Council consisted of colonial officials, settlers and a few Asians appointed by the Governor. Since the Governor chose the members of the government and the other appointees from among those whom he could safely rely on, the majority was on the side of the colonial administration both in the Legislative and in the Executive Council. The whole reform was intended to be a gesture to calm liberal public opinion in Britain and in Uganda after the upheaval caused by the Kabaka scandal. LENNOX-BOYD, however, described this meaningless reform as a big step towards African self-government and declared that since it would take time to effect those important reforms, no further essential constitutional changes would be made before 1961.

The same year a new agreement, similar to that reached with Buganda, was concluded with another tribal state of Uganda, Bunyoro. The Mukama (king), who had so far been absolute ruler of his country, was made to accept a new constitution, under which Bunyoro should be governed by ministers and a tribal parliament called the Native Council.

Elections in 1958

Ten members of the Legislative Council were directly elected in October 1958. In March, when the voters' registration began, the Lukiko passed a resolution demanding the postponement of elections till the favourable conclusion of negotiations on the relationship of the Kabaka with the colonial administration of Uganda, on the introduction of a common electoral roll, and on increased African representation. This having failed, Buganda kept out of the elections. Ankole and Bugisu also refused to participate, so only about half the electorate went to the poll. As a result of the elections, the Uganda National Congress won five seats, the Democratic Party obtained one, and four seats were gained by independents. Later, however, a shift occurred in this breakdown, when the district council nominated two members for Ankole which did not take part in the elections, and the Governor nominated a member for Bugasi, and the independents founded the Uganda Peoples' Union, which was then joined by some members of the National Congress. Eventually, the breakdown by parties of the elected African representatives (including the three appointed members) was as follows: Uganda National Congress 3, Uganda Peoples' Union 7, Democratic Party 1.

Towards the end of 1958, after the launching of the Pan-African movement in East and Central Africa, there appeared also in Uganda aspirations for co-operation between parties. Attempts were made to unite, on the one hand, the two conservative parties of religious orientation (the Progressive Party and the Catholic Democratic Party) and, on the other, the two progressive parties (the Uganda National Congress and the Uganda Peoples' Union), but to no avail.

On November 17, 1958, the Governor appointed a committee under the chairmanship of his Administrative Secretary, J. V. WILD, to work out recommendations for a system of direct election on a common roll to be introduced in 1961, ensuring adequate representation in the Legislative Council for non-Africans.

The Lukiko refused to take part in the committee or even to discuss the issues, insisting that the question of non-African representation should be decided by a future independent government of Uganda, and it blamed the Uganda Peoples' Union and the National Congress for their participation in the work of the committee.

In December 1958 the Buganda politicians outside the Legislative Council and the WILD committee formed a new party, the Uganda National Movement, headed by MUSAZI of the National Congress and MULIRA of the Progressive Party. The new party founded to safeguard the interests of Buganda managed to absorb all minor Buganda parties, except the Catholic Democratic Party. The principal objective of the Uganda National Movement was to obstruct the forthcoming proposals of the WILD committee. In protest against the government instructions given to the WILD committee to ensure non-African representation, the Uganda National Movement campaigned for a boycott of European and Asian traders. Since it brought with it acts of violence (arson, robbery, etc.), the government in May 1959 banned the Uganda National Movement. During 1959 several attempts were made to revive the party under different names (Uganda Freedom Movement, Uganda League, etc.), but all such efforts failed. With the deportation of the majority of its leaders (among them MUSAZI and MULIRA) to remote places, the party as such ceased to exist. But the boycott movement continued. The Baganda proceeded for months with their boycott actions to protest against the political and economic privileges of Asians.

In August 1959, there was a split in the Uganda National Congress. The majority, headed by OBOTE and MAYANJA, broke with the party, while the minority under JOSEPH KIWANUKA[1] continued operating as the Uganda National Congress.

The Report of the Wild Committee

The WILD committee, most of whose members were Africans, submitted its report in December 1959. This report, reflecting for the most part the views of the African majority of the committee, contained a number of progressive recommendations.

---

[1] JOSEPH KIWANUKA, son of the Kabaka's Minister of Finance ("Omuwanika"), was born at Mengo in October 1915. He studied at Budo and later at Makerere College, where he obtained a diploma in engineering. For a time he served in the colonial administration, and during World War II he was assigned to the engineer corps of the East African Army. After the war he was editor of the government-supporting paper *Matalasi* (Messenger) published by Europeans. During the 1949 riots, as a notorious supporter of the colonial administration, he was assaulted and gravely manhandled by the agitated mob, and he had a narrow escape from a fatal end. Later the government sent him to London to attend a journalists' course, and when he returned to Uganda he founded a newspaper in which, in contradiction to his past activities, he conducted vehement anticolonialist propaganda.

It recommended the Legislative Council to be composed only of members elected on a common roll of African, European and Asian voters, all adults to have the right to vote, and the number of seats in the Legislative Council to be raised to 72.[1]

The committee members proposed that "adequate representation on the Legislative Council for non-Africans should be secured by their full participation in the common roll arrangements. We are satisfied that this is the only way in which adequate representation can, in the long run, be achieved. Any arrangements specifically designed to achieve would harm the relations between the races and would not in practice safeguard their position, perhaps the reverse".

The report emphasized that the formation and operation of well organized political parties was the prerequisite of the viability of the proposed democratic system and the removal of intertribal differences: "It is essential to provide an opportunity for a political party to gain sufficient seats to assume a real share in the responsibility of government, and this is the most important step which can be taken to assist the development of political parties."

Besides such democratic proposals the report contained recommendations for several concessions to be made to the colonial imperialists. It proposed, for example, that the Executive Council should include three ex-officio members in addition to the elected ministers, and that the Governor, whom it recommended to replace with an elected Chief Minister presiding over the Council, should be given the right to veto decisions of the Legislative Council.

New Parties

The Uganda Peoples' Union was formed towards the end of 1958 by anti-Buganda forces, primarily Legco members of other provinces (Bunyoro, Busoga, Bugisu, Toro, Ankole), who were joined also by one of Buganda's five representatives, a member of the Uganda National Congress. The policy statement of the party emphasized respect for the position of traditional rulers and chiefs, and at the same time it condemned imperialism and colonialism. But it regarded as its most urgent practical aim the struggle for the liquidation of Buganda's privileged position, for equal democratic rights of all provinces and all peoples of Uganda. This was the only Uganda party which had no followers in Buganda.

In February 1960 the dissident ex-leaders of the Uganda National Congress held a joint conference in Kampala with representatives of the Uganda Peoples' Union. There it was decided, upon a motion of OBOTE, to enter into talks with leaders of the political parties and accordingly to formulate a programme for Uganda's earliest possible accession to independence. A month later the Uganda Peoples' Congress was formed under the direction of OBOTE by the fusion of the OBOTE-led wing of U.N.C. and the Uganda Peoples' Union. The new party was joined by political leaders of Toro, Busoga and Lango, and it received assurances of support also from the Uganda Trades Union Congress and the Uganda African Railwaymen's Union. The party demanded independence for Uganda at once and stood up for the idea of an East African Federation. Its influence grew rapidly in the whole country except in Buganda.

[1] The committee envisaged one member by every 90,000 inhabitants. On this basis Buganda would have had 20 among the 72 members of the Legislative Council.

In June 1960 a group of Baganda intellectuals, headed by former Uganda Labour Minister APOLLO KIRONDE and the Kabaka's Minister of Education, ABU MAYANJA (both members of U.N.C.), formed the United National Party. Though posing as an all-Ugandan party, it could not win support outside Buganda, and there also only intellectuals backed it. Though it expressed its loyalty to tribal rulers and traditions, yet it stood in opposition to the Kabaka's government, which opposed in general the formation of political parties. The United National Party was in favour of independence as soon as possible and opposed Buganda's policy aimed at secession from the Protectorate.

Consultations about the Constitution in April–May 1960

In the spring of 1960 the British authorities held several consultations (with the Prime Ministers of the tribal kingdoms in April, with the chiefs in May) in an effort to work out a draft constitution acceptable to all interested parties. But this effort of the British authorities produced no result, because of the opposition of the Kabaka of Buganda in the first place. The Kabaka and his legislature, the Lukiko, were afraid that acceptance of the proposed constitution would be the end of the feudal rule of the Kabaka and the traditional chiefs.

In May the Prime Ministers or Secretaries-General of the provinces (the tribal kingdoms and districts) met at Makerere and passed a resolution accepting the majority recommendations of the WILD committee and demanding their immediate implementation in order for Uganda to become independent by June 1961. But the delegates from Buganda and Toro voted against the resolution because they wanted to know what form of government Uganda was to have before they would agree to elections.

In July OBOTE requested the administration to declare before elections what Uganda's future government would be like, and he stated at the same time that it was inadmissible to postpone the elections and that the country should accede to independence in July 1961. He proposed also that the political parties meet to discuss the future form of government, but this proposal got no response.

In August the Kabaka went to London at the head of a Buganda delegation and asked the British government to postpone the elections until the Relationships Committee had submitted its report. He demanded assurances that his sovereign rights and the traditional tribal administration in the Kingdom of Buganda would remain intact also after Uganda became independent. In other words, he wished either Buganda to be allowed to secede from Uganda or all of Uganda to be transformed into a loose federation, with Buganda as a part of it; without such a guarantee Buganda would stay out of the election of the new all-Ugandan legislature which was already in preparation all over the country (except in Buganda). The British government refused to give any guarantee. MACLEOD replied that the existing safeguards were entirely sufficient to avert any interference by the central government with the affairs of Buganda, and that he could agree neither to postpone the elections nor to establish federation.

After five weeks of fruitless talks, on September 20, the Kabaka returned home to Kampala.

On September 14, 1960, Colonial Secretary MACLEOD made public the position adopted by the British government with regard to the WILD report. The government accepted most recommendations of the committee subject to conditions and changes which were really tantamount to their rejection.

It agreed with the system of direct election, the extension of the right to vote, but it opposed the introduction of universal suffrage.

It agreed with the introduction of a common electoral roll and with the idea of an elected majority of the Legislative Council, but it insisted on the guarantee of the civic rights and land titles of non-Africans, and that the Governor should retain the power to appoint members to the Legislative Council.

It agreed that the Council of Ministers should be composed primarily of elected members, that it should not be responsible to the Legislative Council but function as a consultative body under the chairmanship of the Governor, not of a Prime Minister, and it refused to limit the number of ex-officio ministers to three.

Since the British government rejected the greater part of the majority recommendations of the WILD committee, the African committee members explained their position to the Legislative Council and sent a delegation to the Colonial Office. In his reply MACLEOD expressed the hope that Uganda after the elections would rapidly progress towards internal self-government and then reach the final aim, independence. At the same time he announced that the administration would set up an Uganda Relationships Committee to choose the best possible form of government for Uganda and to settle the relations between the central government and the provincial governments. He promised, however, that the elections would not be postponed until the Committee's report (as was demanded by Buganda), and that shortly after the elections he would call a constitutional conference.

Two days before the Kabaka came home, on September 18, MACLEOD arrived in Uganda for a four-day visit. During his stay there he conferred at Entebbe with the Governors of the three British East African colonies (Kenya, Uganda, Tanganyika) and attended the inauguration of the new legislative building at Kampala. The Kabaka and his government ostentatiously kept away from the ceremony.

Ankole, Bunyoro and Toro in September demanded in a joint petition the postponement of elections until the relationships between the provinces and Uganda were settled. The Uganda Peoples' Congress, in a statement of policy issued also in September, declared that the actual form of government was the most appropriate one for Uganda as well, since it gave due scope also to decentralization, thereby preventing the government from interfering with local affairs. According to this statement the institution of tribal kingdoms should be adapted to modern democracy. Bunyoro's claim to the "lost countries" should be settled by a referendum to be held in the areas concerned.

The Lukiko's Decision of September 1960 and the Memorandum of October 5

In the days following MACLEOD's departure (September 24–25) the Lukiko laid down in a decision that Buganda would stay out of the forthcoming all-Ugandan legislative elections and would not nominate representatives to the Council; it demanded abrogation of the Uganda Agreement of 1900 and special independent status for Buganda.

The Buganda government warned the people not to register for vote, and the Lukiko addressed a memorandum to Queen ELIZABETH, with a request for Buganda's secession from Uganda. Since the request was refused, the Lukiko adopted a resolution on the proclamation of Buganda's independence by January 1, 1961. And how groundless this resolution was could be seen from the fact that the Buganda government continued to collect the taxes levied by the Uganda Protectorate Government, and it further made use of the services provided by the Protectorate, and accepted the financial support of the British administration (amounting to about half of the public revenues of the province).

In reply to this action of the Lukiko, MACLEOD and Governor CRAWFORD declared that Buganda had no right to secede from the Protectorate, because the 1900 Agreement could not be terminated unilaterally.

The Lukiko then formed a commission which drafted a memorandum to Queen ELIZABETH. The memorandum stated again that Buganda would not be represented in the Legislative Council of Uganda, demanded that the British Government agree to the Kingdom of Buganda becoming an independent state as of September 1, 1961, and affirmed that thereafter the Kingdom of Buganda wished to maintain good relations with Great Britain. The Lukiko at its meeting of October 5 discussed the draft memorandum and after a ten-hour debate approved it by 76 votes to 6, with 1 abstention, after a modification to the effect that the appointed date of independence should be January 1, 1961. MACLEOD in his statement of October 19 threatened the Kabaka and the Lukiko that, if they persisted in boycotting the all-Ugandan legislative elections called for spring, that would be "too bad".

A Provocative Statement by Governor Crawford

On November 19, 1960, Governor CRAWFORD made another, this time outright provocative, statement. Speaking of the decision of the Buganda legislature, he said that nowhere in the agreements and other documents on British protectorate over Uganda was there any mention of the possibility of secession. And as concerns the delay in the granting of independence to Uganda, he claimed that the only reason for the delay was the Kabaka's inflexible policy. As he said, Great Britain could not give up the administration of Uganda until the Kabaka had changed his mind, because, if Uganda became independent without an agreement of the leaders of all provinces and political groups concerning the form of government and other disputed issues, the inevitable result would be tribal warfare and serious conflicts between the tribes of Buganda and the other three provinces.

The Lukiko's Declaration of Independence and Its Decision on Secession

The threat of the Governor only confirmed the Buganda leaders in their determination. The Lukiko at its meeting of December 31 resolved that Buganda would sever its ties with Uganda at 12.00 p.m. and become an independent state. On January 1, 1961, Governor CRAWFORD repudiated the Lukiko's decision and claimed that it had no legal effect. On January 2 he called in five Ministers of Buganda and stated that he had not received the official text of the Lukiko's decision and had been in no position to examine it, so he could not take a final stand, and for the time being everything would remain as it was both in the administration of Buganda and in its relationship with the Uganda Protectorate as a whole.

Miners' Strike in February 1961

In February 1961 in the western part of Uganda 2,500 workers went on strike in the copper mines. On February 15, representatives of the striking miners and the mining companies conducted talks at Kilembe. A crowd of people sympathizing with the strikers staged a march of demonstration through the streets. The police first tried to break up the crowd with tear gas and later opened fire. There are no data available on the casualties. (The police report on a few lightly wounded people is probably far from the real facts.)

Elections in March 1961

The first general elections to the Legislative Council of Uganda were held at the end of March 1961. The Lukiko called upon the people of Buganda to boycott the elections. The Kabaka and the Lukiko branded participation as treason. Consequently, only about 35,000 out of nearly a million qualified voters in Buganda had themselves registered on the roll.

At the all-Ugandan elections more than 1,200,000 out of 1,330,000 registered voters went to the polls. Of the 81 seats 43 went to the Democratic Party and 35 were gained by the Uganda Peoples' Congress. (The Uganda National Congress won only one seat, independent candidates captured two.) This result did not reflect the real relation of forces between the two parties. (The Peoples' Congress received 652,854 votes, and the Democratic Party polled 457,560.) The numerical difference in legislative seats was shifted yet more in favour of the Democratic Party when the Legislative Council co-opted nine members of its own choice and another seven were appointed by the Governor.

After the elections the Governor formed Uganda's first government, which consisted of 13 members. In addition to Democratic Party President B. K. KIWANUKA,[1] as President of the Legislative Council and Minister of State, the government had twelve members: eight of them African, three European and one Indian. It is characteristic, by the way, that five of the nine African cabinet members came from the Bagandas, the subjects of the Kabaka, and that most of them had graduated from university in England, the United States or India.

---

[1] BENEDICTO KAGIMU KIWANUKA, son of a wealthy chief, was born in Masaka District of Buganda in May 1922. He was educated in Catholic mission schools; from 1942 to 1946 he did military service in Britain's African troops, one year in Kenya, three years in Egypt and Palestine. In 1946 he returned to Uganda and was a clerk and interpreter in the judicial apparatus of the colonial administration. In 1950 he decided to opt for the legal profession: he left his job and, after a year of preparatory studies, matriculated at London University in 1952. After four years he obtained his diploma in law. In 1956, returning to his country, he was a practising lawyer and joined the Catholic Democratic Party.

On June 20, 1961, the report of the MUNSTER Commission was made public. On the assumption that Buganda was not free to secede from Uganda, the report recommended that Uganda be proclaimed a federal state, in which self-government should be granted to the four kingdoms (Buganda, Bunyoro, Ankole and Toro). It proposed that some matters — first of all, foreign affairs and control of the defence force and the central police — remain within the competence of the central (this time "federal") government.

The Commission recommended that the Legislative Council be superseded by a unicameral National Assembly composed of members elected through direct and universal adult suffrage; that the right to vote be granted to Africans and non-Africans alike; that the National Assembly might decide upon any amendment to the constitution only by a two-thirds majority and to the constitutions of the several kingdoms only with their respective consent.

The Commission took a stand against the establishment of any kind of "council of chiefs" or "upper house", but recommended the formation of a Council of State, which should have the right to veto the unconstitutional proposals that might be submitted to the National Assembly.

The administration of the federation, in the view of the Commission, should be entrusted to a federal government formed in accordance with the rules of parliamentary democracy.

The Commission was strongly critical of the government of the Kabaka and the Lukiko for their wanton conduct and the functionaries of the Bugandan government for various financial anomalies. It recommended that the members of the Lukiko be elected indirectly, and that the Lukiko have the right to send its representatives to the Federal National Assembly, and the powers of the local councils of the other three kingdoms be identical with those of all other district councils.[13]

As for the head of state, the Commission made no proposal, but expressed the opinion that it would be better to have the post filled by a British Governor-General instead of the Kabaka.

In the matter of the territorial dispute between Uganda and Bunyoro, the Commission recommended that the controversy be settled by a plebiscite to be held in the disputed areas.

In accordance with the recommendation of the MUNSTER Commission, the British Governor on July 3 appointed KIWANUKA to the post of Prime Minister.

The London Conference in September–October 1961

The constitutional conference was held at Lancaster House in London between September 18 and October 9. The conference was attended by KIWANUKA, heading a government delegation, by leaders of the opposition with OBOTE at their head, and by representatives of the four kingdoms, the Kabaka among them.

Colonial Secretary MACLEOD in his opening address expressed his satisfaction that the Buganda leaders, who not long before had still pressed for secession from Uganda,

---

[1] These district councils were not traditional African authorities, but agencies of the colonial administration and were controlled by Provincial or District Commissioners and their subordinates.

had changed their minds and had come to the conference to take part in the drafting of an all-Ugandan constitution. With reference to the sad example of the Congo, he called on the participants to do their utmost to settle their differences by means of negotiation, and assured them at the same time that in the judgement of the British government Uganda should be granted complete independence in a year or two.

Disputes at the conference arose mainly from two issues: (1) the position of the Kingdom of Buganda within the new independent state of Uganda, namely the procedure of the election of members of the Lukiko and of the Bugan dan representatives to be sent to the federal legislature; and (2) the so-called "lost countries" which Bunyoro was demanding back from Buganda.

After heated debates (during which KIWANUKA and his entire delegation walked out and remained absent from the conference for a few days) a compromise came about on the basis of which the new draft constitution was worked out.

Under the new constitution, independent Buganda as a federal state was to be governed by the Kabaka and to have a legislative body of its own with 61 members elected directly on the basis of universal adult suffrage, further six members being appointed by the Kabaka, twenty by the tribal rulers, and another six chosen by the legislature itself.

The representation of Buganda in the National Assembly was arranged so that 21 of its 81 elected members were delegated by Buganda. The question of whether these representatives should be elected directly or appointed by the Lukiko was left to the Lukiko to settle. No decision was reached on the matter of the Bunyoro "lost countries", but it was agreed that the question would be further considered. (The tribal headmen of the "lost countries" disagreed with this idea.)

Under the new constitution, executive power over internal affairs after independence was to be exercised by a Cabinet of Ministers appointed by the National Assembly and headed by the Prime Minister. However, foreign affairs and defence (including control of both the army and the police) would remain within the competence of the British Governor appointed by the Queen of England.

After accepting the new constitution the conference fixed the schedule of independence. It was decided that Uganda would obtain self-government on March 1, 1962, hold general elections in April and be proclaimed an independent state on October 9.

The Elections in April and Change of Government in May 1962

By virtue of the London agreement of September 1961, Uganda received self-government on March 1, 1962. The former government, which was presided over by the British Governor and had three colonial officials among its members, was replaced by a new government headed by Prime Minister KIWANUKA and composed of twelve Ministers — 10 Africans, 1 British and 1 Indian.

The legislative elections were held, this time with the participation of Buganda, on April 25. The majority was won by OBOTE's Uganda Peoples' Congress in league with the Kabaka's party ("Kabaka Yekka Movement"). The Peoples' Congress itself captured 37 out of the 82 seats, so that, together with the 21 seats ensured to Buganda by the London agreement, it had a larger than two-thirds majority in the National Assembly. KIWANUKA's party obtained all in all 22 seats. His government had to resign and his Democratic Party went into opposition. The new government under OBOTE was formed on May 1.

The London Conference in June 1962

On June 12, 1962, leaders of the Uganda parties, including representatives of Buganda, again met in conference in London to discuss the controversial problems (the proposed federal form of government and the "lost countries") and the details of accession to independence. After two weeks of bitter disputes they again managed to arrive at some compromise on almost all questions. The only disputed issue that could not be settled to the satisfaction of all interested parties was the question of the so-called "lost countries", although the majority of the participants (among them the representatives of the Kabaka and of the British government) were inclined to agree to a compromise that the disputed areas should remain for at least two years under the administration of the central government, after which time a plebiscite should decide whether those parts should belong to Buganda or reannexed to Bunyoro, or whether they should remain definitively under central administration. While the tribal headmen of the disputed areas disagreed with the proposition, Prime Minister OBOTE and British Colonial Secretary MAUDLING agreed that the pending dispute should not prevent Uganda from being proclaimed an independent state at the appointed date, October 9.

The conference was closed on June 28. The British Parliament voted the Uganda Independence Bill on July 19.

Independent Uganda

On October 5, four days before the proclamation of independence, Prime Minister OBOTE announced that the day following independence 2,500 (mostly political) prisoners would be granted amnesty and be released.

A few hours before the independence celebration began at Kampala a mass rally was held with the participation of the political leaders of the three East African countries — Uganda, Kenya and Tanganyika. At the meeting OBOTE delivered a speech, in which he promised to spare no effort to support the demand for independence of neighbouring Kenya.

Uganda was proclaimed independent at a festive ceremony on October 9, 1962. The ceremony was held in the presence of 40,000 people and delegates from seventy countries. Great Britain was represented by the Earl of Kent and his wife. The representative of the United States conveyed the felicitations of President KENNEDY and offered $ 2 million in aid for the purchase of industrial and agricultural equipment. The governments of the Soviet Union and the People's Republic of China sent Prime Minister OBOTE telegrams of felicitation, with the solemn expression of their recognition of Uganda as an independent sovereign state and of their readiness to establish diplomatic relations with her. The attending representatives of the People's Republic of China, however, walked out of the ceremony, because the delegation of the Chiang Kai-shek regime was also present among the guests.

After the ceremony the Prime Minister gave a news conference. In his statement he strongly condemned the racist policies of the Republic of South Africa, the Central African Federation and Portugal, and announced that this government would recognize neither the government of the Republic of South Africa nor that of the Central African Federation.

BIBLIOGRAPHY

A. H. Cox, "The Growth and Expansion of Buganda", *Uganda Journal*, Vol. 15 (1950).

The Way to the West: Economic and Railway Survey of Certain Areas of West Uganda, Entebbe, 1951.

A. B. Mukwaya, "Land Tenure in Buganda: Present-day Tendencies", *East African Studies* No. 1, Kampala, 1953.

J. V. Wild, *The Uganda Mutiny*, London, 1954.

N. T. K. Parma, *Deposition of H. M. the Kabaka of Buganda*, London, 1954.

A. I. Richards, *Economic Development and Tribal Change: A Study of Immigrant Labour in Buganda*, Cambridge, 1954.

J. E. Goldthorpe, "An African Elite: A Sample Survey of Fifty-two Former Students of Makerere College in East Africa", *British Journal of Sociology*, Vol. VI, No. March 1955), pp. 31–47.

A. Low, "The British and the Baganda", *International Affairs*, Vol. 32, No. 3 (July 1956), pp. 308–317.

R. Mukherjee, *The Problem of Uganda: A Study in Acculturation*, Berlin, 1956.

D. E. Apter, "Political Development in Uganda", *Current History*, May 1956.

Uganda: Colonial Regime Versus National Aspirations, Cairo, 1957 (?).

P. G. Powesland, "Economic Policy and Labour: A Study in Uganda's Economic History", *East African Studies* No. 10, Kampala, 1957.

"Power in Uganda 1957–1970: A Study of Economic Growth Prospects for Uganda with special reference to the potential demand for electricity", in *The Economist Intelligence Unit*, London, 1957.

W. Elken, *Migrants and Proletarians: Urban Labour in the Economic Development of Uganda*, London, 1960.

Ю. ТОМЛИН, "Независимость Уганды и интrиги колонизаторов" [The Independence of Uganda ahd the Colonialist Intrigues], Международ Жизнь 11/1961.

D. A. Low, *Political Parties in Uganda 1949–62*, London, 1962.

[The Independence of Uganda and the Colonialist Intrigues], 11/1961.

L. A. Fallers (ed.), *The King's Man: Leadership and Status in Buganda on the Eve of Independence*, New York, 1964.

HISTORICAL MONOGRAPHS

C. C. Wrigley, "Buganda: An Outline of Economic History", London, 1958 (University of London Institute of Commonwealth Studies, reprint series No. 1). Reprinted from *Economic History Review*, August, 1957.

K. Ingham, *The Making of Modern Uganda*, London, 1958.

H. Ingrams, *Uganda*, London, 1960.

A. Low and C. Pratt, *Buganda and British Overrule*, London, 1960.

D. E. Apter, *The Political Kingdom in Uganda: A Study in Bureaucratic Nationalism*, Princeton, 1961.

The Kabaka of Uganda, *Desecration of My Kingdom*, London, 1967.

H. S. Morris, *The Indians in Uganda*, London, 1968.

A. R. Dunbar, *A History of Bunyoro-Kitara*, Oxford, 1970.

MEMOIRS BY FORMER BRITISH GOVERNORS

P. E. Mitchell, *African Afterthoughts*, London, 1954.

C. Dundas, *African Crossroads*, London, 1955.

OFFICIAL PUBLICATIONS

Uganda Protectorate. Withdrawal of Recognition from Kabaka Mutesa II of Uganda, 1953 (Cmd. 9028).

Uganda Protectorate. Buganda, 1954 (Cmd. 9320).

The Story of the Legislative Council: What It Is and What It Does, 9th ed., 1958.

Uganda. Report for the year 1958. H.M.S.O., London, 1959.

Uganda. Report of the Uganda Constitutional Conference 1961. H.M.S.O., London, 1961.

Report of the Uganda Independence Conference 1962. London, 1962.

Uganda Report of a Commission of Privy Counsellors on a Dispute between Buganda and Bunyoro. H.M.S.O., London, 1962.

CHAPTER XVIII

TANGANYIKA

The status of Tanganyika was changed on paper after the war, but no essential change was to come for the next ten years or so.

Under the trusteeship agreement endorsed by the United Nations General Assembly the British administering authority accepted the obligation to promote in that territory the progressive development of free political institutions. It undertook to develop the participation of the African inhabitants of Tanganyika in advisory and legislative bodies and in the government of the territory. This was in accordance with the UN Charter, under which the trust territories were supposed to develop "towards self-government or independence".

In reality, however, policy and administration in general did not change at all: the United Nations simply took over the role of the League of Nations, and the UN Trusteeship Council, to which the colonial powers had to submit their reports, replaced the Mandates Commission of the League.

Under the pressure of world public opinion Great Britain undertook to observe the provisions of the trusteeship agreement, but she continued to uphold the existing system of "indirect rule" and did her utmost to hold back political development and to delay the granting of independence. Accordingly the British administration was compelled to introduce certain reforms that would give a semblance of democratic advancement: by manipulating the principles of racial equality and parity it managed for about a decade and a half to water down every reform so as to prevent the legitimate masters of the territory, the Africans, from having a decisive say in the political life and government of their country.

As to the post-war situation of the African population, characteristic data are to be found in the annual report for 1947 submitted to the UN Trusteeship Council by the United Kingdom special representative, Sir JOHN LAMB, who wrote that Africans in Tanganyika felt better in prison than at liberty, and that the officially established form of penalty for Africans was flogging. LAMB stated himself that had it not been for corporal punishment the natives would not have respected the law. According to the report 91.3 per cent of the African population was illiterate.

In addition to political oppression the African peasantry suffered much from economic difficulties. The British administering authority, which had the duty under the UN Charter to promote the economic advancement of the African population and the rise of its standards of living according to appropriate economic plans, was still engaged in devising economic plans and land schemes that served the interests of European capitalists and landlords. (See the plan for the mechanized production of groundnuts and the alienation of the Meru land below.)

In the post-war years the British government was faced with a difficult dilemma. By signing the trusteeship agreement it had undertaken to show respect for the interests of the African population. However, its own interests, or rather the interests of British big capitalists it represented, and its established policy, in view of the inescapable collapse of the colonial system, required the intensification of colonial exploitation, that is, economic development in accordance with the interests of British capitalists and settlers, not of the Africans. "The fundamental problem lies in the conflict between the obligation to protect the land rights of the native inhabitants and the obligation to develop the Territory economically."[1]

The British government was fully aware of this. Its delegate to the Trusteeship Council formulated the problem as follows: "On the one hand, they press us to proceed with economic development. They press us, quite rightly, to proceed with the expansion and improvement of education, which itself depends on economic development. But some of them say also: but you must not alienate land except in the most exceptional circumstances. Here is a contradiction and dilemma. A great deal can be done by peasant farming, but this, as I have said, can be supplemented by plantation agriculture, by mining and secondary industries— all of which require the alienation of land."[2]

True to itself, the British government resolved the dilemma by forcing economic plans to the advantage of European capitalists and settlers. A most typical example was the Ten-Year Development and Welfare Plan for Tanganyika Territory, adopted in 1947.

The First "Reforms" after the War

The reforms introduced in the latter half of the forties brought no change. Up to the end of World War II there had been not a single African member either in the Legislative or in the Executive Council of Tanganyika.

Before 1945 the Legislative Council, with the Governor presiding, had 12 European official members appointed by the Governor and 10 unofficial members (7 European settlers and 3 Asians) who were also appointed by the Governor. The more than eight million African inhabitants of the country had no representative in the legislature. The colonialists took the view that African interests were represented by the British Governor and the officials appointed by him. The composition of the Legislative Council was determined by the British government, which had accepted the obligation under the trusteeship agreement to develop the participation of African inhabitants in the government of the territory.

Two African unofficials were first added to the Legislative Council in 1945, and another two in 1946. The Governor appointed all four from among chiefs loyal to the government. The number of appointed unofficial members was raised to 14, including 7 European settlers and 7 non-Europeans (4 Africans and 3 Asians). At the same time the number of official members was raised to 15, in order to make sure that the Africans, even if supported by all European and Asian unofficials, were unable to enforce their will against the official majority of the colonial government.

[1] B. T. G. CHIDZERO, *Tanganyika and International Trusteeship*, London–New York–Toronto, 1961, p. 233.
[2] *Trusteeship Council Official Records*, T/PV. 822, p. 97.

Prior to the war the Executive Council had been composed of British colonial officials, and only during the war were a few European settlers added as "unofficials". The Council thus had eight official members (three of them ex officio and five Europeans appointed by the Governor) and four unofficial European members. From 1948 onwards each official member was in charge of a department of the government, but he was answerable to the Governor, not to the Legislative Council.

The Question of Tanganyika in the United Nations from 1948 to 1951

The first Visiting Mission went to Tanganyika in 1948. In the absence of political organizations the Mission heard practically only the most conservative elements of the African population—chiefs who, being dependent on the colonial administration for their existence, usually refrained from criticizing the government's policies. Yet the Mission found a great deal to object to and in its report to the General Assembly it pointed out many shortcomings. It objected to the total absence of African representation in the Executive Council and the insignificant number of Africans in the Legislative Council. It criticized that Africans were almost entirely barred from important posts in the civil service: "Positions in the higher grades of the administrative and technical departments are filled by members of the British Colonial Service, which is common to all British Colonies, Protectorates and other dependencies. Africans and Indians may occupy subordinate posts, although it is the express desire of the Government to appoint Africans to positions of higher responsibility as and when they secure the necessary qualifications." Therefore the Mission recommended the expansion of educational facilities for Africans to enable them to take a substantive and active part in the government and political life of the territory. The Mission's main objection was against the political backwardness of the territory, because progress towards independence was conditional first of all on speedier political development.

In urging speedy political development the Mission pointed out that "lack of political planning beyond immediate steps, even in general terms, cannot but have an adverse effect on the progress towards the goal of self-government or independence".

The report discussed in detail the clear and resolute stand of Africans in opposition to the plans of an East African federation. It concluded that representatives of different strata of Africans and Asians whom the Mission had contacted were unanimously against the establishment of inter-territorial institutions.

The administering authority agreed only with the recommendations for better educational facilities and referred to the steps it had already taken in this respect, but it added that any improvement can be made only within the limitations of the existing resources and tasks.[1] To the recommendation for speedy political development and planning it replied flatly that "the development of democratic institutions among the indigenous inhabitants must inevitably be gradual if they are to rest on a solid and lasting foundation. . . . The method and the direction of further advance must be largely determined by the experience gained during this initial stage . . . the first stages of the advance must be erected on the foundations of their own

---

[1] The Ten-Year Plan of 1947 appropriated (really within "limitations") £5,393,000 for the expansion of primary education for Africans. Considering the eight-million population, this expenditure amounted to hardly more than a few shillings per year and per child.

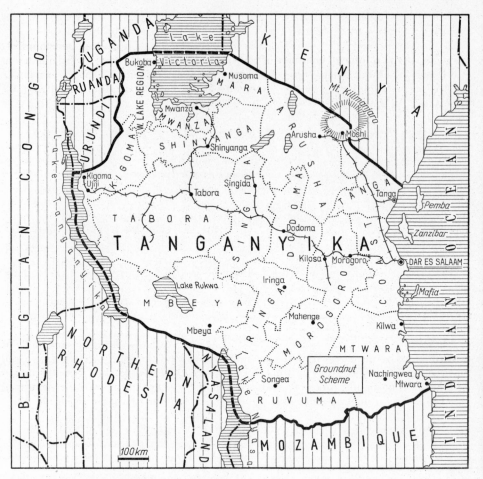

political conceptions and traditions, which must be modified and adapted to the new order by a steady process of education and guidance."[1]

The colonial administration informed the UN Visiting Mission of its large-scale plans for the mechanized production of groudnuts. The Mission's report described it as "a bold economic undertaking ... which may in the long run be of great benefit to the inhabitants of Tanganyika", and stated the opinion that the Governor should consider the measures and conditions which might make it possible to let the Africans enter into possession of the installations built under the groundnut scheme.

Relying on the recommendations of the Visiting Mission the UN General Assembly in its resolution 226 (III) of November 18, 1948, provided that the progressive development of trust territories "should be achieved at the earliest possible date" and that those territories "should attain self-government or independence as soon as possible" and recommended that "the Administering Authorities ... take all possible steps to accelerate the progressive development towards self-government or independence of the Trust Territories they administer".

[1] CHIDZERO, *op. cit.*, pp. 164–165.

130

In response to the recommendations of the UN Visiting Mission and to the General Assembly resolution of 1948 the British colonial administration set up, under the chairmanship of the Attorney General, a Committee on Constitutional Development, including all 14 unofficial members of the Legislative Council and the official member for Local Government. That this committee did not represent African interests was to be seen clearly from the recommendations it made concerning the two most crucial issues, the composition of the Legislative Council and the system of elections. Its report published in 1951 proposed that an official majority should be retained in the legislature, and that the unofficial seats should be divided equally among the three races (7 Europeans, 7 Africans, 7 Asians), that is on a parity basis. Direct elections were proposed for Europeans and Asians, and indirect elections for Africans by means of electoral colleges. The committee claimed hypocritically that the Africans did not desire direct elections, nor any reform of the Legislative Council; it stated in its report: "In respect of Africans, even among their leaders, the political conceptions of most are limited to local units ... There is no instant clamour for reform. The pace of political and constitutional developments must be matched with the capacity of the bulk of the population to absorb change."[1]

The truth, however, was that already at that time the Africans wanted general elections and majority representation in the Legislative Council, or at least equal representation with non-Africans (Europeans and Asians). But the colonial administration found even these moderate demands excessive.

Meanwhile, in its resolution 322 (IV) of November 15, 1949, the UN General Assembly laid down that in the economic policies of the powers administering trust territories "the interests of the indigenous inhabitants must be paramount", and next year, in resolution 438 (V) of December 2, 1950, it stated that "Equitable distribution of land and proper utilization of it together constitute one of the essential conditions in promoting the economic advancement of the inhabitants of Trust Territories".

In 1951 another UN Visiting Mission went to Tanganyika. It heard delegates of the Tanganyikan African Association, who presented a proposal, previously submitted to the Committee on Constitutional Development, for the Legislative Council to have equal numbers of official and unofficial members, the latter including as many African representatives as Europeans and Asians had all together. They added that if their request should be ignored, the parity proposal of the committee would be accepted only temporarily. The Chagga Cultural Association also formulated a proposal, demanding proportionate representation for Africans in the legislature, but eventually it settled for less, accepting the parity formula as a temporary measure. Also the Meru tribe presented a complaint against the alienations (carried out or under way) of tribal lands by the government.

By its resolution 558 (VI) adopted in 1951 the UN General Assembly invited the administering authority of each trust territory to report on "The measures, taken or contemplated, which are intended to lead the Trust Territory, in the shortest possible time, to the objective of self-government or independence ... The period of time in which it is expected that the Trust Territory shall attain the objective of self-government or independence".

---

[1] A. J. HUGHES, *East Africa: The Search for Unity*, London, 1963, p. 60.

True to its policy of procrastination, the British government in 1952 appointed Prof. W. J. M. MACKENZIE as Constitutional Commissioner to examine matters arising out of the report of the Committee on Constitutional Development.

At the same time the British Colonial Secretary, in order to reassure, or rather deceive, the United Nations and world public opinion, made the following mendacious statement to the House of Cmmoons: "First, it is the intention to continue to administer the territory in accordance with the terms of the Trusteeship Agreement until the ultimate goal of self-government has been reached. Her Majesty's Government confidently hope that when that goal has been attained Tanganyika will be within the British Commonwealth. Her Majesty's Government attach importance, for the interests of the inhabitants of Tanganyika, to the maintenance and promotion of British traditions and the British connexion with the territory. Secondly, Her Majesty's Government interpret the Trusteeship Agreement and Article 76 of the United Nations Charter as imposing on the Administering Party an obligation to provide for the full participation of all sections of the population, irrespective of racial origin, in the progressive development of political institutions and in the economic and social advancement of the territory. Each section of the population must be enabled and encouraged to play its full part in the development of the territory and its institutions, in complete confidence that the rights and interests of all communities, both indigenous and immigrant, will be secured and preserved."

The MACKENZIE report was submitted in 1953. It proposed that the unofficial members of the Legislative Council obtain their seats by election, not by appointment, and their number be raised from 21 to 30; that they be elected on a common roll of the three "race" groups (Europeans, Africans, Asians); that every constituency elect three members, one for each race, every voter casting his vote for three candidates, one of the three race groups each. The report proposed ten constituencies: the nine provinces of the country and Dar es Salaam. To the nine unofficial members of each group was to be added a tenth member, elected also on a common roll, to represent general interests of the respective race group.

Accordingly the Legislative Council was to be composed of 10 European, 10 African and 10 Asian elected unofficial members.

Prof. MACKENZIE thought his proposal would ensure racial parity. This word itself was a mere deception. The fact is that, in order that a government majority might be retained in the Legislative Council, the report proposed that the number of official members be raised from 15 to 31.

The government accepted in principle the proposals of the MACKENZIE report, except the most important one — that providing for the election of the unofficial members of the Legislative Council. After two or three years' hesitation it put into force the provision raising the number of unofficials and introducing "parity", of course, by securing at the same time the government majority as proposed by MACKENZIE. Until 1951 the Executive Council had had eight official members and only four nominated European unofficial members, who were then joined by a fifth unofficial, Chief KIDAHA, a trusted man of the government. In 1954 the number of unofficials was raised to six (two Europeans, two Africans and two Asians, to comply with the "parity" principle), while the number of the ex-officio members (all of them high colonial officials) was raised to nine. The unofficial members were nominated by the Governor and took responsibility for a government department under the control of the official member in charge.

Also in accordance with the MACKENZIE proposals the government decided, already in 1953, that the Legislative Council should be presided over, instead of the Governor, by a Legco member appointed by him.

Local Administration

Before 1945 the functions of local government were also exercised by officials of the colonial administration, directly on the provincial, district and municipal level, and indirectly through tribal authorities in the villages. Besides the provincial administrations there were so-called "councils of headmen", but the African population had no elected representative on any level in the local administration. It was in 1945 for the first time that a few unofficials were added to the councils of headmen of the Tanga and Eastern Provinces.

Despite its obligation under the trusteeship agreement, the British government obviously had no intention of changing the well tried system of "indirect rule" for the time being. Proof of this is the following sentence from its 1947 report to the United Nations: "The consolidation of tribal constitutional authority is encouraged as necessary to the establishment of a healthy, efficient, and progressive system of local government, the first essential step in the process of development towards the ultimate objective of self-government."[1]

In 1947–48 the UN Trusteeship Council stated that "the now existing tribal structure is an obstacle to the political and social advancement of the indigenous inhabitants" and proposed to the administering authority the introduction of elective representative institutions.

The first step towards elective institutions of local government was taken in 1949: the first municipal council composed of elected members was set up in Dar es Salaam.

In 1950 the British administration issued the Native Authority (Amendment) Ordinance. While the previous ordinance (1926) meant "native authority" to imply only chiefs and specified their powers, the 1950 amendment broadened the concept by defining "native authority" as "any chief or any other native or natives or any council or group of natives declared to be or established as a native authority under this Ordinance for the area concerned".[2]

At the further insistence of the United Nations the British administration enacted the Local Government Ordinance, 1953, providing for the establishment of county councils, town councils and local councils, designed gradually to replace the existing "native authorities". The new ordinance, however, created only the possibility of establishing new councils, without making it mandatory, and permitted a good number of alternatives for the election of the council members, for the ratio of official and unofficial members, and for the powers of the councils.

The British administering authority declared that the aim of the ordinance was one of "bringing about a transition from the traditional to a modern system of administration, particularly in the establishment of councils".[3] How little this assertion coincided with the real intention of the administering authority was clearly shown by the fact that at the same time as the Local Government Ordinance, also another one, the African Chiefs Ordinance, was enacted, defining again the powers

[1] HUGHES, *op. cit.*, p. 58.
[2] CHIDZERO, *op. cit.*, p. 150.
[3] *Op. cit.*, pp. 150–151.

and functions of the chiefs in order to preserve and strengthen their position and prestige in the areas desirous of making use of the opportunities offered by the Local Government Ordinance. The avowed purpose of the African Chiefs Ordinance was to conserve "the powers of chiefs in local council areas to make orders regulated by and enforcing native law and custom in respect of certain public purposes scheduled in the ordinance".[1]

The duplicity of the administering power was also borne out by Governor TWIN-ING's following statement before the Legislative Council: "It is the intention of the Government of Tanganyika to maintain the tribal system, but to ensure that such changes as may be desirable to meet modern conditions are made when the people feel themselves able to agree. It is Government's intention, too, to maintain the authority of the chiefs, but to ensure that there can be no tyranny, and, indeed, that they are guided and advised by a council which has wherever possible a majority of representatives of the people elected in a democratic way."[2]

In the next few years the councils provided for by the Local Government Ordinance were established by hundreds at district and lower levels.[3] But these councils could not be taken for really democratic local government organs, on the one hand, because their powers were very limited and, on the other, because in them there was no elective majority and the members were not directly elected, and because the appointed members included conservative chiefs and their men, officials of the British administration, and in many places even invited European settlers.

The only really positive step before 1957 towards local self-government was the establishment of municipal councils. By 1957 Dar es Salaam and nine townships had received municipalities of local government status.

In 1957 the powers of the district councils were enlarged to some extent by an amendment to the 1953 ordinance.

Progress towards local self-government being extremely slow, the UN Trusteeship Council in 1957 again urged the administering authority to promote, as rapidly as possible, the establishment of efficient local government units at district and lower levels, and to ensure that such development proceeded on a non-racial basis and that direct, democratic elections were based on the widest possible suffrage.

As appears from the foregoing, the British government pursued the usual double-dealing policy on the issue of local government, too. The United Nations had repeatedly called upon the administering authority to speed up progress, but it did nothing more; in the course of fifteen years it passed not a single decision censuring the administering power.

Characteristically, in the works on post-war development in Tanganyika we can find entirely different evaluations of the British government's policy on this question. All-out supporters of the British policy exaggerate the actual results and praise the administering power. CHIDZERO writes, for example: " . . . there is clear evidence that tremendous progress is being made. Traditional institutions are being gradually and constructively transformed into elective, representative institutions of local government. Purely native authorities are being gradually changed on the district and county level into non-racial councils—institutions which transcend racial inter-

[1] *Op. cit.*, p. 151.
[2] *Ibid.*
[3] Out of 56 districts in the country 51 had district councils, while at higher level only one county council was formed, in Lake Province in 1955, but this was an organ rather of the central government than of the local administration, just like the Provincial Advisory Council established in the province.

ests and differences ... In all this, local people are being prepared not only for local government on modern lines, but for self-government generally."[1]

The liberal A. J. HUGHES, who takes a critical approach, holds a quite different view: "Although the decision to replace indirect rule with more democratic local government was taken a decade before independence, no alternative was firmly established by 1962. Year after year Governors, UN Visiting Missions, administrative officers, T.A.N.U. officials, and, latterly, unofficial ministers repeated the need for the development of institutions at the local level more in keeping with changes at the centre. Yet too little was done."

The Holmes Commission

In 1947 the British government appointed a commission under the chairmanship of MAURICE HOLMES to review and adjust the salaries of civil servants in the East African colonies. In its report the commission differentiated between higher and lower posts, and suggested that non-European employees in the higher posts should receive three-fifths of the salaries paid to Europeans and recommended three pay categories for the lower grades: the highest salary for Europeans, a lower pay for Asians, and the lowest category for Africans. The Africans and Asians vehemently protested, and when the problem of the African civil servants was taken up by the UN Visiting Mission in 1948 and subsequently was discussed by the UN General Assembly in 1952, the Secretary of State for the Colonies saw fit to state in the House of Commons on December 2, 1952: " ... I dislike the system and I hope to live to see it abolished."[2] Afterwards, in 1953, the British Governors of Kenya, Uganda and Tanganyika, and the British Resident in Zanzibar set up a commission under DAVID LIDBURY "to review the whole range of salaries and conditions of the Civil Services ... of the East African Territories and of the East Africa High Commission". The commission's recommendations were accepted by the Tanganyika Legislative Council as well. The LIDBURY commission proposed the fixing of the rates of pay according to personal qualities and responsibility of duties instead of racial disctinction. It rejected the three-fifths rule recommended by the HOLMES commission, and proposed an additional pay to the basic salary, in all grades and regardless of race, for qualified employees recruited from abroad. The commission envisaged the gradual replacement of British officials by Africans, so that the entire personnel of the civil service should ultimately be recruited locally.

In 1954 the British administration accepted the LIDBURY recommendations, and in its 1954 report it made the following statement: "The civil service is established on a non-racial basis. Appointment is governed by the qualifications, experience, competence and general suitability of the candidate and there is nothing to prevent a member of any section of the population being appointed or rising to any post in the service. As far as possible the civil service is staffed from among the inhabitants of the territory, but, where no suitable candidate is available locally, officers are recruited from external sources."[3]

By its resolution on this report the Trusteeship Council instructed the administering authority to submit progress reports on the Africanization of the civil service.

---

[1] CHIDZERO, op. cit., p. 153.
[2] Op. cit., pp. 155.
[3] Op. cit., p. 156.

Accordingly the next report of the British government told of the enactment of a Public Service Commission Ordinance, setting up a commission charged with the duty of "ensuring that all posts that fall vacant are filled locally if possible, and that recruiting from outside the Territory only takes place when there is no suitable local candidate available".[1]

The number of Africans in the civil service did really grow in the next few years, occasionally even in the higher grades, and there was some progress also in the abandonment of racial distinction, but:

(a) Africanization proceeded slowly, and the number of European officials grew at the same pace as that of African employees. In 1956 the Governor still complained that "Government finds it difficult to obtain a sufficiency of locally educated Africans to fill the Clerical Service which still has over 300 vacancies".[2]

(b) There was some improvement also as concerns the inequality of salaries, but the LIDBURY system of additional pay enabled the government to give higher pays to Europeans than to Africans in one and the same grade.

The Groundnut Scheme

In 1947 the British government adopted a large-scale plan for the cultivation of groundnuts in Tanganyika. (Originally outlined in "A Plan for the Mechanized Production of Groundnuts in East and Central Africa", the scheme was practically intended to be carried out in Tanganyika.) The purpose of the scheme was to clear over 3 million acres of unproductive land and to lease it for periods of 99 years to those wishing to grow groundnuts, with the proviso that the land should eventually revert to the indigenous inhabitants. The groundnut scheme was to be operated by the Overseas Food Corporation founded in 1948.

Government propaganda emphasized that the scheme would be "a great catalyst of development" in Tanganyika, promoting the construction of roads, bridges and ports, as well as community centres, hospitals, schools, etc. It described the plan as a primary source of benefits to the African population. The truth, however, is that the scheme, if it could have been carried out, might really have yielded large economic benefits — to the colonial administration (which would have for a hundred years been profiting by leasing the land and sharing in the earnings of the groundnut growers and traders) and to settlers and capitalists who had interests in the production and sale of groundnuts. The Africans (or rather a small section of them) would have been given only a new opportunity to sell their labour for starvation wages and to help the parasitic European capitalists and landlords to wax richer.

With its deceptive propaganda the British government managed to mislead the United Nations, too, making it believe that the plan served the interests of the Africans. The colonial administration kept the UN Visiting Mission informed of the large-scale plan for the improved and mechanized cultivation of groundnuts. The Trusteeship Council was of the opinion that "in the case of Tanganyika the Administering Authority should formulate a plan indicating possible steps by which and the necessary conditions under which the scheme of mechanized production and its complex financial and managerial structure may be transferred to the Africans".

[1] *Ibid.*
[2] *Op. cit.*, p. 157.

However, as CHIDZERO put it, "the grandiose scheme ... proved economically a liability and productively a failure".[1] It turned out that the soil of the chosen area was unfit for the production of groundnuts. Eventually the British government in August 1950 ordered the undertaking to be closed upon a loss officially estimated at £25 million[2] (the total investment had been £36 million).

When the scandal provoked by this failure had subsided, the allegedly £ 11 million worth of assets left of the undertaking (buildings, equipment, etc.) was taken over from the Overseas Food Corporation by the Tanganyika Agricultural Corporation founded in 1953 by Africans. The corporation chairman, Chief HARUN MSABILE LUGUSHA, admitted that Africans had derived some benefits from the groundnut scheme inheritance (farm equipment, machinery and experienced labourers), but he added right away: " ... in view of Tanganyika conditions, all this could have been achieved for a fraction of the £11 million which were profitably invested, if—and I repeat if—Mr. Strachey[3] is right that only £25 million were lost. Frankly, I would find it impossible to account for more than about £7 million worth of assets, including the training of Africans, at 1950 prices. In my view the loss was nearer to £ 30 million than to £25 million."[4]

The Africans, who had not been asked to state their opinion on the launching of the groundnut scheme, were from the outset suspicious of it, and when it ended with failure, they thought of the wasted 25 to 30 million which could have been used for the modernization of the African peasant farms of Tanganyika.

The Eviction of the Meru Tribe

The government of Tanganyika in 1947 appointed the so-called Arusha-Moshi Lands Commission "to examine and consider the present distribution of alienated lands and tribal lands in the Moshi and Arusha districts (Kilimanjaro and Meru Mountains area), and to make comprehensive plans and recommendations for the re-distribution of such lands with a view to—

"(a) improving the homogeneity of alienated and tribal lands respectively; and

"(b) affording relief to congestion of the native population in tribal lands with particular reference to the question of providing them with adequate means of access to other areas suitable for the grazing of stock, the cultivation of annual crops and eventual settlement ..."[5]

Already in 1947 the commission submitted its report, in which it suggested, starting from the economic desirability of forming continuous blocks of European-owned lands, that the Meru and other tribes be excluded from settlement and grazing cattle within a definite area (which covered considerable portions of Meru land).

The duplicity of the commission is characterized by the fact that, while refraining from recommending the eviction of the Meru people, it admitted and stressed the advisability of constituting large expanses of racially homogeneous African or European settlement areas, both with a view to increased effectiveness in the work of local government organs and from the economic and sanitary points of view. The

[1] *Op. cit.*, p. 235.

[2] The shameful story of the groundnut scheme is discussed in detail by JUDITH LISTOWEL, *The Making of Tanganyika*, London, 1965 (ch. 14: "Groundnut Interlude", pp. 142–155).

[3] JOHN STRACHEY, the British Minister of Food.

[4] LISTOWEL, *op. cit.*, p. 155.

[5] CHIDZERO, *op. cit.*, p. 237.

report stated that " . . . it is doubtful if this ideal of homogeneity is one which should be pursued in Tanganyika. Should not the Government of a mandated or trust Territory avoid doing anything which contributes to the perpetuation of tribal, racial and colour divisions? Should it not rather so arrange matters that all who live in the Territory within the King's peace can live side by side and be treated equally under the laws as inhabitants of the Territory irrespective of their native or non-native origin? Should not the same amenities be allowed and the same anti-disease measures be applied to all? Is it necessary or desirable to segregate races, each of which has something to contribute to the welfare of the other and to the common good?"[1]

But the British government did not share this doubt expressed by the commission. On June 7, 1949, after obtaining the consent of the Meru chief, the government announced at a Meru tribal meeting that it had decided to resettle the Meru villages of the Sanya Corridor between Kilimanjaro and Meru Mountains to new lands in the Kingori area. The lands situated north-east of Mount Meru and north-west of Mount Kilimanjaro were owned by European settlers, the dividing strip of land provided room for Meru settlements and estates of white settlers, Boer farmers originating from South Africa. The evictions meant to the Meru people the loss of valuable tribal lands most suitable for cattle grazing, in exchange for less cultivable and tsetse-infested lands. This amounted to the pillage of an African people, in a territory placed under United Nations trusteeship in the middle of the 20th century, by the British administering authority which thereby grossly violated its obligations undertaken in the trusteeship agreement.

The Meru people heard about the announcement with indignation and refused to move. They denounced the chief's consent given without their knowledge as null and void, and the tribe disavowed the chief and forced him to resign. They complained to the 1951 UN Visiting Mission and the British Colonial Secretary, but uselessly. The UN representatives told them to petition the Trusteeship Council and promised to report on their case. And the British government, without deigning to answer, referred the case to the Legislative Council, in which its men wielding the majority passed an eviction ordinance.[2]

The eviction of the Meru people was carried out by force of arms (with police assistance) between November 17 and December 12, 1951.

According to the records kept by the British government, "330 Meru taxpayers" and their families, altogether 1,000 men, women and children, were evicted, 492 huts and store-houses were burnt, 400 cattle and 1,200 sheep impounded, 25 people were arrested and sentenced to imprisonment from two weeks to six months. According to the Meru the losses were much more considerable. EARLE SEATON, the Jamaican lawyer of the Meru, testified before the Trusteeship Council that more than twenty times as many buildings were destroyed: 724 huts, 489 store-houses and 234 stables were consumed by fire, 707 cattle, 1,440 sheep and 1,941 fowls perished; a man died and seven women miscarried. (The last two facts were denied by the government.)

Upon the advice of the 1951 UN Visiting Mission, EARLE SEATON and KIRILLO JAPHET, a Meru farmer, in the summer of 1952 appeared before the Trusteeship Council to petition on behalf of the Meru tribe. After hearing the two petitioners and a representative of the British government, the Council passed a resolution

---

[1] *Op. cit.*, pp. 241–242.

[2] Typically enough, all in all two unofficial Legco members took part in the discussion. One of them, a Boer settler personally interested in the evictions, Major DU TOIT, urged the implementation of the ordinance in order to bring "the bigoted and selfish Meru" to heel and defeat "communist propaganda" '!).

deploring that the administering authority should have found it necessary to evict the Meru people. It admitted, though, that the scheme was "advantageous to the majority of the indigenous inhabitants of the Arusha-Moshi area", and only invited the British government to take the necessary steps to indemnify the Meru and reminded the administering authority that it "should be guided by the principle that African communities settled on the land should be moved to other areas unless a clear expression of their collective consent had been obtained".

The petitioners were not satisfied with this meaningless resolution, and the question was brought to the 1952 session of the General Assembly of the United Nations. The Fourth Committee of the Assembly considered the issue and voted a resolution 32 to 17, recommending the administering power to return the alienated lands to the Meru immediately. At the plenary meeting of the General Assembly the committee resolution was passed by only 28 votes to 20, and in the absence of a two-thirds majority it was not carried.

In 1953 the petitioners again submitted the question to the Trusteeship Council, but the Council decided to postpone its consideration and formulate a stand only on the basis of the findings of the next (1954) Visiting Mission to Tanganyika.

The 1954 UN Visiting Mission found that the Meru put up "stubborn but passive resistance", and therefore it decided that, considering "the consistent attitude of the Meru people, the failure of some of the European farmers to make a success of the land alienated, the increasing pressure of population and the worsening of race relations in that part of Africa", the eviction scheme must be stopped.

The campaign continued for years. Part of the evicted Meru had settled at Kingori and accepted a flimsy compensation,[1] but the majority of the Meru people still resisted. The dogged resistance of the Meru tribe, on the one hand, and the failure of the milk farms established in the Sanya Corridor, on the other, finally led the British government to give some of the alienated land back to the Meru.

During many years, both in the United Nations and in the Tanganyika Legislative Council, as well as in the House of Commons, the British government had to face serious charges on account of the Meru eviction case. But the British government, disavowing its former statements and promises,[2] shamelessly refused all charges.

To the criticisms of the forcible eviction the British government responded with similar hypocritical statements. Governor TWINING, for example, said in the Legislative Council: "Owing to these people's refusal to comply with the law and leave the area, it was necessary to use compulsion. The Administration carried out its unpleasant duties with the utmost consideration to the people concerned . . . Government has taken note of the terms of the resolution passed by the Trusteeship Council.

---

[1] The cash compensation paid until 1957 was only £7,437.

[2] A White Paper of 1930 on policies regarding the indigenous population of the East African territories stated that the British government "adhere to the principle of opportunity in the disposal of all Crown lands irrespective of race, colour or religion—a principle in effect imposed in the Mandated Territory of Tanganyika on His Majesty's Government by the terms of the Mandate upon which administration of the territory is based, and one which they have no idea of abandoning." (CHIDZERO, op. cit., p. 247.) Also in 1930 the then Governor of Tanganyika, DONALD CAMERON, declared: "You must either refuse to grant land which is available and suitable, because it is surrounded by natives, or, alternatively, you will have to move the natives; and . . . if you attempt to do the latter, you will have to use armed force, and you will not succeed even then." (Op. cit., p. 246.) And a year later, when asked by Lord LUGARD whether it was possible to establish separate areas for Africans in Tanganyika, Governor CAMERON replied emphatically: "Not in Tanganyika. As I tried to point out, there cannot be any geographical cleavage." (Ibid.)

There is nothing in the resolution which conflicts with the policy which Government is already pursuing and Government is already taking action on the very lines urged by the resolution."[1]

In reply to the charge that the evictions were aimed at racial segregation the British government claimed mendaciously that the establishment of homogeneous settlement blocks separated not Africans from Europeans but tribal lands from alienated lands, and asserted that anyone who had the necessary means might buy such land for himself. When speaking of this scholastic argument of the British government, even CHIDZERO, a staunch advocate of the government's policy, was compelled to admit that, as "the facts of economic capability between Africans and Europeans suggest, this homogeneity was bound to mean in fact the creation in that area of geographical segregation of the races".[2]

Colonial Secretary LENNOX-BOYD himself had to admit that the whole scheme was devised in the interests of the European settlers. His evasive reply to a question by Labour M.P. JOHN PATON is characteristic of the official British attitude:

"*Mr. John Paton:* Would the Minister inform the House who are the beneficiaries of this newly formed ranch land, and whether it is the case that some of the new lands offered to the tribesmen are tsetse-infested?

"*Mr. Lennox-Boyd:* All those questions were gone into by the native authorities, and they are fully satisfied with proposals of the late Government, which this Government fully endorse.

"*Mr. John Paton:* Would the Minister please answer my question? Who are the beneficiaries in respect of the land?

"*Mr. Lennox-Boyd:* I hope the beneficiaries are those people who will bring prosperity to the whole territory. (*Hon. Members:* Will they be Europeans?) Yes, no doubt they will be Europeans."[3]

The Tanganyika African National Union

Before 1954 the peoples of Tanganyika had no political parties. From 1929 there had existed the Tanganyikan African Association, and inter-tribal society, whose members were mainly civil servants and teachers, and which practically abstained from politics. The society had a number of tribal organizations of local character, which were engaged in cultural and social activities as well as in politics. In 1953 JULIUS NYERERE was elected President of the Association. He worked out a plan to transform the organization into a popular political party. After discussing the plan with a group of members, he arranged on July 7, 1954, a meeting in Dar es Salaam of delegates from all local branches of the Association. The meeting decided to change the name of the society to the Tanganyika African National Union (T.A. N.U.), and adopted the programme of the new party.

The primary aim of the party was (*a*) to prepare the people of Tanganyika for self-government and independence, to struggle relentlessly for the achievement of this goal; (*b*) to combat tribalism and isolationism among Africans, and to build a unified nationalism instead. The party demanded that all local and central govern-

[1] CHIDZERO, *op. cit.*, p. 243.
[2] *Op. cit.*, p. 242.
[3] *House of Commons Debates*, vol. 494, col. 2371.

140

ment bodies be elected, that universal suffrage be introduced and the privileges of immigrants abolished. It declared that it would struggle to achieve African majorities in all organs. It emphasized the necessity of providing the African farmers with loans and machinery, and of encouraging the growth of an African business community. It opposed the alienation of land to non-Africans and objected to the levies on African cotton and coffee production. Finally, the party emphasized its firm opposition to "any move to join Tanganyika in a union or federation with the other East African territories, until the demand for such a federation comes from the African inhabitants of those territories."

The government used every means to obstruct the activities of T.A.N.U. and to prevent its growth.

In its official report for 1954 the administering authority spoke disparagingly of T.A.N.U.'s claim to be considered a national party. It stated with sarcasm that the party had an insignificant number of supporters in only four of the eight provinces and that its ties with the provincial branches were very loose, because these all strove for autonomy in the tradition of the Tanganyikan African Association.

It accused the party of fomenting opposition to the salutary measures of the government, held it responsible for all wrongful acts of African elements, and claimed that the party incited the popular masses against traditional tribal authorities and local government bodies. In his 1956 report the Eastern Province Commissioner claimed that T.A.N.U.'s activities prevented the dam construction and the insecticide spraying ordered by the government. In the same year the Tanga Province Commissioner said the malcontents influenced by T.A.N.U. stirred up trouble against the local administration in several areas. The Western Province Commissioner reported that political actions occurred usually in places where people were discontented with the chiefs.

The growth of T.A.N.U. really was not all plain sailing. From the outset the party had grown and expanded rapidly in Dar es Salaam, in the Northern Province, and along the Central Railway line. Party branches emerged slowly in Tanga, Northern and Lake Provinces, but development was still slower in the remote Southern and Western Provinces. The party executive in the initial years had difficulties in controlling the activities of scattered rural branches. The fact was that leaders of the local branches, for lack of regular contact with the party leadership, often caused tribal disputes, or started political action on account of local issues of little importance instead of promoting the political objectives of the national movement (the local administration also had a share in it, inasmuch as it tried to direct the political activity of Africans towards intertribal struggles around local interests, to obstruct their struggle against the colonial system). It happened also that, for want of regular instruction or experience, the local party leaders made any slight manifestation of African discontent a pretext for launching a political drive against the government or the local authorities, often even against useful measures which some of them mistook for anti-African action.

The initial success of T.A.N.U. was obvious, and the government, despite its disparaging comments on it, was aware of the threat posed by the party. Proof of this was the enactment, shortly after the formation of T.A.N.U., of the Societies Ordinance, which made it possible for the government to ban the T.A.N.U. branches. Section 6 of this ordinance (No. 11 of 1954) read: "It shall be lawful for the Governor in Council, in his absolute discretion, where he considers it to be essential in the public interest, by order to declare to be unlawful any society which in his opinion

(a) is being used for any purpose prejudicial to, or incompatible with, the maintenance of peace, order and good government; or (b) is being used for any purpose at variance with its declared objects."[1]

The 1954 UN Visiting Mission

Shortly after the formation of T.A.N.U. a new UN Mission went to Tanganyika.

T.A.N.U. submitted to the UN Visiting Mission a memorandum written in a moderate tone, describing the appalling poverty of the African population and putting forth the political demands of the Africans. It did not demand a time-table for independence, nor an African majority in the Legislative Council, it was satisfied for the moment with parity of the three races (Africans, Asians, Europeans), and wanted a democratic system only for the election of the local councils. It stated, however, its principled position: "The Africans of this country would further like to be assured both by the United Nations Organization and by the Administering Authority that this territory, though multi-racial in population, is primarily an African country and must be developed as such." Among the African grievances the memorandum emphasized the eviction of the Meru tribe as a most typical example of the duplicity of the administering power.

The Visiting Mission, in its majority report,[2] identified itself with the T.A.N.U. position on almost every point. In a diplomatic though unmistakable phrasing it criticized the policies of the administering authority,[3] and in its recommendations it went even farther than T.A.N.U.: it not only demanded that the administering authority should relinquish the principle of parity and proclaim that the country would be granted independence, but it also proposed that parity of the three races should be abandoned within three years from the first meeting of the Legislative Council, and a time-table of progress towards independence should be worked out so that Tanganyika might attain complete independence in twenty to twenty-five years.

These far from radical recommendations of the UN Mission,[4] and its endorsement of the T.A.N.U. position, practically infuriated the British colonialists. The London government declared that the Mission's proposal for a time-table of twenty to twenty-five years was "based on erroneous assumptions" and that T.A.N.U.'s claim to represent the people of the territory as a whole was "without foundation".

[1] CHIDZERO, op. cit., p. 203.

[2] The pro-British chairman of the Mission, a delegate from New Zealand, disagreed with the majority and refused to sign the report.

[3] For example: " ... the lack of a definite policy of integration, as well as the lack of a clear understanding of the meaning of 'multi-racial society', seems to the Mission to be at the root of some of the Territory's present difficulties, and in particular of the grievances and uncertainties which agitate the minds of Africans ... While the meaning of the terms 'multi-racial society' and 'multi-racial government' has suffered elsewhere in the continent not only through ambiguity but also from abuse, these same expressions are being freely used in the Trust Territory with obviously good intentions, but the unfortunate impression created is that they already represent something very different from the real situations to which they apply ... The present racial representation should not be allowed to obscure the fact that the only form of society which can be developed in a Trust Territory, in conformity with the principles and objectives established by the Charter, is one which integrates all of its racial components on the basis of the equality of all of their individual members."

[4] As is known, Tanganyika actually acceded to independence in seven years from these events.

In violation of its obligations under the terms of the trusteeship agreement, the British government refused to accept the findings and recommendations of the UN Visiting Mission.

In its reply to the report of the Visiting Mission the British government stated: "The Administering Authority is unable to accept the recommendation by the Visiting Mission that a time-table should be fixed for the successive phases of constitutional development and that a date (which would of necessity have to be arbitrary) should be specified by which the Territory would be granted self-government. The declared policy of the Administering Authority is that constitutional development of Tanganyika should be by stages, the ground being consolidated and the future reviewed in the light of the experience gained before each important stage is undertaken. The rigidity of a fixed time-table would be inimical to the harmonious development of political institutions corresponding to consecutive stages of economic and social evolution. This does not mean that political and constitutional progress will be slow."

The United Tanganyika Party

Early in 1956 the colonial government, to counteract the influence of T.A.N.U., formed the United Tanganyika Party (U.T.P.). The new party was formally constituted by unofficial members of the Legislative Council, but was in reality backed up by the government, and its political platform was almost identical with the government's policy. This is convincingly demonstrated by its programme and its entire activity. The party did not cease to call upon the Africans to respect and obey the established government and the traditional authorities. Like the government itself, it also harped upon the equality of races (and, to win the favour of the Africans, it even demanded the lifting of racial differentiation), emphasizing at the same time the existence of different races in the country and upholding their "rights" as separate communities. Accordingly, it opposed the introduction of universal suffrage (and thereby the enforcement of the will of the African majority!) on the grounds that that "would lead to the domination of one racial group by the others", and that the existing situation should continue "until such time as the main races are more nearly formed into one whole as responsible citizens".

In its propaganda the U.T.P. was guided by three objectives: to enhance the prestige of the British colonialists, to undermine the prestige of the United Nations, and to stop the Africans from supporting the T.A.N.U. policy. It endeavoured to make the Africans believe that they had to rely on the British government, not on the United Nations, for Tanganyika's progress towards independence.

At the first convention of the U.T.P. its chairman, IVOR BAYLDON, vigorously attacked the United Nations, declaring that the world organization had no right to interfere in the administration of Tanganyika.

But he concentrated the main effort on an attack upon T.A.N.U. He asserted that T.A.N.U. advocated violence, that its leaders used nationalist catchwords to promote selfish interests and exploited every real or supposed grievance to foment racial hatred. And to mislead the Africans he claimed, as did the government, that T.A.N.U. had very little influence among the ordinary people, because it had practically no following among the populous, large tribes of the country. It is characteristic that these accusations and slanders against T.A.N.U. took up four-fifths of the U.T.P. memorandum submitted to the 1957 UN Visiting Mission to Tanganyika.

Right from the beginning, of course, T.A.N.U. turned categorically against the new party and denounced it as a toady of the government. T.A.N.U.'s counter-propaganda, and the evidently opportunistic policy of the U.T.P. betraying the African interests, had as a consequence that the new party deceived only very few Africans, chiefly the most backward elements. As compared to the 250,000 T.A.N.U. members, the U.T.P. membership, even at its peak of barely 10,000, was made up as follows: Africans 67 per cent, Asians 23 per cent, Europeans 8.5 per cent.

This circumstance as well as the gradual change in the political scene moved the U.T.P. to revise its propaganda. The conspicuous fact that all the government-appointed ("unofficial") members of the Legislative Council came from the U.T.P. clearly belied the official claim that the government favoured neither of the two parties, but that it stood above them. Therefore the government saw it fit to promise that in the near future the unofficial members would be elected by the popular electorate. This announcement was designed to achieve two aims at a time. Namely T.A.N.U., as it was gaining strength, abandoned its moderate policy (acceptance of parity as a temporarily satisfactory principle) and included in its programme the demand for democratic general elections. The government thought that the introduction of an electoral system based on the far from democratic MACKENZIE recommendations might be made to appear as a concession to the Africans, and that thereby it would deceive part of them, even T.A.N.U.'s followers, and induce them to drop their radical demands without making any essential change in the conditions of the oppressed Africans against the privileged Europeans.

In view of the forthcoming elections and of the new tactics of the colonial administration, the U.T.P. already in its memorandum to the 1957 UN Visiting Mission gave evidence of some advances in comparison to its previous policy. It stressed that in the future the Tanganyika government should be "largely African" and demanded "self-government at the earliest possible moment".

As the elections were approaching, the U.T.P. programme became even more radical, at least in words, in order to win African votes. In its policy statement issued in September 1957, the party spoke (though with some reservations) about universal suffrage and went so far as to demand a "time-table" (true, for the attainment of self-government, not of independence):

"The party believes in universal adult franchise achieved gradually on the basis of a qualitative vote.

"The U.T.P. calls on Government to declare their policy for the step-by-step evolution towards self-government for Tanganyika as a Dominion member of the British Commonwealth under which economic, educational and political progress would be linked together and a realistic target date set for the achievement of self-government."

As will be seen below, this proved insufficient for the U.T.P. to escape its doom.

The Persecution of T.A.N.U.

The government did everything in its power to hinder the activities of T.A.N.U. It ordered restriction to be imposed on the freedom of movement of NYERERE who had left his job as a teacher to devote all his time to political activities. The government-influenced press and radio carried on a campaign of slander against the entire action. They incited the chiefs against the party and tried to persuade them to keep their people from joining any T.A.N.U. action.

At a conference of chiefs in Mzombe on May 14, 1957, the Governor argued that tribalism was the mainstay of African society and that T.A.N.U.'s membership was made up of people who broke the tribal ties and did not respect the traditional authorities.

Political meetings of the party were banned or the announced speakers were prohibited from participating.

In 1957 in many places the Provincial or District Commissioners arbitrarily, without giving any reason, banned the local T.A.N.U. branches or refused to permit new branches to operate. The Iringa branch of the party, for example, was banned because its chairman encouraged the African peasants to boycott the veterinary regulations for "cattle dipping", although the party executive had publicly denounced the chairman's action and even expelled him from the party.

NYERERE complained to the Governor against the banning orders, declaring that the party organizations had in several cases been punished unjustly for irresponsible acts of persons who had acted without the knowledge and consent of the party executive committee, in other cases the punishment had been meted out under the influence of non-Africans hostile to the party. He added that the government obviously wished to ruin the reputation of responsible leaders and to find some pretext for stifling the movement.

In spite of all efforts of the government the party grew rapidly in the years 1956 through 1958, and its activity could not be paralyzed. The banned organizations continued operating underground. Their functionaries used co-operative societies, trade unions and private persons (traders, etc.) to keep in touch with the organizations which were free to work in other districts, they circulated the instructions of the executive committee and the party publications, and their representatives and delegates attended the executive meetings and the party conferences.

But the bans failed to achieve the intended aim.

In Dar es Salaam and the surrounding Eastern Province, which were closely watched by the outside world, the wisdom and moderation of the party leaders protected T.A.N.U. against the danger of having its branches banned. The party was supported by trade unions and co-operatives, which participated in its work of organization and propaganda, arranged collections for its purposes, etc.

The executive committee entered into contact with British progressive organizations sympathizing with the African cause (among them the left wing of the Labour Party). OSCAR KAMBONA, who studied in London at the time, forwarded the complaints of Africans to those sympathetic personalities, who then later, when speaking in Parliament, exposed them to British and world public opinion. It was partly due to this that the British colonial administration withdrew some of its banning orders.

The government denied having any connection with the United Tanganyika Party and persecuting T.A.N.U. because of its policy, and said that it had been compelled to use its powers under the 1954 Societies Ordinance because some T.A.N.U. branches endangered "law and order". The British delegate to the Trusteeship Council, JOHN FLETCHER-COOKE, in reply to the allegation that the U.T.P. was the "government party", declared: "The Government has never favoured, and never will favour, the United Tanganyika Party to the detriment of any other political party ... The Government welcomed the formation of T.A.N.U. in 1954 in the hope that it would develop into a strong political party dedicated to a programme of political advancement by constitutional means. That basic attitude remains unchanged, and it is only the Government's primary obligation to take all action necessary to avoid the danger of breaches of the peace that has led the Government to take the action it has had to take . . . Government . . . [is] . . . most anxious to promote the maximum political freedom."[1]

Nyerere's Struggle in the United Nations

JULIUS NYERERE as a petitioner submitted the complaints of the peoples of Tanganyika, in words and in writing, to the Fourth Committee of the UN General Assembly in 1956 and to the Trusteeship Council in 1957. He explained the demands of the people — first of all for a concrete time-table for independence — and his party's resolute but sensible and moderate policy, and refuted the slanders heaped upon his party. His political wisdom and sensible conduct are best characterized by his statements on the privileged position of Europeans and Asians and on their relations with the Africans:

" . . . in all the plural societies in Africa which are or have been under British control the tendency is towards domination by a minority. What is actually happening in Tanganyika ? It is true we have the Trusteeship Agreement, but in Tanganyika what is staring us in the face at present is domination by a minority. If we combine this with the historical facts we are frightened. There will be no harm in giving a statement that our country is going to be democratic if that is the intention of the British but another thing that makes us suspicious is the silence of the Administering Authority on this issue . . .'

"The minorities are now in a privileged position in the country. The Africans are fighting against this privileged position of the minorities in Tanganyika. The Government of Tanganyika seems to be the advocate of the minorities. We believe that the best opportunity we can get is for the Government to promise us this thing that we have been asking, so that the African has no longer any need to feel that the minorities are in a privileged position."

" . . . I have repeatedly said . . . that I do not want racial bitterness in the country . . . (I have told) the Africans why they should not quarrel with the Asians and the Europeans in the country. I emphasized the fact that these are our neighbours and they are going to be permanently our neighbours."

" . . . We believe that since the Asians and the Europeans have settled in Tanganyika, democracy is as much a matter of guarantee to them as to us and that we could all go ahead and demand democracy without feeling that we were doing so to the detriment of the interests of the Asians and Europeans."

On his return from New York in September 1957 NYERERE issued a statement saying: "We have never advocated, and I hope we shall never advocate, that self-governing Tanganyika should be governed by Africans alone."

Another Tanganyika petitioner who appeared together with NYERERE before the Trusteeship Council in 1957 was THOMAS MAREALLE, a highly respected chief of the Chagga, who advocated the same political principles. Speaking of the minority question, he said among other things: " . . . Europeans and Asians have got to accept a minority position in Tanganyika; but if they do not, then . . . there will be no political stability, since the Africans will not accept any other formula of a future government." On another occasion he said: "We need to think of ourselves not as Africans, Asians or Europeans, but first and foremost as Tanganyikans, with

---

[1] CHIDZERO, op. cit., pp. 203–204.

a common pride in our country and with privileges and obligations which we share in common."[1]

In November 1956, during the annual Chagga Day celebrations, Chief MAREALLE stressed the same idea: "There is no doubt that we shall all have a say in the affairs of this country, whatever our skin colour, but there is equally no doubt that, eventually, this territory will be governed by an African majority. We sincerely hope, of course, that it will be a wise and reasonable majority. What we need even more than the vote, I think, is mutual respect and tolerance. Without them, equality can be sheer mockery."[2]

The UN General Assembly in its resolution adopted on February 26, 1957, recommended the Administering Authorities to "take the necessary measures to ensure that the Trust Territories of Tanganyika, the Cameroons under British administration, the Cameroons under French administration, Togoland under French administration and Ruanda-Urundi achieve self-government or independence at an early date", and invited them "to estimate the period of time required for the attainment of self-government or independence by all Trust Territories in conformity with General Assembly resolution 558 (VI) of 18 January 1952 and the present resolution".

British Duplicity. Split in T.A.N.U.

The British government obstinately defied the resolutions of the Trusteeship Council and the General Assembly alike. Its perfidious attitude was reflected in the statement of both the United Kingdom delegation to the United Nations and the British Governor of Tanganyika.

At the Trusteeship Council meeting of April 2, 1956, the United Kingdom delegate, Sir ALAN BURNS, argued against a concrete time-table on the grounds that preparation for self-government "depends on the interplay of numerous imponderables", and he added: "It is unthinkable that those responsible for carrying on Her Majesty's Government could, in the discharge of their duties under the Trusteeship System, plot out a timed course of political development for a Trust Territory based on nothing more than guesswork."

BURNS's successor, Sir ANDREW COHEN, a year later repeated to the Council the same argument, but in a more diplomatic manner: " . . . there is much virtue in proceeding step by step, neither too quickly nor too slowly; judging the exact nature of each step in the light of experience of the last one; and consulting the representatives of the people on the Legislative Council at each stage."

Governor EDWARD TWINING, on the other hand, was harping upon the same point in the Tanganyika Legislative Council. In 1956 he told the Council that the government would follow "our usual practice whereby the pace of change is decided in the light of experience gained at each stage and the readiness of people for the next step forward". And in May 1957, following the example of the British diplomatists, he struck a sharper tone: "If twenty or even ten years ago we had set ourselves a time-table, it would have had to be constantly altered and would have served no purpose but to demonstrate its uselessness."

In the hope of checking the resistance of T.A.N.U. the Governor nominated NYERERE and RASHIDI KAWAWA (the general secretary of the Tanganyika Federa-

---

[1] Op. cit., pp. 198, 199, 200–201.
[2] Africa Digest, Jan.-Feb. 1957, p. 123.

tion of Labour) to be unofficial members of the Legislative Council. But in December 1957 NYERERE resigned, giving as a reason that the government had rejected his constitutional proposals.

At the annual conference of T.A.N.U. in January 1958, however, NYERERE changed his policy. He proposed that the party, while being against the tripartite vote recommended by the MACKENZIE commission, should take part in the elections and open its ranks to Europeans and Asians. The conference decided not to boycott the elections, but opposed the admission of non-Africans. With his change of heart on the latter issue NYERERE antagonized many of the delegates. Jumping to the occasion, T.A.N.U.'s organizing secretary, ZUBERI MTEMWU, left the party, and his group of ten formed the African National Congress (A.N.C.). The new party, while voicing too radical demands on certain points (citizenship rights for black Africans only, Africanization of the civil service and the Legislative Council), followed a more conservative line than T.A.N.U. on other issues with a view to obtaining support from the Muslim population.

Elections in 1958–1959

In the first round of the elections, held in September 1958 in five out of ten constituencies (Eastern, Southern, Tanga, Northern and Western Provinces), the African T.A.N.U. candidates were elected in all five constituencies, T.A.N.U.-backed European candidates were elected in three constituencies and Asians again in all five. Neither the U.T.P. nor the A.N.C. gained a single seat.

On October 14, 1958, Governor TURNBULL addressed the newly elected Legco members and promised that self-government would bring Tanganyika an African majority both in the legislature and in the government.

In the election campaign before the second round of the elections T.A.N.U. demanded an elected majority in the Legislative Council and in a Council of Ministers which should replace the Executive Council, the abolition of "racial parity" and the tripartite vote, and the introduction of universal adult suffrage.

The second round of the elections, held in February 1959, ended with the total victory of T.A.N.U. All five African candidates as well as four European and three Asian candidates of the party were elected unopposed, and T.A.N.U.-supported candidates won everywhere in a canter.

In March the Governor, in reply to T.A.N.U.'s demands, announced that the Executive Council would remain but part of its functions would be taken over by a twelve-man Council of Ministers, in which five places would be held by elected members, and that a committee would be set up, under Sir RICHARD RAMMAGE, to ascertain the popular opinion and to work out recommendations for an electoral reform, for the possible abandonment of the principle of "racial parity", and for a broadening of the electorate, on the understanding that universal adult suffrage was out of the question.

The Rammage Committee. Tanganyika Wins Self-Government

The committee, which was appointed in May 1959, was composed of 14 members, including seven Africans, five Europeans and two Asians. After touring the country for several weeks, the committee prepared its report, which then the Governor forwarded to the Colonial Secretary. Consideration by the Colonial Office, however, was delayed because of preparations for the coming parliamentary elections in England.

On October 20, 1959, the Governor informed the Legislative Council that in 1960 (two years before the expiry of its term) it would be dissolved, and in September general elections would be held in accordance with the Colonial Secretary's decisions to be based on the recommendations of the RAMMAGE committee.

On December 15, 1959, the Governor announced at last that the RAMMAGE recommendations had been accepted with minor changes by the Colonial Secretary, and that accordingly in the course of 1960 Tanganyika would be granted internal self-government, with elected majorities in the Legislative Council and the Council of Ministers. At the same time he made public the envisaged reforms, the main points of which were the following:

1. The Legislative Council would have an elected majority, including 50 seats left "open" for African, European and Asian candidates alike, 10 seats for only Europeans, and 11 for only Asians.

2. The country would have a responsible government, called the Council of Ministers, with a majority of elected members.

3. The tripartite vote was to be abolished, and a common roll of voters introduced instead. Most constituencies would elect one representative each, but where there were reserved seats for Europeans or Asians, the votes should be cast separately for candidates of the two races; every voter would have as many votes as the constituency concerned was to elect representatives, but the three votes should be given for three different candidates.

4. Elective franchise was extended: franchise qualifications had until then been 21 years of age and three years of residence in the country, including six months within the constituency, as well as an income of £150 a year, or the holding of functions with any organ of the colonial administration or with any African authority. From now on the income qualification was reduced to £75 a year, and the knowledge of English or Swahili could substitute for the formerly required official functions.

5. To determine the composition and the powers of the Council of Ministers, and to discuss other constitutional issues, a conference was to convene in London in May 1960.

Elections in August 1960. The Nyerere Government

In accordance with the British government's above decisions based on the recommendations of the RAMMAGE committee, elections were held under the new constitution in August 1960. This was the first time in Tanganyika that no kind of racial distinction was applied in the nomination of candidates and in the voting. T.A.N.U. won a sweeping victory: it gained 70 out of 71 seats. Among the elected members, as provided by the constitution, there were non-Africans, too (11 Asians and 10 Europeans). But also they were either nominated or supported by T.A.N.U. The party's candidates were unanimously elected in 58 out of the 70 constituencies.[1]

---

[1] It is interesting to note that the Tanga constituency elected a Swiss woman to the Legislative Council, Mrs. MARKWALDER, wife of the manager of the Amani sisal plantations. She had been invited by the local Africans to stand for election, and she was elected unanimously with the support of T.A.N.U.

On the basis of the election results, the Governnor asked JULIUS NYERERE to form the government. On September 3 the NYERERE government was formed of 12 members: seven Africans (all elected Legco members), four Europeans (one elected member, one appointed by the Governor, and two officials), and one Asian.

In his radio address to the people of Tanganyika after taking office NYERERE declared that the country would accede to independence in the near future, but that would not yet be the end of the struggle. On the contrary: the struggle must be intensified to combat the colonial heritage, to overcome poverty, disease, ignorance, prejudice and fear. At the same time he called upon the population, including all three races, to break with racial hatred and prejudice, to co-operate among them and to have mutual respect. Speaking of the relationship of Africans and Europeans, he said: "We must learn to forget the arrogance and prejudices of the past. The people of Tanganyika have become fervent nationalists without becoming racialists." A few days later at a mass meeting in Dar es Salaam he declared: "A man's skin is no sin in Tanganyika."[1]

Early in 1961 NYERERE visited England, the United States and West Germany, and upon his return he sent a letter to the London *Observer*, which published it on March 5. In the letter NYERERE stated that the admission of South Africa as a republic to the British Commonwealth of Nations would betray the principles of the Commonwealth and therefore would bring with it the inevitable withdrawal of Tanganyika. Tanganyika as an independent state would like to become a member, but if South Africa remained Tanganyika would keep out. The country would rather do without the aid offered by Britain than abandon its principles.

Later, on a trip in West Africa, NYERERE appealed to the fraternal African countries to boycott the products of South Africa. He said also that Tanganyika supported the proposal for the establishment of a joint African military high command and was in favour of developing communications, trade and economic ties among the independent African states to serve as a basis for future political federation.

Constitutional Conference in March 1961

In his speech to the Legislative Council on October 11, 1960, Governor TURNBULL confirmed the British government's support for the efforts of the people of Tanganyika to win independence at the earliest possible date, and announced the convocation of a constitutional conference in London to discuss the introduction of complete internal self-government and the preparations for independence. Then he made known that the government was working out a three-year plan of economic development and intended to speed up the Africanization of the civil service and of the commercial and industrial organizations.

In the debate NYERERE said that, to do away with the existing imbalance in the composition of the civil service, African candidates would be given preference over Europeans and Asians, who had so far been preferred. He declared that now independence was not a matter of demand but one of planning, since the preparation of internal self-government was a serious task. "Nothing stands in our way," he said, "except the time to do properly and thoroughly the work that requires to be done."

[1] HUGHES, *op. cit.*, pp. 8–687.

Instead of holding the promised London constitutional conference in March, Colonial Secretary MACLEOD with his advisers went to Dar es Salaam, where he and Governor TURNBULL conferred with the NYERERE government to fix a schedule of independence for Tanganyika. The three-day talks were successful: on March 29 it was officially announced that it had been agreed that Tanganyika would obtain full internal self-government on May 1, 1961, and be granted independence on December 28.

As was agreed at the Dar es Salaam conference, internal self-government was accorded to Tanganyika on May 1, 1961.

Under the agreement the Legislative Council was renamed the National Assembly, and NYERERE, who until then was Chief Minister in the government presided over by the Governor, became Prime Minister at the head of the government; at the same time the Governor and other colonial officials ceased to be cabinet members. The Governor relinquished his powers, except those related to defence and foreign affairs, but these questions also were taken up by the Cabinet and the National Assembly during preparations for independence.

The National Assembly Meeting of June 16, 1961

On June 16 the National Assembly passed a unanimous resolution requesting Great Britain to grant Tanganyika's independence in December at the latest. Afterwards the legislature debated and adopted the constitution to be put into force after independence, providing that:

1. The National Assembly should be composed of elected members only, universal adult suffrage should be extended to those who were born in Tanganyika, provided that at least one parent had also been born in the country; those who did not qualify might request the granting of citizenship (this did not apply to those born after independence).

2. The Prime Minister would be appointed by the Governor from among the M.P.s of the majority party, the other ministers would be appointed by the Prime Minister from among the National Assembly members; the government would be collectively responsible to the National Assembly; the constitution might be amended only by a two-thirds majority of the National Assembly.

Later during the legislative session NYERERE explained in detail that his external policy was intended to serve world peace and the right of all nations to self-determination and independence. He stressed that in the initial period his government would, "for historical and practical reasons", be represented only in Western states, and wished to pursue a strictly neutral policy.

Towards the end of June 1961 the British and the Tanganyika government held new discussions, after which, on July 6, 1961, Colonial Secretary MACLEOD announced to the House of Commons that his government had decided to advance the date of Tanganyika's independence from December 28 to December 9, and that the Queen would be represented at the independence celebrations by Prince PHILIP, the Duke of Edinburgh.[1]

---

[1] It is not without interest to note that in this decision the British government was not led by the desire to speed up accession to independence. Rather it had to comply with the desire of the Duke of Edinburgh, who did not wish to spend the Christmas season in Africa.

The First Steps of the Nyerere Government

In the half year following the introduction of self-government the NYERERE cabinet was preoccupied with the finances of the country. At the June session of the National Assembly Prime Minister NYERERE had managed after long debates to have the budget passed, allocating £24 million for plans of economic development. The members found this insufficient, but life vindicated NYERERE's moderation.

For a long time the financial negotiations with the British government, despite the latter's former promises, had led to no result. This prompted NYERERE to go to West Germany and the United States and ask for their financial assistance. Thereupon the British government felt compelled to raise considerably the amount of it original insignificant offer, while the United States and West Germany each promssed to grant £3 million in aid.

To improve the financial conditions of the country, the government reviewed the concesisions agreed to by the colonial administration. (On December 1, for example, it terminated unilaterally the contract by which the Belbase firm of Belgium enjoyed privileges incompatible with the sovereignty of Tanganyika.)

In October the government decreed the readjustment of the salaries of civil servants. (Pay rise in lower grades, promotion according to competence.)

When the government in the same month submitted to the National Assembly a Bill on citizenship abolishing all differentiation between Africans and non-Africans, NYERERE declared that if the proposal should not be accepted as it was, he would resign. The Bill was passed without change.

Independence for Tanganyika

Already before the introduction of self-government (April 21), the UN Trusteeship Council adopted a resolution, sponsored by the United Kingdom and ten other British Commonwealth countries, laying down that the British administration of Tanganyika would be terminated by December 28, 1961, and recommended at the same time that Tanganyika be admitted to membership of the United Nations.

The independence celebrations started at Dar es Salaam on December 9, 1961. The event was attended by the Duke of Edinburgh representing the Queen. Another distinguished guest was the great old man of the East African revolution, JOMO KENYATTA, the Prime Minister of Kenya. The celebrations attracted a crowd of 75,000 people. On this occasion there were two moments that distinguished the event from other similar functions.

The four-day celebrations began with the unveiling of an independence monument erected in a main square of Dar es Salaam.[1] In the presence of three thousand people the unveiling was performed by NYERERE himself, who appeared in the company of KENYATTA and made a festive speech, in which he said in particular:

"The genuine monument of independence is still to be erected. That monument will be the nation we shall create, and we may proudly bequeath it to the future generations of our country. May the torch which we have lighted on the top of this modest monument remind us that we have not yet attained this goal."

---

[1] The monument was put up in the square which the Tanganyikans named *Mnazi Mnoja* (Swahili for "Square of the Lonely Coconut Palm"), where for long years the Tanganyikan peoples fighting for independence had held big political rallies.

The other outstanding moment of the festivities is still more memorable, but it had its antecedents:

Still in 1959 NYERERE had said in a speech before the legislature: " . . . we, the people of Tanganyika, would like to light a candle and put it on top of Mount Kilimanjaro which would shine beyond our borders giving hope where there was despair, love where there was hate, and dignity where there was only humiliation."

This symbolic statement of the leader of the people of Tanganyika was carried into effect by a young sub-lieutenant of the Tanganyika national army, ALEXANDER NYIRENDA, who climbed the peak of Mount Kilimanjaro and, at the exact minute of the proclamation of independence, hoisted there, in a violent snowstorm, the flag of independent Tanganyika and lighted the symbolic torch of independence.

BIBLIOGRAPHY

G. PADMORE, "Tanganyika, Trusteeship Territory", in *Africa: Britain's Third Empire*, London, 1949, pp. 67–70.

A. K. DATTA, *Tanganyika: A Government in a Plural Society*, The Hague, 1955.

J. GUNTHER, "The Wonderful World of Tanganyika", in *Inside Africa*, New York, 1955, pp. 396–420.

J. HATCH, "African Policies in Dar-es-Salaam", in *New from Africa*, London, 1956, pp. 45–57.

M. L. BATES, *Tanganyika under British Administration 1920–1955*, London, 1957.

J. HATCH, "Tanganyika", in *Everyman's Africa*, London, 1959, pp. 84–95.

"Tanganyika Today", *International Affairs*, Vol. 36, No. 1 (January 1960).

G. M. CARTER, "Partnership Works in Tanganyika", in *Independence for Africa*, New York, 1960, pp. 23–30.

KATHLEEN M. STAHL, *Tanganyika: Sail in the Wilderness*, The Hague, 1961.

B. T. G. CHIDZERO, *Tanganyika and International Trusteeship*, London, 1961.

DEREK BRYCESON, "Tanganyika, the Challenge of Tomorrow", in J. DUFFY and R. A. MANNERS, *Africa Speaks*, New York, 1961, pp. 99–106.

The Economic Development of Tanganyika. Report of a Mission organized by the International Bank for Reconstruction and Development at the request of the Governments of Tanganyika and the United Kingdom. Oxford, 1961.

J. C. TAYLOR, *The Political Development in Tanganyika*, Stanford, 1963.

JUDITH LISTOWEL, *The Making of Tanganyika*, London, 1965.

UN PUBLICATIONS

Reports of the United Nations Visiting Missions to Tanganyika, 1948, 1951 and 1954.

Tanganyika: Its Present and Its Future (Jan. 28, 1952).

Tanganyika: Land in Transition (Jan. 10, 1955).

Survey of Political Events and Development in Tanganyika (TT/1956/2).

PUBLICATIONS OF THE TANGANYIKAN GOVERNMENT

MARK WILSON, *Arusha-Moshi Lands Commission* (1947).

Report of the Committee on Constitutional Development (1951).

The Constitutional Debate (1951).

W. J. M. MACKENZIE, *Report of the Special Commissioner appointed to examine matters arising out of the Report of the Committee on Constitutional Development* (1953).

OFFICIAL BRITISH DOCUMENTS

Development of African Local Government in Tanganyika (Col. No. 277), 1951.

Tanganyika: A Story of Progress. H.M.S.O., London, 1961.

Report of the Tanganyika Constitutional Conference 1961. H.M.S.O., London, 1961.

Before and during the war the people of Zanzibar had no say in the public affairs of the island, nor did they play any active part in politics. From 1925 Zanzibar had had its Legislative and Executive councils. The Executive Council comprised, besides the Sultan and his heir, eight officials of the British administration and six appointed "unofficial" members. Of the latter six members three were Arab, two Indian and one European. The Legislative Council had no elected members, and the Africans — the majority of the population — had not a single representative. The colonial administration added one appointed African member to the Legislative Council in 1946, and another in 1947, while raising the number of ex-officio members accordingly in order to ensure them the majority.

Political activity among the people of Zanzibar started on a racial basis, early in the thirties. Various groups of the population formed "associations", such as the African Association, the Shirazi Association (composed of Africans who claimed descent from African immigrants who had interbred with Persians settled in the island about a thousand years ago), the Arab, Indian and Muslim associations. The principal demand of the Africans was that the administration should include more officials from among the local, mainly African, population; on the other hand, the Arabs demanded that the Legislative Council consist of elected members instead of appoint-ed ones.

In March 1954 the British administration wanted to raise the number of the appointed unofficial members of the Legislative Council from six to twelve: four Arabs, four Africans, three Indians and one European. The Arabs opposed this plan and insisted that the unofficial members must have the majority in the Legislative Council, demanded that they be elected and not nominated, that elections be held under general suffrage (not through vote by race groups), and called for the introduction of a ministerial system. One of the leaders of the Arab Association, ALI MUHSIN,[1] went to London to persuade the Colonial Secretary, but it was to no avail.

In November 1955 the colonial administration promulgated an amendment to the Constitution. The number of the unofficial members of the Legislative Council was raised from eight to twelve, so that six of them should be elected and six appointed by the Sultan on the recommendation of the British Resident. At the same time

[1] ALI MUHSIN was born of an Arab Muslim family in Zanzibar in 1919. His family had lived on the island for over a hundred years. His father was a religious leader. ALI took a degree in agronomy at Makerere University College in Uganda. Upon his return to his country he taught at the local Teacher Training College. After the war he took an active part in politics and became a leader of the Arab Association. In 1951 he was appointed to the Legislative Council, where his oppositionist attitude won him numerous adherents.

the number of ex-officio members was raised to thirteen, so they continued to have the majority. To the Executive Council, which had until then consisted of ten ex-officio members, were added an African, an Arab and an Asian (Indian) unofficial member; these were, however, nominated by the British Resident. At the same time a "Privy Council", composed of the British Resident and five other British colonial high officials, was established to advise the Sultan.

To this step of the colonial administration MUHSIN responded by founding the Zanzibar Nationalist Party in December 1955. The party, which consisted mainly of young and educated Arabs, called for struggle against the colonial administration and demanded self-government for Zanzibar immediately. The Africans, being afraid that the immediate introduction of self-government would cause political power to pass into the hands of the economically powerful class of wealthy Arabs and of the Arab intellectuals having an Arab education, took a stand against the demand of the Zanzibar Nationalist Party. In early 1957, before the elections under the constitutional reform, the African Association and the Shirazi Association, to ensure the success of the anti-Arab struggle, merged and formed the Afro-Shirazi Party under the leadership of ABEID KARUME.[1]

At the elections to the Legislative Council in 1957 the Afro-Shirazi Party polled 60 per cent of the votes, gaining five of the six seats in the Council, while 21 per cent was cast for the Zanzibar Nationalist Party, which obtained no seat. Thus MUHSIN himself was defeated, but he could get in as an appointed member by the grace of the British Resident. The following year he resigned from both the Legislative and the Executive Council and spent all his time strengthening his party and campaigning for immediate independence.

After the elections the parties renewed their activity, and also the broad masses increasingly engaged in the political struggle. The Senior Commissioner of the colonial government stressed in his 1958 report: "Traders, cultivators, fishermen, even housewives are affected. Villagers in the rural area argued among themselves . . . Women even pawned their clothing in order to raise the bus fare to political meetings . . ."[2]

This growing activity brought with it the sharpening of conflicts between African and Arab. Africans boycotted the Arab traders, so that hundreds of shops had to close down, while the Arab landlords chased away their African squatters. The hostility between Arabs and Africans also set members of the two parties against one another. In September 1958 both parties sent delegates to the first conference of the Pan-African Freedom Movement of East and Central Africa (P.A.F.M.E.C.A.). Delegates from other African countries managed to persuade the two parties to co-operate at least in some matters, chiefly in those concerning Africa as a whole. To lessen inter-party disagreement, leaders of the two parties met at a round-table conference and set up a joint arbitration committee, members of which regularly attended political meetings where their presence helped to calm down the atmosphere; or, for example, when it came to a dispute between African and Arab workers at the wharves, they achieved that alternate days of attendence were instituted for Africans and Arabs. Thereafter the two parties established a joint Freedom Committee, which succeeded in reaching a unified standpoint: the two parties agreed that full independence should be achieved by 1960.

[1] ABEID KARUME came to Zanzibar in his youth from the Congo. For many years he had been a sailor on a cargo boat and thus had seen many parts of the world. Later he was employed by a motor-boat company in Zanzibar port. After the war he became involved in politics and soon was elected President of the African Association.

[2] L. HUGHES, *East Africa: The Search for Unity*, London, 1963, p. 204.

This unity of determination, however, did not last long.

In 1959 the administration carried out another partial reform: it raised the number of the unofficial members of the Executive Council from three to five, and kept promising to raise the number of elected members in the Legislative Council from six to eight, and to extend the franchise by giving women also the voting right. With this meagre "reform", or rather with the promise of it, which was intended to check the discontent of the masses, the administration attained just the opposite result. The activity of the two parties gained fresh vigour. Although, for the time being, both parties dropped the demand for immediate independence, yet they did not stop clamouring for further reforms. ALI MUHSIN charted a scheme for civil disobedience unless self-government was granted by 1960, but his party declared at the same time that it had no objection to leaving the external affairs, financial and security matters in the hands of the British Resident. The leader of the Afro-Shirazi Party, ABEID KARUME, said that his party demanded the establishment of a Legislative Council composed solely of elected members by 1960 and full independence by 1963.

In March 1960 the Afro-Shirazi Party split. Led by Sheik MOHAMMED SHAMTE, a group of young Africans, among them three of the five elected African members of the Legislative Council, left the party and formed the Zanzibar and Pemba People's Party (Z.P.P.P.).

After the split the Afro-Shirazi Party, whose leaders were keeping in close touch with JULIUS NYERERE and the Tanganyika African National Union, formed a united front with the Zanzibar Nationalist Party. They demanded elections on the basis of universal suffrage and full independence at once. The Z.P.P.P., on the other hand taking the view that immediate independence would help the Arab ruling class to power, wanted independence only by 1963. The party demanded the abolishment of the system of voting by race groups, the introduction of a bicameral legislature, a lower house of 30 elected members without any ex-officio and appointed members, a 10-member Council of Ministers headed by the parliamentary majority leader as Chief Minister, and an upper house consisting of members nominated by the Sultan on the advice of the Chief Minister.

The British government in 1960 appointed a Constitutional Commissioner to draw up reforms after consultation with leading Zanzibar politicians. But the Commissioner had received in advance the principles on which he was to base his proposals. He presented his report in August 1960 and his proposals were approved by Colonial Secretary MACLEOD.

The report contained some positive suggestions: (1) The majority would be ensured to elected members both in the Legislative and in the Executive Council; the Legislative Council would choose its own Speaker. (2) The distribution by race groups of the seats to be filled by election in both Councils would be abandoned, and candidates from all race groups would be allowed to run for election in all districts. (3) The report proposed a five-member Council of Ministers with a Prime Minister designated by the British administration from members of the majority party, and with another four Ministers appointed by the Legislative Council on the recommendation of the Prime Minister.

On the other hand: (1) Three colonial chief officials would continue to be ex-officio members in both the legislature and the executive. (2) Besides 21 elected members, the Legislative Council would continue to have five appointed "unofficial" members nominated by the Sultan on the advice of the British Resident. (3) The Resident would continue to preside in the Executive Council. (4) The proposals said no word about extension of the suffrage.

Acceptance of the Commissioner's proposals sharpened the inter-party conflicts again. The Zanzibar Nationalist Party and the Z.P.P.P. were opposed to the proposals; the Indian Association and the Muslim Association handed the administration a memorandum, demanding that even after the introduction of the uniform electoral system a few seats be reserved for representatives of the Indians; the Afro-Shirazi Party accepted the Commissioner's proposals with certain reservations, which it explained in a memorandum stressing mainly three points: (1) The party agreed to the introduction of partial self-government, but only for a period of three years on the expiration of which the country should accede to independence. (2) The party agreed that the franchise should not be extended "for the present", on the understanding that this decision should apply to the coming elections after which there should be universal adult suffrage. (3) Not even during the transition period of three years should seats be reserved for the particular race groups either in the Legislative or in the Executive Council.

In the second half of 1960 the island's political life bore the marks of the elections scheduled for January 1961. The parties stated their position and displayed vigorous election propaganda. The Afro-Shirazi Party demanded universal suffrage, called for a fight against corruption and nepotism, and took a stand for the creation of an East African Federation. The Zanzibar Nationalist Party demanded full independence for Zanzibar, likewise in the framework of an East African Federation; it emphasized at the same time that, if the party came to power, it would accept financial aid from anyone, but with no political strings attached. The Zanzibar and Pemba People's Party also demanded full independence, but rejected the idea of federation, and wished to achieve Zanzibar's independence within the British Commonwealth of Nations. In the economic field the party proclaimed that, in addition to the import of foreign capital, a larger scope should be ensured to domestic capital investments. It demanded introduction of general compulsory education and abolition of school fees.

The broad masses also became highly active. They were especially alarmed by the fact that the United States was building rocket bases on the island — with the permission of the British government — under the guise of "scientific research".

In this connection both the Afro-Shirazi Party and the Zanzibar Nationalist Party made vigorous propaganda against the colonial administration, and organized a protest march, in the course of which the demonstrators burnt a rocket model as a sign of their protest The colonial administration branded the mass demonstration as an upshot of Communist propaganda, with reference to the visit which some political figures of Zanzibar had made to the Soviet Union and China.

Death of the Sultan

The Sultan of Zanzibar, SEYYID SIR KHALIFA BIN HARUB, who had reigned in the island 49 years (since 1911), died at the age of 81 on October 9, 1960. He was succeeded on the throne by his 50-year-old son, SEYYID SIR ABDULLAH BIN KHALIFA.

Elections in 1961 and the Ensuing Complications

In 1960 the British administration gave Zanzibar a new "Constitution", which raised the number of Legislative Council members to thirty, eight of whom only were nominated and twenty-two elected by the islanders on the basis of universal suffrage. The new Constitution provided that after the elections a ministerial government should be formed by members of the majority party. The election took place in January 1961, but none of the parties won an absolute majority: 10 seats went to the Afro-Shirazi Party, 9 to the Nationalist Party, and 3 to the People's Party. Since, however, two of the three People's Party members favoured the Nationalists and one decided to support the Afro-Shirazi Party, the British administration ordered that, there being no way of forming a majority government, new elections should be held, which then it called for June of the same year.

Shortly after the January elections, on a Sunday afternoon in late February, U.S. Assistant Secretary for African Affairs MENNEN WILLIAMS arrived at Zanzibar to make a few hours' visit on the island during his tour of Africa. He was met there by demonstrators who protested against the U.S. Government's plan to build a satellite launching station in Zanzibar. The demonstration was organized by the trade unions affiliated to the Nationalist Party. The protesters carried posters saying: U.S. imperialists, you made the wrong choice, go home.[1]

During the new elections held on June 1 violent clashes began between voters belonging to the various parties, accusing one another of electoral malpractices. The situation was aggravated by the fact that the British authorities immediately proclaimed the "state of emergency" and called in the police to suppress the disturbances. The police used tear gas and arrested many people, and later troops were dispatched from Kenya and Tanganyika to help the police. The result was that not only the "disturbances" did not stop but new clashes followed for days on end between the police and troops, on the one side, and some armed groups of the outraged population, on the other, so that the number of dead, wounded and arrested persons increased day by day.[2]

As the result of the elections, the two principal parties (MUHSIN's Nationalist Party and KARUME's Afro-Shirazi Party) obtained equal numbers of seats (10 each), and SHAMTE's People's Party won three. ALI MUHSIN managed to persuade the People's Party to enter into coalition with the Nationalists for the purpose of forming the government, but he had in exchange to let the leader of the People's Party, MOHAMMED SHAMTE, take the post of Chief Minister.

The London Conference in March 1962

In March 1962, at the time of the conference on the future of Kenya, the Colonial Secretary invited to London the Sultan of Zanzibar and representatives of the Zanzibar political parties. Prior to the conference the leaders of the opposing parties in Zanzibar agreed that, despite the difference of opinion between them, they would take a common stand at the conference and demand that the country be proclaimed

[1] *Neue Zürcher Zeitung*, March 1, 1961 (UPI, Dar es Salaam).

[2] The report issued at the end of the election day still mentioned only three dead, 140 wounded and 50 arrests. Two days later 17 dead and 200 wounded were reported. The *Daily Express* of June 5 knew of 50 dead and 300 wounded. On the same day ROBERTSON, Secretary of the British colonial administration, spoke of 57 dead, 70 seriously wounded and more than 600 arrests. The official report published on June 6 mentioned 57 dead, 360 wounded and 598 arrests. The *Tribune* of Paris, in its June 8 issue, on the basis of information received from "reliable sources" on the 7th, wrote about 64 dead and 745 arrests, and a day later, referring to the "official source", reported 65 dead and 794 arrests. Finally, the most competent "official authority", British Secretary for the Colonies MACLEOD, in his statement on June 13 admitted that 66 people had died, 320 had been wounded and more than 1,200 arrested.

an independent state, which as a constitutional monarchy should be a member of the British Commonwealth and of the East African Common Services Organization created by the British government; should the three other East African colonies of Great Britain form a federation, Zanzibar would also join it. In his speech at the opening meeting of the conference on March 10, Colonial Secretary MAUDLING praised the agreement reached by the Zanzibar parties, yet at the close of the talks (April 7) that had lasted for almost three weeks, he said Great Britain was still prepared to grant independence to Zanzibar, but he declared also that, since the various parties were unable to agree upon a single programme for the gradual attainment of independence, there was for the time being no possibility of forming a unified and stable government that could realize internal self-government, which was the primary condition of independence.

Plans of the British Government. Party Struggles in Zanzibar.
Introduction of Internal Self-Government

The London conference of March–April 1962, which had been convened to decide the independence of Zanzibar, thus deferred this decision for an indefinite time. What the British government intended to achieve by this delay was soon to come to light. Before granting self-government to the island country, it wanted to sound out which one of the two principal parties would gain the majority at a clean election, and which one of them, once in power, could assure the permanence of British influence after the granting of self-government or independence. To this end, under the pretext of preparing the new elections, it ordered the official registration of all qualified voters. This was done so that officials of the colonial authorities talked personally with every one of the 307,000 voters and took photographs of them. As the talks made it clear that the large majority of the electorate were in favour of the Afro-Shirazi Party, the Colonial Secretary resorted to a trick. In early March 1963 the Dar es Salaam newspaper *Tanganyika Standard* published a communiqué announcing that the new elections would take place in July, but that the British government would previously grant self-government to the coalition government in power at the time. The Afro-Shirazi Party violently protested, stating that the coalition government had gravely violated the law when registering the voters,[1] and in case of self-government it would be in a position to falsify the election results by force, and this would have as a consequence that even after independence the Arab minority would wield power over the African majority of the island's population. Colonial Secretary SANDYS went in person to Zanzibar and talked three days with the party leaders. He then declared that he would meet the demand of the Afro-Shirazi Party that elections be held first and self-government come after. The coalition parties, which were aware that this would be the end of their rule, came to see the point and sought an understanding with the British colonialists. The Secretary for the Colonies, after making sure that he was able to put the coalition in the service of his policy, early in April announced officially that two weeks before the election to be held in July the actual cabinet would be granted self-government.

---

[1] KARUME, President of the Afro-Shirazi Party, and Sheik OTHMAN SHARIFF, a representative of the party, in the Legislative Council repeatedly protested against the unlawful act of the coalition parties' registering as voters many citizens of Goa and of the Comoro Islands, while arresting and taking into custody, for the time of registration, voters of the Afro-Shirazi Party on a charge of illicit immigration to the island.

Accordingly, Zanzibar received internal self-government on June 24, 1963. MOHAM-
MED SHAMTE and his Ministers solemnly took the oath of office as members of the
first "constitutional" colalition government of the now self-governing country.

*Death of the Sultan Abdullah and Enthronement of Seyyid Jamsid. Elections in July
1963 and the Formation of the New Government*

After less than three years of reign, on July 1, 1963, the Sultan SEYYID ABDULLAH
died and was succeeded by his eldest son, 33-year-old SEYYID JAMSID.

The elections were held on July 7 to 9, exactly two weeks after the introduction
of self-government and a few days after the new Sultan had come to the throne.
To prevent a recurrence of the bloodshed which had taken place at the time of the
elections of June 1961, the British authorities dispatched two companies of Scots
Guards, airplanes and helicopters to the island for the duration of the elections.
Although the Afro-Shirazi Party obtained the absolute majority of votes (54 per
cent), it won only 13 out of 31 seats, and 18 seats were secured by the coalition of
the Nationalist Party and the People's Party. The new government, headed by
MOHAMMED SHAMTE, was again formed by this coalition.

The London Talks in September 1963

Two months following the elections, September 20 through 24, 1963, Colonial
Secretary SANDYS met in conference in London with representatives of the Zanzibar
coalition government and reached an agreement that Zanzibar would accede to
independence on December 10, with the Sultan remaining ruler of the new, sovereign
state and having the right to appoint his own successor, and that the country would
join the British Commonwealth of Nations.

Accord with Kenya

After the end of the conference Prime Minister MOHAMMED SHAMTE conducted
talks with the Kenyan delegation which was also meeting in conference at London,
and on behalf of the Sultan entered into an agreement with Prime Minister KENYATTA
on the future of the coast strip of Kenya which had belonged to Zanzibar until 1920,
when Great Britain annexed it to Kenya colony in exchange for an annuity to be
paid to the Sultan of Zanzibar. By virtue of the agreement the Sultan relinquished
his sovereign right to the coast strip and waived his claim to the annuity once and
for all in favour of the young state of Kenya being on the eve of independence.
KENYATTA in turn made the binding promise that independent Kenya would guarantee the Zanzibar citizens living in the coast region equal rights, freedom of religion
and freedom of speech.

Independent Zanzibar

In accordance with the agreement concluded at London in September 1963, the
independence of Zanzibar was ceremoniously proclaimed on December 10. The instru-

ments of independence were handed to the Sultan by Prince PHILIP, the Duke of Edinburgh, on behalf of the Queen of England. In their telegrams sent on the occasion of the proclamation of independence, the governments of the Soviet Union and of the People's Republic of China recognized the new independent state and expressed their readiness to establish diplomatic relations with it. Prime Minister MOHAMMED SHAMTE in his speech delivered at the independence festivities promised in the name of his government that he would do everything possible to make the country a prosperous, strong, democratic state. He stressed the unity of the African, Arab and Indian populations of the island and declared that the government would make efforts to ensure equal rights and duties to all.

BIBLIOGRAPHY

Report of a Commission of Inquiry into Disturbances in Zanzibar during June 1961, London, 1961.
Report of the Zanzibar Constitutional Conference 1962, London, 1962.
Zanzibar Independence Conference 1962, London, 1963.
M. F. LOFCHIE, *Zanzibar: Background to Revolution*, Princeton, 1965.
J. MIDDLETON and J. CAMPBELL, *Zanzibar: Its Society and Its Politics*, Oxford, 1965.

CHAPTER XX

BRITISH SOMALILAND

The British colony of Somaliland remained for three years after the war's end under a military administration the British set up there after having reoccupied the territory from the Italians in 1941. The establishment of "civil government" in 1948 meant keeping the pre-war colonial regime unchanged. After 1948, just as prior to the war, the country had neither a legislative assembly nor an executive council: the laws were passed by the British Governor and implemented under his instructions and control by the colonial administration. The "Protectorate", as it was called, had an Advisory Council including even a few elected members, but this body had no other functions than to give advice (without binding force upon the colonial authorities).

In the post-war years several political parties were formed in British Somaliland. The most important of them were the Muslim Somali National League which was keeping in touch with Egypt and Aden (its predecessor was the Somali National Society which had been founded in 1935 as a social organization and constituted into a political party in 1951), and the United Somali Party which maintained contact with the Somali Youth League functioning in former Italian Somaliland. Until 1955, however, these parties had displayed no particular activity.

In November 1954 the British government signed an agreement with Ethiopia on the reannexation to Ethiopia of the southern portion of British Somaliland (the Reserved Areas and the Haud).[1] The agreement guaranteed that the Somali tribes living in British territory use the reannexed areas beyond the border as grazing grounds, and even that the British government dispatch British liaison officers to protect the grazing rights of Somalis coming from British Somaliland when staying in Ethiopian territory. Nevertheless, the detachment of the area roused great indignation among the Somali tribes living in British Somaliland. This mood was so general that all political parties of British Somaliland rallied in a National United Front for the struggle to recover the disannexed area, and sent delegations to the United Nations and the British government on several occasions, but without success.

In 1957 the world's events and above all the considerable changes on the African continent compelled also the British government to make some shift in its policies.

[1] The territory in question had been arbitrarily ceded to Ethiopia by the British government in 1897, when the Somali population still had no say in the affairs of their country. In 1936, during the Italo-Ethiopian war, it came under Italian rule as part of Ethiopia. When the British reoccupied it in 1941, it was placed under military administration together with British Somaliland, and after 1948 was administered as part of the "Protectorate".

11*

The British colonialists came to understand at last that they could not delay the introduction of at least some reforms in British Somaliland at a time when representatives of seven independent African states (Morocco, Tunisia, Libya and the Sudan in addition to Ethiopia, Liberia and Egypt) were sitting in the United Nations, when a government consisting of Somalis had formed in former Italian Somaliland and there was born the Greater Somali League demanding the unification of all Somali territories, and when in the French colony of the Somali Coast the government that had been constituted after the introduction of the *loi-cadre*, the so-called Governing Council, already had four Somali members.

The turn took place rather slowly.

In 1957 a Legislative Assembly and an Executive Council were set up, but the Assembly had solely nominated members, and the Council consisted of ex-officio members only. The colonial administration employed very few Somalis, and none of them in leading posts.

In the course of 1958 a Commission appointed by the Legislative Assembly drew up a reform, on the basis of which the British administration decided that: (1) elections to the Legislative Assembly should be held in May 1959; the Assembly should consist of 33 representatives (17 official members, 3 nominated and 13 elected unofficial members) and presided over by the Governor; (2) the Executive Council should continue to consist of only ex-officio members, but the unofficial members of the Legislative Assembly should get acquainted with the work of the Executive Council and be consulted; (3) the elections should take place through vote by secret ballot in the three urban electoral districts, and by acclamation in the provinces; (4) the right to vote would be granted to every male over 21 years of age who had any one of the eleven franchise qualifications.

This rather meagre constitutional reform roused so great indignation that the British Secretary of State for the Colonies saw it necessary to calm down the people by promising further reforms. Still before the elections, in February 1959, during his visit to Hargeisa, the seat of the colonial government, he declared in a public speech that he regarded the announced reform as a first step which in 1960 would be followed by further measures, according to which the Legislative Assembly would have a majority of elected members, and the Executive Council would include also Somalis as Ministers with full powers. He promised self-government for 1960, to be followed by the necessary steps to prepare the country for independence. Finally he promised that if, after Somalia (former Italian Somaliland) became independent, the British Somali Assembly should decide to conduct talks on the unification of the two countries, and if independent Somalia should be ready for such negotiations, the British government would promote the conduct of such talks. He also made known that a new Commission would be appointed to work out the details of further reforms and to find out what measures would be fit to ensure the participation of the greatest possible number of Somalis in public affairs.

On the eve of the elections a split occurred in the National United Front. The Somali National League had already accused MARIANO,[1] a leading figure of the United Front, of having failed to press energetically enough for the unification of all Somalis, and of wishing to take the British-administered territory into the

---

[1] MICHAEL MARIANO was born of a Catholic family in British Somaliland in 1914. He was educated in Aden and afterwards taught there for a time. Later he entered the service of the colonial administration of British Somaliland and then switched over to business. From 1955 on he was active in the National United Front and was a member of its delegations sent to the British government and the United Nations.

Commonwealth. These accusations proved true after the promulgation of the 1958 Constitution. The Somali National Legaue indignantly rejected the new "Constitution" and decided to boycott the elections, while MARIANO called upon the United Front to endorse the Constitution and participate in the elections. Thereupon the Somali National League quit the United Front, which MARIANO then changed to a political party under his leadership.

The elections took place in May 1959, but neither the Somali National League nor the United Somali Party put up candidates because they were unwilling to send representatives to a legislature in which elected members did not have the majority. Of the Somali parties only the National United Front took part in the elections and obtained seven of thirteen seats.

The new Commission which the British had promised to appoint before the elections presented its report in 1959. It proposed that every male over 21 years should have the right to vote at the elections to be held in February 1960; the Legislative Assembly should consist of 33 elected members having school education and of three ex-officio members; an Advisory Body composed of the established chiefs or their representatives should be formed to help the Legislative Assembly, which would have to hear its opinion; the Executive Council should consist, in addition to the presiding Governor, of four elected Ministers and three colonial officials, the decisive say being reserved for the Governor.

The colonial administration accepted the proposal and organized the new elections on its basis in February 1960. Before the elections the Somali National League and the United Somali Party entered into a pact. The programmes of the two parties hardly differed from each other, since both demanded independence as soon as possible, and unification of the country with former Italian Somaliland (now Somalia), with the French colony of the Somali Coast, as well as with the Somali-inhabited areas of Ethiopia and Kenya. Of the 33 seats 20 went to the Somali National League; 12 to the Somali United Party and one to the National United Front. The Governor ensured to the National League and the United Party two Ministries each in the new united government (Executive Council), which was headed by M. EGAL[1] as "Leader of Government Business" (that is, deputy of the British Governor).

In April 1960 EGAL led a parliamentary delegation of British Somaliland to Mogadishu, where he conducted talks with parliamentary leaders of the Italian trusteeship territory. On April 17 they issued a communiqué, in which they demanded that the merger of the two countries "under one Flag, one President and one Government" take place on July 1 at the latest (the day of Somalia's accession to independence).

Afterwards EGAL led a delegation to London to obtain the consent of the Colonial Secretary to the immediate accession to independence of the territory and to the unification of the two countries. Secretary of State for the Colonies MACLEOD a few days before the talks, on April 25, stated that the decision passed at Mogadishu by the local leaders of the two countries was not official and not binding upon the British government. He declared at the same time that the future of British Somaliland would be decided during the forthcoming talks in London between the British Colonial Secretary and the representatives of British Somaliland, but "represent-

---

[1] MOHAMMED HAJI IBRAHIM EGAL was born the son of a rich family of merchants at Berbera in 1921. He went to Muslim primary and secondary schools in the country and studied in England for five years. Returning home, he took over his father's business. From 1954 on he was active in the Somali National League and became its Secretary in 1958.

atives of other countries" (meaning, of course, Somalia) would not be allowed to join in the negotiations; and that, if the talks should result in an agreement on the granting of independence to British Somaliland at an early date, the British government would seek contact with the government of Italy because the foreign affairs of Somalia for the time being — until July 1 — fell within the competence of the Italian government.

It soon appeared, however, that the spokesman of the Colonial Office had misjudged the situation. The London talks, indeed, began in the early days of May (the delegation of British Somaliland was led by the same EGAL who had signed the Mogadishu communiqué). But shortly afterwards the delegation of Somalia appeared on the scene, and public opinion forced the British government to change its mind. The participation of the representatives of Somalia in the negotiations was no longer opposed, and on May 5 MACLEOD said that the British government was willing to agree that British Somaliland become independent at the same time as the Italian trusteeship territory.

The talks were successfully concluded on May 12. The British government gave its consent that British Somaliland should accede to independence as early as June 26 in order to be able to unite as an independent state with Somalia on July 1. It was agreed also that following independence a certain number of British officers and colonial officials would remain in the country for six months, and that Great Britain would grant the new state of Somalia, for the time being, £1.5 million a year in aid.

Pursuant to the London decision British Somaliland became independent on June 26, 1960, and formed a united government headed by Prime Minister EGAL and composed of members of the Somali National League and the United Somali Party.

On the day of independence the two parties issued a joint statement, outlining the policy which, in their view, the united state of Somalia ought to follow in the future: Somalia should adopt a neutral stand, support and implement the resolutions of the Bandung Conference and of other Afro-Asian conferences, establish diplomatic relations with all countries, except Israel and South Africa, recognize the Algerian government fighting for independence, provide assistance to all countries struggling for liberation from the colonial yoke, strengthen at the same time her own defences and accept no aid subject to conditions.

On July 1, 1960, the two countries merged in the Somali Republic, in whose first independent government EGAL became Minister of Defence.

CHAPTER XXI

THE EASTERN SUDAN

After the suppression of the Mahdist war of independence the British colonialists administered the Eastern Sudan as an "Anglo-Egyptian Condominium". In 1924, as we have seen,[1] they terminated even this specious division of power, but in 1936 the pressure of the international situation made them to come back to it. At the end of World War II the Eastern Sudan still was styled "Anglo-Egyptian Condominium".

Anglo-Egyptian "joint possession" of the Eastern Sudan was a pure fake. Power was divided only on paper; in fact, the country was entirely under the sway of British colonial rule. This situation was vividly depicted by the American journalist JOHN GUNTHER, who was to the Eastern Sudan in 1952–1953:

"In fact the local administration in Khartoum had extraordinary—almost autonomous — powers. It was run by Englishmen, of course, but these constituted a Sudanese government...

"The condominium agreement states that the Governor-General shall always be appointed by the Egyptian government with the concurrence of the British government, but this formula was nothing but a fiction. The Governor-General was always British ...

"The chief representative of Egypt in the Sudan is still the British governor ...

"There were also 130 Sudanese in the Sudan Political Service, but their jobs were minor. All nine governors (of the nine provinces) were British ... so were the deputy governors and the top-level administrators in Khartoum itself. These men were the steel brace that held the Sudan together and made it function as a state.

"The Sudan Political Service was probably the best paid body of its kind in the world ... Members got eighty days' *annual* leave (think by comparison of Foreign or Colonial Office officials who do not get home more than once every two or three years at best) with free transportation to England and back not only for themselves but for their families; and they could retire at forty-eight ...

" ... It took a junior officer ten years to rise to the status of District Commissioner. Boys not more than a few years out of Oxford might rule a territory the size of England ..."[2]

The legend of "joint possession" is not the only delusive propaganda trick of the imperialists in connection with the Sudan. Another trick is the canting glorification of the civilizing activities of the British colonialists. While the American journalist sympathizing with the British imperialists denounces the legend of "joint possession"

[1] Vol. II, p. 248.
[2] J. GUNTHER, *Inside Africa*, pp. 233, 237, 238.

as a lie, as we have just seen, he nevertheless accepts this glorification unscrupulously in his work *Inside Africa* by extolling British colonial rule in the Sudan:

"Perhaps their regime was archaic and expensive and it was imposed on the country by force in the first instance, but what magnificent job the British did! For fifty years their administration gave the Sudan education, justice, public order, and almost complete political tranquillity, with opportunity for development, even during periods of the most effervescent crisis. There has never been a revolt; there has never even been a sign of overt unrest."[1]

As far as "opportunity for development" is concerned, GUNTHER himself points out in his book that, "Almost half the administrative budget went to salaries, . . . moreover in half a century . . . the British did not spend a total of more than £ 17,000,000 on Sudanese improvements."[2]

Recalling his visit to Khartoum in 1953, GUNTHER writes that the city "has no sewage system . . . Even in important British houses there are no flush toilets . . night clubs exist drearily in Khartoum, with girls of assorted nationalities."[3]

As far as "education" is concerned, the British colonialists, just as in all other colonies, gave a wide scope to the "educational" activity of missionaries, and established Gordon College, where about 500 Sudanese students took degrees in medicine, law, engineering, agriculture and public administration. After World War II a million pounds sterling was allocated for the expansion of the school system, intended to educate the Sudanese youth to be meek servants of the British colonialists and to forget about their national goal, the achievement of independence.[4]

The colonialists, however, did not achieve their aim. The independence aspirations of the Sudanese people were not to be suppressed either by mission schools or by Gordon College or by delusive colonialist propaganda. Mr. GUNTHER's allegation that "there has never been a revolt; there has never been a sign of overt unrest" is a blatant lie. In other places we have told about the risings of the Sudanese people in the times after the Mahdist revolt (1900–1914),[5] and we have also pointed out that the reason why we have no information on the popular movements in the inter-war years is that the British colonialists had isolated the country from the outside world.[6] They tried to maintain this policy even after World War II, but they succeeded only in part, owing to the changed international situation. The Omdurman demonstrations of February 1953 and the uprising of August 1955 will be related below. GUNTHER himself makes mention of the assassination of three British district commissioners. But the independence aspirations and "overt unrest" became manifest not only in demonstrations and revolts: the entire post-war history of the Eastern Sudan is a history of the Sudanese people's *political struggles* for independence.

[1] *Ibid.*, pp. 240–241.
[2] *Ibid.*, p. 239.
[3] *Ibid.*, p. 234. The author stresses that he met no English women at those places, for "*English* women are not allowed to be night-club entertainers or prostitutes in the Sudan".
[4] How much the British colonialists despised the Sudanese aspirations for independence is best illustrated by the following: When in the early years of this century they reconstructed the city of Khartoum destroyed during the Mahdist revolt, its main street was named after General KITCHENER, the defeater of the revolt, and it bore this name, as a deep contempt of the Sudanese national sentiment, for years after World War II. When GUNTHER was in Khartoum, his talks with British colonial officials revealed to him that most of them regarded the 1953 agreement as premature, as a necessary evil, for they did not contemplate granting independence to the Sudan until after 1966.
[5] See Vol. II, p. 59.
[6] *Ibid.*, p. 250.

The 1945 Common Platform of the Sudanese Political Parties
and Their Negotiations in Cairo

Immediately after the war's end, late in 1945, the British government, on the initiative of the Egyptian government, declared its willingness to start negotiations on a revision of the 1936 Anglo-Egyptian Treaty. Independent members of the General Graduates' Congress, for fear that Great Britain and Egypt would again reach an agreement at the expense of the Sudanese people, made efforts to unite all Sudanese parties in a single bloc. They worked out a common platform in which:

1. They demanded a "free democratic government" for the Sudan to decide upon the form of union with Egypt and the kind of alliance they wanted with the United Kingdom.

2. They proposed a joint commission consisting of equal numbers of representatives of the British and Egyptian governments, on the one hand, and of the Graduates' Congress, on the other, to work out recommendations for the government of the country to be handed over to the Sudanese within the shortest possible time.

3. They demanded freedom of the press, freedom of assembly, and freedom of movement and trade for the Sudanese people.

All parties accepted this platform, and a delegation comprising their representatives went to Cairo to explain the demands of the Sudanese people to representatives of the British and Egyptian governments.

The delegates first entered into negotiations with the Egyptians, but they met with flat refusal. The Egyptians insisted that the Sudanese recognize the supremacy of the Egyptian Crown and agree in advance, without conditions, to union with Egypt. Representatives of the Umma Party and of similar-minded minor independence groups rejected this demand and, breaking off the negotiations, left Cairo. Representatives of the "Unionists"—the Ashigga Party and others — remained in Cairo and continued the talks.

The Promises of the British Government

In the meantime the Advisory Council for the Northern Sudan had requested the Governor-General to declare that the future of the Sudan would not be decided without consulting the Sudanese people. Complying with the request, the Governor-General on November 5, 1945, made a statement assuring the Council of "the Government's firm intention to consult the people of the Sudan regarding the future of the country".[1]

A statement to the same effect was made in the United Kingdom Parliament by BEVIN on March 26, 1946: "His Majesty's Government look forward to the day when the Sudanese will be able finally to decide upon their political future for themselves." He emphasized that the aim of the Sudanese administration was to establish organs of self-government as a first step towards independence, and promised the Sudanese that no change would be made in the status of the Sudan without consulting them through constitutional channels.

This promise of BEVIN was reaffirmed by the Governor-General at the April 17 meeting of the Advisory Council for the Northern Sudan.[2]

---

[1] *Proceedings of the Advisory Council for the Northern Sudan*, 4th Session, 3rd Nov. 1945.
[2] *Ibid.*, 5th Session, 17th Apr. 1946.

A few days later, on April 21, 1946, the Governor-General appointed a group to make recommendations for the "closer association of the Sudanese with the Administration of the country"[1] and invited the political parties to nominate their representatives for co-operating with the group. This set to work, and its meetings (which were called the "Sudan Administration Conference") worked out proposals for a constitutional reform.

Unsuccessful Anglo-Egyptian Negotiations

The 1936 Anglo-Egyptian Treaty was concluded for twenty years with the proviso that upon expiration of that period either contracting party might initiate negotiations on a revision of the treaty, but such negotiations might be started by common agreement already after the first ten-years' period. Already a few months prior to the expiry of ten years the Egyptian government proposed a revision of the treaty, and the British government consented. The talks began at Cairo in 1946 but brought no result because the Egyptian government, claiming that the Sudan was part of Egyptian territory, demanded abrogation of the 1899 Condominium Agreements and recognition of Egypt's sovereignty over the Sudan; on the other hand, the Wafdist Party, whose leader, NAHAS PASHA, had been dismissed by King FAROUK in 1944, was not willing to participate in the negotiations.

The negotiations having failed, BEVIN and SIDKY PASHA, who had prepared a new draft of the Anglo-Egyptian Treaty at London, reached a compromise in the question of the Sudan and laid it down in a protocol annexed to the draft treaty (October 1946). This document, which is known as the "Draft Sudan Protocol", formulated the compromise agreement in the following terms:

"The policy which the High Contracting Parties undertake to follow in the Sudan within the framework of the unity between the Sudan and Egypt under the common Crown of Egypt will have for its essential objectives to assure the well-being of the Sudanese, the development of their interests and their active preparation for self-government and consequently the exercise of the right to choose the future status of the Sudan. Until the High Contracting Parties can in full common agreement realize this latter objective after consultation with the Sudanese, the Agreement of 1899 will continue and Article 11 of the Treaty of 1936 . . . will remain in force..."[3]

This compromise seemed to satisfy all three parties. Egypt was satisfied that it guaranteed a provisional unity between the Sudan and Egypt, postponing the decision on definitive union. The agreement also tried to satisfy the Sudanese by recognizing their right to self-government and self-determination. And Great Britain achieved by it the maintenance of the status quo, and by satisfying Egypt, she obtained SIDKY PASHA's consent to the proposed Anglo-Egyptian treaty of alliance.

The British government, however, was disappointed in its calculations. In the Sudan alarming rumours were spreading that the British government agreed to the definitive unity of Egypt and the Sudan without ensuring the Sudanese the right to secede from Egypt in the future. To calm down the people, the British Prime Minister on October 28, 1946, made a statement in the House of Commons

---

[1] J. S. R. DUNCAN, *The Sudan's Path to Independence*, p. 134.

[2] *Papers regarding the Negotiations for a Revision of the Anglo-Egyptian Treaty of 1936.* — Cmd. 7179 (1947), p. 4.

in which he said: " . . . no change in the existing status and administration of the Sudan is contemplated and no impairment of the right of the Sudanese people ultimately to decide their own future."

This announcement, however, did not dissipate the concern of the Sudanese people and of the independence groups, since the Egyptian press interpreted the agreement to its own taste, and what is more, NOKRASHY PASHA declared in the Chamber of Deputies: "When I say unity of Egypt and the Sudan under the Egyptian Crown, I mean permanent unity."[1]

It was thus obvious that the Draft Sudan Protocol could be incorporated in the Anglo-Egyptian Treaty of Alliance only if the parties agreed with regard to its interpretation. The British government even made an attempt to bring the Egyptian government to take a more moderate stand, offering "the support of the United Kingdom in the maintenance of a Sudan friendly to Egypt, and in particular to safeguard the position of Egypt with regard to the waters of the Nile". Furthermore, it proposed the establishment of a joint Anglo–Egyptian–Sudanese body to review the progress of the Sudanese towards self-government. But the Egyptian government was adamant and refused to recognize the right of the Sudanese to self-determination, and rejected the British proposal. The British Foreign Secretary on January 27, 1947, was compelled to announce in Parliament that the Egyptian government had broken off the negotiations for a revision of the Anglo-Egyptian Treaty of 1936.

The Question of the Sudan before the UN Security Council
(August 5 to September 10, 1947)

After breaking off the negotiations the Egyptian government took the dispute over the Sudan to the Security Council of the United Nations. NOKRASHY PASHA appeared before the Council on behalf of the Egyptian government, and Sir ALEXANDER CADOGAN represented the British position. NOKRASHY PASHA argued that Egypt and the Sudan had always formed a unit "physically, economically and racially."[2] He said that MOHAMMED ALI's Sudan campaign[3] in 1820 had been not a conquest but a "consolidation of the various parts of Egypt and a unification of its governmental institutions",[4] and that the boundary between Egypt and the Sudan was an invention of the British. From all this he drew the conclusion that the question of self-determination of the Sudanese people did not even arise, the relations between the peoples inhabiting the Nile Valley was an internal affair of Egypt and the Sudan which had to settle it without any interference from the "invading British". He accused the British government of using the question of Sudanese self-government and future self-determination only as an excuse for prolonging its rule over the Sudan in its own selfish interests. The British, he said, were in every respect alien to the Sudanese and were not qualified to guide the social and cultural development of the Sudanese and their preparation for self-government. "I must reiterate the intention of the Egyptian Government", he said, "to work in season and out of season to protect the Sudan from dismemberment, to make it possible for our Sudanese brethren to direct their own affairs within the framework

---

[1] Ibid., p. 6.
[2] As to how far this allegation was from the truth, see Vol. I, pp. 160 – 161.
[3] See Vol. I, p. 266.
[4] S.C.R., 175th meeting, 5 Aug. 1947, sections 35–38.

of the unity of the Nile Valley under the Crown of Egypt." Accordingly, he asked the Security Council to put an end to the British rule forced upon the Sudan since 1899.

In what NOKRASHY PASHA said of British hypocrisy and selfish interests there was a great deal of truth. On the other hand, he himself was no less a hypocrite when, denying the facts of history, spoke of the long-standing unity of Egypt and the Sudan, while at the same time he tried to conceal the selfish interests of Egypt in the question of the Sudan by empty and lying phrases about the fraternal ties between the Egyptian and the Sudanese peoples.

The Security Council unanimously rejected the Egyptian plea and took a stand in favour of the right of the Sudanese people to self-determination. The reasons which induced the particular members of the Security Council to adopt this stand were not all identical. Some members stood on the principle of the right of self-determination and on the denial in principle of the right of conquest (Soviet Union, China, Poland, Syria, Brazil, Colombia), while the position of others was nothing else than support to British imperialism against Egypt (United States, France, Australia). In practice, however, the resolution adopted by the Security Council was so unambiguous that NOKRASHY PASHA was forced to give up his position and recognize the right of the Sudanese to self-determination, with the reservation, though, that its exercise should not take place under British rule and with British aid. "I am confident", he said in his last speech in the Security Council, "that when the Sudanese are free to express themselves they and the Egyptians will reach mutually satisfactory solutions which will accord with the democratic principles of the Charter."

In this way the Security Council recognized the right of self-determination of the Sudan and even made the official representative of Egypt recognize it, but it left open the question of how Britain and Egypt should settle their differences between them.

New Abortive Negotiations. The British Government's Arbitrary Step. Establishment of a Legislative Assembly and an Executive Council

The Security Council was still considering the Sudan question when, on August 22, 1947, the British Governor-General of the Sudan presented to the British and Egyptian governments his proposals for the establishment of a Legislative Assembly and an Executive Council. Upon instructions from his government the British Ambassador in Cairo on October 23 informed the Governor-General that "His Majesty's Government have no comments to offer on these proposals which are, they consider, well calculated to achieve the proclaimed purposes of the Co-dominium, namely the progressive development of self-government in the Sudan."[1]

In his letter of November 26 the Egyptian Prime Minister accepted the proposals in principle but disagreed with the Governor-General about the details and proposed certain modifications (he demanded extension of the suffrage; objected that the Legislative Assembly would not be the last instance with regard to the approval of the budget and the enactment of laws; that the proposals made no mention of Egyptians participating together with the British in preparing the Sudanese for self-government). He wrote in his letter:

[1] No. 207, Cairo, 23 Oct. 1947 (463/34/47).

"Since the Royal Egyptian Government are sincerely desirous — as emphasized on several occasions—to enable the Sudanese to govern themselves and are not willing that the Sudanese should lose any opportunity of having the maximum share of responsibility of government accorded to them, the Royal Egyptian Government, notwithstanding that the Anglo-Egyptian dispute is still pending, deem it their duty — while fully maintaining their position which had been clearly defined before the Security Council—to accept participation, for the time being, in drawing up a regime which would pave the way to self-government, provided this regime be free from the defects pointed out in the attached note and provided that it fulfills the requirements outlined in the said note. Thus the delay in settling the Anglo-Egyptian dispute will not retard the progress of the Sudanese, for any period, on the road to self-government."

Since a repeated exchange of letters between the Governor-General and the Egyptian Prime Minister led to no accord, the two governments agreed that the British Ambassador in Cairo and the Egyptian Minister of Foreign Affairs conduct talks on the ways of preparing the Sudanese for self-government. These talks took place in May 1948, and the negotiating parties, with the consent of the Governor-General, proposed that a tripartite Anglo–Egyptian–Sudanese Committee be set up to supervise the progress of the Sudanese towards self-government, and an Anglo-Egyptian Committee to supervise the elections to the Legislative Assembly. The Governor-General agreed that two of the Egyptian officials serving in the Sudan be included in the Executive Council and that the senior staff officer of the Egyptian forces stationed in the Sudan attend the Executive Council meetings where matters of defence were under discussion. The Foreign Affairs Committee of the Egyptian Senate, however, did not accept the agreement, objecting that Egypt had received few seats in the Executive Council and had been given no guarantee that the two Egyptian members of the Executive Council would hold ministerial functions in the future government.

The negotiations thus got into a deadlock, and the British government decided to take an arbitrary step. On June 14, 1948, the Under-Secretary for Foreign Affairs made a statement in Parliament saying:

"His Majesty's Government . . . feel that they can no longer stand in the way of the Governor-General doing as he thinks fit regarding the promulgation of the Ordinance in accordance with his duties and obligations for the good government of the Sudan under the Agreement of 1899."

The Governor-General received from his government the authorization for the implementation of the constitutional reform. Meanwhile the report of the Sudan Administration Conference had been prepared and submitted to the Governor-General. It contained essentially the following recommendations:

1. The Advisory Council for the Northern Sudan, which had achieved its purpose of introducing the Sudanese in the government of the country, should be abolished.

2. A Legislative Assembly should be established of 100 Sudanese members, of whom 85 should be elected from the provinces (including the three southern provinces) and 15 nominated by the Governor-General.

3. The "Governor-General's Council" should be replaced by an Executive Council of 18 members, of whom 9 should be elected by the Legislative Assembly from among its own members, and 5 should be appointed by the Governor-General (from among the British or Sudanese), while the Governor-General's Civil, Financial and Legal secretaries and the Army Officer Commanding Troops should be ex-officio members as before.

The Governor-General agreed to these proposals with some modifications, and still in the middle of June promulgated the Legislative Assembly and Executive Council Ordinance.

Pursuant to the ordinance, the Executive Council had twelve members, among them six Sudanese, and the Legislative Assembly consisted of 95 members, of whom 89 were Sudanese; 65 of the latter were elected (10 directly and 55 by electoral colleges), 10 were nominated by the Governor-General, and 14 were ex-officio members of the Assembly. The Executive Council was appointed by, and answerable to, the Governor-General, who was empowered to change any decision of the Council and substitute for it his own decision, with the only restriction that he was bound to have his reasons entered in the records of the Council and to report on his action to the British and Egyptian governments. He was obliged to report also in case he had approved a bill in regard of which no agreement has been reached between the Legislative Assembly and the Executive Council.

Both the Legislative Assembly and the Executive Council were formed in December 1948 and immediately set to work.

In this Legislative Assembly the Umma Party played the leading role, since the pro-Egyptian Ashigga Party refused to participate. Also of importance was the part played by the National Front which had been founded in 1949 by moderate elements of the Ashigga Party, and which was in favour of some kind of looser relations with Egypt (a status similar to the dominions of the British Commonwealth) instead of total union. The Legislative Assembly included also thirteen representatives of the four million inhabitants of the Southern Sudan; but they had not yet developed a unified political line and were wavering between the different parties.

Anglo-Egyptian Negotiations in 1950. Unilateral Abrogation of the Condominium. Agreement by the Egyptian Government and New Promises of the British Government

In the summer of 1950, preliminary talks began, on British initiative, between the British Ambassador in Cairo and the Egyptian government to prepare resumption of the negotiations for a revision of the 1936 Anglo-Egyptian Treaty. The talks took place in a "cordial atmosphere" until King FAROUK in a Speech from the Throne (read by Prime Minister NAHAS PASHA) said: "My Government considers that the 1936 Treaty has lost its validity as a basis for Anglo-Egyptian relations, and it deems it inevitable that it should be abrogated." He added that these relations in the future should be founded upon new principles approved by the Egyptian Parliament: immediate and complete withdrawal of British troops and unification of the entire Nile Valley under the Egyptian Crown.

The Egyptian government's intention to abrogate unilaterally the 1936 treaty and the 1899 agreements caused an uproar in the British Parliament. Foreign Secretary BEVIN in his speech to the House of Commons on November 20, 1950, said that the treaty of 1936, which had been ratified by the Parliaments of both countries, could not be modified without common accord. He reiterated his statement made earlier, in March 1946, that the people of the Sudan should in the future freely decide their status. He declared at the same time that despite the existing difficulties he would not abandon his efforts to reconcile the differences with Egypt through friendly negotiations.

In December 1950 Egyptian Foreign Minister MOHAMED SALAH EDDIN BEY proposed a transition period of two years for the Sudan to prepare for self-government and for the plebiscite deciding the future status of the country. This proposal, which he made to the British Ambassador in Cairo, he repeated in July 1951.

But the Egyptian government did obviously not for a moment take seriously this proposal of its Foreign Minister. On October 8, 1951, Prime Minister NAHAS PASHA in Parliament declared the unilateral abrogation of the 1936 treaty and the 1899 agreement. On this occasion he submitted to Parliament three bills on the termination of the condominium status and an amendment to the Sudan Constitution, proclaiming thereby King FAROUK "King of the Sudan". The Legislative Assembly was replaced by a Constituent Assembly, and the Executive Council by a Sudanese Cabinet, whose members were appointed by the King of Egypt who could at any time dismiss them. The King, however, reserved himself control over foreign affairs, defence and finance. He was also empowered to sanction the laws passed by the Constituent Assembly, and could dissolve the Assembly at any time if he wished.

This Egyptian move did not come as a surprise to the British government, which the resumed and unsuccessful negotiations had convinced that the Egyptian government was not willing to back down. In the days preceding Egypt's unilateral step another British attempt was made to bring pressure to bear upon the Egyptian government by winning the favour of the Sudanese parties and public opinion. Early in October 1951 HERBERT MORRISON on behalf of the British government made to the Egyptian government the following five-point proposal for a solution of the Sudan problem:

1. Appoint, in agreement with the Sudanese, a mixed Anglo–U.S.–Egypto–Sudanese commission to supervise the constitutional development of the Sudan and provide advice to the British and Egyptian governments.

2. Issue a joint Anglo-Egyptian statement of principle regarding the Sudan.

3. Provide an international guarantee of Nile waters agreements.

4. Establish, if possible with assistance from the International Bank, a Nile Waters Development Authority to develop the Nile.

5. Fix an "appointed day" for the entry into force of Sudanese self-government as a prelude to the choice by the Sudanese of their final status.

As a basis for the joint statement referred to in point 2, the British government laid down four principles:

(a) In view of the dependence of both Egypt and the Sudan on the waters of the Nile and in order to ensure the fullest co-operation in expanding the supplies available and in sharing them, it is essential that the friendliest relations should link the two peoples.

(b) It is the common aim of Egypt and Great Britain to enable the people of the Sudan to attain self-government as soon as possible and thereafter choose freely for themselves their form of government and the relationship with Egypt that will best meet their needs as they then exist.

(c) In view of the wide differences of culture, race, religion and political development existing among the Sudanese, the process of attaining full self-government requires the co-operation of Egypt and the United Kingdom with the Sudanese.

(d) The two Governments therefore agree to set up forthwith an International Commission in order to help the Sudanese towards the goal in (b) and to assist them in formulating their future Constitution.

Ten days after the unilateral abrogation of the Condominium Agreements, on October 25, 1951, the British Governor-General of Egypt (through his deputy) announced to the Legislative Assembly that the Sudan would receive "a self-governing Constitution which will satisfy the immediate aspirations of the Sudanese people before the end of 1952". This announcement by the Governor-General was confirmed also by the British Labour government, and after the Tory cabinet had taken office, Foreign Secretary EDEN on November 15, 1951, said in Parliament:[1]

"In view of the uncertainty caused in the Sudan and elsewhere by the Egyptian Government's unilateral action in purporting to abrogate the 1936 Treaty of Alliance and the two Condominium Agreements of 1899, His Majesty's Government find it necessary to reaffirm that they regard the Governor-General and the present Sudan Government as fully responsible for continuing the administration of the Sudan.

"His Majesty's Government is glad to note that the Sudan has for some time been and is now moving rapidly in the direction of self-government. In their view this progress can and should continue on the lines already laid down. His Majesty's Government will, therefore, give the Governor-General their full support for the steps he is taking to bring the Sudanese rapidly to the steps of self-government as a prelude to self-determination, and now await the recommendation of the Constitution Amendment Commission. His Majesty's Government are glad to know that a Constitution providing for self-government may be completed and in operation by the end of 1952.

"Having attained self-government, it will be for the Sudanese people to choose their own future status and relationship with the United Kingdom and with Egypt. His Majesty's Government consider that the attainment of self-government should immediately be followed by active preparations for the ultimate goal of self-determination. They will support the Governor-General in his efforts to ensure that the Sudanese people shall be able to exercise their choice in complete freedom and in the full consciousness of their responsibilities.

"His Majesty's Government, with whose support the Sudan Government have brought the Sudanese people to their present stage of progress, are confident that they will work with united enthusiasm towards their goal. His Majesty's Government meanwhile guarantee to ensure the defence and security of the Sudan during the intervening period."

The Legislative Assembly at Work. The "Self-Government Statute"

While the British and Egyptian governments were discussing between them, and while the latter tried to shelve the question of Sudanese independence by taking a unilateral measure, and the British government, instead of granting independence, made new promises to reassure the Sudanese people, the Legislative Assembly of the Sudan did not look on with folded arms either. On December 5, 1950, the Umma Party submitted a draft resolution proposing that the Assembly send a message to the Governor-General in these terms:

"We, the members of the Legislative Assembly of the Sudan, are of the opinion that the Sudan has now reached the stage at which self-government could be granted, and request Your Excellency to approach the Condominium Powers with a request that a joint declaration of the grant of self-government be made before the end of the Third Session of this Assembly."

The proposal, which was discussed in the Legislative Assembly on December 13, gave rise to a heated debate. Opponents of the proposal moved an amendment whose adoption would have signified practically the renouncement of the demand

[1] *House of Commons Debate*, Fifth Series, vol. 493, colls. 1176–1178.

176

for self-government.[1] The proposal came to the vote, after two full days of debate, in the early morning hours of December 15. The draft was adopted in its original form by a majority of one vote (39 votes to 38).

Four days later the Legislative Assembly adopted another resolution, requesting that the Governor-General appoint a commission, at least half of whose members should be Sudanese, to revise the Governor-General's Ordinance of 1948 on the establishment of the Legislative Assembly and the Executive Council, and to make recommendations for making the Assembly and the Council "a practical instrument of democratic government with a full measure of parliamentary control . . ."

This body, called the "Constitutional Amendment Commission", came into being on March 26, 1951, and in January 1952 it presented its report giving the outlines of full Sudanese self-government. The Legislative Assembly considered the report from April 7 to 23, 1951, approved a draft Self-Government Statute prepared on the basis of the report, and in May 1952 forwarded it to the British and Egyptian governments.

The British government was pleased with the Statute from the beginning. Not that it was enthusiastic about the idea of Sudanese self-government, but it regarded the act as a step which proved that the Legislative Assembly did not take note of the unilateral termination by Egypt of the condominium status of the Sudan. On the other hand, the Egyptian government, whose intentions were basically opposed to the Statute, made its utmost to block it, the more so since the pro-Egyptian Sudanese, the leaders of the Ashigga Party, were in a difficult position. Although they were the only ones who abstained from voting for the Statute, they would hardly have been able to justify before the masses backing them their refusal of an instrument aimed at the long-awaited introduction of self-government. Also, they found it difficult to accept the Statute after having supported the abrogation of the Condominium Agreements and having insisted for months that the Governor-General's action was illegal.

The Egyptian government tried to amend the situation with a compromise solution: it invited ABDEL RAHMAN to discuss the matter. ABDEL RAHMAN did not go in person, but at the end of May he sent his "personal representative" to Alexandria, underlining also thereby that the agreement that might be reached would not be binding upon the Umma Party. At the talks a compromise was indeed worked out to the effect that if the Sudanese recognized the suzerainty of King FAROUK, the Egyptian government would consent to a revision of the 1951 Egyptian decision on the Sudanese Constitution. But the Egyptian government, which would have been ready to accept this compromise, was thrown out immediately after the talks. The new government sent ABDEL RAHMAN another, this time personal, invitation for the end of July. Owing to the rapidly succeeding changes of government, however, this invitation remained unanswered, and the revolutionary change of July 23 created an entirely new situation.

---

[1] An amendment was moved to rephrase the resolution as follows: "We, the members of the Legislative Assembly of the Sudan, are of the opinion that the Sudan has made good progress *towards* the stage at which full self-government can be granted, and request Your Excellency to press on urgently with such measures which, while consistent with *the maintenance of good government* throughout the country, will ensure that not only shall self-government be full and complete, but also that, in *working towards* that end, all sections of the community and all parties may co-operate in developing the institutions of government so as *to hasten the day* when the goal is attained." (Italics by the author.)

The Effect upon the Sudan of the 1952 Egyptian Revolution.
The Anglo-Egyptian Agreement of February 12, 1953

Unlike the royal government, the new Egyptian administration was willing to recognize the right of the Sudan to self-government and self-determination, with the reservation that the Sudan should exercise this right "in a free and neutral atmosphere" (that is, with no interference from the British), and that, in one or another form, the independent state of the Sudan should remain in close contact with Egypt. The negotiations which General MOHAMMED NAGUIB started with the leaders of the Sudanese parties held out good prospects from the very beginning. The British government, which (although, as we have seen above, it had for years on end made promises to recognize the right of the Sudan to self-government, and even to self-determination later) for five months after presentation of the Statute had not a word to say about its acceptance, was in the end compelled, in face of the change in Egyptian policies, to "put a good face on a bad business" and to declare its official acceptance of the Self-Government Statute.

This happened in October 1952. On November 2 the Egyptian government informed the British government of its proposed amendments to the Statute. Talks began between them, and the result was decided by the circumstance that the negotiations between General NAGUIB and the leaders of the parties, and those between the party leaders, had been successfully concluded by early January 1953. The Umma Party and the Socialist Republican Party allied with it willingly accepted the Egyptian reservations, and a definitive agreement was reached on this basis by the three great Sudanese parties on January 12, 1953. After this nothing was left to the British but to agree with Egypt on the same line.

Egypt and the United Kingdom signed an agreement on the Sudan question on February 12, 1953. The agreement declared the condominium terminated, and guaranteed the right of the Sudan to decide by itself within three years' time whether she wished to be an independent sovereign state or to join Egypt.

The agreement provided for the establishment of three mixed commissions. The task of one of them was to supervise the Governor-General's activities in the transfer of certain power functions to the Sudanese bodies of self-government, the other had to organize and supervise the parliamentary elections, and the third was instructed to carry out the Sudanization of the whole administration.

The Sudanese attached special importance to this latter—the so-called Sudanization Committee—for it was clear to them, irrespective of party affiliations, that as long as different posts were filled by British and—though in smaller number—Egyptian officials, they could not expect the agreements to be implemented fully and with due regard for the interests of the Sudanese people. The agreement laid down as a task of the Committee "to complete the Sudanization of the Administration, the Police, the Sudan Defence Force, and any other Government post that may affect the freedom of the Sudanese at the time of Self-Determination. The Committee shall review the various Government posts with a view to cancelling any unnecessary or redundant post held by British or Egyptian officials . . ."

The agreement provided that the Committee's decisions taken by majority vote should be submitted to the Sudanese Council of Ministers. If the Governor-General should not agree with any such decision or with the views of the Council of Ministers, then he could—with the approval of his own Commission[1] withhold his assent, but in event of disagreement between them, the case should be referred to the two (British and Egyptian) governments. The decision of the Governor-General's Commission would be reversed only in case both governments agreed to the contrary. The Sudanization Committee had to discharge its duties, pursuant to the provisions of the agreement, within a period not exceeding three years.

On February 20, a week after the signing of the agreement, a crowd of more than a hundred thousand people marched in the streets of Omdurman celebrating the great event of the coming of independence. The American journalist JOHN GUNTHER, who watched the demonstration, pertinently points out that the Prophet's black flags, the Mahdi's black-yellow-green flag and the red-white-black flags of the Egyptian National Liberation Rally flew by the thousand peaceably together, but he saw no Union Jacks.[1]

New Opposition Parties in the Sudan

Early in the fifties three new opposition parties appeared in the political life of the Sudan.

In 1951 there formed the left-wing party called the Anti-Imperialist Front which started as a branch of the Sudan Movement for National Liberation launched as far back as 1946. The party took a stand against the agreement concluded between leaders of political parties and the Egyptian government. At the elections of November 1953 it returned to Parliament only one member; but outside Parliament, mainly in the towns, it gained great influence, partly owing to the fact that it had maintained close relations with the largest trade union of the country, the railwaymen's union, further with the Sudan Workers' Trade Union Federation and various youth and women's associations.

The right-wing Socialist Republican Party also came into being before the 1953 elections, in 1952. The new party followed the cautious conservatism of the tribal leaders who were influenced by neither of the two sects of EL-MAHDI and EL-MIR-HANI. As a distant goal, it demanded independence free from Mahdist domination, and for the time being it did not press for self-government, but only called for improvement of the colonial administration, and insisted on the necessity of defending the Southern Sudanese against exploitation by the Northerners. The pro-independence parties (N.U.P. and Umma) regarded the new party, not without good reason, as a tool of the British imperialists who had created it in order to undermine the unity of the independence movement. At the November 1953 elections the party won three seats in Parliament.

It was after the 1953 elections that the non-Arab and non-Moslem tribes of the Southern Sudan formed the Liberal Party, which rallied the existing splinter groups of the Southern Sudan (Southern Party, Southern Political Association). The party demanded local self-goverment for the Southern Sudan on a federal basis. It rapidly gained ground in the country towns and villages of the Southern Sudan (for example, in Equatoria province). By 1955 it had local branches in most of the towns and villages. The leaders of the party stood up against the AZHARI government, demanded greater share for the Southerners in government affairs, and followed a pro-Egyptian policy.

---

[1] *Inside Africa*, p. 235

The 1953 Electoral Campaign and the Opening of Parliament

The first general election was held in November 1953. The National Unionist Party advocating union with Egypt gained the absolute majority—with fifty seats in the House of Representatives against the Umma Party's twenty-three seats, and with twenty-one out of the thirty-one seats in the Senate.

The first Sudanese Parliament elected under the new Constitution met on January 1, 1954, to elect its President and the Prime Minister. ISMAIL EL-AZHARI was elected Prime Minister.

On January 9 the Governor-General stated officially that the Cabinet, the House of Representatives and the Senate were constitutionally formed. It was on this day that, according to the agreement of February 12, 1953, the transition period of three years began during which the system of self-government had to be completed.

Parliament set the date of March 1 for its inauguration and to start discussing. But the turn of events caused it to delay its working. Broad masses of pro-independence Sudanese thought that the appointment of a government supporting the Egyptian government's efforts at annexation was tantamount to giving up the idea of independence, and scheduled a mass demonstration in Omdurman for March 1 under the auspices of the Umma Party. As the government banned the Omdurman demonstration, the crowd gathered in Khartoum and marched in procession toward the Government House. The government sent out police to disperse them. A clash between the unarmed people and the police carrying firearms resulted in 34 dead and hundreds of wounded.

General NAGUIB, who arrived by plane at Khartoum on the morning of March 1, was also met by a demonstrating crowd at the Khartoum airfield, so he was escorted to the city by a roundabout route and he flew back to Cairo on the following day leaving his business unfinished.

Parliament was opened on March 10, this time without any special ceremony.

The Policy of the Azhari Government. British Withdrawal from the Sudan

From its first day in office the AZHARI government followed a definite political line. Its programme could be summed up briefly: to complete Sudanization within the shortest possible time and oust the British colonialists from the country. The Sudanization Committee held its first meeting on February 24, 1954, set to work immediately and prepared one after another the proposals for the replacement of British civil servants in high functions by Sudanese officials.

The smooth implementation of the government's policy and notably the work of the Sudanization Committee were blocked by the fact that the government had no solid majority on the Governor-General's Commission. Therefore the government proposed, and Parliament on April 24 decreed, a change in the composition of the Commission. One of the Umma Party members was relieved from the Commission and replaced by a Southern Sudanese member of the National Unionist Party.

The opposition protested and sent representatives to London to raise an objection. But London advised them to try to work through normal constitutional channels in Parliament. The majority of Parliament, however, backed up the government. On July 8 an act was passed on compensation or pension for dismissed British officials. Shortly afterwards the mass dismissal of British officials began. On August 15 the last British high officer—the Commander-in-Chief of the Sudan Defence

Force, Major-General R. D. SCOONES—surrendered his office to his Sudanese deputy and returned to England. The last British police officer left the country on October 9, followed by the chief of the Political Service, G. K. BELL, on December 14.

Azhari's Policies after the British Withdrawal

The AZHARI government essentially completed the task of Sudanization in the first year of the three-year period envisaged by the 1953 agreement for this purpose. By early 1955 already the Governors of all nine provinces and the heads of all civil government offices in Khartoum were Sudanese, and the withdrawal of the junior British officials and functionaries went on at a quick pace.

AZHARI's rapid success was in no small degree due to the fact that his measures to oust the British were both tacitly and overtly supported by the Egyptian government. But the reason why AZHARI pushed the ousting of the British was not to play the country into the hands of Egypt. His first and foremost task was to part from the British colonialists, and to this end he made use of the support of Egypt; the settlement of relations with Egypt, the safeguarding of Sudanese independence against Egypt, was to come later.

In the government just as in the Ashigga Party there were intransigent elements belonging to the Khatmia sect who entertained different ideas, who regarded the ousting of the British as the first step towards union with Egypt. Already during 1954 they repeatedly proposed, both in the government and in the press, that the government lay down its position on the matter of the relations with Egypt. But AZHARI was fully aware that the majority of the Sudanese people wanted full independence, not union with Egypt, so he took a guarded attitude and refrained from stating his views. If the question was put direct to him, he gave an evasive answer and said that the policy to be followed regarding the relations with Egypt would be determined by the National Unionist Party at the proper time.

AZHARI's and his party's switching over to the policy of full independence became gradually manifest.

In November 1954, following an invitation from the British government, AZHARI made a visit to London, where he was received by Prime Minister CHURCHILL and also the Queen. What AZHARI had to talk about with the British government was not made public. But from further developments it may be inferred that, even though no formal agreement was entered into, AZHARI on his part assured the British government that the Sudan, once independent, would not join Egypt; and that the British government, in the awareness that Great Britain would by no means get back her old positions in the Sudan, tried at least to save face and declared its willingness to consent to the Sudan's independence in exchange for renunciation of union with Egypt.

The main facts in support of the above inference are the following: After returning from his visit to London on December 3, AZHARI was so confident in the support of his party and of the majority of the people that still in December he relieved three cabinet members (those belonging to the Khatmia sect and the Ashigga Party) who were in favour of close ties with Egypt, and thus he secured his freedom of action.

In a speech he delivered on the second anniversary of the 1953 Anglo-Egyptian agreement, February 12, 1955, he practically sang the praises of the British colonialists who had left the country. A month later, on March 16, he already took a stand openly for Sudanese independence. In April he took part in the Bandung Conference, and upon returning home, on May 25, Bairam Day, he declared that he was going to do all in his power to achieve the country's independence and total sovereignty.

This action of AZHARI met with no insignificant resistance within his own party, but he succeeded in winning the majority, and this support made it possible for him to dismiss from the cabinet his principal antagonist, SAYED MOHAMMED NUR EL-DIM, who accused him of having betrayed the programme on which he had been elected. This was done on June 19. When a month later he went to Cairo to attend the anniversary celebration of the July 23 Egyptian revolution, the Egyptian government virtually boycotted him.

But AZHARI held to his new line. On July 31 the Sudanization Committee announced the completion of its mission. The next day, August 1, in a speech delivered during a religious holiday, AZHARI reaffirmed his party's policy in favour of independence.

In the meantime he untiringly toured the country and spoke up for independence. The masses met him everywhere with enthusiasm, and since he advocated just what the Umma Party had stood up for in advance, adherents of this party could not afford to oppose him, no matter how much they disliked him personally.

Then, after almost half a year of preparation, he turned to Parliament. On August 16 Parliament on his proposal adopted a resolution unanimously, demanding, with reference to Article 9 of the 1953 agreement, that the necessary steps be taken to implement the right of the Sudan to self-determination.

Uprising in August to October 1955

Immediately after the passage of the August 16 resolution, when AZHARI stood on the peak of popularity, and when there was every indication that the country was inevitably and rapidly progressing towards independence, an uprising broke out in a province of the Southern Sudan on August 18.

It is still difficult to form an opinion of the causes and the character of the uprising. The scanty reports published in the press at that time are but conjectures at the best (if not deliberate falsifications). According to J. S. R. DUNCAN (who, at the time of the rising was still an adviser to the Governor-General in Khartoum) the uprising was started by the troops spread over the whole of Equatoria province, except Juba, the province seat, and the troops were joined also by the civil population and the police. In his opinion, "There was no single cause for this tragedy. There were many contributory causes: the historic distrust of the south for the north; wild [?] electioneering promises by northern politicians; the dispute over 'safeguards' for the south in the months preceding the Agreement of 1953; the Egyptian radio campaign of the previous year and more; the excessively fast rate of Sudanisation; the almost complete lack of interest in southern affairs by Azhari's predominantly northern Sudanese Cabinet; our [that is, the British government's] dilatoriness in ending a policy of protection and in introducing experienced northern administrators; and the unsuitability of some of the northerners for the task of handling these different people. These were the main causes. A forged telegram, exhorting the administrators to harshness and purporting to be from Azhari, provided the tragic spark" [which touched off the uprising].[1]

23 DUNCAN, *op. cit.*, pp. 191–192.

That this account of Duncan's is a pack of lies cannot be doubted. This explanation was fabricated evidently for the purpose of providing an alibi to the British government and to shift responsibility upon the Egyptian government and the northern Sudanese themselves, but the lies prove just the contrary: this account gives palpable evidence that the uprising was a result of British provocation, for which responsibility rests on the British colonial authorities and, in the last analysis, on the British government.

It is a fact of history that it was the British colonizers who had striven from the outset to divide the country, to separate the southern from the northern provinces. Already from 1902 onwards they applied in six northern provinces different measures from those instituted in the three southern provinces. In the north, for example, they reckoned with the people's allegiance to the Islam and did not allow Christian missions to function, while they flooded the southern provinces with all manner of Christian missionaries. Trade between north and south was made subject to hardly obtainable special licences, and so forth. Duncan himself mentioned that the British officials had the—according to him—"not unreasonable thought" that the provinces of the Southern Sudan might best be united with Uganda or Kenya(!).[1] The fact is that until 1938, that is throughout four decades, the British colonialists did practically nothing to develop the southern provinces, and not until 1947 did they adopt officially the position that the northern and southern provinces should be treated uniformly as one country. Duncan himself states that "There is a tendency now for both northern and southern Sudanese to lay the blame on the British for the fact that the southerner lags behind the northerner. That is reasonable up to a point."[2]

If anyone still doubts whether the uprising was the product of British provocation, he can be enlightened by the following commentary of Duncan:

"The task facing the Sudanese Government was to defeat the mutineers or obtain their surrender. It was their task; not ours any longer. This was mutiny against the Sudanese Government. The Governor-General flew back from England where he had been on leave. As the days went by, the pathetic aspect of the mutiny became apparent: the mutineers would not be persuaded that the British would fail to come to their aid. They had captured the wireless transmitting set at Torit and sent out signals to Nairobi (which were all intercepted) reporting their position, strength, ammunition, etc., and asking when British reinforcements would come. It was the Governor-General's duty to tell them curtly that no British troops would be forthcoming and to call upon them, as Commander-in-Chief of the Sudan Defence Force, to surrender. They did surrender: though, in fact, the form of surrender was flight, many hundreds to Uganda and others to the hills. By the end of October northern administrators had, with courage which cannot be too highly praised, taken up the uneasy strings of administration again."[3]

A much more objective explanation of the causes and nature of the uprising is given in the book of Professor P. M. Holt of London:[4] "The troubles . . . were the inevitable result of over-hasty political change. The British administrators who, if alien, were at least familiar to the unsophisticated southerners, had gone and their places had been taken by the no less alien northern, Arabic-speaking, Muslim Sudanese. For the most part new to the higher responsibilities of ad-

[1] *Ibid.*, p. 61.
[2] *Ibid.*, p. 62.
[3] *Ibid.*, pp. 193—194.
[4] *A Modern History of the Sudan*, pp. 166—167.

ministration, the northerners were particularly at a disadvantage in dealing with the south, from which they had been virtually excluded until less than ten years previously. The southern political leaders, conscious of their weakness under the new regime, adopted Azhari's own former tactics and began to seek Egyptian support. They announced that they were aiming to establish an autonomous South, linked only in a federation with the North. When mutiny broke out in the Equatoria Corps of the Sudan Defence Force, the mutineers were buoyed up by the impossible hope of receiving British help. The governor-general, Sir Knox Helm, who had succeeded Sir Robert How in March 1955, could only order the mutineers to lay down their arms. They surrendered on 27 August, but by this time disorder had spread through the southern provinces and many northerners lost their lives. The new rulers acted on the whole wisely and temperately in this very dangerous crisis."

As regards Professor HOLT's estimate of the casualties, it can be questioned. According to DUNCAN, the mutiny resulted in nearly 300 dead among the northerners, while afterwards 200 southerners were sentenced to death, 500 to imprisonment for more than two years and 550 to imprisonment for shorter periods.[1] (Among those imprisoned were numerous leaders and members of the Liberal Party accused of having participated in organizing the mutiny.)

Party Struggles during and after the Uprising. Inter-Party Agreement. Birth of the Independent Republic of the Sudan

Under the terms of the 1953 Anglo-Egyptian agreement an elected Constituent Assembly ought to decide whether the Sudan would become an independent state or unite with Egypt in some form. The idea of AZHARI's majority party was that the existing Parliament should transform into a Constituent Assembly. This solution was, for understandable reasons, unacceptable to the Umma Party. This party proposed that a plebiscite be held instead. This proposal was met with great enthusiasm all over the country. Two days before the above-mentioned parliamentary meeting of August 16, public opinion made ALI EL-MIRGHANI himself stand up for the plebiscite. On August 29 Parliament passed a resolution unanimously demanding the British and Egyptian governments to consent to a modification of the 1953 agreement and the organization of a plebiscite. The British government gave its assent on September 13, and the Egyptian government on October 2.

Notwithstanding this, the plebiscite did not take place. The mutiny and its drowning in blood had impaired the prestige of the government and the majority party. Taking this opportunity, the opposition proposed the formation of a coalition government. The struggle between the parties came to a head. AZHARI found himself opposed also by ALI EL-MIRGHANI. He had also antagonized many members of his party. The result was that on November 11, during the budgetary debate, he was outvoted in Parliament and had to tender his resignation to the Governor-General. A few days later, however, the majority again took his side and Parliament re-elected him on November 15.

The events of those few months, the mutiny and the party quarrels, had not gone without leaving their marks. The leaders had to understand that their dissension jeopardized the cause of independence. The situation prompted the two religious leaders—for the first time in their life—to meet and see each other.

[1] DUNCAN, *op. cit.*, p. 199.

Azhari saw the time had come for action. On December 15, 1955, he announced that he was going to submit to Parliament a draft declaration of independence. He did it four days later, on December 19, and Parliament adopted the declaration, of which then the British and Egyptian governments had to take note.

The solemn proclamation of independence took place on January 1, 1956. Sitting on the grandstand at the ceremony side by side with the two religious leaders of the Sudanese people, Ali el-Mirghani and Abdel Rahman el-Mahdi, were Under-Secretary of State for Foreign Affairs Douglas Dodds-Parker on behalf of the British government and Deputy Minister Sayed Abdul Fattah Hassan representing the Egyptian government, who previously in Parliament had ceremoniously handed over to Prime Minister Azhari the formal letters of recognition by the United Kingdom and Egypt respectively.

But their presence could not stop Azhari from mentioning in his solemn address the horrors of colonial oppression, the centuries-long suffering of the Sudanese people and their struggle for independence. In his speech he said among other things:

"It will remain a source of great pride for the nation for many years to come that it was able, by wisdom, firmness and good faith, to extract its liberty, independence, and sovereignty from the teeth of colonisation . . . without having to resort to heavy bloodshed to achieve its freedom and undo the shackles of slavery . . . Colonisation sat heavily upon the land for fifty-seven years, tyrannizing over its population, destroying its peculiarities, and spreading hatred and separation between its people in order to acquire a long stay."[1]

BIBLIOGRAPHY

The Sudan: The Road Ahead. Fabian Colonial Bureau, London, 1945.

Y. Osman and M. A. Mahgoub, "The Sudan for Liberty", *Pan Africa*, Vol. 1, No. 3.

M. F. Perham, "The Sudan Emerges into Nationhood", *Foreign Affairs* (New York), Vol. 27 (1947).

M. F. Shukry, *Egypt and Sovereignty over the Sudan (Arabic)*, Cairo, 1946.

J. D. Tothill (ed.), *Agriculture in the Sudan*, New York, 1948.

A. H. Marshall, *Report on Local Government in the Sudan*, Khartoum, 1949.

H. A. R. Gibb, *Anglo-Egyptian Relations*. Royal Institute of International Affairs, Vol. XXVII, No. 4 (October 1951).

J. S. R. Duncan, *The Sudan: A Record of Achievement*, Edinburgh, 1952.

H. E. Hurst, *The Nile*, London, 1952.

R. El Badawy, *Egypt, Britain and the Sudan*, Cairo, 1952.

Mekki Shibeika, *British Policy in the Sudan*, London, 1952.

Mekki Abbas, *The Sudan Question: The Dispute over the Anglo-Egyptian Condominium 1884–1951*, London, 1952.

D. Newbold, *Making of the Modern Sudan: The Life and Letters of Sir Douglas Newbold*, London, 1953.

J. Marlowe, *Anglo-Egyptian Relations*, London, 1954.

H. Macmichael, *The Sudan*, London, 1954.

Sudan Almanac 1954, Khartoum, 1954.

H. C. Jackson, *Sudan Days and Ways*, London, 1954.

H. C. Jackson, *Behind the Modern Sudan*, London, 1955.

Saad ad-Din Fawzi, *The Labour Movement in the Sudan 1946–1955*, London, 1957.

A. Gaitskell, *Gezirah: A Story of Development in the Sudan*, London, 1959.

[1] *Ibid.*, p. 207.

ABD EL-FATTAH IBRAHIM EL-SAYED, *Sudanese-Egyptian Relations*, The Hague, 1960.

L. A. FABUNMI, *The Sudan in Anglo-Egyptian Relations*, New York, 1960.

P. M. HOLT, *A Modern History of the Sudan*, New York, 1961.

B. M. SAID, *The Sudan: Crossroads of Africa*, London, 1965.

C.P. СМИРНОВ, История Судана *(1821—1956)* Moscow, 1968.

M. A. AL-RAHIM, *Imperialism and Nationalism in the Sudan: A Study in Constitutional and Political Development, 1899–1956*, London, 1959.

CHAPTER XXII

FRANCE'S POST-WAR COLONIAL POLICY AND
THE INDEPENDENCE MOVEMENTS

The French Constituent National Assembly elected on October 21, 1945, was composed of 522 deputies, including nine from Black Africa: LAMINE GUÉYE and LÉOPOLD SENGHOR from Senegal, FILY DABO SISSOKO from the French Sudan, YACINE DIALLO from Guinea, FÉLIX HOUPHOUËT-BOIGNY from the Ivory Coast, SOUROU MIGAN APITHY from Dahomey, GABRIEL D'ARBOUSSIER and FÉLIX TCHICAYA from French Equatorial Africa, and MANGA BELL DOUALA from the Cameroons. The population of the African territories also had taken part in the election, with separate rolls for "full French citizens" (European settlers and the citizens of the four Senegal *communes* who constituted a majority of the electorate) as voters belonging to the "first college" and for "subjects" (Africans from other colonies) belonging to the "second college". Of the 17 million population 117,700 African "subjects" were qualified to vote, and only 70 to 80 per cent of them went to the poll (79 per cent in French West Africa, 75 per cent in French Equatorial Africa, 82 per cent in the Cameroons).

LAMINE GUÉYE alone of the nine Africans was elected by the "first college", the other eight (among them SENGHOR in Senegal) were elected by the "second college".

In the beginning, at the initiative of LAMINE GUÉYE, the nine African representatives joined the French Socialist Party (S.F.I.O.) and united in the *Bloc Africain* which, however, did not last long. A few months later the Bloc broke up, and its members were divided between three anti-fascist parties: LAMINE GUÉYE, SENGHOR and DIALLO stood by the Socialist Party, HOUPHOUËT-BOIGNY, D'ARBOUSSIER, SISSOKO, TCHICAYA and APITHY joined the Communist Party, and DOUALA chose the M.R.P.

The Constituent National Assembly did not consider the question of the colonies as a separate issue, but during the constitutional debate it took up several questions relating to the colonies, namely:

1. the participation of the African deputies in the French National Assembly;
2. the institution of Chambers in the colonies;
3. the establishment of a Federal Parliament of the French Union;
4. the need to reduce the purview of high colonial officials or to replace them with responsible politicians in the executive organ and the legislature.

Positive decisions were made on all these issues, and they were included in a draft constitution. It was a natural consequence of the composition (different party affiliations) of the Constituent Assembly that these decisions did not reflect a uniform view, they were rather contradictory and confused. The draft was pertinently characterized by ANTOINE LAWRENCE from the point of view of the African colonies:

"The draft put side by side expressions like 'one and indivisible republic' and 'free union', which latter implied of course the right to secede. It provided for a Grand Council of the Union, with merely advisory capacity, and for local assemblies based upon general elections, but the laws of the metropolitan country continued to be in force in the overseas territories. This obvious contradiction created confusion, a mix-up of federative and assimilative trends . . ."[1]

The constitution passed on April 19 was rejected by a referendum on May 6, 1946. (In the Constituent Assembly only the Communists and the Socialists voted for it.)

The African populations accepted the draft, despite its contradictory provisions regarding the colonies, and voted for it in the referendum. But in view of the small number of Africans who had the franchise, their votes did not affect the outcome of the referendum. Regardless of the provisions concerning the Africans, the draft constitution was rejected by a majority of the European voters.

Despite the defeat of the draft constitution the first Constituent National Assembly still produced some positive results. In addition to some legislation of an economic character,[2] the Assembly passed also two acts of political importance: on April 11, 1946, an act proposed by HOUPHOUËT-BOIGNY on the abolition of forced labour in the colonies, and on May 7 an act moved by LAMINE GUÉYE granting French "citizenship" to the Africans thus far regarded as "subjects". The first one, which was not meant to protect the interests of the poor peasants compelled to do forced labour, but intended to secure the competitive interests of the African planters against the European settlers profiteering by African labour, failed to define the scope of forced labour, with the result that, in spite of the law, various forms of forced labour were applied for many years to come. And the declaration of citizenship was nothing but an empty phrase, because for the next decade it did no entail either the introduction of universal suffrage or the suppression of the election system of the dual college.

The second Constituent National Assembly was elected, after the referendum, on June 2, 1946. In the nine months since the elections of October 1945 the forces of reaction gained new strength and reorganized. The relationship of political forces in the metropolitan country had shifted in favour of the right wing: the M.R.P. became the strongest political party in France. The right wing of the European settlers in the French colonies (especially in the Ivory Coast and the Cameroons) also started to organize. (Their organization formed at a convention in Douala, the Cameroons, held another gathering in Paris from July 30 to August 24, 1946.) The number of African voters had grown by a few thousand in the meantime, but the actual election turnout decreased (71.5 per cent voted in West Africa, 73 in Equatorial Africa, 62 in the Cameroons). In spite of this all previous African deputies, except D'ARBOUSSIER, were elected to the second Constituent Assembly.

In the overseas constitutional committee of the second Constituent National Assembly the African deputies prepared a draft of their own which contained among others the following clause providing for the complete liquidation of the colonial system:

"France condemns the system of colonialism based on annexation, conquest and domination over overseas territories. She waives all one-sided sovereignty

[1] ANTOINE LAWRENCE, "Renaissance politique de l'Afrique noire", *Cahiers Charles de Foucauld* 31/1953, pp. 74–85.
[2] A decree introducing the *franc C.F.A.* as the French African territories' own currency (December 25, 1945), and an act of April 30, 1946, establishing F.I.D.E.S. (Fonds d'Investissement pour le Développement Economique et Social).

over the colonized people. She recognizes their freedom to govern themselves and settle their own affairs in a democratic manner."

Apart from the declaration of principle the proposed draft was not at all radical. Instead of independence for the colonial territories it only demanded that within twenty years they should be allowed to decide whether to remain in the French Union or to become an independent sovereign state. The draft contained no provision for the organs of the Union on the grounds that the Constituent National Assembly had no right to decide this issue, that it was up to a Union conference in which all members would have equal representation, that is, in which the overseas territories had the majority. Besides the above declaration of principle another radical motion was aimed at the suppression of the duality of electoral colleges (European and African). After a long debate the constitutional committee could be made to accept this draft provision, but the plenary meeting, owing to a number of counterproposals by right-wing French deputies, was unable to agree on a definitive text of the constitution. Finally, the Assembly referred the case to the government and charged the Minister for Overseas France with formulating the final text. The constitution thus drawn up bore little resemblance to the African-proposed draft of the overseas constitutional committee. Though it took over the declaration which repudiated colonialism, it did so with essential changes. Let us see, for example, this provision:

"France and her overseas people form a Union based on equality of rights and duties, without distinction as to race or religion. The French Union is composed of nations and peoples which combine or co-ordinate their means and efforts to develop their various civilizations, to raise their well-being and safeguard their security. True to her traditional mission, France has the intention of leading the peoples for whom she has assumed responsibility to free self-government and democratic administration of their own affairs. France rejects every system of colonialism based on arbitrariness, and guarantees everybody's right to the holding of public office and to the individual or collective exercise of the rights and freedoms proclaimed or confirmed in this constitution."

The draft mentioned the African colonies as "overseas territories" of the "one and indivisible French Republic", for which the right to self-determination, independence and secession from the Republic was entirely ruled out, and which — except the trust territories of the Cameroons and Togoland — were members of the French Union not as states but as integral parts of France.

Despite the African proposal the constitution provided in detail for the organs of the state apparatus, namely the Grand Council of the French Union, in which the "overseas territories" as not independent states had no place, and the Assembly of the French Union. Taking part in this fake of parliament were also the African colonies as territories of the French Republic, though not through directly elected representatives, but through delegates sent by their respective territorial assemblies. It could pass neither laws nor decisions, it was not even entitled to meet on its own, it could be convened only by the President of the French Republic at the same time with the session of the French National Assembly. Its powers were limited to advancing opinions on overseas subjects touched upon in the Bills under discussion by the National Assembly, making relevant recommendations to the Paris government or the National Assembly.

As regards the original proposal of the most practical importance to the Africans, the suppression of the dual college, all the constitution did was that it introduced a single college (for the election of the French Assembly) in the countries of French

West Africa and Togoland, while it retained the two colleges in the countries of French Equatorial Africa and the Cameroons, and for local elections everywhere.

This constitution, which fell way short of the African expectations, was passed by the Constituent National Assembly on September 28, 1946, by 440 votes (Socialists, Communists and M.R.P.) to 106. Despite the defects of the constitution the African deputies voted for its passage, since they saw in it a small measure of progress. In the referendum held on October 13, 1946, it was rejected in the overseas territories by a slight margin (335,000 to 258,000 — because the majority of the electorate, the Gaullist settlers, who followed the intentions of their retired leader, voted against it), but the overall result of the referendum, in spite of the great number of opponents, and owing to a mass abstention of voters, was positive (9,297,000 voted yes, 8,165,000 voted no, and 8,519,000 were absent).

The Status of the African Territories in the French Union

The 618 members of the French National Assembly included 23 deputies from Black Africa (exclusive of Madagascar), among them 18 Africans, 2 West Indians and 3 Europeans. (The countries of French West Africa, where a single electoral college had been introduced, returned 14 Africans, the countries of French Equatorial Africa sent 3 Africans, 1 West Indian and 1 European, the Cameroons elected 1 African, 1 West Indian and 1 European.) The 315-member Grand Council of the Union had 32 "African" senators (19 from West Africa, 8 from Equatorial Africa, 3 from the Cameroons, and 2 from Togoland), including several Europeans. In the Economic Council composed of 169 members there were seated 13 representatives of economic groups and trade unions from African and other overseas territories, either delegated by the respective organizations or appointed by the French Assembly.

The constitution made it possible also to include African deputies in the French government. Already in 1946–47 LAMINE GUÈYE was an assistant secretary of state in the BLUM government, but the first African to be a full cabinet member was HOUPHOUËT-BOIGNY in the GUY MOLLET government in 1956. The Ministry of the greatest concern to Africans (Overseas France), however, was always headed by a French statesman who was responsible for France's overseas policies only to the French National Assembly and the Prime Minister.

Such African participation in the parliamentary bodies of France and in the organs of the French Union brought no substantive change from the point of view of the situation of Africans and their independence aspirations. The territories continued to be governed by French Governors appointed by Paris under the supreme authority of the Governors-General in French West Africa and in French Equatorial Africa, respectively, with the only difference that the two Federations were renamed "Groups of Territories", and the Governors-General became "High Commissioners", who in turn were responsible not to a Minister of Colonies but to the Minister of Overseas France. Each territory had its own Territorial Assembly, in which, however, the leading part was invariably played by the French settlers, even though they were the minority, and the activity of which body — in addition to the adoption of the territorial budget — was practically confined to helping the Governor in the performance of his administrative functions. In the exercise of supreme power each High Commissioner relied on a Council of Government composed of appointed colonial officials. It is true that in August 1947 each Council of Government received a new agency slightly reminiscent of parliament, the so-called Grand Council. This body was composed of 40 territorial council delegates in French West Africa, and 20 in Equatorial Africa. This gave some African politicians an opportunity to voice their opinions, but the powers of these "parliaments" was not broader than those of the Territorial Assemblies: in addition to discussing and adopting the budget of a Group of Territories submitted by the High Commissioner (such budgets were naturally of greater importance than those of the individual territories), they played a passive role just like the Territorial Assemblies—they assisted the High Commissioner and his Council of Government in the work of administration.

With the adoption of the constitution the French "Fourth Republic" was born. In the changed international situation after the war the French bourgeoisie gained new strength, forgetting everything (the crimes which it had committed before and during the war by letting France come into German fascist occupation, and the big promises it had made during the war to the workers and the subjected colonial peoples), and learning nothing. It pursued the old imperialist and colonialist policies, with some changes in methods and slogans, but unchanged in essence. In the first ten years (1946-1955) of the Fourth Republic the French government, like its British rival, professed neocolonialist principles in words, but used every means to maintain its old-style colonial rule. In those years it paid relatively little attention to the African colonies, because it was concerned mostly with the Far and the Near East (the dirty colonial wars in Indochina and Algeria). In Africa at that time France was not yet in danger of losing her colonies, since—as we shall see soon—the independence movements of the French African colonies did not yet get rid of the war-time illusions about the good intentions of the French colonialists (Brazzaville!), and most of their leaders were under strong French influence (LAMINE GUÈYE, SENGHOR, HOUPHOUËT-BOIGNY). The French colonialists were aware that sooner or later they would have inevitably to introduce democratic reforms, but they were in no hurry. In ten years they passed only two noteworthy laws of some importance to the Africans. The Labour Code, whose draft was submitted to the legislature on April 12, 1949, was made law only three and a half years later, on December 15, 1952. Even this was "outdistanced" in delay by the Municipal Law, which was initiated on November 16, 1948, and was adopted a round seven years after, on November 16, 1955.

The Labour Code was practically nothing else than the practical implementation, with a considerable time lag, of the regulations of 1946 prohibiting forced labour and granting the Africans' civil rights. It was really of some help to improve the conditions of African labourers, but it did not do away with the enormous disproportion between wages and the rising consumer prices.

The Municipal Law *(loi municipale pour les territoires d'outre-mer)* provided that the status of *commune de plein exercice*, which three towns of Senegal (Dakar, Saint-Louis, Rufisque) had obtained long before, should be granted to an additional 35 towns of the French African colonies: 6 new *communes* were created in Senegal, 5 in Guinea and Dahomey each, 4 in the French Sudan, 3 in the Ivory Coast and the Cameroons each, 2 in Upper Volta, the Middle Congo and Gabon each, 1 in Chad and Ubangi-Shari each. The *communes* chose their mayors and their municipal councils through general elections extending to all adult inhabitants regardless of race. This can account for the fact that in the municipal elections held a year later (November 18, 1956) all *communes* elected African mayors, and that a great number of African political leaders (LAMINE GUÈYE in Dakar, SÉKOU TOURÉ in Conakry, MODIBO KEITA in Bamako, GABRIEL LISETTE in Fort-Lamy, FULBERT YOULOU in Brazzaville, SOUROU MIGAN APITHY in Porto-Novo, DJIBO BAKARY in Niamey, BARTHÉLEMY BOGANDA in Bangui, etc.) got elected, and this enhanced their influence among the popular masses.

Mention should be made also of the law passed by the French National Assembly on May 22, 1951, widely extending African franchise by including women in the electorate. The original Bill, which was introduced by a woman deputy from the M.R.P., intended to enfranchise only mothers of four or more children. The Communists demanded extension of the franchise to all women who met the African voting qualifications. But the French National Assembly endorsed only the original version, extending the franchise to mothers of at least two children. The Bill even in this form met with stubborn right-wing opposition in the Senate, but after long debates the National Assembly adopted it by 447 votes to 291.

Until 1956 the elective franchise was not extended further. Nevertheless, the number of African qualified voters grew from year to year, from election to election. Before 1947 the electoral registers listed almost exclusively names of officials and employees, clergymen and lawyers, merchants, handicraftsmen and ex-servicemen. As the activity of the masses grew, however, an ever increasing number of workers and mainly peasants obtained the right to vote. By 1951 the voters among the rural population had outnumbered the urban voters.

Formation of the R.D.A. and Its Initial Years

In September 1946 the African deputies in Paris issued a manifesto addressed to the Africans, calling upon all the trade unions, cultural and religious associations to send their delegates to a conference to be held in Africa with a view to forming an interterritorial political party of Africans, designed to direct the struggle for the liberation of African countries and peoples. "In spite of all machinations of the reaction", they wrote in the manifesto, "we call a big rally of all organizations whose rapid development is a sure indication that they strive to realize political and social democracy in Black Africa."

The conference, which met in Bamako on October 18, 1946, was attended by 800 delegates from African countries, who were enthusiastically welcomed by a crowd of 15,000 Sudanese on the opening day. Although the conference was convened by an agreed decision of all political leaders representing Africans in the French Constituent National Assembly, only the communist deputies (HOUPHOUËT-BOIGNY, D'ARBOUSSIER, APITHY, TCHICAYA and SISSOKO) took part, since LAMINE GUÈYE and SENGHOR, under pressure from the French Socialist Party (which saw a "communist peril" in the formation of a single party of all African nationalists), and the M.R.P.'s DOUALA kept away from the conference.

The conference formed the proposed united interterritorial party, the R.D.A. *(Rassemblement Démocratique Africain)*, which elected HOUPHOUËT-BOIGNY President and D'ARBOUSSIER Secretary-General.

In the first few months the R.D.A. was joined by broad masses of Africans. In the elections of November 1946 six members of the party were already returned to the French Assembly. In 1948 HOUPHOUËT-BOIGNY and D'ARBOUSSIER made a propaganda tour of French West and Equatorial Africa, canvassing for new members, and with good success. At that time local political parties affiliated to the R.D.A. were operating almost everywhere in those territories, and their membership numbered over 700,000. And this was so despite the fact that the parties maintaining relations with the French Socialist Party and the M.R.P. were everywhere in sharp opposition to the R.D.A., and the colonial administration left no stone unturned to hamper the activities of the R.D.A. parties.

The opportunist French Socialist Party was gradually losing its influence in Africa, and in 1948 this induced SENGHOR to break with it. His party, the *Bloc Démocratique Sénégalais*, joined the group of African deputies of the French Assembly, the *Indépendants d'Outre-Mer* (I.O.M.), which maintained no regular contact with any French party.

The R.D.A. convened its second conference to Bobo-Dioulasso, in Upper Volta, for January 1, 1949. Since the authorities refused to permit the holding of the meeting, the conference was held at Treichville, a suburb of Abidjan. Owing to official pressure, only 167 delegates could get to the meeting place, as against 800 participants at the first conference held in October 1946, although the R.D.A. membership had since risen to several times its previous strength. From France only four communist deputies and a few communist newspapermen were present. But the mood of the majority of the delegates was more enthusiastic and determined than ever, and the resolutions of the conference reflected the revolutionary determination of D'ARBOUSSIER rather than the vacillation of HOUPHOUËT-BOIGNY and some of his associates. The conference condemned "the reactionary and colonialist policies of the parliamentary majority of the present government", and its resolution submitted by LISETTE, and adopted unanimously, stated:

"The conference confirms its faith in the alliance of the peoples of Black Africa with the great French people who, headed by the working class and its Communist Party, struggle courageously and confidently for national independence, against American imperialism. In the spirit of this alliance the conference expresses its will: to promote the creation of such a democratic and anticolonialist government of the Union which equally relies on all manner of French democrats and the overseas peoples."

At the same time the conference emphasized the leading role of the party organizations, as against that of the parliamentary deputies who, in its view, ought to serve the mass movement.

Towards the end of 1949 and early in 1950, under the pretext of mass upheavals in the Ivory Coast, the government launched a strong police campaign against the R.D.A., which it accused of organizing the disturbances. The action took a toll of 52 lives and hundreds of wounded people, and was followed by more than 3,000 arrests. (A warrant was issued also against HOUPHOUËT-BOIGNY, who was saved only by his parliamentary immunity.) Persecution by the authorities, and the ever more violent campaign which the government, the French colonists and the reactionary parties of France conducted on account of the R.D.A.'s relations with the French Communist Party, impelled many R.D.A. members to desert. Under the impact of these developments HOUPHOUËT-BOIGNY, the former vocal "revolutionary", made a sharp turn and assumed the role of leader of the loyal opposition. In October 1950 together with all fellow deputies of his party, except D'ARBOUSSIER, he severed all relations with the French Communist Party and declared that the aim of the R.D.A. policy was to build up mutual understanding and co-operation with France, that is, with the French government and its authorities. D'ARBOUSSIER and a number of other leading party politicians refused to follow this opportunist line of HOUPHOUËT-BOIGNY. As a consequence—in several countries during the next few years—local parties broke their affiliation with the R.D.A.; the desertion of its leftist members steadily weakened the R.D.A., and in many places even new left-wing parties were formed.

HOUPHOUËT-BOIGNY's political activity after his volte-face was characterized by an endeavour to ingratiate himself with the French government in power, and to channel the independence movements of the Africans from the road of the anti-imperialist struggle to the path of appeasement with the colonialists. All his public actions were indicative of this endeavour. All his speeches and writings were essentially protestations of his anti-Communism and his loyalty to France. For instance, in an appeal to the people of the Ivory Coast during the elections for the French National Assembly in June 1951, he declared:

"We are not Communists and we never were, we serve the betterment of our African land and the social advancement of its inhabitants ... We never were anti-French, nor are we now, and nor do we intend to become in the future ... We want to develop the Ivory Coast into the most beautiful country of the French Union. Long live the R.D.A.! Long live the Ivory Coast! Long live France! Long live the French Union!"

HOUPHOUËT-BOIGNY's new policy, however, met with sharp opposition on the part of many of his old followers. For example, SÉKOU SANOGO, who had been an R.D.A. supporter from 1946 to 1949, and who now ran for election as a member of the Gaullist R.P.F. (and was elected second deputy for the Ivory Coast to the French Assembly), spoke of the R.D.A. leaders in his election appeal in such terms:

"The trust which the country had placed in its representatives (the former R.D.A. deputies) has been betrayed. They used the five-year mandate as deputies in the metropolitan country for mere oppositionism to the republican government and in our own country for the establishment of a political movement which undermined the sacred rights of the citizens and sank to terror acts, looting, arson, killing, and to the organization of an uprising ... The deputies elected in 1946 have led the country to the brink of ruin. Neither the apparent break with the Communist Party, nor the parody of rapprochement with the republican government, nor the shameful submission to certain politicians and political parties they have publicly castigated before, can give them back the trust of the country they have betrayed."

But HOUPHOUËT-BOIGNY reckoned well. Formerly pursuers of the R.D.A., the French government and the local French colonial authorities turned into its partners. It was due to this that at the re-election of the Territorial Assemblies in March 1952 the R.D.A. managed to have 28 of its members elected in the Ivory Coast, 13 in the Sudan, 8 in the Middle Congo and 6 in Chad.

Also after the elections HOUPHOUËT-BOIGNY took every occasion to assure the colonialists of his loyalty. In March 1952, for example, his welcoming address to the Minister of Overseas France on a visit to Abidjan was larded with phrases about "coexistence of the French and of the Africans of the Ivory Coast" and "interdependence of France and Africa".[1]

How much the official attitude towards the R.D.A. had changed was shown by the fact that JEAN-BAPTISTE MOCKEY, an R.D.A. leader who had been arrested on the charge of having organized the riots in the Ivory Coast in February 1949 and got a heavy sentence of imprisonment, was acquitted and released in April 1953, and the sentences of his co-defendants were suspended.

---

[1] *La Côte d'Ivoire*, May 31, 1952.

The principal opponent of HOUPHOUËT-BOIGNY was D'ARBOUSSIER, who continued to regard himself as the elected Secretary-General of the R.D.A. In this capacity he demanded on April 25 the convening of the R.D.A.'s committee of co-ordination. HOUPHOUËT-BOIGNY declined on the grounds that D'ARBOUSSIER had long before ceased to be Secretary-General of the R.D.A. Thereupon D'ARBOUSSIER, in LAMINE GUÉYE's paper *(L'A.O.F.)* on July 6, 1952, wrote an open letter to HOUPHOUËT-BOIGNY, which he signed "Gabriel D'Arboussier, Secretary-General of the R.D.A." In the July 24 issue of *Afrique Noire* HOUPHOUËT-BOIGNY also wrote an open letter after he had got the R.D.A. parliamentary group in Paris to pass a resolution, on July 12, expelling D'ARBOUSSIER from the party.

D'ARBOUSSIER's effort to persuade certain parties to oppose the policy of HOU-PHOUËT-BOIGNY succeeded only in part: he managed to divert the largest party of the Cameroons, the *Union des Populations du Cameroun* led by UM NYOBÉ, and the minority party of Senegal, the *Union Démocratique Sénégalaise*. But he failed in his effort to organize an opposition inside the R.D.A. relying on the radical-minded R.D.A. youth. This can be accounted for mainly by the fact that the two most radical politicians of the R.D.A., SÉKOU TOURÉ and MODIBO KEITA, did not find it opportune for the time being to break with HOUPHOUËT-BOIGNY. (Later developments proved how well they behaved from the point of view of the movement. By supporting HOUPHOUËT-BOIGNY they could continue to play a leading part in the R.D.A. and strengthen the R.D.A. left wing, protecting at the same time the movement from the persecution of the authorities at home, while SÉKOU TOURÉ in Guinea could rebuild his party, which had disintegrated as a result of the persecutions, and get himself elected to the Territorial Assembly in 1953.)

The "Overseas Independents"

The R.D.A.'s successes following HOUPHOUËT-BOIGNY's turnabout and the resulting decline of the prestige of the parties which were influenced by SENGHOR and maintained relations with the I.O.M. induced the parliamentary deputies of these parties to rally their own respective parties in interterritorial groupings like the R.D.A. To carry out this idea, in February 1953 they met at Bobo-Dioulasso, in Upper Volta.

This "congress" was nothing more than a get-together of the leaders of parties and their deputies sitting in the Paris Assembly. The leading part in the deliberations was played, besides SENGHOR who initiated the gathering, and MAMADOU DIA, by LOUIS-PAUL AUJOULAT of the French Cameroons, HUBERT MAGA of Dahomey, SÉKOU SANOGO of the Ivory Coast, and JOSEPH CONOMBO and NAZI BONI of Upper Volta. The congress was not a meeting of elected party delegates. Most of the participants other than parliamentary deputies came from among the minor local parties. The whole congress proceeded according to SENGHOR's principles. His idea was realized by combining all African I.O.M. parties in an all-embracing I.O.M. Movement. Also the resolution of the congress reflected SENGHOR's ideas who, already in 1950, said in a speech at a UNESCO Assembly:

"The age of nationalism is over. I am of the opinion that the French African territories have to work towards a 'French Federation' whose members would have autonomy. But political autonomy cannot preclude close co-operation with France and other European countries. Africa has to use the technological thinking and inventions of Europe, just as it used Christianity, to develop its own organizations primarily in the fields of culture and music . . . The aim I set myself is the complete independence and autonomy of the spirit."[1]

In the congress resolution the participants, true to the Senghorian spirit, talked of the "interdependence of peoples and nations" instead of independence and declared that they preferred "fundamental freedoms" to liberty, and the "material and moral independence" of the individual to the independence of their country. In a pathetic tone the resolution demanded the putting into practice of the constitutionally proclaimed principles "justice, freedom, equality" and a reform of the French Union in the spirit of "active federalism".

In his speech to the congress SENGHOR made the following profession of allegiance to the French colonialists:

"We still have much to learn. It will take many years to build up our home on solid foundations. I declare once again that we don't want to secede from France. On the contrary: we have to regard ourselves as young pages who are fit only to be train-bearers of the noble lady—France. We have to work to do honour to the train of our protectress sometime. In any case we want only the protection of France and will never permit the United Nations to interfere with our quarrels and worries. By comparing our situation to what is happening in neighbouring countries, we can state that France is the only one who had fulfilled her civilizing mission, and we feel that, compared to our companions of the Gold Coast, Liberia and British Gambia, we are in a more advantageous situation."

R.D.A. Co-ordinating Committee Meeting in July 1955

HOUPHOUËT-BOIGNY was more and more worried by the intensifying activity and mass influence of the parties opposing his opportunism, especially the Union des Populations du Cameroun. He therefore tried to persuade the leaders of those parties, notably UM NYOBÉ and BAKARY, to accept his policy. Since he failed in this effort, he finally brought himself to do what he had for years been reluctant to do: he called a meeting of the R.D.A. co-ordinating committee. (Owing to HOUPHOUET-BOIGNY's sabotage the highest organ of the R.D.A. had not met since 1949.)

The meeting which opened at Conakry on July 7, 1955, and was attended by the committee members and the R.D.A. deputies of the French National Assembly, dealt with internal affairs of the R.D.A. movement in the first place. The meeting expelled from the R.D.A. those parties which opposed HOUPHOUËT-BOIGNY's policy (among them the Union Démocratique Sénégalaise and BAKARY's Union Démocratique Nigérienne). In his statement to the committee, HOUPHOUËT-BOIGNY, true to his opportunist policy, defined the aim of the movement as being a struggle for higher living standards, not for independence:

"Leading quarters of the metropolitan country as well as responsible members of the overseas élite are aware that real independence is feasible only in the framework of conscious and organized interdependence . . .

"Unitary republic or federal republic? What is important to us is not the institutions themselves but the spirit that pervades them. It is important that the institutions satisfy the Africans . . .

---

[1] *Paris–Dakar*, June 8, 1950.

"The African must eat better, live better and dress better every day. The spiritual future has to be prepared by a steady broadening of the mass culture. Legal privileges have to be accompanied by real economic and social advancement ... In the present historical circumstance we build the future of Africa in a realistic manner if we struggle for higher standards of living of Africans. We cannot build up Africa if we enthuse about great ideas which go ahead of the events, we shall rely upon the welfare of the peasants and the productive labour of skilled workers."

The same spirit pervaded LISETTE's report on economic policy and MODIBO KEITA's on social policy. Though disagreeing in principle with HOUPHOUËT-BOIGNY's opportunist line, MODIBO KEITA and SÉKOU TOURÉ still found it better to keep up a semblance of their support for him in order to preserve the unity of the movement and to facilitate the party's resistance to official persecutions.

After this the R.D.A.'s influence, despite the dissent of the opposition parties, went on increasing. At the election of the (third) French National Assembly on January 2, 1956, R.D.A. candidates from six countries of French Africa obtained eight seats: HOUPHOUËT-BOIGNY and OUEZZIN COULIBALY won in the Ivory Coast, MODIBO KEITA and MAMADOU KONATÉ in the French Sudan, HAMANI DIORI in Niger, GABRIEL LISETTE in Chad, FÉLIX TCHICAYA in the Middle Congo, and SÉKOU TOURÉ in Guinea. The R.D.A. had relatively strong minority parties, which were joined in 1956 by the respective local majority parties, in three (Dahomey, Upper Volta, Gabon) of those territories where there was no R.D.A. majority.

The "loi-cadre"

In ithe January 1956 elections to the French National Assembly the majority was obtained by the republican front formed by GUY MOLLET's Socialist Party and PIERRE MENDÈS-FRANCE's Radical Socialist Party. The first thing the new government did was work out, under the impact of the Bandung Conference and the events of Algeria, a Bill which (in order to drain off the revolutionary spirit of the African independence movements) empowered the government to decree the introduction of political reforms in the colonies and fixed the scope of such reforms. The draft of this so-called loi-cadre was tabled in the National Assembly by GASTON DEFERRE, the Minister for Overseas Territories, on February 29, 1956, and it was promulgated on June 23, 1956, after it was passed by the French Assembly as well as by the legislature of the French Union.

The reforms envisaged in the loi-cadre boiled down to the following:

To introduce universal suffrage extended to cover all males and females over 21 years of age.

To replace the system of the dual college of "citizens" and "subjects" with a single college in the election of the Territorial Assemblies and the National Assembly alike.

The centralized government of the two Groups of Territories (French West Africa, French Equatorial Africa) would be replaced by territorial governments of the individual colonial entities.

Each colony would have its own territorial government, and the Territorial Assemblies would become legislatures of a parliamentary character.

The two Groups would continue to exist, each with a French Governor and a Grand Council, but without a central executive body (the former "Council of Government"). Their functions would be "to co-ordinate the work of the territories in the economic, financial, social and cultural fields and to promote and foster their common interests".

A number of bodies and authorities, which had until then been functioning as central organs at Dakar or Brazzaville, would be broken up into territorial bodies and authorities.

The reforms provided for in the *loi-cadre* were implemented by decrees issued within the stipulated one-year period. That the reforms meant no real autonomy for the territories could be seen from the fact that, under the terms of the *loi-cadre*, each territorial government was headed, not by an African Prime Minister, but by a French Governor[1] appointed by and responsible to the Paris government, furthermore some of the African ministers of the territorial government were nominated by the French Governor, and the territorial government was not responsible to the legislature of the territory.

AFRICANUS pertinently described the *loi-cadre* as a "compromise that satisfies nobody and whose internal contradictions already appear", because "it raises more questions than it resolves".[2] Nonetheless, the *loi-cadre* received an enthusiastic welcome from public opinion both in France and in Africa. Sharp criticisms came only from a few young African intellectuals.[3]

The overwhelming majority of the Africans, however, received the *loi-cadre* favourably. This was only natural to opportunist African politicians who professed that "real independence is feasible only in the framework of conscious and organized interdependence",[4] and that their aim was not political and economic independence but "the complete independence and autonomy of the spirit".[5] It was two months before the promulgation of the *loi-cadre* that SENGHOR declared:

"We spell out clearly: to talk of independence today, in the historical and geographical situation we are in, means to put the cart before the horse, it means to think in an upside-down manner, it means not to think at all and to raise a false problem . . . Even if we had all the necessary means, cadres and solid wealth, available for independence, it would still remain questionable whether to be independent is in our interest. Against the damagogues we shall also in the future demand internal autonomy by stages for the overseas territories."[6]

Not only the opportunist train-bearers of the colonialists, but at first also such genuine fighters for independence as SÉKOU TOURÉ and MODIBO KEITA, welcomed the *loi-cadre* as a step towards independence.

But the parties influenced by SENGHOR and LAMINE GUÈYE, though they had enthusiastically applauded the *loi-cadre* upon its promulgation, soon came to realize

---

[1] The Governor was assisted by one of the African ministers styled *vice-président du Conseil*.
[2] AFRICANUS, *L'Afrique noire devant l'indépendance*, Paris, 1958.
[3] "The sluice-gate of legal formulas will not long resist the storm of freedom" (FRANÇOIS SENGAT-KUO). "The *loi-cadre* is a calculated adaptation of the regime whose overrule it is intended to save" (NICOLAS ATANGANA). "The *loi-cadre* is dying." "Instead of a federal executive organ they introduce a fantastic interterritorial gathering, with a tremendous waste of money and time for hotels and receptions. Let's admit that these gatherings are good for politicians to get acquainted with one another. But in the participating ministers they develop first of all a sort of micro-nationalism, a feeling that they are commissioned to represent the interests of a restricted community" (JOSEPH KI-ZERBO). Cf. the collection of articles under the title "La loi-cadre" in *Présence Africaine*, Feb.-March 1958, pp. 69–124.
[4] See HOUPHOUËT-BOIGNY's speech of 1955 in Conakry.
[5] See SENGHOR's statement to UNESCO in June 1950.
[6] *Condition Humaine*, April 4, 1956.

that it favoured rather their antagonists, the steadily growing R.D.A. and its leader, HOUPHOUËT-BOIGNY, whose policies involved the danger of Africa being "balkanized", and therefore they thought it necessary to join forces against this danger.

The I.O.M. Congress of 1957 in Dakar

The African politicians declaring themselves socialists, who had rallied in the I.O.M. Movement under SENGHOR's leadership, met in Dakar on January 11–13, 1957. They resolved to unite their political parties operating in the several territories into an interterritorial political union. The congress was attended, besides the initiators SENGHOR and DIA, among others by NAZI BONI (Upper Volta), MAGA (Dahomey), ZODI (Niger), GRUNITZKY (Togoland), AUJOULAT (Cameroons), AUBAME (Gabon), and as observers by YOULOU (Middle Congo) from the R.D.A., BARRY DIAWADOU (Guinea) and OUÉDRAOGO (Upper Volta). The latter drew tempestuous ovations by his address, in which he called upon the "Big Three" (LAMINE GUÈYE, SENGHOR and HOUPHOUËT-BOIGNY) "to offer on the altar of Black Africa a bit of their self-love and prestige to let Africa be free".

As a result of the congress deliberations, the participants formed the proposed interterritorial party, called the *Convention Africaine*, with a combined programme containing the following essential points:

1. They favoured the idea of a "Federal Republic of France" comprising a "confederate union of free and equal nations".

2. They demanded a "reorganization and fusion of the African parties" as well as the creation of a common group of all overseas parliamentary deputies.

3. They protested against the "Balkanization" of France's African colonial empire, and demanded autonomy for the territories of French West Africa and French Equatorial Africa which, while maintaining their federal status, would constitute two states with the necessary joint official agencies and might be members of the Federal Republic.

4. They swore by socialism, in its Senghorian interpretation, which meant a socialism (!) corresponding to the "Negro-African spirit" and the "Negro-African reality of the twentieth century".

The African socialist deputies, who since 1953 had not followed SENGHOR but continued to keep in close touch with the French Socialist Party, precisely at the same time (January 11 to 13) as the I.O.M. congress was held, assembled in Conakry under the direction of LAMINE GUÈYE and also formed an interterritorial organization of unity of their local parties under the name of *Mouvement Socialiste Africain* (M.S.A.).

Attending the congress were among others LAMINE GUÈYE, SISSOKO (French Sudan), BARRY IBRAHIMA (Guinea), DJIBO BAKARY (Niger), JACQUES OPANGOULT (Middle Congo), CHARLES OKALA (Cameroons). The Secretary-General of the French Socialist Party (S.F.I.O.), PIERRE COMMIN, was also present.

The programme of the new organization, as laid down in the congress resolution, was differing from the stand adopted in Dakar in the following points:

1. As against the Dakar group, the M.S.A. did not demand autonomy for the African territories, it advocated only a "free association of metropolitan France and the overseas territories".

2. It rejected the single-party system and opted for a multi-party system on the grounds that "political democracy supposes the existence of several parties and

the guarantee of opposition rights". (No doubt, this stand was influenced as much by the "principle" as by the circumstance that the M.S.A. parties were almost everywhere the minority facing the parties of the R.D.A. and the Convention.)

3. Unlike the Convention, the M.S.A. did not break with the French Socialist Party; on the contrary, it stated that "the M.S.A. will take part in the Socialist International through its representatives included in the French delegation".

In accordance with this latter conception, the 21-men M.S.A. executive elected at the congress (with LAMINE GUÈYE as Chairman) included ex officio three members of the S.F.I.O. leadership, and vice versa, three M.S.A. leaders took part in the S.F.I.O. Executive Committee.

The Elections of March 1957

Elections under the *loi-cadre* were held in all territories in March 1957. This was the first introduction of universal suffrage in French colonies, with a common electoral roll of Africans and non-Africans; consequently Africans had a sweeping majority everywhere, so that they could send their own elected representatives to the Territorial Assemblies.

The elections were conducted amidst enthusiasm over the *loi-cadre*. Not only the R.D.A. parties, but also those affiliated to the M.S.A. and the Convention, conscious of their strength, looked confidently forward to the elections. Indeed, the R.D.A. scored much success, but the M.S.A. and the Convention attained relatively poor results. The R.D.A. gained nearly half of the seats (236 out of 476) in West Africa, obtaining the majority and coming into power in four territories (Ivory Coast, Sudan, Guinea, Upper Volta), while in Equatorial Africa it won a sweeping victory (46 seats against 15 won by the local party) in Chad, where it also took over the government. Among the West African territories, SENGHOR's Convention won only in Senegal, obtaining not even an insignificant minority in other territories. And in Equatorial Africa it gained a majority of two in Gabon (18 seats against 8 won by the R.D.A. and 8 by the local party), and obtained not a single seat anywhere else. The M.S.A. managed to win a majority in Niger alone. Local parties obtained the majority and formed the governments in Mauritania, Dahomey, the Middle Congo and Ubangi-Shari.

The brilliant election results of the R.D.A. were taken by HOUPHOUËT-BOIGNY for a triumph of his own policy which would guarantee his future success. SÉKOU TOURÉ, though his political views were different from the ideas of the "leader", was also pleased with the movement's success, because he thought that the new positions would provide a broader basis for the party to struggle for independence. In an interview given after the elections he said:

"We hope everybody understands the decisive change achieved by the people, and that all would reach an honest agreement on a sensible programme, after leaving behind victories and defeats, to set about the constructive work which alone can fulfil the great hope born of the March 31 elections. In this way we offer our fraternal hands to all. We want a harmonious rallying, not round one man, but round the higher interests of Africa."

How much of this optimism of SÉKOU TOURÉ became reality was revealed by the R.D.A. conference six months later.

The third conference of the R.D.A. took place at Bamako from September 25 to 30, 1957. In contrast to the first two conferences (1946 and 1949), which the R.D.A. had to put through as a persecuted party, under difficult conditions, the third conference was held by a political movement which was not only officially recognized, but which enjoyed the support and esteem of the French government and the bourgeois parties. Participating in the conference, in addition to 254 delegates of R.D.A. parties (80 from the French Sudan, 31 from Guinea, 30 from the Ivory Coast, Senegal, Niger and Upper Volta each, 8 from Chad, 7 from Dahomey, 5 from the Middle Congo and 3 from Gabon), were leaders of non-R.D.A. parties and trade unions as guests (among them LAMINE GUÈYE and MAMADOU DIA), as well as representatives of the M.R.P. and other French bourgeois parties, and even the Prime Minister of France himself (MENDÈS-FRANCE) with two French cabinet members (FRANÇOIS MITTERRAND and EDGAR FAURE). Characteristically, the 254 delegates included all in all 53 "workers and employees", 17 peasants and 17 "businessmen and artisans", and as many as 162 officials and civil servants, plus 5 chiefs.

The conference took place in the spirit of HOUPHOUËT-BOIGNY's increased prestige and of the unity of the movement. There was no visible opposition. Instead of making an open general attack on HOUPHOUËT-BOIGNY's prestige as "leader" and his policy, the opponents chose to raise certain concrete questions in support of their position. D'ARBOUSSIER, for example, who at the time was a member of the Niger Territorial Assembly and Vice-President of the Grand Council of French West Africa, had made peace with HOUPHOUËT-BOIGNY in the meantime, and appealed to the delegates "to put aside for the moment the demand for independence when the question is of how to improve the situation of the popular masses". The other great theoretical opponent, SÉKOU TOURÉ, also called the members for unity: "Join forces for Africa to hold out more proudly in union with France."[1] It was but an exception that the conference had to hear a dissonant voice from an invited guest from the African students' association in Paris (F.E.A.N.F.), EMMANUEL BATIEBO, who called the *loi-cadre* a "colonialist bluff" and accused the R.D.A. of "having entirely left its policy line and betrayed the African masses"[2].

The deliberations of the conference bore evidence, on the other hand, that many delegates were opposed to HOUPHOUËT-BOIGNY's opportunist policy on several points, and this was reflected by the resolution passed by the conference. A typical example was the way they treated the most burning problem of France, the question of Algeria. HOUPHOUËT-BOIGNY raised the idea of calling upon the Algerian freedom fighters to surrender and to join the French Union. The conference, however, in a resolution moved by SÉKOU TOURÉ, requested the French government to enter into talks with "competent leaders of the Algerian people".

The conference resolutions might serve as typical examples of a flexible revolutionary diplomacy. Without repudiating the policy of HOUPHOUËT-BOIGNY in outspoken and explicit terms, the resolutions expressed the ideas of SÉKOU TOURÉ and D'ARBOUSSIER, either by flexibly recasting HOUPHOUËT-BOIGNY's words to suit their interpretation, or by mixing the two conceptions, thus giving them an entirely different meaning.

[1] ANDRÉ BLANCHET, *L'itinéraire des partis africains depuis Bamako*, Paris, 1958, p. 30.
[2] *Op. cit.*, p. 9.

The resolutions reiterated, for example, the theses of HOUPHOUËT-BOIGNY about "interdependence" as "the golden rule of life of the peoples" but stressed at the same time "the inalienable right of peoples to independence". Or, for example, his idea that the overseas territories as states enjoying internal autonomy should unite with France, under French direction, in a large federation with a common parliament and a common government, was given expression in the political resolution of the conference as follows:

"The conference is of the opinion that Black Africa's belonging to a large political and economic community is for all members a factor of power and real independence, therefore it proposes the strengthening of a democratic and fraternal Franco-African community based on equality."

Instead of endorsing HOUPHOUËT-BOIGNY's idea of a federation comprising France and all the African and other overseas territories, the conference took a stand in favour of establishing a democratic federation of the territories — amassed in federal groups by the colonialists, that is, the countries of French West Africa and French Equatorial Africa — within the Franco-African community:

"The Conference authorizes the parliamentary groups to submit at the earliest possible time a draft bill on the establishment of a federation made up of autonomous states, with a federal government and a federal parliament as the supreme authority of the federated states.

"Aware of the fact that the territories are linked by strong economic, political and cultural ties, and in the interest of the future of the African community, it authorizes the parliamentary deputies to submit a draft bill on democratization of the existing federal executive organs..."

The conference resolutions thus chimed in with the contradictory spirit characteristic of the R.D.A. at the time: complete unity in appearance, swing to the left in essence. This is borne out also by the evaluation of the *loi-cadre* given in the political resolution ("The Conference considers the *loi-cadre* to be an irreversible step on the road towards the liberation of the African population") and still more by the decision of the conference (against HOUPHOUËT-BOIGNY's intentions) to point out the timeliness of uniting all African parties in a single front. On this point the political resolution stated:

"The Conference welcomes the historic meeting of all African political organizations and their representatives taking part in its work as well as the presence of the parties of the metropolitan countries who make joint efforts to secure the creation of a large popular community uniting the people of France with the peoples of the overseas territories.

"The Conference confirms that the R.D.A. continues to regard it as its mission to combine all living forces of the movement and notes with satisfaction the proposals, supported by all African political parties, for a meeting with a view to regrouping the parties, and authorizes the R.D.A. co-ordinating committee to organize that meeting."[1]

In the eye of the outside world the highly respected HOUPHOUËT-BOIGNY remained the leader of the movement. He was elected President unanimously, the Vice-Presidents were SÉKOU TOURÉ and MODIBO KEITA, and D'ARBOUSSIER again became one of the secretaries of the movement. Characteristic of the situation was what SÉKOU

---

[1] For the full text of the political resolution, see F. ANSPRENGER, *Politik im Schwarzen Afrika*, Appendix, pp. 463–465.

Touré said in his address at the closing meeting of the conference: "Félix Hou-phouët-Boigny continues to be our President, but in the French government he will represent, not his own ideas, but the ideas of the R.D.A."

The Regrouping Conferences of 1958

The R.D.A.'s resounding success in the March elections and the third conference held with the participation of delegates from almost all African political parties and of leading French politicians, a gathering which was followed with wide interest and which outwardly demonstrated the unity of the R.D.A. movement, impelled the leaders of the Convention Africaine to take an initiative for the establishment of a united front of all African parties.

On October 19, 1957, SENGHOR and DIA offered the R.D.A. leaders to take a joint action. On November 2 the R.D.A. co-ordinating committee gave its assent in principle. SENGHOR then proposed as a minimum programme the creation of a "united political movement socialist in spirit". Subsequently, in an exchange of letters between LISETTE and SISSOKO, the R.D.A. recommended the union, also within each territory, of all parties operating there. At the Regrouping Conference which met in Paris on February 15, 1958, the politicians representing different currents of opinion and thus far opposed to one another(among them SÉKOU TOURÉ and BARRY DIAWADOU, DJIBO BAKARY and HAMANI DIORI, OUEZZIN COULIBALY and NAZI BONI) not only took part but they all subscribed to SENGHOR's fundamental idea of a "Federal Republic of France" whose every member should be given the "right to independence". The conference proclaimed the union of the attending parties, and an agreement was arrived at even on the details. Only one point remained undecided: what should be the name of the new united party. And, strange and even ridiculous as it may seem, this turned out to be the banana skin on which the formation of the united party slipped up in spite of the alleged agreement in principle. The participants of the conference again met in Dakar on March 26, with a view to finding an agreed name, but this second Regrouping Conference also failed. The R.D.A. leaders insisted on retaining the already traditional name of their movement, but the others showed no inclination to agree, because acceptence of the name R.D.A. would have made the African masses believe that all politicians recognized HOU-PHOUËT-BOIGNY as their leader.

De Gaulle's 1958 Constitution and the African Colonies

After coming into power in May 1958, General CHARLES DE GAULLE received from the National Assembly on June 3 a mandate to work out a new constitution. On July 30 the government published the provisional draft, which was first to be discussed by a constitutional committee formed of parliamentary deputies. On August 14, the committee proposed some modifications, and the government on August 21 announced its decision, which actually was DE GAULLE's personal decision, and submitted the draft to the Council of State. The same day DE GAULLE set out on a surprise visit to the French African colonies, in order to use his personal influence to persuade the African political leaders to accept the constitution under preparation. On August 29, two days after his return home, the Council of State finished its business by endorsing the draft. On September 3 the government definitively approved the text of the draft, which was published officially the next day with the proviso that a referendum to be held on September 28, with the participation of the entire population of France and the overseas territories, should decide on its final adoption and enactment or on its rejection.

The original draft contained a number of points which would have been entirely unacceptable to the Africans. But the constitutional committee, which included also African members (SENGHOR, LAMINE GUÈYE, LISETTE as representatives of HOUPHOUËT-BOIGNY, and PHILIBERT TSIRANANA), proposed substantial changes which came nearer to the views of the Africans. President DE GAULLE's statesmanship is evidenced by his acceptance of most of those changes. He even went further than the committee had proposed, while on some other details he remained adamant.

The most essential differences from the first draft were the following:

The original version mentioned a "federation" whose members "enjoy autonomy and are free to handle their affairs", but the members were not styled states. In the final text the members were called states and the federation a "community of free peoples". This was a concession from DE GAULLE.

The original draft envisaged no separate federal parliament, but the overseas territories were to send representatives to the French Senate. The constitutional committee proposed an Assembly of the Community composed of parliamentary deputies from the member states, having competence mainly in external affairs and economic matters. President DE GAULLE consented instead to the establishment of a special assembly called the Senate of the Community with reduced powers: it could pass mandatory decisions only if authorized by the legislatures of all member states.

The original draft envisaged no executive organ (government) of the Community. The constitutional committee proposed an Executive Council composed of the Prime Ministers of the member states and of departmental ministers in charge of the common affairs. President DE GAULLE agreed to this, too.

Originally the common affairs were: foreign affairs, defence, joint economic and financial policies, production of strategic materials, justice and higher education. The constitutional committee added to them also transportation and telecommunications, and laid down that the African states might conclude separate bilateral agreements with France only for matters concerning justice, higher education and transportation. President DE GAULLE accepted the distinction between common affairs and those which might be regulated by separate agreements, but gave wider scope for the conclusion of such agreements.

Under the terms of the original draft the African countries were to become members of the French Community of their own free will, by adopting the constitution, but thereby they waived their right of self-determination and could not claim independence. The draft mentioned, beside the "French Community", also the "Community of free peoples", but thereby it understood France's relations, not with the African countries, but with the already independent ex-colonies (Morocco, Tunisia). On the other hand, the constitutional committee proposed that, once the Community constitution was adopted, the African countries should be entitled, after five years, to choose the status of an autonomous state belonging to the Community. President DE GAULLE recognized the Community members' right to choose their own status (not even after five years, but any time), and stated in the final text of the constitution that a member state of the Community had the right to be granted independence, but he added that "by acceding to independence it shall cease to be a member of the Community".

In spite of these concessions the constitution served the neocolonialist aspiration of the French imperialists, DE GAULLE included. Its primary aim was to prevent the

African countries from becoming independent states, and the newly established Community served to ensure the political and economic leading role of the French colonialists, the priority of the interests of the French monopoly-capitalist bourgeoisie. Consequently the constitution was unacceptable not only to those who refused to give up the main aspirations of the African peoples, the achievement of independence, but it was diametrically opposed to all conceptions and requirements which the African politicians adhering to different political views raised in their memoranda when waiting for the publication of the constitutional proposals. Here are a few excerpts from such documents.

From LÉOPOLD SENGHOR's memorandum of June 28 to President DE GAULLE:
"The constitution has to create equality between the metropolitan country and the overseas territories. It has to establish their association (or federation) and proclaim their right to independence and also to internal reorganization. The overseas territories have to obtain a share in the organs of the association, their delegates together with the delegates of the metropolitan country should elect the common head of state, who should be their leader and arbiter at the same time, and their deputies should take part in the government of the association and in both chambers of its parliament."

From SENGHOR's and DIA's joint memorandum of July 9:
"The constitution has to establish a Federal Republic . . . but classical federalism is out of the question. The Federal Republic must not deter the constituent republics with strong legislative powers. The most important authority is the President of the Federation. The powers recognized by general agreement as powers of the federation should be vested primarily in the executive. But beside the President of the Federation there may function a Congress as a liaison organ where delegates from the parliaments of the overseas territories and of the metropolitan country would meet. This Congress, even without major legislative powers, may play an important part from the point of view of the cohesion of the Federal Republic."

From HOUPHOUËT-BOIGNY's draft constitution of July 16, 1958:
"The peoples of Africa and Madagascar . . . know well that they will for a long time need close co-operation with France. They are aware that they live in a century in which only large political and economic entities count. In the free exercise of their right to self-determination they have declared through their elected representatives that they will renounce the right to secede in order to form a federation with France based on the absolute equality of rights and duties."

On July 17 the R.D.A. and the opposition P.R.A. *(Parti du Regroupement Africain)* addressed to DE GAULLE another joint memorandum (signed by LISETTE and YACÉ on behalf of the R.D.A. and by SENGHOR and MAMADOU DIA on behalf of the P.R.A.),[1] and with reference to the resolution of the Regrouping Conference held in Paris in February, laid down the principles upon which in their view the constitution should be built. The main points of their proposal were as follows:

"1. The association of the peoples of France and the overseas territories, in the form of a Federal Republic, is based on the recognition of the right of self-determination of the overseas peoples. All inhabitants have equal rights and freedoms guaranteed by the federal constitution which shall be observed by all member states.

"2. The Federal Republic is composed of autonomous states. These states may form groups and as such become a member of the Federal Republic.

[1] It was signed also by MAURICE LENORMAND, the representative of New Caledonia.

"3. The Federal Republic has a unicameral federal parliament and a federal government."

But the federal parliament was not intended as a legislative organ. Point 5 of the proposal provided in this respect as follows:

"5. The federal parliament is made up of representatives of the member states of the Federation on an equal basis. The federal parliament shall deal with the common affairs. It may recommend the passage of uniform laws and may accept commissions for working out such legislation."

The scope of authority of the Federation would be limited to foreign affairs, defence, common economic and financial matters, higher education and justice.

In contrast to the well-sounding but essentially more or less compromising views, SÉKOU TOURÉ stated with unambiguous determination on July 24:

"Public opinion must know that we unanimously and definitely reject any constitutional proposal which does not break deliberately and resolutely with the impossible old policy of assimilation and integration, which does not recognize the right of the overseas peoples to independence and does not lay down the principle of the equality of peoples."

A week after the presentation of the joint memorandum in Paris, immediately before the provisional draft was referred to the constitutional committee, another African contribution was made, in Cotonou, at the inaugural congress of the P.R.A., at the initiative of SENGHOR and LAMINE GUÈYE, but not in their spirit .

Formation of the P.R.A.

After the failure of the Regrouping Conferences of the African parties in Paris in February 1958 and in Dakar in March, the parties affiliated with the Convention Africaine and the M.S.A. continued their negotiations for the creation of a unitary interterritorial organization. The successful conclusion of the discussions was decisively promoted by the change of regime in France (DE GAULLE's coming into power). The parties rivalling with one another within their respective territories, in order to join forces in the new situation, created unified parties in each territory, and the leaders of the Convention and the M.S.A. called all the parties under their influence to a joint congress to form a unitary interterritorial organization.

Held in Cotonou (Dahomey) from June 25 to 27, 1958, the congress succeeded, by an agreement of all parties present, in establishing the *Parti du Regroupement Africain* (P.R.A.).

On this single issue the congress displayed complete unity, but the political aspect of the congress was indicative of a gap between the policy of the leaders (notably SENGHOR) and the delegates' views expressing the will of the masses.

In his report to the congress SENGHOR stressed that "we first want an African community before the Franco-African community!", but his idea of the latter was a transformation of "one and indivisible" France into a "Federal Republic of France", in which the African countries would also be members, but not as independent states, and which would constitute a confederation (a commonwealth French fashion) with all former French colonies (Morocco, Tunisia, Indochina). "The division of powers between the federation and the member states is simple: all matters of international importance — like diplomacy, defence, finance, higher education, judiciary — should be dealt with by the federation."

In this congress SENGHOR definitively threw off the mask: he disclosed that what he regarded as the objective of the movement was not independence for the African countries, but only internal autonomy under the neocolonialist rule of French imperialism. Further on in his speech he made a confused and demagogic statement against demanding independence:

"Real independence cannot be introduced from above, it must be deserved and won. It is high time for us to face the realities reasonably ... to get down to our concrete problems ... Independence has no positive content. To be independent means to be dependent on no one. By the way, this is only a grammatical definition of the concept, for nowadays every state is largely dependent on another state, even though not on all other states, including the United States and the Soviet Union... It stands to reason that, for a nation to live and thrive, it is not enough to be dependent on no one. It has to control itself, to organize and to work ... Let us guard against misusing the word independence. It is too comfortable a word, which may hide cowardice or lack of imagination. Therefore we prefer such positive concepts as are self-determination and autonomy. Not that we refuse independence. We have proclaimed our right to independence. The final form of our political evolution will necessarily be nominal independence. And it is well like this. But I declare that this legalistic formula does not give us the content, which is effective independence ... Independence is a victory which we win, not so much over others as rather over ourselves, not so much by force of arms as rather by the sweat of our brows."[1]

The majority of the delegates, however, were unwilling to accept this policy of compromise. In the debate following SENGHOR's speech impassioned statements were made by delegates one after another. BAKARY and SISSOKO, DIAWADOU and NAZI BONI spoke in terms of vehement criticism about the "horror regime" of the French colonialists and their atrocities, the "cynical exploitation" of the colonies. And speaker after speaker stood up to demand independence: "It is time to put a stop to idle talk and word-splitting. Independence for French West Africa immediately! Or else we, the people of Niger, will join other states which will soon become independent, Nigeria for instance" (BAKARY). "Today the possibility exists for us to demand independence at once. But we accept a multinational confederation with France" (ABDOULAY LY). "We cannot divide ourselves between our two countries. We cannot teach our children to be African and French at the same time. We want to be African in the first place" (Mme QUENUM of Dahomey).

These oppositionist elements got the upper hand in the congress. The political resolution did not reflect SENGHOR's opportunistic ideas, but gave expression to the radical demands of the opposition: the congress demanded independence, and community with France only after independence:

"The Congress adopts the slogan of immediate independence and decides to take all necessary measures to mobilize the African masses in support of this slogan and to realize this desire for independence. It takes a position in favour of creating a strong, progressive African community before undertaking political co-operation with any other community on the basis of equality . . . It proposes negotiations with France on the establishment of a multinational confederation of free and equal nations without renouncing the African desire to unite all former colonies in a Federation of the United States of Africa."[2]

[1] The text of SENGHOR's speech was published, still before it was delivered, by the Paris weekly *France-Observateur* in its issue of July 24 under the title "Les mouvements africains devant la constitution".

[2] Cf. ANDRÉ BLANCHET, "Cotonou — le congrès de la rupture?", *Marchés Tropicaux*, Aug. 9, 1958.

SENGHOR and LAMINE GUÈYE, although this resolution was passed against their intentions, saw it better not to oppose it, lest they should jeopardize the unity just achieved. They let the congress adopt the resolution unanimously, by acclamation, neither did they object to the election of BAKARY as Secretary-General of the P.R.A.

But the triumph of the supporters of the idea of independence did not last long. Back in Paris, the leaders, in spite of the resolution they themselves had applauded, persistently pursued their policy of opportunism. It took them only two months (August–September) to win back to their policy the majority of those who had so enthusiastically stood by the Cotonou resolution, and so they managed to win them over to voting "yes" in the referendum.

Yet the Cotonou congress had some positive result, too. The resolution in question really mobilized broad masses of Africans to support the demand for independence, and its impact made itself strongly felt even after the backing down of a number of parties. Party members abiding by the Cotonou resolution left the dissident parties and in several places formed new minority parties to fight for independence.

The public mood that was reflected in the Cotonou congress resolution had doubtless been instrumental in the fact that during his tour of Africa in August DE GAULLE was compelled to revise his unflexible position to some extent.

De Gaulle's Tour of Africa

CHARLES DE GAULLE's six-day propaganda tour of Africa provided two convincing bits of evidence: (1) it was a demonstrative illustration of the General's amazing capability of quickly recognizing the realities and flexibly changing his policy by taking these realities into consideration; (2) it gave incontestable evidence that the great democratic and antifascist fighter and French patriot, for all his high-falutin speeches, essentially pursued, though in a different garb, the antidemocratic and colonialist policy of his predecessors.

At the first stop on his journey, in Tananarive (Madagascar), he said on August 20 that each territory was entirely free to decide whether or not to accept the proposed new constitution, but if it voted "yes" it would commit itself for ever to be a member of the French Community, and if it voted "no" it would mean a complete break with France and the other members of the Community. In his speech he did not even utter the word "independence". At the second station of his tour, in Brazzaville, he spent two days (August 23–24) and conferred with the President of the Grand Council of French Equatorial Africa, BARTHÉLEMY BOGANDA, who let him know that if he insisted on this rigid standpoint he would have to reckon with the secession of several territories. Prompted by this hint, DE GAULLE used a different language in his speech at Brazzaville on August 24:

"You say: we have the right to independence. Of course, you have. Whoever wants independence may get it at once. The metropolitan country will not object. Any territory can get it immediately if it votes 'no' on September 28. This will mean that it wants to go its own way, in isolation, on its own account and at its own risk. In other words, it chooses secession. The metropolitan country will draw the necessary conclusion but, I guarantee, it will not object . . . And what is more, if in the course of time a territory . . . feels capable of undertaking all burdens and responsibilities of independence, all right, it will be its business to decide through its own elected representatives . . . I guarantee in advance that the metropolitan country will not object in this case either."

On August 25 at the next stop, in Conakry, Sékou Touré, in his address of welcome to de Gaulle, categorically stated that Guinea wanted independence:

"We only work hard to secure our own future and the happiness of our people ... More important to us than anything is our human dignity, which we refuse to renounce. But this is conditional upon freedom, because any oppression, any coercion, frustrates the human dignity of him who is oppressed, compulsively humiliates him into an inferior being. We prefer poverty in liberty to riches in slavery!"

He emphasized at the same time that they did not wish to sever relationship with France, they considered it necessary, provided that it was free from all coercion:

"Our hearts and our minds — and what is more, our obvious interests — command us to choose independence and freedom. We do not want to secure our position either with France or against France.

"Today, considering the evolution of the international situation, and especially the enormous progress made in dependent countries by the anticolonialist movement, we can state that the military power of a country threatening the freedom of another can guarantee neither the prestige nor the interests of the metropolitan country. The future guarantee of France's interests and evolution in Africa can be only in free association with the overseas countries. The economic and cultural activities of France will continue to be indispensable to the harmonious and rapid development of the overseas territories. However, Guinea demands the freedom to leave, so that the Franco-African marriage will not in time seem to be an arbitrary construction imposed upon the rising generations."

Having understood that his game was lost in Guinea, de Gaulle, to "save face", in his reply made the following hypocritical statement:

"France compels nobody to enter into the Community ... The talk here has been on independence. I declare, more loudly here than in other places, that independence is available to Guinea. She may win it, she may obtain it on September 28 by voting 'no'. I guarantee that the metropolitan country will not object. It will draw the necessary conclusions, of course, but it will not oppose."

He was more frank with his other reply, which he gave by excusing himself from going to dinner with Sékou Touré in the evening "in view of the terms used by Sékou Touré in his speech".

On taking his leave next morning de Gaulle wished Guinea good luck ("Bonne chance pour la Guinée!"), he was insincere again, because he was determined, should Guinea choose independence which he "will not oppose", to do everything in his power to make life worse for Guinea.

At the last station of his journey, in Dakar, de Gaulle was received on August 26 by a demonstrating crowd of thousands of Africans (among them the rank and file of the P.R.A.) demanding independence at once and shouting slogans vilifying the General and the French Community.

The Referendum of September 1958

The African political leaders utilized the month that went by between de Gaulle's visit and the referendum (August 27 to September 27) for preparing the masses for the voting: Houphouët-Boigny and Senghor encouraged their followers to vote "yes", Sékou Touré and Bakary called upon them to vote "no".

On his arrival in Paris on August 29, Houphouët-Boigny made a statement expressing his conviction that "every responsible African and the working African population will vote 'yes' ... All the territories will vote 'yes'." And in a campaign speech in Abidjan on September 9, arguing with SENGHOR's supporters, he said mockingly:

"In Cotonou they raised the issue of immediate independence forcibly. They thought they would confound the R.D.A. delegates and could present them as traitors to Africa. They themselves believed not a word of what they talked about in Cotonou. General de Gaulle pledges them plainly that on September 28 they can win independence at once. Let them take it. But they won't ..."

Further on in his speech he stepped up mockery contesting the well-known view of SÉKOU TOURÉ (without calling him by name for obvious reasons):

"The time has come when certain formulas ... are no longer valid. In former times they said: 'I prefer to be first in my village rather than be second in Rome.' Now I tell you: 'I prefer to be the millionth member of a solid, powerful, rich community which is respected by the world, and which is able in itself, with the enormous resources available, to ensure man's balanced development, to raise his humanity to a higher level, rather than be first in a miserable state.'"[1]

At a P.R.A. executive meeting in Niamey on September 14, SENGHOR, who like HOUPHOUËT-BOIGNY was canvassing for "yes" votes, responding to the latter's attack against the Cotonou congress, repudiated the charge that the P.R.A. actually wanted independence:

"The opponents of voting 'yes' rely on the sentence of the resolution beginning with 'It accepts the slogan of immediate independence ...' The argument is weak. In French the words have precise meanings. The resolution does not say: 'It demands immediate independence', but it says: 'It accepts the slogan of immediate independence', namely the question is only a formula which lends wings to imagination. In other words, it is a slogan intended 'to mobilize the African masses'."

In the same breath he also gave the reasons why his party did not demand independence at once:

"Independence must be paid for. Independence implies also that groundnut prices should be adjusted to world market prices, that wages and salaries should perhaps be lowered, as was done in Morocco and Tunisia. This is no reason for renouncing independence, but reason enough to organize it well."[2]

The only one of the political leaders who resolutely advocated voting "no" was SÉKOU TOURÉ. On September 14 at a territorial meeting of his party he said:

"Guinea cannot afford to be told some day: 'You missed independence, you must now submit to dependence.' We shall be an independent nation as of September 29. We shall take over all responsibility for our own affairs ... We pay respect to the present government of France for its gesture of great international, moral and political significance. ... We shall thus keep up our fraternal relations with the French people. From now on, with the Europeans living in this country we shall form a community of free and equal people. Capital investments made now or in the future will enjoy increased security."[3]

In the referendum held in September 28, 1958, Guinea — alone among all French colonies — voted "no" and became an independent state on October 3.

BAKARY's government party on Niger, the *Union Démocratique Nigérienne*, was defeated by the opposition R.D.A. party, the *Party Progressiste Nigérien*, which

[1] *Discours à Abidjan*, Sept. 7, 1958.
[2] SENGHOR, "Parfaire l'unité africaine", *Afrique Nouvelle*, Sept. 26, 1958.
[3] SÉKOU TOURÉ, *L'expérience guinéenne*, pp. 176–182.

voted "yes" and gained 78 per cent of the vote, thereby bringing about the fall of the BAKARY government.

This was how, despite the African majority's dreaming about independence everywhere, and as a result of the compromising policy of the party leaders, none of the French colonies except Guinea made use of the opportunity to win it.

General DE GAULLE failed to keep the promise he had made in his speech at Conakry. After the proclamation of independence France broke all connections with Guinea. The French specialists employed in Guinea (officials, doctors, engineers, technicians, teachers, etc.), who numbered more than four thousand, left the country precipitately, taking with them everything that could be moved.

The Birth and Demise of the French Community

Following the referendum, during November and December, all the former French colonies that had voted "yes" asked for admission to the French Community. Subsequently each new republic drew up its own constitution, under which it would have a unicameral parliament and a parliamentary government headed by a Prime Minister who, following the American example, was also head of state. Thereby the ex-colonies seceded from France and chose to belong to the Community on the same basis as the French Republic. Since accordingly they sent no more deputies to the French National Assembly and Senate, the French government, to secure its close relationship with the African political leaders, on May 27, 1959, issued a decree by which each member state of the Community delegated to the Paris government an African "minister-councillor". At the end of July DE GAULLE appointed HOUPHOUËT-BOIGNY Minister-Councillor for Foreign Affairs, LISETTE for economic and social policy, SENGHOR for cultural affairs, and TSIRANANA for national defence.

With the adoption of the DE GAULLE constitution there was born the "Fifth Republic", together with the much talked-of French Community, whose short history of a year and a half eloquently demonstrates that it was, though not still-born, unfit to live. The Executive Council of the Community, which included the Prime Ministers and departmental ministers of the African member states as well, met for a couple of days seven times in a year and a half,[1] to discuss the work of the public agencies, financial matters, joint defence, higher education, radio frequencies and the like, and primarily to co-ordinate as far as possible the political aspirations of the member states. But those discussions were of no practical consequence, because the decisions were subject to President DE GAULLE's authoritative and non-appealable opinion.

Still more pitiable is the operetta-like story of the Senate of the Community. This pseudo-parliament of the French Community met only twice — as was put pertinently by GEORGES BIDAULT — first to celebrate its birth, and again to attend its own funeral.

As early as December 1958, half a year before the first meeting of the Community Senate (July 15 to 31, 1959), African federalists had started an action which was to lead to the establishment of the Federation of Mali and then of the Entente

---

[1] During 1959 such meetings took place in February, March and May at Paris, in July at Tananarive, in September again at Paris, in December at Saint-Louis, and the last meeting was held at Paris in January 1960.

Council during 1959, when later the Federation of Mali and Madagascar raised their demand for independence. Ultimately it led to the independence of all former French colonies in the course of 1960, thus burying the French Community in its form received from the 1958 referendum.

Delegations of federalists from Senegal, the French Sudan, Dahomey and Upper Volta — headed by SENGHOR and LAMINE GUÈYE on behalf of the P.R.A., and by MODIBO KEITA and D'ARBOUSSIER on behalf of the R.D.A. — held a conference at Bamako on December 29 and 30, 1958. The conference, under the chairmanship of SOUROU APITHY of Dahomey, decided to unite the four countries in the Federation of Mali. They called together delegates from the Territorial Assemblies of the four countries to a constituent meeting in Dakar for January 14, 1959. On the 17th, the meeting proclaimed the formation of the Federation of Mali. However, HOU-PHOUËT-BOIGNY managed to dissuade Dahomey and Upper Volta from participating in the new federal state. APITHY announced Dahomey's withdrawal early in February, and YAMÉOGO followed suit on behalf of Upper Volta early in March. Consequently the Federation of Mali subsisted for a while as an association of two states, Senegal and the French Sudan. In Dakar on March 24, 1959, after leaving the P.R.A. and the R.D.A. respectively, the leading parties of the two federated countries, joining with the opposition parties of Dahomey, Niger and Upper Volta, formed a new inter-territorial organization, the *Parti de la Fédération Africaine* (P.F.A.).

The federal parliament of the new state, composed of twelve delegates each from the Territorial Assemblies of Senegal and Sudan, met in Dakar on April 4 to elect the President and the government of the federal state. SENGHOR was elected head of state and MODIBO KEITA was appointed Premier of the federal government made up of eight members (four for each federal state).

As early as December 4, 1958, HOUPHOUËT-BOIGNY announced a claim of the Ivory Coast to membership in the French Community, and stressed at the same time that he opposed the creation of a regional African community, because in his view "the establishment of such a community would impose a needless burden and would ultimately lead to a confederation with France, which would thus comprise two communities instead of one". Whereas now, to counterbalance the Federation of Mali, he succeeded in persuading Dahomey, Niger and Upper Volta (the three countries where he was in a position to exercise his influence, since the R.D.A. parties wielded the majority in their Territorial Assemblies and governments) to form the Entente Council, though not a political federation, but a loose association with the Ivory Coast under its leadership and guidance. The Entente was definitively formed at a meeting of the Prime Ministers (as well as parliamentary presidents and departmental ministers) of the four countries in Abidjan on May 29, 1959. No joint political agencies were set up, but the Entente Council composed of the Prime Ministers and other competent ministers of the member countries only dealt with economic and social questions.

SENGHOR's and MODIBO KEITA's new common front, the P.F.A., held its first congress from July 1 to 3, 1959. The composition of the elected executives of the party expressed a stable equilibrium of Senegal and Sudan (SENGHOR was President, MODIBO KEITA Secretary-General, BAKARY and ZINSOU Vice-Presidents, and the other leading functionaries were elected on a fifty-fifty basis from among Senegalese and Sudanese members), and the political resolution of the congress reflected an alloy of the programmes of SENGHOR and MODIBO KEITA: it took a stand in favour of African unity, national independence, the "interdependence of nations", as well as the "African road to socialism".

In the following months, after managing to lure the three other West African countries taking his advice into a loose association under his control and in accordance with the interests of the Ivory Coast, HOUPHOUËT-BOIGNY used every effort to silence the still restless oppositionist faction of the R.D.A. parties in the Entente countries, and he succeeded for the time being. Having satisfied himself that he had nothing to fear from any serious opposition within the party, he summoned the congress of the R.D.A.

At the congress, which was held at Abidjan from September 3 to 5, HOUPHOUËT-BOIGNY, who thought he was absolute master of the movement after SÉKOU TOURÉ and MODIBO KEITA had left the R.D.A., spoke in biting terms about the "sensation-mongering loud-mouthed militants" who were campaigning from behind the screen of "African federation, African unity":

"Our opponents lay emphasis on the word 'freedom' and on the word 'independence'. What matters to us are not the words, but the 'reality' of freedom and independence . . . Our ultimate aim is to create a great federation or confederation (the word means little!) which is made up of autonomous states, including the French Republic. These states should settle their affairs by themselves, as is done in Canada, Switzerland, the United States or in the Soviet Union, but with a genuine federal (or confederate) government and a genuine federal (or confederate) parliament. We deliberately make no distinction between federal and confederate. We are not worried about the words, provided that both have the same content."

The orations of the other speakers at the congress were characterized by flattering verbiage extolling HOUPHOUËT-BOIGNY and DE GAULLE.[22]

The R.D.A. congress flowing with loyalty was already meeting when the September 4 issue of Le Monde published a statement by MAMADOU DIA declaring that "Senegal and Sudan wish the Community to be transformed into a multinational confederation". A few days later, on September 11, Senegal and Sudan informed the Executive Council of the Community of their determination to make use of their constitutionally guaranteed right to independence.

On September 29 SENGHOR, as head of the Mali delegation, presented a memorandum to DE GAULLE, stating that the Federation of Mali even as an independent state wished to remain a member of the Community. At first DE GAULLE adopted a negative attitude but the current political transformations in Africa (the existence of newly independent states bordering on the former French colonies — Eastern Sudan, Ghana, Guinea — and the forthcoming independence of the trust territories of the Cameroons and Togoland), and the increasing activity of the African independence movements whose representatives more and more frequently appeared before the international forum of the United Nations to put forward their complaints and demands, finally convinced the General that Paris could maintain its influence and positions in the ex-colonies only if it gave up its inflexible attitude.

In December 1959 DE GAULLE went to Saint-Louis in Senegal to attend the sixth session of the Executive Council of the Community. In his speech at the meeting of December 12, and next day in the federal parliament in Dakar he solemnly acceded to the demand of the Federation of Mali, feigning that the September 1958 constitution had provided for this contingency.

[22] From YAMÉOGO's closing speech: "Our General is President Houphouët-Boigny . . . Christ himself, the first revolutionary in the world, said: *Ecce qua bonum et qua jucundum habitare fratres in unum.* [Behold how good and pleasant it is to see brethren dwell together in unity.] With his humane law General de Gaulle reminded us of our common descent. Follow the teaching of the President of the R.D.A. and foster the community spirit."

Encouraged by the example of the Federation of Mali, PHILIBERT TSIRANANA, while in Paris on his way home from a voyage to America, on December 27 let DE GAULLE know that Madagascar also demanded independence but wished to remain in the Community. President DE GAULLE agreed to this, too.

On January 1 the French trust territory of the Cameroons became an independent state. It was followed by Togoland on April 27.

On January 18 negotiations began in Paris between France and Madagascar. France signed an agreement with Madagascar on April 2 and with the Federation of Mali on April 4, granting them independence by June 20. At the same time another agreement was initialled providing for co-operation with France after independence.

The agreement with the Federation of Mali stirred even HOUPHOUËT-BOIGNY, although thus far he had spoken only mockingly and disparagingly of those who advocated independence. On the day the agreement was signed he declared: "No matter what the outcome of the current developments may be, the Ivory Coast and her friends will never be willing to accept an inferior position either in Africa or in the formation which is now called the renewed French Community." On April 16 the Entente commissioned HOUPHOUËT-BOIGNY to submit to DE GAULLE the demands of the Entente countries. HOUPHOUËT-BOIGNY had a talk with DE GAULLE on June 1, and two days later the Prime Ministers of the four countries made a formal application.

On June 20 the Federation of Mali and Madagascar (the Malagasy Republic) became independent states, whereupon their respective Prime Ministers signed the already initialled agreement on co-operation with France.

HOUPHOUËT-BOIGNY now went to the other extreme. Before accession to independence he had refused to sign even a preliminary arrangement for co-operation, and DE GAULLE deferred. It was in the absence of such an arrangement that the Prime Ministers of the Entente countries signed an independence agreement on July 11, and all four countries were granted independence in the early days of August.

The changes in the status of the countries of French West Africa produced similar developments in the countries of French Equatorial Africa, too. After the dissolution in June 1958 of the two federations (of West and Equatorial Africa) established by the French colonialists, the Prime Ministers of the four territories of French Equatorial Africa made several attempts to bring their countries closer together, if possible in the form of regional federation, but these attempts failed in consequence of the differences in the conditions of their countries, on the one hand, and owing to disagreement between their political leaders.

The federal links connecting the countries of French West Africa and those of French Equatorial Africa were terminated by the colonialists on June 30, 1959. Already a few months before (January 1959) the Prime Ministers of the four countries of Equatorial Africa met in conference to discuss their future co-operation in financial, economic and cultural questions. They decided to hold such conferences regularly in the future and to establish a permanent secretariat in Brazzaville to deal with common affairs.

When early in 1960 the existing form of the French Community began to disintegrate, the Prime Ministers and parliamentary presidents of the countries of Equatorial Africa at their conference in Bangui decided "to raise their relations in the field of economic, social and cultural co-operation to a political level" and "to study the institutional forms necessary to couple internal political autonomy with joint inter-

214

national sovereignty".[1] However, Gabon was unwilling to undertake obligations beyond the introduction of a customs union and a common currency and the co-ordination of defence and foreign policy. Therefore, at a meeting in Fort-Lamy on May 17, 1960, the Prime Ministers of the Middle Congo, Ubangi-Shari and Chad decided that the three territories should form a single state *(Union des Républiques de l'Afrique Centrale)* and as such join the renewed French Community.

But the new state could not be formed because FULBERT YOULOU changed his mind in the last minute, and the four territories won independence as four separate states in the course of August. (The four countries maintained relations among them, and their heads of government met regularly also after independence. The former Governor of French Equatorial Africa, YVON BOURGES, remained in his place and continued as "special representative of the President of the Community in the states of Equatorial Africa".)

The Senate of the Community met in its second (and last) session on June 3, 1960, two weeks after the French Parliament (the National Assembly on May 11, the Senate on May 18) had enacted a reform of the French Community on DE GAULLE's proposal. The Community Senate's only business at this session was to pass the reform into law, that is to accept the new form of the French Community, amounting to a declaration of its own dissolution.

The renewed French Community was substantially different from its original version. The former Executive Council was replaced by an informal conference of the heads of state and government of all member states, and the Senate of the Community was superseded by an interparliamentary senate, which held regular meetings of delegates sent by the parliaments of the Community states. The head of state of France (General DE GAULLE) continued to be President of the Community, but neither he nor the Prime Ministers' conference could make obligatory decisions without the consent of all heads of state. And the interparliamentary senate was only an advisory body, not a legislative organ.

That was how by the end of 1960 all former French African colonies (with the single exception of French Somaliland, which had not demanded independence) became independent states[2] and as such applied for and obtained membership of the United Nations.

However, the federation of Senegal and Sudan, which was not based on political unity, was short-lived. Precisely two months following the day of independence, on August 20, 1960, the Federation of Mali fell apart. Senegal and Sudan, the latter under the name of Mali, continued to exist as separate independent states. But their later history, just like that of all former French colonies which have become independent, does not belong in the story of the disintegration of the colonial system, it is already part of the history of independent African states.

BIBLIOGRAPHY

ROBERT LEMAIGNEN, L. S. SENGHOR and Prince SISOWATH YOUTEVONG, *La Communauté impériale française*, Paris, 1945.
P. GEORGES, "Le colonialisme contre l'industrialisation", *Servir la France*, July 1946.

[1] Cf. FULBERT YOULOU's article in *Afrique Nouvelle*, March 2, 1960.
[2] Apart from the Federation of Mali which was granted independence on June 20, the other territories became independent between August 1 and 20. Mauritania alone, around which vehement debates erupted in the United Nations, acceded to independence with some delay, on November 28.

HENRI BENAZET, *L'Afrique française en danger*, Paris, 1947.

EMMANUEL MOUNIER, *L'Eveil de l'Afrique noire*, Paris, 1948.

Le Rassemblement Démocratique Africain dans la lutte impérialiste, Paris, 1948.

C. ASSALE, "Le bilan de la colonisation française en Afrique noire", *Cahiers Internationaux*, March-April 1949.

R. PLEVEN, *The Evolution of the French Empire towards a French Union*, London, 1949.

RAOUL MONMARSON, *L'Afrique noire et son destin*, Paris, 1950.

O. MANNONI, *Psychologie de la colonisation*, Seuil, 1950.

MAJHEMOUT DIOP, "Contribution à l'étude des problèmes politiques en Afrique noire", *Présence Africaine*, 1950.

HUBERT DESCHAMPS, *L'Union française*, Paris, 1952.

GEORGES BALANDIER, "Le développement industriel et la prolétarisation en Afrique noire", *L'Afrique et l'Asie*, No. 20, 1952.

HUBERT DESCHAMPS, *L'Eveil politique africain*, Paris, 1952.

MAMADOU DIA, *Réflexions sur l'économie de l'Afrique noire*, Paris, 1952.

JEAN DRESCH, "Les investissements en Afrique noire", *Présence Africaine*, April 1952.

WILLIAM TOP, "La valeur du travail des salariés africains", in *Le travail en Afrique noire*, Paris, 1952.

GASTON LEDUC, *L'économie de l'Union française*, Paris, 1952.

HENRI LABOURET, *Colonisation, colonialisme, décolonisation*, Paris, 1952.

Le travail en Afrique noire, Paris, 1952.

HUBERT DESCHAMPS, *Les méthodes et les doctrines coloniales de la France — du 16ᵉ siècle à nos jours*, Paris, 1953.

GEORGES LEBRUN KÉRIS, *Mort des colonies?* Paris, 1953.

JEAN ROMIEU, *Les mouvements coopératifs en Afrique noire*, Montpellier, 1953.

MARIE-ANDRÉ DU SACRÉ-COEUR, *La condition humaine en Afrique noire*, Grasset, 1953.

KADER FALL, "Problème de l'élite en Afrique noire", *Présence Africaine*, No. 14, 1953.

I. DU JONCHAY, *L'industrialisation de l'Afrique*, Paris, 1953.

R. GUTERMUTH, *Die Krise des französischen Imperialismus nach dem zweiten Weltkrieg*, Berlin, 1953.

GASTON JOSEPH "Réflexions sur la réforme politique outre-mer", *L'Afrique Française*, Nov.-Dec. 1954.

L. S. SENGHOR, "L'avenir de la France dans l'outre-mer", *Politique Etrangère*, Oct. 1954.

GASTON JOSEPH, "Décentralisation et déconcentration", *L'Afrique Française*, March–April 1955.

LAMINE GUÈYE, *Etapes et perspectives del'Union française*. Ed. de l'Union française, 1955.

P. NORD, *L'Eurafrique notre dernière chance*, Paris, 1955.

K. ROBINSON, "French Africa and the French Union", in C. HAINES (ed.), *Africa Today*, Baltimore, 1955, pp. 311–336.

RAOUL MONMARSON, *L'Afrique franco-africaine*, Paris, 1956.

FRANÇOIS MITTERRAND, "Présence française et abandon", *Tribune Libre* 12/1957.

PIERRE MOUSSA, "Les chances économiques de la communauté franco-africaine", *Cahiers de la Fond. Nat. des Sc. Pol.* 83/1957.

JEAN-JACQUES POQUIN, *Les relations économiques extérieures des pays d'Afrique noire de l'Union française 1925–1955*, Paris, 1957.

JEAN-MARC LÉGER, *Afrique française — Afrique nouvelle*, Ottawa, 1958.

ANDRÉ BLANCHET, *L'itinéraire des partis africains depuis Bamako*, Paris, 1958.

"France in Africa". Special number of *Current History*, New York, Feb. 1958.

AFRICANUS, *L'Afrique noire devant l'indépendance*, Paris, 1958.

F. BORELLA, *L'évolution politique et juridique de l'Union française depuis 1946*, Paris, 1958.

ALBERT TEVOEDJRE, *L'Afrique révoltée*, Paris, 1958.

JEAN SURET-CANALE, *Afrique noire*, Paris, 1958.

WALTER REICHHOLD, *Westafrika*, Bonn, 1958.

"La loi-cadre", *Présence Africaine*, Feb.–March 1958, pp. 69–124. (Articles by L. S. BÉHANZIN, N. ATANGANA, NENE KHALY, MAMADOU TOURÉ, F. SENGAT-KUO and JOSEPH KI-ZERBO.)

A. Autra, *Considérations sur la loi-cadre*, Porto-Novo, 1958.

Jean Ehrhard, *Le destin du colonialisme*, Eyrolles, 1958.

François Luchaire, *Droit d'outre-mer*, Paris, 1959.

P. F. Gonidec, *Constitutions d'Etats de la Communauté*, Sirey, 1959.

H. Goldberg, *French Colonialism: Progress or Poverty?* New York, 1959.

M. E. Morgaut, *Un dialogue nouveau: l'Afrique et l'industrie*, Paris, 1959.

Leo Hamon, *Introduction à l'étude des partis politiques de l'Afrique française*, Paris, 1959.

Georges Balandier, "Remarques sur les regroupements politiques africains", *Revue Française de Science Politique*, Dec. 1960.

G. Lisette, "L'évolution politique et l'avenir des pays d'Afrique noire d'expression française", *Les Cahiers Français*, Jan. 1960.

Albert Garand, "L'outre-mer français et la Communauté économique européenne", *Politique Etrangère* 1/1960, pp. 33–51.

Franz Ansprenger, *Politik im Schwarzen Afrika*, Bonn, 1961.

M. Hamon, *Le Parti Fédéral Africain et le Rassemblement Démocratique Africain de la querelle fédéraliste à l'indépendence (1959–1960)*. Paris, 1961.

Les Constitutions des Etats d'expression française, Paris, 1961.

В. В.Гаврилюк. *Распад французской колониалрьной имевии* [Collapse of the French Colonial Empire], Moscow, 1962.

Jean Suret-Canale, *Afrique noire occidentale et centrale*, Paris, 1964.

Jean Rous, *Chronique de la décolonisation*, Paris, 1965.

Lamine Guèye, *Itinéraire africain*, Paris, 1966.

Edward Mortimer, *France and the Africans 1944–1960*, London, 1969.

CHAPTER XXIII

FRENCH WEST AFRICA

Senegal

As early as 1928 a socialist party formed in the four privileged towns of Senegal (the "Quatre Communes"). From 1936 it functioned as the Senegal section of the French Socialist Party (S.F.I.O.) without showing any noteworthy activity. On the morrow of World War II AMADOU LAMINE GUÈYE[1] and LÉOPOLD SÉDAR SENGHOR[2] founded a new political party, the *Bloc Africain,* which also maintained relations with the French Socialist Party. At the 1945 election both of them won seats in the French Constituent Assembly as members for Senegal, and SENGHOR played an active part in the drafting of the new French Constitution. Yielding to pressure from the Socialist Party, neither SENGHOR nor GUÈYE attended the Bamako Conference of 1946, which gave birth to the *Rassemblement Démocratique Africain* (R.D.A.), and they did not join this organization later either.

Co-operation between SENGHOR and GUÈYE did not last long. Although their political aims were completely identical (both declared themselves socialists and proclaimed struggle "against capitalist imperialism"), yet they thought they could achieve their goal, not by revolution, but through peaceful evolution, by means of progressive reforms; both stood up for an extension of the powers of the Territorial Assembly and the establishment of an Executive Council answerable to the Territorial Assembly, still — in contrast to the militant nationalists — they did not go beyond demanding that half of the members of the Executive Council be elected and only half be nominated by the Governor. What separated them was the difference of mentality between the two politicians. Unlike GUÈYE, an ex-magistrate and privileged big-city bourgeois detached from tribal life and the toiling masses, SENGHOR, who was an offspring of an underprivileged tribe, in spite of his Catholic education and complete integration with European culture, was aware that a successful popular movement was inconceivable without paying regard to the tribal customs and cultural heritage of the African peoples, to the needs and aspirations of the toiling masses of African workers and peasants, villagers and townspeople. Starting

---

[1] AMADOU LAMINE GUÈYE was born at Medine, in the French Sudan, in 1891. He rated as a French citizen, for his parents were resident at Saint-Louis, one of the four *communes* of Senegal. He qualified as a lawyer in Paris in 1921. In 1924 he was elected Mayor of Saint-Louis. Later he served as a magistrate in Réunion and Martinique. In 1937 he became the political director of the Senegalese group of the French Socialist Party. During the Vichy regime he kept aloof from politics.
[2] See Vol. III, p. 104.

from this conviction, he considered it the task of the party to achieve equality of political rights for the entire people, to espouse the organizations (unions, co-operatives) formed to improve the material conditions of the labouring masses.

In February 1948 SENGHOR launched the periodical journal *Condition Humaine*, in which he set forth his ideas, attacked the policies of GUÈYE and the democratic bloc, and demanded decentralization of the party and participation in politics of the Africans without French citizenship.

In October 1948 SENGHOR definitively broke with LAMINE GUÈYE. Together with his adherents he withdrew from the Bloc Africain and founded a new party, the *Bloc Démocratique Sénégalais* (B.D.S.). In Paris he broke with the French Socialist Party and joined the group of French overseas parliament-arians (*Indépendants d'Outre-Mer* — I.O.M.) which had been formed in September 1948.

The new party gained ground rapidly throughout the country, mainly in the vil-lages, so much so that at the French parliamentary elections of June 1951 it suc-ceeded in defeating GUÈYE: the two seats reserved for Senegal thus went to SEN-GHOR and one of his followers. At the March 1952 elections to the Territorial Assembly (where until then the Socialist Party had wielded the majority) SEN-GHOR's party obtained 41 out of 50 seats, the remaining 9 seats going to the party of LAMINE GUÈYE. The 1953 municipal elections in Dakar and Saint-Louis brought victory to GUÈYE's S.F.I.O. group.

In the first half of the fifties the influence of SENGHOR's party in Senegal was growing, while he himself was active mainly in the French Parliament where, as one of the leaders of the I.O.M. group, he spoke up for a federation of the countries of French West Africa. In November 1952 he had no small part in the I.O.M.'s success in getting Parliament to pass an act (Overseas Labour Code) which ensured the workers in the colonies the right to enter into collective bargaining and intro-duced some labour-safety and welfare measures. In February 1952 he initiated the proposal which the Bobo-Dioulasso congress of the I.O.M. adopted for the creation of a federal African republic within the French Union. On this basis, SENGHOR in the following years worked out a detailed plan for the countries of French West Africa to form two federal republics with seats at Dakar and at Abidjan, respectively. This sparked off a political struggle which went on for years between partisans and opponents of federalism.

SENGHOR's attitude towards the *loi-cadre* of 1956 was ambiguous. As a champion of the unity of French West Africa, he sharply criticized the *loi-cadre*, objected that it provided for no real self-government but was trying to "Balkanize" French Black Africa. At the same time, however, he demanded the consistent implementation of the *loi-cadre*, regarding it as a prelude to self-government.

At the 1956 general elections Senegal again sent him and one of his adherents to the French National Assembly.

When the *loi-cadre* came into force in June 1956, the B.D.S. merged with two splinter groups and changed its name to *Bloc Populaire Sénégalais* (B.P.S.). One of the two groups was the Senegal Democratic Union, which had formerly been the Senegal section of the R.D.A. until it was expelled for "leftism" by the Conakry meeting of the R.D.A. in 1955; the other was a socialist group.

At the elections to the Territorial Assembly held under the *loi-cadre* in March 1957, the B.P.S. obtained 47 of 60 seats, and thus its members formed the government

(Executive Council) with MAMADOU DIA[1] as Vice-Chairman. (Chairman of the Council was invariably the French Governor.)

In January 1957 the I.O.M. was superseded by two new inter-territorial parties, the *Convention Africaine* founded by SENGHOR and the *Mouvement Socialiste Africain* (M.S.A.) formed by LAMINE GUÈYE. From that time on the B.D.S. functioned only as a territorial section of the Convention Africaine.

The unity of the B.P.S. did not last long. At the end of 1957 the revolutionary anticolonialist elements led by MAHJMOUT DIOP and OUMAR DIALLO, who disagreed with SENGHOR's ambiguous policy, left the B.P.S. and founded the *Parti Africain de l'Indépendance* (P.A.I.).

Early in 1958 LAMINE GUÈYE's M.S.A. and SENGHOR's Convention Africaine united to form a new inter-territorial organization called the *Parti du Regroupement Africain* (P.R.A.), and at the same time GUÈYE's socialists merged with SENGHOR's B.P.S. in a new party, the *Union Progressiste Sénégalaise* (U.P.S.). Shortly after the merger the U.P.S. decided to call upon the electorate to vote "yes" at the referendum offered by President DE GAULLE of France. This decision of the party caused a new split. Dissenting members of the party, headed by ABDOULAYE LY,[2] resigned, and they formed the *Parti du Regroupement Africain Sénégal* (P.R.A. Sénégal). This party accused SENGHOR of undue submission to French influence; it demanded complete independence and therefore campaigned for voting "no".

In the referendum held in September 1958 the P.A.I. and the P.R.A.–Sénégal, which were both in opposition to the U.P.S., made propaganda for voting "no", but the majority of the electorate, following the call of SENGHOR's party, voted "yes". SENGHOR himself and some of his adherents were undecided for a while, they criticized the way General DE GAULLE had risen to power, were not satisfied with the new Constitution, so much so that when in August 1958 DE GAULLE paid a visit to Dakar, SENGHOR happened to go on holiday at that time and was absent from Dakar to avoid meeting the General, and leftist elements of his party staged a demonstration against DE GAULLE. In the end, however, they voted for the adoption of the Constitution.

In December 1958 political leaders from Senegal, Sudan, Dahomey and the Upper Volta held a congress at Bamako, where they resolved to unite the four countries in a federation under the name of "Mali". The Federal Constitutional Conference was held at Dakar in January 1959. (This induced the right wing of the U.P.S. to withdraw and form the *Parti de la Solidarité Sénégalaise.)*

In January 1959 Senegal became a republic, and at the legislative election in March the Union Progressiste Sénégalaise gained all of the 80 seats.

During March, at the insistence of HOUPHOUËT-BOIGNY, Dahomey and the Upper Volta changed their minds and left the federation. On the other hand, SENGHOR's U.P.S. and MODIBO KEITA's *Union Soudanaise* merged in the *Parti de la Fédération Africaine* and carried out the two countries' union in a federation.

[1] MAMADOU DIA was born at Khombole, Senegal, in 1910. He went to school at Saint-Louis and Dakar (William Ponty College). He became a teacher and journalist. After the war he was elected to the Territorial Assembly of Senegal, and in 1948 to the French Senate. In Paris he made studies in economics. First in Paris and later in Dakar he was one of SENGHOR's closest political associates. He is the author of several scientific works, mainly on economic subjects: *Réflexions sur l'économie de l'Afrique noire*, Paris, 1953; *L'Economie africaine: Etudes et problèmes nouveaux*, Paris, 1953; *Nations africaines et Solidarité mondiale*, Paris, 1960.

[2] ABDOULAYE LY, historian, a founding member of the *Fédération des Etudiants d'Afrique Noire en France*, from 1956 a member of the B.D.S., in 1957–1958 Minister of the Interior in Senegal.

Immediately after the war, in 1945, MODIBO KEITA[1] and MAMADOU KONATÉ[2] (deputy for the French Sudan in the French National Assembly of that time) founded the *Bloc Soudanais* as the Sudan section of the French Socialist Party. Both were also founding members of the R.D.A. constituted at Bamako in October 1946. After the Bamako Conference the two of them organized the *Union Soudanaise* as the Sudan section of the R.D.A. That year, to counterpoise the militant anticolonialist Union Soudanaise, FILY DABO SISSOKO[3] with the support of reactionary chiefs (and with the tacit support of the government) founded the *Parti Soudanais Progressiste* (P.S.P.), a conservative party leaning to tribal traditions. At the 1946 elections to the French National Assembly two members of SISSOKO's party and only one of the Union Soudanaise were elected.

In 1947 KEITA and KONATÉ went to Paris. There the police arrested them and kept them in detention for a month. Upon their return home they led further their party's struggle, in keeping with the political line of the R.D.A., against the ruthless colonial regime.

In 1948 MODIBO KEITA was elected General Secretary of the Union Soudanaise and also a member of the Territorial Assembly. In 1950, when the colonial authorities started to persecute the R.D.A., MODIBO KEITA was accused of being a Communist and deported to a remote region, where for a time he organized schools. When towards the end of 1950 HOUPHOUËT-BOIGNY and his R.D.A. broke with the French Communist Party, the Union Soudanaise remained affiliated with the R.D.A. in opposition to HOUPHOUËT-BOIGNY's leadership.

In 1952 MODIBO KEITA returned to Bamako and was re-elected to the Territorial Assembly.

During the years that followed the leaders of the Union Soudanaise made every effort to build up a massive basis for their party, and their effort was crowned with success.

In January 1956 MODIBO KEITA was elected a deputy for the Sudan and became the first African Vice-President of the French National Assembly. After KONATÉ's death in 1956 the leadership of the Union Soudanaise passed entirely into MODIBO KEITA's hands, who was elected Mayor of Bamako in November next. In 1957 he became a member of the French cabinet as Under-Secretary of State for France Overseas (in the BOURGÈS-MAUNOURY government), and later Under-Secretary of State in the Prime Minister's office (in the GAILLARD government).

At the elections to the Territorial Assembly held in March 1957 after the introduction of the *loi-cadre* the Union Soudanaise won 64 out of 70 seats, and thus the first government (presided over by the French Governor) of the country was formed

---

[1] MODIBO KEITA, an offspring of one of the most powerful families of the Bambara tribe (the family traces its ancestry to the rulers of the Mali Empire that existed in the 13th century), was born at Bamako in May 1915. He was educated at Bamako and Dakar. At Bamako he taught in school and later became a school inspector. In 1937 he was one of the founding members of the Bamako cultural youth society "Arts et Travail". Afterwards he was transferred to Sikasso, where he engaged in political propaganda against the colonial system.

[2] MAMADOU KONATÉ, school principal, born in the French Sudan in 1897. One of the founders, and from 1949 Vice-President, of the R.D.A. From 1946 to 1956 he represented the Sudan in the French National Assembly. Died in 1956.

[3] FILY DABO SISSOKO, teacher, was born in the Sudan in 1900. Deputy for the Sudan in the French Assembly from 1945, later he was a UN delegate, Minister of State and President of the Territorial Assembly.

by leaders of the Union Soudanaise: the post of Deputy Prime Minister was occupied by JEAN-MARIE KONÉ,[1] and the office of the Minister of the Interior was taken by MADEIRA KEITA.[2] MODIBO KEITA was in charge of the country's external relations (relations with France and the other countries of French West Africa).

In the 1958 referendum the Sudan voted "yes". MODIBO KEITA and his party were led to this decision by a twofold consideration: on the one hand, the effort to preserve the unity of the countries of French West Africa and, on the other, the fear that in case of voting "no" the party could not poll the majority of the vote and would thus lose face and influence among the masses.

After the referendum, the Sudan became an autonomous republic within the French Community in November 1958. President of the Republic was JEAN-MARIE KONÉ, and MODIBO KEITA remained a member of the French cabinet.

In December 1958, upon the initiative of MODIBO KEITA, representatives of the Union Soudanaise, the Union Progressiste Sénégalaise and the Parti Progressiste Dahoméen held a conference at Bamako and decided to establish a Federation under the name of Mali.

In January 1959 MODIBO KEITA was elected President of the Grand Council of French West Africa by 15 votes with 11 abstentions. This seemed to indicate that the idea of federation got support from some of the countries of French West Africa. But leaders from Dahomey and the Upper Volta, upon pressure from HOUPHOUËT-BOIGNY, changed their position and refused to join the federation. Nevertheless, the federation came into being: in April 1959 the Union Soudanaise and the Union Progressiste Sénégalaise merged to form the *Parti de la Fédération Africaine*, and the two countries, Senegal and the French Sudan, united in the Federation of Mali.

Prior to this, at the territorial elections held in the Sudan in March 1959, all seats were captured by the Union Soudanaise. After the elections the Parti Soudanaise Progressiste and all other minor opposition groups merged into the Union Soudanaise (SISSOKO himself had joined MODIBO KEITA's party already in December 1958), and thus the Union Soudanaise became the single political party of the country, whose government was taken over by MODIBO KEITA.

The Federation of Mali

The Federal Assembly of the new state met on April 4, 1959. It consisted of twelve representatives[3] of each of the two federal states, Senegal and the Sudan. SENGHOR was elected President of the Federal Assembly, MODIBO KEITA was appointed Prime Minister of the federal government, and MAMADOU DIA became Deputy Premier.

---

[1] JEAN-MARIE KONÉ was born of the Moslem Bambara tribe at Sikasso in October 1913. He went to school at Sikasso, Bamako and Dakar. From 1935 he taught in school at Gao and Koumandou. After 1942 he was active in the trade-union movement. From 1946, as secretary of a local R.D.A. branch, he was persecuted by the colonial authorities. In 1949 he was sentenced to three years' imprisonment. Later the Court of Appeal in Dakar acquitted him, but the colonial administration in 1951 transferred him to a country girls' school. In the fifties he was one of the most active members of the Union Soudanaise.

[2] MADEIRA KEITA was born at Kita in the French Sudan in January 1917. He went to school in Dakar. In 1946 he founded the Democratic Party of Guinea. He was arrested nine times for his political activities, and the French authorities deported him on a number of occasions to different countries of French West Africa. Returning to the Sudan, he became a member of the Political Bureau of the Union Soudanaise.

[3] The Federal Constitution adopted on April 24 raised the number of the representatives of each federal state to twenty.

The government had six more Ministers, three from Senegal and three from the Sudan.

For the time being the French government simply ignored the establishment of the Federation of Mali.

The leaders of the new state, to demonstrate to the world the popularity of the idea of federation and the vitality of the Federation of Mali, summoned the congress of the Parti de la Fédération Africaine, which met on July 1, 1959. In addition to 50 delegates from Senegal and the Sudan each, the congress was attended by 29 delegates from other African countries, representing the parties which had embraced the idea of an association of African countries (10 from Mauritania, 7 from Dahomey, 6 from the Niger, and 6 from the Upper Volta).

The principal report to the congress was presented by SENGHOR. In his speech he developed his idea of federation, his concept of a unified African Negro nation in the making, which he set against the notion of "homeland" ("the homeland of the African is the land where the tribe he belongs to is living: that is, Serereland, Mossiland, and so on"); of the state, which in his view was nothing more than a sort of executive organ of the nation ("the state is to the nation what the contractor is to the architect"); of the federal state as the state formation most convenient to the Africans, and finally of what he called "African socialism".

MODIBO KEITA, in his report on questions of organization, tried to make the organizational principles of the R.D.A. prevail also in the Parti de la Fédération Africaine: this party being a co-ordinator of the parties functioning in the several countries, it should rely, not upon the leaders, but upon the membership, strict organization and moderate centralism; the territorial sections being realizers of the party's unified policy, divergences could be only in the tactical line; where the party was still in opposition the tactics might be different from that applied where it was in power or had a share in the government. (As will be seen below, it was mainly the disagreement just on organizational matters that led to the disintegration of the Federation of Mali one year later.)

The congress adopted a political resolution in which it took a stand in favour of the idea of national independence, of interdependence of the African peoples, and of African unity, and embraced the slogan about an "African road to socialism", which, however, it failed to outline concretely.

The congress elected the party's nine-member Executive Bureau, of which SENGHOR became President with the Dahomeyan ZINSOU and the Niger refugee BAKARY as Vice-Presidents.

In September 1959 Senegal and the Sudan informed the Executive Council of the French Community that the two countries wished to use their right laid down in the Constitution of the Fifth Republic and to become a sovereign state under the name of Federation of Mali without ceasing to belong to the French Community.

The 1958 Constitution introduced by DE GAULLE had offered every French colony the opportunity to decide, by way of referendum, to withdraw from the French Community and become a sovereign republic, but it denied them full independence within the Community. There was, however, a provision in the Constitution (Art. 78) which made it possible for any member state of the Community to enter into a special agreement with France on the transfer of some constitutional powers to the Community and vice versa. It was with reference to this provision that the leaders of the Federation of Mali demanded full independence within the Community. Their idea was that the Community should transfer the totality of sovereignty to the new state, which would thus become independent within the Community and as an independent state should conclude with the Community an agreement on the transfer of part of its sovereignty.

This loose interpretation of the Constitution was contrary to DE GAULLE'S conception, and at first he was reluctant to accept it.

On November 26, 1959, the leaders of the Federation of Mali — MODIBO KEITA, MAMADOU DIA and LÉOPOLD SENGHOR — had talks with DE GAULLE in Paris. They proposed that the two countries be granted full sovereignty, which they then would transfer to the Federation, and the Federation as an independent state should negotiate and conclude an agreement with France regarding their future relations. At that time DE GAULLE took the position that the independence of the Federation of Mali and agreement on its relationship with France should be simultaneous and be included in a single act. Hardly had two weeks passed, however, before DE GAULLE changed his mind. He had found that the way proposed by Mali actually was to the advantage of French neo-colonialism, since it made it possible to keep the ex-colonies politically and economically dependent on French imperialism by satisfying their increasingly pro-independence nationalists with a show of transfer of "sovereignty" and with the aid of agreements concluded with them as sovereign states.

This changed position of DE GAULLE was first given voice on December 10, 1959, at the sixth session of the Executive Council of the French Community at Saint-Louis, where DE GAULLE in his inaugural address indicated for the first time that the French government was ready to recognize the Federation of Mali, by saying: "Je salue Saint-Louis, je salue ici ceux du Sénégal, et d'avance, comme je le dirai à Dakar, je salue ceux du Mali!"

Three days later, on December 13, before the Federal Assembly of Mali at Dakar, DE GAULLE delivered a speech, in which he announced that the Federation of Mali would become independent "with the assistance, consent and help of France". He made it appear as if the independence of the country corresponded to the intentions of the French government as a development envisaged by the Constitution of the Fifth Republic. At the same time he unequivocally disclosed that what he understood by "independence" was by no means an end to dependence upon France, it was no real independence. Here are a few passages of DE GAULLE'S speech:

"France, Mali and the states constituting the Federation of Mali will conduct talks on changes in their relations. The Constitution of the Community, which we have all voted for, explicitly provided for this. These talks will create a new situation for the Federation of Mali and the states of Senegal and the Sudan forming this Federation . . .

" . . . Independence implies desire, attitude, intention. In today's world, in this so small, so narrow and so interdependent world, real independence, complete independence, exists in reality for no one. Not a single state, however big and powerful, can do without the others. And since there is no state that could do without the others, no manner of policy is possible without co-operation . . .

" . . . In the world there has always been struggle. This is the fate of man, the law of the human race. At present the struggle is waged between those who want freedom and those who give it up."

And to avoid any misunderstanding, DE GAULLE in his speech warned the Federation of Mali that the whole world would fix its eyes upon it and watch which camp of this struggle it would join, "the camp of freedom, or the other".[1]

[1] For DE GAULLE'S speech see *Chronique de la Communauté*, Dec. 1959.

SENGHOR replied to DE GAULLE's speech. He extolled the General as "the anti-colonialist revolutionary of the twentieth century" and declared: "We want to win our national sovereignty, and this not against France, but together with France, within the great Franco-African community. This independence will be effective, for its effectiveness will be served by co-operation."

The proposed talks again took place in Paris, between January 18 and April 4, 1960. As a result of the talks an agreement was reached, by which the Federation of Mali should become an independent state on June 20, 1960, but would remain a member of the French Community. Here are a few characteristic provisions of the agreement:

The new state shall obtain the right to set up armed forces of its own with the aid of France, but at the same time it shall allow France to station troops and build military bases in the territory of the country.

The Federation of Mali has the right to introduce a national currency, but shall renounce this right and remain in the franc zone.

The Federation of Mali shall establish normal diplomatic relations with France, whose diplomatic representative in Mali shall every time be acting as doyen of the Diplomatic Corps, and it shall in the future, too, co-ordinate its external policies with the French government.

The new state shall have the right to send its own diplomatic representatives to other countries, but in the countries where it does not maintain diplomatic missions its interests shall be protected by France.

The essence of the agreement is perhaps best characterized by SENGHOR's statement made after the signature: "I think this is rather France's victory than ours. But it is also a victory of the Community. We have proved that we can be fully independent and yet remain together."

The agreement signed at Paris was ratified by the Federal Assembly of Mali on June 8, 1960, and by the French Parliament on June 16, 1960. The instruments of ratification were exchanged at Dakar on June 19, and the next day the Federation of Mali was proclaimed an independent state. The festive meeting of the Federal Assembly called on this occasion, which was attended also by diplomatic representatives of the Soviet Union, the United States and West Germany, was inaugurated by SENGHOR as President of the Assembly, who in his speech solemnly proclaimed the independence of the country. (SENGHOR remarked that independence for the country would not be an inexpensive thing, and therefore the government would have to practise economy from the very beginning.) After that MODIBO KEITA, the Prime Minister, took the floor and declared that the new state wished to maintain close relationships with the French Republic "in the framework of the renewed Community, the revival of which has been made possible by de Gaulle's sagacity and understanding". Every time DE GAULLE's name was mentioned a tumultuous ovation followed.

French Guinea

The struggle for independence in Guinea was started by the Democratic Party of Guinea founded by MADEIRA KEITA[1] in 1946 under the name of *Parti Progressiste de Guinée*. In 1947 the party joined the R.D.A. and, as its Guinea section, changed

---

[1] See footnote on p. 222.

its name to the *Parti Démocratique de Guinée*. For years following its formation the party under MADEIRA KEITA waged a fight on three fronts: it was persecuted by the Franch administration; in the political arena it came up against the *Union Franco-Guinéenne* led by YACINE DIALLO,[2] which was supported by the French colonial authorities and was currying their favour, and which maintained relations with the French Socialist Party; and within the African community it met with hostile opposition on the part of the established chiefs and local rulers throughout the country. During the six years of his tenure as General Secretary of the party MADEIRA KEITA was brought to trial nine times by the colonial authorities and was sentenced to shorter or longer terms of prison and deported from one country to another in French West Africa.

In 1952 the general secretaryship of the party was taken over by SÉKOU TOURÉ.[3] As party leader, he concentrated mainly on developing his party into a large, nation-wide mass organization, which he managed to achieve by building up local branches in a very short time. This as well as his activity in the 1953 strike made him popular to the workers all over the country. At a by-election in 1953 he was elected to the Territorial Assembly. In June 1954 he stood for the French National Assembly but was defeated owing to the election being rigged by the colonial authorities. This unlawful action of the administration raised an uproar in the country and only added to SÉKOU TOURÉ's popularity. By January 1956, when new elections to the French National Assembly took place, the Democratic Party of Guinea had grown so strong that the colonial authorities could no longer prevent SÉKOU TOURÉ from being elected. In November of the same year he was elected also Mayor of Conakry.

SÉKOU TOURÉ pursued his activities with unabated energy for restoring the unity of the labour movement. To this end, in April 1956, he founded a trade-union centre, called *Confédération Générale des Travailleurs Africains* (C.G.T.A.), rallying in it the local organizations affiliated with both the C.G.T. and the W.F.T.U., and in January 1957, in order to promote the unity of the trade-union movement, he brought into existence the *Union Générale des Travailleurs d'Afrique Noire* (U.G.T. A.N.), free from all European or international affiliations. SÉKOU TOURÉ summed up the aim of this organization in these words: "To unite and organize the workers of Black Africa, to co-ordinate their trade-union activities in the struggle against the colonial regime and all other forms of exploitation."

[2] YACINE DIALLO, an offspring of a Fulah chief's family, was born at Labé, Guinea, in October 1896. He was a school teacher. From 1945 until his death in 1954 he was a member of the Territorial Assembly and a deputy for Guinea in the French National Assembly.

[3] SÉKOU TOURÉ, grandson of SAMORY, the great figure of the African independence struggle, was born in the village of Faranah in Guinea. After completing primary school, in 1936 he entered the Conakry French technical school. The next year, however, he was expelled for leading a student strike. He completed his secondary school education by correspondence. In 1940 he was employed by a French firm, and a year later he qualified in telecommunication. While working in this line he displayed great activity in the labour movement. In 1945 he was elected General Secretary of the Guinean Postal Workers' Union, and in this capacity he was one of the founders of the Federation of Workers' Union of Guinea, which was affiliated to France's C.G.T. and, through it, to the World Federation of Trade Unions (W.F.T.U.). In 1946 he attended the Bamako founding conference of the R.D.A. In 1947 he entered the service of the Ministry of Finance and became General Secretary of the Treasury Employees Union. Because of his political activities he soon lost his office, and afterwards he devoted all his energy to the trade-union movement. In 1948 he became General Secretary of the Guinea section of the C.G.T., and in 1950 he occupied the same post in the co-ordinating committee of C.G.T. sections in French West Africa.

At the elections held under the *loi-cadre* in March 1957 the Democratic Party of Guinea won a sweeping victory, so that the French Governor was compelled to let members of the party form a government and to appoint SÉKOU TOURÉ its head (Vice-President of the Executive Council). Two months later, in May 1957, SÉKOU TOURÉ was elected also a member of the Grand Council of French West Africa.

As Vice-President of the Executive Council, SÉKOU TOURÉ had greater freedom of action than anyone else in the other French colonies, because — thanks to his organizational work of many years — his party had strong local branches not only in the capital, but all over the country, in the villages as well, and took an active part in political life. This made it possible for him, once at the helm of the government, to start creating the necessary preconditions for self-government. This activity proceeded in three directions:

(*a*) He placed an increasing number of Africans in the administrative apparatus;

(*b*) he paid special attention to the economic development of the country, stepped up the construction of railways, bridges and roads, and started the production of aluminium;

(*c*) with a view to completely destroying the power of chiefs, he established village councils and promoted the organization of peasant co-operatives.

SÉKOU TOURÉ's consistent efforts to lay the foundations of independence were not at all intended to put an end to co-operation with France. In July 1957, for instance, he said in a talk with the French Governor: "Even though there have been differences between our movement and representatives of the administration, the leaders of the movement have never had the intention of violating the national interests of France." But the French government distrusted SÉKOU TOURÉ for his work of organizing the party and building the labour unions as well as for his governmental activities. SÉKOU TOURÉ further incurred the enmity of the French government by his vigorous propaganda for a federation of the countries of French West Africa, and mainly by his success in winning for his conceptions the majority of African leaders, first at the Bamako Conference of the R.D.A. in September 1957 and then at the March 1958 meeting of the Grand Council of French West Africa.

It was obviously the intrigues of the French government which were responsible for the absurd occurrence that SÉKOU TOURÉ, while working in Guinea with devotion and success for preparing his country for independence, was the main target of fierce attacks on the part of the young radical intellectuals of Black Africa living in Paris. The paper *l'Etudiant d'Afrique Noire* of the "Fédération des Etudiants d'Afrique Noire en France" in several articles accused him of demagoguery and betrayal of the African national movement.

But SÉKOU TOURÉ went his way unwaveringly, and when DE GAULLE offered the former French colonies the choice between limited autonomy and full independence, that is either membership in the French Community or withdrawal from it, SÉKOU TOURÉ chose the latter without hesitation. "We prefer poverty in liberty to riches in slavery", was the slogan he issued on the eve of the referendum, and the huge majority of the people of Guinea agreed with him.

In the referendum held on September 28, 1958, Guinea—alone among the French African colonies—said "no" to DE GAULLE with 1,136,000 votes to 57,000 and chose complete independence.

On October 2, 1958, Guinea became independent with SÉKOU TOURÉ as President of the Republic.

Mauritania held a peculiar place in the French colonial empire. When crossing the threshold of the new era following the war, Mauritania was both economically and culturally the most underdeveloped and most neglected country in France's African empire. Mauritania is the most sparsely inhabited country of Africa: it has an area of 415,000 square miles (1,086,000 sq. km.) and a population of 615,000 (two-thirds of them being nomadic Moors), that is less than one person per square kilo-metre. And though it is rich in natural resources, the French imperialists had not even started to exploit them before the war.

Mauritania is a typical example to show that, during the partition of the world, the imperialists occupied not only those backward countries which could immediately provide a source of primary materials or profitable capital markets, but also those which might in the future serve such purposes. This is why the French imperialists neglected this colony even more than all the rest of their African possessions. Until the entry into force of the *loi-cadre*, they had not drawn the population into the political affairs in any form (even the seat of the colonial administration was outside the country, in Saint-Louis, Senegal); they had not cared for the economic develop-ment of the country, they had done practically nothing in the field of public health and education: there were in the country all in all two schools (of the secondary-school type) that provided something more than elementary education.

After the war Mauritania was gaining importance both economically and strategi-cally. First, because rich iron-ore deposits were discovered in the northern regions, and for the purpose of their extraction an international consortium called "Miferma" was established with French, English, West German and Italian capital. Second, because in the post-war international situation, when the African countries set out on the road to independence, it became particularly important for France to possess, or at least to control, this territory which might in the future serve as a strategic base in three ways: against the two great independent Maghreb states (Morocco and Algeria), the independent (French) Sudan and Senegal, as well as the Spanish possessions in West Africa.

In view of her geographical position Mauritania is an intermediate area between the Sudan and the Maghreb countries, but also ethnographically she forms a transi-tion between the Sudanese and the mixed Arab-Berber peoples (the Moors) inhabit-ing the northern part of the continent. These latter live in the larger, northern, area of the country, while the southern portion is inhabited by the Sudanese tribes related to the peoples of Senegal and the French Sudan. This accounts for the fact that the territory of Mauritania was coveted by even three of the neighbouring independent countries: first and most vigorously by Morocco (claiming kinship with the majority of the tribes living in the two countries), and also, though less vigorously, by the French Sudan and Senegal (equally with reference to the ethnic ties linking their peoples).

This was how the absurd situation arose in which, in opposition to the expansionist policies of these African countries, it was the French imperialists who, in order to maintain control over their former colony and to use it as a strategic base, stood up for the independence and sovereignty of Mauritania and supported in the country those forces which demanded that Mauritania become an independent republic.

The first political party in Mauritania was the *Entente Mauritanienne*, founded by a small functionary, HORMA OULD BABANA,[1] who in 1946 was elected a deputy

[1] HORMA OULD BABANA was born in Mauritania in 1912.

for Mauritania in the French National Assembly. In 1947 the established tribal chiefs of Mauritania, who disliked BABANA's political activity, formed the *Union Progressiste Mauritanienne* (U.P.M.) with the help of the French colonial administration. In 1951, despite the popularity of BABANA and the Entente Mauritanienne, the new party managed to disseat BABANA and elect to the French National Assembly its own leader, MOKHTAR N'DIAYE.[1]

A year later, at the election of the Territorial Assembly, the U.P.M. gained 22 out of 24 seats. At the 1956 elections to the French National Assembly N'DIAYE again defeated BABANA.

After his election defeat in 1956 BABANA fled to Morocco, whose government and leading parties had declared a few months before that they considered Mauritania a part of Morocco and demanded its reannexation. BABANA himself also favoured the Moroccan position.

Towards the end of 1956 and at the beginning of 1957 the Liberation Army organized by Moroccan political parties made incursions into Mauritanian territory, but the attacks were every time repelled by the French troops stationed in Mauritania, with the aid of reinforcements dispatched from Dakar and Algiers by the French colonialists. The armed conflicts demanded numerous victims on both sides.

The Grand Council of French West Africa, by its unanimous decision of June 23, 1957, rejected as "unfounded" Morocco's claim to Mauritania and, solemnly confirming that Mauritania was an integral part of French West Africa, invited the French government "to take action in all national and international bodies to support and defend Mauritania's membership both in the Federation and in the French Union".

However, BABANA's party, the Entente Mauritanienne, did not acknowledge defeat. When at the elections to the Territorial Assembly held a year after the introduction of the *loi-cadre*, in March 1957, the U.P.M. won a hundred per cent victory (capturing all 34 seats), the Entente complained of fraud, demanded invalidation of the election and called for new elections under strict supervision. But its efforts were to no avail. As a result of the elections the leader of the U.P.M., MOKHTAR OULD DADDAH[2] (who took over from N'DIAYE in 1957), as Chairman of the Executive Council formed a government of members of his party only, and this government, following the political line of the French colonialists, was against union with Morocco and also against joining the Federation of Mali.

The first business of the government was to establish a capital for the country, which until then the French had governed from Saint-Louis in Senegal. DADDAH managed to have the seat of government transferred to the township of Nouakchott situated on the seacoast, where—for lack of appropriate buildings—the first meeting of the cabinet was held in a tent.

---

[1] SIDI EL MOKHTAR N'DIAYE was born at Atar in 1916. His father was Mauritanian, his mother came from a Wolof tribe. After finishing his studies at the Saint-Louis school for chiefs' sons, he served in the French colonial administration of Mauritania. He was one of the founders and leaders of the Union Progressiste Mauritanienne.

[2] MOKHTAR OULD DADDAH, a descendant of chiefs of the Ould Biri tribe, was born in Mauritania (Traza district) on December 27, 1924. Graduating from the Saint-Louis school for chiefs' sons (Senegal), he first worked as an interpreter. In 1948 he went to Paris, where he took his degree in law and pursued studies in the school of Oriental languages. During his years in Paris he was one of the organizers of the student group rallied behind SIDI EL MOKHTAR N'DIAYE, then deputy for Mauritania in the French National Assembly. Returning to Mauritania, he took an active part in politics as a member of the Union Progressiste Mauritanienne. In 1957 he was elected to the Territorial Assembly.

Remaining without a leader, the Entente Mauritanienne did not endure long. In May 1958 DADDAH engineered a merger of the Entente and the U.P.M. The united party was named the *Parti du Regroupement Mauritanien* (P.R.M.).

In the referendum held in September 1958 the P.R.M., which campaigned for voting "yes", was confronted with a new opposition party, the *Parti de la Renaissance Nationale Mauritanienne* ("Nahdah"), which pressed for union with Morocco. However, the P.R.M. assisted by the colonial authorities again won by a large majority.

On November 28, 1958, the Territorial Assembly proclaimed the country the Islamic Republic of Mauritania.

The new Constitution, drafted after the proclamation of the Republic, was enacted by the National Assembly on March 22, 1959. The Constitution lays down that Mauritania is a democratic republic in which all men have equal rights, but it does not affect the feudal institutions of the existing tribal system, the prerogatives of chiefs. It recognizes the Islam as official religion, while guaranteeing every citizen liberty of conscience and freedom of religion. Under the Constitution the Prime Minister is elected by the National Assembly for a period of five years, and the Ministers are appointed by the Prime Minister. Any amendment to the Constitution shall be decided by the National Assembly upon the motion of the Prime Minister, but this does not apply to the territorial integrity of the country and to the republican form of government which are unchangeable under the terms of the Constitution.

b In April 1959, a month before the elections, a new opposition party was formed y the Sudanese living in the south of the country, the *Union Nationale Mauritanienne* (U.N.M.), which kept in close contact with SENGHOR's and MODIBO KEITA's Parti de la Fédération Africaine. Its main political goal was to achieve Mauritania's union with the Federation of Mali. This party blamed the leaders of the P.R.M. for serving as blind tools the interests of France, and demanded that, besides Arabs (Moors), the Sudanese also should have a say in the national affairs. At the May 1959 elections, however, DADDAH's P.R.M. gained all seats in the Assembly, since both the "Nahdah" and the newly formed U.N.M. kept out of the elections.

Early in 1960 the Moor chiefs of the Adrar district, being dissatisfied with DADDAH's policy, formed a new opposition party, the *Union des Socialistes Musulmans Mauritaniens* (U.S.M.M.).

At the end of June DADDAH went to Paris, where he had talks with Prime Minister MICHEL DEBRÉ, with JEAN FOYER, Secretary-General of the French Community, and with President DE GAULLE. The talks resulted in an agreement on Mauritania's accession to independence on November 28, the second anniversary of the proclamation of the Islamic Republic of Mauritania.

In August 1960 the Sultan of Morocco, who had not given up regarding Mauritania as a detached province of Morocco, appealed to the United Nations, requesting it to put the question of Mauritania on the agenda of the next session of the General Assembly.

During September and October the Moroccan government in declarations and radio broadcasts accused the French and Mauritanian governments of provoking incidents on the Moroccan frontier and of persecuting and oppressing Mauritania's population, which was "unanimously for the withdrawal of the French troops and the resignation of the Daddah government". The French and Mauritanian governments rejected the charges as false.

As for the border incidents, we are not in a position to substantiate or to refute the charges. As regards the other accusation, however, the fact is that late in September the Mauritanian government enforced the arrest of four "Nahdah" leaders and a month later banned the party. (The U.N.M., since its goal had become meaningless with the disintegration of the Federation of Mali, entered a united front with the government party.)

In mid-October DADDAH again went to Paris to talk with DE GAULLE, and definitively agreed with the French government on the details of Mauritania's accession to independence.

Shortly after DADDAH's visit to Paris, Prince MOULAY HASSAN of Morocco went to see President HABIB BOURGUIBA of Tunisia to win his support for the Moroccan claim to Mauritania, but his mission proved unsuccessful.

In the night of November 8 Mayor ABDELLAHI OULD OBEID of the town of Atar, a member of the Mauritanian National Assembly, was assassinated by persons unknown. In the communiqué published in this connection the government of Mauritania laid the murder at the door of the Moroccan government. The communiqué said among other things: "The Moroccan government attempts to intimidate the population of Mauritania by acts of terrorism. Such acts incur general condemnation and will attain the contrary of what they are aimed at: they confirm the people of Mauritania in their determination to defend their national independence."

The question of Mauritania was discussed in the First Political Committee of the United Nations General Assembly during the fourteenth session in November 1960. The Moroccan representative pleaded that Mauritania was historically an integral part of Morocco, and that the peoples of the two countries were linked by religious, political and cultural ties. He censured the French who, in his view, insisted on making Mauritania an independent state because they needed that country to build a military base there for their nuclear tests in the Sahara and to secure the colonial exploitation of the country's mineral resources by monopoly capitalism. He referred to the 1956 agreement between France and Morocco, under which the frontiers between Morocco and French West Africa had to be established by way of negotiations. He also blamed the French government for its colonial practices of repressing and persecuting the political groups which advocated Mauritania's union with Morocco, and for its use of unlawful methods to influence the referendum of September 1958, the result of which did not reflect the real will of the people.

There ensued a heated debate during which the Afro-Asian countries could not agree. The Asian and the Arab countries—with the only exception of Tunisia—endorsed the Moroccan claim, while the countries of Black Africa—with the sole exception of Guinea—argued for the independence of Mauritania, that is in support of the position of France. As there was no hope for having the Moroccan position accepted, Indonesia, Jordan and Libya proposed that the United Nations invite France and Morocco to settle the question of Mauritania by way of peaceful negotiations on the basis of the 1956 agreement. Afghanistan moved an amendment proposing that the settlement of the question be discussed, not between France and Morocco, but between the "interested parties", that is Morocco and Mauritania, and this through a new plebiscite under UN supervision. Another amendment[1] went even farther than that: the United Nations should invite the interested parties

---

[1] The amendment was originally presented by India, and after India withdrew it, it was moved by Iraq.

to conduct negotiations, expressing the hope only that the questions would be settled by negotiation, and the paragraph on a new plebiscite should be omitted. Under the rules of procedure, this latter proposal was first put to the vote, and since the Committee rejected it (by 39 votes to 31, with 25 abstentions),[1] the original sponsors withdrew their draft. Thus the question was removed from the agenda of the Political Committee, and the plenary session of the General Assembly did not take it up.

In the meantime, without awaiting the proclamation of independence, the United Kingdom on November 22 and Tunisia on November 23 announced officially their recognition of the new independent state and promised to support its admission to membership in the United Nations. The Moroccan political leaders branded this Tunisian step as a betrayal of Arab unity.

On November 28, 1960, the former French colony became independent as the Islamic Republic of Mauritania. The ceremony was attended by 1,500 foreign guests, including heads of state and government from independent African countries (except Guinea, Mali and Morocco). The French government was represented by Prime Minister DEBRÉ himself. At the festive meeting of the National Assembly DEBRÉ and DADDAH signed the document on the independence of Mauritania. After reading DE GAULLE's personal message, DEBRÉ in his speech emphasized that Mauritania could always count upon the assistance of France "on both the civil and the military line". DADDAH in turn pledged Mauritana's eternal gratitude to the French people and spoke in praiseful terms of President DE GAULLE.

The government of Morocco declared the day of Mauritania's independence the "Day of Protest". Business life stood still, coffeehouses, movies and other places of entertainment kept closed, and prayers were said in the mosques "for the unity of Morocco, for Mauritania's return to the mother country". The government issued a manifesto saying among other things the following: "France has brought herself to carry out a plot against our country by granting sham independence to a large part of our territory. By instituting a puppet government and imprisoning the true representatives of Mauritania she tries to secure a hold over Mauritania for ever, violating thereby international agreements and her obligations arising therefrom." The French Ambassador to Morocco made representations to the Moroccan government on the very same day.

The governments of West Germany and Switzerland recognized the new independent state by cable on the day of independence.

Ivory Coast

The single political party of the Ivory Coast, the *Parti Démocratique de la Côte d'Ivoire* (P.D.C.I.), was established by FÉLIX HOUPHOUËT-BOIGNY[2] in 1946, as

---

[1] The proposal was voted by the Arab and the socialist countries as well as by Burma, Ceylon, India, Indonesia, Nepal, Guinea, the Sudan, Austria, Ireland, Panama, Paraguay and Cuba; those voting against were most of the countries of Black Africa and Latin America, the United Kingdom, France, the United States and the other NATO countries; abstaining from the vote were Ghana, Mali, Tanganyika and Togo among the countries of Black Africa, and Tunisia alone of the Arab countries.

[2] See Vol. III, p. 104.

a result of the reorganization of the "Syndicat Agricole Africain" which he had founded in 1944. After the R.D.A. was formed at the Bamako Conference in 1946, the P.D.C.I. functioned as its Ivory Coast section.

In November 1945, and again in June 1946, HOUPHOUËT-BOIGNY was elected a deputy for the Ivory Coast and the Upper Volta[1] in the French Constituent Assembly, and in November 1946 he was elected to the French National Assembly. In Paris he entered into relations with left-wing parties of France, the French Communist Party among them. When the Communist Party went into opposition the French colonial authorities accused they P.D.C.I. of making communist propaganda, and tried every means to annihilate it: they persecuted members of the party, banned their meetings and demonstrations, used unlawful means to defeat the party's candidates at the elections, and dismissed from office the chiefs and officials sympathetic to the party. At the same time they sponsored the organizations opposed to the P.D.C.I. The party responded by intensifying its activity: it organized a boycott of European shopkeepers and a strike of African domestic servants which was joined by workers of the Abidjan Niger–Railway, it staged women's demonstrations, etc. The party became especially active in 1949–1950. The reaction of the colonial administration was the cruelest kind of police terror.

Although the participants of the aforesaid actions refrained from every form of violence, and no harm came to any European, the rumour was spread among the population that HOUPHOUËT-BOIGNY's followers wanted to kill all French inhabitants of Abidjan. On January 24, 1950, a warrant was issued for the arrest of HOUPHOUËT-BOIGNY. The arrest could not be carried out because of his parliamentary immunity, yet the news of the warrant caused great excitement in Abidjan. On January 30, 1950, in the market place of the district seat Dimbokro a crowd of 3,000 demonstrators gathered with the purpose of presenting to the colonial authorities a petition in favour of HOUPHOUËT-BOIGNY. The police ordered out to disperse the demonstrators opened fire on the people, killing 13 and wounding 50 of them.

On February 1, the French government banned all meetings of R.D.A. branches throughout French West Africa, and dispatched troops to the Ivory Coast from Senegal. Relying on their help the colonial administration started another campaign of terror, killing 52 Africans, wounding hundreds of them, and making about three thousand arrests. On March 2, thirty-seven of the arrested people were brought to trial at Grand-Bassam on the charge of having organized an uprising "on instructions from distant places", and 21 of them were sentenced to various prison terms. (The groundlessness of the charge is shown by the fact that in January 1951 the High Court in Dakar repealed all those sentences.)

The repressive measures the colonial administration applied against the R.D.A., and the slandering propaganda spread against HOUPHOUËT-BOIGNY and his party by the authorities and their African agents as well as the French settlers, discouraged a number of the leaders of the party, first of all many chiefs and religious leaders. The party's influence was declining, and there was a constant increase in the membership of minor political groups[2] aided by the administration and directed in part by French settlers, in part by Africans in the pay of the colonial authorities. This change was borne out clearly by the subsequent elections. At the election to the Senate in June 1950, when the President of the Ivory Coast Territorial Assembly

[1] The French government in 1932 annexed the Upper Volta to the Ivory Coast.
[2] See *Afrique Nouvelle*, Dec. 6, 1951.

233

was re-elected, the former holder of this function, AUGUSTE DENISE[1] of the R.D.A., was defeated. To put a stop to his party's disintegration and to win the favour of the colonial administration, HOUPHOUËT-BOIGNY decided to dissociate himself publicly from the French Communist Party and, by making a complete political about-face, to give up oppositionism and follow a policy of collaboration with the French government and the local colonial administration.

In October 1950 HOUPHOUËT-BOIGNY made a declaration in the French National Assembly that the R.D.A. broke with the French Communist Party and would function as a "purely African party". A year later, in a newspaper article he gave as a reason for his break with the Communists that Communism was based on class war, and it did not make sense to speak of class war in a country where classes were non-existent. He stated in the same article that the aim of his party was "to make Africa flourish and to turn it into the most loyal country of the French Union".

The colonial administration and the French settlers at first were suspicious of HOUPHOUËT-BOIGNY's change of front, but they soon became convinced that his conversion was not a tactical move, and that his former revolutionary line had been insincere. In the first half of the fifties HOUPHOUËT-BOIGNY managed to establish close co-operation both with French business quarters and with the colonial administration. He succeeded in doing so by adapting the political activities of his party, on the one hand, to the policies of the French government and, on the other, to the business interests owned by large French firms and French settlers in the Ivory Coast.[2] As a result of his co-operation with French capitalists, the exports of the Ivory Coast increased to a considerable extent (amounting in 1956 to 44 per cent of the total exports of all countries of French West Africa), and his stand for the French government secured the P.D.C.I. (and the R.D.A. in general) the support of the colonial authorities in every election (to the French National Assembly, the Territorial Assembly and the municipal councils). It was due to this support that while in 1951, when HOUPHOUËT-BOIGNY was re-elected, the R.D.A. sent to the French National Assembly only three members for the whole of French West Africa, yet in January 1956, in addition to HOUPHOUËT-BOIGNY and COULIBALY[3] as deputies for the Ivory Coast, another seven R.D.A. candidates were elected to the National Assembly for other countries of French West Africa, and that the P.D.C.I. won a sweeping victory everywhere in the Ivory Coast territorial elections held on Novem-

[1] AUGUSTE DENISE, a member of the Baoulé tribe, was born in the Ivory Coast village of Tiassale in 1906. He went to school at Dakar, where he graduated in medicine. He practised as a doctor first in Senegal, then at Abidjan, and won great reputation. In 1945 he was one of the founders of the P.D.C.I., which in 1946 elected him General Secretary. In October 1946 he attended the R.D.A. conference at Bamako as a delegate of his party. In 1946 he became a member of the Ivory Coast Territorial Assembly, of which he was President from 1947 to 1950. In 1957 he became Vice-Premier and then Prime Minister in the government established under the loi-cadre.

[2] Characteristic of the way HOUPHOUËT-BOIGNY matched his policy to the intentions of the French government was the attitude he took at joint conferences of the R.D.A. parties and during the talks with leaders of sister parties, regarding the question of federation between the countries of French West Africa. The creation of a federation, which would have strengthened the position of the West African countries, ran counter to the interests of the French government, and it was HOUPHOUËT-BOIGNY, who endeavoured to make the antifederal policy of the French government prevail against the large majority of the political leaders of the fraternal countries.

[3] DANIEL OUEZZIN COULIBALY, one of the founder members of the R.D.A., was born in the Upper Volta in 1909. He graduated from William Ponty College, where he took a master's

234

ber 18, 1956, and March 31, 1957. In the meantime, in November 1956, HOUPHOUËT-BOIGNY was elected also Mayor of Abidjan.

Still in 1956 HOUPHOUËT-BOIGNY became Minister attached to the Prime Minister's Office in Paris, and he then remained a member of the cabinet for three years. In this capacity he had a share in the launching of aggression against Egypt, and in January 1957 he represented in the United Nations the French government's colonialist position in the question of Togoland.

As a member of the French government, HOUPHOUËT-BOIGNY took an active part in the preparation of the *loi-cadre*. The Ivory Coast government formed under the *loi-cadre* after the elections of March 1957 passed into the hands of the P.D.C.I., which practically meant HOUPHOUËT-BOIGNY himself. In his place and under his control, the post of Vice-Premier (later Prime Minister) was filled by AUGUSTE DENISE.

In the September 1958 referendum the majority of the electorate, heeding the propaganda of HOUPHOUËT-BOIGNY and his party, voted "yes". But the unified stand which the party showed during the referendum did not reflect the real situation within the party. Young members of the party had from 1956 increasingly voiced their discontent with the party leadership, accusing it of yielding to the influence of the well-to-do conservative planters and merchants. This discontent was especially growing when, at the Bamako conference of the R.D.A. in September 1957, DENISE, in opposition to the majority of the delegates, was against the formation of a federal government of French West Africa. DENISE was also later the foremost champion of this position within the P.D.C.I. (When the Grand Council of French West Africa passed a decision on the establishment of a French African Executive Council, DENISE most resolutely declared that if this should be realized the Ivory Coast would conclude a separate agreement with France.) Although the party's submission to the colonialists as well as its opposition to the idea of federation tallied with HOUPHOUËT-BOIGNY's political line, the critics cast the blame for the inadequate policy not upon the absent HOUPHOUËT-BOIGNY but upon DENISE who was heading both the party and the government. The oppositionist mood was so prevalent in the party that it led to open attack against the leadership at the party congress which took place from March 19 to 21, 1959. Leadership by DENISE was sharply criticized, and the delegates were unwilling to re-elect him as General Secretary. Instead they elected JEAN-BAPTISTE MOCKEY,[1] who was known to disagree with HOUPHOUËT-BOIGNY's submissive policy towards the French government, the colonial authorities and the French colonists. Seeing that MOCKEY was favoured by public opinion, HOUPHOUËT-BOIGNY also consented to DENISE's replacement by MOCKEY.

---

degree. From 1935 till 1942 he taught at William Ponty College. Between 1946 and 1951, and again from 1956 to 1958, he was a member of the Ivory Coast Territorial Assembly, and from 1947 to 1953 a member of the French National Assembly.

[1] JEAN-BAPTISTE MOCKEY was born in the Nzima tribe (of which also KWAME NKRUMAH came) in 1915 in the Ivory Coast, near the Gold Coast border. He graduated in pharmacology at the Dakar school of medicine. Returning to his country, he became head of the laboratory of the Abidjan central hospital. After the war he took an active part in politics. In 1946 he was elected to the Territorial Assembly. In 1949 he was arrested and sentenced to two years in prison. After serving his term he resumed his political activities. In 1956 he became Chief of the Secretariat to HOUPHOUËT-BOIGNY and Administrative Secretary of the P.D.C.I. In the same year he was elected Mayor of Grand-Bassam. In 1957 he was re-elected to the Territorial Assembly and appointed Minister of the Interior in the DENISE government formed under the *loi-cadre*.

Despite the inner-party troubles, the parliamentary elections held on March 22, 1959, resulted in the P.D.C.I.'s gaining all seats. Having drawn the lesson, HouPHOUËT-BOIGNY resigned from his post in the French government. In April 1959 he returned to the Ivory Coast and began to make order in the affairs of his party and to consolidate the position of the government. First of all, in order to break the resistance of the young people, he summoned a youth conference and reshuffled the government in May to include in it MOCKEY (as Vice-Premier) and several representatives of the youth, among them AMADOU KONÉ.[1]

HOUPHOUËT-BOIGNY's plan was carried out in May 1959: on the 29th the Prime Ministers, Parliamentary Presidents and competent Ministers of the Ivory Coast, Dahomey, Upper Volta and Niger met at Abidjan and formed a loose alliance of the four countries, the so-called Entente Council *(Conseil de l'Entente)*. This first meeting of the Council discussed the questions of economic co-operation. It was decided to set up a Solidarity Fund (into which each member country had to contribute 11 per cent of its real revenue, while only 1/16 part of the basic receipts went to the Ivory Coast and 5/16 to each of the other three countries), to maintain the customs union introduced by the French colonialists, and also to co-ordinate their economic and social policies. The conception of a common political body did not come up.

In July 1959 DE GAULLE appointed HOUPHOUËT-BOIGNY Minister of State as a minister-counsellor of the French Community.

HOUPHOUËT-BOIGNY and MOCKEY did not co-operate long. MOCKEY, who stood up for full independence and wished to follow the example of the Federation of Mali, being unwilling to accept HOUPHOUËT-BOIGNY's opportunist policy, in September 1959 resigned from his post of Vice-Premier and in October stepped down as General Secretary of the party as well. (Shortly afterwards he lost also his office of Mayor, since HOUPHOUËT-BOIGNY dissolved the town council of Grand-Bassam.)

In spring of 1960 HOUPHOUËT-BOIGNY performed his second about-face. When in December 1959 DE GAULLE agreed that the Federation of Mali become independent without leaving the French Community, HOUPHOUËT-BOIGNY angrily realized that his opportunist policy was in an impasse: he had given up the demand for independence because he had wanted his country to remain within the French Community. Now that membership in the French Community was no longer inconsistent with independence, it made no sense for the Ivory Coast and the other countries of the Entente Council to demand autonomy within the French Community instead of independence. On April 4, 1960, the day the independence agreement between France and the Federation of Mali was signed, HOUPHOUËT-BOIGNY declared: "No matter what the outcome of the current developments may be, the Ivory Coast and her friends will never be willing to accept an inferior position in Africa or in the formation which is now called the renewed Community."

Two weeks later, on April 16, the Entente Council instructed HOUPHOUËT-BOIGNY to submit to DE GAULLE the request for independence of the four countries. On

---

[1] AMADOU KONÉ was born at Tabou in 1926. He received secondary and university education in Paris, where he obtained a doctor's degree in surgery. He displayed great activity among the African students in Paris. From 1953 to 1956 he was President of the Association of Ivory Coast Students in Paris. Returning to his country, he was an active member of the "Ivory Coast R.D.A. Youth" which was combating the opportunist policy of the P.D.C.I. and the DENISE government. In March 1959 he was elected General Secretary of the youth organization.

June 1, HOUPHOUËT-BOIGNY went to see DE GAULLE and obtained his consent in principle. On June 3 the four Prime Ministers handed DE GAULLE the formal request of their governments that the French Community, without any preliminary agreement regarding future co-operation, should transfer all powers to the governments of the four territories. On June 11 Prime Minister DEBRÉ of France and the Prime Ministers of the four countries signed in Paris the agreement on the transfer of sovereignty. The agreements were ratified by the French Parliament on July 20 and by the legislatures of the Entente countries on July 27. In early August independence was granted to the four Entente countries, of which the Ivory Coast came last — on August 11.

Dahomey

SOUROU MIGAN APITHY[1] founded the Dahomey section of the R.D.A., the *Union Progressiste Dahoméenne* (U.P.D.), in 1946.

The U.P.D. recruited its membership almost exclusively in the South of Dahomey controlled by Roman Catholic missionaries. Yielding to pressure from the missionaries, the party broke soon with the R.D.A. on account of the latter's connections with the French Communist Party.

At the 1951 elections to the French National Assembly, when Dahomey elected two members, Southern Dahomey again elected APITHY, while Northern Dahomey sent HUBERT MAGA[2] to the National Assembly. APITHY became one of the secretaries of the Assembly and held that post until 1955.

In 1951 the U.P.D. split: the Southerners led by APITHY left the party and founded the *Parti Républicain du Dahomey* (P.R.D.), while the Northerners formed a party of their own, the *Groupement Ethnique du Nord-Dahomey* (under MAGA's leadership).

At the 1952 elections to the Territorial Assembly APITHY's party gained 19 out of 32 seats; MAGA's party, which had in the meantime changed its name to *Mouvement Démocratique du Dahomey* (M.D.D.), formed the minority.

In November 1955 a new party appeared in the political scene. JUSTIN AHOMADEGBÉ's[3] *Union Démocratique Dahoméenne* (U.D.D.). This party absorbed also the U.P.D., which had shrunken to a minor group after the withdrawal of APITHY and MAGA, and from 1956 functioned as a section of the R.D.A.

---

[1] SOUROU MIGAN APITHY was born at Porto-Novo in April 1913. He went to a local mission school, then studied in Bordeaux and Paris, where he qualified as an accountant. First he was employed by a French company, and later he ran an office on his own. In 1945–1946 he was a member for Dahomey and Togoland in the French Constituent Assembly. In October 1946 he attended the Bamako founding conference of the R.D.A. and was elected Vice-President of the organizing committee. In November of the same year he was elected a deputy for Dahomey to the French National Assembly. In 1948 APITHY was among the founders of the I.O.M. (Indépendants d'Outre-Mer).

[2] HUBERT MAGA was born the son of a peasant family at Parakou in Northern Dahomey in August 1910. He graduated from a teacher's college in Dahomey and taught in school for years, then became a headmaster and acquired great reputation in the North of the country. He founded the first boy-scout group in Dahomey. In 1951 he was elected a deputy for Dahomey to the French National Assembly, where he joined the I.O.M. group.

[3] JUSTIN AHOMADEGBÉ was born in the Fon tribe's ruling family at Abomey in 1917. He studied in Senegal, first at William Ponty School, then at the Medical College in Dakar, where he qualified as a dentist and then practised dentistry for years in the service of the colonial administration. In 1952 he became a member for Abomey in the Territorial Assembly.

In January 1956 MAGA was re-elected to the French National Assembly, and from November 1957 until April 1958 was Under-Secretary for Labour in the GAILLARD cabinet.

At the elections in March 1957 the P.R.D. obtained 35 of the 60 seats in the Territorial Assembly, while 14 seats went to MAGA's M.D.D. and 7 to AHOMADEGBÉ's U.D.D. After the elections the P.R.D. and the M.D.D. formed a pact, and the coalition government set up under the *loi-cadre* was headed by APITHY. At first MAGA was reluctant to accept a Minister's portfolio, but later he took over the Ministry of Labour. In 1958 the new party elected Dr. EMILE DERLIN ZINSOU[1] its General Secretary. He was Minister of Commerce from July 1958 till April 1959. APITHY and MAGA merged their parties in the *Parti Progressiste Dahoméen* (P.P.D.), which from then on functioned as the Dahomey section of SENGHOR's P.R.A. (Parti du Regroupement Africain).

In the 1958 referendum, thanks to the concurrent agitation of the P.P.D. and the U.D.D., the overwhelming majority voted "yes".

In December 1958 the P.P.D., together with the leading parties of Senegal, Sudan and Upper Volta, stood up for the creation of the Federation of Mali. The U.D.D. closely related to HOUPHOUËT-BOIGNY, however, campaigned against the federation, and organized mass demonstrations against the APITHY government. These demonstrations, on the one hand, and, on the other, the pressure which the French government applied by threatening to withhold the economic aid in case of union with the Federation of Mali, in early March 1959 led APITHY to give up the idea of joining the Federation. But this step of his resulted in a split of the U.P.D. APITHY restored his former party, the P.R.D., and MAGA reorganized his Moslem democratic movement into the *Rassemblement Démocratique Dahoméen* (R.D.D.). But ZINSOU, who consistently favoured union with the Federation of Mali, broke with APITHY and maintained the local branch of the P.R.A., and when in late March 1959 the P.R.A. was replaced by the Parti de la Fédération Africaine (P.F.A.), ZINSOU became its President. (ZINSOU and his group stayed away from the 1959 elections.)

At the legislative elections in April 1959 APITHY's governing party managed to gerrymander the constituencies so that it gained 37 seats by polling 144,038 votes, and MAGA's R.D.D. obtained 22 seats with 62,132 votes, while the 172,179 votes cast for AHOMADEGBÉ's U.D.D. brought this party only 11 seats. This election trick caused public indignation and provoked mass demonstrations, so that the government called in troops from the Niger to calm down the people. In such circumstances APITHY saw fit to agree to hold new elections in nine constituencies (formally the new elections were decreed by the Supreme Court of Dahomey), and to come to terms with AHOMADEGBÉ on a common stand of the two parties to vote for the U.D.D. candidates. As a result, the new legislature consisted of 28 members from the P.R.D., 22 from the R.D.D. and 20 from the U.D.D. Afterwards the three parties agreed that they would form a coalition government under MAGA, in which each

---

[1] ÉMILE DERLIN ZINSOU was born at Ouidah in March 1918. He was educated at William Ponty School and at the Medical College of Dakar, then graduated from university in Paris, where he took his degree in medicine. In 1945 he again went to Paris and became APITHY's secretary. In 1946 he was a founder member of the R.D.A., but later broke with it, and in 1955, becoming a member for Dahomey in the French Senate, he joined the I.O.M. group. In 1958, when the P.R.A. was formed, he as a follower of SENGHOR's joined that organization, which elected him Joint Federal Secretary. ZINSOU was one of the most ardent champions not only of the federation of Senegal, Sudan, Dahomey and Upper Volta, but he advocated the union of all countries and all political parties of French West Africa.

of the three parties received four portfolios. AHOMADEGBÉ became President of the Assembly.

Shortly after the elections, in May 1959, MAGA's government joined the Entente Council established by HOUPHOUËT-BOIGNY.

Dahomey won independence on August 1, 1960.

Upper Volta

The first political association in the Upper Volta after the war was brought to life by a feudal ruler of the Mossi tribe, MOGHO NABA; it was called the *Union pour la Défense des Intérêts de la Haute-Volta*. The organization set itself a single aim: to obtain administrative autonomy for the Upper Volta, which had been annexed to the Ivory Coast in 1932, that is to restore the pre-1932 territorial status. The Union was founded prior to the 1945 elections to the French Constituent Assembly. HOU-PHOUËT-BOIGNY tried to persuade MOGHO NABA that the Mossi should also support the candidate of the Ivory Coast R.D.A., but NABA proposed the candidacy of a member of his party, who made propaganda for the country's separate status. The R.D.A. candidate won by a slight majority, but the many votes cast for the Mossi candidate showed that the overwhelming majority of the Mossi were for MOGHO NABA's policy.

In 1946 the organization was transformed into a political party and was named the Volta Union *(Union Voltaïque)*. Members of the party were recruited mainly from Mossi chiefs and young Catholic intellectuals, and this ensured the party the support of both MOGHO NABA and the Catholic missionaries. In its policy the party followed SENGHOR's line and entered into relations with the I.O.M. (Indépendants d'Outre-Mer). In 1947, when President AURIOL of the French Republic made a tour of French West Africa, MOGHO NABA availed himself of the occasion to convince the President of the rightfulness of his people's demand. That the French government met the Mossi demand may have been due to this conversation between MOGHO NABA and the President, but still more to the French government's intention to prevent by this step the R.D.A. from spreading into the Upper Volta. Thus it was that on September 4, 1947, the Upper Volta regained its former status and was re-established as a separate colonial entity.

In 1948 two followers of HOUPHOUËT-BOIGNY's, DJIBRIL VINAMA and ALI BAR-RAUD, formed in the Bobo-Dioulasso district the Upper Volta section of the R.D.A. called the *Parti Démocratique Voltaïque* (P.D.V.). The party relied mainly on the western districts of the country, first of all on Bobo-Dioulasso, inhabited by minor tribes other than Mossi (Gourounsi, Lobi, Fulah), which, after the restoration of the separate status of the Upper Volta, came to be at a disadvantage in view of the numerical superiority of the Mossi, and were therefore dissatisfied with the adminis-tration. The colonial authorities, including the Governor himself, did their utmost to disrupt the party's activities. In spite of this several candidates of the P.D.V. were elected, and one of them was even made President of the Grand Council. After the elections, however, the party was rapidly losing its influence. This may be ascribed, on the one hand, to persecution by the authorities,[1] and, on the other hand, to the

---

[1] The inter-territorial R.D.A. headed by HOUPHOUËT-BOIGNY chose Bobo-Dioulasso as the venue of its second conference, but the Upper Volta colonial administration denied the permission, and the conference was held at Abidjan.

fact that a great part of the chiefs had been discouraged by the slanderous anti-R.D.A. propaganda in which the other parties — and the colonial administration — represented the R.D.A. as a communist organization. The decline of the party's influence was already manifest during the by-elections to the Grand Council in November 1948, and still more at the elections in June 1951 and in October 1953, when even the only candidate of the party was defeated.

In 1954 a new political party appeared in the political arena in the district of Bobo-Dioulasso: the *Mouvement Populaire d'Evolution Africaine* (M.P.E.A.) founded by NAZI BONI.[1] The party was sharply opposed to the local R.D.A. section, the P.D.V., and established contacts with the I.O.M. The main point of its programme was the demand that the country be divided into two parts: a Mossi and a non-Mossi territory. Since the colonial administration had always followed the policy of "divide and rule" and was interested in pushing back the R.D.A., it gave its support to the new party.

After the separation was completed, the prestige and influence of the Volta Union increased considerably. The Union gained ground especially during the elections of June 1951 and October 1953. From 1953, however, there were within the party ever growing differences between the conservative older chiefs and Catholic-influenced educated young people, on the one hand, and, on the other, the politicians who represented with the party leadership the interests of various parts of the country and were influenced by different tribal rulers. These internal conflicts in January 1955 led to the disintegration of the Volta Union. JOSEPH CONOMBO,[2] whose influence and authority had considerably grown since he had been Under-Secretary of State for the Interior in the French cabinet, founded the *Parti Social d'Education des Masses Africaines* (P.S.E.M.A.), which in its programme promised reforms and emphasized its opposition "to any party striving to debar the Africans from the handling of their own affairs, and to any movement whose existence is only due to the conflict of local interests, to the instigation of hatred among families and races". By January 1955 the party had about 500,000 members, holding the majority in the Territorial Assembly and having two members in the French National Assembly.

In November 1956 the P.D.V. and the P.S.E.M.A. were merged into the *Parti Démocratique Unifié* (P.D.U.) under the presidency of OUEZZIN COULIBALY and under the patronage of MOGHO NABA as honorary president.

Simultaneously with the birth of the P.D.U., MICHEL DORANGE[3] and KANGO, GÉRARD OUÉDRAOGO[4] founded the *Mouvement Démocratique Voltaïque* (M.D.V.), which represented the interests of the western districts hostile to the Mossi chiefs. One of the leaders of this party was MAURICE YAMÉOGO.[5]

---

[1] NAZI BONI was born in the Bobo-Dioulasso district in 1912. He came from a tribe independent of the Mossi ruler. He graduated from William Ponty School in Dakar, and then taught in school at home. In 1946, and again in 1951, the Bobo-Dioulasso district elected him to the French National Assembly. In 1950 he founded a social organization called the *Amicale Voltaïque.*

[2] JOSEPH CONOMBO, was born of a Roman Catholic family in the Upper Volta in 1917. He graduated from William Ponty College in Senegal and qualified as a doctor in Paris. In 1951 he was elected to the French National Assembly, where he joined the I.O.M. group.

[3] MICHEL DORANGE, a French army officer and member of the French National Assembly was born in 1917.

[4] KANGO GÉRARD OUÉDRAOGO, a scion of the Mossi rulers' family, a finance official, was born in the Upper Volta in 1925.

[5] MAURICE YAMÉOGO, a member of the Mossi tribe and a Catholic, was born in the locality of Koudougou of the Upper Volta. He graduated from secondary school in Pabret, and then

At the elections to the Territorial Assembly in March 1957 the P.D.U. gained 37 seats, the M.D.V. won 27 and the M.P.E.A. obtained 7 seats. After the elections the P.D.U. and the M.D.V. formed a coalition government under OUEZZIN COULIBALY who was a close acquaintance of HOUPHOUËT-BOIGNY. But the coalition did not last long, it was dissolved in December 1957. The M.P.E.A., the M.D.V., and a third opposition party, the P.S.E.M.A., merged into a new party called "Volta Solidarity" and formed a unified opposition of COULIBALY's governing party. The unified opposition managed to obtain a majority and to have NAZI BONI elected President of the Assembly by 37 votes to 31 cast for the R.D.A. But COULIBALY refused to resign, and after winning over a few Assembly members, he soon succeeded in regaining the majority, and in April 1958 he even managed to depose NAZI BONI from the parliamentary presidency. After that NAZI BONI and his party entered into close relations with SENGHOR's and KEITA's party (P.F.A.), and pursued propaganda, in and out of the legislature, for union with the Federation of Mali.

On September 7, 1958, COULIBALY died. After some delay YAMÉOGO was appointed to succeed him as Prime Minister. YAMÉOGO formed the new coalition government, in which he included seven members of his party and only five members of the opposition party associated with SENGHOR's organization.

In the September 1958 referendum the Upper Volta voted "yes".

In January 1959 the U.D.V. decided to join the nascent Federation of Mali together with Senegal, the Sudan and Dahomey. Under pressure from HOUPHUËET-BOIGNY, however, YAMÉOGO gave up this plan and prepared a draft Constitution, the adoption of which was tantamount to rejection of union with the Federation. On March 15, 1959, he organized a plebiscite in which "yes" meant adoption of the draft Constitution and "no" meant union with the Federation. By bringing pressure to bear upon the electorate, YAMÉOGO managed to secure for the draft 1,011,804 out of 1,265,805 valid votes, while only 254,001 votes were cast for joining the Federation. The parties that had stood by the Federation withdrew from the coalition.

A month after the plebiscite the new legislative elections were held under the new Constitution. To win the absolute majority for its parties the government enacted an electoral law securing this aim[1] (as a consequence, the U.D.V. by polling only 62 per cent of the votes gained over 90 per cent of the seats — 70 out of 75). The new government, which now consisted entirely of YAMÉOGO's followers, could without difficulty join the Entente Council which had been established by HOUPHOUËT-BOIGNY in May and whose members were thus the Ivory Coast, Dahomey, the Upper Volta and Niger.

NAZI BONI, who still favoured rapprochement with Mali, in March 1959 founded the *Parti National Voltaïque* (P.N.V.), as a member of the inter-territorial P.F.A., at the same time as the Federation of Mali. The YAMÉOGO government banned this

---

became a civil servant. In 1946 he was elected to the Territorial Assembly, and in 1948 he became a member of the Grand Council of French West Africa. For years he was a member of the French Christian trade-union centre, the Confédération Française des Travailleurs Chrétiens (C.F.T.C.).

[1] In the two main constituencies, which together elected 59 members, a majority slate system was introduced, that is all seats were given to the party (the U.D.V.) which, by counting all votes cast in all districts, obtained the majority; on the other hand, in the two urban constituencies (Ouakigouya and Ouagadougou) the proportional system was applied, which meant that in Ouagadougou, despite the majority secured by NAZI BONI's M.P.E.A., three of eight seats were captured by YAMÉOGO's Union Démocratique Voltaïque. (The P.D.U. associated with the R.D.A. took up this name in 1958.)

party in October 1959. A few days later NAZI BONI formed the *Parti Républicain de la Liberté*, likewise affiliated with the P.F.A. This party was not long-lived either: it was also banned by YAMÉOGO in January 1960. But the party continued functioning underground. Immediately before independence, in July, jointly with another opposition organization, the "Peasant Action Group", it addressed an open letter to the government, criticizing its policies and demanding the calling of a round-table conference with the participation of representatives of the opposition to discuss the matters concerning accession to independence. YAMÉOGO called the authors of the letter "ill-willed agitators representing no one" and had them arrested — except NAZI BONI who managed to flee to Mali.

The Upper Volta became independent on August 4, 1960. Characteristically, YAMÉOGO in his speech on the occasion of the independence festivities extolled DE GAULLE to the skies as the one to whom the country was indebted for its freedom.

The Niger

The first political party in the Niger, the *Parti Progressiste Nigérien* (P.P.N.), was founded by two young African teachers, DJIBO BAKARY[1] and HAMANI DIORI,[2] in 1946, shortly after the R.D.A.'s Bamako conference as the Niger section of the R.D.A. BAKARY was elected General Secretary of the party, and DIORI became deputy for the Niger in the French National Assembly.

When in 1960 the R.D.A. changed its policy and broke with the French Communist Party, a split occurred in the ranks of the P.P.N. HAMANI DIORI took the side of HOUPHOUËT-BOIGNY, but DJIBO BAKARY could not agree with the new policy of the R.D.A., resigned from the P.P.N. and founded a new party, called the *Union Démocratique Nigérienne* (U.D.N.). The general secretaryship was taken over by DIORI. But the withdrawal of BAKARY's followers weakened the P.P.N. considerably, while the U.D.N., relying on the trade unions and thus on a broad mass basis, grew ever stronger. As a result, DIORI was not re-elected at the 1951 elections to the French National Assembly. In the next few years, however, DIORI's P.P.N., which enjoyed tacit support from the colonial authorities, regained vigour and at the following elections in 1956 DIORI again became deputy for the Niger in the French National Assembly, although BAKARY as his opponent polled only a few votes less than was cast for him.

At the 1956 municipal elections 13 seats were gained by DIORI's party, 10 by BAKARY's and 4 by the *Bloc Nigérien d'Action* (B.N.A.), a new party, which maintained relations with the French Socialist Party and was headed by ISSOUFOY SEYDOU DJERMAKOYE. BAKARY was elected Mayor of Niamey.

In January 1957 BAKARY and DIORI merged their parties in the *Mouvement Socialiste Africain* (M.S.A.), which regarded itself the Niger section of LAMINE GUÈYE's party functioning under the same name in Senegal.

At the March 1957 elections to the Territorial Assembly the M.S.A. obtained the absolute majority (41 seats against 19 for DIORI's P.P.N.), and thus the new government headed by BAKARY was formed of M.S.A. members.

[1] DJIBO BAKARY was born in the Niger in 1922. He was educated in Dakar. After his return, from 1941 onwards, he taught in school.

[2] HAMANI DIORI was born at Soudouré (Niger) in 1916. He went to school at Niamey, Porto-Novo and Dakar. From 1936 to 1938 he taught in school in his country, first at Niamey and then at Maradi. In 1938–1939 he taught at the "Ecole de la France d'Outremer" in Paris, and when he returned to his country he became a headmaster at Niamey.

Early in 1958, after the inter-territorial P.R.A. led by SENGHOR had formed, BAKARY's party also joined it and changed its name to "Sawaba" (Freedom) Party.

The BAKARY government remained in office only one year and a half. In the September 1958 referendum BAKARY and his party, following SÉKOU TOURÉ's example, took a stand for complete independence from France, and called upon its members to vote "no". But DIORI's P.P.N., with the aid of reactionary chiefs (and the colonial authorities), and owing to the deserter DJERMAKOYE's breaking with BAKARY and going over to DIORI, succeeded in making sure that the huge majority of the electorate votes "yes", including a few members of the BAKARY government who had left their posts. After this the BAKARY government resigned on October 29. As more than half of the Assembly members stood down, the French government dissolved the Territorial Assembly and called new elections for December 14. This time DIORI's party, which had in the meantime changed its name to *Union pour la Communauté Franco-Africaine* (U.C.F.A.), gained 54 of 60 sets, the remaining 6 seats, all of them in the Zinder district, were won by BAKARY's party.

After the elections BAKARY continued campaigning for union with the Federation of Mali, and his party became the territorial section of the P.F.A. At the same time BAKARY, just as SENGHOR and GUÈYE, protested against illegal practices during the elections and demanded that new elections be held, but naturally to no avail. To the protest DIORI responded by having the Assembly pass a resolution on the exclusion of the six members of BAKARY's party, and for June 27 called new elections in the Zinder district, but BAKARY's party was debarred from participation, and so the seats were given to DIORI's men.

In accordance with the election results, the new government was formed of DIORI's followers with him as Prime Minister. The first thing the new government did was to dissolve the Niamey municipal council, which was headed by BAKARY as Mayor. The DIORI government had from the outset rejected the idea of union with the Federation of Mali, and in May 1959 announced its joining the Entente Council established by HOUPHOUËT-BOIGNY.

In July 1959 the DIORI government disbanded the Niger section of the Labour Union of Black Africa and in October banned also the Sawaba Party and arrested many of its members. BAKARY fled and took refuge in Bamako.

Getting rid of all organized opposition, and enlisting thus the support of the French government and of the reactionary chiefs (a special governmental department was set up for the protection of the chiefs' interests), DIORI became absolute master of the situation.

The Niger was proclaimed independent on August 3, 1960.

BIBLIOGRAPHY

FRENCH WEST AFRICA

G. SPITZ, *L'Ouest africain français*, Paris, 1947.

E. GUERNIER (ed.), *L'Afrique Occidentale Française*, Paris, 1949, Vols I–II.

E. LANTENOIS, "L'urbanisme en A.O.F.", in GUERNIER, *L'Afrique Occidentale Française*, Vol. II.

R. DELAVIGNETTE, *Freedom and Authority in French West Africa*, New York, 1950.

K. E. ROBINSON, "Economic Development in French West Africa", *World Today*, Dec. 1950.

A. GOUILLY, *L'Islam dans l'A.O.F.*, Paris, 1952.

CH. A. MASSA, "Notes sur les conditions de vie du travailleur africain en A.O.F.", *L'Afrique et l'Asie* 19/1952.

H. LABOURET, *Paysans d'Afrique occidentale*, Paris, 1953.

T. L. Hodgkin, "Political Parties in British and French West Africa", *Information Digest* (Africa Bureau) 10/1953.

Hommage à Jacques Richard-Molard, Paris, 1953. (A selection published by *Présence Africaine* in memory of the author.)

T. L. Hodgkin, "Background on French West Africa", *West Africa*, Jan.–April 1954.

J. Pouquet, *L'Afrique Occidentale Française*, Paris, 1954.

E. Berg, *Trade Unions in French West Africa* (M. A. thesis, Columbia Univ.), New York, 1954.

K. E. Robinson, "Political Development in French West Africa", in *Africa in the Modern World*, Chicago, 1955.

J. W. Saxe, "The Changing Economic Structure of French West Africa", in *Annals of the American Academy of Political and Social Science*, March 1955, pp. 52–61.

Г. Скоров, *Французский империализм в Западной Африке* [French Imperialism in West Africa], Moscow, 1956.

J. Richard-Molard, *Afrique Occidentale Française*. Berger-Levrault, 1956.

W. Reichhold, "Wirtschaftsfragen Französisch-Westafrikas", in *Afrika heute*, Bonn, 1957, pp. 187–190.

P. H. Siriex, *Une nouvelle Afrique — A.O.F. 1957*. Plon, 1957.

W. Reichhold, *Westafrika*, Bonn, 1958.

J. Richard-Molard, "Problèmes humains en Afrique occidentale", *Présence Africaine* (1958).

R. Schachter, *Some Aspects of the Development of Political Parties in French West Africa*, Oxford, 1958.

V. Thompson and R. Adloff, *French West Africa*, London, 1958.

Ernest Milcent, *L'A.O.F. entre en scène*, Paris, 1958.

B. Davidson, "France and West Africa", *New Statesman*, Aug. 9, 1958.

Gray Cowan, *Local Government in West Africa*, London, 1959.

S. C. Easton, *The Twilight of European Colonialism*, New York, 1960, pp. 346–375.

Н. Е. Гаврилов, *Западная Африка под гнетом франции (1949–1959)* [West Africa under the Yoke of France (1949–1959)], Moscow, 1961.

Annuaire des Républiques de l'Ouest Africain, Dakar (Havas Afrique), 1960.

D. T. Niane and J. Suret-Canale, *Histoire de l'Afrique occidentale*, Conakry, 1961.

A. Летнев, "Аграрные отношения в Западной Африке" [Agrarian Conditions in West Africa], *Мировая экономика и международные отношения*, Moscow, 7/1962.

Colin Newbury, "The Government General and Political Change in French West Africa", in K. Kirkwood, *African Affairs*, Carbondale, Ill., pp. 41–59.

Philip Neres, *French-Speaking West Africa: From Colonial Status to Independence*, London, 1962.

I. Kende, *A francia gyarmatbirodalom felbomlása Nyugat-Afrikában* [Disintegration of the French Colonial Empire in West Africa], Budapest, 1964.

Ruth Morgenthau, *Political Parties in French-Speaking West Africa*, London, 1968.

J. D. Hargreaves, *West Africa: The Former French States*, London, 1968.

SENEGAL

Thompson-Adloff, *op. cit.* (1958), pp. 108–117.

E. Séré de Rivière, *Sénégal–Dakar*, Paris, 1953.

Rapport général sur les perspectives de développement du Sénégal (1960).

Territoire du Sénégal: Procès-verbaux des séances du Conseil Général (1946–52) et de l'Assemblée Territoriale (1952–60), Saint-Louis du Sénégal, 1946–60.

M. Crowder, *Senegal: A Study in French Assimilation Policy*, London, 1962.

FRENCH SUDAN

Thompson-Adloff, *op. cit.* (1958), pp. 146–154.

G. Spitz, *Sansanding*, Paris, 1949.

J. Delval, "Le R.D.A. ou Soudan Français", *L'Afrique et l'Asie* 16/1951.

G. Spitz, *Le Soudan Français*, Paris, 1955.
Territoire du Soudan Français: Procès-verbaux des séances du Conseil Général (1947–52) et de l'Assemblée Territoriale (1952–60), Bamako, 1947–60.

FRENCH GUINEA

Thompson-Adloff, *op. cit.* (1958), pp. 132–139.
Roland Pré, *L'avenir de la Guinée Française*, Paris, 1946.
G. Balandier, "L'or de la Guinée Française", *Présence Africaine* 4/1948.
J. Aurillac, *Régime politique et administratif de l'A.O.F.*, Dakar, 1949.
M. Houis, *La Guinée Française*, Paris, 1953.
Territoire de la Guinée Française: Procès-verbaux des séances du Conseil Général (1947–52) et de l'Assemblée Territoriale (1952–56), Conakry, 1947–56.
Etudes guinéennes, Conakry, 1947–1955.
Guinée — Prélude à l'indépendance, Paris, 1958.
F. Gigon, *Guinée, Etat pilote*, Paris, 1959.
Sékou Touré, *L'action politique du Parti Démocratique de Guinée*, Paris, 1959.
Sékou Touré, *African Independence and Unity*, New York, 1959.

MAURITANIA

Thompson-Adloff, *op. cit.* (1958), pp. 162–170.
J. Beyries, "Evolution sociale et culturelle des collectivités nomades de la Mauritanie", *Bulletin du Comité d'Etudes Historiques et Scientifiques de l'A.O.F.*, Dec. 1937.
Jamal Sa'd, *The Problem of Mauritania*, New York, 1960.
White Paper on Mauritania. Kingdom of Morocco: Ministry of Foreign Affairs. Rabat, 1960.
Territoire de la Mauritanie: Procès-verbaux des séances du Conseil Général (1947–52) et de l'Assemblée Territoriale (1952–60), Saint-Louis du Sénégal, 1947–60.
A. G. Gerteiny, *Mauritania*, London, 1967.

IVORY COAST

Thompson-Adloff, *op. cit.* (1958), pp. 122–132.
F. J. Amon d'Aby, *La Côte d'Ivoire dans la cité africaine*, Paris, 1951.
E. Avice, *La Côte d'Ivoire*, Paris, 1951.
B. Badie, "Le sort du travailleur noir de Côte d'Ivoire", in *Le travail en Afrique noire*, Paris, 1952.
G. E. Carter, "The Ivory Coast Expels 'Stranger' Africans", in *Independence for Africa*, New York, 1960, pp. 106–118.
Territoire de la Côte d'Ivoire: Procès-verbaux des séances du Conseil Général (1947—52) et de l'Assemblée Territoriale (1952–60), Abidjan, 1947–60.
I. Wallerstein, *The Road to Independence: Ghana and the Ivory Coast*, Paris, 1964.

DAHOMEY

Thompson-Adloff, *op. cit.* (1958), pp. 139–146.
R. Grivot, *Réactions dahoméennes*, Paris, 1954.
A. Akiendélé and C. Agnessy, *Dahomey*, Paris, 1955.
Territoire du Dahomey: Procès-verbaux des séances du Conseil Général (1947–52) et de l'Assemblée Territoriale (1952–60), Porto-Novo, 1947–60.
R. Cornevin, *Histoire du Dahomey*, Paris, 1963.
R. Cornevin, *Le Dahomey*, Paris, 1963.

UPPER VOLTA

THOMPSON-ADLOFF, *op. cit.* (1958), pp. 171–179.
Territoire de la Haute-Volta: Procès-verbaux des séances du Conseil Général (1947–52) et de l'Assemblée Territoriale (1952–60), Ouagadougou, 1947–60.

NIGER

THOMPSON-ADLOFF, *op. cit.* (1958), pp. 155–162.
E. SÉRÉ DE RIVIÈRE, *Le Niger*, Paris, 1952.
Territoire du Niger: Développement social, Niamey, 1952.
Territoire du Niger: Procès-verbaux des séances du Conseil Général (1947–52) et de l'Assemblée Territoriale (1952–60), Niamey, 1947–60.
P. BOUARDI, *La République du Niger*, Paris, 1960.
ANDRÉ CLAIR, *Le Niger*, Paris, 1965.

CHAPTER XXIV

FRENCH EQUATORIAL AFRICA

The Middle Congo

In the French colony called the Middle Congo two political parties were formed in 1946: in the northern part of the country JACQUES OPANGOULT[1] set up the territorial section of the French Socialist Party (S.F.I.O.), and the *Parti Progressiste Congolais* (P.P.C.) was founded by FÉLIX TCHICAYA[2] in the south. The latter party in 1948 joined the R.D.A. and functioned as its territorial section. While both parties kept in touch with their respective mother parties in France, they were in fact tribal organizations: OPANGOULT's party recruited its members from the Mbochi tribe in the first place, and TCHICAYA's from the Vili tribe. The two parties were active chiefly during elections, when from time to time other tribal factions were also formed which, once defeated at the elections, went out of existence.

Up to 1956 the main factors in the political life of the Middle Congo were not Africans but Gaullist deputies elected to the French National Assembly by the European settlers. Backed up by most of the chiefs and big business interests and having the tacit approval of the colonial administration itself, TCHICAYA from 1946 was on every occasion elected to the French National Assembly by the African voters, but all he did there was to demand that the duality of the electoral system be ended. In the Territorial Assembly, where Africans held the majority (in the Assembly elected in 1952 there were 17 members from the P.P.C. and 7 from OPANGOULT's party), members hardly did more than criticize the colonial administration for disregarding the Assembly's decisions, submitting unfinished bills for consideration and referring delicate matters to select committees, thus bypassing the plenary sessions of the Assembly, and they stood up against proposed tax increases.

The Bakongo, the largest tribe of the Middle Congo, up to 1956 had taken no active part in politics. They had kept aloof from political parties and labour unions, for they took these for agencies of the colonial authorities. Even in the post-war years the greater part of the Bakongo were under the influence of the Matswanist sect,[3] stayed away from the elections, or if they went to the polls at all, they wrote

---

[1] JACQUES OPANGOULT was born in the Mbochi tribe at Ikagna, in the north of the Middle Congo, in December 1907. He went to mission schools and from 1938 was employed at the Brazzaville law court.

[2] FÉLIX TCHICAYA was born in the Vili tribe at Libreville (Gabon) in November 1903. He was a tradesman.

[3] According to BALANDIER, though the sect in 1949 had only 4,000 active members, ninety per cent of the tribe sympathized with the movement. (See *Sociologie actuelle de l'Afrique noire*, p. 403.)

the name of the late ANDRÉ MATSWA on the ballot paper. They protested against the assessment and imposition of taxes, but did not go beyond passive resistance.

In 1956 FULBERT YOULOU[1] formed a new party under the name of *Union Démocratique de Défense des Intérêts Africains* (U.D.D.I.A.). As this party also joined the R.D.A., it took over from the weaker P.P.C. the functions of the R.D.A. section. Several of the P.P.C. leaders, among them S. TCHICHELLE,[2] Vice-President of the Party and Mayor of Pointe-Noire, went over to YOULOU's party.

In 1957, when the African sections of the S.F.I.O. merged into the independent inter-territorial party called the *Mouvement Socialiste Africain*, the Congo section took up the same name (M.S.A.).

At the March 1957 elections 21 members of the M.S.A. and the U.D.D.I.A. each and 3 independents were elected to the Territorial Assembly. Since two of the independents supported OPANGOULT's party, the Governor appointed him to form the government. YOULOU became Minister of Agriculture.

In the referendum held on September 28, 1958, all parties stood by the French Community, and 99.1 per cent of the electorate voted "yes".

Two months later, on November 28, 1958, the Territorial Assembly passed a resolution unanimously, proclaiming the country a Republic and an autonomous member state of the French Community. The country changed its name to the Republic of the Congo.

A the same meeting, however, a shift occurred in the power relations between the two parties: a member of OPANGOULT's party went over to YOULOU's party, which thereby obtained a majority of one vote (23 to 22). Thereupon YOULOU formed a new government, submitted a new draft Constitution and proposed that the seat of government be transferred from Pointe-Noire to Brazzaville. OPANGOULT's followers then provoked a veritable free-for-all in the Assembly. Though the police and the gendarmerie managed to restore order, the M.S.A. members refused to discuss YOULOU's proposals and left the meeting. Being left without opposition, the 23 U.D.D.I.A. members of the Assembly elected YOULOU Prime Minister and passed a decision on the transfer of the capital to Brazzaville. Thereafter the members of the Assembly and their families left Pointe-Noire.

On the same day riots broke out in the city, resulting in four dead and sixteen injured. The riots lasted until December 1, when YOULOU and TCHICHELLE also left for Brazzaville. Upon his arrival there, YOULOU held a press conference at which he promised to include in his new government also representatives of the opposition. But he went back on his word: the government formed on December 8 consisted of members of his party only. The M.S.A. members demanded new elections and

---

[1] FULBERT YOULOU, a member of the Lari tribe, went to mission schools at Brazzaville and in the French Cameroons, and studied theology at Libreville and Brazzaville. In June 1946 he was ordained a priest and became Vicar of the St. Francis Parish in Brazzaville. He was active as an organizer of Catholic youth movements and a hospital chaplain, and as such he became widely known. In 1956, together with TCHICAYA and OPANGOULT, he stood for election to the French National Assembly, and was elected Mayor of Brazzaville. For his political activities, the ecclesiastical authorities suspended him, but he continued to wear the priestly garb and retained the title of *Abbé*.

[2] STÉPHANE TCHICHELLE, a member of the Vili tribe, was born in 1915 at the coastal township of Kouilou. He was educated in mission schools, from 1930 he worked as a railwayman, in 1936 he became station master in Pointe-Noire and an active member of the Railwaymen's Union. From 1946 he was a leader of the Parti Progressiste Congolais and a member of the Territorial Assembly. From 1947 to 1957 he was a member of the Grand Council of French Equatorial Africa. In 1956 he became Mayor of Pointe-Noire.

said that until then they would not attend the Assembly meetings. For weeks on end they staged large-scale demonstrations against the YOULOU government in the suburbs of Brazzaville. This agitation led to bloody tribal conflicts between the Mbochi and the Lari living in the suburbs Poto and Bacongo, respectively. The tribal war that was raging for two days, February 19 and 20, 1959, caused heavy casualties: 130 dead and 170 wounded. To put an end to the massacre, the French authorities dispatched 1,300 troops, whose appearance stopped the fightings — allegedly without bloodshed. Three hundred and fifty rioters, among them OPAN-GOULT, were arrested.

On February 21 the Territorial Assembly (attended only by members of the U.D.D.I.A.) unanimously adopted the draft Constitution tabled by YOULOU and approved the Paris agreement concluded a month earlier on a customs union of the countries of French Equatorial Africa.

On April 30, 1959, YOULOU dissolved the Territorial Assembly and called new elections for June 14. In order to ensure his party the majority in the Assembly, he raised the number of seats to 61 and redivided the constituencies to suit the purposes of his party. By these measures, and with the tacit approval of the French colonial authorities, he managed that this party (while polling only 64 per cent of the votes) gained 51 out of 61 seats. The beheaded party of OPANGOULT won the remaining 10 seats.

Immediately following the elections Brazzaville was the scene of "disturbances": "militants" of YOULOU's party started a hunt after followers of the Matswanist sect who still lived in large numbers in the city and on its outskirts and who ignored the assessment orders of the government and refused to pay taxes. (Later the YOULOU government presented the affair as though the action of the U.D.D.I.A. militants had been called for by violent clashes between various Bakongo groups.) According to the official version, the disturbances were put down in 48 hours, and afterwards the sect members reported *en masse* for tax assessment. There is no information available either on the casualties or on the number of arrests.

The newly elected Territorial Assembly held its first meeting on June 30, 1959, when it passed a unanimous resolution on the release of a good number of political detainees (including OPANGOULT). This, of course, did not apply to the Matswanists. In early July YOULOU formed his new government, including in it two members of the opposition, but the posts of Vice-Premier and Minister of the Interior were occupied by TCHICHELLE, and the other key positions were filled by three of YOU-LOU's European followers: JOSEPH VIAL as Minister of Finance and Planning, HENRI BRU as Secretary of Economics, Agriculture and Forestry, and CHRISTIAN JAYLE as Secretary of Information.

The YOULOU government's version of the submission of the Matswanists was proved entirely false by the events of July — August 1959, when new clashes occurred between sect members and U.D.D.I.A. militants. After "curbing" again the Mat-swanist sect, the government deported about 500 of its members to the district of Fort Rousset. But the sect put up resistance, in the course of which the police killed 35 and wounded 17 people. On October 1, YOULOU made the Territorial Assembly pass an act on the state of emergency, empowering the government to impose a curfew and to forbid more than five persons to assemble, and providing for the establishment of a special court that could render an unappealable judgment against "those participating in any kind of activity of a group, organization or sect which attempts by advice, instruction, slogan or by any other means to disrupt the existing system, internal peace or public order, or to provoke disobedience to the laws and other governmental measures" (including those advocating the non-payment of taxes).

On November 21, 1959, YOULOU had the Territorial Assembly adopt an amendment to the Constitution. Accordingly, he was elected President of the Republic while remaining head of government (after the model of the United States of America).

Early in 1960 YOULOU apparently changed policy. He relieved his three European ministers and replaced them by two M.S.A. members; and immediately before the proclamation of independence (August 15, 1960) OPANGOULT and YOULOU agreed to merge their parties. By this agreement OPANGOULT became a member of the government as Minister of State.

The former French colony was proclaimed an independent state on August 15, 1960. Characteristically, it was on the occasion of the independence festivities that a statue of General DE GAULLE was unveiled in Brazzaville, and huge posters protested the people's "gratitude and loyalty" to France.

Gabon

The oldest party of Gabon, the *Mouvement Mixte Gabonais* (M.M.G.), was founded in 1946 as the Gabon section of the R.D.A. by LEON M'BA,[1] who was one of HOU-PHOUËT-BOIGNY's closest associates. Two years later, in 1948, there was formed, in opposition to the M.M.G., the second Gabonese party, the *Union Démocratique et Sociale Gabonaise* (U.D.S.G.), whose founder, JEAN-HILAIRE AUBAME,[2] deputy for Gabon in the French National Assembly, was in close touch with SENGHOR and the I.O.M. group. The party functioned as the Gabon section first of SENGHOR's *Convention Africaine* and later of the P.R.A.

In 1953 M'BA's party changed its name to *Bloc Démocratique Gabonais* (B.D.G.). In that year M'BA was elected Mayor of Libreville.

At the elections held after the introduction of the *loi-cadre* in 1957 M'BA's party won the majority, and the government was headed by M'BA as Vice-President of the Gabon Executive Council.

At the 1957 Bamako conference of the R.D.A., M'BA sided with HOUPHOUËT-BOIGNY and took a stand against the federal aspirations.

New elections to the Territorial Assembly were held in July 1958, when M'BA's party again came out victorious, and he himself became President of the Executive Council.

Before the 1958 referendum, when both the B.D.G. and the U.D.S.G. were in favour of the new Constitution offered by DE GAULLE a third party was formed, the *Parti de l'Unité Nationale Gabonaise* (PUNGA), which rallied in its ranks all those who not only were dissatisfied with the policy of the M'BA government but also demanded full independence for the country, and therefore campaigned for a vote of "no" in the referendum. Their activity was, however, confined to the south of the country, a relatively small area, and thus they polled only 15,000 votes against

---

[1] LEON M'BA, a member of the Fangi tribe, was born at Libreville in February 1902. He went to Catholic mission schools, and from his early youth was an accountant in the French colonial administration.

[2] JEAN-HILAIRE AUBAME was born at Libreville in 1912. Like M'BA, he came from the Fangi tribe and worked for years in the colonial administration.

91,000 "yes" votes. Under the new Constitution adopted this way M'Ba was appointed Prime Minister on February 27, 1959.

For a time after the referendum M'Ba tried to put down the internal opposition (in October 1958 he accepted a proposal of the U.D.S.G. for a government reshuffle), and showed indulgence also towards the federal aspirations of the other three countries of French Equatorial Africa: during October his plenipotentiary discussed the issue of federation with their representatives; he himself declared in Paris a few weeks later that "Gabon does not object to the countries of French Equatorial Africa forming a closer national union", and on January 17, 1959, he consented that the four countries conclude a transport and customs agreement.

This change of policy by M'Ba, however, was only apparent. During 1959 he concluded with France a number of bilateral agreements which strengthened the positions of the colonialists.

And in spring of 1960, when on Fulbert Youlou's initiative the question of federation was brought to an issue, it was M'Ba who on behalf of Gabon flatly refused, thus frustrating the creation of the federation. (Aubame had campaigned for the federation.)

At the elections to the district councils in June 1960 M'Ba's party won another victory: the B.D.G. gained 244 seats of 330, while Aubame's opposition party (several members of which had in the meantime gone over to the government party) obtained only 82 seats.

Immediately before independence, in August 1960, the General Students Union of Gabon sent the government a telegram protesting against the agreements concluded with France and demanding "total and immediate independence".

On August 17, 1960, Gabon was proclaimed an independent republic.

Ubangi-Shari

The political movement of the peoples of Ubangi-Shari after the war was launched by two brothers, Georges and Antoine Darlan. Both were members of the first Territorial Assembly of the colony. In 1949 Georges Darlan was elected President of the Territorial Assembly and a member of the Grand Council of French Equatorial Africa. At the outset both followed a moderate political line. But it was not long before Antoine — who in 1947 had proposed that French Equatorial Africa change its name to Equatorial France — joined the R.D.A. and formed its territorial section, the *Union Oubanguienne*, and adopted the R.D.A.'s radical policy.[1] This was why the colonial authorities and the French representatives branded him as a Communist and persecuted him. Nevertheless, Antoine Darlan remained loyal to the R.D.A. policy of that time and pursued it consistently even after Houphouët-Boigny's about-face. In the Territorial Assembly he fought against the colonial administration and the settlers[2] backing it — until 1952. He sharply criticized the administration for disregarding the Territorial Assembly (the French authorities failed to ask for the Assembly's consent to the use of public funds, presented im-

---

[1] Georges Darlan, however, held to the moderate line and played no noteworthy part in the political life of the country.

[2] The overwhelming majority of the representatives elected by Europeans to the Territorial Assembly were members of the *Union pour la Défense des Intérêts Oubanguiens*, a branch organization of France's R.P.F. (*Rassemblement du Peuple Français*).

portant matters for consideration not to the plenary session of the Territorial Assembly but to a five-member "standing committee" consisting of supporters of the government) and for unlawful intervention in the conduct of elections. He demanded an end to land seizures for European concessionaires and to the restriction of the hunting rights of Africans, and claimed just distribution of imported goods and approval of public expenses by the Territorial Assembly. He censured the colonial administration for arbitrary actions of its officials and for neglect of the interests of Africans, charging it with having regard for the interests only of those Africans who backed up its policy.

On October 14, 1949, ANTOINE DARLAN said in the Territorial Assembly:

"You, gentlemen of the administration, use the basest methods to delay the evolutionof Oubangui-Chari. You employ intimidation and corruption to induce people to leave one party and join another."[1]

DARLAN waged a desperate struggle against the colonial administration and the settler representatives for the right of the Territorial Assembly to appoint a commission of inquiry to supervise the activities of the local organs of administration in the provincial districts.

Right in the first year of its existence the Union Oubanguienne grew into a mass party. In 1948 it had already 18 district branches with more than 20,000 members.

With the unanimous support of all African members of the Territorial Assembly, ANTOINE DARLAN in 1948–1949 managed to persuade the Assembly to withhold from the government-influenced "standing committee" the right to take measures on its own between parliamentary sessions, and obtained from the French government a confirmation of the right of the Territorial Assembly to appoint commissions of inquiry. Also it made the Assembly allocate 300,000 francs for the establishment of schools, medical relief stations and stores catering for workers.

From the end of 1949 DARLAN's popularity went on declining. Many of his proposals were rejected in the Territorial Assembly, because even leaders of his own party voted against him, partly out of jealousy, but mainly since they found his radicalism overdone, particularly after 1950, when the R.D.A. in other countries had switched over to an opportunist policy. DARLAN definitively lost his leading role in 1952 when the more moderate politician BOGANDA[2] came to the front.

In 1952 BOGANDA founded a political party, the *Mouvement pour l'Evolution Sociale de l'Afrique Noire* (M.E.S.A.N.). At the elections held in March 1952 his party obtained the majority of African seats in the Territorial Assembly (17 out of 20). BOGANDA, in addition to becoming a member of the Territorial Assembly, was elected in April to the Grand Council of French Equatorial Africa.

BOGANDA, unlike ANTOINE DARLAN, pursued an ambiguous policy: he attacked the colonial administration, but he did it in a less sharp tone than DARLAN, and demanded independence for the country, stressing every time that after independence he wanted friendly relations with France, not separation from her. He had

[1] THOMPSON-ADLOFF, *The Emerging States of French Equatorial Africa*, p. 391.

[2] BARTHÉLEMY BOGANDA was born on April 10, 1910. He graduated from the Catholic Seminary of Yaoundé (William Ponty School). He was ordained a priest in 1935. In 1946, as a candidate proposed by the bishop of Bangui, he was elected to the French National Assembly, where he joined the M.R.P. *(Mouvement Républicain Populaire)*. In 1950 he threw off the cassock, got married, and resigned from the M.R.P. From that time on the colonial authorities treated him as a rebel and arrested him on the eve of the 1951 elections to the French National Assembly. He was detained in prison for 45 days. All the same, he was elected to the French Parliament, where he joined the Independents.

partly this, partly his repeated anti-Communist pronouncements, to thank for the fact that the French colonial authorities raised no obstacles to his political activity.

The Territorial Assembly elected in March 1952 had 19 members from BOGANDA's M.E.S.A.N., and 9 independents. The Union Oubanguienne, ANTOINE DARLAN's party, vanished from the political arena. DARLAN himself joined the M.E.S.A.N. but played no considerable role there. He was politically active mainly in Paris as a member of the French National Assembly, to which he was re-elected in 1953. Fourteen European (French settler) members of the Territorial Assembly belonged to the R.P.F. of metropolitan France. BOGANDA, while being also a deputy in the French National Assembly, spent little time in Paris, devoting all his time and energy to winning the masses of his country, to developing the M.E.S.A.N. into a mass party. His attractive personality and oratorical power made him very popular in a short time. BOGANDA's position, popularity and authority were especially enhanced after the Berbérati events in 1954.

On April 30, 1954, the dead bodies of two Africans were discovered on the estate of a French settler by the name of BONTEMPS in the village of Berbérati. The Baya population of the neighbourhood clamoured for the arrest of BONTEMPS. The local French authority refused. The angry crowd attacked the settler, injured him and two of his assistants, stoning another European coming to their aid; this man died of his wounds. The French Governor rushed in troops to suppress the riot, and 102 Africans were arrested. BONTEMPS was acquitted of the charge of murder, and the 102 arrested Africans were tried on the charge of "armed rebellion". The court sentenced ten of them to forced labour ranging from five to ten years, and another 67 people to prison from six months to three years.

BOGANDA had nothing to do with these events, except that he accompanied the Governor visiting the place of the disturbances and admonished the rioters to refrain from violence. The Bayas heeded the popular leader's advice, and the disorders stopped. This enhanced BOGANDA's prestige in the eyes of the authorities. On the other hand, despite the harsh sentences meted out, the response of the Africans, who followed BOGANDA's instructions, was that they joined in large numbers the independence movement led by BOGANDA and his party. BOGANDA's popularity soared so high that in 1955 he was elected Mayor of Bangui, and at the elections of January 2, 1956, in which twice as many voters took part as in 1951, he was elected to the French National Assembly (receiving 155,952 votes while his opponent polled 20,230).

At the elections to the Territorial Assembly held under the *loi-cadre* in March 1957 all M.E.S.A.N. candidates were elected, so that the Executive Council, now headed by BOGANDA, had no opposition.

In June 1957 BOGANDA was again elected, by 19 votes against one abstention, President of the Grand Council of French Equatorial Africa. In the Grand Council he angrily criticized the colonial officials and the Governor himself for their unbending colonialist attitude. He stressed that if there were still insufficient numbers of Africans qualified for administrative functions, it was due to the neglect of public education; the country needed political self-government, fewer officials and more technicians. He demanded an end to the division of the country into administrative units, for these regions, he said, "have become screens erected between ourselves and the French Republic and between the territorial government and our toiling African populations". "Decolonialization" was his constant slogan, but in none of his speeches did he fail to assure France of his loyalty. His radical diatribe roused the indignation of some French colonial officials, but the Council members stood up for him as one man: the Council at its meeting of November 16, 1957, unanimously voted him total confidence and requested the Governor to punish the officials who refused to comply with the spirit of the *loi-cadre*.

After DE GAULLE came to power in France, BOGANDA continued his double-faced policy: he demanded independence for his country but did not miss a single opportunity to express his pro-French feelings. At the time of DE GAULLE's visit to Brazzaville on September 1, 1958, BOGANDA cordially thanked him "for having kept his promises", but at the same time he handed him a petition requesting the French government to recognize in the new Constitution the right to independence of the African colonies.

In the September 1958 referendum 98.8 per cent of the electorate, following BOGANDA's advice, voted "yes", that is, chose autonomous status within the French Community instead of real independence. After the referendum BOGANDA, heading his government as Prime Minister, concentrated first of all on the drafting of the new Constitution of the country and on the preparations for the general election to be organized under that Constitution.

*

BOGANDA's political programme was not confined to the demand for independence, he was also the most ardent champion of uniting the four colonies of French Equatorial Africa in an independent federal state. Already in 1952, by naming his party the "Mouvement pour l'Evolution Sociale de l'Afrique Noire", he gave expression to his aspirations in this direction. Having come to power after the electoral success in March 1957, he began talks with the head of government of Chad, GABRIEL LISETTE, whom he tried to persuade into forming a Chad section of the M.E.S.A.N. And when a sweeping majority elected him President of the Grand Council of French Equatorial Africa in June 1957, he regarded the unanimous support he enjoyed on the part of representatives of the associated countries of Equatorial Africa as full powers to take the lead in all French Equatorial Africa. Still before the 1958 referendum, partly through correspondence, partly by sending out personal representatives, he established contact with the governments of the countries of French Equatorial Africa, inviting them to create a unified federation of states in Central Africa. But his initiative failed. The political leaders of the Middle Congo and Gabon, YOULOU and AUBAME, who also cherished the idea of federating the countries of Equatorial Africa, took him for a rival and rejected his proposal, while LISETTE refrained from taking a definite position. BOGANDA's initiative met with favourable response only on the part of the Middle Congo opposition leaders, OPANGOULT and TCHICAYA, but this circumstance even more envenomed his relations with YOULOU and with the R.D.A. in general. In early November it became clear that for the time being he could expect none of the countries of Equatorial Africa to take his side.

But BOGANDA did not acknowledge defeat. Encouraged by the support of OPANGOULT and TCHICAYA, he said in a speech before the Assembly in November 1957:

"In making our proposal for the formation of a Central African state we pursue the aim of restoring the Congo State, creating a Great Congo which would be open to all and which would have Brazzaville for its capital. We intend further to maintain French Equatorial Africa, but in a more effective form and at less costs than hitherto . . . As we have met with reluctance on the part of the governments of Chad and Gabon, the new state will for the moment be confined to a union of Ubangi-Shari and the Middle Congo."

Since he soon had to see that he could not count upon the Middle Congo either, he decided to establish at least in his own country the "Central African Republic", which might in the future become the basis of the federal state of Central Africa he proposed to create.

*

On December 1, 1958, the Territorial Assembly, at the motion of BOGANDA, unanimously passed a resolution changing the name of the country to the Central African Republic.

On December 6, 1958, the Constituent Legislative Assembly installed into office the first government of the new Republic with BOGANDA as Prime Minister. Included in the government were two of BOGANDA's closest associates, his cousin DAVID DACKO[1] as Minister of the Interior and ABEL GOUMBA[2] as Minister of Finance.

The number of BOGANDA's enemies grew in proportion as his popularity was increasing and his power position strengthening. After his militant speeches in the Grand Council the colonial authorities and the French settlers, who had considered him a moderate politician, again viewed him as dangerous man and turned against him. What was of great consequence for him was that an opposition against him and his policies was brewing among the Africans, and even within his own party, mainly in the ranks of the African élite. The latter objected that BOGANDA, instead of letting a larger number of Africans participate in the administration, surrounded himself with foreigners; they accused him (not without reason, as we have seen) of striving for absolute government. Later, under the pressure of his party, he drew more and more domestic cadres into the leadership, but his dictatorial aspirations estranged many even of his followers and induced them to leave the M.E.S.A.N. and join the opposition.

His increasing radicalism in the Grand Council during 1957 and 1958, as well as his efforts with a view to federation, turned against him part of the leading politicians of the other countries of Equatorial Africa, too. In April 1958 he was elected again President of the Grand Council, but this time by a majority of one vote only (10 votes to the 9 cast for the R.D.A. candidate). The proclamation of the Central African Republic caused great alarm among the leaders of the neighbouring countries.

On December 15, 1958, leading politicians of the countries of French Equatorial Africa, on BOGANDA's fresh initiative, met in Paris at a round-table conference to discuss the question of federation. But this conference brought no result: the majority of the participants were against federation and favoured only the idea of economic and technical co-operation.

---

[1] DAVID DACKO, a cousin of BOGANDA's, was born in March 1930 at Bouchia, in the Mbaiki district in the south of the country. He went to school at Bambari, then in the Middle Congo, where he qualified as a teacher. He was an elementary school headmaster in Bangui, and was active in the trade unions affiliated to the French socialist labour federation. Until 1957 he did not take part in politics. In March 1957, as a member of the M.E.S.A.N., he was elected to the Territorial Assembly. In BOGANDA's government he was Minister of Agriculture, Cattle-breeding and Forestry from May 1957 till August 1958 and Minister of Administrative Affairs from August till December.

[2] ABEL GOUMBA, a member of the Bondziri tribe, was born at Grimari in 1927. He graduated from the Medical College of Dakar. During World War II he practised as a doctor at Rufisque in Senegal, and later in the Middle Congo. In 1957 he returned to Ubangi-Shari and in March he was elected to the Territorial Council as a member of the M.E.S.A.N. In 1958–1959 he was Vice-President and President of the Executive Council.

The Constituent Assembly, which consisted solely of members of BOGANDA's party, invested him with almost absolute power pending the entry into force of the new Constitution in preparation. Making use of the opportunity, BOGANDA began carrying out his economic and other plans (for example, in order to force back to agriculture the unemployed Africans gathering in growing numbers in Bangui, he got the Assembly to pass an act against "vagrancy"; another legislative act prohibited people from going unclothed). Moreover, before presenting, on February 9, 1959, the draft Constitution prepared by a specially appointed commission, he modified it to the effect that, concentrating in one hand the functions of head of state and head of government, it invested a single person with full power, so as to sanction by law his absolute rule he had established in practice.

The elections were set for April 5, 1959, but BOGANDA did not live to see that day: on March 28, 1959, he was killed in an air crash. In spite of this the elections ended in total victory for the M.E.S.A.N., whose candidates polled 343,866 out of 352,259 votes (this number amounted to 58 per cent of the electorate) and gained 48 seats out of 50. This sweeping victory of the M.E.S.A.N. was due to the fact that BOGANDA had prevented the opposition (R.D.A. and M.S.A.) candidates from taking part in the elections in three of the four constituencies.

After BOGANDA's death GOUMBA took over as Acting Premier, and in May 1959 the legislature, after a heated debate, elected DACKO to succeed BOGANDA as Prime Minister. GOUMBA became Minister of State in charge of economic planning.

In his inaugural address after his appointment DACKO, following BOGANDA's line, spoke of the necessity of putting an end to tribal and racial conflicts, of uniting the countries of French Equatorial Africa in a federal state, and in the next two months he introduced a number of administrative and economic measures (dividing the country into four provinces instead of the "administrative districts" established by the colonial regime; stepping up the replacement of European officials by Africans; drawing up a new plan of economic development, establishing agricultural co-operatives, etc.). The measures caused discontent not only among his political opponents but also within his own party. General indignation followed his action by which he levied taxes on shotguns, and certain leading members of his party objected to the inflated administrative apparatus and to the frequent abuses of authority. The oppositionist mood rose especially high when DACKO presented to the Assembly a bill investing him with the same full powers as were accorded to BOGANDA. The Assembly rejected the bill unanimously.

During the subsequent months the opposition movement grew still stronger. Two members of the M.E.S.A.N. leadership, N'GOUNIO, Mayor of Bangui, and MALCOM-PHO, President of the Assembly, persuaded 18 representatives to sign a declaration, in which they demanded DACKO's resignation, accusing him of abusing his authority and intending to dissolve the legislature. In October 1959, a motion of no confidence was tabled in the Assembly on this account, but DACKO managed to make it defeated and to get the Assembly to vote him confidence. Five days later DACKO reshuffled his government. Although GOUMBA was not openly in favour of the motion of no confidence, DACKO viewed him as his principal adversary and left him out of the new government.

In June 1960 GOUMBA and his followers withdrew from the M.E.S.A.N. and founded a new party under the name of *Mouvement d'Evolution Démocratique de l'Afrique Centrale* (M.E.D.A.C.), which stood up against the dictatorial regime of the DACKO government.

On August 13, 1960, the Central African Republic became an independent state.

At the war's end in 1945 there was in Chad only one political party, that of the ettlers, the *Union Démocratique Tch adienne* (U.D.T.), the Chad section of France's R.P.F. It also had African members, but these were only sultans, chiefs and officials of the administration. At the elections in October 1945 both electoral colleges voted for the candidates of this party, who thus became deputies for Chad in the French National Assembly. Although they both came from the ranks of the Resistance and declared themselves "democrats", they professed ultra-conservative views. The representative of the first (the European) electoral college, RENÉ MALBRANT, who was re-elected in November 1946, in the French National Assembly consistently was against bills of liberal tendencies (for example, he opposed the labour law to be introduced in the colonial countries).

It was in 1946 that GABRIEL LISETTE[1] founded the first political party of Africans as the Chad section of the R.D.A., the *Parti Progressiste Tchadien* (P.P.T.), which rapidly gained ground among the African masses. At the elections held in November 1946 the second electoral college (in which a small part of the African population also had the right to vote) elected LISETTE against the U.D.T. candidate. In the French National Assembly LISETTE joined the R.D.A., which made him parliamentary secretary of the party.

The French government, the colonial administration and the settlers looked askance at the new party's affiliation with the R.D.A. and its growing popularity. The conservative parties in the French Assembly attempted to unseat LISETTE on the ground that, because of his service of recent date in the colonial administration, he was not eligible. LISETTE, however, succeeded in getting confirmed in his seat with the help of the French Socialist Party and mainly of LAMINE GUÈYE.

The colonial administration did all in its power to counterbalance the influence of the P.P.T. It dismissed from office or transferred to remote districts those African officials in its employ whom it knew to be members of the party or its sympathizers. This could easily be done, since in the early post-war years the Territorial Assembly consisted entirely of government-supporting elements. Of 30 members of the Assembly 27 belonged to the U.D.T. (10 Europeans as well as 17 African chiefs and the like), and they supported every measure of the administration. The P.P.T.had only three members in the Territorial Assembly. How the administration kept a hold on the Territorial Assembly is shown by the fact that, when in 1947 the P.P.T. proposed abolishment of the system of the dual college, the majority voted in favour of its maintenance. This was a unique experience, for the territorial assemblies of all the other French African colonies favoured the introduction of a single electoral list.

The anti-P.P.T. policy of the French colonial administration had no small part in the birth of two new rightist African parties in opposition to the leftist P.P.T, In 1948 AHMED KOULAMALLAH,[2] who thought LISETTE's party was too radical. withdrew from the P.P.T. and founded the *Parti Socialiste Indépendant du Tchad* (P.S.I.T.), and in 1950 there was formed the Chad section of the *Union Démocratique*

---

[1] GABRIEL LISETTE, whose parents hailed from Guadeloupe, was born in Panama on April 2, 1919. He went to school in Guadeloupe and in France. He married a French girl. From 1939 till 1942 he served in the Army of Free France. In 1944 he moved to Brazzaville and worked in the colonial administration. In 1946 he was transferred to Chad colony.

[2] AHMED KOULAMALLAH, a Muslim trader, head of the Tidjaniya sect, was born of an Arab chief's family at Baguirmi in February 1912. From 1945 he was a member of LISETTE's P.P.T.

et Sociale de la Résistance[1] (U.D.S.R.). This latter kept in touch with the P.P.T. but just for the purpose of pushing it to the right. This effort of the U.D.S.R. was not without success. When HOUPHOUËT-BOIGNY changed policy and the R.D.A. broke with the French Communist Party, LISETTE held to HOUPHOUËT-BOIGNY's R.D.A. line and even said something about his readiness to co-operate with the colonial administration. This notwithstanding, during the 1951 elections to the French National Assembly the authorities used strong pressure to defeat LISETTE, and they succeeded.

At the elections to the Territorial Assembly in March 1952 the U.D.T., which had in the meantime changed its name to *Action Sociale Tchadienne* (A.S.T.), gained 33 seats out of 45, the P.P.T. won four, and eight seats were divided among the P.S.I.T., the U.D.S.R. and the "Independents".

After the elections the colonial authorities dismissed some African officials employed in the administration, together with certain local tribal leaders who had voted against the U.D.T.–A.S.T. In several places the population organized marches of demonstration to protest against the dismissals and the unlawful practices of the colonial authorities which had falsified the election results. The authorities resorted to force of arms against the demonstrators. In some places it came to cruel incidents, thus in April 1952 in Bébalem, where police fired into a crowd which was assembling in front of the administration building and staging a peaceful sit-down strike to protest against the unlawful arrest of an African. As to the casualties and the number of arrests no reliable data were published, but the court in December 1952 convicted 22 of the arrested persons of the crime of participating in an "armed rebellion".

Early in 1953 a group of A.S.T. members, led by BÉCHIR-SOW, quit the party and formed an independent political group called the *Union de la Défense des Intérêts Tchadiens* (U.D.I.T.).

The elections to the French National Assembly in October 1953 brought another regrouping of the parties. When a former Governor of the colony, ROGUÉ, offered himself as a candidate, his candidacy was opposed not only by the P.P.T., but by the A.S.T. and even by the French administration. To prevent ROGUÉ from being elected, the P.P.T. brought itself to support the A.S.T. candidate, an ultra-conservative French settler. KOULAMALLAH, who could not agree with this move, again broke with LISETTE and revived his former organization, the P.S.I.T.

After the elections a Mulatto tradesman, JEAN BAPTISTE, formed a new rightist party, the *Union Démocratique Indépendante du Tchad* (U.D.I.T.);[2] the principal adviser of this party was ROGUÉ, the ex-Governor who had won a seat at the elections.

The Territorial Assembly elected for a period of five years in 1952 was characterized by an intensifying activity of the African members. Although a great deal of discussion consisted of personal bickerings and inter-party quarrels, the Territorial Assembly during the five years passed a number of meaningful resolutions on the improvement of the administration, on control over the authorities, on the development of primary and professional education, etc. But hardly anything came of these resolutions, because the colonial administration disregarded most of them. The only important result of the work of the Assembly was a resolution adopted by a large majority, and passed into law in December 1955, on the introduction of the single electoral list.

---

[1] PLEVEN's and MITTERRAND's party in the French National Assembly.
[2] Not to be mistaken for the other U.D.I.T. (Union de la Défense des Intérêts Tchadiens), the small group of BÉCHIR-SOW which had separated from the A.S.T. early in 1953.

Before the January 2, 1956, elections to the French National Assembly KOU-
LAMALLAH changed the name of his party to *Mouvement Socialiste Africain* (M.S.A.)
and entered into relations with the French Socialist Party (S.F.I.O.). But some of
the former leaders of his party dissociated themselves and continued under the name
of P.S.I.T.

This time the winner at the elections was LISETTE, who after an absence of five
years became again a deputy in the French Parliament. At the end of the same year
LISETTE was elected Mayor of Fort-Lamy, and 18 representatives of his party were
elected to the 33-member municipal council.

On March 11, 1957, the Territorial Assembly was re-elected. For the time of the
elections the P.P.T. concluded with the U.D.I.T. and part of the U.D.S.R. a pact
called the *Entente Républicaine*. LISETTE's P.P.T. won a sweeping victory: it gained
46 out of 65 seats, while JEAN BAPTISTE's U.D.I.T. obtained 11 and the A.S.T.
7 seats, but KOULAMALLAH's M.S.A., though polling 31,000 votes out of 544,000,
suffered total defeat, because none of the election districts gave it a majority of the
vote. Neither BÉCHIR-SOW nor any other member of his group got elected, and this
faction was never again to play a role in politics.

This victory of the P.P.T. was due, on the one hand, to its good organization
(in the South, where the party was strongest, 79 per cent of the electorate went
to the polls, while only 59 per cent did so in other districts) and, on the other hand,
to the fact that the A.S.T., conscious of the support of the colonial administration
and the chiefs, had not bothered about party organization. This victory was also
promoted by the more than threefold increase in the number of qualified voters
since 1952 (rising from 308,000 to 1,196,000).

After the elections LISETTE, as leader of the majority party, formed the govern-
ment, including in the ten-member cabinet four representatives of other parties as
well (the leader of the U.D.I.T., JEAN BAPTISTE, as Minister of Planning, two
European members of the A.S.T. as Ministers of the Interior and of Public
Works, and the leader of the A.S.T., ALI DJIBRINE KHERALLAH, as Minister of
Finance).

In September 1957 LISETTE attended the Bamako conference of the R.D.A.,
where he was elected President. Though he remained one of the most loyal followers
of HOUPHOUËT-BOIGNY's, he played the role of mediator (in respect of the countries
of French Equatorial Africa) between proponents and opponents of a federation
of the four countries, and he was the promoter of the several meetings of the four
Prime Ministers. (Before his defeat in February 1959, one of LISETTE's last acts was
the formation of an economic and customs union with the other three countries
of French Equatorial Africa.)

In spite of the fact that LISETTE had made JEAN BAPTISTE a member of his
government, the coalition of the P.P.T. with the U.D.I.T. did not last long. From
that time on the Territorial Assembly, which had until then been occupied mainly
with criticism of the colonial administration, became the scene of inter-party struggles.
In autumn of 1957 the main objective of the opposition was the formation of a
government by Africans, and the debates turned around the distribution of the
different positions, delegations and committees among the political parties. The
P.P.T. and the U.D.I.T. fell out, the P.P.T. joined forces with the U.D.S.R., and
the U.D.I.T. as opposition allied with the A.S.T. The criticism of the colonial administration and the struggle for independence were relegated to the background.

After the elections KOULAMALLAH challenged the validity of the election held in
the Chari-Ba district (which was counted his and his party's most reliable con-

stituency), levelling the accusation that the P.P.T. candidates had won by trickery, and demanded new elections. The Council of State confirmed the charges and called new elections in the Chari-Ba district. During the election campaign conducted in April–May 1958 KOULAMALLAH gained much help from the popularity he had won by his efforts to put an end peacefully to armed clashes between Arab peasants and the nomadic Foulah in that district in August 1957 and in April 1958.[1] He made use of his popularity for political purposes, accusing the LISETTE government of being unable to maintain order in the country. It was partly due to this move that all seven seats for the district were obtained by his party, the M.S.A., which now fused with the A.S.T. and the U.D.I.T. to form the opposition bloc *Union Socialiste Tchadienne* (U.S.T.). Thus the opposition in the Territorial Assembly had 26 votes against the P.P.T.'s 39 votes.

In September 1958 nine members of the Assembly — chiefs for the most part — formed a new political group headed by SAHOULBA,[2] the *Groupement des Indépendants et Ruraux du Tchad* (G.I.R.T.).

In summer of 1958 LISETTE's government got in a difficult position. While in the French National Assembly LISETTE was busy representing the R.D.A. line by the side of HOUPHOUËT-BOIGNY against SÉKOU TOURÉ, at home as Prime Minister he had to tackle the increasingly aggressive opposition. In June the U.S.T. demanded removal of one of LISETTE's European right-hand man, Minister of the Interior VAZEL, whom KOULAMALLAH could not forgive his having led the P.P.T. campaign against the M.S.A. in the Chari-Ba by-election; LISETTE refused to comply, but, to halt the opposition, he offered the U.S.T. two ministerial seats and several committee posts. KOULAMALLAH flatly rejected the offer, and on June 30 he announced that the U.S.T. would withdraw from all committees and start an over all struggle against the government's programme. LISETTE, in order to consolidate his position, looked for a new ally in SAHOULBA, the G.I.R.T. leader, and his nine-member group. Considering, however, that the majority of this group consisting of chiefs did not look avourably upon the government's policy, LISETTE could not be quite sure of their support. A grave government crisis was about to break out when DE GAULLE's visit to Chad in August and the preparation of the forthcoming referendum created an entirely new situation. In view of the referendum the party struggle stopped for a while, as all political leaders were in favour of remaining in the French Community. In the referendum held in September 1958 with a 98.7 per cent participation, Chad fvoted "yes".

Exactly two months later, on November 28, the Territorial Assembly proclaimed Chad to be a Republic within the French Community. At the same time it manifested its readiness to co-operate with the other three countries of French Equatorial Africa. The Territorial Assembly did not enter into the question of how far this co-operation should go and what form it should take, thus allowing a free hand to LISETTE who, following HOUPHOUËT-BOIGNY's lead, was against the establishment of any federal legislative or executive body.

The position of LISETTE's government, however, became less and less stable. The U.S.T. demanded that the Territorial Assembly be dissolved and new elections

---

[1] There were 31 dead and 41 injured during the August 1957 incidents and 19 dead in April 1958.

[2] GONTCHOME SAHOULBA was born at Lévé in Chad on October 16, 1926. From 1951 until 1959, as deputy for Chad, he was a member of the Council of State of the French Republic, and from 1957 to 1959 he was President of the Territorial Assembly.

held, and campaigned ceaselessly for this end. In November, as a result of his propaganda, mass demonstrations were held on two occasions to keep the Territorial Assembly from meeting. On both occasions the government called out police to disperse the demonstrators, but LISETTE, yielding to the pressure of the opposition, promised to hold new elections and took some opposition members into his government. This, however, was not enough to avert the crisis.

In January 1959 the opposition parties, led by AHMED KOULAMALLAH, rallied in a drive called the *Mouvement Populaire Tchadien* (M.P.T.). When later this movement was joined also by the G.I.R.T., and when nine M.P.T. members of the cabinet resigned, the Territorial Assembly at its meeting of February 10 defeated the LISETTE government by 33 votes to 17. G.I.R.T. leader SAHOULBA, President of the Territorial Assembly, was then elected head of government. A month later, on March 13, Prime Minister SAHOULBA was replaced by KOULAMALLAH, who in turn kept his post only for ten days, because in the meantime LISETTE had managed to win over the great majority of the opposition. (Only four members stood by KOULAMALLAH.) But LISETTE, whom the events of the last few months had convinced that he was unwelcome to many because of his non-African origin and his past activities in the service of the colonial administration, thought it better to give both the party leadership and the premiership over to one of his closest associates and followers, FRANÇOIS TOMBALBAYE,[1] who then included in his cabinet one member of both the G.I.R.T. and the U.D.IT. (KHERALLAH and JEAN BAPTISTE).

At the election of the Legislative Assembly on May 31, 1959, the P.P.T. now led by TOMBALBAYE obtained the absolute majority, gaining 57 of 84 seats.[2]

After the elections TOMBALBAYE tried hard to bring the opposition parties nearer to the P.P.T., but his efforts failed. What is more, during the summer it came to serious clashes — in June between P.P.T. and G.I.R.T. members at Bongor, and in July between P.P.T. and M.S.A. members at Fort-Lamy. In September KOULAMALLAH made it known that the M.S.A. would remain in opposition, and in October his party conducted an antigovernment campaign among the Muslim population because TOMBALBAYE was leading a government delegation to Israel. By early 1960 the inter-party struggle had so much aggravated that in February the government coalition broke up and the three Muslim opposition parties (M.S.A., G.I.R.T., U.D.IT.) under KOULAMALLAH's leadership united to form a new opposition party, the *Parti National Africain* (P.N.A.), whereupon TOMBALBAYE ousted from his cabinet KHERALLAH and JEAN BAPTISTE who joined the new party.

On August 11, 1960, Chad became independent. The independence festivities took place with great ceremony on January 11–12, 1961.

---

[1] FRANÇOIS TOMBALBAYE was born of a Protestant family of traders at Bedaya in the South of Chad in 1918. Having completed his studies he was an assistant teacher for a time, and then became president of the labour union "Syndicat Autonome du Tchad". In this capacity he founded the local branch of the P.P.T. in Fort-Archambault. In March 1952, as a P.P.T. candidate, he was elected to the Territorial Assembly. In 1957 he was re-elected and also became a member and Vice-President of the Grand Council of French Equatorial Africa.

[2] How shrewdly the government organized the elections to cheat the opposition is shown by the fact that neither the M.S.A., which polled 10 per cent of the votes (55,000), nor the M.E.S.A.N., which polled 2.5 per cent (11,041), could win a single seat, and the G.I.R.T. by obtaining 8 per cent (44,438) gained only two, that is, 2.5 per cent of all seats.

BIBLIOGRAPHY

FRENCH EQUATORIAL AFRICA

A. Lauraint, *Les problèmes de transport de l'Afrique Equatoriale française*, Brazzaville, 1945.
A. F. Éboué, *La nouvelle politique indigène pour l'Afrique Equatoriale française*, Paris, 1945.
P. Gamache, *Géographie et histoire de l'Afrique Equatoriale française*, Paris, 1949.
A. Lauraint, "Le plan décennal de développement économique et social", in *Afrique Equatoriale française*, Paris, 1950.
E. Trézenem and B. Lembezat, *La France équatoriale*, Paris, 1950.
H. Zieglé, *Afrique Equatoriale française*, Paris, 1952.
L. Gray Cowan, "French Equatorial Africa", *Journal of International Affairs*, 1953.
Louis Sanmarco, "Harmonisation et stabilisation entre l'A.E.F. et la Métropole", *L'Exportateur Français*, Dec. 1953.
E. Trézenem, *L'Afrique Equatoriale française*, Paris, 1955.
Georges Balandier, *Sociologie actuelle de l'Afrique noire: Changements sociaux au Gabon et au Congo*, Paris, 1955.
R. Delavignette, *Afrique Equatoriale française*, Paris, 1957.
V. Thompson and R. Adloff, *The Emerging States of French Equatorial Africa*, Stanford, 1960.
"Post-Colonial Reunion", *The Economist*, May 28, 1960.
G. Balandier, *Sociologie actuelle de l'Afrique noire*, Paris, 1963.

MIDDLE CONGO

Thompson-Adloff, *op. cit.* (1960), pp. 476–526.
S. C. Easton, *The Twilight of European Colonialism*, New York, 1960, pp. 387–393.
"La République Congo", *Les Cahiers Français*, May 1960.
G. M. Carter, "Tribalism Erupts in the French Congo", in *Independence for Africa*, New York, 1960, pp. 90–95.
Jean-Michel Wagret, *Histoire et sociologie politique de la République du Congo (Brazzaville)*, Paris, 1963.

GABON

F. Grébert, *Au Gabon*, Paris, 1948.
G. Balandier and Ch. Pauvert, *Les villages gabonais*. Inst. d'Etudes Centrafr. Mémoire n°5, 1952.
Thompson-Adloff, *op. cit.* (1960), pp. 343–384.
Easton, *op. cit.*, pp. 385–387.

UBANGI-SHARI

J. P. Lebeuf, *Banghi*, Paris, 1952.
A. Teulieres, *L'Oubangui face à l'avenir*, Paris, 1953.
Thompson-Adloff, *op. cit.* (1960), pp. 385–425.
Easton, *op. cit.*, pp. 383–385.

CHAD

J. P. Lebeuf & A. Masson-Detourbet, *La civilisation du Tchad*, Paris, 1950.
J. P. Lebeuf & A. Masson-Detourbet, *Du Cameroun au Tchad*, Paris, 1954.
J. P. Lebeuf, *Fort Lamy* (n. d.).
P. Hugot, "Tchad et Soudan", *L'Afrique et l'Asie* 37/1957.

THOMPSON-ADLOFF, *op. cit.* (1960), pp. 426–475.
EASTON, *op. cit.*, pp. 380–383.
JACQUES LE CORNEC, *Histoire politique du Tchad 1900—1963*, Paris, 1963.

OFFICIAL PUBLICATIONS

Le Gabon et le Moyen-Congo. Gouvernement français, Ministère des Colonies. Paris, 195
Territoire du Moyen-Congo: Débats de l'Assemblée Territoriale (1947–60).
Territoire du Gabon: Débats de l'Assemblée Territoriale (1947–60).
Territoire de l'Oubangui-Chari: Débats de l'Assemblée Territoriale (1947–60).
Territoire du Tchad: Débats de l'Assembléee Territoriale (1947–60).

263

CHAPTER XXV

MADAGASCAR

Three important political changes took place in Madagascar after the end of World War II.

In October 1946 the French colonial administration carried out a constitutional reform. The Council of Representatives established in March 1945, which had been but a consultative and advisory organ, was superseded by a 36-member Representative Assembly, and Provincial Councils composed of a Madagascan and a European section were set up in the five provinces of the colony. Each of these Councils sent to the Representative Assembly three European and four Madagascan members (except Tuléar province which had the right to five Madagascan representatives). In this way 15 European and 21 Madagascan members constituted the Representative Assembly. The island country sent two French and three Madagascan representatives to the French National Assembly, and two French and six Madagascan members to the Council of the Republic.

The second major reforms was the abolition of the *indigénat* regime immediately after the war's end.

A change of no less importance for the political life of the country was the birth of political parties. Since the banning of the "Vi Vato Sakelika" no political parties had existed in the island, but four parties were formed there during 1946.

At war's end there lived in Paris a noted Malagasy writer and poet, JACQUES RABEMANANJARA.[1] Immediately after the end of war, in 1945, Madagascar sent to the French Constituent Assembly two deputies, Dr. RAVOAHANGY and Dr. RASETA. The three of them in February 1946 founded the first political party, the *Mouvement Démocratique de la Rénovation Malgache* (M.D.R.M.). The party had no fixed programme. Its moderate right wing, to which also the leaders belonged, demanded for Madagascar, not independence, but merely equal rights with metropolitan France within the French Union, that is internal self-government. The left wing, however, which was constituted for the most part by members of the youth organizations affiliated with the party — the *Jeunesse Nationale* (J.N.) and the *Parti Nationaliste de Madagascar* (PANAMA) — demanded independence at once.

Opposed to the M.D.R.M. was the *Parti des Déshérités Malgaches* (PADESM). This party had been formed by tribes which had in olden times been oppressed and exploited by the Merina tribe ruling over the Hova State. The party did not deem

---

[1] JACQUES RABEMANANJARA was born in 1913 in the Betsimisàraka tribe at Maroantsetra in Tamatave province. He was educated in France, where he graduated from art school. He stayed in France and made a name for himself as a writer and poet.

it necessary to engage in political fight against the colonial administration and for independence. Instead it fought for the abolishment of the prerogatives of the Merinas in social and economic matters. As an antagonist of the M.D.R.M., which represented the pro-independence aspirations, the party depended on the support of the colonial administration.

The third party, the *Parti Démocratique Malgache* (P.D.M.) led by the Rev. RAVE-LOJAONA, stood against both the PADESM and the M.D.R.M. It opposed the PADESM because its own members came mostly from the upper strata of the Merina tribe, and it set itself against the M.D.R.M. because it found the policy of this party all too radical. In spite of its name, the P.D.M. did not strive to win the hearts of the masses, it relied only on the educated minority of the Merinas. Though it regarded independence as the primary goal of the political struggle, yet instead of independence it demanded, for the time being at least, that the country be declared a United Nations Trust Territory (under French adminis-tration!), and insisted that the most urgent task, "the first condition of freedom", was to improve the economic and political situation for the Malagasy people, to raise the living standards, to defend the Malagasies against exploitation (either French or domestic), to open the avenues of education to the broadest strata of the people.

Finally the fourth party, the Catholic-founded and Catholic-influenced *Mouve-ment Social Malgache* which counted very few members, did not consider the PADESM an adversary and stood in opposition not only to the radical M.D.R.M., but also to the Protestant-influenced P.D.M., although in its programme, like the P.D.M., it demanded fundamental freedoms for the people and self-government.

As the result of the elections of 1946 the M.D.R.M. won the majority in the Mada-gascan sections of four of the five Provincial Councils (altogether 64 out of the 92 seats reserved for Madagascans on the five Councils), yet the party sent only 9 members to the Representative Assembly (because the votes cast in the two sec-tions were counted together), while the PADESM had 12 seats. The M.D.R.M. candidates — RABEMANANJARA, RAVOAHANGY and RASETA — were elected deputies to the French National Assembly, and three members of the two parties (M.D.R.M. and PADESM) each were elected to the Council of the Republic.

The 1947 Uprising

On the night from March 29 to 30, 1947, an uprising against French rule broke out in Madagascar. The insurgents assailed the barracks and police stations, and even captured several of them. In some places they tore down Christian churches and mission buildings. Throughout the country they occupied entire townships and even regions. They fought bloody battles with the troops and police dispatched against them. Communication stopped in several places all over the country. One of the strongest French military bases, 118 miles north of Tananarive, was com-pletely cut off from the rest of the island. During the uprising numerous European settlers (and still more Malagasies who stood by the French) were beaten up, some of them (mostly Malagasies) were tortured or killed. It took the French three months to put down the uprising on the whole, but in some places guerrilla warfare lasted another year and a half, until the end of 1948.

The colonial administration and its troops made a bloody reckoning with the defeated insurgents. All the prisoners kept in the jails of Farafangana, Manakara and Mananjary were massacred in the prison yards. In the vicinity of Maromanga the captured insurgents crammed in a prison wagon were killed to the last man. Similar massacres were carried out in other places as well. For example, the population of the town of Fianarantsoa, which in 1941 had had 21,000 inhabitants, numbered only 19,000 in 1950.

As to the total death toll, estimates made at different times by the colonial administration showed entirely different figures: an official statement published in 1948 admitted that 90,000 people had died, while another version, published in 1950, mentioned only 11,342 dead.[1] For the difference between the two official estimates, RAYMOND K. KENT gives the explanation that in 1948, when the revolt had just come to an end, the colonial authorities were not interested in concealing the number of victims, while in 1950, when the regional chiefs had to establish the number of m ssing persons, they reported low figures in order to minimize the importance of the uprising.[2]

The massacre resulting from the defeat of the revolt did not mean the end of reckoning. There followed then mass trials in which over 5,000 people were sentenced to death, or to prison each for more than one year and a half. Among those condemned to death were M.D.R.M. leaders RASETA and RAVOAHANGY, while RABE-MANANJARA got a life sentence.[3]

The French government took the Madagascar revolt as an unexpected storm brought about by the islanders for no serious reason. The French colonialists boasted Madagascar as a model colony whose population during fifty years of French rule had embarked upon the road of peaceful economic and cultural advancement.[4] Accordingly, the only explanation the French government could devise for the uprising was that it had been organized by foreign-inspired Communist elements. And as it was unable to find Communists in the island, it branded as Communists unleashing the revolt the leaders of the M.D.R.M., the party which had advocated the overthrow of the colonial regime and the fight for independence. This accusation was a deliberate lie. In fact, it was public knowledge that twenty members of the Political Committee of the party had held a meeting in Tananarive on March 27, three days before the outbreak of the uprising. In that meeting they discussed the situation in the light of the government's policy of terror and of the revolutionary preparations made by extremist elements (PANAMA, J.N.) of the movement. As the party condemned the use of violence, in order to prevent the outbreak of the revolt it sent telegrams on behalf of the party leaders to all party branches, instructing them "to keep calm and composed in the face of all maneuvers and provoca-

---

[1] According to this 1950 report the breakdown of the 11,342 victims was the following: 140 French, 2 Indians, 19 Chinese, 2 Syrians, 17 Senegalese and 11,162 Malagasies. Of the latter, 1,646 were killed by the insurgents, 4,126 by the government troops, and 5,890 fled into the jungle where they starved or froze to death.

[2] *From Madagascar to the Malagasy Republic*, London, 1962.

[3] The sentences of the three party leaders were later repealed under the pressure of French public opinion, and all three were exiled to Europe.

[4] This hypocritical propaganda was so successful that the legend of the prosperity of Madagascar was accepted by a large part of international public opinion. The British scholar RAYMOND K. KENT wrote: "Under French rule, Madagascar became more advanced than most of the European possessions in Africa south of the Sahara." (*Op. cit.*, p. 97.) According to another British author, STEWART C. EASTON, after World War II the Malagasy people "set in motion a rebellion against the French which appears to have had no reasonable object in view, no program to be attained, ... when there were no grievances sufficient to explain the outbreak". (*The Twilight of European Colonialism*, p. 399.)

tions designed to arouse disturbances among the Malagasy people and to sabotage the peaceful policies of the MDRM". But the French colonialists were not to be disconcerted. They simply said that the telegram had been nothing else than a coded message for the rebellion to be started.

The Causes of the 1947 Uprising

That the French colonialists in Madagascar did in some respects more than in other African colonies is a fact. Illiteracy ratios in the island amounted to *only* 60 to 65 per cent; the different mission schools initiated a larger number of young Malagasies into the philosophy of French colonialism, and even a college was established for them, the *Académie Malgache*; the colonial administration was successful in combating the tropical diseases which in the past had demanded lots of victims, etc. All this, however, did not alter the fact that the agricultural concessionaires monopolized 1.5 million hectares of forest, the mining companies had seized another million or more, and that less than one-third of the tillable land owned by the concessionaires was under crop, thus stripping the Malagasy peasants of one million hectares of land on which to produce the food they needed for their subsistence; nor did it alter the situation in which the French concessions profited billions every year from timbering, while the Malagasy workers who did the job had to work for starvation wages.

In addition to economic exploitation, the discontent of the Malagasy people was kindled by the tyranny and terror of the colonial administration as well as by the privileged position accorded to the French colonists and by their provocative, hostile attitude. In the last two years of the war, after the liberation of the island, the local colonial authorities of "Free France", disregarding the "Brazzaville spirit", continued the practices of the Vichy regime and did not stop resorting to arrests, imposing fines and exacting compulsory deliveries of produce. (The "rice distribution agencies", for example, practised the requisitioning of most of the rice produced by Malagasy peasants for two years after liberation.)

Under the impact of world events following the war there started in Madagascar just as in all African countries — mainly owing to the influence of the students returning from overseas and of Malagasy ex-servicemen of the Armies of Free France — the process of the people's awakening to national consciousness and engaging in struggle for independence. The obstinate colonial administration was unwilling to notice this: it refused even to talk with the M.D.R.M. leaders, and at the same time it gave its full support to the PADESM which, being an obedient tool of the colonialists, sabotaged the struggle for independence. One of the main sources of the political discontent of the masses was just the fact that, after the 1946 elections where the M.D.R.M. candidates had polled the huge majority of the votes, the fraudulent electoral system introduced by the administration ensured the PADESM a two-thirds majority in the legislature.

The opposition quarters on the whole held the view that the revolt had been provoked by the colonial administration itself. If there is no evidence to support this assertion, it is a fact that the administration had had knowledge of an uprising in the offing and had done nothing to prevent it. On March 18, that is twelve days before the outbreak of the uprising and nine days before the M.D.R.M. leaders sent out their circular telegram, the Governor of Fianarantsoa province, VINCENT DOLOR, wired to the French High Commissioner, informing him of the revolt in the making, and stated even the day of its proposed outbreak. He repeated his warning on March 25, but the High Commissioner took no precautions.[1]

Madagascar after the Revolt of 1947

Hard times came upon the people of Madagascar after 1947. While in Paris, in the National Assembly and in the Ministry of Overseas France, the causes of the revolt and the lessons to be drawn were argued about, the police terror reigned in the island.

In the early years following the uprising the attention of the colonial administration was absorbed first of all by the efforts to find out and liquidate the "politically dangerous" or "unreliable" elements. Arrests were made continually, the courts made no scruples to mete out sentences of forced labour for months and years to those whom the colonial authorities brought before them on the charge of participation in any political movement. (Freedom from persecution was enjoyed only by members of the PADESM which, however, had also been banned together with all the other parties.)

Besides persecuting the patriots the colonial administration from 1949 on paid increased attention to the economic development of the island with a view to "modernizing" agriculture. This "economic development", however, was an entirely one-sided affair: the ten-year plan of economic development launched in 1949, just like the rest of the economic measures taken by the administration, was intended neither to improve the conditions of the Malagasy peasantry nor to promote their economic advancement, but served to increase the income of European farmers and planters, buyers and exporters.

The terror regime established after the uprising paralyzed the independence movement for years. The formation of legally functioning parties, or overt struggle for independence, or any open action against the colonial administration was doomed. Yet the patriots did not sit back: they organized underground and prepared to resume the struggle. In 1950 students coming home from French universities set up local underground groups which later formed a political party, the *Parti de l'Union du Peuple Malgache*. That same year there emerged in Tananarive a Solidarity Committee, which propagated the idea of independence and demanded amnesty for those who had been sentenced for participation in the 1947 uprising.

In 1951 a young leader of the M.D.R.M., who happened to be left at liberty after the suppression of the uprising, won at a local by-election in spite of every effort of the colonial authorities, the French settlers and their Malagasy helpers.

Between 1948 and 1956 no political party existed legally in Madagascar. On the other hand, the trade-union movement became active as early as 1949, and in November 1949 the different unions established close relations at a trade-union congress held near Tananarive with the participation of 180 delegates from various parts of the country. The successful 22-day wage strike of the Diégo-Suarez dockworkers in December 1950 gave rise to a veritable strike wave: official government reports mentioned four strikes in 1951, 15 in 1952, and 21 in 1953.

---

[1] The wire of March 18 said: "According to information given me in confidence by the military authorities, certain Malagasy are about to launch a revolt against Frenchmen on March 29, beginning in Tananarive. Take measures to alert all posts to prepare for any eventuality." (KENT, *op. cit.*, p. 107.)

Characteristic of the political atmosphere of the early fifties was the changing attitude of the clergy. During and immediately after the revolt Catholic and Protestant clergymen alike unreservedly took sides with the colonial administration and its terror regime, thereby discrediting themselves and estranging the Malagasy masses. In view of the spread of national consciousness and the idea of independence in larger and larger masses of the Malagasy people, the clergy brought themselves to pose as promoters and supporters of Malagasy national aspirations in order to restore their flagging authority and former influence. When in 1953 the Solidarity Committee issued an appeal demanding amnesty for participants of the 1947 uprising, the Catholic paper *Lumière* expressed agreement with the demand as a "just claim" (though refusing to join the signers of the appeal on the ground that, in its opinion, the authors of the appeal were under Communist influence), and the bishops of Madagascar issued a joint statement declaring that the Church recognized the Malagasy people's national aspirations as just and did not disapprove of political activity.

The Independence Movement after 1956

In 1956 a new stage began in the political life of Madagascar. The introduction of the *loi-cadre* restored the people's right to form political parties and engage in politics. And the people made use of this right; not less than 18 parties and fractions were founded between the introduction of the *loi-cadre* and the 1957 elections. Most of them represented tribal or local interests and nearly all of them rallied behind three big parties: the leftist *Union des Démocrates Malgaches*, the rightist *Parti Social Démocrate de Madagascar* (P.S.D.), and the centrist group of "Progressive Nationalists".

The left wing of the Progressive Nationalists, the *Union des Intellectuels et Universitaires Malgaches*, was directed by Dr. RAMANGASOAVINA, and the right wing, called the *Union Nationale Malgache* (UNAM), was led by RABEMANANJARA who was ʾiving in Paris and by one of his close associates, ALEXIS BEZAKA,[1] at home. The "Progressives" accepted the *loi-cadre* as a prelude to "total and definitive" independence, which they did not think inconsistent with membership in the French Union. They demanded only that the question be decided after accession to independence. What separated the left wing from the right wing was that the former was in favour of co-operation with the Communists, while the latter was against it. Close to the Progressive group stood RAKOTONIRINA's party, the *Union des Indépendants*, which, in addition to being against co-operation with the Communists, did not regard independence as a primary condition of remaining within the French Union.

The leftist party *Rassemblement des Peuples Malgaches* (R.P.M.), which later changed its name to *Union des Démocrates Malgaches* (U.D.M.), had been founded by ANDRIAMANJATO,[2] a Protestant pastor. The party considered the *loi-cadre* unac-

---

[1] ALEXIS BEZAKA, a member of the Betsimisàraka tribe, was born in March 1916 at Ambatokintana in Tamatave province. He went to school in Tamatave and became a businessman. In 1945 he was elected to the Provincial Council of Tamatave. As one of RABEMANANJARA's closest associates, he was an original member of the M.D.R.M.

[2] RICHARD ANDRIAMANJATO, a member of the Merina tribe, was born at Mahitsy near Tananarive in July 1930. He studied theology and philosophy in France (Montpellier, Strasbourg and Paris). In 1957 he returned to Madagascar and served at one of the biggest Protestant churches of Tananarive.

ceptable, demanded independence at once and was against remaining in the French Union. The main body of the party was constituted by the Diégo-Suarez workers.

The extreme right wing of the independence movement was represented by the P.S.D. (Social Democrats), which was founded late in 1956 in Majunga province by PHILIBERT TSIRANANA[1] with the help of the French Socialist Party. The P.S.D., though posing as a socialist party, pursued an ultra-conservative policy. It was against co-operation not only with the Communists but with any party standing more to the left than itself, and branded the demand for immediate independence as "agitation by a minority of malcontents". Instead it voiced the need for gradual progress towards independence, and considered membership in the French Union not only desirable but even absolutely indispensable. It rejected also the demand for amnesty, claiming that "the majority of the Malagasies are against an amnesty". When at the elections of April 1957 the party obtained the majority in the Provincial Council of Majunga, the General-Secretary of the party, TSIRANANA, was elected to the presidency.

Before the referendum of September 1958 the P.S.D. took a stand for voting "yes", while several opposition parties campaigned for voting "no". In May 1956 the latter parties convened an Independence Congress in Tamatave, where they brought into existence the "Délégation Permanente du Congrès de l'Indépendance" (D.P.C.I.) to organize and influence the referendum campaign. However, their action failed. Seventy-seven per cent of the electorate voted in favour of the Constitution offered by DE GAULLE. (Characteristically, the majority in the two biggest towns of the island, Tananarive and Tamatave, voted "no".)

Under the new Constitution the provisional government, headed by TSIRANANA as Prime Minister, was formed in October 1958.

In the months following the referendum several new political parties sprang up. In October, after its defeat in the referendum, the D.P.C.I. split. Militant nationalist and socialist elements of the movement, led by the Abbé RICHARD ANDRIAMANJATO, formed an independent political party, the A.K.F.M. ("Antokon' ny Kongresin' ny Fahaleovantenan' i Madagasikara"), and the moderate elements, headed by MANJA GAONA, founded the *Mouvement National pour l'Indépendance de Madagascar* (MONIMA). The A.K.F.M., which recruited its members principally from the urban workers and intellectuals, demanded independence immediately and amnesty for all the politicians imprisoned or exiled since the 1947 uprising. The MONIMA, without giving a clear programme of its own, took a middle position between the TSIRANANA government and the militant nationalists of the A.K.F.M. who formed a strong opposition.

It was also after the referendum that another party of such middle-of-the-roaders was formed — the *Union Démocratique Socialiste de Madagascar* (U.D.S.M.), which was not to last long. The founders originally claimed that the Malagasy traditions should be reconciled with the idea of Christendom, and insisted that the political leaders in exile since 1947 should come back into political life. However, the U.D.S.M. members in the Provincial Council voted in unison with the government on

---

[1] PHILIBERT TSIRANANA was born the son of a peasant family of the Tsimihety tribe in the locality of Ambarikorano in 1912. When a child he guarded his father's flocks. He first went to school at the age of twelve; in 1930 he was sent to Tananarive, where he took his master's degree and then taught in school for twelve years. In 1946 he went to France, where he studied education in Montpellier. In 1950 he returned to Madagascar, and taught theory of education in Tananarive. In 1952 he was elected to the Majunga Provincial Council.

the matter of constitutional reform, and the party soon entered into the alliance of the rightist bloc *Cartel des Républicains* formed at TSIRANANA's initiative.

In December 1958 the Christian parties, to counteract the influence of the militant A.K.F.M., merged into a single Christian organization, the *Rassemblement Chrétien de Madagascar*, with a moderate nationalist programme. The party, which thus united various Christian organizations, was especially active among the peasants, first of all in Fianarantsoa, Tananarive, Tamatave and Diégo-Suarez.

In October 1958, following the referendum, the Assembly convened by the French High Commissioner proclaimed Madagascar the "Malagasy Republic" as a member state of the French Community. Then, without new general elections being held, a Constituent Assembly was summoned, consisting of members of the Provincial Councils. It discussed the new "Republican Constitution" proposed by TSIRANANA and on May 1, 1959, adopted it by 1,368,059 votes to 392,557.

According to the Constitution the country is headed by the President of the Republic, whose post is filled by election to be held every seven years through indirect vote. The President appoints the members of the government, is empowered to dissolve the National Assembly upon consultation with the Senate (the first Senate was composed of TSIRANANA's followers who had sat on the committee drafting the Constitution). The Constitution also empowers the President to declare, in case of need, the state of emergency during which he governs the country by decrees.

Two days after the adoption of the Constitution PHILIBERT TSIRANANA was elected President of the Republic, while he retained also the office of Prime Minister.

With the coming to power of TSIRANANA and his government a new situation arose. Being in power, they also were now for the building of a unified state instead of a federation, and, considering the people's ever louder demand for amnesty and their aspirations for independence, they talked more and more about the progressive attainment of independence within the French Community, and even promised an amnesty. The overwhelming majority of the opposition parties — the "moderate" opposition — which also thought it possible for the country to attain independence with the material help of France, now had no serious reason to oppose the government. Owing to personal, tribal and similar dissensions, they formally continued to pose as opposition parties, but in fact — now tacitly now overtly — they supported the government's policy.

In the new situation, largely also under the impact of the highly significant changes that had occurred in Black Africa (the Sudan, Ghana and Guinea having acceded to independence), the only consistent opposition party, the A.K.F.M., stepped up its activity demanding an amnesty and full independence at once. In the meantime the centrist parties which had shifted to the right lost numerous members, who, remaining loyal to the idea of independence, joined the A.K.F.M. (Among them was RABEMANANJARA, who had incurred TSIRANANA's hatred because, contrary to all expectations, he voted "no" at the referendum.) After its congress in August 1959 the party worked out a detailed programme, which demanded, among other things, nationalization of private business interests, replacement of non-Malagasy officials of the local and central administrations by Malagasies, and withdrawal of the country from the franc zone.

This militant action of the A.K.F.M. was not in vain. Since its policy expressed the real will of the masses, the moderate opposition parties, which were otherwise against the A.K.F.M., were compelled in certain matters, particularly in that of the amnesty, to endorse the demands of the A.K.F.M. It may have been due to this change that in October 1959 ANDRIAMANJATO, President of the A.K.F.M., was elected Mayor of Tananarive, and the Malagasy Assembly passed by a huge majority a resolution pressing for the promulgation of a law on amnesty.

But TSIRANANA's policy did not change. His party, the P.S.D., at its congress held in Fianarantsoa in August 1959, adopted a programme, under which it conducted for months on end a propaganda campaign in favour of "gradual independence within the French Community". The party declared itself a champion of "socialism", but instead of proposing concrete steps towards socialism, it confined both its programme and its propaganda to phrasemongering about socialism, emphasizing that it aimed "at liberating the human being from every servitude that oppresses him, and in consequence at ensuring to every man, woman and child [?], in a society founded on equality and fraternity, the free exercise of their rights, of their natural abilities and religion".

In reality this party and the government posing as socialist did their utmost to push the country on to the capitalist road of economic development. In November 1959 TSIRANANA went to New York and Washington, where he had talks with representatives of the United States government. Thereupon Madagascar joined the European Economic Community, and after the Madagascar conference of the Economic Commission for Africa held in February 1960, the TSIRANANA government became busy getting big U.S. monopolist companies to make investments in Madagascar (in spring of 1960 the Minister of Industry and the Under-Secretary for Economic Affairs of the TSIRANANA government conducted talks with big capitalists in the United States, and later representatives of U.S. concerns — Westinghouse, Koppers, and others — went to Madagascar for the same purpose) and trying to obtain loans and credits from international capitalist organizations (E.E.C., *Fonds d'Aide et Coopération*).

In December 1959, on returning from the United States, TSIRANANA had a talk in Paris with President DE GAULLE, and — encouraged by DE GAULLE's speech in Saint-Louis on December 12 — he requested and received his consent that Madagascar, following the example of the Federation of Mali, might ask for independence without ceasing to be a member of the French Community.

In January 1960 the TSIRANANA government, with a view to popularizing its policy, conducted a large-scale campaign in the course of which TSIRANANA visited eleven cities and delivered speeches. In February the Malagasy Assembly empowered TSIRANANA to discuss the conditions of independence with the French government. In the same months RABEMANANJARA and RAVOAHANGY, still in exile, declared that they endorsed TSIRANANA's policy.

In mid-February the Franco-Malagasy talks began in Paris on the question of Madagascar's independence. As a result, Prime Ministers DEBRÉ of France and TSIRANANA of Madagascar on April 2 signed two agreements: the one providing for Madagascar's accession to independence on June 26, 1960, and the other to the effect that the country, once independent, will remain a member state of the French Community. At the same time they initialled a number of other agreements to be signed after the granting of independence. In accordance with those agreements France should have the right, even after Madagascar had become an independent state, to maintain strategic bases and station troops in the island, but would at the same time assist the Malagasy Republic in building up a national army, and the country would remain within the franc zone.

Pursuant to the agreement of April 2, 1960, Madagascar became independent as the Malagasy Republic on June 26, 1960.

BIBLIOGRAPHY

HENRI DE CASSEVILLE, *L'Ile ensanglantée*, Paris, 1948.

"Insurrection malgache". *Bulletin des Missions*, Abbaye Saint-André-les-Bruges, XXIV, 1950

R. W. RABEMANANJARA, *Madagascar: Histoire de la nation malgache*, Paris, 1952.

R. W. RABEMANANJARA, *Madagascar sous la rénovation malgache*, Paris, 1953.

PIERRE STIBBE, *Justice pour les Malgaches*, Paris, 1954.

HILDEBERT ISNARD, *Madagascar*, Paris, 1955.

PIERRE NORD, *L'Eurafrique notre dernière chance*, Paris, 1955 (ch. II., III, IV; pp. 13–33.

JACQUES RABEMANANJARA, "Témoignages malgaches et colonialisme", *Présence Africaine*, Paris, 1956.

GEORGES BRUN-KERIS, "Madagascar à l'heure de la Loi-Cadre", *Marchés tropicaux du Monde*, No. 626, 1957.

CHARLES ROBEQUAIN, *Madagascar et les bases dispersées de l'Union française*, Paris, 1958.

ROBERT BOUDRY, "Décolonisation à Madagascar?" *La Pensée* 78/1958.

JACQUES RABEMANANJARA, *Nationalisme et problèmes malgaches*, Paris, 1958.

J. RABEMANANJARA, "Les fondements culturels du nationalisme malgache", *Présence Africaine*, Feb. 1958.

WILLIAM A. HANCE, "Madagascar and Tropical Africa: Similarities and Contrastes", in *African Economic Development*, London, 1958.

PHILIBERT TSIRANANA, *Discours*, Tananarive, 1959.

HUBERT DESCHAMPS, *Histoire de Madagascar*, Paris, 1960.

Madagascar: Birth of a New Republic, 1949–59, Paris, 1960.

R. K. KENT, *From Madagascar to the Malagasy Republic*, London, 1962.

CHAPTER XXVI

FRENCH TRUST TERRITORIES

French Cameroun

In 1947 REUBEN UM NYOBÉ[1] founded a party named *Union des Populations du Cameroun* (U.P.C.). The party demanded unification of the French and British Cameroons and independence for the united country.

The French colonial authorities, being alarmed by the activities of the U.P.C., promoted the formation of opposing parties. In 1950 the African CHARLES OKALA formed the *Union Sociale Camerounaise* (U.S.C.), and in 1951 LOUIS-PAUL AUJOULAT, a French doctor born in Algeria, founded the *Bloc Démocratique Camerounais* (B.D.C.). Both held that unification and independence were a mere utopia.

In 1951, after the R.D.A. broke with the French Communist Party, the U.P.C. withdrew from the R.D.A. and continued as an independent party, but at the March 1952 elections to the Territorial Assembly it was unable to obtain a seat when facing the government-assisted opportunist parties.

In 1952 NYOBÉ went to New York and presented to the United Nations General Assembly a petition demanding immediate unification of the country, the establishment of a legislative assembly and a governing council with an African majority, universal and equal suffrage for all adults, and the fixing of a date for the country's accession to independence.

NYOBÉ's militant attitude in New York added to his personal authority and popularity, and was highly instrumental in the rapid growth of his party. At the end of 1952 the U.P.C. had about 30,000 members, and early in 1955 its membership was already over 100,000.

The growth of the party and its revolutionary effect on the masses prompted the colonial administration to start an over-all attack against the U.P.C. The new French High Commissioner of the territory, ROLAND PRÉ, who took office in January 1, 1955, pursued the attack on two lines. A great part of the U.P.C. activists were employed in various provincial organs of the colonial administration. To paralyze the work of the party throughout the territory, the High Commissioner transferred these people to central posts in towns where the authorities could check their every move. At the same time he started a campaign of slander against the U.P.C., accusing its leaders of being Communist, of using nationalist slogans and striving

---

[1] REUBEN UM NYOBÉ was born of Protestant parents at Boumnyebel in the Cameroons in 1913. He graduated from law school and became an office clerk. From 1944 he was active in the trade-union movement as a functionary of the local union affiliated to the French C.G.T. In 1946 he attended the constituent conference of the R.D.A. in Bamako.

to overthrow the system under cover of the trade unions. The colonial administration found a willing helper in the Roman Catholic Church. In April 1955 the Catholic bishops of the Cameroons issued a joint pastoral letter calling upon the faithful to keep away from the U.P.C. which propagated the ideas of Communism. The High Commissioner in his report to the French government had the self-confident assurance to promise that he would soon put down the "Communist actions".

What happened, however, was just the contrary. In reply to the episcopal letter, FÉLIX-ROLAND MOUMIÉ[1] issued a mimeographic pamphlet entitled *Religion or colonialism?*, in which he unmasked the church dignitaries as allies of the secular authorities—the colonialists; and the people responded by starting a counter-move. On April 22, 1955, the U.P.C., the Cameroons Women's Democratic Union, the Cameroons Democratic Youth, and the trade unions affiliated to the C.G.T. held a joint rally. This meeting issued a call for the ending of trusteeship, the creation of a sovereign Cameroun, and general elections to a Constituent Assembly before December 1, 1955. The appeal found a nation-wide response and stirred up large masses. The colonial authorities ordered out police and troops against the demonstrating people, and a veritable massacre began, in which thousands of people were killed.[2] In July 1955 the colonial authorities, referring to a 1936 law (designed at that time to be applied against fascist organizations), banned the U.P.C., the Cameroons Women's Democratic Union and the Cameroons Democratic Youth, and arrested the trade-union leaders.

The U.P.C. went underground. MOUMIÉ left the country and directed the party's antigovernment propaganda first from the British Cameroons and later from Cairo, where he published a newspaper entitled *Voix du Cameroun*. NYOBÉ, who at the time of the ban was in Nigeria, returned home to lead the clandestine movement.

Although the United Nations Visiting Mission to the Cameroons in autumn of 1955 took an unfavourable view of the U.P.C., the Cameroons politicians opposed to the U.P.C.'s policy, and even the French High Commissioner and the French government, were fully aware that the policy of the U.P.C. represented the will of the people of the Cameroons, and that sheer force was insufficient to counteract the party's influence. The "moderate" parties found it necessary to make some change of tone.

The B.D.C. issued an appeal in which, while opposing the claim for immediate independence by raising the slogan of "realistic nationalism", it demanded self-government. AUJOULAT insisted that "reforms" were needed. High Commissioner PRÉ talked about the dangerous "political vacuum" brough about by the elimination of the U.P.C. And the French government, to avert this danger, worked out a "statute" holding out to the Cameroons at least some minor elements of self-government. Characteristically enough, at the French parliamentary elections in January 1956, AUJOULAT who had been a member of the French Assembly without interruption since 1945, and who ran for election in a Central Cameroons constituency,

---

[1] FÉLIX-ROLAND MOUMIÉ was born at Bamun, in the Cameroons, in 1926. He qualified as a doctor in Dakar. From 1947 he was a member and later President of the U.P.C.

[2] The U.P.C. claimed that the death toll was about 20,000. According to official reports there were only 24 dead and 114 wounded among the Africans, while the armed force lost one dead and 62 injured, and Africans killed two Africans and one European. (*Afrique Nouvelle*, June 14, 1955.)

was defeated by M'BIDA,[1] a candidate advocating self-government. (M'BIDA polled 64,397 votes, while AUJOULAT obtained only 18,915.)

The independence aspiration of the Cameroonian people, the political fight waged underground by the U.P.C., could not be put off either with the high-sounding phrases of "moderate" politicians or with the sham concessions of the French government.

In summer of 1956 the U.P.C., led by MOUMIÉ, started armed resistance in form of guerrilla warfare against the French colonial administration. At the same time, in June 1956, SOPPO PRISO,[2] who had been a member of the French National Assembly since 1947 and of the Cameroons Territorial Assembly since 1952, and who in March 1956 had said that "the U.P.C. is the only movement expressing the true opinion of the Cameroons population", formed a new political party, the *Union Nationale*, with the purpose of uniting all political organizations of the territory. The new party demanded independence for the Cameroons but was against any kind of the use of force, demanding restoration of the U.P.C.'s rights and a general amnesty. Since the Union admitted to its ranks followers of the U.P.C. and various groups which sympathized with them, the U.S.C. and the B.D.C. broke with the Union at the first congress of the party on August 4, 1956.

Three months later, in November 1956, a new split took place in the Union. Municipal elections were called for November, and the election of the Territorial Assembly was scheduled for December. The second congress of the Union Nationale, held at Douala from November 6 to 8, discussed the question of participation in the elections. SOPPO PRISO was in favour of participation, but his followers insisted on boycotting the elections. Thereupon they parted.

That the true will of the people was represented by the banned U.P.C., not by the legally existing parties, became evident at the municipal elections in November, when the majority of the voters just in the most important constituencies, following the U.P.C. call for boycott, stayed away from the vote (in Yaoundé 30 per cent, in Douala only 12 per cent of the electorate went to the polls).

The election of the Territorial Assembly took place on December 23. On December 8 NYOBÉ, in an interview he gave to the Paris neswpaper *La Dépêche du Midi*, explained that his party and its adherents would not take part in the elections until the administration had granted general amnesty to the imprisoned fighters of the national movement and until it had restored the democratic liberties, notably, by repealing its decree of July 13, 1955, which had banned the U.P.C.

At the elections the administration resorted to unbridled police terror to get the largest possible number of voters to go to the poll; the guerillas in turn responded to the government terror with counteractions. Nowhere did more than 50 to 60 per cent of the electorate participate in the election (in some constituencies participation hardly even amounted to 10 – 20 per cent), but the government attained its goal: it succeeded in setting up a Legislative Assembly which, apart from a few independent peasant members, consisted of adherents of the legally authorized moderate parties loyal to the administration. The B.D.C., which was already at

---

[1] ANDRÉ-MARIE M'BIDA was born the son of Roman Catholic parents in Endinging, Southern Cameroons, in 1917. He qualified in theology, and worked as a clerk from 1945 to 1950. In 1951 he opened a shop in Ebolowa. In 1952 he was elected to the Territorial Assembly. From 1953 till 1956 he was a Councillor of the French Union. In 1956, as a leader of the Catholic B.D.C. ("Christian democrats"), he was elected to the French National Assembly.

[2] SOPPO PRISO, a building contractor, was born in 1913 at Douala. In 1948 he founded the youth organization called the Jeunesse Camerounaise.

that time led by M'Bida, and which had been joined by Ahmadou Ahidjo's[1] newly formed *Union Camerounienne*, obtained the majority, and the first government of the Cameroons was formed by M'Bida. For this "success" of the government, however, the people of the Cameroons had to pay a stiff price. The death toll of the police terror and the guerrilla actions amounted to about 1,500.

In the newly elected Assembly the Union Camerounienne headed by Ahidjo had 38 members, M'Bida's B.D.C. had 20, and Soppo Priso's Union Nationale had 8 members. First thing the Assembly did was to discuss the "Cameroons Statute" made public towards the end of 1955, and the debates lasted a whole month (February 1957). Soppo Priso took a stand against the draft statute and insisted on the adoption of a declaration that the Cameroons should become an independent sovereign state. Ahidjo, President of the Assembly, and the Moslem nobility who set the tone in his party, as well as M'Bida's "Christian democrats", were against the demand for independence. They accepted the statute, only they proposed that the term "territory" be changed to "Trust State" and the powers of the Cameroons government widened to some extent, and they voted to accept the statute with these modifications. In May 1957 the Assembly installed the new coalition government, with M'Bida as Prime Minister and Ahidjo as Deputy Premier and Minister of the Interior.

The activities of the M'Bida government boiled down to conducting a nationwide campaign to counteract the influence of the U.P.C., and bombarding the French government with requests to send troops to wipe out the guerrillas. But the French government, certainly on the ground of what it had learnt from its Indochina experience, refused. On the contrary, starting from the consideration that in the new international situation it might gain more by peaceful compromise than by force to keep its colonial positions, it made attempts to persuade Nyobé and the U.P.C. into stopping the guerrilla war and co-operating with the government. Newspapers in Paris and in the Cameroons published article after article written in a conciliatory tone (and obviously inspired by French government circles), and then Bishop Thomas Bongo of Douala (who in early 1957 had rudely attacked Nyobé and the U.P.C. in an open letter published in the Cameroons press) called on Nyobé in person with a view to bringing him to make peace with the government. As all this was to no avail, the French government resorted to new tactics: having realized that the M'Bida government's former policy of terror applied against the U.P.C. made it unsuitable for a rapprochement with Nyobé, it replaced this government by one which it thought fit for the purpose.

On February 18, 1958, the Cameroons Assembly removed the M'Bida government, and appointed Ahmadou Ahidjo to form the new cabinet. M'Bida and his "Christian democrats" went into opposition, while Soppo Priso and his Union Nationale joined in forming the government.

The French government's reliance on Ahidjo can well be explained. The influence of the U.P.C. prevailed mainly in the South of the country, where the guerrilla war was going on. Ahidjo, who failed from the North and represented the interests of

[1] Ahmadou Ahidjo, son of a Fulah chief, was born at Garoua, the capital of the Northern Region, in May 1922. He went to primary and secondary school at Yaoundé. From 1945 he was a radio operator in the Post Office. As a member of the "Moslem Youth" organization, he took part in political activities. From 1947 he was an elected member of the Territorial Assembly. In 1953 he was elected to the Assembly of the French Union, of which he was a Secretary in 1954 and Vice-President in 1956.

chiefs and feudal rulers of the Northern Region, did not see in the U.P.C. such a direct threat to himself and to his masters as did M'BIDA.

Upon coming to power, AHIDJO set himself the aim, on the one hand, to secure the support of the French government for himself and his cabinet, and, on the other, by stressing the demand for independence and granting minor concessions, to calm down the opposition, including the U.P.C., and to consolidate his power position by putting an end to the civil war. For this reason he promised amnesty to the U.P.C. guerrillas in case they stopped fighting and abandoned their underground activities. On June 12, 1958, he submitted to the legislature a draft decision inviting the French government to recognize the right of the Cameroons to independence, and to transfer the rights it exercised under the Trusteeship Agreement to the High Commissioner of the Cameroons without, however, terminating the trusteeship status of the territory before the proclamation of independence. On the strength of this decision he conducted talks with the French government, and managed to have a new Cameroons Statute drafted. The new statute recognized the Cameroons' right to independence, giving the territory "full internal autonomy", and leaving only foreign affairs, defence and finance in the hands of the French government. The Cameroons Assembly adopted the new statute (by 45 votes to 4, with one abstention) on November 22, 1958.

In the meantime, however, two months before the adoption of the new statute, important changes had taken place in the political life of the Cameroons. On September 13, 1958, REUBEN UM NYOBÉ was shot dead by a military patrol; and MAYI MATIP,[1] accepting AHIDJO's offer of amnesty, gave up the fight in the same month and returned to the political scene with his maquis organized into a legally functioning opposition party, called the *Front de Réconciliation*. The party regarded itself as the real successor to the "Union des Populations du Cameroun", in contrast to the U.P.C. led by MOUMIÉ, which remained underground and continued the guerrilla war against the government. On January 23, 1959, M'BIDA left the country for Guinea, where he contacted MOUMIÉ at the U.G.T.A.N. Congress in Conakry.

At a by-election in April 1959 MATIP got himself elected to Parliament. At the same time his party, which had been joined by other opposition groups, was renamed the *Front Populaire pour l'Unité et la Paix*.

In spring of 1959 the French government announced to the United Nations that the Cameroons would become independent on January 1, 1960. The UN General Assembly on March 14, 1959, gave its approval by 56 votes and with 23 abstentions, disregarding the demand of the Cameroonian opposition that before accession to independence general elections be held under international supervision. The abstentions included the socialist countries and a number of Asian and African countries (Ghana, Guinea, Tunisia and others).

AHIDJO jumped to the occasion. Being sure of the support of the French government and the United Nations, and aware that he had succeeded in regimenting those members of the U.P.C. whom he could at all expect to get hold of (MATIP and his followers), AHIDJO thought the time had come to throw off his mask. From May 1959

---

[1] THÉODORE MAYI MATIP was born the son of a chief at Eséka near Douala in June 1917. In his youth he served in the colonial police, and then became a journalist. After the war, he engaged in political activities within the U.P.C., and became president of the party's youth wing, the Cameroons Democratic Youth. In 1955, when both the party and the youth organization were banned, MATIP was imprisoned and was not released until two years later. Being set at liberty, he took an active part in the underground work of the U.P.C. as secretary to NYOBÉ.

onward he forced through Parliament bill after bill building up his full powers: he became empowered to suspend the freedom of assembly and organization at his discretion, to introduce the state of emergency and curfew , censorship of the press and correspondence, passport regulations, to set up special summary courts, to prohibit the circulation and importation of certain printed publications, to order the arrest of anyone whom he deemed dangerous to public order.

And under the pretext of combating the guerrillas AHIDJO started his reign of terror with the aid of French High Commissioner XAVIER TORRE.[1]

In the months preceding the proclamation of independence (in the second half of 1959) there was in the Cameroons no end of arrests and tortures, of trials at which the martial law courts passed sentences in complete disregard of legality on the basis of confessions extracted by torture, and public and secret executions were in the order of the day.[2] All opposition papers were suppressed and the papers in the service of the government conducted an unscrupulous campaign of slander against the liberation fighters, branding their guerrilla warfare as "banditry" and the patriots as "terrorist brigands".

The legally functioning parties, even though they disagreed with AHIDJO's policy, displayed no serious resistance. SOPPO PRISO criticized AHIDJO's "tactics", but he did not withdraw his men from the government. MATIP and his followers posed as an opposition party, but showed their oppositionism only in words; MATIP still wanted to be regarded as the only executor of NYOBÉ's political will, but at the same time he condemned the guerrilla war and vilified MOUMIÉ, while refraining from raising his voice against AHIDJO's reign of terror. In October 1959 he published his programme, in which he demanded restoration of the U.P.C. to full rights, amnesty for the political prisoners convicted in 1955, and the release of those languishing in jail (but not, for the time being, the return home of the political emigrees !). He proposed that the U.P.C. summon its congress to elect its leadership, that a government of national unity be formed, and parliamentary elections be organized under the control of this new government.

AHIDJO, while ruthlessly repressing every dissenting view within his own party,[3] tolerated MATIP's pseudo-militancy without further ado. This fact clearly shows how right MOUMIÉ was when he called MATIP the traitor to the U.P.C.'s and NYOBÉ's policy.

The only veritable opposition of the AHIDJO government was the underground U.P.C. led by MOUMIÉ, which reacted to the institution of the reign of terror by stepping up the guerrilla war.

On August 13, 1959, M'BIDA and MOUMIÉ issued a joint statement, proposing the convocation of a round-table conference of all political organizations of the Cameroons.

Neither AHIDJO nor the French government nor the United Nations responded to the call. Arrests, tortures, courts martial, and executions did not for a moment stop in the country.

---

[1] In August 1959, the French government paper *Le Figaro* carried an article entitled "Growing Terror in Cameroun", in which it wrote among other things: "The fight waged against terrorism in defence of the people [?] is conducted at present almost exclusively by the French army and police dispatched from the metropolitan country."

[2] As to the details of the atrocities, see the pamphlet entitled *Rape of Cameroons* (Committee of African Organisations, London) and the petitions submitted to the United Nations.

[3] It was for such dissensions that, for example, he dismissed Vice-Premier and Minister of Education MICHEL NYINE on September 12, 1959, and got Parliament to remove its President, DANIEL KÉMAJOU, on October 15.

During the fourteenth session of the United Nations General Assembly, on September 29, 1959, the Fourth Committee heard the U.P.C. representatives, who informed the international organization of the atrocities going on in the Cameroons (their hearing was opposed only by the French delegation). A few days after this hearing, on October 9, AHIDJO staged further executions in public—with the knowledge and consent of the French administration[1]—in the market places of Douala, Yaoundé, and Dschang.

On the deeds of horror carried out by the AHIDJO government during 1959, the "Committee of African Organisations" published a pamphlet entitled *Rape of Cameroons*, which, together with an enumeration of the most heinous facts, contained the appeal which the U.P.C. had addressed to world public opinion the day following the executions.

In the UN General Assembly in November 1959 India, Ghana and several other Afro-Asian countries proposed that still before the proclamation of independence the United Nations send a Visiting Mission to the Cameroons to examine the situation, but the General Assembly rejected this proposal (by 44 votes to 33). By this decision the United Nations sanctioned AHIDJO's reign of terror and was instrumental in making the French Cameroun, with the antidemocratic AHIDJO government, an independent state without enabling its people to express their will through democratic elections.

During December AHIDJO conducted talks with the French government, and on December 25 he signed an agreement by which:

The French troops and police remained in the country, and France would help the Cameroonian government to build up its own army; France would continue providing financial and technical aid to the country; the French currency should be the legal tender, and the country remained in the franc zone; France would support the country's admission to the United Nations.

Three days before the declaration of independence the Executive Committee of the U.P.C. adopted a resolution calling for total revolutionary struggle to win real independence for the Cameroons.

On January 1, 1960, the former Trust Territory under French administration was proclaimed an independent state. The proclamation of independence took place amidst cruel incidents. To demonstrate against AHIDJO's reign of terror, the U.P.C. guerrillas made surprise attacks upon the Douala airport and police stations, and the patriots staged mass protests against sham independence. In the streets and at the airport of Douala violent clashes occurred between the guerrillas and patriots, on the one hand, and AHIDJO's police force, on the other.

AHIDJO's press, like the French bourgeois papers, reported on the guerrilla actions and the demonstrations by the patriots as "atrocities of terrorist gangsters". How far this interpretation of the events was from the truth is shown by the fact that even according to official reports of the AHIDJO government all in all five people were killed in the clashes between police and the civil population, and the "terrorists" lost 25 dead and the same number of wounded. (In reality the police terror resulted in far bigger casualties.[2])

In such circumstances it is not surprising that the celebration of independence took place without the participation of the population.

---

[1] French High Commissioner TORRE came back from Paris the day before the executions.
[2] The *Neue Zürcher Zeitung* of January 3 estimated the casualties at "about one hundred."

"Contrary to all expectation, the ceremony in which the French Tricolour was replaced by the national flag of the Cameroun was witnessed by only a small group of spectators", wrote the paper *La Croix* on January 4, 1960. And *Le Monde* in its January 5 issue reported as follows:

"Afraid of disturbances, the government in the very last minute cancelled the brass concert and torchlight procession scheduled for midnight ... Never before had the capital city of any country presented such a tragically empty spectacle as Yaoundé at this most exciting moment of the history of the country ... As night was falling, the population left the streets of Yaoundé and Douala ... At the dinner given by the President of the Assembly soldiers in arms six feet away from the guests guarded the entrances to the building, and prominent figures of Yaoundé reassured their guests by producing the revolvers they had been carrying upon them since the July riots."

Characteristically, UN Secretary-General HAMMARSKJÖLD was among the guests of the independence celebrations, while Ghana and Guinea stayed away.

The Cameroonian patriots were not alone with their opinion of the AHIDJO regime and their appraisal of the independence achieved by it. On January 1, 1960, the French Catholic paper *Témoignage Chrétien* published an article entitled "Restless Cameroun", in which it made the following comment:

"What is the value of a political independence which right at the outset sanctions complete economic, psychological, social and cultural dependence? What is the value of an independence whose pseudo-engineers are personages devoid of any self-reliance and abilities ...? When all is said and done, Cameroun is looking forward to independence amidst the decay of order and a general confusion, and this confusion may possibly have the worst of consequences."

French Togoland

Before and during World War II political parties were non-existent in Togoland. In 1946, however, when Togoland, like the rest of the French colonies, was given a Territorial Assembly, SYLVANUS OLYMPIO[13] formed a political party out of the *Comité de l'Unité Togolaise* (C.U.T.), a cultural society organized by the French Commissioner in order to help the administration's influence to prevail upon the African intelligentsia.

OLYMPIO and his party set themselves the aim of uniting in a single independent "Ewe State" the Ewe tribes living in isolation from one another in three different colonies (British Togoland, French Togoland, Gold Coast). The French colonialists, whom the Ewe movement threatened with the loss of their colonial positions, stopped supporting the C.U.T., and the French administration, to counteract the organization's activity which it held dangerous, and to prevent its possible advance in the forthcoming elections, lent assistance to NICHOLAS GRUNITZKY[2] and PEDRO OLYMPIO (a relation of SYLVANUS OLYMPIO's) in founding a new party, the *Parti*

---

[1] See Part Seven, ch. VII, footnote 14.

[2] NICHOLAS GRUNITZKY was born in an influential family of Atakpamé in Togoland on April 4, 1913. His father was a merchant of mixed German and Polish descent, his mother was African. NICHOLAS was educated in France, where he obtained a diploma in engineering. He returned to Togoland in 1937. During World War II he joined DE GAULLE's resistance movement. After the war, from 1945 to 1949, he was an engineer of the State Railways. In 1949 he set up a transport business.

Togolais du Progrès (P.T.P.), which labelled the Ewe movement as a manouevre of the British colonialists. Instead of demanding independence, the party was in favour of maintaining French domination as the only safeguard of the future progress of Togoland.[1]

The French government contemplated eliminating the influence of the C.U.T. with the help of the P.T.P., but this scheme failed for the time being. In November 1946 the C.U.T. candidate (Dr. MARTIN AKU) was elected to the French National Assembly by 4,726 votes, while GRUNITZKY as candidate of the P.T.P. received only 1,637 votes. At the December elections to the Territorial Assembly the P.T.P. put up no candidates, and thus of the 24 seats 15 (in the South) were gained by the C.U.T., while the northern constituencies elected 9 "independent" representatives of the chiefs. OLYMPIO was elected President of the Territorial Assembly.

In autumn of 1947 OLYMPIO went to New York. Before the UN Trusteeship Council he eloquently expounded the Ewe demand for unification and independence.

In 1951 two new political organizations were formed in Togoland, one to the right from the P.T.P., the other to the left from the C.U.T.

In July 1951 the chiefs' representatives in the Territorial Assembly formed a political party named the *Union des Chefs et Populations du Nord* (U.C.P.N.). This party, which had no regional branches and whose political line tallied with that of the P.T.P., essentially was an organization representing the interests of conservative chiefs.

In September 1951 there formed a youth association called "Juvento",[2] which, while figuring as the youth cultural organization of the C.U.T., had a rather different political programme. In contrast to the C.U.T., which actually represented the Ewe interests, the Juvento rejected tribal policies, regarded the aims of the Ewe movement as outdated aspirations, and strove for the attainment of independence instead of the unification of the Ewe tribes.

However the political line of the Juvento may have differed from that of the C.U.T., OLYMPIO thought it better not to take notice of it for the moment and not to bother about the affiliation of the youth organization with his own party, because he needed the votes of the young people in the elections against the P.T.P. and the U.C.P.N. These two rightist parties, in fact, were steadily gaining ground with the help of the colonial administration, which accorded them every lawful and unlawful assistance. When in June 1951 the members of the French National Assembly were re-elected, GRUNITZKY won (by 16,255 votes to 10,768) over the C.U.T.'s Dr. AKU, who had been a deputy for Togo in the French National Assembly since 1946. At the election of the Territorial Assembly held barely a year later, in March 1952, the U.C.P.N. received 20,316 votes, the P.T.P. 12,030, and the C.U.T. only 9,073.

In the meantime two wings had taken shape also within the Juvento: the militant, radical left wing was led by MESSANE AIDHSON, the moderate right wing by ANANI IGNACIO SANTOS. AIDHSON having fled to the Gold Coast after his arrest in 1952, the left wing for a time displayed no activity of any importance, but the right wing

---

[1] The P.T.P. paper *Le Progrès* wrote in July 1952: "Sylvanus is working for the Gold Coast, not for Togoland . . . Only in common with France can we solve the many problems facing our country in a peaceable, clever and intelligent manner and with a firm hand. To build up Togoland we shall need France for some time. Understanding and friendship between France and Togoland, if we join forces zestfully and frankly, will make our efforts still more effective."

[2] Some say that the word "Juvento" is a contraction of the Latin word *juventus* ("youth") and the word "Togo"; others claim that it is an abbreviation made of seven French words: Justice — Union — Vigilance — Education — Nationalisme — Ténacité — Optimisme.

did all the more so under one of OLYMPIO's close associates, SANTOS, who in 1954 and 1955 represented, together with OLYMPIO, the position of the C.U.T. before the UN Trusteeship Council.

In April 1955 the French Parliament adopted a new statute for Togoland, enlarging somewhat the powers of the Territorial Assembly and setting up a nine-member Governing Council, but legislation continued to be controlled practically by the colonial administration; the Territorial Assembly in reality exercised no legislative function but was only a consultative body, and the Governing Council was presided over by the French High Commissioner, who nominated four of the nine Council members, only five of them being elected by the Territorial Assembly.

Under the new statute the elections to the Territorial Assembly were held on June 12, 1955. In spite of the C.U.T.'s call to boycott the elections, of 190,053 qualified voters 156,590 went to the poll. A sweeping majority of the votes were cast for the U.C.P.N. (92 per cent) in the northern constituencies, and for the P.T.P. (95 per cent) in the South.

The newly elected Territorial Assembly by its decision of July 4 solemnly declared that Togoland was in favour of close co-operation with France but wanted by no means unification with British Togoland, which in its view would entail loosening this co-operation. The decision stressed at the same time that while the country wished to remain in the French Union and to delegate its representatives to the French National Assembly, yet it wanted internal reforms and full autonomy.

In December 1955 the United Nations General Assembly decided that a plebiscite should be held in both French and British Togoland.

In the meantime the French government, as it were, to meet the demand of the Territorial Assembly, had drawn up a new statute for Togoland. The new statute was already about an "autonomous republic", not about an "autonomous territory", it nevertheless meant no essential step forward. However, the Territorial Assembly, after a short debate, accepted it in August 1956. On the day of the entry into force of the new statute GRUNITZKY was installed as the first Prime Minister of the "Autonomous Republic of Togo", and he took into his cabinet two young U.C.P.N. members (who both were engineers educated in France).

In the plebiscite held pursuant to the United Nations General Assembly resolution on October 28, 1956, the voters had to choose between acceptance of the statute and maintenance of the trusteeship status. In spite of the C.U.T. campaign for boycotting the elections, the majority of the electorate went to the polls (the number of those abstaining from the vote amounted on an average to 35.3 per cent in the South, and to only 12.3 per cent in the North) and voted 313,532 to 22,266 to accept the statute.

In June 1957 another United Nations Visiting Mission went to Togoland. Upon its recommendation the UN General Assembly invited the French government to hold new general elections for the Territorial Assembly and to widen the powers of the Togolese government.

This UN resolution and the fact that OLYMPIO, in the Fourth Committee of the United Nations General Assembly at its twelfth session in November 1957, raised the demand for the independence of Togoland, induced GRUNITZKY to adopt a new policy, particularly in view of the elections due in spring of 1958: giving up his former position, he also began to voice the demand for independence, and urged the French government to implement the UN resolution, pressing for extension of the powers of the Togolese government. Upon his insistence the Togoland Statute was again revised in February 1958, and the French government accorded the territory a larger measure of self-government, retaining *only* the handling of foreign affairs, finance and defence.

On April 4, 1958, new elections were held under United Nations supervision. Sixty-four per cent of the electorate took part in the voting, and OLYMPIO's C.U.T. received 190,220 votes, thus gaining three-quarters of all seats (33 out of 46). The U.C.P.N. obtained 10, the P.T.P. 3 seats. Accordingly, the French government had to appoint OLYMPIO Prime Minister in place of GRUNITZKY and charged him to form the new government.

Having come to power, OLYMPIO at once changed policies. While up to that time he had most insistently demanded independence and criticized the French government for its reluctance to grant independence, he now took a course towards co-operation with France and did not consider it urgent to proclaim independence any more. In November 1958 OLYMPIO again went to the United Nations, this time not as a petitioner but in his capacity of official representative of Togoland—as a member of the French delegation. The UN General Assembly in its meeting of November 14, 1958, on a motion from France, gave its consent to Togo's becoming an independent state two years after the C.U.T.'s coming to power, on April 27, 1960.

The consequences of OLYMPIO's turn to the right made themselves felt in the party. In addition to GRUNITZKY's P.T.P. and the chiefs' U.C.P.N., OLYMPIO came up against a third opposition—this within his own party. Young leaders of the C.U.T.'s youth organization, the Juvento, began to rise against OLYMPIO's opportunist policy. They took him to task for concentrating all his attention on petty practical, economic matters instead of giving his party and the country a political programme of action, and for not seeking contact with the national movements of other African countries, notably with the unfolding movement of African unity. "What happened after the victory?", one of the leaders of the organization put the question in his report to the Juvento Congress in March 1959, and gave the answer right there: "The most conspicuous thing is the lack of a programme of action . . . This is all the more deplorable since such a programme would have prevented distrust, incomprehension, rivalry and even hostility from gaining ground in our relations with the C.U.T." In the resolution passed by the Congress the organization assured the government of its support, but at the same time called upon it to make every effort to create the militant unity of action of the entire Togolese people.

As OLYMPIO did not respond to the call, soon it came to an open split. One of the Juvento leaders, ANANI IGNACIO SANTOS, who held a key post in the government as Minister of Justice, Public Works, Mining, Transport and Communications in one person, on May 9, 1959, resigned from the government, but soon afterwards (on June 21) it was OLYMPIO who announced that his party was breaking with the Juvento, which in his opinion was "striving for disruption and instigating against the government", and that members of the Juvento could no longer have a place in the C.U.T.

At the same time a gradual split began in the Juvento itself: the moderate right wing with SANTOS in the lead separated from the radical left wing headed by AIDHSON. (The radical group did not endure long, because in April 1960 AIDHSON, upon returning from Ghana, was arrested at the frontier and interned at Lomé.)

The opposition parties having boycotted the district elections held in August 1959, the candidates of the C.U.T. were everywhere elected to the district councils. Independent opposition candidates ran for election in only one district (Lama-Kara), but also there the C.U.T. list received the majority of the votes (15,791 as against the 5,642 cast for the opposition). The influence of the opposition, however, was shown by the fact that barely more than half the electorate went to the polls (272,264 out of 470,493).

In October 1959 the P.T.P. and U.C.P.N. amalgamated in one party under the name of *Union Démocratique des Populations Togolaises* (U.D.P.T.). The new party, however, did not pursue the former policy of the two parties, but, learning from the defeat by the C.U.T. and following OLYMPIO's example, shifted in the opposite direction. Having until then followed a pro-French policy while demanding only autonomy instead of independence, now it stood up against the moderate policies of the OLYMPIO government and claimed independence and democratic liberties, voicing the slogan of African unity.

In November 1959 municipal elections were held in six towns of the country. Although the U.D.P.T. put up no official party candidates, the "Independents" standing for election in three of the six towns included a number of U.D.P.T. members and others closely related with the party. Where only the government party set up candidates, very few people went to the poll (in Lomé, for example, 67 per cent of the qualified voters). In the other three towns the independent candidates received a relatively large percentage of the votes (40 in Atakpamé, 48 in Sokodé, 39 in Anécho). Eventually the C.U.T. gained 136 out of the 160 seats on the municipal executive committees, while the "Independents" received only 24. OLYMPIO was elected Mayor of Lomé.

In December 1959 the relations between Togo and neighbouring Ghana became strained; OLYMPIO accused NKRUMAH of plotting against the independence of the territory and wanting to annex it just like British Togoland. NKRUMAH, on the other hand, thought that Ghana was threatened by the policy of OLYMPIO who, when acceding to power in summer of 1958, that is more than a year after the union of British Togoland with Ghana, openly voiced his intention to separate British Togoland from Ghana.[1]

On the last day of December 1959 HAMMARSKJÖLD, Secretary-General of the United Nations, went to visit Togoland and conduct talks with OLYMPIO. At the special meeting of the National Assembly held in honour of the prominent guest, OLYMPIO took the floor and emphasized that the government and people of the Republic of Togo would never agree to their country's union with Ghana. Further he expressed the hope that, with the aid of France and the United Nations, the country would be able to achieve independence in a peaceful and orderly manner, and that the attainment of independence would result in rising standards of living for the population.

In March 1960 OLYMPIO went to Paris to discuss the details of accession to independence with the French government. During his stay there he held a press conference, of which he made use to attack NKRUMAH and to denigrate him in the eye of world public opinion.

Shortly before the proclamation of independence, on April 8, 1960, OLYMPIO in an interview given to the press[2] emphasized that after independence his government would concentrate mainly on the economic advancement of the country, on the raising of the living standards of the population, and that he intended to attain this goal with the material help of the Federal Republic of Germany which had expressed readiness to render assistance to Togo in her economic development.

---

[1] He said in a statement to the press: "I have to say that my country opposes any integration, thus also former British Togoland's integration." (See *Le Monde*, Aug. 2, 1958.)

[2] See *Neue Zürcher Zeitung*, Apr. 9, 1960.

In the same interview he declared that Togo intended to set up an army for the defence of her frontiers with the aid of France, and that he had discussed the matter in detail with the French government during his visit to Paris in March.

The proclamation of the independence of Togo took place amidst great celebrations in Lomé, on April 28, 1960, in the presence of representatives from over eighty countries. In his speech at the special meeting on the National Assembly OLYMPIO expressed his thanks "to the states which have handled our affairs", first to the former German colonialists "who first introduced our country to modern life" (?), then to France "which for forty years of domination over Togoland has remained loyal to her traditional liberalism and generosity" (?), and specially to General DE GAULLE who "is one of the first to have understood that Africa cannot remain in immobility". Further he explained that his government wished to follow a neutral foreign policy, joining none of the great power blocs. Characteristically, in his statements made during the weeks immediately preceding the declaration of independence, so among others in his aforesaid interview of April 8, he had said several times just the opposite. He had asserted that he was unwilling to pursue "a shuttlecock policy between East and West", he rejected "every socialist experiment", and stated his determination to shape a West-oriented foreign policy, that his country after independence would remain in the Western camp.

BIBLIOGRAPHY

J. C. FRÖHLICH, Cameroun-Togo, territoire sous tutelle, Paris, 1956.
A. TEVOEDJRE, L'Afrique révoltée, Paris, 1958.
S. C. EASTON, The Twilight of European Colonialism, New York, 1960, pp. 406–423.
MARCEL NGUINI, La valeur politique et sociale de la tutelle française au Cameroun, Aix-en-Provence, 1956.

TOGOLAND

F. ANSPRENGER, Politik im Schwarzen Afrika, Bonn, 1961, pp. 209–216, 406–409.
ROBERT CORNEVIN, Histoire du Togo, Paris, 1959.

CAMEROONS

The Kamerun at Accra, Cairo, 1958.
Rape of Cameroons, London, 1959.
"Le Cameroun devant l'indépendance", France-Observateur, Dec. 30, 1959.
ANSPRENGER, op. cit., pp. 192–208, 392–404.
R. SEGAL, "The Test of Cameroun", in African Profiles, London, 1962, ch. 12, pp. 187–195.
La révolution kamerounaise: Ses objectifs, sa signification et ses répercussions dans le continent africain. Bureau du Comité Directeur de l'U.P.C. Cairo, 1960.
DAVID E. GARDINIER, United Nations Challenge to French Policy, London–New York–Nairobi–Oxford, 1963.
VICTOR T. LE VINE, The Cameroons from Mandate to Independence, Cambridge, 1965.
WILLARD R. JOHNSON, The Cameroon Federation: Political Integration in a Fragmentary Society, Oxford, 1970.

CHAPTER XXVII

THE BELGIAN CONGO

In the 20th century up till World War II, just as before, the fate of the Congo was largely determined by its geographical isolation.

This made it possible, ever since King LEOPOLD's private property had been renamed what it really was, a colony of Belgium, for the Belgian colonialists to go on — without interference from liberal public opinion at home or in other civilized countries of the world — keeping the African population in political subjection and extracting enormous profits from the rich natural resources of the territory.

It was also due to this circumstance that the African population isolated from the outside world, and even from the kindred peoples of neighbouring territories, put up no noteworthy, organized resistance, and that in the Belgian Congo there were no conscious, political independence movements, but only primitive sectarian actions and spontaneous peasant risings.

The oppression and exploitation of the African masses was carried out hand in hand, in close co-operation and peaceful coexistence, by three arms of the colonialists: the colonial regime upheld by the Belgian government, the Belgian monopoly interests, and the missionaries of various Christian churches.

In their pursuit of exploiting the rich natural resources of the territory with the help of millions of toiling Africans the colonialists were hiding behind two high-flown hypocritical slogans: "civilization" and "paternalism".

Belgian Governor-General PIERRE RYCKMANS formulated the civilizing mission of the colonialists in these terms: "To dominate in order to do service .... This alone can be an excuse and complete justification for the occupation of colonies. We do service to Africa by civilizing it."

What the Belgian colonialists meant by civilizing was, while letting an insignificant section of the African population live a life of relative ease, to provide cheap labour to European capitalists and monopoly companies and, by building a broad network of mission schools, to teach the African masses, deprived of the possibility of acquiring real knowledge and culture, to serve meekly the colonial system of oppressors and exploiters. They made all this appear to the Africans as the rich and cultured European colonialists' paternal care of the poor backward Africans. By ensuring a relative well-being to the few and promoting the spread of a pseudo-culture through the missionaries they could split the African population (workers' settlements, the training of an "African élite") and prevented the African masses for a long time from seeing the real face of the colonial system, awaking to political consciousness and starting to fight for democracy and independence.

The Belgian imperialists boastfully proclaimed that, in contrast with the other colonial powers, they succeeded in creating welfare for the Africans and securing the "peaceful development" of the colony. The truth is, however, that they did nothing of the sort for the Africans, but they made it possible for the European monopoly capitalists to proceed with the unhindered exploitation of the wealth of the country and to pocket immense profits. At the end of World War II the vast majority of the Africans lived in poverty and backwardness just as in the early decades of the century.

But a new situation arose after the war. The war-time experiences, the events that had occurred in the colonial countries during and immediately after the war led to substantial changes in the thinking of the Congolese people.

The war-time economic difficulties hit the African population in the first place. The colonial administration made the Africans work hard to supply the raw materials required for the war efforts. Forced labour, which in the pre-war decades the Belgian colonialists had tried to replace with more modern forms of exploitation, was reintroduced and grew to great proportions. The destitute African peasants flocked in large numbers to the cities and industrial centres where paid jobs were available. Thousands of African peasants, who had so far secluded themselves from the Europeans, now came to see the great difference in the living conditions, e conomic and political opportunities and treatment of European and African la bourers.

Further thousands of Africans did military service in the war, many having participated in the Allied campaigns abroad (Egypt, Middle East, Burma, etc.). In the army they saw many things which did much to change their views of the "white people" and to discredit these in their eyes (they saw "whites" killing one another, they were themselves ordered to kill white people, to guard white prisoners, whom they had to shoot in case of an escape attempt, they met American Negroes who, unlike the Africans, were treated in the army on an equal footing with whites, consorted with white prostitutes, etc.).

To force the Africans to increase the extraction of minerals needed for war purposes and to step up the production of rubber, the Belgian colonialists conducted propaganda against the racist ideas of Nazism and operated with democratic slogans and promises of reform.

African awakening to political consciousness was hastened by the war-time events in the neighbouring French colonies (Brazzaville !) and by the establishment, in the last stage of the war, of the United Nations Organization whose Charter envisaged the liquidation of the colonial system.

All this was instrumental in the fact that towards the end of the war thousands of Africans in the Congo were already dreaming of political rights, an end to racial discrimination, participation in the government of the country, and improvement in their material conditions.

Not only the thinking of Africans but also the political attitude of the European colonists changed. In the Congo prior to the war the European settlers had only material and social advantages over the Africans, they also had no political rights and were entirely dependent upon the Brussels government. The war loosened this dependence considerably. Their isolation from the mother country owing to the war roused them to action, urging them to do away with their dependent status. The settlers longed for political rights and self-government. They did not want to enjoy political rights in the mother country (as did settlers of other colonial powers in Africa), but they wished to introduce settler autonomy in the administration, and,

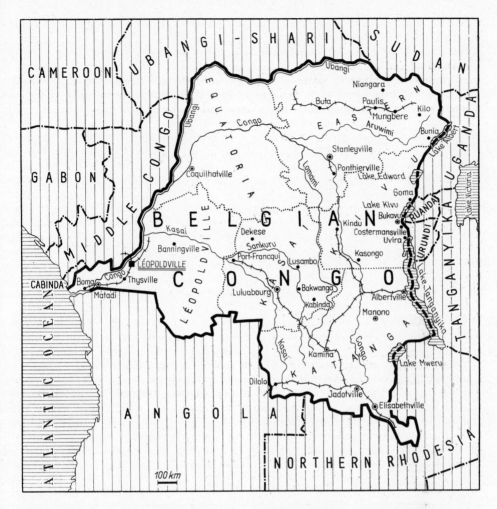

since it was evident that the Belgian government, under pressure from the change of wind of the times, was prepared to make some concessions to the Africans, the colonists were inclined even to go into opposition, to take an anti-African stand.

True, the colonial policies of Belgium did not essentially change, but the changes taking place in the international relations and in the life of the Congo itself compelled the colonial masters to resort to falsehoods and deceiving promises with a view to checking the rising African aspirations for democratic rights, and to revising to a small extent the oppressive colonial regime.

The post-war history of the Belgian Congo can be divided into three stages: 1945 to 1954; 1954 to 1958: 1958 to 1960.

In his inaugural address to the Government Council in 1949 Governor-General Eugène Jungers said that to expunge racial discrimination from the laws is not enough, the people's minds must be purified, and he added: "It is not possible to conceive of a country in which there is no social hierarchy. But when the present evolution reaches its full development, this hierarchy must be based solely on differences of competence, of efficiency and of education."[1]

Another advocate of Belgian colonialism said this at about the same time: "Never up till now has the word 'colony' taken on a pejorative sense in Belgium, and we shall probably be the last to replace it in our own terminology."

As early as 1892 in the Congo Independent State of King LEOPOLD a system of *immatriculation* had been introduced. This measure created a special African class of *immatriculés* (or *évolués*); persons who had reached a certain standard of education and moral development could apply to enter this class. Members of this "civilized" class enjoyed the same civil status as any European. This was of no practical consequence, however, because the law made no distinction between *immatriculés* and *non-immatriculés*, the only distinction was between Europeans and "natives". In 1948 another step was feigned towards the elimination of racial discrimination: some Africans received a good-conduct certificate *(carte de mérite civique)*, but this provided no advantage in practice. Finally in 1949 a commission was appointed to study the question of the "civilized status" that might be accorded to Africans. The commission submitted its recommendations. In 1951 Governor-General JUNGERS accepted some of them and in 1952 issued a new decree on *immatriculation*, establishing "juridical assimilation" for Africans who had adopted the "Western civilization". It was recommended by the commission that Africans ought to be assimilated not only juridically but also socially and economically, but JUNGERS rejected the suggestion as too far-flung. Equality before the law was of little interest to the Africans, who were just dreaming about the suppression of economic and social disparities, about possibilities for their living standards to come nearer to those of Europeans, and for themselves to enjoy the same treatment and respect in society as did the Europeans. The "reform" failed to redress the most serious grievances of the Africans, nor did it create equality of rights, and so it was no wonder that the *immatriculés* viewed the reform with resentment, because they found it utterly unsatisfactory, and so did all those who saw in *immatriculation* a forcible measure to divide the African community and threaten the solidarity they needed to bring the struggle for their rights to success. This explains why many of those who would have qualified, among them most of the African clergymen, never applied for *immatriculation*.

In 1953 the colonial administration took another step. It allowed Africans in general (regardless of their status) to acquire landed property, either in the tribal areas or even in urban communities, called *centres extra-coutumiers* (extra-tribal centres), and to live there like the settlers, undisturbed by the fear of eviction.

Until 1947 Europeans had represented the interests of Africans in the Government Council functioning under the colonial administration as well as in the Provincial Councils attached to the provincial governments. In 1947 two of those European members were replaced by Africans, and from 1951 onwards African interests were represented in the Government Council by eight Africans nominated by the administration.

Before 1947 African children could go only to government-subsidized Catholic schools or to Protestant mission schools, which received no government aid. (They were barred from higher qualifications, except in theological colleges.) The children

[1] Cf. G. MALENGREAU, *Principles and Methods of Colonial Administration*, London, 1950, p. 41.

of European settlers had separate schools. In 1946 the administration granted financial aid also to Protestant mission schools and established an undenominational public school for European children. From 1948 onwards, schools which had thus far admitted only European children were allowed to accept Asian children as well as any mulatto child whose paternity had been acknowledged by the white father. In 1950 the reform went further: admission was granted to Africans and to any mulatto child even if not owned by the European father. After 1950 racial discrimination in principle was thus stopped in elementary schools in the Congo, but in practice there was still a point of discrimination in admission: African children had to pass a severe entrance examination covering not only their intelligence levels but also their family background and health conditions, while European children were not required to go in for such examinations.

The majority of the European colonists were averse to the idea of the assimilation of Africans, but there were also several who made attempts to form some connection with Africans. For instance, a social organization of Europeans, the *Fédération des Colons*, in 1953 changed its name to *Fédération des Colons et des Classes Moyennes du Congo*, and invited middle-class Africans (shopkeepers, small contractors, clerks) to join the various settler organizations. But these attempts failed, because the ordinary African could not be convinced that their interests were identical with those of Europeans.

Similar attempts by certain Catholic and other friendship societies also failed. Although their members tried to draw Africans into their circles, they still kept aloof from "natives" when outside of those premises. The Africans resented that the Europeans, after amiably shaking hands with them in their gatherings, pretended not to know them when they met in the street and other public places.

In the first ten years following the war the situation of the Africans underwent hardly any change, yet a considerable shift occurred in their mentality. Accelerating urbanization brought with it the growing discontent of the masses. Their own experiences made during the war (the Elizabethville strike of Union Minière workers in 1941, the soldiers' mutiny at Luluabourg in 1944, the Matadi strike in 1945, etc.), on the one hand, and the events taking place in the neighbouring French colonies in the war years as well as the post-war development of the independence struggle in a number of colonies (Gold Coast, Kenya, etc.), on the other, prompted also the peoples of the Congo to launch a struggle for rights and economic betterment. Indicative of the backwardness of their thinking was that they could not even come upon the idea of independence in those years. They only made efforts to improve their lot under the existing colonial system. They demanded an end to racial discrimination, claimed equal pay for equal work, regardless of the colour of skin, and facilities of higher education and qualifications.

At the time the Africans still had neither trade unions nor political parties. Before the war not even European workers were allowed to form trade unions (European workers and employees who showed dissatisfaction were sent home forthwith to Belgium by the monopoly companies), only during the war (1942) did they obtain the right to form unions and two years later (1944) the right to strike. From that time on the Africans also demanded the same rights, but the Belgian authorities permitted them (in 1946) only to set up "consultative councils" to negotiate on the workers' behalf with the employers or the colonial authorities, but Africans were not allowed to strike.

The first mass organization of Africans in the Congo was the Abako cultural society *(Alliance des Bakongos pour l'Unification, Conservation et Expansion de la Langue Kikongo)* formed in 1950 by the Bakongo tribe with the permission of the colonial administration. In its first years the organization did not deal with politics, it served only to promote cultural aims.

Change of Wind in 1954

The year 1954 brought a turn in the life of the Congo. The change of government in Belgium in the wake of the 1954 parliamentary elections was a promise of considerable changes in the Congo as well. The reactionary Social Christian (Catholic) government was superseded by a coalition of Socialists and Liberals, and the clericalist SCHEYVEN was succeeded in the Colonial Ministry by AUGUSTE BUISSERET, an anticlericalist. The fact of the change of government itself impressed the Africans, since it made it obvious to them that the apparent concert of the three groups of colonialists — administration, monopoly companies, missionaries — had been but a pooling of interests which now collapsed. Colonial Minister BUISSERET pursued a strongly liberal, anticlerical policy: he established a network of undenominational schools for Africans (who had until then been permitted to go to mission schools only) and considerably reduced the financial aid provided to missions. This made him very popular among the Africans but antagonized the missionaries and the churches. The government's policy and the spread in the colony of liberal (and socialist) propaganda in the wake of the change of government incited to opposition the monopoly companies and the settlers, who feared that the cultural and political advancement of the Africans imperilled their capitalist interests.

A certain relaxation of the severity of the colonial regime was brought about by the visit in 1955 of King BAUDOUIN, whose affability towards the Congolese came as a surprise not only to the African people but to the King's own men, too. He jovially talked with people, shook hands with many, inquired about their worries and complaints, and in general made the impression that, in contrast with the colonial officials, he had the welfare of Africans at heart. (For example, he made a special fund set up for the improvement of African housing from which to grant loans to Africans who wanted to build their homes outside the extra-tribal centres.) This appearance was kept up by the King's speech, upon his return to Brussels, before the Royal African Circle where he said among other things:

"I want to insist on the fact that the basic problem which now confronts the Congo is that of human relationships between black and white. It is not enough to equip the country materially, to endow it with wise social legislation, and to improve the standard of living of its inhabitants; it is imperative that the whites and the natives should show the widest mutual understanding in their daily contacts. The time will then come — the date cannot yet be determined — to give our African territories a status which will guarantee, for the happiness of all, the continuing existence of a true Belgo-Congolese community, and which will assure to each, white or black, his proper share in the country's government, according to his own qualities and capacity. Before we realize this high ideal, Gentlemen, much remains to be done."

The King's attitude and words brought even Governor-General LÉO PÉTILLON, who really did not share the government's liberal policy, to make similar statements in the weeks following the royal visit. In his inaugural address in the Government Council, for example, he asserted that henceforth Belgium's policy in the Congo would be a policy, not of segregation, nor of assimilation, but one of association.

On another occasion he declared that the time was approaching when Africans and Europeans in the Congo would look upon each other as brothers. In official texts from 1957 onwards the term "emancipation" occurred more and more often. On October 23, 1957, for example, Colonial Minister BUISSERET told the *Académie Royale des Sciences Coloniales* that the aim of Belgium's colonial policy was "to humanize, to develop, to associate and finally to emancipate in the framework of that association."

Those well-sounding statements let the Africans hope that the privileges of the European settlers and the anti-African discriminations would soon be ended, and thus their situation would improve considerably. But the statements remained what they were, and the "reforms" of the four years of liberalization did nothing to change the abject situation of the Africans.

In 1955 Africans got permission to buy and drink liquors (up to that time they could drink only beer) and to frequent European-owned cafés, which they had also been forbidden to enter before.

In 1957 Africans (to the exclusion of workers and employees of the administration) were allowed to form unions for the defence of their interests together with the right to strike, but every new organization had to obtain a permit from the administration.

In December 1957 a law was enacted making it a crime to incite to racial hatred, and providing that those who "showed racial or ethnic aversion or hatred" should be fined or imprisoned. This law was made to appear as a progressive measure to curb the white racists, but in practice it was a means of intimidating the Africans. (After the riots of January 1959, for example, many Africans were thrown in prison under that law.)

The year 1957 witnessed a reform of the Government Council. Formerly this was an advisory body composed of Europeans and a few African members specially appointed by the Governor-General to represent African interests. From 1957 on the members of the Government Council represented different segments of the population (the independent middle classes, rural interests, employers, employees, etc.) regardless of race. This reform increased the number of African members, but the Council preserved its essentially advisory character. The powers of the Government Council were broadened to an insignificant extent: until then its activities had been confined to considering the proposals formulated by the Brussels government, and now the reform empowered the Council to formulate proposals of the colonial budget. However, this was of no practical significance, on the one hand, because the administration accepted only trusted persons as advisory members, and, on the other, because the Government Council still had no right to make decisions.

The true nature of the colonial policy of the Belgian coalition of Liberals and Socialists was clearly shown by the fact that the coalition government also failed to redress one of the main African grievances (the shocking difference between European and African workers in respect to their working conditions and wages), it only continued the former practice of trying to pacify the discontented Africans with partial reforms. In 1956, for example, pensionability and sickness insurance were made available for certain categories of African labourers. The main issue (the inequality of wages) remained unsolved throughout the four years of the new regime, and the working conditions of Africans were in many respects comparably disadvantageous even as late as 1958 (Africans were not legally entitled to holidays, they could be dismissed at any time, etc.). In February 1958 graduates from the Congo University of Lovanium (established near Léopoldville in 1956) sent the Belgian government a memorandum requesting the enforcement of "equal pay for equal work". Since they received no reply, in April they addressed a letter to the Colonial Minister. They referred to the minister's recent visit to the Congo and the talks they had had with him, during which he had promised that the measures of discrimination between Europeans and Africans would be abolished. And they put the question: On what grounds does a Belgian worker receive higher wages for the same job than an African having the same qualification?[1]

But the "liberal and socialist" government of Belgium did not deign to reply.

In 1958 two substantive reforms were introduced on paper: restrictions on the movement of Africans were removed by law, and legislation was made on the unification of criminal procedure, extending the jurisdiction of all courts to Africans and Europeans alike. (Until then minor offences of Africans were handled by police courts, which could not judge the cases of Europeans.)

The practical value of these reforms, however, was almost nil, since the authorities, whenever they saw fit, could restrict the movement of Africans without any legal provision, and the enunciation of equality before the law was no guarantee that European magistrates would use the same standard in administering justice to defendants and litigants of both races.

The only field in which the liberal regime made considerable progress in foutr years was the schooling of Africans. In addition to creating a network of undenominational primary and secondary schools, the government made it possible, even though in a modest measure, for Africans to receive higher education in Belgium. The first Congolese student graduated from the Belgian University of Louvain in 1956, and the same year saw the opening of the first university of the Congo, the Catholic University of Lovanium, a branch of the Belgian Catholic University of Louvain.

In all other fields the "reforms" and "progressive measures" of the liberal regime were either only sham reforms, intended to check the discontent of Africans, or at most only minor revisions of the repressive laws and institutions of the existing colonial system.

The Belgian government's flirtation with liberalism, however, produced no change in the colonial policies of the Belgian imperialists. The profits squeezed out of the colony by the Belgian and British monopoly interests in the Congo continued to grow as before,[2] and at the same time the "liberal" Belgian government, unlike its predecessors, opened the door wide to penetration by U.S. monopoly capital.[3]

The change of government brought no turn for the better in the conditions of the Africans. But the process which had started in the thinking of Africans during the war years considerably accelerated from the mid-50's under the impact of various

---

[1] They concluded the letter by declaring that, unless the differentiation between Europeans and Africans was ended, they were ready to turn the Congo into "a second Algeria". A week later, however, under pressure from above they withdrew this threat.

[2] In six years (1947–1952) the net profits of the joint-stock companies having interests in the Congo amounted to $430 million, of which $250 million went to dividends. (Cf. *West Africa*, May 5, 1956.) Union Minière stockholders pocketed more and more money every year. The company's net profit was $19 million in 1948 and $84 million in 1955, while the dividend per share was $9.60 in 1948 and $44 in 1955.

[3] As we have seen (vol. III, p. 109), already during the war the United States procured its uranium supply from the Congo. In the post-war years the exports of the Congo's most essential minerals (uranium, thorium, cobalt) to the United States increased steadily. A big stride ahead was made, thanks to the "liberal" Belgian government, in the year 1955. The value of cobalt exports in 1955 was around $30 million. In the same year an agreement between Belgium and the U.S.-controlled Combined Development Agency secured to the latter 90 per cent of the uranium and thorium production of the Congo for 1956 and 1957, and 75 per cent for 1958 and 1959.

factors — the appearance in the United Nations of newly independent countries of Asia and North Africa, the advance of independence movements in the British and French colonies in Black Africa, the change of government in Belgium and the ensuing liberal policies.

In the growth of the political consciousness of the Africans no small part was played by the educated class *(évolués)* emerging from African society and enjoying a privileged position as compared to the popular masses. This privileged class, which the Belgian colonialists hoped would help them in the unhampered exploitation of the country, ultimately promoted even from two sides the fall of the colonial regime. The new Belgian government's liberal policies helped this class to grow in numbers and in standards (school reform, Congolese students at Belgian universities). With the widening of the horizon of the *évolués* grew their discontent. Detached from their tribal communities, they stood between Africans and Europeans. They were separated from the Africans by their privileged position, wider horizon and better education, but the Europeans did not receive them into their midst. This awkward situation made them responsive to liberal propaganda, but they interpreted liberalism to their own liking: they were dreaming of the equality of Africans and the future independence of the Congo.

At the same time the existence of this privileged group of Africans aroused in broad masses a desire to improve their lot, and prepared the ground for them to launch a political struggle for their rights and for independence.

The Bakongo organization, the Abako, which had so far been operating as a cultural society with the approbation of the government, in 1955 elected a new president, JOSEPH KASAVUBU,[5] who, by setting the society political tasks (unification of the

<hr>

Capital investments in the Congo by U.S. monopoly interests also went up in the post-war years. The Pacific Iron and Steel Company had a steel works in Léopoldville, ROCKEFELLER's International Basic Commodity Corporation acquired interests in a textile factory of Albertville, the United States Plywood Corporation controlled timber production in the southern Congo, etc., etc. As the result of negotiations in 1950 between Brussels and a financial group controlled by Chase Manhattan Bank of New York, the Congo mining industry in 1951 was granted a loan of $70 million by the World Bank and $15.5 million by the Eximbank. In the first ten years following the war, owing to the obstinate opposition of Belgian monopoly interests, American capital had been unable to penetrate into the mining industry itself. But the "liberal" government started to break the ice also in this field for U.S. interests: a group of American capitalists, supported by BUISSERET despite objection from Belgian companies, among them Société Générale and Union Minière, worked out a large-scale plan to build, with a fund of $1,500 million provided by U.S. capitalists, a huge hydroelectric plant utilizing the Inga Falls (on the Congo river between Léopoldville and Matadi), whose abundance of water is four times that of Niagara Falls. This would have been the largest power plant in the world, which could have supplied power for the purpose of operating different processing industries and making navigable the Congo from Léopoldville to Matadi. The plan was frustrated by the political events of the years that followed.

[5] JOSEPH KASAVUBU, a member of the Bakongo tribe, was born in 1910 at the township of Tshela in the Province of Léopoldoille. (One of his grandfathers was an immigrant Chinese railway worker.) He was educated in mission schools and then studied for priesthood a couple of years. Finally he abandoned his studies and acquired a teacher's diploma in 1940. Having taught in school for two years, he became a civil servant in the financial administration of the colony. During the war and in the first few post-war years he played an active part in the missionary-influenced organizations of the *évolués*. Already at that time he was longing for a political career and making plans for the unification of the Bakongo tribes scattered in three colonial countries (Belgian Congo, Middle Congo, Angola). In 1946 he presented to the society called *Union des Intérêts Sociaux Congolais* a memorandum entitled "The Right of the First Inhabitants", explaining that the Congolese, notably the Bakongo, were entitled by ancient right to possess and govern the Congo. He was one of the most active members of the Abako founded in 1950.

Bakongo living in different colonial countries), practically changed it to a political association.

. The "liberal" Belgian colonialists, to restrain the aspiration of the privileged minority of Africans and also to prevent the eruption of a mass struggle for independence, avoided resorting to force and tried a roundabout way. Prof. A. J. VAN BILSEN drafted and published a scheme holding out the prospect of a united Congolese nation of Africans and Belgians and of an independent state of the Congo thereafter (in thirty years !). The good professor set up a mixed team of Belgians and Africans to study the problems of the future of the Congo and Ruanda-Urundi. The magazine *Conscience Africaine*, which had been launched in Léopoldville in 1953 by *évolués* influenced by missionaries, fully endorsed BILSEN's conceptions and propagated them. In 1956 it published a manifesto proposing the formation of a unitary political party of Africans and Europeans as a means leading to the final aim of creating a united Congolese nation. It gave also a detailed sketch of a thirty-year plan for the political, economic and social development of the Congo.

To the manifesto of the *Conscience Africaine* the Abako replied with a memorandum outlining its political programme. It described the idea of a Congolese nation comprising Europeans as a utopia and ridiculed the thirty-year plan of preparation for independence. It demanded political rights — complete freedom of opinion and the press, freedom of organization, conscience and religion — at once, not thirty years after. And for this end it proposed, not a political party in common with Europeans, but a variety of parties to be formed by tribes, it demanded the right for every tribe to form its own party.

In 1957 the political activity of Africans followed the policy defined in those two documents. But the two documents widely differed in their effect. The Abako programme formulated expressly the demands and goals of the Bakongo tribe, but the aims it set expressed the interests and aspirations of other African tribes, too, so that the programme ensured the Abako the support of many other tribes. On the other hand, the *Conscience Africaine* manifesto, although its authors also belonged to a single tribe (the Bangala), did not express the wishes and demands of that tribe, it was only a programme which was formulated by Bangala *évolués* and which was not attractive, if it was known at all, to the masses of their own tribe either. Thus it happened that this manifesto did not at all influence the masses, though having a certain impact upon *évolués*, while the Abako programme found supporters not only in the Bakongo masses but also among other tribes, the Bangala included.

Municipal Elections in 1957—58

Under a decree issued by the colonial government in 1957 the adult male inhabitants (over 25 yeart) of each city in the Congo had to elect a municipal council, which should be headed by a mayor chosen by the council and confirmed by the respective Belgian provincial governor.

The first municipal elections were held in Léopoldville, Elisabethville and Jadotville at the end of 1957, and in Stanleyville, Luluabourg, Bukavu and other places in 1958. In Elisabethville a group of *évolués*, joining forces with broad-minded settlers, formed a political party, the *Union Congolaise*, which set itself the aim of uniting in a single party Africans and those Europeans who intended to remain in the country after independence. But the candidates ran for election not on behalf of the party, but as representatives of some tribe or another, and not even with a specific political programme (except the Union Congolaise), but with practical demands of local concern at most, for promoting the interests of their own respective tribes. The elections took place so much on a tribal basis that many Africans, primarily the older generations, did not even go to the poll if they found none of their tribesmen listed among the candidates.

Another Change in 1958

The year 1958 brought about a new, decisive turn in the Congo. The deep-going transformation which had gradually affected the thinking of the African peoples and their political life during the fifties, and which had reached a crucial stage by that time, did not fail to make itself felt in the Congo either. The appearance and public activity of the first three young African states recently liberated from colonial status (Sudan, Ghana, Guinea), joining forces with other newly independent Asian and African countries in the United Nations Organization, brought into the focus of attention of world public opinion the problems and independence movements of the countries still living in colonial subjection, including the countries of Black Africa. The peoples of the Congo followed with particular attention the events in the neighbouring French colonies. The circumstance that President DE GAULLE of France let the French colonies have the choice between autonomous status within the French Community and independence, and that this offer was made in the immediate vicinity of Léopoldville, in Brazzaville inhabited by kindred Bakongo people, inflamed the desire of freedom that was alive but dormant in the minds of the Congolese peoples.

At the same time another circumstance helped considerably to widen the horizon of the Congolese. Students from the Congo had already been studying in Belgium; it happened also that smaller groups made a brief visit to Brussels. But it was in 1958, during the World's Exhibition of Brussels, for the first time that hundreds coming from different parts of the Congo stayed in Belgium together for a longer time. Being accommodated in quarters reserved for Africans, members of different tribes from different regions of the Congo came closer together, got acquainted with one another's problems, and suddenly realized that Africans, regardless of tribal differences, all had the same problems everywhere in the Congo, that they all wished to improve their situation, to shake off the yoke of colonialism, to achieve freedom and independence. Together they familiarized themselves with European living conditions, and comparison with their own circumstances of life at home revolted even those who had so far been loyal servants of the Belgian administration.

At this critical moment, in the summer of 1958, the liberal Belgian government was overthrown and the coalition of Liberals and Socialists was replaced by the Social Christian Party. In the Colonial Ministry the Liberal BUISSERET was succedeed by a member of the Social Christian Party, L. PÉTILLON, who, when holding the office of Vice-Governor-General of the Congo, had only half-heartedly backed the policy of the liberal government and therefore was not popular with the Africans. But now, as head of the new Colonial Ministry, he had to face the changes in the international arena as well as in the Congo, and was compelled to make certain concessions to the Africans.

Upon taking office, he proclaimed the policy of "decolonization" and renamed his office the "Ministry for the Belgian Congo and Ruanda-Urundi". He appointed a study group of Belgian government officials to examine the situation in the Congo and formulate recommendations for future governmental policies.

Also in 1958, two years after the foundation of the Catholic University of Lovanium near Léopoldville, PÉTILLON established an undenominational University at Elisabethville. Both universities were equally open to Europeans and Africans, but during the academic year 1958–59 Africans constituted two-thirds of the student body at Lovanium and only a quarter at Elisabethville University.

As has already been mentioned, lower-grade schools after 1950 admitted African and European children alike, but still in 1958 the Africans had to pass a severe entrance examination and were tested also regarding family background and physical condition, while such examinations were not obligatory for European children. (In Elisabethville many African parents complained because their children had been rejected for "unsatisfactory physical condition" while they were told at the same time that the children needed no medical care.)

In part at the initiative of the Lovanium graduates (see p. 1884), in part under pressure from the trade unions, the government in 1958 decided that, as of January 1, 1959, Africans in the civil service should receive equal pay with Europeans having the same qualifications and should get equal opportunities for promotion. (Settlers and mining companies also took some steps to remove the discriminatory restrictions. In happened in the summer of 1958 for the first time that an African family could move into the European quarter of the city, and in 1959 Africans in the Katanga mining area were allowed to leave the workers' settlement and buy homes elsewhere.)

These measures which were intended to pacify the Africans, however, produced the opposite result: the African leaders awakening to political consciousness felt prompted to start an organized political struggle for their rights.

In August 1958, under the influence of DE GAULLE's tour of French Africa, a group of Congolese intellectuals, with PATRICE LUMUMBA[1] at their head, sent the Belgian Governor-General a memorandum defining their final goal as complete independence for the Congo, and demanded for the time being that political leaders of the Congolese people be invited to join the working group appointed by the Belgian government to work out a new Congo policy.

In the second half of 1958 two new parties emerged in the Congo: Cerea *(Centre du Regroupement Africain)* was founded by ANICET KASHAMURA[2] in August, and the other, called the *Mouvement National Congolais* (M.N.C.), was formed by PATRICE LUMUMBA in October.

The activities of Cerea were limited to Kivu Province, where the party was born. It stood against the domineering Belgian colonists, for stricter control over the central government, and demanded a radical land reform. KASHAMURA declared himself

---

[1] PATRICE LUMUMBA, a member of the Batetela tribe, was born in 1925 in the Sankuru district of Kasai Province. He went to Catholic mission schools until 14 years of age, when he converted to Protestantism, and later to free-thinking. After completing his studies he entered the service of the Belgian colonial administration, where he worked eleven years (first in the revenue office, then in the post office). At the same time he took up politics in a Stanleyville African employees' union, which elected him president. After eleven years as a civil servant he was brought to trial and sentenced to prison for malfeasances committed by his subordinates. Being set at liberty in 1957, he settled in Léopoldville, where he was sales manager of a brewery.

[2] ANICET KASHAMURA was born in 1928 in the locality of Kalehe in Kivu Province. From 1948 till 1956 he worked as accountant with different agencies of the colonial administration. After 1956 he became a journalist and engaged in politics.

socialist and regarded the progressive building of a socialist state as the final aim of his movement.

LUMUMBA set his party the task of achieving independence for the Congo, which he wished to attain by means of "peaceful negotiations" with the Belgian government, by implementing the Universal Declaration of Human Rights, by democratizing the administration and preparing broad masses of Africans for the civil service. In contrast to the other large Congo parties, which were organized on a tribal basis, LUMUMBA's party repudiated every kind of tribal or provincial separatism and advocated the unity of the country.

In October 1958 PÉTILLON was on a short visit to the Congo, where he received among others a delegation of the recently formed M.N.C., which demanded that its representatives be allowed to form part of the working group on Congolese problems. The minister rejected this demand.

PÉTILLON was in office only a few months. In November 1958 the Belgian government was succeeded by another coalition under the premiership of the Social Christian GASTON EYSKENS, and PÉTILLON's office was taken over by the liberal politician HEMELRIJCK of the Social Christian Party.

The working group submitted its report to the new government, and the Prime Minister promised in late November that the Congo policies would soon be worked out and made public.

In December 1958 LUMUMBA and two other M.N.C. leaders attended the Accra Conference of African Peoples. In his speech at the conference LUMUMBA stated among other things: "This historic conference which brings us together, politicians of all the countries of Africa, shows that in spite of frontiers and ethnic differences, we are of one mind and have the same desire to make our continent a happy one, free from anxiety, and from the fear of colonial domination. Down with colonialism and tribalism! Long live the Congolese nation! Long live an independent Africa!"

Back from the Accra conference, at a mass rally held in Léopoldville on January 3, 1959, LUMUMBA rejected the VAN BILSEN recommendations, espoused by the Belgian government and the other Congolese parties, for "gradual progress" towards independence. He categorically demanded independence at once.

Under the influence of the events in the French Congo, the Abako intensified its activity. KASAVUBU had also prepared to go to the Accra conference, but he did not obtain the necessary travel documents. After the return of the Congo delegates (LUMUMBA and his associates) the Abako called a mass meeting for January 4, but the authorities refused to give permission. A demonstrating crowd of about 30,000 people which was gathering to attend the meeting proceeded through the streets of the city, giving occasion to manhandling Europeans, damaging churches, mission schools and other buildings. The colonial authorities called out the police and soldiers, who then opened fire upon the demonstrators. (The Belgian parliamentary commission set up to investigate the "riots", in its report published in March, estimated the casualties at 49 African dead, 330 African and 49 European wounded.) The colonial administration and the Belgian press accused the Abako and the Kimbangist sect of having unleashed the "riots", although they had nothing by which to substantiate the charge, and it was even public knowledge that KASAVUBU tried to calm the demonstrators. On January 8 KASAVUBU and two of his associates were arrested, and on January 12 the Abako was proscribed. The Belgian "Minister for the Congo" used his influence to have KASAVUBU and his men released from prison and taken to Belgium.

Influenced by the deliberations of the Accra conference and the latest events in the Congo, the King of the Belgians and his government in Brussels tried to pacify the Africans with reassuring statements. In his radio message on the Congo policy the King said on January 13: "It is our firm intention, without undesirable procrastination but also without undue haste, to lead the Congolese population forward towards independence in prosperity and peace." A government statement issued also in January used a slightly different formula: "Belgium intends to organize the Congo as a democracy, capable of exercising the prerogatives of sovereignty and of deciding the question of independence for itself." What real intentions were concealed behind these fairly well sounding declarations became clear when Foreign Minister PIERRE WIGNY in April 1959 published a reform plan, pretending that the Belgian government had the serious intention of granting freedom to the Congolese in due time. To explain what he understood by freedom, he added right away: ". . . When the time comes the Belgians and Africans will be living in such a relation of mutual amity that the two countries will remain closely linked forever."

The plan envisaged a whole hierarchy of "councils" of various levels. Most of the inferior, local (borough, urban district, town, district, territorial) councils were to be directly elected, while the majority of the members of the high-level councils (the Provincial Councils, a preliminary sort of lower house called the General Council, and an upper house known as the Legislative Council) would be indirectly elected after March 1960 (by electoral colleges composed of elected territorial and municipal councillors). The powers of the inferior councils would include the right of decision in local matters, while the higher councils' right of decision would be limited to a small scope for the time being (in spite of the fact that their loyalty to the government was guaranteed also by the system of indirect election).

If we add to this that the plan left the executive power, for the moment at least, in the hands of the Belgian colonial administration, which was accountable neither to the "General Council" nor to the "Legislative Council", we can only agree with the evaluation given of this scheme by the American author STEWART C. EASTON (otherwise an ardent champion of colonialism): "The whole is an entirely different system from the British . . . The structure is the same one which the Belgians themselves had been using for fifty years in the Congo. No radical changes were contemplated save the gradual devolution of power to the Africans but within the same structure."[1]

But this policy of the Brussels government, already half a century overdue, proved to be untenable in the light of the international events and the turbulent advance of African political movements in the year 1959.

In April 1959 the Congo leaders met in a conference in Luluabourg. The conference, in which the leading part was played by LUMUMBA and his M.N.C., after heated debates adopted moderate resolutions requesting autonomy for the Congo by 1961 as well as the restoration of freedom of speech, and took a position in favour of preserving the unity of the country.

During the same month CLEOPHAS KAMITATU[2] and ANTOINE GIZENGA[3] formed

---

[1] *The Twilight of European Colonialism*, New York, 1960, p. 472.

[2] CLEOPHAS KAMITATU was born in 1931. He was educated in a Jesuit seminary and prepared for priesthood, but later changed his mind and flung himself into politics. For a time he was secretary at a local agency of the Belgian colonial administration.

[3] ANTOINE GIZENGA was born at Mushiko in 1925. He finished his studies at a Catholic mission school in Kinzambi, and later he worked in the offices of the Catholic mission in Léopoldville.

the *Parti de la Solidarité Africaine* (P.S.A.). The party recruited its members mainly from among peasants and agricultural labourers, and found considerable following in over twenty-five tribes of two districts (Kwango and Kwilu) in the Lower Congo. Like LUMUMBA's party, this new party advocated the unity of the Congo.

After his return from Belgium in May 1959, KASAVUBU reorganized the Abako into a political party. In June he submitted to the Belgian Minister for the Congo a detailed plan, demanding the establishment of a separate Bakongo state, and declared that from January 1, 1960, the Bakongo would stop to recognize the supreme authority of the colonial administration.

In July 1959 a split occurred in the M.N.C. Moderate elements of the party, who found LUMUMBA's policy too radical, joined with JOSEPH ILÉO[1] and ALBERT KALONJI[2] and left the party. They formed a new party, the *Mouvement National Congolais* (Kalonji wing) under KALONJI's chairmanship.

LUMUMBA, at the conference of his M.N.C. held late in October 1959 in Stanleyville, issued the slogan "independence at once". Although he intended to achieve independence not by force but by terminating co-operation with the Belgian colonialists, by launching a campaign of "civil disobedience", after the conference disturbances occurred in many places, resulting in the death of twenty people and the arrest of LUMUMBA.

An additional two parties made their appearance in the Congo political arena during the latter half of 1959. In Katanga Province MOISE TSHOMBÉ formed the *Confédération des Associations Ethniques du Katanga* (Conakat). In the capital of Equatorial Province, Coquilhatville, representatives from 25 splinter groups active in different areas of the colony formed the *Parti National du Progrès* (P.N.P.). Both parties were of definitely Western orientation, and as such they enjoyed support from the Belgian colonialist government (as TSHOMBÉ's party did from Union Minière, too!). Common features of the two parties were that (1) both stood for the decentralization of government and conceived of the future independent Congo state as a federation of autonomous republics, and (2) both admitted Africans and Europeans as members. In contrast to Conakat, whose activities were limited to Katanga Province, the P.N.P. was constituted as a national party and wished to achieve the Congo's independence through non-violence, without even passive resistance.

Still in November 1959 KASAVUBU managed to combine his Abako together with two other parties (KAMITATU's and GIZENGA's P.S.A. and KALONGI's M.N.C.) in a bloc named the "Abako Cartel". On the other side, before the forthcoming Brussels round-table conference, Conakat, the P.N.P. and LUMUMBA's M.N.C. formed a league to counteract the Abako Cartel.

In the first half of December the leaders of the large Congolese parties (with the sole exception of LUMUMBA, who was in prison at that time) went to Brussels, where they had unofficial talks for ten days with members of the Belgian government and

---

[1] JOSEPH ILÉO was born in Léopoldville in 1922. He studied philosophy and sociology in Europe.

[2] ALBERT KALONJI, a member of the Baluba tribe, was born in 1929 at Hemptinne in Kasai Province. He was educated at the Lusambo Catholic mission school and at the Kisanto agricultural college. For a time he was employed by the Belgian colonial administration. In 1954 he attended an accountants' course and from that time on he was an insurance broker. In 1957 he was made a member of the Kasai Provincial Council. In 1958 he went to see the World's Exhibition in Brussels, where he formed the Congolese National Movement to oppose the Abako policy. Back in the Congo he left his organization and joined LUMUMBA's Mouvement National Congolais.

leaders of Belgian political parties. Before their departure, on December 14, they issued a joint communiqué, stating that the talks ended in failure, for which the Belgian government was to be blamed, and that upon their return home they would start the struggle for independence at once.

On December 15 Minister SCHRIJVER told the Belgian Parliament that in mid-January a round-table conference would be held in Brussels, to discuss the Congo's independence, with the participation of members of the Belgian government and legislature as well as political leaders and chiefs from the Congo, that thereafter, still in the first half of the year, general elections would take place in the Congo to elect the members of the Congo Chamber of Representatives and the Senate, to form a parliamentary government, and that the country would win independence in 1960.

Local Elections

Elections for municipal and rural councils were held in the Congo during December 1959. The elections passed off quietly, only at Luluabourg in Kasai Province were there skirmishes between the Lulua and Baluba tribes early in the month. No reliable data on the casualties of those incidents are available. (Official reports spoke of 16 dead and "over thirty" injured.) KASAVUBU and KALONJI, who had just returned from Brussels, demanded postponement of the elections for a date following the round-table conference to be held in January. Since their demand went unheeded, they called upon their parties to boycott the elections but to refrain from disorders. The municipal elections were conducted smoothly in the absence of those two parties, but in the Léopoldville and Boma constituencies, where the large majority of the electorate were Bakongo, only 10 to 30 per cent (mostly European settlers) went to the poll (in Boma only 102 out of 5,686 registered voters). LUMUMBA's party, although he and several other party leaders were in prison, won a sweeping victory in Stanleyville, and so did TSHOMBÉ's party in Elisabethville.

King Baudouin's Visit to the Congo

The elections were not yet over when King BAUDOUIN arrived in the Congo for a two-week stay. The first stop of his visit was Stanleyville. He was received at the airport by demonstrators clamouring for independence, although the police had forbidden the gathering of more than five persons on this occasion and used tear gas against the people. Police had much difficulty in clearing the way for the King to drive on. Many arrests were made. In the evening hours a huge crowd assembled in front of the city jail, where LUMUMBA was imprisoned. The people were again dispersed with tear-gas grenades. Thereupon the demonstrators scattered in the streets and showered volleys of stones at the houses and cars of Europeans. In the night policemen were stationed on the Congo riverside to prevent further groups of demonstrators from coming into the city.

In the evening the King delivered a radio address, in which he stressed that he came to endorse the aspirations of those whose interests he had at heart. Although he admitted that the time had come to understand and satisfy the rightful aspirations of the Congolese, he emphasized that the people of the Congo envisaged their future in unity and brotherhood with Belgium.

Besides the high colonial officials and African dignitaries, the King received and heard also leaders of the political parties, who all demanded independence at once and immediate release of the political prisoners, first of all LUMUMBA.

After his visit to Stanleyville the King spent a few days in Ruanda-Urundi and after the elections he visited Bukavu (Kivu Province), Elisabethville (Katanga Province), then Luluabourg (Kasai Province) on December 26 and finally Léopoldville on the 28th. He was met everywhere by crowds demanding independence and the release of the prisoners. When he arrived in Luluabourg, tribal warfare between Lulua (LUMUMBA's followers) and Baluba (KASAVUBU's supporters) was culminating, and an investigation of mass poisonings in Bushongo villages was under way. In Léopoldville the people receiving the King ostentatiously cheered KASAVUBU. In the Governor-General's office the King talked for more than an hour with African party leaders, headed by KASAVUBU and KALONJI, who handed him the resolutions of the Kishantu conference held a few days before (see below) and requested the immediate convening of the promised constitutional conference. They said that for this end they would go to Brussels on January 5, because otherwise their followers, who demanded independence immediately, would rise in revolt and sweep them away. The King promised that the conference would take place in January and that three members of the Abako Cartel would be drawn into the discussions. On the other hand, Minister SCHRIJVER told a news conference that January 5 was an impossible date, because the King and he would not return to Brussels until early in January.

The last stop of the royal visit was Coquilhatville (Equatorial Province), where King BAUDOUIN arrived on December 31. This was the only city where the Africans received him with no hostile manifestations, though voicing their demands for independence. The next day the King, after receiving the African political leaders of the province, said good-bye to the Congo population by conveying his new year's greetings and flew home to Belgium.

A week after his return home, on January 10, King BAUDOUIN made a broadcast statement in Brussels, in which, following the spirit of the Kishantu conference resolution, he adopted the view that the Congo after independence should be a federation of autonomous republics. On January 14, however, the Belgian Minister for the Congo emphasized in a radio address intended for the Congo that independence must not lead to the breaking up of the country. At the same time he explained at length that, from the point of view of the country's future, it was of utmost importance to increase Belgian and other foreign capital investments, and therefore the most essential task of the future government of an independent Congo would be to guarantee "political stability" and "social peace". He advanced the opinion that the Congo government would have to strive in the future to encourage the inflow of American and West German as well as Belgian capital. He announced that the granting of a loan of $ 40 million to the Congo was being discussed with the International Bank for Reconstruction and Development.

The Inter-Party Conference at Kishantu

KASAVUBU's Abako Party and the parties allied with it, the M.N.C., the P.S.A., the *Parti Populaire Africain* (P.P.A.) and the Bayanzi Association, held a conference at Kishantu near Léopoldville from December 26 to 28, 1959. The five parties succeeded in formulating an agreed programme for the future of the Congo. In accordance with the resolutions passed at the conference the Congo was to become the *Union des Républiques d'Afrique Centrale* (U.R.A.C.), an independent federal state comprising six autonomous republics with separate constitutions, the actual six provinces of the Belgian Congo. With a view to forming the government of the independent federal state, elections should be held urgently and the election campaign should be started immediately. It was stressed in the resolution:

"We point it out to Belgium that the government to be formed as a result of the elections will get down to work immediately. Until this government is formed, we shall reject any futile discussion of relationships between Belgium and the Congo."

At the same time the resolution proposed that representatives of Belgium come together with political leaders of the Congo to talk over the details of the transfer of power.

In a separate resolution the five parties took a firm stand against the plan of the colonial administration to establish a so-called Belgo-Congolese joint-stock company, in which the Belgian government would participate with its existing capital interests in the Congo, and they demanded that the Belgian government's shares of Congolese capitalist enterprises should be transferred to the government of the independent Congolese federation immediately after accession to independence.

In another resolution, considering the increasing outflow of private capital from the Congo, the participating parties demanded the immediate introduction of stringent foreign exchange controls and state regulations for the hitherto free capital exports.

The Kishantu resolutions were worked out as a result of compromise. Shortly before the conference KASAVUBU's party still declared that the Lower Congo would be proclaimed an independent state by January 1, 1960. After the opening of the conference it was still rumoured that a Congolese émigré government would soon be formed in Brazzaville. In the interest of unanimity among the parties demanding federation, however, these extremist plans were abandoned, and the Abako also subscribed to the demand for a government to be formed on the basis of elections, and even dropped the demand for fixing a date for independence.

The Belgian government welcomed the compromise resolutions of the Kishantu conference, because the federal solution tallied with its own conception, and the demand for elections made it possible to delay further the granting of independence.

The Brussels Conference of January 1960

On January 8, 1960, the Belgian Cabinet decided to convene the round-table conference for January 20.

The conference met on schedule. Participating in it on behalf of Belgium were three ministers and ten M.P.s (representing all Belgian parties, except the Communists) and ten alternate delegates. The Congo was represented by 44 delegates and 38 alternates. The number of delegates from the Congolese parties was fixed by the Governor-General in the light of the results of the recent local elections. The Abako Cartel sent eleven delegates, the P.N.P. also eleven, the M.N.C. only two (it had achieved no big success at the elections because its leader, LUMUMBA, was in jail), the Conakat party three, and minor parties altogether six. Besides, the chiefs were represented by eleven delegates. Three of the delegates of the small parties joined the Abako Cartel delegation which professed to be radical, and three more took sides with the P.N.P. which was held moderate. When the conference opened, nobody counted with the M.N.C. as an opponent of any importance in the absence of LUMUMBA. In the first few days KASAVUBU, who was in general regarded as head of the entire Congolese delegation, behaved provokingly and operated with demagogical phrases. He rehashed his old scheme of separating the Lower Congo from the Congo state and transforming it into an independent republic joined with the French Middle Congo and Angola. At the same time he vociferously demanded independence for the Congo at once and the adoption of a constitution to be respected also by the Belgian government. When the delegates of the Belgian government rejected this demand, KASAVUBU walked out of the conference and did not put in an appearance for a long while.

KASAVUBU's behaviour annoyed all the Congolese delegates and disappointed even his own followers. The Congolese delegation did not miss him, and so KASAVUBU was not restored to chairmanship of the delegation even after he showed up again later towards the end of the conference.

KASAVUBU's secessionist schemes worried the Belgian government, too, all the more because the Conakat party and its leader, TSHOMBÉ threatened with the secession of Katanga, the richest province of the Congo.

All these circumstances had a share in the fact that the atmosphere of the conference changed in a couple of days. The change was promoted also by the reappearance of LUMUMBA in the political arena.

On January 21, the day following the opening of the Brussels conference, LUMUMBA was sentenced in Stanleyville to six months' imprisonment on the charge of having organized the disturbances at the end of last October. Since his party refused to attend the conference without him, and because all the Congo delegates to the conference as well as the Belgian Socialists demanded his freeing, the colonial authorities released him from prison. So on January 26, the day following KASAVUBU's withdrawal, LUMUMBA arrived in Brussels and took part in the further proceedings of the conference. From the very moment that he entered the conference hall, his hands still bruised by the manacles worn in jail, everyone there looked upon him as head of the entire Congolese delegation. The Congo delegates did so because he had the greatest prestige among all political leaders, and the Belgian representatives because his demand for a strong central government agreed with the conception promoted also by Brussels.

On January 27 a compromise agreement was reached on the date for independence. The Congo delegates proposed June 1, the Belgian government suggested the end of July. Finally they agreed for June 30. At the beginning of the conference there was much debate over procedural questions. The Congolese delegates demanded to be permitted to invite foreign experts, but the demand was declined.

The Congolese delegates declared in advance in a joint statement that their objective was independence, and stressed the desire that the decision of the conference should be binding also upon Belgium, but the Belgian government insisted that any decision to be passed should be submitted to the Belgian Parliament for approval. The Congolese accepted this after KASAVUBU's walk-out.

The conference deliberated in two committees. One discussed the structure of the future independent state, the other considered the electoral system to be introduced.

The conference passed altogether sixteen resolutions. These laid down first of all that all people should be equal before the law and everyone had the right to freedom, personal safety and material security.

Minister SCHRIJVER suggested a unified central government for the Congo, but with decentralized public services and broad provincial autonomy. This coincided by and large with the views of LUMUMBA and his followers. The suggestion was accepted by all Congolese delegations but Conakat, and the powers of the central government and the provincial governments were defined. Now as before TSHOMBÉ insisted on changing the Congo into a federal state, and emphasized again that the Congo after independence should maintain close relations with Belgium.

On January 31 SCHRIJVER said that the Congo would negotiate on an equal footing with Belgium. And on February 10 Vice-Premier LILAR declared that the Congo would enjoy full sovereignty without any reservation. It was decided that Belgium would provide technical and financial assistance to the young independent state, and that an economic conference would be held in Brussels in April.

SCHRIJVER proposed the conclusion of a treaty of friendship between Belgium and the Congo still before July 1. At the end of the conference TSHOMBÉ made the solemn promise that the Conakat party would guarantee the security of capitalist property in Katanga.

It was resolved that the first parliamentary elections would take place in 1960. The first Congo Parliament, which would consist of two chambers and function as a constituent assembly, would sit in Luluabourg, and its working language would be French. Its term was to be three to four years. The two chambers should hold a joint sitting to adopt the definitive constitution of the country, by taking separate votes on the particular articles, and by a two-thirds majority. Also a joint sitting should elect the head of state for the period till the entry into force of the constitution. In case no agreement would be reached the presidential functions would be exercised by the President of the Senate or the Chamber of Representatives. But the Congolese delegates were agreed that for the time being, until the day of independence, the King of the Belgians should remain head of state, and that he should nominate the first government of the Congo after the elections. Detailed arrangements were made to fix the number of members to be elected to parliament by the provinces in proportion to the size of their population. The suffrage would be universal and the voting obligatory.

The conference showed that the Belgian government had really changed its policy. Considering the real situation, it had to see that the Congo's independence could only be delayed but could not be prevented, and if it wished to save what it could (the lion's share in the resources of the country), it would have to agree with the future masters of the Congo. Therefore it made some concessions in political matters, too, even more than the Congolese might have expected in view of the past attitude of the Belgian government, in order to make sure that the most important economic issues would be taken up for discussion in a favourable atmosphere.

The conference demonstrated at the same time that the Belgian government made the political concessions with the ulterior motive that it would be able to sabotage them later or to postpone their implementation for a long time to come. This was to be seen clearly from the conference resolution which fixed the term of the provisional parliament in three to four years, although the Belgian government had promised to grant independence by June 30 (giving the young independent state the right to elect a new parliament under its new, definitive constitution).

Another resolution, evidencing the fraudulent intentions of the Belgian government, reserved for Brussels the right to appoint the first government of the Congo. The Belgians obviously were hopeful that they would have no particular difficulty in passing the government of an independent Congo peacefully, by money and propaganda, into the hands of African leaders who would continue to be held in leash by the Belgian government.

But they had to be disappointed in their calculations. They attained their goal only in part and at the cost of serious complications. Their policy made the Congo a scene of bloody events already before, and still more after, accession to independence.

The Provisional Constitution

After the Brussles conference the Belgian government began to draw up a constitutional text in accordance with the conference resolutions. Minister SCHRIJVER tabled the first draft in parliament on February 26. The draft was prepared with the participation of a political committee set up of six Africans at the Brussels conference. The draft regulated the composition and the powers of the Government Council *(Collège exécutif général)*. This executive body was to include the Governor-General as President and, to comply with the demands raised by the conference delegates, six African members to be appointed by the King of the Belgians on the recommendation of the Minister for the Congo. The Provincial Councils were to be composed of the Provincial Governor concerned and three African members. The duty of the Government Council would be to exercise until independence day (June 30) the functions which had thus far fallen within the purview of the Governor-General, except control of the armed forces and military bases as well as the colonial administration and urgent matters regarding the budget. Among the members of the Government Council were also KASAVUBU for Léopoldville, LUMUMBA for Oriental Province, and P.N.P. leader BOLYA for Equatorial Province.

The draft was unanimously approved by the Belgian Parliament on March 2. The Communists proposed, though, omission of the provision transferring some functions to the Governor-General, but after their motion was rejected they also voted for the draft.

On March 12 the Belgian Parliament dealt with the report of SCHRIJVER, Minister for the Congo, on the January round-table conference. It approved the report and voted confidence to the government. The resolution, proposed by the Communists and passed unanimously, expressed the hope of parliament that with the assistance of Belgium the Congo would make good progress on the road of development.

Parliament unanimously adopted also another resolution approving the government's declaration against foreign interference in the affairs of the Congo.

At its meeting of March 27 the Belgian cabinet approved the provisional constitution drawn up in accordance with the resolutions of the round-table conference of January. The same cabinet meeting approved the decree issued by the Governor-General of the Congo prohibiting the political parties from organizing armed units.

The final text of the provisional Congo constitution of 253 articles was published on April 18. It was based essentially on the sixteen resolutions of the Brussels conference, covering also some additional questions which had not been dealt with there, but which the six African members of the political committee agreed to include in the constitution.

The constitution laid down also that the head of state should be elected by the two chambers of parliament at a joint sitting. The presidential powers included the right to conclude international treaties in the name of the Congo state, with the proviso that the treaty of friendship, assistance and mutual co-operation with Belgium should be signed before independence by the first Congo government to be appointed by the King of the Belgians.

The provisional constitution provided further that the Congo government might be deposed only by a two-thirds majority of one of the chambers of parliament or by a simple majority of both chambers. The election of the head of state also required the vote of a two-thirds majority of parliament, and the adoption of the final constitution to be drawn up after independence was made subject to the assenting vote of a two-thirds majority of the Provincial Councils as well.

A highly important constitutional provision, which was made without previous discussion at the conference, was for the establishment of a Constitutional Court besides the ordinary courts of law. The function of this Court was to prevent the abuse of authority by government bodies and judicial organs during the transitional period. Therefore it had powers to supervise any act of parliamentary legislation before promulgation, to make sure that it was not contrary to any provision of the constitution, and to confirm all government decrees.

The provisional constitution laid down that French should be the language of deliberations in parliament and the main working language of the government bodies.

The host of about twenty thousand Belgian colonial officials was very worried by the Congo developments, because they thought of the forthcoming independence of the Congo as a threat to their very existence. Minister SCHRIJVER, who was entrusted with studying the economic and political problems of the Congo, tried to reassure the Belgian officials that after independence they would be entitled to be employed by any other department of the state machinery of Belgium, but that it might be also that the young independent state of the Congo would invite their further services, either in their present assignments or elsewhere. Similar assurances were given also by other members of the Belgian government.

The colonial officials, chiefly those of the lower grades, could not be reassured by such statements. Their discontent rose so high that on April 1 a group of small functionaries of the Belgian colonial administration staged at Stanleyville airport a demonstration against Minister for the Congo SCHRIJVER. Thereupon the minister, in a speech at the exclusive Royal Africa Club in Brussels, harshly reprimanded the grumbling colonial officials and settlers. "After June 30 life in the Congo will be different from what it is now", he said. "If the ordinary Belgian does not like it, let him come home. The Belgians in the Congo have to adapt themselves to the new conditions. Those who stubbornly cling to the old conditions cannot be of use there. There is no more room for conservatism in the Congo." Not to frighten his distinguished audience, however, he added at once that Belgium, though granting independence to the Congo, would not abandon the country but would "assist" it also after independence.

On April 20 LUMUMBA, while talking with NKRUMAH in Accra, stated that after independence the Congo would introduce a democratic system and pursue, as a non-aligned country, the policy of positive neutralism in international relations, but she would gladly welcome foreign capital and foreign technicians. He said: "We want to be on friendly terms with all nations, so we welcome those who come here to help our country to raise the standard of living." He took a stand in favour of the idea of a "United States of Africa", explaining that by it he understood an association of independent and sovereign states.

At its meeting of May 4 the Government Council decided that the proclamation of independence should be issued in Léopoldville on June 30. It was also decided that the two chambers of the newly elected legislature would meet in Léopoldville to vote confidence to the Congo's first government appointed by the King of the Belgians.

Claims of France and the Central African Federation

A week after the closing of the Brussels conference Paris informed the Belgian government through diplomatic channels that France still maintained her right of preference, as recognized in the 1885 convention and confirmed in 1908, over the Congolese possessions of Belgium in case of their alienation. The Belgian government responded with an energetic protest.

A few days later, on March 4, the Prime Minister of the Central African Federation, Sir ROY WELENSKY, disclosed in an interview given to the London *Daily Express*, that he would deem it desirable to annex Katanga, this Congo province rich in copper and cobalt, to the Federation. The Belgian government immediately protested against WELENSKY's statement both in Salisbury and in London.

The claims raised on the part of France and the Central African Federation were taken up also in the Belgian Parliament. Prime Minister EYSKENS and Foreign Minister WIGNY reiterated their protest. With reference to United Nations resolutions they rejected all foreign claims and stood up for the continued territorial integrity and unity of the Congo.

Then the French government hastened to let Brussels know that it waived its right of preference. WELENSKY remained silent. This was also a reason why in March the Belgian government dispatched day after day airborne troops to the Congo.

The Brussels Economic Conference in April–May 1960

In the spring of 1960, in pursuance of the resolutions of the January conference, the Belgian government convened an economic conference on the Congo. This conference lasted from April 26 till May 16. The Congolese leaders, who were busy preparing for the elections scheduled for May, now showed less interest than they had during the constitutional conference of January. Of all political leaders only TSHOMBÉ as head of the Conakat delegation was present. During the discussions he spoke in favour of economic and financial autonomy and demanded safeguards for the freedom of capitalist enterprise in Katanga. (This demand was supported also by his political opponents, delegates from the Balubakat political group.)

The conference passed a resolution providing that after independence the Congo would receive financial, technical and economic aid from Belgium, that the first Congo government and Belgium would conclude a treaty of friendship, assistance and co-operation. The delegates voted for these arrangements but stated once again that they could not guarantee that the resolutions would be approved by the government to be formed in mid-June, before accession to independence.

The Belgian ministers attending the conference (EYSKENS and SCHEYVEN) talked volubly about the Belgian government's sincere willingness to help, and submitted recommendations for the settlement of different economic and financial matters. They suggested notably that the Congo should join the European Economic Community, and that the interests which the Belgian colonial administration had in the Congo companies should be invested in a future Belgo-Congolese Development

Corporation in which — in the view of the Belgian government — other countries might also take a share. No resolution was passed on these issues, however.

The three-week conference reached agreement neither on the dismantling of Belgian military bases nor on the 1960 budget. At the last meeting a 15-member commission was appointed to study these problems.

The conference adopted altogether fifteen resolutions, which were regarded as recommendations for substantive negotiations between the Congo and Belgium. They were not expressly endorsed by any one of the attending members of the Congo Government Council on the grounds that after June it would be the sovereign right of the central Congolese government to decide on the economic and financial matters of the country.

The hypocrisy of the Belgian government was evidenced by the fact that, while at the conference its representatives speechified about the solution of the problems of the independent Congo, the government sent further units to reinforce its troops in the Congo (a battalion withdrawn from West Germany was flown to the Congo from Brussels) and urgently sent there a "minister-resident" with full power in the person of General GANSHOF VAN DER MEERSCH. Characteristically enough, the Belgian Socialists, who had for months attacked the government because of the troop transports to the Congo, now defended the government's action. Their representative attending the conference, Senator ROLIN, gave as a reason that Belgium in the United Nations had assumed responsibilities to do her best to prevent any chaos that might be caused by tribal conflicts in the Congo.

The conference clearly demonstrated, on the one hand, how great interest foreign states were taking in the independent Congo and, on the other, how hard the Congolese politicians tried to establish foreign contacts. One or another Congo delegate often disappeared for days to make short visits either to America or to the capital of some European socialist country, while others again were approached on the spot by official and unofficial representatives of foreign countries, who tried to influence them with advice (especially on economic and financial matters).

Tribal Conflicts and Party Struggles

While the African political leaders in Brussels were discussing political issues (in January) and economic questions (in April), trying to reconcile the opposing views by negotiation, in the Congo recurrent strifes between tribes as well as political differences in some places led to bloody incidents from time to time. The hostilities which had been set loose several months earlier between Baluba and Lulua tribes in Kasai Province continued throughout January. In the early days of that month bloody clashes occurred between the two tribes in the African district of Luluabourg, resulting in serious injuries to more than twenty people. The police made many arrests. A few days later similar brawls took place in some villages of Kasai Province. The Lulua pillaged a number of Baluba villages and burned many huts.

In the middle of January leaders of the two tribes, having met by Lake Mukamba some 100 kilometres from Luluabourg, signed an agreement for the removal of 90,000 Balubas from Lulua country, where they lived at the time, to another area. But the agreement was objected to by tribal and political groups both on the Baluba and on the Lulua side, and therefore two Baluba leaders withdrew their signatures. Governor-General CORNÉLIS said that the scheme endangered the economy of Kasai Province, and prohibited the plan from being carried out. He declared a state of emergency in the province and sent his lieutenant, LAFONTAINE, to restore order, which he did.

For a while there was peace in Kasai Province, but towards the end of March the Baluba-Lulua conflict broke out again. At Luluabourg on March 28, the police fired upon the rioters, wounding several Africans. Over 60 Africans were arrested. The rioters set fire to two houses. The authorities imposed a curfew. On March 29, Lulua and Baluba at Ndesha, Kasai Province, clashed during a religious ceremony where large numbers had assembled. Two policemen and twelve Africans were seriously wounded, more than sixty Africans suffered minor injuries. Here also a curfew was imposed.

As the elections scheduled for May were approaching, in the middle of March the intensifying electoral campaign in Katanga led to bloody scuffles between followers of the Balubakat and Conakat political groups. In Elisabethville at a weekend in mid-March supporters of the two parties rushed at one another, armed with poisoned arrows, spears and home-made rifles. They looted and tore down many houses or set fire to them. The troops were called out to put down the riots, the state of emergency was declared and a curfew was ordered.

The casualties of the two-day fighting and military action included 18 dead, 150 seriously and numberless lightly wounded. The police arrested over five hundred Africans.

TSHOMBÉ and SOUENDE, the leaders of Conakat and Balubakat, respectively, met in a Sunday evening and issued an appeal to their followers inviting them to stop fighting, but the appeal was of no avail. They could not go on the air, because the cables of the broadcasting station had been cut off. A small airplane was hired for dropping leaflets containing the appeal, but when circling over the city it flew against a power line and crashed, killing the pilot.

A few days later the conflicts flared up both in Elisabethville and in its environs, and new mass arrests followed. On March 18, in the African-inhabited Katuba quarter of Elisabethville 58 Africans were taken in custody. In Kasenga district all bars and taprooms were closed down, a curfew was imposed and all gun-licences cancelled.

The African sections of the city were an appalling sight: houses in ruin and burnt down everywhere, smashed furniture and broken glass on the streets, etc.

The state of emergency was ended in Kasai Province on April 4, in Katanga on April 11. But in the latter half of April the Lulua-Baluba skirmishes flared up again. On April 18 and 19, the scuffle took a toll of six dead in the Luluabourg area.

In the African quarter of Luluabourg the Baluba burnt down thirty houses. In a lorry the police discovered the decapitated bodies of two Luluas. Three mutilated bodies were found in a nearby village. Forty-seven Baluba youths were arrested. The troops and colonial police were called out to restore order. At Demba a military detachment held up a Lulua gang of a hundred men getting ready to fight. A Lulua tribesman who resisted the police was shot dead.

Baluba warriors in the suburbs of Luluabourg killed ten Luluas, a woman and a child among them. They crossed the river and burnt down 300 Lulua huts at Nganza, then raided the village of Ndesha, where they gravely wounded thirty Luluas. The troops dispatched under Belgian officers arrested eighty Baluba tribesmen. According to an official report the chiefs of the Lulua tribes living in the areas of Demba, Dibaya and Kasumba addressed an ultimatum to the Belgian authorities, demanding that all Baluba tribes be removed from those areas within three days, else all Lulua fighters would march upon Luluabourg.

On April 22 the Governor of Kasai Province, to meet a demand of the Provincial Council composed of Africans, again declared a state of emergency in the Lulua quarter of Luluabourg and in the area of the Bakwanga and Gandajka tribes.

The Issue of International Treaties before the Belgian Senate

The Belgian Senate on May 9 started discussing the foreign affairs committee report on Belgium's commitments undertaken in international treaties on behalf of the Congo State. The Senate took the position that the Berlin agreement of 1885 defining a conventional basin of the Congo and securing freedom of navigation of the Congo and all its affluents, as well as the 1919 treaties of Saint-Germain which confirmed those conventions, and which had been signed by the administering powers on behalf of the dependent territories, were not binding upon the independent successor states. The sovereign state of the Congo would therefore be free to terminate the agreements and to conclude new conventions concerning navigation on the Congo river. It was stressed at the same time that the treaties concluded by Belgium fixing the boundaries of the Congo, as well as the multilateral international treaties entered into by Belgium, such as the Geneva Convention on the prohibition of forced labour, should continue to remain in force.

Protests from the Rhodesia Racists

The coming independence of the Congo threw the racists of Southern Rhodesia into panic. Prime Minister EDGAR WHITEHEAD of Southern Rhodesia on May 10 delivered a speech, in which he described the action of the Belgian government granting independence to the Congo as "ill-advised and irresponsible": "I cannot imagine anything as ill-advised as to govern a people for sixty years without giving them a minimum of political responsibility, and then to withdraw."

Parliamentary Elections in May 1960

The elections were held between May 12 and 23. The right to vote was granted to all males over 21 years who had permanent residence in the country. Women were eligible but were not allowed to vote.

The colonial police and the 5,000 Belgian soldiers stationed in the colony, as well as the African troops under the command of Belgian officers, were put on the alert in order to keep up order and prevent or put down any possible disturbances. But the Belgians doubted the reliablility of African soldiers (clashes between African troops and the police were everyday occurrences; African commanders in many places did not give out ammunition to the men), so the Belgian government kept dispatching Belgian reinforcements by air (infantry from West Germany, parachutists from Belgium). The Belgian authorities released false reports to deceive public opinion. In spite of the fact that during the elections the Belgian armed forces in the Congo grew to a considerable size, after the election the Belgian authorities insisted that their strength was below 5,000.

For fear of possible rioting, the Belgian government introduced severe precautions for the duration of the elections. Early in May Defence Minister GILSON of Belgium went to the Congo to size up the situation, and Governor-General CORNÉLIS flew to Brussels for instructions. In Léopoldville a curfew was imposed from 8 p.m. till 5 a.m., political gatherings were banned and, just in case, 1,500 police and 3,000 troops were kept in readiness day and night.

The elections were conducted under the supervision of members of the Belgian Colonial Council. LUMUMBA charged that the Belgian inspectors manipulated the ballot in favour of certain parties toadying the colonialists.

The 137 parliamentary seats were contested between 28 parties, which can be divided into three categories:

First, LUMUMBA's party, the M.N.C., and its allies, the Union Nationale Congolaise (U.N.C.), the Balubakat and a coalition of Kasai tribes (Coaka), together with two other left-wing parties, the P.S.A. and Cerea, favoured a united independent Congo state with a strong central government.

Second, KASAVUBU's Abako party and the Conakat in league with it, as well as the KALONJI wing of the M.N.C. wanted federation and a loose central government (in fact, KASAVUBU schemed towards the secession of the Province of Léopoldville, and TSHOMBÉ wished Katanga to secede from the Congo).

The third category was made up of moderate parties representing primarily rural and tribal interests; these parties voiced the necessity of a peaceful and gradual transition to independence, and favoured the unity of the Congo, but demanded decentralization of the government (P.N.P., Parti de l'Unité Nationale — PUNA, Kivu Popular Rally — REKO, and Association Rurale Progressiste — A.R.P.).

LUMUMBA's party came out victorious from the elections. It won 36 seats, of which 21 in Oriental Province (in Stanleyville it polled 95.8 per cent of the vote, 23,270 out of 24,278), six in Kivu and Kasai Provinces each, two in Equatorial Province and one in Léopoldville. (The parties allied with the M.N.C. obtained an additional 13 seats.) Next came the P.N.P. with 14 seats in four provinces. The left-wing P.S.A. and KASAVUBU's party gained seats only in Léopoldville, 13 and 12 respectively. As to their allies, KALONJI obtained 8 seats in Kasai Province, TSHOMBÉ seven in Katanga. The other left-wing party, Cerea, grabbed 10 seats in Kivu Province. From among the moderate parties, in addition to the P.N.P. only PUNA obtained seven seats in Equatorial Province and REKO four in Kivu. The minor parties shared the remaining 13 seats among themselves.

The members of the Provincial Councils were elected at the same time. In these elections LUMUMBA and his allies won a sweeping victory in three provinces (Oriental, Kasai, Kivu), and KASAVUBU in Léopoldville.

Although the elections demonstrated unmistakably that LUMUMBA's party and the other left-wing parties enjoyed the confidence of the majority of the population, the Belgian authorities went to all lengths to prevent LUMUMBA from coming into power. In the last days of the elections, when LUMUMBA's victory was already evident, the police impounded copies of his party's paper, Uhuru, for its criticism of the Belgian administration, and, on the pretext that LUMUMBA was preparing a coup, strong Belgian armed forced were concentrated in Stanleyville.

During the elections LUMUMBA gave several interviews. Thus on May 14 at a press conference he demanded that the Belgian government transfer power immediately to the provisional government of the Congo, claiming that this was the only possibility of maintaing order and putting a stop to the further shedding of blood. At his news conference in Stanleyville on May 19 he protested against the delay of Belgian troop withdrawals and criticized the appointment of a "minister-resident" in charge of general political affairs. He declared that neither he nor KASHAMURA would accept the place they had been offered in the Government Council until the "minister-resident" returned to Brussels and the Government Council took over all executive functions. Finally he demanded that a commission be formed to settle the controversial issues between Belgium and the Congo.

On the same day King BAUDOUIN signed in Brussels the provisional constitution of the Congo, which entered into force on independence day, July 1.

Returning from the Congo after the elections, Minister SCHRIJVER stated with satisfaction that the elections had taken place in a calm atmosphere. But this was very far from the truth.

The official reports themselves put the death toll of the month-long pre-election campaign at fifty at the least. In Léopoldville still in the days before the elections a good number of people were killed in the bloody incidents between Lulua and Baluba. Many arrests were made. Three LUMUMBA followers were found dead in the street, and several others vanished without leaving a trace.

In the Léopoldville area clashes occurred on May 9 between African police and off-duty unarmed African soldiers. The brawl originated from the differences due to the fact that in the course of a previous incident the police had killed two Bayaka tribesmen and wounded four, and the soldiers raided two police stations with sticks and stones. Both sides suffered casualties. Another conflict was reported from Yafolo in Oriental Province. The police fired upon the rioters and killed a man.

On the occasion of the arrival in Stanleyville of Governor-General CORNÉLIS on May 4 a large group of Africans organized a street demonstration. The police clashed with the crowd and arrested several people. Some of these, however, managed to escape with the help of the demonstrators. The official report said that the demonstration had been staged by extreme elements of the M.N.C.

The relationship between Governor LEROY of Oriental Province and the M.N.C. enjoying great popularity in that province became so tense that the Belgian government felt compelled to recall the Provincial Governor. LUMUMBA took over responsibility for the maintenance of order in Stanleyville.

On May 6 in Elisabethville the police used tear gas to disperse the striking railway workers who demanded a pay rise. Several African workers were injured in the ensuing riot. Railway traffic came to a complete halt. Any gathering of more than five persons was prohibited, and the troops were ordered to be in readiness.

At the same time a strike movement started in Katanga among the low-paid African employees of the colonial administration and mining companies. In keeping with the growing cost of living, the salaries of Belgian employees had been raised threefold in a few months, while the Africans still received the old wages. The latter feared that after independence the prices would go up further, therefore they demanded a pay rise of 5 per cent from July 1 and another 10 per cent rise from December 1. On the other hand, some African trade-union executives, who had attended the Brussels economic conference, proposed that the salaries of high-paid Belgian officials should be reduced.

Serious incidents were reported from several provinces. In Kinshasa, the African section of Léopoldville, a curfew was imposed because of new Lulua-Baluba clashes on May 13. The Baluba killed a number of Lulua, pillaging and burning down their huts.

Four people were killed and fourteen wounded in skirmishes in the town of Kamina.

At Goma, Kivu Province, in the vicinity of the Ruanda boundary, on May 13 the mob looted and burnt down the house of the commandant of the town. Troops armed with tear-gas bombs were sent against the rioters.

At the locality of Luebo in Kasai Province the Baluba set fire to 200 Lulua huts. Police were sent to the scene and killed two Baluba raiders. Many mutilated bodies were found in the burning ruins, and 25 wounded Lulua were taken to hospital. Thereupon the Lulua attacked a Baluba village ten kilometres from Luebo, with the result of many casualties on both sides. The two incidents together were officially reported to have demanded a death toll of 18 (the actual figure might well have been much higher).

The Crucial Stage of the Independence Struggle

On June 1 LUMUMBA's M.N.C. issued in Stanleyville a communiqué, laying claim to power with reference to its sweeping election victory. At the same time LUMUMBA declared that the government to be formed by the M.N.C. would guarantee the protection of the person and property of all African and non-African citizens of the Congo, and that the party based its policy on sincere friendship among tribes and races.

On June 2 LUMUMBA gave a press conference in Léopoldville. In connection with the forthcoming accession of the Congo to independence he summed up the demands of his party as follows:

1. The Belgian armed forces to be withdrawn from Congo territory immediately, still before independence.

2. The Belgian government to recall at once its "minister-resident", General VAN DER MEERSCH, who had been commissioned to put down any possible disorders at the time of the proclamation of independence.

3. The chief of state to be elected directly, not by the future National Assembly and Senate as had been planned.

4. A new flag to replace the proposed flag of the new state, because this bore the marks of colonialism (a golden star on a blue background surrounded by six small stars symbolizing the provinces).

At the same time he announced that he demanded to form the new government and to be appointed Prime Minister, and that he intended to form a coalition in league with the other progressive parties.

In his statement he assured the European colonists that they might safely stay on after independence; that, in case his party came to power, they and their property would not be harmed. He added that he had made the political leaders and chiefs promise to protect the lives and property of Europeans. (The number of Belgian settlers who had left the Congo in the first five months of 1960 was officially estimated at about 100,000.) At the same time a paper of LUMUMBA's party wrote this: "We ask Europeans to remain with us in our country. We ask their sincere co-operation. We need them as technicians and teachers. They mustn't be afraid—we will obey those who will obey our laws. We ask them to help us; we want to live together with everybody. To those who are packing, we'll simply say that they have outdated feelings."[1]

But the settlers were not reassured. They were worried by LUMUMBA's demand that the Belgian troops be withdrawn before independence was granted. They applied for airplane tickets in so large numbers that Sabena Belgian World Airlines had to charter 80 aircraft from other companies, for the period until June 30, to meet

[1] The New York Herald Tribune, June 7, 1960.

at least part of the increasing demand. (Immediately before independence the settlers' flight from the Congo took still larger proportions. In the last few days of June the 2,500 Portuguese settlers living in the Congo also left the country. Some of them settled in Angola, others flew back home to Portugal.)

Early in June KASAVUBU had conversations in Brussels with members of the Belgian government, whom he tried to persuade to appoint him to form the government. But the Belgian minister-resident, in accordance with the election results, put LUMUMBA in charge. Owing to the wrangling of the parties over the distribution of ministerial places, LUMUMBA could not form his government on schedule. He was then given more time, so that he might manage to agree with the parties. The Belgian minister-resident, however, not waiting for LUMUMBA to report on his talks, commissioned KASAVUBU, who had only 12 votes in parliament, to establish a government. This step roused a violent outcry, and since the general elections held in the meantime had returned LUMUMBA's candidates to the National Assembly and the Senate by an overwhelming majority, the Belgian government was compelled to recognize LUMUMBA's right to form the government. LUMUMBA succeeded in getting an agreement accepted, under which KASAVUBU recognized the LUMUMBA government on the understanding that he would take over the presidential functions himself. The government was formed on June 23. It comprised 21 ministers besides LUMUMBA who as Prime Minister held also the portfolio of defence. Seven out of 21 ministerial seats were taken by LUMUMBA's M.N.C., two were given to P.S.A., P.N.P., Cerea, Abako and Conakat each, and one to the Balubakat, UNIMO, U.N.C. and PUNA parties. The post of Deputy Premier was filled by ANTOINE GIZENGA of the P.S.A.

In the evening of June 23 the 137-member National Assembly of the Congo voted confidence to the LUMUMBA government. At the same meeting LUMUMBA put forward his programme. He stated that the independent Congo intended to maintain friendly relations with all countries, but without joining any bloc, and that the main concern of his government would be to ensure social justice and progress.

On June 24 a joint sitting of both chambers of parliament elected KASAVUBU President of the Republic. (KASAVUBU obtained 158 votes, while his opponent, JEAN BOLIKANGO of the Bangala tribe, won 43.) The next day in Léopoldville KASAVUBU's supporters celebrated on this occasion. It came to street brawls between the Bakongo cheering KASAVUBU and the Bangala supporters of BOLINKANGO. The two sides rushed upon one another with knives, seriously wounding 13 people. The police made 44 arrests.

On June 27 KASAVUBU took the oath as President of the Republic at a joint meeting of both chambers of parliament. During the ceremony an anti-government demonstration was held before the parliament building. About 1,000 supporters of KALONJI, the Baluba chief, gathered there to protest against their leader's being left out of the government. KALONJI himself, standing in an open car, made a speech demanding the division of Kasai Province and the unification in an autonomous state of the Baluba living in different provinces of the Congo.

On June 28 two large groups of people, hostile to each other and both demonstrating against the government, proceeded through the streets of Léopoldville: KALONJI's 2,000 men who demanded for their party three ministerial seats and a post of under-secretary, and BOLIKANGO's 500 Bangala followers, who demanded for their leader the defence portfolio (which was retained by LUMUMBA). The fifty policemen called out to restore order succeeded in driving KALONJI's adherents into back-streets, preventing thereby a direct clash between the two camps, and the Bangala crowd which was reluctant to disperse was broken up with tear-gas bombs.

At its meeting of June 27 the LUMUMBA government decided that the country after independence would be named the Republic of the Congo. Also it formed a committee to draw up the text of the treaty of friendship to be concluded with Belgium. The text was finalized in great haste, and the Treaty of Friendship, Assistance and Co-operation was signed by the Foreign Ministers of the two countries still before independence, as scheduled, on June 29.

FULBERT YOULOU, the President of the former French Congo, which in November 1958 had been renamed the "Republic of the Congo", having been apprised of the decision of the LUMUMBA government concerning the name of the new independent Congo state, issued in Brazzaville a statement to the press, protesting against the ex-Belgian Congo being named also the "Republic of the Congo", a name which the former French Middle Congo had already bearing for almost two years, and under which his country was a member of the World Health Organization and the International Labour Organization. He sent his protest by wire to President DE GAULLE of France as well as to KASAVUBU and LUMUMBA of the Congo.[14]

Independence was proclaimed in the presence of representatives of 60 countries on June 30. Among those attending was a five-member delegation of the United States, headed by President EISENHOWER's personal representative, ROBERT D. MURPHY, who warmly greeted LUMUMBA and assured him that the United States wished to maintain "friendly and mutually beneficial" relations with the independent Congo and would do all in its power to promote their co-operation. King BAUDOUIN of Belgium took part personally in the celebration. On his arrival in Léopoldville, a minor incident took place. A young African jumped onto the running-board of the open car of the King, unsheathed the King's sword and brandished it over the monarch's head shouting "Independence!" until he was apprehended.

The granting of independence was declared by King BAUDOUIN in the National Assembly. In his speech he characterized the Congo's accession to independence as "an event of decisive consequence for the future, not only of this country, but of all Africa". Further on he talked about three dangers the young independent state would have to face: its people's unpreparedness for governing the country, the tribal conflicts raging in various provinces, and the fact that certain areas of the Congo were very attractive to some foreign states, which were ready to use the slightest indication of weakness to their own advantage (?!).

Speaking after the King, LUMUMBA sharply criticized the Belgian colonial administration which had brought oppression, humiliation and suffering to the African population.

BIBLIOGRAPHY

TOM MARVEL, *The New Congo*, New York, 1948.
BASIL DAVIDSON, "The Congo and Angola", *West Africa*, May 22 and 29, 1954.
"La révolution industrielle au Congo Belge", *Eurafrique* (Algeirs) 14/1954, pp. 38–43.
Synthèses, No. 121, June 1956 (special issue on the Congo).

[1] The protest proved unavailing; the question was later solved provisionally by the United Nations, which registered the two Congo states by these different names: Republic of the Congo (Brazzaville) and Republic of the Congo (Léopoldville).

Situation économique de la Belgique et du Congo Belge, Courtrai, 1958.

R. DE MEYER, *Introducing the Belgian Congo and the Ruanda-Urundi*, Brussels, 1958.

T. R. KANZA, *Le Congo*, Brussels, 1959.

JULES CHOMÉ, *Le drame de Luluabourg*, Brussels, 1959.

A. A. МАРТЫНОВ, *Конго под гнетом империализма* [The Congo under the Yoke of Imperialism], Moscow, 1959.

Synthèses, Nos 163–4, Dec. 1959–Jan. 1960 (special issue on the Congo).

Congo 1959: Documents belges et africains. Brussels, 1960.

Congo—Prelude to Independence, London, 1960.

PATRICE LUMUMBA, "The Independence of the Congo", in DUFFY-MANNERS (ed.), *Africa Speaks*, Princeton, 1961.

M. N. HENNESSY, *The Congo*, New York, 1961.

RUTH SLADE, *The Belgian Congo*, London, 1961.

J. GÉRARD-LIBOIS & B. VERHAEGEN, *Congo 1960*, 2 vols., Brussels, 1961.

JANE ROUCH, *En cage avec Lumumba*, Paris, 1961.

PATRICE LUMUMBA, *Congo My Country*, London, 1962; New York, 1962.*

*LUMUMBA wrote this book in 1956, but it was not published until after his death. Its original title, under which it was published in Brussels in 1961, is: *Le Congo, terre d'avenir, est-il menacé?*

R. C. KAMANGA, *A Short Biography of Patrice Lumumba*, Cairo, 1962.

TIBOR KÖVES, *Feketék és fehérek Kongóban* [Blacks and Whites in the Congo], Budapest, 1962.

Ю. Н. ВИНОКУРОВ, *Трудный путь к независимости* [Difficult Road to Independence], Moscow, 1967.

HISTORICAL WORKS

CHARLES D'YDEWALLE, *L'Union minière du Haut Katanga de l'âge colonial à l'indépendance*, Paris, 1960.

ROBERT CORNEVIN, *Histoire du Congo*, Paris, 1963.

GEORGE MARTELLI, *Leopold to Lumumba*, London, 1963. (An imperialist propaganda pamphlet.)

RENÉ LEMARCHAND, *Political Awakening in the Belgian Congo*. U. of Cal. Press, 1965.

MICHEL MERLIER, *Конго от козонизации до независимости* [The Congo from Colonization to Independence], Moscow, 1965.

H. LOTH, *Kongo, heisses Herz Afrikas: Geschichte des Landes bis auf unsere Tage*, Berlin, 1965.

ROGER ANSTEY, *King Leopold's Legacy: The Congo under Belgian Rule 1908–1960*, Oxford, 1965.

PROPAGANDA AND APOLOGIA OF BELGIAN COLONIALISM

V. VERMEULEN, *Déficiencies et dangers de notre politique indigène*. Impr. I.M.A., 1953.

G. MALENGREAU, "Political Evolution in the Belgian Congo", *Journal of African Administration* 6/1954, pp. 160–166.

G. MALENGREAU, "Recent Developments in Belgian Africa", in C. G. HAINES (ed.), *Africa Today*, Baltimore, 1955, pp. 337–357.

W. UGENX, "Commentary", in C. G. HAINES (ed.), *Africa Today*, Baltimore, 1955, pp. 357–365.

G. HOSTELET, *L'œuvre civilisatrice de la Belgique au Congo, de 1885 à 1953*, Brussels, 1954. Vol. II: "Les avantages dont les Blancs et les Noirs ont bénéficié et bénéficieront de l'œuvre civilisatrice de la Belgique au Congo".

PIERRE RYCKMANS, "Belgian Colonialism", *Foreign Affairs*, Oct. 1955.

GEORGES BRAUCSH, "The Problem of Elites in the Belgian Congo", *International Science Bulletin*, Vol. VIII, No. 3 (1956).

G. BRAUSCH, "Origines de la politique indigène belge en Afrique", *Revue de l'Institut de Sociologie Solvay* 3/1955, pp. 455–478.

G. Brausch, "Le paternalisme, une doctrine belge de politique indigène", *Revue de l'Institut de Sociologie Solvay* 2/1957, pp. 191–217.

Jean Labrique, *Congo Politique*, Léopoldville, 1957.

J. Stengers, *Combien le Congo a-t-il coûté à la Belgique?* Brussels (Académie Royale des Sciences Coloniales), 1957.

Jean Sépulchre, *Propos sur le Congo politique de demain: Autonomie et fédéralisme*, Elisabethville, 1958.

A. A. J. van Bilsen, *Vers l'indépendance du Congo et du Ruanda-Urundi*, Brussels, 1958.

Le Congo Belge, 2 vols., Brussels (Office de l'Information et des Relations Publiques pour le Congo Belge et le Ruanda-Urundi), 1959.

Teaching and Education in Belgian Congo and in Ruanda-Urundi, Brussels, 1959.

King Baudouin, *The Political Future of the Belgian Congo* (Speech on the reforms on January 13, 1959), Brussels, 1959.

Thirteen Million Congolese, Brussels, 1959.

W. C. Ganshof van der Meersch, *Congo, mai-juin 1960:* Rapport du Ministre chargé des affaires générales en Afrique. Brussels, 1960.

Paul van Reyn, *Le Congo politique: Les partis et les élections*, Brussels, 1960.

Congo, July 1960: Evidence. Statement by Mr. Merchiers, Belgian Minister of Justice, at the Press Conference 28.7.60.

Fernand van Langenhove, *The Congo and the Problems of Decolonization*, Brussels, 1960

Georges Brausch, *Belgian Administration in the Congo*, London, 1961.

CHAPTER XXVIII

RUANDA-URUNDI

Ever since the end of World War I, when the Belgian government, thanks to the great colonial powers and the League of Nations, had received the mandate for these two tribal kingdoms (Ruanda and Burundi), it regarded and even treated the territory of Ruanda-Urundi as a colony, an appendage to the Congo. Legislative and executive powers were here also entirely in the hands of the King of the Belgians, the Belgian government and parliament. The laws passed in Brussels with respect to the Congo were applicable also in the mandated territory of Ruanda-Urundi. Parliament in Brussels approved the budget and the Belgian government had the last word in all affairs of the territory. Not even a Governor was appointed specially to the mandated territory, but the Vice-Governor-General of the Congo acted as Governor of Ruanda-Urundi and even had emergency legislative powers.

Nothing changed for a time following World War II. On behalf of the United Nations the Belgian government undertook the obligations of trusteeship, that is, preparation of the territory for independence, but it did nothing to change the pre-war situation which fell short of the requirements of the League of Nations mandate. The Belgian colonial imperialists made use of the UN trusteeship system for delaying the granting of independence, in order to maintain their neocolonialist influence over Ruanda-Urundi even after independence and to enable their capitalist companies to continue the economic exploitation of the territory.

This determined Belgium's entire post-war colonial policy, which can be summed up as follows: to foment the internal conflicts of the peoples of the territory, thereby weakening them and tying down their energy for the struggle among themselves, and to divert their attention and prevent their independence aspirations from taking shape in an organized fight for freedom.

Those internal conflicts, which already in the inter-war years had made it easier for the colonialists to carry out their schemes, continued and even intensified after the war. Of utmost consequence was the class and tribal antagonism between the Hutu poor peasants (descendants of the indigenous inhabitants of the territory) who owned no land or only possessed small plots at most and the Tutsi (a pastoral people who had come as conquerors and subjugated the Hutu), owners of vast lands and many cattle. The war years brought growing wealth to the Tutsi and growing poverty to the Hutu, thus fanning their enmity.

Besides chiefs the Hutu tribal society developed another privileged stratum, the so-called "notables", who, by doing services for the Tutsi lords, could acquire land and cattle or, by rendering services to the colonialists, could win the confidence of the Belgian authorities and thus secure various benefits.

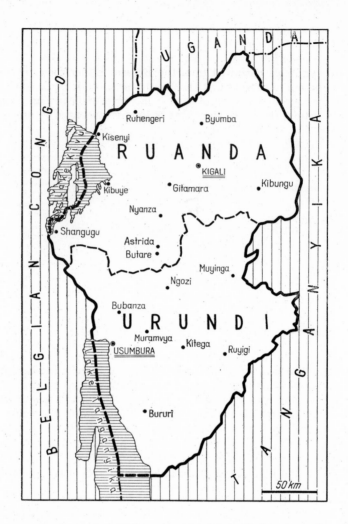

And a new source of growing difference within the tribal society after the war was the slow but progressive spread of democratic ideas.

Side by side with the activities of the United Nations and its Trusteeship Council, efforts were being made in the tribal society of the territory to achieve liberation from the yoke of colonialism, to win independence. This struggle for democratic government and freedom had not yet taken an organized form, but the tribal communities were divided by the differences between promoters of democracy and independence, on the one hand, and the conservatives stubbornly clinging to tribal traditions, on the other.

Finally, after the war, when Ruanda-Urundi was made a trust territory and the question of independence was raised, the rivalry and hostility which had been rampant between the two tribal kingdoms of Ruanda and Burundi since time immemorial, and which had been relegated to the background during the years of colonial rule, acquired major significance. The question arose as to whether the two countries should unite in a single independent state or whether they should form two separate independent nations. The rulers of the two countries, as well as the majority of the peoples, wanted separation.

The Belgian colonialists exploited these differences by applying the time-tested divide-and-rule principle borrowed from the British. Either they upheld the privileges of the Tutsi oppressors against the Hutu masses trying to shake off the yoke of oppression, or they posed as apostles of democratic evolution and supported the Hutu struggle against the Tutsi. They always opposed and tried to prevent the division of the territory, because they expected the conflict to promote their neocolonialist schemes in a future unitary independent state.

In the first ten years following World War II the Belgian colonialists did nothing essential to comply with their obligation undertaken in the trusteeship agreement to establish democratic administrative bodies (legislative and executive organs). The so-called democratization of the existing customary tribal authorities also did not start until 1952. Their status and powers were "regulated" by ordinance as early as 1943, during the war. The ordinance provided nothing new but "sanctioned" the actual situation. It recognized the tribal state headed by the king *(Mwami)* and composed of chiefdoms and sub-chiefdoms. The king was elected according to tradition but had to be invested by the Belgian Governor. The chiefs and sub-chiefs were appointed by the king but had to be confirmed by the Belgian administration. The king was assisted by a Council of State, and the chiefs by chiefdom councils, but the composition and functions of the councils were not regulated by the ordinance. In 1947 a Council of the Vice-Government-General was established, but it had nothing to do with democracy either as to its composition or its functions. It was composed of colonial officials as ex-officio members and other Europeans (merchant and settler representatives) appointed by the Vice-Governor-General, who had the right to appoint also three Africans to the Council, or if he saw fit, to replace them with further settler representatives. In 1949 this Council was further "democratized": its membership was enlarged to include the two tribal kings. In fact the composition of the Council was inconsequential, because it met in a brief session only once a year and was merely an advisory body. In 1950 an African priest and three chiefs were invited to attend the meetings but were excluded from a voice in the Council; in 1951 the priest was included in the membership, but the two other African seats were given to representatives of Catholic and Protestant missionaries.

The UN Trusteeship Council reminded the Belgian government that the measures taken were insufficient and that the Council of the Vice-Government-General must be given legislative functions with larger African participation. In 1951 the UN Visiting Mission stated that the Council had no political importance, because it was not made up of popular representatives, and expressed the view that the Council could be politically significant only if the customary tribal institutions were developed in a democratic direction, in which case — provided that African representation would be considerably increased — the Council as an advisory body might play an important part in fostering the contacts between the customary tribal authorities and the central colonial administration and in preparing the Africans for managing their own affairs.

To comply at least formally with the requirements defined by the United Nations, the Belgian government began to "democratize" the customary tribal authorities to its own liking.

When the decree of July 14, 1952, was issued, "the Belgian Administration considered the time had come to try and democratize the political institutions of the two countries".[1] Essentially, the much advertised democratization provided for measures to be taken in two opposite directions, which in no way made the regime more democratic; on the contrary, they strengthened its anti-democratic character. The reform was not aimed at the introduction of really democratic institutions (elected legislative and executive organs), but first of all, as was claimed, it was an attempt at the democratization of customary tribal administration. It curtailed the absolute powers of the two kings and of the chiefs and the Tutsi oligarchy by building a whole network of advisory bodies on different levels. These councils were the following (from the lowest level upwards): sub-chiefdom councils, chiefdom councils, district councils, High Council of State.

The composition of these councils was different. The decree fixed their memberships, among them the number of sub-chiefs, chiefs, and other notables, in part ex officio, in part by nomination. Other people than those included in these three categories only had some insignificant part to play in the indirect election of the sub-chiefdom councils. Each sub-chiefdom council comprised 5 to 9 elected members (one for every 500 inhabitants) in addition to the sub-chief. These members were chosen by an electoral college consisting of notables whose names were selected from a list, prepared by the sub-chief "taking into account the preferences of the inhabitants", and containing at least twice as many names as the number of the members of the council; this list had to be approved by the chief and accepted by the colonial administration. Under this system of election the Hutu could expect to have any meaningful representation only in the local sub-chiefdom councils, since they were elected to the three higher-level councils only in small numbers and as a rare exception.

These councils had their powers confined to acting as advisory bodies to the Mwami, the chief, or the sub-chief, respectively, without having a voice in the decisions of any of them. But even as advisory bodies they were not representative of the popular will, since most of their members came from among the Tutsi oppressors, not from the Hutu farmers who still made up the overwhelming majority of the population.

The organization of the councils thus meant no kind of democratization; on the contrary, it only buttressed the absolute power of the Mwami and the chiefs by giving a semblance of democracy.

The same goes for another democratic-looking reform. This referred to the Mwami and to the chiefs part of the internal affairs of local concern which had until then been within the purview of the colonial administration. In other words, the reform, far from curbing the power of the Tutsi ruling class, still encouraged it under the pretext of "democratic evolution".

Elections in 1953 and 1956

Pursuant to the 1952 reform the election of the various councils was held both in Ruanda and in Urundi in 1953. As could be expected, the Hutu constituted an insignificant minority of elected members everywhere, except in the sub-chiefdom councils, that is, at the lowest level. The results of the 1953 elections were as follows:

---

[1] Quoted from a Belgian government paper, *Memo from Belgium, Ruanda-Urundi*, published in September 1961.

| | Ruanda | | Urundi | |
	Tutsi	Hutu	Tutsi	Hutu
Chiefdom councils	613	79 (11.4%)	273	99 (26.6%)
District councils	185	19 (9.3%)	140	27 (19.3%)
High Councils of State	29	3 (9.4%)	26	4 (13.3%)

The Hutu obtained more seats only in the 5-to-9-member sub-chiefdom councils: they captured 1,995 seats (47.65%) out of 4,187 in Ruanda, and 2,285 seats (60.3%) out of 3,789 in Urundi.

As appears from the above figures, the difference between Tutsi and Hutu as well as the subjection of the Hutu was less pronounced and maybe less severe in Urundi than in Ruanda.

The next election of council members took place in 1956. A novelty on this occasion was that the members of the sub-chiefdom electoral colleges, instead of being put on a list prepared by the sub-chiefs, were elected by secret ballot by the entire adult population.

Nevertheless, this was no improvement towards democratization either, because traditional fear and subservience, despite the secrecy of the vote, compelled the backward Hutu farmers to vote for their Tutsi lords.

The 1956 elections in the trust territory brought the following results:

| | Ruanda | | Urundi | |
	Tutsi	Hutu	Tutsi	Hutu
Sub-chiefdom councils	1,895	2,261 (54.3%)	1,664	2,240 (57.4%)
Chiefdom councils	597	107 (15.2%)	301	85 (22.0%)
District councils	163	21 (11.4%)	120	20 (14.3%)
High Councils of State	31	1 (3.1%)	28	2 (6.7%)

Characteristic of the collusion between the colonialists and the Tutsi aristocracy was the delusive trick they played in 1954 on the UN Visiting Mission. The principal means for the Tutsi lords to oppress and exploit the Hutu poor peasants was the *ubuhake*, a contract by which the landless and cattleless Hutu undertook to do labour and other services to the Tutsi landlord in return for the use of land and cattle. At its meeting of March 1, 1954, in the presence of the members of the UN Visiting Mission, the High Council of Ruanda, at an initiative of the colonialists and upon a motion from the Mwami, decided to suppress the *ubuhake* system and distribute part of the cattle among the Hutu farmers, and later to terminate the land-use contracts and distribute the pastures. The colonial administration as well as the Mwami and the Tutsi presented this measure as a generous concession on the part of the Tutsi lords in favour of the Hutu masses. The fact is that about 200,000 head of cattle were distributed in the next four years, but this was of little use to the Hutu as long as they possessed no pasture and the promised land distribution failed to come. (A similar "reform" was introduced in 1955 in Urundi, too, where all in all 700 head of cattle were distributed.)

The Start of the Independence Movement (1956–57)

In April 1956 a European settler, ALBERT MAUS, a member of the Council of the Vice-Government-General of Ruanda-Urundi, proposed that the Hutu should receive separate representation in the Council. The Mwami opposed, claiming that there was no ground for distinguishing between "Tutsi" and "Hutu". MAUS's proposal was rejected unanimously by the Council. (He alone voted for it.) Then MAUS submitted his resignation in a letter to the Council, charging that the Mwami was a foe of democracy who opposed the proposal because he favoured the Tutsi and was aware that separate Hutu representation would precipitate the collapse of Tutsi domination. This went to say, wrote MAUS in conclusion, that "the conflict of interests between the Tutsi and Hutu communities, which is the most pressing social problem and the most poignant human drama in the Territory, will therefore continue to be officially ignored by our institutions . . ."

MAUS's prediction was vindicated by the events. In February 1957 the High Council of Ruanda issued a "statement of views", stressing that the accession of Ruanda to self-government should be realized through the full use of the African *élite*, and urged the training of an *élite* for participation in the management of public affairs. This conception was essentially aimed at the perpetuation of Tutsi domination and the continued exclusion of the Hutu from the state's affairs.

On March 26, 1957, a royal decree replaced the Council of the Vice-Government-General with a 45-member General Council. This comprised seven high officials of the colonial administration and the two kings of Ruanda and Urundi as ex-officio members, 32 members were appointed to it by the Governor, and four representatives of rural communities, two for Ruanda and two for Urundi, were chosen by the two High Councils of State from among their own members. There was no provision for the numerical ratio of European and non-European members, but a European majority was ensured, since the unofficial members were appointed by the Governor. (In 1957 the General Council consisted of 26 Europeans, 16 Africans and one Asian.) Like its predecessor, the new Council was no legislative assembly but an advisory body. It signified a step forward in so far as it included more African members. (Among the 22 members of the former Council of the Vice-Government-General there were only 5 Africans.)

Still in March 1957 a group of members of the High Council of State published a manifesto demanding democratization of the Mwami's regime and independence for Ruanda. A Hutu group then responded with another manifesto, demanding an end to Tutsi domination and democratic rights for the Hutu, and taking a stand in favour of the continuation of the trusteeship status.

Shortly after the publication of the Hutu manifesto, in June 1957, KAYIBANDA and MULINDAHABI started the Hutu Social Movement to give impetus to the Hutu manifesto, to combat Tutsi abuses and demand the democratization of institutions. When the High Council of Ruanda decided to banish the terms "Tutsi" and "Hutu" from official documents, the Hutu Social Movement objected, claiming that there was nothing hurtful about such racial descriptions, and that without such distinction it would be impossible to assess the true social advance of the country and the progress of the underprivileged majority of the population.

In November 1957 JOSEPH HABYARIMANA GITERA founded the *Association pour la Promotion Sociale de la Masse* (Aprosoma) and started a newspaper *(The Voice of the Common People)*, in which he made vehement attacks against the social system, the privileges of the Tutsi, and the court of the Mwami.

The 1958 Events

In January 1958 GITERA requested the Mwami to convene the High Council of Ruanda to study the problem of relations between the Hutu and the Tutsi. Mwami

Mutara III complied by establishing in April a special commission to study the problem and submit recommendations to the High Council.

Before the commission's report was taken up for consideration, Tutsi chiefs complained to the Mwami of alleged attacks made on them by Aprosoma supporters. Then a group of elderly Tutsi at the Mwami's court submitted a protest note to the Mwami and the High Council, demanding punishment for the supposed "troublemakers" who advocated the distribution of land. Later the same authors addressed a note to the members of the special commission, protesting against any revision of Hutu–Tutsi relations. They argued in their note that "the relations between the Tutsi and the Hutu have always hitherto been based on servitude, so that there is no foundation for brotherhood between us ... As our kings conquered the country of the Hutu and killed their petty kings, how can they now claim to be our brothers?"

In June the High Council considered the report of the special commission. The Hutu spokesmen in the commission requested equal rights and opportunities for the Hutu to hold public offices and for their children to have the same educational facilities as Tutsi children. The High Council evaded consideration of the request on the grounds that public appointments were subject to certain requirements which the Hutu did not meet, and that the insufficient education of Hutu children was the fault of the Belgian administration and the missions. The High Council admitted, though, that there was a need for social reforms, but asserted that its proposals had been ignored by the administration. The Mwami also evaded the issue by stressing that the Hutu-Tutsi problem was not a racial issue, it was a matter of social reforms, so that those who raised this problem were "dividers of the people, enemies of their country, and disturbers of public order".

The Tutsi accepted the views of the High Council and of the Mwami as being an expression of political wisdom and realism, but the Hutu interpreted them as meaning a negation of the problem. Their leaders stated their disappointment at the Mwami's attitude, whom they had expected to find a solution, and others said that from then onwards they regarded the very institution of kingdom as rejectable.

In the latter half of 1958 Mwami Mutara made a long visit to Belgium. His relations with the Belgian administration, excellent at the beginning but increasingly deteriorating in recent years, had utterly worsened by the end of 1958 — allegedly because of the cool reception he had been given during his visit to Belgium. It was rumoured that shortly after his return he had said: "There will not be a single European in Ruanda at the end of a year."

At the opening meeting of the General Council on December 2 the Governor of Ruanda-Urundi dealt at length with the Hutu–Tutsi problem. His speech was a typical example of sly circumlocution.. He said that the problem really existed but was not a problem of Tutsi and Hutu, it was rather a conflict between rich and poor. Large masses of the population lived in poverty and were politically, socially and economically oppressed by certain representatives of the local authorities. The latter were preponderantly Tutsi, while the poor were Hutu. This would not mean, however, that there was an oppressive Tutsi class and there were exploited, defenceless Hutu masses, but it meant that there was a peasant class insufficiently protected from the arbitrary actions of certain local representatives of authority who, because of circumstances and not by the nature of the political system, came for the most part from the ethnic group of the Tutsi. The Belgian administration hunted down abuses, no matter who committed them, but did not condemn the Tutsi as a whole.

The Governor said in this connection that 152 sub-chiefs had been removed from office between 1955 and 1957, but the administration was against appointing Hutu to replace systematically the removed Tutsi chiefs, judges, etc. Such a policy would rouse righteous indignation among a large and deserving segment of the population, because it would mean replacing one injustice by another. This would lead to a civil war, confirming the erroneous view that the problem was a racial one rather than a misuse of local authority. It could not be denied that the vast majority of the rich dominating groups were Tutsi, but the Hutu lacked adequate training, and so it was difficult to find a sufficient number of qualified persons among them. What should be done therefore was to improve the position of the Hutu, to reform the political structure, and to combat poverty.[1]

During the December session GITERA, as a member of the General Council, again requested discussion of the Hutu–Tutsi problem. But the Governor, recalling that he had dealt with it in his opening speech and reminding the Council that certain members were already preparing a report on the question, opposed consideration of the issue. So the question was not discussed during the session.

Towards the end of 1958 three Hutu members of the General Council and the European settler A. MAUS sent a report to the King of the Belgians, to the "Minister for the Congo and Ruanda-Urundi", and to the Governor-General. Later they sent it also to the 1959 Working Group and the 1960 Visiting Mission of the United Nations. The report dealt with the Hutu–Tutsi problem as one having two aspects. che first was that customary African authorities, who were for the most part Tutsi, committed abuses and that certain steps intended by the Belgian administration to improve the position of the Hutu peasants were turned against them. The second aspect of the problem was that the Hutu were politically, economically and culturally backward owing to Tutsi domination, which was growing stronger thanks to the Belgian administration, and that the gap between Tutsi wealth and Hutu poverty was steadily widening. The report proposed radical steps to resolve the problem: abolition of chiefdoms, constant supervision of the lower-level African authorities, separation of administrative and judicial powers, education of the Hutu masses in their rights, numerical parity between Tutsi and Hutu in the distribution of public positions, and similar radical reforms. The final conclusion of the report was this: "To avoid revolution, a revolution must be carried out. The Administration must not be faced with the dilemma of either supporting the oppressors in the name of public order or of supporting the revolt in the name of justice."

In February 1959 GITERA transformed Aprosoma, the social organization he had founded in 1957, into a political party. In a letter to the Belgian government, a copy of which was sent simultaneously to the United Nations, he requested that Ruanda-Urundi be granted independence before the introduction of the reforms demanded by the Hutu.

The 1959 Working Group

On April 16, 1959, the Belgian government set up a Working Group composed of government officials and politicians to study the problems of Ruanda-Urundi. The Working Group arrived in the territory on April 22 and stayed there for a month.

[1] However, on a later occasion, in a speech before the UN Visiting Mission on March 3, 1960, the Governor declared that he had changed his views expressed in his earlier statement and said: "The Tutsi–Hutu problem certainly had an economic basis but, as I had tried to emphasize, it also had a politico-social basis and the administration would have to take it into account".

Both the Tutsi and the Hutu stated their points of view in writing. Right on the day when the Working Group arrived, the Mwami called together the Tutsi leaders (chiefs, judges, etc.) to formulate their opinion. They demanded internal autonomy and democratic reforms, but stood by a hereditary constitutional monarchy and Tutsi overrule. Their document dealt primarily with the Hutu–Tutsi conflict which was coming to a head, in their view, because of inflammatory writings by Hutu politicians, GITERA in the first place. They alleged furthermore that the Catholic missionary press incited the ethnic groups against each other (obviously because they were against the subjection of the Hutu masses), and criticized the Belgian administration for its failure to intervene and to suppress the "incitements to racial hatred". The only Hutu representative at that meeting protested against the documents which quoted only writings by Hutu authors without mentioning the provocative and slanderous pamphlets of Tutsi writers, a proof that the documents represented one-sidedly the interests of the Tutsi overlords.

Partly the same position was expressed by the Commission on Political Reform, whose conclusions were approved by the High Council and submitted to the Working Group on April 28, 1959. This document proposed profound reforms (separation of legislative, executive and judicial powers, establishment of ministries, elective principle at lower levels, etc.), but it also did not affect the monarchical institution and Tutsi domination. It regarded the Hutu–Tutsi dispute as an outcome of misunderstanding, of instigating propaganda and of malicious statements, and put the blame on the passivity of the Belgian administration. In their conclusions, however, the authors of the document accused the customary Tutsi authorities of oppressing and exploiting the people, and did not propose autonomy for the Tutsi authorities but demanded stricter control by the Belgian administration over the customary Tutsi authorities, and the transfer of power to the people by gradually Africanizing the territory's government. For this end they proposed better facilities for broad masses of the people to learn and acquire political and professional qualifications, to hold public offices. They recommended the dismissal of traditional chiefs and appointed judges, the abolition of the non-elective chiefdom councils, and the introduction of universal suffrage at all levels.

The two Hutu groups, the Aprosoma party and the Hutu Social Movement, also stated their views to the Working Group. In their memorandum they attacked the Tutsi regime, blaming it for abuses and the exploitation of the people. They wanted the Belgian administration to retain and strengthen its control of the country for a long time to come. They advocated the gradual transfer of powers to the people through Africanization. They demanded the introduction of universal suffrage (also for the appointment of judges), the complete elimination of heads of chiefdoms who upheld the feudal system, access to education for all, and the right to hold public positions for those who had the necessary qualifications.

The Working Group left the territory at the end of May. After its departure the Tutsi distributed anonymous leaflets vilifying Aprosoma and the Hutu leader, especially GITERA, whom they branded as traitors, as enemies of Ruanda, of the Mwami and of independence, and whom they threatened to destroy.

In June, simultaneously with the propagation of those leaflets, it was rumoured throughout the country that the epidemic spread of the tsetse fly and certain cattle diseases had been caused by the Belgians. Having given up his hostile position adopted with regard to Belgium at the end of the preceding year, the Mwami again took a course for co-operation with the Belgian authorities, and in order to regain the confidence of the colonial administration, he vehemently refuted those rumours at public meetings.

Events Following the Mwami's Death

On July 25, 1959, the Mwami of Ruanda, CHARLES MUTARA, died of cerebral hemorrhage. The rumour went among the Africans that he had been poisoned by Europeans, and this created unrest in the country and led even to riots in some places. In the absence of a direct descendant of the Mwami, the Tutsi leaders were afraid that the Hutu might proclaim the republic. Therefore they dispatched armed troops to attend the funeral. Under the protection of the troops, and without consulting the people, they proclaimed the late Mwami's brother, KIGELI NDAHIN-DURWA, to succeed him.

On September 3, 1959, supporters of the Tutsi government formed a political party, the *Union Nationale Ruandaise* (UNAR), under the chairmanship of FRANÇOIS RUKEBA, a businessman at Kigali.

The new party held its first public meeting on September 13. The meeting, at which the main speaker was RUKEBA, was attended by about 2,000 people.

RUKEBA and nine more speakers, chiefs for the most part, assured the new Mwami, KIGELI V, of their loyalty and criticized his enemies. They also vehemently attacked the Belgian administration and the missions which they accused of having divided the country and its people. The party appealed to all Ruandese to unite, expressing the hope that its programme would ensure a sweeping election victory which would make UNAR the single political party, all-powerful in the country.

The speeches were made public in French translation, but the opponents said it all was falsified, that the passages attacking the Belgians and all foreigners in general and the Ruandese of differing views had been omitted.

UNAR leaders denied that such statements had been made at the meeting, although the audience was impressed by the unusually strong language the speakers used against the Belgian administration.

RUKEBA first had set out his party's programme in a manifesto at the meeting. The documents called for the union of all Ruandese "without ethnic, social or religious distinction", enumerating in a demagogical manner all the demands the fulfilment of which was a dream of all Africans desirous of freedom and independence: internal autonomy by 1960, independence by 1962, a constitutional monarchy with responsible ministers, universal suffrage for the election of legislative organs, separation of the executive and judicial powers, an economic and social programme, revision of the agreement with the missions, democratic educational reforms on a nationwide basis, elimination of racial discrimination between "white" and "black" and between the Ruandese tribes, maintenance of peace and order based on non-violence.

UNAR held two more meetings in September, one at Astrida on the 20th and another at Gitarama on the 27th. A numerous group of Aprosoma supporters showed up at the Astrida meeting and staged a vocal counter-demonstration against the UNAR leaders.

On September 14 progressive Tutsi intellectuals (mostly young government officials and other employees) founded a new party, the *Rassemblement Démocratique Ruandais* (RADER). This party was in reality established under the auspices of the Belgian administration to counteract the existing parties (Aprosoma and UNAR). This was to be seen from the party's programme which, just like UNAR, was not sparing of promises (constitutional monarchy, "establishment of a social, economic and cultural order", authentic democracy "in harmonious relationship" with the various groupings of the Ruandese people, the election by universal suffrage of chiefs, sub-chiefs and councillors, land reform, etc.), but it revealed at the same time that the party was practically promoting the interests of the colonialists when it demanded internal autonomy only by 1964 and independence by 1968, affirming its "friendly feelings" towards Belgium and pledging its full support to "the spreading of the Gospel" in Ruanda.

The growing activity of the parties prompted the two Catholic bishops of Ruanda to send circular letters to all Catholic priests in the territory.

In the first circular, dated September 24, 1959, they strongly attacked UNAR, which they described as being akin to fascism and displaying pro-Communist and pro-Islamic influences. This apparent contradiction was resolved by the authors themselves in their letter, stating frankly that their biting criticism was not directed against the political views and demands of the party but was provoked by the fact that UNAR wanted the schools removed from mission influence and put in the care of public authorities.

Their second letter, dated October 11, accused Aprosoma of incitement to racial hatred. Therefore the bishops, to prove their "impartiality and neutrality", later (in April 1960) submitted the circulars to the UN Visiting Mission.

On October 9 Mwami KIGELI V was sworn in at Kigali in the presence of the Belgian Governor of Ruanda-Urundi. The same day saw the birth of a party sharply opposed to both Tutsi parties, the *Parti du Mouvement de l'Emancipation Hutu* (Parmehutu), which developed from the Hutu Social Movement under the leadership of GRÉGOIRE KAYIBANDA, and which differed from all other parties in that it had local branches (cells) established all over the country. In its manifesto the party called for an end to the feudal regime and the Tutsi hegemony. It accepted the constitutional monarchy and the Mwami as head of state, but demanded the separation of the legislative and executive powers, an end to the abuses of the ruling classes, the recognition of individual landed property, and the access of the Hutu to education at all levels. It stressed that Ruanda could not attain independence until it had been democratized.

By the early days of October the situation had come to a head. The activities of the parties and their rivalries often resulted in violent incidents. False rumours were circulated again. It was rumoured, for example, that vaccinations caused sterility. Of course, this was a serious setback to the anti-tuberculosis programme. To the tension was added the excitement with which the people looked forward to the Belgian government's statement based on the report of the Working Group.[1]

The Belgian Governor tried to prevent the further aggravation of the tense situation by issuing on October 10 an order prohibiting all political meetings.

On October 14, leaders of the Hutu parties of Ruanda (together with some advanced Hutu of Urundi) wrote a letter to the Belgian Minister for the Congo and Ruanda-Urundi. They gave expression to their fear that the internal autonomy under consideration for Ruanda would in practice mean a return to the despotic rule of the Tutsi. They protested against the formation of anti-democratic and reactionary parties like UNAR, which were supported by the Tutsi authorities, and whose demagogical propaganda was misleading or intimidating the ignorant Hutu masses with a view to winning their votes at the elections. They requested the Belgian

---

[1] The Working Group submitted its report three months after schedule, on September 20.

government "not to terminate its trusteeship until the Hutu people were sufficiently emancipated to be able to defend their rights effectively".

During the entire month of October acts of terrorism and violence were organized by UNAR against those Tutsi leaders who had not joined the party, as well as against members and sympathizers of RADER, and against Hutu leaders, among them those of the Aprosoma party. The assaulters beat up their victims, often even killed them or threatened their lives, destroyed their farms, pillaged their shops, slew or mutilated their cattle, damaged their vehicles, etc. The attacks were intended to lure into UNAR those who hesitated and to frighten the members of opposing parties into joining UNAR. The campaign of terror brought results: to avoid being attacked, almost all members and supporters of RADER went over to the UNAR camp.

In excuse of its actions UNAR levelled charges against the Hutu parties, asserting that they organized attacks on the Tutsi lords and the monarchy, allegedly with the support of some colonial officials and missionaries. Of course, the Hutu counter-actions provoked by the Tutsi terror were inevitable, but the campaign of terror was undoubtedly organized and directed by the Tutsi leaders of UNAR.

On October 25 an anonymous leaflet was posted on trees in the Nyanza district. It listed the names of ten RADER and Hutu leaders, charging them with plotting to kill the Mwami and overthrow the monarchy in Ruanda, to keep the people in slavery under the Belgians. It called upon the people to unite their forces and exterminate "these snakes, the enemies of Ruanda", and their offspring.

On October 27 a RADER delegation handed the Governor and the Mwami a memorandum entitled "Grave political situation in Ruanda: Terrorism". After citing various cases of attacks against people and property, they charged that the passivity of the authorities encouraged the terrorist campaign, and they warned the administration that in case they would not be given protection against such attacks, they would have to resort to violence, too.

In a letter of October 29 addressed to the UN Trusteeship Council, UNAR asserted that the Belgian administration utilized the Hutu–Tutsi problem to delay the emancipation of Ruanda, and complained that the local authorities impeded the UNAR activities.

In a letter of November 3 to the Belgian Governor, the UNAR leaders protested against the allegations that they were responsible for the incidents, and stated that the accusation was part of a systematic campaign of slander against their party.

The tension was further aggravated when, more than a month after the Kigali meeting of UNAR, the administration removed and transferred to less important posts in distant places three reputed and very popular chiefs, KAYIHURA, MUNGA-LULIRE and RWANGOMBWA. This action was intended to be a disciplinary measure to punish them for having participated at the Kigali meeting and having endorsed by their presence the attacks on the Belgian administration. At the same time the administration published a circular letter stating that the chiefs and other customary tribal authorities were not prohibited from joining a political party as private persons, but in the exercise of their functions they were not permitted to engage in propaganda against the Belgian administration nor to join a party whose programme tended to discredit the administration.

On October 15 the three chiefs wrote a letter to the Governor, in which they protested against the charges made against them, and they accused the local administrative authorities of bias and illegal action against them. They stated that they would give up their career rather than abjure their political views. They ended their letter by saying: "If you do not provide a remedy, this policy may lead to a disastrous breach, resulting in a stinging defeat for Belgian policy in Ruanda."

On October 16 the Mwami KIGELI addressed a note to the Governor, declaring that the transfer of the three chiefs was illegal, that any attack on them was an attack on the Mwami himself, and that under the circumstances the period of mourning, which lasted from the death of the preceding Mwami till the enthronement of the new king, would continue, and the enthronement festivities would not take place until law and order had been restored in the country. He stated that he was bound to let public opinion know the reasons for the abnormal situation.

The Governor invited the three chiefs to see him at Kigali on October 17. The meeting, however, was disturbed by a mass demonstration. Despite the ban on public gatherings hundreds of people assembled around the Governor's residence and cheered the deposed chiefs, demanding an abrogation of their transfer. The Governor received a delegation of four demonstrators, and told the chiefs that he had not accepted their resignation but would give them eight days to think it over. But the crowd continued demonstrating, and the police used tear-gas bombs and hand grenades to disperse the people. One demonstrator was killed and four were wounded. Similar demonstrations took place in a number of places in the chiefs' own districts.

On October 24 the Governor again conferred with the three chiefs, after taking security measures this time to avoid incidents. He maintained his decision, but they came to an agreement that the chiefs would postpone taking over their new posts until the current negotiations with the Mwami were ended. In the meantime the sub-chiefs of MICHEL KAYIHURA's chiefdom had submitted a collective resignation.

After October 24 the customary authorities continued their efforts to persuade the Belgian administration to withdraw the disciplinary measure, and the Mwami again wrote a note to the Governor. The latter was adamant but agreed to withhold the appointment of new candidates to the three "vacant" chiefdoms until the publication of the government statement in preparation.

The case of the chiefs who chose to go into voluntary exile preluded a break between UNAR and the Belgian authorities and greatly contributed to the aggravation of the situation.

The Disturbances of November 1959

In November 1959 bloody riots occurred in Ruanda. The commission of inquiry set up by the Belgian government and, relying mainly on information provided by that commission, the UN Visiting Mission that went to Ruanda in the spring of 1960 presented world public opinion with a completely false and distorted picture of those events. Their reports stated that the disturbances had been started by the Hutu, who attacked the Tutsi and went on pillaging and killing, whereupon the Tutsi reacted by way of "self-defence", and many Hutu were killed in the fighting that ensued. The Mwami tried in vain to stop the incidents, the fighting was brought to an end by the Belgian police and troops. Afterwards large numbers of the Tutsi, for fear of revenge from the Hutu masses, chose to flee to neighbouring countries. The Belgian administration was said to have been careful with the use of force and to have displayed moderation in treating the rioters and handling the affairs of the refugees.

The facts, however, as can be seen also from the above-mentioned two reports, speak differently.

The allegation that the Hutu started the incidents does not square with the facts. True, the UN Visiting Mission says that "From 6 November onwards, the Tutsi leaders took a series of counter-measures to stop the revolt of the Hutu", but the fact is — and this appears also from the UN report (par. 198–199) — that the Hutu actions were first started by the Tutsi provocations of November 1 and 3.

On November 1 a band of young Tutsi in the Gitarama district attacked a Hutu sub-chief, DOMINIQUE MBONYOMUTWA, a leader of Parmehutu. This caused great agitation among the local Hutu population. The next day the Hutu staged a demonstration against UNAR. On November 3 the false rumour was spread that MBONYOMUTWA had died. UNAR alleged that he himself had launched the false rumour of his death. The Hutu sub-chief strongly denied this, pointing out that Hutu indignation over the attack made on him was all the more understandable as UNAR leaders since October 29 had been spreading the rumour that he and other Hutu leaders would not live to see the end of the week because they would be killed. On November 3 the Hutu again assembled to demonstrate in front of the house of the local Tutsi chief, GASHAGAZA. Owing to Tutsi provocation, this quiet demonstration ended in an attack on the chief's house and caused the death of two Tutsi.

What could have been described as "counter-measures" were therefore not the Tutsi actions but what the Hutu did in response to them. The disturbances were started by the Tutsi, not by the Hutu. The Tutsi themselves provided the direct cause for the Hutu revolt. But the real causes of the events did not lie in those provocations. The Hutu were stirred to action by the bitterness which had accumulated in them over the centuries because of the Tutsi terror and tyranny, looting and violence, because of endless poverty and suffering. The violent action of the Tutsi, on the other hand, was motivated by the danger of losing their privileged position, a danger which they wanted to prevent by exterminating the Hutu leaders and terrorizing the Hutu masses.

If we wish to get a true picture of the events, we must not leave out of consideration the essential differences between the Hutu and Tutsi actions.

It is a fact that the Hutu masses in their despair resorted to violence, they pillaged and set fire to huts, but they did it with no intention of killing. It is stated in the UN report (par. 203): " . . . the incendiaries, who were often unarmed, did not attack the inhabitants of the huts and were content with pillaging and setting fire to them. The most serious incidents involving tragic wounding and death occurred when the Tutsi were determined to fight back, or when there were clashes with the forces of order." The Hutu did not intend to exterminate the Tutsi, all they wanted was to do away with their privileges and dominant position. The Tutsi, on the other hand, started an organized campaign of deliberate genocide against the Hutu population, and it was not their fault if they failed.

To illustrate the methods of the Tutsi massacre, let us quote from the relevant part of the report of the UN Visiting Mission (par. 208): "From 6 to 10 November 1959, a number of commando raids were organized to arrest or kill certain Hutu leaders. On 6 November, Secyugu, a Hutu trader known to be a supporter of PARMEHUTU, was attacked and killed in his house near Nyanza by an armed band led by the Twa Chief Rwevu. During the two succeeding days a number of other Hutu, among them Nsokana, Habarugera, Barekeraho, Tirizibwami, Gatabazi, Nebuzishi, Ntagobwa and Callixte Kabayisa were assassinated in similar circumstances in the Nyanza and Gitarama districts. On 8 November, the riots spread to the Astrida district, where a councillor of APROSOMA, Innocent Mukwiye Polepole, was attacked and killed, while in the Nyanza district several other Hutu leaders were killed, including 'monitors' Sindibona and Munyandekwa. On 10 November, the same fate befell Joseph Kanyaruka, secretary and treasurer of APROSOMA, who had fled the day before with his family and livestock to take refuge with a relative, Elias Renhazo, residing in Urundi near the Ruanda boundary. An armed band, raised in the chiefdom on the borders of Ruanda, crossed the boundary and after encircling the house where Kanyaruka had taken refuge, killed him and his relative Renhazo with spears."

And further on (par. 211): "The Tutsi attacks were fairly clearly a series of organized actions. At the very beginning of the disturbances, the customary authorities had collected armed troops totalling several thousand men ... The majority of commando groups which took part in the attacks against the Hutu were formed of those armed troops ... The group would set off in mission with very definite instructions. In other cases, emissaries were sent out from Nyanza with verbal orders instructing them to bring back or kill certain persons, and permitting them to appeal to local authorities for armed forces to be assembled on the spot to help them in their mission. It seems to be an established fact, moreover, that in many cases a commando group set out with orders only to arrest a person, but in effect killed him, either because he resisted arrest or because some attackers had the instinct to kill."

That the Tutsi actions had been motivated by political considerations was stated later by the Belgian Resident-General in his speech of March 3, 1960. He explained that the UNAR leaders apparently had seized the occasion to intimidate the masses by striking actions and paralyzing the anti-UNAR movements and depriving them of their most prominent representatives and spokesmen. (UNAR Chairman RUKEBA and Vice-Chairman KAYIHURA were tried by court-martial and sentenced to six and nine years' imprisonment, respectively, for having organized assassinations.)

The allegation that the Mwami tried to stop the revolt is also false. Indeed, the Mwami tried to intervene — in defence of the Tutsi lords, against the Hutu. He did his utmost to crush the anti-Tutsi actions, but he did nothing to prevent the Tutsi atrocities. On November 5 he issued a proclamation condemning the riots, no matter which tribe had started them, and affirming that he was the Mwami of all nationals of Ruanda without distinction. On the same day he had a talk with the Governor, to whom he said that the Belgian authorities had failed to take appropriate steps to protect the Tutsi and their property against the Hutu attacks. He demanded permission for himself and his (Tutsi) chiefs to take the measures necessary to maintain law and order. Since the Governor refused this permission, on November 6 the Mwami addressed a telegram simultaneously to the King of the Belgians, the Belgian Parliament and the Governor and repeated the same demands. The Governor again rejected the demand and placed the entire country in a state of "military operation". Thereafter, on November 9, a joint proclamation of the Mwami and the Governor appealed to the population to stop the fratricidal struggle. The actual attitude of the Mwami clearly contradicted these sanctimonious pronouncements. As we have seen above, right at the outset of the disturbances, under the pretext of protecting the Mwami the Tutsi chiefs assembled several thousand armed men around the Mwami's residence, which continued to serve as Tutsi headquarters. The Tutsi sent out their commando groups from there and they took there the Hutu captives (who were said to have been horribly tortured) — all this under the wings of the Mwami who together with UNAR leaders actively participated in the direction of the vicious actions against the Hutu.

As far as the local Belgian authorities are concerned, they used all the police force and troops available to them (troops were called also from the Congo and even Belgium), to curb the perpetrators of the atrocities, whether Hutu or Tutsi, but in calling them to account as well as in handling the affairs of refugees they were clearly biased in favour of the Tutsi.

The riots were not yet over when the colonial administration's Legislative Order No. 081/225 of November 12, 1959, proclaimed martial law and made all persons subject to the jurisdiction of the Military Court whose decisions were unappealable, except in cases of death penalty.

The Military Court passed sentences on 1,238 persons. About 85 per cent of these cases involved pillaging and arson, the remainder were murder cases. The defendants, with few exceptions, were all Hutu, since more than twenty thousand Tutsi, including first of all the leaders and active participants of the Tutsi actions, avoided prosecution by fleeing to remote places of the country or abroad (Urundi or the Congo). The resettlement of these refugees was organized, in the words of the UN Visiting Mission, "at great cost and with much care" by the Belgian administration, but not in order to bring them to trial. Temporary refugee camps were constructed for them where they received food, blankets, medical care, and special assistance in building homes in new settlement zones, recovering their livestock, and getting compensation of the damage they had suffered owing to the loss of their land, produce and other assets. In brief, while the starving Hutu poor peasants were imprisoned for having revolted, the resettlement and rehabilitation of the Tutsi lords and killers were organized "with much care".

A detailed chronology of the events, of the Hutu and Tutsi actions, would seem needless here, since no objective information is available, and the official records of the Belgian authorities or the relevant data supplied by the UN Visiting Mission's report can hardly be credited. (See par. 194 to 222 of the report.)

According to official records about two hundred persons were killed and 317 wounded. These figures are also unreliable, because the Africans, whenever they could, carried off their dead and buried them silently, behind the back of the authorities, and the published figures covered only those who were treated in hospitals.

The Belgian Government Statement of November 10, 1959, and the Subsequent Reforms

The Working Group established by the Belgian government in April submitted its report on September 2, 1959. It stressed the necessity of radical political and administrative reforms and made concrete recommendations. The report was made public on September 10, simultaneously with the Belgian government statement explaining the proposed reforms. The Belgian government accepted practically all recommendations of the Working Group, except one: while the Working Group deemed it absolutely necessary for Ruanda-Urundi to follow the road towards autonomy as a unitary state, the Belgian government, although it had repeatedly expressed the conviction that the unity of the two territories was essential, did not wish to commit itself to this course of action, but proposed their unification for some time in the future. The government statement was in fact nothing else but an official reiteration of the recommendations of the Working Group. The main points of the proposed reforms were the following.

The chiefs would cease to exercise political powers. The chiefdoms would be changed to administrative *circonscriptions*, and the chiefs would become officials of the general administration.

The sub-chiefdoms and the extra-tribal centres would be reintegrated as communes into the administration of the country and constitute the only basic decentralized political entities below the national level. The organs of these communes would be a mayor and a communal council. Until they were created in their final form, the existing sub-chiefdoms, extra-tribal centres and urban *circonscriptions* would become provisional communes which would elect their councils during the first half of 1960. These councils would elect the head of the provisional commune.

At the state level the legislative powers would be exercised temporarily, until a system better suited to the wishes of the people was adopted, jointly by a new state council and the Mwami. The great majority of the members of the state council would be elected by an electoral college composed of the councils of the provisional communes. These elections should take place early enough for the state council to begin functioning in the second half of 1960.

Beside the legislature of each state a government would be formed whose members (its head and the departmental heads) would be appointed or removed from office by the Mwami in agreement with the Belgian Resident.

As constitutional head of the state, the Mwami would remain outside the government and above the parties. He would not govern, and his public enactments should be countersigned by the government.

An important measure provided for the rapid fusion of the tribal administration and the general (trusteeship) administration, the result being that a number of responsible offices would be taken over by Africans.

At the time the government statement was issued, the riots in Ruanda were still in full swing, and so the reforms were of no actual interest.

When law and order had been restored by and large in the country, the Belgian government issued decrees and ordinances on the implementation of the reforms outlined in the statement of November 10.

The interim decree of December 25, 1959, described the organs of the provisional communes, the interim chiefdoms and the two states, laid down the principles for the election of the members of the different councils, and defined the trusteeship to be exercised by Belgium over the administration of the territory.

The royal interim order of January 25, 1960, prepared the fusion of the tribal administration and the colonial administration. It provided that the Residencies of Ruanda and Urundi should be replaced by states of the same name, and that the Resident-General of the trust territory should transfer to the respective governments such powers of the two Residents and of the Vice-Governor-General as were only of regional interest.

Ordinance No. 221/51 of February 6, 1960, provided that the High Council of Ruanda and its permanent delegation to the General Council should be dissolved, and that the powers of those bodies should be transferred to a "provisional special council" composed of six members appointed by the Resident-General. The membership was later raised to eight, thus permitting each of the four principal parties to have two representatives on it.

On February 15, 1960, in view of the approaching date of the Congo's accession to independence, the Belgian government decreed the decentralization of the trust territory to the state level. The Governor of Ruanda-Urundi, who thus far had resided in Léopoldville, moved to Usumbura and placed the administration under the authority of a "secretary-general".

Ordinance No. 221/73 of March 10 provided that the communal elections should be held after June 7, 1960, the precise date being determined by the local administration.

On February 26 the Belgian government submitted a proposal to the UN Trusteeship Council that a UN observer group be sent to supervise the communal elections to be held in June.

After the Disturbances

During and after the disturbances altogether 1,143 persons were arrested. The Military Court dealt with 207 cases, and by March 30, 1960, it had decided 135 cases involving 1,013 defendants. About 85 per cent of the cases involved pillaging and arson, the remainder were killings. Two death sentences were pronounced. Characteristically, the Court always used two interpreters, one Hutu and one Tutsi, and had the interpretations supervised by a European. A number of UNAR leaders fled to Tanganyika or Uganda to avoid persecution, some of them were sentenced *in absentia*. After the disturbances the Military Resident invested with emergency powers placed several persons under a system of prescribed residence. By March 22 such restrictions had been imposed on 42 people.

During the disturbances more than 5,000 dwellings were burned. More than 7,000 unsheltered people (almost all were Tutsi) found refuge with missions and in administrative buildings. The number of refugees was growing. The Belgian authorities tried to help the mass of refugees to return home or resettle in new areas. But these efforts brought little result. Part of the Tutsi refugees refused to go to camps or elsewhere, they demanded to be re-established in their own lands. Their parties, RADER in the first place, demanded also that those who had ousted them should be punished and obliged to pay damages. The Hutu, on the other hand, opposed the re-establishment of the Tutsi and argued that by ousting them and seizing their property they had only recovered what the Tutsi had taken from them by force in the past. Also they threatened more violence in case the Tutsi were allowed to return.

The situation was complicated by the fact that the Tutsi chiefs made the refugee problem a political issue and sabotaged the government actions in the hope of exploiting the case politically. Another trouble was that armed fighting between Hutu and Tutsi had been again frequent occurrence over several months. According to the Belgian administration's report submitted at the request of the UN Visiting Mission the number of refugees (concentrated in camps or scattered all over the country) was about 22,000 at that time.

During the riots the Hutu, particularly in the north and north-west of the country, chased away many Tutsi chiefs and sub-chiefs. And the attacks made against the Hutu were joined in by a good number of Tutsi chiefs, who were then killed in the clashes with the security forces or sent to prison, while others were removed from office by the administration, and again others resigned voluntarily in view of the opposition of the Hutu population. The Belgian administration filled the vacant posts provisionally by appointing Hutu by preference to replace the Tutsi. The related changes in the distribution of chiefdoms and sub-chiefdoms between Tutsi and Hutu after the events were summed up by the report of the UN Visiting Mission (par. 236) as follows:

	1 November 1959	1 March 1960
Total number of chiefdoms	45	45
Vacant chiefdoms	2	1
Tutsi chiefs	43	22
Hutu chiefs	—	22
Total number of sub-chiefdoms	559	531*
Vacant sub-chiefdoms	—	17
Tutsi sub-chiefs	549	217
Hutu sub-chiefs	10	297

* Twenty-eight sub-chiefdoms disappeared when they were merged in November with neighbouring sub-chiefdoms.

As the Resident-General stated in his speech, these replacements were made necessary by the agitated mood of the Hutu majority. They were only temporary measures, and as soon as the situation permitted, the final appointments would be decided by the population in the next elections.

Mass arrests began on November 14, 1959, when the disturbances were already over. This again led to scattered incidents in the next few days, whereupon the Military Resident prohibited all private and public meetings. Towards the end of November order was restored so that two companies of parachutists were withdrawn from the territory, and in early December the curfew was lifted and the ban on gatherings removed.

King BAUDOUIN, who was staying in the Congo at that time, went to Ruanda-Urundi on December 19, 1959. At the airport of Usumbura he was welcomed by the Governor of the trust territory (the Vice-Governor-General of the Congo), the two Mwami and a group of Tutsi chiefs. The King, who was lodged at the Governor's residence, went sightseeing incognito and then had talks with leaders of the political parties, representatives of ex-servicemen and a delegation of the Chamber of Commerce. The next day, after conferring with the two Mwami, the King flew back to the Congo.

During December new incidents occurred between Tutsi and Hutu, causing large numbers of Tutsi to flee to Uganda. In the middle of the month, for example, Ankole reported the arrival of 800 Tutsi refugees with 4,000 head of cattle.

At the end of December the Belgian government appointed a commission to inquire into the November riots. The commission, which was composed of three trusted Belgian personalities (an honorary provincial governor, a professor of university, and a lawyer), visited Ruanda from January 7 to 17, 1960. On February 26 it submitted its report, which on February 29 was communicated also to the next UN Visiting Mission then staying in Brussels on its way to Africa.

Armed clashes between Tutsi and Hutu flared up time and again. An AFP report dated from Usumbura on April 2 was about a series of skirmishes in the Gabiro district which had taken a toll of dozens of lives. Another report by the same new agency, dated April 16, said that a large band of Tutsi had carried out a "terrorist raid", killing two Africans and a European, and causing serious injuries to an African and a European.

The 1960 UN Visiting Mission

The UN Mission visited Ruanda from March 2 to April 1. On its way to Africa it stopped at Brussels on February 29, and the Belgian government informed the members of the Mission that it would make a formal request to the UN Trusteeship

Council to send an observer group to supervise the elections to be held in the trust territory during that year.

During the Visiting Mission's stay in Ruanda the political parties organized mass demonstrations clamouring for democracy and independence.

In the first half of March, while the Mission was touring the country, several violent incidents took place. Between March 9 and 12 the Hutu made successive attacks on Tutsi villages in the district of Biumba. More than a thousand huts were burned, and about 700 Tutsi families fled to seek refuge with Catholic missions or went elsewhere. On March 13 the UN Mission leaving Kabgayi for Kigali was greeted by nearly 30,000 Hutu gathered on the roadside. In other places along the road various groups, some of them supporting Parmehutu and others UNAR, stopped and greeted the Mission's convoy. The demonstrators threw letters, leaflets and placards into the vehicles. In a place the gendarmes patrolling the road were assailed with stones by some 300 demonstrating people, and, trying in vain to disperse them with tear-gas grenades, they fired into the crowd. Two women were killed and two men wounded, several gendarmes suffered injuries. In another place, near the village of Runda, a group of 500 people attacked the district administrator of Gitarama and his staff on their way back after parting from the Mission's convoy. The administrator's men used their firearms and wounded eight people, one of them fatally.

Being apprised of the incidents, the Mission first talked with the Belgian Special Resident and then made an appeal to the people of Ruanda to remain calm and help to maintain law and order. It called an emergency meeting for the following day, March 15, with the participation of representatives of the Belgian authorities, the Mwami and leaders of the political parties. The chairman of the Mission at this meeting called upon the political leaders to renounce the use of violence and provocation, to make their supporters observe law and order and co-operate with the authorities. The Mission managed to have the leaders of the political parties sign a joint communiqué drawn up in this spirit, which was then countersigned also by the chairman of the UN Mission, the Mwami, representatives of the Belgian administration and the African members of the special council. This was the first time that a formal agreement was reached between the political leaders, the Mwami and the Belgian administration.

In the second half of March the Mission continued its tour of the two countries of the trust territory. In several places (Kisenyi, Kitega, Usumbura, etc.) it had further discussions with Belgian officials (thus with the Resident-General in Kitega on March 24, and with Minister SCHEYVEN, who was in the territory at the time, in Usumbura on March 27), with the two Mwami and representatives of the opposing parties of the two countries, with several chiefs and private persons. During these conversations demonstrating groups from different parties were around almost everywhere. They all clamoured for democracy and independence, voicing the demands of their respective parties, distributing leaflets and submitting memorandums to the Mission. It came also to minor incidents, it happened even that the police had to step in to check or disperse the people, but no serious clashes took place.

Before leaving the territory, on March 31, the UN Mission released a communiqué, and after its return to New York it prepared a voluminous report which it submitted to the United Nations on June 2.[1]

---

[1] *United Nations Visiting Mission to Trust Territories in East Africa, 1960: Report on Ruanda-Urundi* (T/1551).

Both the communiqué and the conclusions and recommendations of the report clearly demonstrate that—

(a) the Mission was not unprejudiced, it was partial towards the Belgian administration, praised its policies and even deferred to it as far as it could; in the introduction of its report it expressed its thanks to RAYMOND SCHEYVEN, Minister for Economic and Financial Affairs of the Belgian Congo and Ruanda-Urundi, and to other high colonial officials for their "cordial co-operation . . . in assisting the Territory";

(b) on the most essential points the Mission was mistaken in its judgement of the situation in Ruanda and the positions taken by the African parties;[1]

(c) it saw the future political evolution of the territory with undue optimism.[2]

That the Mission's report is a slipshod and clumsy job can be clearly seen from its conclusions and recommendations summed up under the sub-title "Sequel to the November disturbances in Ruanda".[3]

To resolve the refugee problem the Mission proposed that "efforts should be made, as far as possible, to reintegrate refugees in their region of origin" (a scheme which the Belgian administration had started before the arrival of the UN Mission and which had been in progress for months), and it added: "The Mission fully realizes that the success of such an undertaking depends essentially on the co-operation of the local Hutu populations and of the Tutsi refugees themselves. It hopes that the laders of all the political parties will co-operate fully with the territorial authorities in order to facilitate the reintegration of refugees" (par. 467).

About filling the vacant chiefdoms the report stated: " . . . the replacement of Tutsi chiefs and sub-chiefs by Hutu had caused bitterness among the Tutsi and consequently had not helped to diminish antagonism between the two races" (par. 468). Considering, however, that "the Resident-General . . . gave the Mission the assurance that the Administration would act extremely prudently in that field and would not proceed with new replacements except when absolutely necessary", the Mission "hopes that, with the introduction of the elective principle, the problem of provisional authorities will disappear" (par. 468).

---

[1] " . . . there are very clear indications that the majority of Africans of the two territories, especially among the educated classes and leaders of political parties, wish to maintain more or less close relations between Ruanda and Urundi . . ." (par. 412). " . . . The Mission is confident that the Ruandese and Urundian leaders will be able to find an area of agreement concerning future co-operation and association between them . . . there is little doubt that in the long run the interest of Ruanda and Urundi would be better served by any arrangement which would avoid splitting up the Trust Territory into smaller units" (par. 413). " . . . on many principles the parties appear to agree, or at least their differences in policy do not appear to be fundamental" (par. 439). " . . . There does not appear to be any fundamental opposition to a constitutional monarchy. . . . the opposing [Hutu and Tutsi] sides have a great distrust of the good faith of their adversary [and of the Administration]. . . . it seems that the general population, often misled by false rumours and with little idea of the real situation, is easily excited to violence" (par. 440).

[2] "The Mission hopes that the new plan of action which has been drawn up by the Belgian Government . . . will pave the way for a national reconciliation in Ruanda and a relaxation of tension in Urundi" (par. 458). As regards the Africanization of the civil service, the Mission believed that the measures (being prepared by the Belgian administration, but being far from satisfactory) "will enable the best qualified persons from lower categories to secure appointment to higher posts" (par. 429).

[3] " . . . the Mission believes it will be useful to review briefly a number of the problems arising from the November 1959 disturbances, the solution of which, whether by means of a round-table conference or other forms of negotiation or decision, is essential for the country's future peaceful development" (par. 466).

As concerns the Special Resident invested with emergency powers, the Mission expressed the belief that "any unnecessary continuation" of those extraordinary powers "will in the long run not be conducive to reducing the political tension now reigning in the country . . . For these reasons, the Mission sincerely hopes that the Administration will examine the possibility of ending the emergency régime as rapidly as possible" (par. 469).

The report talked about "national reconciliation which is essential for the execution of the reforms that are envisaged" and broached the idea of amnesty measures that might lead to such reconciliation. "The Mission feels that it is politically highly desirable to adopt as soon as possible amnesty measures with regard to the events of November since it is convinced that without them national reconciliation will be difficult" (par. 470). After stating this the report mentioned the administration's fears of the granting of amnesty (the dangers ensuing from the return of Tutsi leaders involved in the disturbances), and pointed out that UNAR leaders, whom the Mission had met in Tanganyika, requested an opportunity to return home and reintegrate into the normal political life of the country. The Mission itself was in support of this request, revealing its secret sympathies towards UNAR: "The Mission wishes to emphasize the desirability of reintegrating the UNAR leaders into the normal political life of the country, especially as UNAR is accepted by many as the nationalist party of Ruanda" (par. 472).

Most characteristic of the ineffectiveness of the Mission's entire activity is the last paragraph of the chapter "Conclusions and recommendations" in its report (par. 473):

"There are other important problems such as the Ruanda monarchy, the form of the future democratic institutions and the welfare of the peasant masses, upon which the Mission had not commented in detail. It feels that what is the most important is not so much the ideal solutions to these problems as the need to reach agreement on certain basic measures which will be in accordance with the wishes of the majority, which will be as far as possible acceptable to the whole population, and which will be directed towards the establishment of institutions through which the people can peacefully and constitutionally pursue their political, economic and social objectives. The Mission is confident that, once these institutions have been established, the people of Ruanda-Urundi will prove themselves competent to solve their own problems in their own way."

The visit by the UN Mission did not allay the tension reigning in Ruanda. The Hutu parties and a large part of the population were embittered mainly by the postponement of the communal elections. The Mission feared that this bitterness might erupt in new disturbances. This is why at the end of April, when the Mission stopped at Brussels on its way back to New York after a few weeks' stay in Tanganyika, it had talks with the Belgian Minister for the Congo and Ruanda-Urundi, and asked him to advance the date of the communal elections. The minister replied that the Belgian government was so busy preparing the Congo for independence that for the time being it was unable to deal with the problems of Ruanda-Urundi (!), but he promised to hold a restricted discussion at the end of May — and shortly thereafter he would talk with ten to twelve representatives from Urundi — about the preparation of the communal elections and of an enlarged conference; he said that the communal elections would possibly be held in June, and a few months later, perhaps in October, the enlarged conference would be convened to discuss all questions concerning the political future of Ruanda-Urundi and the preparations for general elections in 1961.

The disturbances continued also after the departure of the UN Visiting Mission. In the middle of April, for example, the Belgian news agency reported the arrest of "70 terrorists" who had set fire to 400 huts in the mountain region of the Astrida district.

In its communiqué issued on the eve of its departure from the trust territory, the UN Visiting Mission expressed the hope that Belgium would ask the United Nations General Assembly to discuss at its 1961 session the question of the independence of Ruanda-Urundi; it recommended that a round-table conference be immediately convened with the participation of representatives of the Africans, the Belgian government and the United Nations to decide on the future of the territory; it proposed that general elections be held early in 1961 under UN supervision to establish the bicameral legislature which would draw up the constitution of the country. The Mission recommended that Ruanda-Urundi be granted independence as a unitary state.

Urundi in 1959–1960

At the end of December 1958 ANDRÉ NDABIBONA, speaking on behalf of sub-chiefs, complained to the Mwami of Urundi about certain chiefs whom he accused of treating the sub-chiefs as slaves, and requested that the status of sub-chiefs be defined, that their salaries be raised, and that they be assured of representation in the High Council of Urundi. In January 1959 the sub-chiefs presented to the Mwami a new complaint signed "Hutu and Tutsi of Kitega", protesting against the monopoly of the Ganwa in nominations to higher posts.[1]

The appearance of the Working Group in April 1959 provoked considerable political activity on the part of the customary tribal authorities and the High Council of State. The Mwami MWAMBUTSA, in his speech to the High Council during the visit of the Working Group on April 23, emphasized that Ruanda and Urundi were two separate states, and that each must be allowed to develop according to its own aspirations. He protested against the United Nations recommendation that the administering authority should merge the two states into a single entity, and insisted that this was impossible. At the same time he stated that Urundi wanted autonomy but would still need Belgian assistance for a long time, and so the trusteeship system should not yet be terminated.

On the same day, April 23, Chief BARUSASIYEKO, on behalf of the High Council of State, submitted to the Working Group a draft constitution. The draft laid down that Urundi was a constitutional monarchy, the democratic state of the Urundian people. The High Council stressed that, if a Burundi nation did not yet exist, it was the fault of the United Nations which had made Ruanda-Urundi a single trust territory without making distinction between nationals of the two countries. The draft established fundamental human rights for all citizens and laid down the principle of the separation of legislative, executive and judicial powers. The legislative power would be exercised collectively by the Mwami, the High Council of State and the Legislative Council. The latter two would be composed of representatives elected by the chiefdoms and of co-opted members. The executive power would be held by the Mwami, who would appoint a leader to form the government composed of Urundi and Belgian ministers. The Urundi ministers would be assisted by Belgian experts,

[1] The Ganwa are offspring of Tutsi rulers.

and the Belgian ministers would be assisted by Urundi secretaries of state. The Belgian ministers would be gradually replaced by Urundians according as the number of capable Urundi officials would increase. If a minister raised the question of confidence and failed to obtain the majority vote in the Legislative Council or the High Council of State, he would hand in his resignation to the Mwami. Judges would be appointed for life by the Mwami, either directly or from a list submitted by the High Council and the courts of appeal.

The draft provided in detail for the elections to the chiefdom councils and the sub-chiefdom councils, as well as for the election or appointment of chiefs and sub-chiefs. The sub-chiefdom councils would be elected on the basis of direct universal suffrage, and the sub-chiefs would be appointed by the Mwami from among the council members. The membership of the chiefdom councils would be directly elected from among members of the sub-chiefdom councils, and the chiefs would be appointed and dismissed by the Mwami. As long as Belgian trusteeship existed, Belgian and Urundian officials would have equal status. After independence, on the other hand, Burundi and Belgium would regulate by agreement the questions of administrative and technical assistance to be provided by Belgium and the status of Belgian officials serving in Burundi.

In contrast to Ruanda, in Urundi the relations between the Belgian administration and the customary authorities were normal, and their co-operation was peaceful. The Governor returning from leave in Belgium on September 30, 1959, was welcomed at the airport with impressive cordiality by the Mwami and many chiefs, who thereby demonstrated their loyalty to Belgium, dissociating themselves from agitated Ruanda whose African leaders were not present on the occasion.

Political parties did not exist in Urundi before 1959. The first political party was the *Parti de l'Unité et du Progrès National du Burundi* (Uprona),[1] founded by ANDRÉ NUGU, a Tutsi leader, in September 1959.

In its first manifesto the Uprona party demanded internal autonomy for Urundi by January 1960, to be followed by independence, with the establishment of democratic institutions within the framework of a hereditary monarchy, the introduction of universal suffrage, the economic development of the country, the promotion of social welfare, the advancement of education with state assistance. It took a stand against any form of incitement to racial hatred both between Europeans and Africans and among the different ethnic groups of Urundi. It pledged to respect authority but demanded that the people should be consulted on any matter affecting the future of Urundi, and protested against the Belgian government's issuing its statement on the future of the country without having consulted the responsible local political organs.

In another manifesto, published a few weeks later, the Uprona party deplored the civil war in Ruanda and called upon the people of Urundi to keep calm and remain loyal to the Mwami and the dynasty. At the same time it stressed the importance of recognizing individual land ownership.

Almost simultaneously with the birth of Uprona a second party the *Union Nationale Africaine du Ruanda-Urundi* (U.N.A.R.U.), was formed in Usumbura under the leadership of BARNABÉ NTUNGUKA.

The membership of U.N.A.R.U. comprised many Swahili and Africans from Uganda. On the question of independence this party agreed with Uprona but differed in that it intended to extend its operation to both countries of the trust territory.

---

[1] The party was originally called the *Union Nationale Progressiste*.

For the time being, however, it was active only in Urundi and its influence was confined almost exclusively to the town of Usumbura. During the UN Visiting Mission's tour of Urundi many of the party's members went to Kitega and other places and joined in the demonstrations organized on the occasion of the Mission's passage.

The November events in Ruanda created agitation and unrest in Urundi as well. That no incidents took place was due, on the one hand, to the prestige and authority of Mwami MWAMBUTSA who had reigned for 43 years and, on the other hand, to the relatively peaceful intercourse between the administering authority and the customary African authorities. The November 10 statement of the Belgian government and its consequences, however, spoiled this good understanding.

The King of the Belgians invited the two Mwami to go to Brussels for an audience on November 9 (the day before the publication of the government statement). The Mwami of Ruanda, with reference to the unrest spreading in the country, refused the invitation, but the Mwami of Urundi accepted it forthright and flew to Brussels on the 7th. His month-long stay in Belgium covered the entire period of the disturbances in Ruanda.

As we may recall, a Hutu leader of Aprosoma who had fled from Tutsi bands and taken refuge with a relative in Urundi was assassinated by his pursuers on November 10. After this event the Belgian Resident of Urundi placed the north of the country under "military operation".

In November and December 1959 the Hutu–Tutsi problem of Urundi was a topic of controversy in the press. The story started on October 14, when a number of progressive Hutu personalities of Urundi joined the Hutu parties of Ruanda in signing a letter addressed to the Minister for the Belgian Congo and Ruanda-Urundi, in which they expressed their anxiety that internal autonomy might lead to Tutsi absolutism and requested the continuation of Belgian trusteeship. A letter published in the newspaper *Temps Nouveaux d'Afrique* on November 13 explained that the news stated in the October letter did not concern Urundi because castes did not exist there and the Hutu–Tutsi problem was also non-existent. Thereupon the November 27 issue of the newspaper published a letter from ALBERT MAUS, asserting that the Hutu–Tutsi problem existed in Urundi just as in Ruanda, and expressing the hope that "the Belgian and Urundi authorities were not awaiting a second civil war to open their eyes and would introduce with good grace in Urundi the drastic reforms which were now being carried out in Ruanda under the threat of blood and fire". In reply to this letter one of the Uprona leaders, LOUIS RWAGASORE, the son of Mwami MWAMBUTSA, on December 4 wrote an open letter in which he attacked MAUS and stated among other things: "Your work has borne fruit in Ruanda. Must Urundi go through the same experience before you are fully satisfied? . . . There is a problem, that of the small and weak and they have no race." A few days later MAUS again explained his position that "the rich are nearly always Tutsi and the poor are nearly always the Hutu".

In December several representatives from Usumbura called on the Mwami and requested him to take steps to avoid conflicts between the Hutu and the Tutsi and a repetition of the Ruanda disorders. They suggested that an extraordinary national council should be convened to examine the effects upon Urundi of the disturbances in Ruanda, and that the political parties and leaders should be reminded of their duties and responsibilities in the grave situation of the country.

On January 5, 1960, MWAMBUTSA, the Mwami of Urundi, issued a circular letter addressed to the population with an appeal for unity, stating that "it would be incomprehensible if the people of Urundi were to become divided at the very time when the country was choosing its future political path".

The Belgian government statement of November 10, 1959, which applied to Urundi as well, elicited no immediate response from the African authorities of Urundi. On December 22 the High Council of State set up a political committee composed of its own members to study the government statement. The same committee dealt with the interim decree of December 25, too, and summed up its views on the two documents in a memorandum which was unanimously approved by the High Council on January 20, 1960, and sent to the President of the Belgian Parliament with copies for the United Nations, the Resident-General of the trust territory and the Resident of Urundi.

In the memorandum the High Council of Urundi charged that the administering authority had failed to take into account the wishes that the Council had expressed on behalf of the population for the drawing up of the reform plan. The main points of this criticism were the following:

(a) instead of granting internal autonomy to the country, Belgium was imposing on it a colonial system under the pretext of trusteeship;

(b) the Belgian administration did not recognize Urundi nationality, it did not lay down that the right to vote and the right of being elected should be granted only to Urundi nationals;

(c) it was imposing a truncated democracy instead of a genuine democracy which required that the political authorities should be elected by the people and confirmed by the Mwami;

(d) the methods of Africanization applied by the administering authority were leading rather to Europeanization, as the most capable African civil servants were withdrawn from the direct indigenous administration and transferred to the indirect European administration;

(e) the Belgian administration was abolishing the chiefdoms, these customary political entities of the state, instead of enlarging them and making them provinces with elected provincial councils, which would elect from among their own members the heads of provinces for appointment by the Mwami.

In January–February 1960 an additional five political parties were formed in Urundi: the *Parti du Peuple* (P.P.), the *Parti Démocratique Chrétien* (P.D.C.) the *Mouvement Progressiste du Burundi* (M.P.B.), the *Union Démocratique Paysanne* (U.D.P.) and the *Voix du Peuple Murundi* (V.P.M.).[1]

Of all these parties only two, the P.P. and the P.D.C., acquired considerable importance. In addition of Uprona and U.N.A.R.U., they provided most of the participants of the demonstrations organized during the stay of the UN Visiting Mission.

In contrast to Uprona which adopted a hostile attitude towards the Belgian administration and demanded independence for Urundi at once, the P.D.C., as the second largest and best organized party, saw it necessary to establish democratic institutions first and be granted independence later, and therefore it was in favour of continued Belgian trusteeship. The confrontation of the two parties was due, in addition to differences of political opinion, also to tribal conflicts: Uprona supported the members of the actually reigning dynasty (the Bezi), while the P.D.C. favoured the former ruling family (the Batare).

---

[1] A sixth new party, called Aprodeba, disappeared in a couple of days for lack of supporters.

The P.P. recruited its members from the underprivileged and exploited masses, regardless of whether they belonged to the Hutu, Tutsi or Twa tribes, and its programme proposed their liberation from under the yoke of the Ganwa oppressors.

On January 23 the P.P. sent the United Nations a petition stating its disagreement with the High Council of State. The Resident offered to explain to the High Council the government statement and the interim decree as well as the related plans. Later he proposed that a mixed committee composed of members of the High Council and representatives of the Belgian administration should be appointed to discuss the text of the memorandum. But the High Council maintained its position and rejected the Resident's suggestions.

On January 30 the Resident-General in Usumbura received the Mwami and the members of the High Council's political committee. He repeated the Resident's proposal, but it was again refused.

The memorandum which the High Council adopted on January 20 in response to the Belgian government statement created tension between the High Council and the administering authority. The excitement and tension were further increased in early February by the news of the Belgian government's decision to grant independence to the Belgian Congo on June 30.

On February 3 the High Council of State adopted a motion demanding independence for Urundi by June 21, 1960, and the holding before that date of a round-table conference of representatives of Urundi, Belgium and the United Nations to pave the way for independence. The resolution laid down even a time-table for independence in six stages:

(a) electoral campaign and detailed arrangements for elections;
(b) provincial elections and elections for the constitution of the Lower House;
(c) elections for the constitution of the Upper House;
(d) formation of the government;
(e) meeting of Parliament and proclamation of independence;
(f) transfer of public powers.

The parties felt prompted to action, whereupon the Mwami on February 8 addressed a message to the population, emphasizing that he stood above the parties and that no party could speak in his name. Three days later he appealed to the people of Urundi to remain calm and to co-operate with the Belgian administration. The situation became more tense towards the end of February, when the Resident-General decided to appoint an interim committee of five members to replace the High Council whose three-year term of office had expired. On top of this came the news of the impending visit by the UN Mission. The political parties and leaders made feverish preparations to submit their programmes and proposals to the Mission and through it to the United Nations.

The three-year term of the High Council of Urundi expired on February 17, 1960. The five-member interim committee was established under Ordinance No. 221/60, pending the setting up of the new institutions provided for in the interim decree. The committee, presided over by the Mwami, was charged with the task of exercising the functions of the High Council as required by current business and the examination of urgent problems. By his Ordinance No. 221/79 of March 17 the Resident-General set up three special committees: an electoral committee, a social and educational committee, and an economic and financial committee. The first would include among its members a representative of each of the legally constituted political parties.

An ordinance of March 10 of the Resident-General had provided for the holding of communal elections in Ruanda during June 1960, but no such provision had been made for Urundi. The interim committee and the electoral committee were to examine, in co-operation with the Belgian administration, the problems of the preparation of these elections and to start a campaign of information to explain to the broad strata of the population the electoral operations and the significance of the elections.

During March three new parties were formed: the *Démocratie Nationale du Burundi* (D.N.B.), the *Parti Démocratique des Jeunes Travailleurs du Burundi* (P.D.J.T.B.) and the *Parti Démocratique Rural* (P.D.R.).

In March the parties held three joint congresses. The first took place early in March with the participation of seven parties (Uprona, U.N.A.R.U., P.P., P.D.C., M.P.B., U.D.P. and V.P.M.). It failed to reach agreed conclusions: Uprona and U.N.A.R.U. withdrew in the early days of the deliberations. Following this abortive attempt the various parties divided and held two separate congresses. One such congress was attended by the five parties which continued discussing on the first occasion after the withdrawal of Uprona and U.N.A.R.U. The other was held with the participation of Uprona, and the V.P.M. which took part in both congresses, as well as two of the recently formed parties (D.N.P. and P.D.J.T.B.).

The two congresses were seized of the same problems, first of all the question of franchise and the preparation of elections, independence and the proposed round-table conference. The five-party congress stated its views on these problems in a joint programme adopted on March 19, 1960. The four-party congress summed up its conclusions in a letter which was sent to the UN Visiting Mission a few days after the presentation of the memorandum containing the programme of the five-party congress.

In the question of electoral franchise the five-party congress took the position that only Urundi nationals should have the right to vote, while the congress of four parties requested that the Mwami and the interim committee should fix the conditions on which aliens also should be granted political rights.

With regard to the elections both congresses were of the opinion that the chiefs and sub-chiefs must be prevented from exerting their personal influence upon the electorate. The five-party congress proposed that those authorities should exchange posts during elections, and that control should be enforced to ensure that they did not return to their own *circonscriptions* to conduct electoral propaganda and did not commit abuses in their temporary *circonscriptions*. On the other hand, the four-party congress suggested the suspension of the activities of the territorial and tribal authorities. The five-party congress proposed that the Mwami's son, RWAGASORE, and sons-in-law should be kept out of the electoral campaign and that no one should make propaganda in the Mwami's name. The memorandum of the four parties stressed that the elections should be supervised by a commission composed of representatives of the parties, Belgian officials and UN observers; that the elections should be preceded by an electoral campaign lasting at least two months; that the Mwami should issue a circular explaining the elections to the population, and that the Mwami and the Resident should have this official document distributed widely by a group of independent persons of impartiality.

As to the question of independence, the five parties held the view that independence should be preceded by a period of democratization, and therefore it would be inappropriate to fix an early date for accession to independence. The four parties, on the other hand, considered that the country could accede to independence in the near future, after proper preparations, and it demanded as an urgent reform the pensioning of the customary chiefs and sub-chiefs and their replacement by new chiefs who would be capable of keeping up with developments, and who would be elected by the people and invested by the Mwami. They also requested that immediately before and after independence an international force should stay in the country to ensure public order until a police force was made up exclusively of Urundian nationals.

Both congresses demanded the holding of a round-table conference after the communal elections. But while the five parties were of the opinion that the conference should decide only the questions relating to independence, the four parties considered that, in addition to setting a date for independence, the round-table conference would have to decide the establishment of democratic institutions in the new state, the election of a bicameral legislature and the formation of a government. Accordingly, the four-party congress in its letter to the UN Visiting Mission proposed a detailed time-table as follows:

(a) if the communal elections took place in June the round-table conference should be prepared and held during July and August:

(b) the electoral campaign for the legislative elections should be held in September;

(c) the elections to the two chambers of parliament should take place during October;

(d) the government should be formed in November and make preparations for Urundi's accession to independence;

(e) Urundi should accede to independence on the traditional holiday of the country, December 27.

U.N.A.R.U. took part in the four-party congress but disagreed with its conclusions regarding the voting rights of aliens. The V.P.M. attended both congresses and endorsed the conclusions of both.

Before the Mission's departure the P.D.R., which was formed at the end of March and thus could not take part in either congress, submitted a memorandum formulating its programme, in which it demanded independence for Urundi at the earliest possible date and the right to vote and eligibility for Urundians alone. It demanded further that Belgium and the United Nations, with the participation of representatives from Urundi, should fix the date and conditions for accession to independence, after the formation of the government of the state of Burundi, still before the end of 1960 or, if the establishment of democratic institutions was delayed for unforeseen reasons, in the middle of 1961 at the latest.

The UN Visiting Mission arrived at Kitega on March 21 and spent ten days in Urundi: five days at Kitega, where it split into two groups which went to visit several towns and villages, and five days at Usumbura. As in Ruanda, the Mission encountered hundreds of demonstrators everywhere. (On March 23 at Mgozi, where the Mission was accompanied by the Mwami, two groups, each several thousand strong, waited for the visitors. An Uprona group demonstrated with demands for independence, the other group, led by the P.D.C., clamoured for democracy.) The Mission met and heard everywhere representatives of different political parties, nonpolitical groups and organizations, as well as a number of individual petitioners, including even chiefs and missionaries. The parties described their own respective ideas, and the masses shouted their own slogans, but there was no incident among the supporters of the opposing parties. This can be ascribed, on the one hand, to the relatively quiet mood in the country as compared with Ruanda and, on the other, to the more tactful attitude of the authorities.

The UN Visiting Mission, in addition to hearing representatives of the parties and other African politicians, made sure that it had substantive discussions with officials of the Belgian administration and the customary authorities. On the day of its arrival at Kitega the Mission met and talked with the Belgian Resident and his leading staff, with the Mwami and members of the interim committee. On the next day, before receiving party delegations, it heard the Resident's report on the situation in the country. On March 24 it had a long discussion with the Resident-General who had come from Usumbura for this purpose.

On the 25th the Mission attended a reception given by the Mwami, who handed it a memorandum drawn up jointly with a group of chiefs. On the 27th it had intensive talks with Minister SCHEYVEN of Belgium and the Resident-General. On the 28th it visited missionary establishments and again talked with the Resident-General.

At the March 24 meeting in Kitega the UN Mission informed the Resident-General that it wished to propose that before the communal elections the Belgian government call a round-table conference with representatives of the political parties of the two countries and that elections on the basis of direct universal suffrage be held early in 1961 to elect the members of the legislatures for Ruanda and Urundi; and also that United Nations observers attend the round-table conference and the world organization send a team of experts in order to assist in the development of the territory. The Mission asked for the Belgian government's opinion on these intended proposals.

The Resident-General forwarded this information to Brussels, and the Belgian government's reply came in on March 30. The government generally agreed with the Mission's proposals, but it held that the round-table conference could not be summoned before August, which meant in practice that the communal elections planned for June were postponed to a later date.

Having received the Belgian government's reply, the Mission immediately summoned an informative conference with representatives of the political parties of Ruanda and the next day with those of Urundi (the meetings were attended also by the Mwami of the country concerned). The participants were satisfied with the plan of a round-table conference, but they felt that August was too far off, and most of them regretted the postponement of the communal elections. This opinion was shared by the UN Mission.

After the Mission's departure the Mwami of Urundi, in the company of the Belgian Resident and members of the interim committee, visited all districts of the country. The population received him with enthusiasm everywhere, and he assured the people that he recognized all political parties, but all parties should have equal rights and none of them might claim to be considered "the Mwami's party", and that every Urundi national was free to join the party of his choosing or not to join any party. The Resident accompanying the Mwami explained to the a hudience of the mass meetings the UN Visiting Mission's communiqué of March 31.

In its report submitted in June 1960 the UN Mission expressed the hope that the Belgian government would propose that the independence of the country should be discussed in 1961 by the United Nations General Assembly. It proposed that a round-table conference should be convened immediately to discuss the future of the country with representatives of the African population, the Belgian government and the United Nations, and that communal elections should be held early in1961, under UN supervision, to elect members to the bicameral legislature which would have to draw up the constitution of the country. The Mission recommended the establishment of a Community of Ruanda-Urundi.

In May 1960 the Ministry for the Belgian Congo and Ruanda-Urundi called the representatives of the Ruandese parties to Brussels for a conference in connection with the forthcoming elections. It expected that it would succeed in bringing about a reconciliation of the reactionary UNAR and the three democratic parties (Aprosoma, Parmehutu, RADER). However, this attempt of the Belgian government failed, because KAYIBANDA decided in the last minute that the UNAR delegation should not take part in a conference which would discuss only procedural matters. The representatives of the democratic parties demanded in unison that KAYIBANDA should resign and charged that the Mwami and the UNAR leaders were responsible for the bloody incidents of November 1959, and that a campaign of slander against the democratic parties was still organized by members of the UNAR leadership who had in the meantime fled to Dar es Salaam.

In connection with the approaching independence of the Congo the Belgian government in June introduced a number of precautionary measures. The Belgian Minister of Defence sent Belgian army officers to Usumbura to assist the Resident-General in organizing the security forces (until that time the "maintenance of order", primarily the suppression of "disorders", in the trust territory had been a duty of the Congolese police). Also in June an independent radio station was put into operation in Usumbura (until that time the trust territory had been serviced by the Belgian broadcasting station at Bukavu in the Congo).

On June 21 the Belgian government tabled in Parliament an urgent bill providing that the economic, financial and customs union between the Congo and Ruanda-Urundi should continue after the independence of the Congo pending different arrangements between the government of Belgium and the government of the independent Congo state.

In June–July 1960 communal elections were held in Ruanda. UNAR in the last minute called upon its supporters to boycott the elections on the grounds that the other parties, in collusion with the Belgian authorities, used threats to solicit votes. But the call met with response only in few places. The election turnout was 78.2 per cent; Parmehutu won 70 percent of the vote, Aprosoma 7.4 per cent, RADER 6.6 per cent, while UNAR obtained all in all 2 per cent.

At the beginning of July 1960 Mwami KIGELI went to Léopoldville to pay a call on Secretary-General HAMMARSKJÖLD of the United Nations. After his return he stayed in Ruanda for only a couple of days, and towards the end of July he again went to Léopoldville, giving as a reason that the hostile majority of the legislature made it impossible for him to govern his country.

On August 9, 1960, Prime Minister EYSKENS of Belgium gave a press conference in Brussels, where he announced that Belgium would in all probability withdraw from Ruanda-Urundi. He said that his government was considering this possibility, on the one hand, because the protection of the trust territory had been provided by the troops stationed at a Katanga military base which was now to be dismantled, and, on the other hand, because the trust territory was an enormous material burden on Belgium.

On August 13 UNAR cabled the Security Council, requesting that the Belgian armed forces be withdrawn from Ruanda-Urundi just as from the Congo and replaced by UN forces. At the same time it sent a telegram to Brussels, protesting against arbitrary actions of the Belgian colonial authorities.

On September 15 a delegation of Urundi parties staying in Geneva addressed a cable to the United Nations, demanding the immediate calling of general elections, the termination of Belgian trusteeship and the transformation of Urundi into a sovereign constitutional monarchy, and appealed to the Trusteeship Council to send a permanent UN Mission to the territory to ensure the implementation of the proposed measures. The delegation charged that the Belgian Governor was muzzling freedom of the press and freedom of expression, and finally it stressed the hope that Ruanda and Urundi would take their seats in the large United Nations family as two independent kingdoms.

In the first half of October violent clashes took place between Tutsi and Hutu tribes in the north of Ruanda, near the Congo boundary. According to official reports 130 huts were burned down, six people were killed and ten wounded during the incidents, and the forces of order made more than a hundred arrests. Part of the population (mainly Tutsi) fled from the scene of the incidents to the Congo's Kivu Province bordering on Ruanda-Urundi. The International Red Cross reported about 8,000 refugees (two-thirds of them were women and children).

Mwami Kigeli sent a cablegram to Secretary-General Hammarskjöld and King Baudouin and requested the immediate intervention of the United Nations to restore order and ensure "constitutional freedom". A similar request was addressed to Hammarskjöld by the UNAR leaders staying in London.

On October 20 the Belgian Resident-General issued an ordinance providing for the formation in Ruanda of a provisional government under a Premier to be appointed by the Resident-General, as well as a 48-member council to take the place of the provisional special council. The provisional government and the new council were formed a week later, on October 27. The Resident-General appointed Kayibanda to head the government which had another ten members (six Hutu, two Tutsi and two Europeans). Seventy per cent of the council members came from the Parmehutu and Aprosoma parties, 30 per cent from RADER. (With reference to irregularities committed in the communal elections, UNAR took part neither in the government nor in the new council.)

In Urundi the communal elections were held in November 1960. The preparation of the elections had been entrusted to a committee with the participation of political parties. The report of this committee had been considered in Brussels towards the end of August. On the grounds that by a former agreement the Mwami stood above the parties, the committee had proposed that the Mwami's relatives should be kept out of politics and that aliens (Belgians included) should not be given the right to vote. The Belgian authorities accepted the proposals. Consequently the Mwami's first-born son, Rwagasore, who was an active participant in the political struggle for the country's independence, was placed under house arrest for the period of the elections.

At the elections 83 per cent of the voters went to the poll. The largest number of votes were gained by the P.D.C. (32 per cent), Uprona (18 per cent) and the P.D.R. (17 per cent).

Negotiations in December 1960

From December 7 to 13, 1960, representatives of the Ruanda political parties, the provisional government and the Belgian administration held a conference at Kisenyi. The negotiations resulted in an agreement on the procedures of the coming elections. The parties declared their readiness to take part in the elections and to refrain from disorders and personal invectives. On the other hand, the Belgian authorities promised to remain neutral towards all political parties. Another agreement was reached on expediting the repatriation of refugees to enable them to participate in the elections.

Similar negotiations took place at Kitega, in Urundi, between December 16 and 20. Here also an agreement was arrived at regarding the election procedures and the preparations for the introduction of internal autonomy.

The report of the 1960 UN Visiting Mission to Ruanda-Urundi was discussed by the United Nations General Assembly at its fifteenth session in 1960. Before the opening of the debate, the Fourth Committee of the General Assembly heard a number of petitioners, among them a representative of Aprosoma, who said that the 1959 disturbances had been provoked by the Tutsi leaders' refusal to introduce the democratic reforms demanded by the Hutu. The petitioner protested against amnesty being granted to UNAR members imprisoned or exiled for participation in the riots, and he criticized UNAR for its boycott of the June–July communal elections and charged that UNAR was under the influence of foreign interests.

On December 20, 1960, the General Assembly of the United Nations adopted two resolutions on this subject. Resolution 1579 (XV) laid down that legislative elections should not be held until (1) full and unconditional amnesty measures were implemented, (2) the refugees were enabled to return, and (3) a conference fully representative of political parties was held. The General Assembly set up a three-member UN commission to supervise the preparatory measures preceding the elections, the conduct of the election campaign and the elections to be held in 1961, and to submit an interim report to the General Assembly at its next session. The General Assembly deemed it advisable for Ruanda-Urundi to become independent as "a single, united and composite" state.

Resolution 1580 (XV) concerned only Rwanda and provided that a referendum should be held under UN supervision in order to ascertain the wishes of the people as to the institution of monarchy and the present Mwami of Rwanda.

The Ostende Conference in January 1961

Early in January 1961 a conference was held in Ostende to discuss the future of Ruanda-Urundi. Participating in the week-long discussion were the interested Belgian officials and representatives of the two African kingdoms as well as the members of the UN Commission for Ruanda-Urundi under the chairmanship of Ambassador MAX H. DORSINVILLE. The conference did not pass any resolution, but it heard the different points of view of the two countries regarding the way of obtaining autonomy.

The conference discussed mainly three questions: the preparation and the timetable of elections, the common affairs of Ruanda-Urundi, and the reconciliation of the Rwandese parties. The Hutu parties of Rwanda (Aprosoma and Parmehutu) and all but one of the Burundi parties wanted the elections to take place still during January; UNAR and RADER proposed the postponement of the elections subject to the three conditions set by the United Nations; while Uprona held the view that elections might be held only two months after the arrival of the UN Commission.

The Burundi parties proposed the immediate setting up of a committee to examine the common problems of the two countries. UNAR and RADER agreed. In the opinion of the Rwandese government and the Hutu parties of Rwanda, however, these matters fell within the competence of the legislatures and governments to be constituted on the basis of the election results.

The UNAR delegates abstained from the debate over the question of reconciliation. The other parties confirmed their willingness to respect the resolutions of the Kiseny conference. RADER stressed the need for the administering authority to remain neutral (!).

At the meeting of the UN Security Council on January 12, Soviet representative ZORIN charged that Belgium had gravely violated the trusteeship agreement by utilizing the trust territory for aggression on the Congo, and therefore he proposed that Belgium should be divested of the right to administer Ruanda-Urundi and that the territory should be granted independence immediately. Since the western imperialist powers and Secretary-General HAMMARSKJÖLD took sides with Belgium the Soviet motion was defeated. Thereupon, on January 13, the representatives of Ceylon, Liberia and the United Arab Republic submitted to the Security Council a draft condemning Belgium for having violated the trusteeship agreement, in spite of the explicit prohibition laid down in the December 1960 resolution of the UN General Assembly, by using the trust territory for military operations against the Republic of the Congo, and they demanded that Belgium should forthwith stop making use of the trust territory for actions against the Congo.

The Sequel to the Ostende Conference

At the time of the Ostende conference the Belgian government granted amnesty to those serving prison sentences up to five years. Shortly thereafter, on January 20 1961, it decided also to postpone the elections. It was due to this step of the Belgian government that soon after the Ostende conference serious events erupted in both countries.

Based on the elections held in November of the previous year, the provisional government and the Legislative Assembly of Burundi were formed on January 26 and 28, respectively. The government included representatives of all major parties except Uprona, whose two members also joined the government, though not as representatives of their party.

The Proclamation of Independence and the Rwandese Republic

The Minister of the Interior in Rwanda summoned the local (municipal and communal) representatives to "informative talks" on January 28, 1961. The meeting was attended by 3,200 mayors and communal councillors, who assembled in a place enclosed with a wire fence, surrounded by 10,000 people who attentively listened to the discussions relayed by a public address system. The meeting, which lasted nine hours without interruption, dethroned Mwami KIGELI, proclaimed the republic and the independence of Rwanda. (Representatives of RADER left the meeting, because they did not agree with the abolition of the institution of monarchy.

The meeting then elected a Legislative Assembly to replace the provisional special council established by the Belgian administration. The new legislature consisted of 40 members from Parmehutu and 4 members from Aprosoma. Then a President of the Republic was chosen in the person of MBONYOMUTWA, who obtained 2,391 out of 2,873 votes. The Legislative Assembly elected GITERA its President. The President of the Republic entrusted KAYIBANDA to form the government, which was done right away. The President then announced the establishment of a High

Court and explained the guiding principle of the new state. Accordingly, at the end of the meeting, the constitution of the new state was promulgated, stating that Rwanda was a sovereign democratic Republic which, for the time being, would recognize Belgian trusteeship under the auspices of the United Nations. All nationals of the Republic would be equal before the law. The separation of legislative, executive and judicial powers was enunciated.

The thousands of people who attended the meeting greeted the decisions with great enthusiasm and freedom songs.

Being confronted with the accomplished fact, the Belgian government, to avert new disturbances, saw it better to accept the newly elected bodies, though not the proclamation of independence.

The Usumbura Incident of March 1961

In March 1961 a fatal accident in Usumbura, the capital of Burundi, sparked off a grave incident between the African population and the administering authority.[1] An African nurse in the Usumbura hospital gave quinine pills instead of laxatives to a few children treated there. Nine children died of gastric poisoning. The news of the accident got round swiftly, and the exasperated parents besieged the hospital. The doctor and the police hurrying to the place were received with a volley of stones. The administration then sent troops to restore order, but by the time they arrived a huge crowd of enraged demonstrators had assembled. The troops fired into the crowd, killing two and wounding seven demonstrators. The rumour was spread in town that the European missionaries and doctors conspired to poison the Africans. The administration imposed a curfew and banned all gatherings, but the agitation of the population lasted for several days.

The Issue of the Trust Territory before the United Nations

In April 1961 the UN General Assembly again dealt with the question of Ruanda-Urundi and discussed the DORSINVILLE report. It adopted a draft resolution sponsored by 26 delegations. In the resolution the General Assembly regretted the failure of the Belgian government to implement the previous UN resolutions and to co-operate fully with the DORSINVILLE commission. The Assembly invited Brussels to rescind the order of October 25, 1960, to hold legislative elections in August 1961 and a referendum in Rwanda on the question of the Mwami. It demanded the formation of new, broad-based governments to replace the antidemocratically constituted provisional governments, the granting of general amnesty and the repatriation of the refugees. It called upon the Belgian government "to ensure that there is no unwarranted interference with the exercise of public freedom and that no persons may be removed or detained without recourse to due process of law".

The General Assembly requested the DORSINVILLE commission to return as soon as possible to Ruanda-Urundi and supervise the implementation of the UN resolutions, and invited the Belgian government to help the commission in the discharge

---

[1] The outside world came to know about the case only from reports of Belgian news agencies, so we cannot know whether the subsequent events were provoked really by this accident or by the general discontent and bitterness of the masses.

of its responsibilities, while it authorized the commission, in the event that the performance of its duties were hindered, to request the General Assembly to re convene immediately. (The 15th session of the Assembly was not closed so it might discuss the question of Ruanda-Urundi during summer, before the territory's accession to independence.)

Finally the General Assembly expressed its conviction that "the best future for Ruanda-Urundi lies in the accession of the Territory to independence as a single united and composite State". /

The resolution was adopted by 83 votes to 1, with 3 abstentions. Belgium voted against it, France, Spain and Portugal abstained, the delegations of nine countries (South Africa among them) were absent during the vote. The United Kingdom and the United States voted for the resolution.

The Elections of September 1961

Pursuant to the UN General Assembly resolution adopted in April 1961 general elections were held both in Rwanda and in Burundi during September. As provided by the said resolution, the United Nations sent a group of three observers to the territory for the duration of the elections. The elections were preceded by a violent campaign, in the course of which bloody clashes occurred in Rwanda between supporters of the opposing parties (primarily between Hutu and Tutsi). By August 24 the incidents as well as the intervention of the Belgian troops trying to "restore order", as was stated the same day by Colonel DELPERDANGE, commander of the Belgian troops, had taken a toll of 171 lives, including 44 people killed by Belgian soldiers (this was also stated by the Belgian colonel). At the end of August the Belgian colonialists dispatched new reinforcements to help the 1,500 men of the force of occupation. Information on the number of further casualties resulting from the electoral "campaign" is not available.

The elections took place in two rounds. Burundi went to the poll on September 18 The opposition party whose direction had been taken over by the Mwami's son RWAGASORE, won a sweeping victory by obtaining 58 out of 64 seats. The Front of Unity (a coalition of the P.D.C., the P.P. and the M.P.B.), which enjoyed the tacit support of the administering authority and had been in power since 1960, gained all in all six seats. Consequently the head of the former provisional government JOSEPH CIMPAYE, was forced to resign and went into opposition. The new government was headed by the founder and leader of Uprona, Prince RWAGASORE.

In Rwanda, where the elections were held a week later, a referendum was taken simultaneously to decide the choice between kingdom and republic and the question whether Mwami KIGELI V should be permitted to live in the country.[1] The elections to the Legislative Assembly were won by the governing Parmehutu party, which gained 35 out of 44 seats. (UNAR obtained 7 seats, Aprosoma 2, and RADER none.) Premier KAYIBANDA and most members of his provisional government were re-elected. The vast majority (about 80 per cent) of the voters in the referendum were against the restoration of the monarchy and the return of the Mwami.

[1] Two days before the elections Mwami KIGELI, who had been ousted early in 1961 and had since been staying abroad, crossed the border of Rwanda, but the Belgian authorities arrested him and did not divulge his whereabouts. Brussels said that the Mwami was held in protective custody for the duration of the elections.

At the inaugural meeting of the newly elected Legislative Assembly on October 2 the Belgian Resident-General read a decree proclaiming that in accordance with the election results the monarchy was abolished, and announced that the Legislative Assembly elected the Prime Minister of Rwanda, GRÉGOIRE KAYIBANDA, President of the Republic by 43 votes to 1. Under the American-style constitution the head of the state retained the functions of Prime Minister.

The Haitian chairman of the observer group which the United Nations had sent to Ruanda-Urundi to supervise the elections stopped in Brussels on his way back to New York. He had talks with members of the Belgian government and made a statement on the radio, praising the co-operation of the administering authority with the local governments, and emphasizing that the elections had been in perfect order and that calm was reigning in both countries. But the facts contradicted this statement. In Rwanda the Tutsi, dissatisfied with the election results, provoked disorders, which again led to Tutsi–Hutu conflicts. In the early days of October burnings and killings were everyday occurrences in Usumbura and Kigali. On October 12 the Usumbura radio announced the news of Belgian operations against "law-breaking groups" which, angry about the election results, made attacks against the Hutu population and the Belgian authorities.

Another report, dated from Usumbura on October 15, was about skirmishes between Hutu and Tutsi tribes in the north of the country, near the Uganda border. In a place the Tutsi killed 20 Hutu. The security forces of the administration in that area performed a mopping-up action, in which they unarmed a great many Tutsi tribesmen.

A communiqué of the Rwandese government issued on October 21 spoke of further Tutsi–Hutu fightings, in consequence of which 3,000 Tutsi from the centrally located Nyanza district sought refuge with Catholic and Protestant missions and large numbers living at Kibuye fled to Kivu Province in the Congo.

The Assassination of the Prime Minister of Burundi

On October 14, 1961, Prince RWAGASORE, the Prime Minister of Burundi, was assassinated. The Fourth Committee of the UN General Assembly met on October 17 and, upon a motion from Guinea and representatives of several Afro-Asian countries, requested an urgent inquiry into the circumstances of the assassination. On the same day the Burundi legislature elected ANDRÉ MUHIRWA, a close relative of the assassinated prince, to the office of Prime Minister.

On October 20 the police arrested the assassin, a Greek trader by the name of JEAN KAGEORGIS, and his three accomplices — former Under-Secretary JEAN-BAPTISTE NTAKIYICA, his brother HENRI, and the mayor of Muruta, ANTOINE NAHIMANA, who were all said to have admitted complicity in the assassination.

Delegations from Ruanda-Urundi, headed by Prime Minister KAYIBANDA of Rwanda and Vice-Premier PIERRE NGENDANDUMWE of Burundi, arrived in Brussels on December 4, 1961. The delegations, which came at an invitation from PAUL-HENRI ; SPAAK, Deputy Prime Minister and Foreign Minister of Belgium, had discussions with the Belgian government on the future of the two countries. The conversations lasted more than two weeks and resulted in the signing on December 21 of an agreement ("Brussels Protocol") under which the two countries of the trust territory, as a first step towards independence, would be granted full internal autonomy as of January 1, 1962, on the understanding that they would win complete independence before the end of 1962.

The Question of Ruanda-Urundi in the UN General Assembly

In January–February 1962 the UN General Assembly again took up the question of Ruanda-Urundi to consider the observer group's report on the September elections in the trust territory. It could be seen from the report, which described the events before and during the elections, that it was based for the most part on information supplied by the officials of the administering authority. The debate started with a speech by Belgian Foreign Minister SPAAK, who, hypocritically as befits a typical neocolonialist, asserted that the Belgian government sincerely wished Ruanda-Urundi to become independent, because the territory was a burden on Belgium. He said that Belgium had profited nothing from the trust territory; on the contrary, she spent on it $20 million every year. How many times as much the Belgian capitalists having interests in the territory had cashed in on it, he did not tell. Moreover, he tried to convince the United Nations that the Belgian government had had nothing to do with the division of the territory, that the African populations of the two countries had demanded so.

This latter issue gave rise to a heated debate. Representatives of African countries — first of all Ghana, Guinea, the Sudan and Nigeria — protested against the division of the trust territory and qualified it as a new neocolonialist manoeuvre of the Belgian government in the interest of the Katangese separatists. The representative of Ghana stressed that if there was mistrust between the peoples of the two countries instead of understanding, it was the fault of the administering authority.

The two governments of Rwanda and Burundi, on the other hand, informed the UN General Assembly that they jointly demanded the termination of trusteeship by July 1, 1962. Accordingly the delegations of African and Asian countries submitted a draft resolution providing that the trust territory should be granted independence by July 1.

The Soviet delegation moved an amendment to the Afro-Asian draft concerning the future of Ruanda-Urundi. The motion demanded the withdrawal of all Belgian forces from Ruanda-Urundi as a basic condition for the guarantee of the complete independence of the territory. The United States representative declared that he could not endorse the granting of independence by July 1 if the Belgian troops were to be withdrawn earlier, because if the Belgian forces left the territory before its accession to independence, a situation like that in the Congo would arise there. He insisted on rejecting the Soviet amendment.

The representative of Ghana was in favour of the Soviet motion. The Irish and Swedish representatives introduced an amendment proposing the training of indigenous forces with the help of experts provided by the United Nations in order to achieve as rapidly as possible the progressive replacement of Belgian military forces.

The Fourth Committee of the General Assembly adopted the Afro-Asian text of a resolution by 88 votes to none, with 11 abstentions. The socialist countries and Iraq abstained because of the rejection of the Soviet proposal.[1]

[1] Ghana, Guinea, Mali, Ethiopia, Morocco, the United Arab Republic, Iraq, India, Indonesia and Burma had voted for the Soviet motion, but after its rejection they nevertheless accepted the original draft resolution.

By this resolution the Fourth Committee recommended the General Assembly to establish a five-member commission with the task of proceeding immediately to the territory and ensuring the reconciliation of the various political factions, and trying to find a formula "for the creation of the closest possible form of political, economic and administrative union".

At its meeting of February 23, 1962, the UN General Assembly adopted the resolution without further change. During the debate the delegations of the socialist countries again demanded that the Belgian troops should be withdrawn before the day of independence; they only abstained but did not vote against the resolution because it contained a number of positive elements.

The General Assembly finally set up the proposed five-member commission,[1] and decided to resume its session in the first week of June to consider exclusively the question of Ruanda-Urundi.

The DORSINVILLE commission submitted its report in the middle of March. The report charged that the Belgian government failed to comply with the most essential provisions of the UN resolutions, that it had not granted amnesty, nor had it resettled the refugees, that it had violated the resolution of the United Nations providing that indigenous governments should not be formed until an atmosphere of peace and tranquillity was restored and until the political leaders were set at liberty. Instead, the Belgian government had encouraged the formation of governments by members of the parties which promoted Belgian interests (in Rwanda it had sanctioned the Gitarama coup, and in Burundi it had itself established a provisional government). The report stated that by a legislative decree of October 25, 1960, the Belgian government had given the administrative organs such powers which prevented the inhabitants of the territory from exercising their basic freedoms. Finally it accused both the Brussels government and the local Belgian authorities that instead of co-operating with the UN Commission they had hindered it in the fulfilment of its task: its departure from Brussels was delayed, and in the territory it was received with mistrust and hostility by the local Belgian officials. It was stated in the report: "It is our firm conviction that as long as the trust power persists in sheltering the administration in Usumbura (the territory's capital) for acts taken in formal opposition to the recommendations of the General Assembly and to its own decisions along the same line, there is no possibility of arriving at a solution mutually satisfactory to the different problems of the territory."

The Belgian government denied everything. The representative of Belgium to the United Nations said in his statement that 1,400 out of 2,000 political prisoners had already been released, the cases of the others were open to discussion with members of the UN Commission, and that the majority of the 60,000 refugees had already returned home and the rest were expected to return in the next three to four months. He claimed that the Gitarama coup had to be accepted as an accomplished fact, otherwise a "popular explosion" might have been to be feared. He attempted to explain away the delays experienced by the commission members in seeing officials and in travel by alleging that they were a result of the "tremendous burden of additional work brought about by unexpected events". He declared that the Belgian government was ready for "the fullest and most frank co-operation" with the United Nations, agreed that the world organization should determine the conditions and the time of elections and send its observers to supervise them, because

---

[1] The commission was composed of the representatives of Liberia, Togo, Morocco, Haiti and Iran.

Belgium shared with the United Nations the goal of "bringing independence to the people of Ruanda-Urundi in a peaceful and harmonious fashion".

The Five-member UN Commission (March–May 1962)

The UN Commission for Ruanda-Urundi, composed of five commissioners under the chairmanship of Miss ANGIE BROOKS, the Foreign Minister of Liberia, first conferred with the Brussels government at the end of March and then, on April 8, went to Addis Ababa where it negotiated with high-level delegations of Rwanda and Burundi, each composed of five members. The negotiations lasted ten days and brought no result. The two African delegations insisted upon the division of the territory. The UN Commission was successful in one point: the two African delegations agreed on an economic union between their two countries.

Thereafter the two governments presented to the UN Commission a joint petition requesting that the Belgian troops leave the territory before July 1.

After touring the trust territory for several weeks, the Commission submitted its report to the United Nations on May 26. The report stated the failure of the mission, that the two countries insisted on separation, that both equally demanded independence by July 1 and the previous departure of the Belgian troops. It described the way the UN resolutions were being implemented in the two countries (amnesty measures, the return of all refugees, maintenance of law and order, the guarantee of legality and basic freedoms, etc.).

Still before the General Assembly reconvened, the United States launched an intensive propaganda campaign to prolong the stationing of Belgian troops. The American press published articles spreading alarming rumours of the dangers facing the trust territory in case the Belgians and their armed forces would leave. Not only was the Tutsi–Hutu strife painted in gloomy colours, but a correspondent of *The New York Times*, in an effort to confirm the need for the continued presence of Belgian troops in the territory, concocted the groundless story that the Tutsi actions were backed up by the countries of the Soviet bloc which hoped to penetrate the ex-Belgian colony with the help of the Tutsi.[1] A week later, U.S. Assistant Secretary for African Affairs MENNEN WILLIAMS declared that, since according to the recent UN report Rwanda and Burundi wanted the Belgian troops withdrawn before July 1, it was absolutely necessary in the interest of peace and order for the United Nations to dispatch UN peace-keeping forces there, because "when the Belgians go, it's quite possible that racial antagonisms of the past will flare out and that there'll be fighting which might result in a conflagration".[2]

The UN General Assembly Session in June 1962

The General Assembly met on June 7 to discuss the report of the five-member UN Commission and to reach a decision on the question of Ruanda-Urundi. The first speaker was again PAUL-HENRI SPAAK, who took pains to offer excuses for the actions of the Belgian government. He said that Belgium wanted the territory

---

[1] TAD SZULC, "U.S. Will Ask U.N. to Guard Ruanda", *The New York Times*.
[2] *The New York Times*, May 28, 1962.

to win independence as soon as possible and, in view of the economic difficulties, was ready to assist both countries after independence, too. At the same time he expressed the concern that after the withdrawal of Belgium new disturbances might break out, and therefore he deemed it necessary to station Belgian troops in the territory for at least three months after independence. He referred to a similar view expressed by the UN Commission and denied that the Belgian government had any part at all in the division of the territory. The Africans themselves insisted on division, he said, and the Belgian government could not force them into a community against their will.

In reply to this BENOÎT BINDZI of Cameroon said that what Brussels proposed was tantamount to the continuation of trusteeship.

Foreign Minister CALLIXTE HABAMENSHI of Rwanda and Prime Minister ANDRÉ MUHIRWA of Burundi, answering a question from the delegations of the Soviet Union, Ghana and Guinea, stated their views on the issue of stationing Belgian troops in the territory. This time HABAMENSHI did not repeat his government's former point of view that the troops should be withdrawn before July 1, but declared that his government did not wish to commit itself but reserved the right freely to choose the country with which it was to be associated after July 1. On the other side, MUHIRWA, while stating categorically that Burundi demanded the immediate evacuation of the Belgian forces, expressed his regret that Rwanda did not adopt a similarly firm position, thereby jeopardizing economic co-operation between the two countries.

On June 19 the Belgian delegation presented a time-table of the troop withdrawals in case the UN General Assembly would decide the immediate evacuation of the troops. According to this schedule, it insisted, to arrange the troop withdrawal in less than three months was technically impossible.

The socialist countries and the majority of the African countries persisted in demanding the withdrawal of all troops before July 1.

The representative of Liberia, MARTINUS L. JOHNSON, confuted the Belgian allegation and pointed out that the Belgian forces of 900 men could be withdrawn in a much shorter time, since "one air transport alone can accommodate more than 200 men".

On June 21 the delegate from India, C. S. JHA, proposed a compromise. He accepted that the withdrawal by July 1 was unfeasible, therefore he proposed that after that date the remaining troops should be confined to their barracks, to avoid interfering in the affairs of the two countries, and then they should be removed from there "as quickly as possible".

The General Assembly considered a draft resolution submitted by 19 Afro-Asian countries requesting the withdrawal of the Belgian forces before the date of independence or, if this was impossible, their confinement to barracks and their departure by August 1 at the latest. Joint efforts by the Belgian and U.S. delegations succeeded in getting this provision of the draft amended to the effect that, "as of 1 July 1962 the Belgian troops in process of evacuation will no longer have any role to play and that the evacuation must be completed by 1 August 1963, without prejudice to the sovereign rights of Rwanda and Burundi". This meant, in other words, that the governments of the two independent states might, if they so desired, to request the stationing of Belgian troops in their territory after August 1.

The Soviet delegation proposed reversion to the original wording of the provision, but its motion was defeated. The non-controversial points of the resolution were the following:

Rwanda and Burundi would attain independence as separate states on July 1, 1962;

the United Nations would send a team of experts to Rwanda and Burundi with the task of supervising the withdrawal and evacuation of Belgian forces, helping to secure the implementation of the agreement on economic union between the two governments, drawing up recommendations for economic and technical assistance to be provided to them, and assisting the two governments in the organization of their administrative cadres and in the training of internal security forces;

the United Nations would grant $2 million in 1962 for the purposes of emergency measures to ensure the continuation of essential services in the two countries;

both states would be recommended for admission to UN membership.

On June 27 the General Assembly adopted the resolution presented by the Fourth Committee by 93 votes to none, with 10 abstentions.[1] The Soviet Union again submitted a proposal for the withdrawal of the troops by July 1, but the motion was rejected by 46 votes to 24, with 33 abstentions, that is by a minority decision.

Secretary-General U THANT announced on the same day that he had appointed TAGHI MASR of Iran to assist in organizing the administration of the two young states and that the team composed of at least ten specialists would soon leave for Africa. He said also that the UN troops stationed in the Congo would send out officers to organize the local security forces.

SPAAK expressed his satisfaction with the resolution, describing it as "a fair compromise". But the United States was still not satisfied. The U.S. representative, CHARLES W. YOST, declared that his government could not agree to the deadline of August 1, and that those who had forced this provision were "taking a serious responsibility in the light of the situation in the territory".

The Independence of Rwanda and Burundi

In the evening before July 1, Foreign Minister SPAAK of Belgium issued an appeal to the Belgian settlers living in Rwanda and Burundi to stay on and continue their activities. (During the months before independence 75 per cent of the European inhabitants of Ruanda-Urundi — about 6,000 people, mostly Belgians — had left the territory.)

On July 1, 1962, the countries of the former Belgian trust territory won independence as two separate states: the Rwandese Republic and the Kingdom of Burundi. The proclamation of independence took place in the two capitals — Kigali and Usumbura, respectively — in the presence of a representative of the King of the Belgians, with all solemnity but in a small way.

The celebration in Usumbura was attended by 20,000 Africans, and 21 salvoes were fired — with a single gun. A chorus of African Catholic seminarists sang the national anthem of Burundi, and a military band played a few marches.

Kigali, the Rwandese capital of 2,000 inhabitants, celebrated on an even smaller scale.[2] The ceremony here took place without mass attendance, in the presence of a small number of guests. The considerable amount of money provided by the Belgian government for the purpose of independence celebrations was not used as intended. The KAYIBANDA government offered the guests only a cold buffet and

---

[1] The socialist countries, except Cuba, abstained from the vote.

[2] This village was chosen for capital because it was the ancient seat of the rulers of Ruanda.

saved most of the money for public use (schools, etc.). In connection with the festive occasion the government ordered the bars closed at night for a week.[1]

In their festive address the hosts, President KAYIBANDA in Kigali and Mwami MWAMBUTSA in Usumbura, expressed their gratitude to the King and the government of Belgium, and called upon their own people to keep calm and work hard.

Mwami MWAMBUTSA said among other things: "Our country will now be independent. But I tell you that from now on you will have to work harder than before and to increase your efforts. Many of you think independence means that there is no law any more and everybody may do as they want, steal and rob, with no fear of punishment. This is nonsense, it is time you understood. Greater care must be taken than before to maintain law and order. Certainly there are some among you who have travelled in independent countries; they can testify how hard the independent peoples have to work. Indeed, they often work far into the night. If we fail to make similar efforts, no one will come to our rescue. For no one helps the spongers."

And here are a few sentences from KAYIBANDA's speech: "Our population is like a young couple getting married. We are adult now. On Sunday we should drink and celebrate and then the next day, like any young married couple, we should go to work, for there is more work than ever to do."

As to the evacuation of the Belgian troops, the government of Burundi declared that it expected the Belgian forces to leave the country by August 1 as provided by the UN resolution. On behalf of Rwanda, however, KAYIBANDA stated that the withdrawal of the Belgian troops before August 1 was technically impossible, and that the danger of invasion by the exiled Tutsi feudal lords and their supporters required the presence of Belgian military forces for six months after August 1, and that the training of Rwandese recruits also required the assistance of a limited number of Belgian officers and servicemen. Having drawn a lesson from the Congo example, KAYIBANDA did not request the sending of UN forces to Rwanda.

It is interesting that the greetings of UN Secretary-General U THANT — who cabled the two heads of state on June 30 expressing the hope that both states would soon be admitted to membership of the United Nations — were followed, right on the day of independence, by the telegrams of congratulation from the Presidents of West Germany and Switzerland.

Complications about the Assassination of Rwagasore

In the weeks preceding independence hot debates were going on in Burundi about the execution of KAGEORGIS, the Greek trader sentenced to death for the murder of Prince RWAGASORE. The government insisted that the trial of the assassins should be held before an all-Burundi special tribunal, but Foreign Minister SPAAK of Belgium refused to comply and referred the case to a Belgian court on the pretext that, in the view of UN legal experts, the procedural laws enacted by the newly independent states could not have retroactive force. This step of SPAAK seemed to substantiate the suspicion of the Burundi government, and of part of the popu-

---

[1] It was characteristic of KAYIBANDA's frugal regime that the monthly salary of his cabinet ministers was about $100, that is one-fifth of the pay in Burundi and one-tenth as much as in the Congo. KAYIBANDA's wife did regular work in the fields like any other peasant woman. The shops and other premises left vacant after the mass departure of Belgian settlers were put to use. A butcher's shop was outfitted for the U.S. Embassy, a grocery store for the Belgian Embassy, and the premises of a pharmacy were occupied by the new National Bank.

lation, that the Belgian colonialists had had a hand in the assassination of RWAGA-SORE. The Burundi Legislative Assembly at its meeting of February 17, 1962, branded SPAAK's action as an unlawful step violating the provisions of the Brussels Protocol of December 21, 1961, which had introduced internal autonomy in Burundi. It passed a resolution stating that Burundi refused to recognize the competence of the Belgian court in the case of the murder of Burundi's Prime Minister, a crime against the country and its people. Brussels did not respond.

The Belgian court opened the trial on March 5. Besides the actual perpetrator of the murder, the Greek trader JEAN KAGEORGIS, an additional eight persons were put in the dock, among them the masterminds behind the crime: a leader of the P.D.C. which enjoyed Belgian support but had been utterly defeated in the last elections, former Minister of the Interior JEAN NTIDENDEREZA, who had hired KAGEORGIS to commit the murder; the former president of the P.D.C., JOSEPH BIROLI; and ANTOINE NAHIMANA, an accomplice of KAGEORGIS's. The close relatives of the assassinated Prime Minister were represented as plaintiffs by Belgian left-wing attorneys. These demanded on the first day of the trial that the one-man Belgian court should disclaim competence and refer the case and the defendants to an African tribunal. When the Belgian judge refused, the attorneys walked out of the trial.

The defence attorneys of the accused, also Brussels lawyers, pleaded that in the days following the assassination their clients had been tortured by the police into confessing to having committed the crime.

The Belgian public prosecutor demanded the death penalty for five defendants in addition to KAGEORGIS, whom he qualified as the ringleader of a band of murderers, but the judge meted out the death sentence only to KAGEORGIS, NTIDENDEREZA and NAHIMANA, while he sentenced BIROLI to life imprisonment and the others to different terms in prison. The penalty of two of those condemned to death (NTIDENDEREZA and NAHIMANA) was commuted to a life sentence by the Belgian court of appeal.

The sentences roused great indignation both in and outside Burundi, since they pointed to the complicity of the Belgian government. The African delegates to the United Nations branded the trial as a farce intended to cover up that the main responsibility for the assassination lay upon the officials of the administering authority. Partisans of the late Prime Minister declared that after independence the case would be retried because they could not be content to see simple imprisonment being meted out to NTIDENDEREZA and BIROLI.

With the day of independence approaching, the Belgian government was facing a dilemma.

1. Being aware of the anti-Belgian mood of the agitated people in Burundi, the Brussels government was afraid that after the transfer of power all nine convicts detained in the Usumbura penitentiary, among them those sentenced to prison only, might be killed. On the one hand, this would make a bad impression on Belgian public opinion and result in the Belgian Parliament's refusal to vote financial assistance to independent Burundi, and this in turn would seriously endanger the African interests of the Belgian capitalists. On the other hand, the killing of the prisoners, including the P.D.C. leaders whom as faithful servants of Belgium the Belgian government had managed to save from execution, would turn even the P.D.C. followers against the Belgian government, which, however, needed their support in order to further strengthening its influence over independent Burundi.

Therefore the Belgian authorities first contemplated taking the prisoners to Brussels. But they had to give up this plan, for such a move would have proved the charge made against them that they had had a finger in the assassination and now tried to cover up. Then the idea came up that the prisoners might be placed under UN protection. But this would have been impossible even if the Burundi government had agreed, because the United Nations had no armed forces stationed in that country.

2. The second problem arose in connection with the execution of the condemned assassin KAGEORGIS. A few days before independence the Greek's attorneys lodged a complaint with the chief public prosecutor in Brussels, accusing the officials of the Belgian trust administration that they had hired KAGEORGIS to commit the murder. The chief public prosecutor, as an authority competent to investigate criminal cases of the colonial officials, initiated an inquiry, but rejected the attorney's request that the execution of KAGEORGIS be postponed pending the conclusion of the inquiry.

The Belgian government was interested in seeing KAGEORGIS executed still before the proclamation of independence, because it feared that the Greek, if he was still alive when the government of independent Burundi would take office, might find a way to reveal the complicity of the Belgian authorities. But some difficulties still stood in the way of the execution. Neither in the Congo nor in Ruanda-Urundi had a single death sentence been carried out since 1945. Such sentences had consistently been commuted to forced labour for life. SPAAK now had to find excuses for dissuading the King of the Belgians from exercising the customary right of pardon. First he argued that, if the death sentence was not carried out before the evacuation of the territory, the Belgian government might have to face the charge that it failed to respect the sentences pronounced by its own courts. Then he put forward the argument that the Belgians living in Burundi who wished to remain there after independence deemed it desirable to make a clean sweep of the case, because they were afraid that the undecided attitude of the Belgian government might encourage the Africans to revenge themselves on the Belgian colonists.

The act of clemency was left undone. A few hours before the proclamation of independence KAGEORGIS was executed in the Usumbura prison yard. It nevertheless did not happen without complications. Under the Belgian law the way of execution was hanging by the neck. But the Belgian officials were reluctant to have a gallows erected in the prison yard on the eve of the independence celebrations. Then Colonel HENNEQUIAU, the Usumbura representative of the Belgian government, ordered execution by shooting, but the Belgian gendarmes refused to obey the order. In the last resort, a firing squad had to be formed of soldiers of the African troops.

The news of the execution caused consternation in Belgium and roused deep indignation among the African delegates to the United Nations. The African population of the country, however, did not consider the "embarrassing affair" closed. To solve the mystery of the assassination of RWAGASORE was left to the young independent state as an item of the onerous heritage of Belgian colonialism.

BIBLIOGRAPHY

A. A. J. BILSEN, *Vers l'indépendance du Congo et du Ruanda-Urundi*, Brussels, 1958.
PHILIPPE LEURQUIN, *Le niveau de vie des populations rurales du Ruanda-Urundi*, Louvain, 1960.

Jacques Lefèbvre, *Structures économiques du Congo Belge et du Ruanda*, Paris, 1962.

"Тройная ставка" [Treble Stakes], Азия и Африка сегодня (Moscow), 3/1962. (Belgian' monopoly interests in Ruanda-Urundi. The strategic importance of the territory fo NATO.)

Philippe Leurquin, *Agricultural Change in Ruanda-Urundi 1945–1960*. Stanford University, 1964.

OFFICIAL PUBLICATIONS

Renseignements commerciaux relatifs aux principales productions du Congo Belge et du Ruanda-Urundi, Brussels, 1959.

La situation économique du Congo Belge et du Ruanda-Urundi en 1959, Brussels, 1960.

United Nations Visiting Mission to Trust Territories: Report on Ruanda-Urundi, New York, 1948 *(idem,* 1952, 1955, 1958, 1960).

CHAPTER XXIX

ITALIAN SOMALILAND

The former Italian colonies were the subject of disputes for years after World War II, but the most complicated of all was the problem of ex-Italian Somaliland, because it was where most of the controversial interests and demands were conflicting. The successor to Italian colonial imperialism, the young "democratic" Italian Republic, used every legal and illegal means to recover this territory, the most valuable of its former colonies.

The Emperor of Ethiopia laid claim to Somalia and Eritrea, as parts of the ancient Ethiopian empire, to annex them "by historical right".

The British imperialist government, on the other hand, intended to make use of the occasion, under the pretext of uniting the Somali tribes, to annex to British Somaliland both ex-Italian Somaliland and the Somali-populated Ogaden Province of Ethiopia occupied by Britain years before, and to keep the whole as a "trust territory" under British administration. The two other Western imperialist great powers, the United States and France, to forestall the British scheme and to facilitate their own penetration of the former Italian territories, made efforts to have the ex-Italian colonies (including Somaliland) placed under United Nations trusteeship (proposed by the United States) or under direct Italian administration (proposed by France).

While the rivalling imperialists could not agree among themselves or with the Emperor of Ethiopia, the Somali people also lacked unity. As we have seen before,[1] ever since the British armed forces had overthrown the rule of Italian colonialism, part of the Somalis gravitated towards Ethiopia, and others were dreaming of independence. In the first few years following the war, however, while the great powers disputed Somalia among them, the Italians, many of whom — thanks to the British occupiers — retained their places, managed to deceive a not numerous but rather vocal segment of the Somalis (former employees of the Italian colonial administration) and bribe them with promises and money into demanding the return of the Italian colonialists.

The British government, being convinced that it would not succeed in preserving the Somali territories, saw it better to come to an agreement with the Italians (to the detriment of the Somali people) that Italy should get the colony back as a trust territory and the Ogaden should be returned to Ethiopia. This agreement was joined in by the U.S. imperialists, who could expect greater possibilities from the rule of a weak Italian partner than from that of either the British imperialists or anti-impe-

---

[1] See Vol. III, Chapter X.

rialist Ethiopia. French imperialism had from the outset supported the Italian claim, and the Soviet Union also accepted the agreed view of the three Western powers.

After such antecedents the General Assembly of the United Nations, in its resolution concerning the former Italian colonies, decided to declare ex-Italian Somaliland a trust territory and charged Italy with its administration.

If we take into consideration that the return of Somaliland was demanded on the Italian side not only by the Italian bourgeoisie but by all political parties of Italy, including the left-wing parties; that the British government which pursued in this case a shameful, double-dealing policy was the Labour government pretending to be socialist; that among those backing this decision there were also left-wing parties in the countries then members of the United Nations, including the great powers; and that the United Nations which had written on its flag the right of peoples to self-determination, and whose Charter made any decision affecting the future of a given country subject to the majority opinion of the population concerned and to respect for the interests of other countries, had passed this resolution against the express wishes of the vast majority of the Somali population and in spite of the strong protest of Ethiopia as an interested party — we have to regard this decision on the future of Somaliland as one of the darkest points thus far in the history of the United Nations, and as one of the most disgraceful acts of the great powers and the other states members of the United Nations as well as of the political parties supporting or approving this attitude of their respective governments.

The First Negotiations (1946—47)

At the Potsdam conference in July 1945 the victorious great powers (the Soviet Union, the United States and the United Kingdom) formed the Council of Foreign Ministers of four powers (France included) to prepare the peace treaties to be concluded with the former European allies of Nazi Germany (Italy, Finland, Hungary, Rumania and Bulgaria).

The Council of Foreign Ministers first met at London in the second half of September 1945. Prior to this, on August 28, the Emperor of Ethiopia received the envoys of Great Britain, the United States and the Soviet Union in Addis Ababa and declared that Ethiopia, as the first victim of Italian aggression, expected the Council of Foreign Ministers to consider Ethiopia's claims against Italy. But the Emperor was disappointed of his expectations. The Council of Foreign Ministers invited the representatives of Canada, Australia, New Zealand, South Africa and India to take part in the meetings and made it possible for a representative of Yugoslavia and Prime Minister DE GASPERI of Italy to attend, take the floor and put forth their demands, but refused to hear the representatives of either allied Ethiopia or the peoples of the former Italian colonies. Ethiopia, although she had twice asked to be heard in the debate, was permitted only to present her views in writing. In a statement to a correspondent of Reuter's on September 21, HAILE SELASSIE said that his government had addressed a memorandum to the Council of Foreign Ministers demanding that Somalia and Eritrea should not be returned to Italy but reannexed to Ethiopia, of which they had been part from time immemorial until the Italians had occupied them. He protested at the same time that his country was denied the right to be represented and speak in the debate while the representative of the defeated Italian aggressor was permitted to participate and submit freely his point of view.

At their first conference held at London in September 1945 the Foreign Ministers of the great powers failed to agree on a number of issues, including the question of the ex-Italian colony of Somaliland, and they entrusted their deputies with continuing the negotiations. Afterwards the question was again discussed at the second meeting of the Council of Foreign Ministers in Paris during April 1946. The negotiations which had been going on for months before the Paris meeting brought no solution to the question of Somaliland. The four great powers submitted four different plans. The British government proposed that former Italian Somaliland be united with the "Protectorate" of British Somaliland and with Ethiopia's Somali-inhabited Ogaden Province into a single trust territory under British administration.[1] The United States proposed collective UN trusteeship, and France proposed Italian trusteeship under UN supervision for all former Italian colonies. The Soviet Union, like the United States, recommended collective trusteeship, but on May 10 Soviet Foreign Minister V. M. MOLOTOV announced that the Soviet Union had assented to the French proposal.

Since agreement could not be reached on several points of the treaties of peace this time either, the Foreign Ministers instructed their deputies to prepare a draft for the peace treaties and, putting aside the controversial matters for the time being, to submit the draft treaties to the next meeting of the Council of Foreign Ministers to be held again in Paris.

At this meeting, on June 14, 1946, the Foreign Ministers decided to call a conference of representatives of twenty-one former belligerent states to consider and approve the drafts of the peace treaties. Having failed to agree on the issue of the Italian colonies, the Foreign Ministers adopted a single draft article containing the following provisions: (a) Italy to renounce all right to her former colonies, (b) these territories to remain under British Military administration pending their final disposal, (c) their future to be decided by the Council of the four Foreign Ministers within a year of the signing of the peace treaty. The Foreign Ministers promised, in case no agreement would come in one year, to submit the problem to the UN General Assembly and accept its decision as binding.

The four Foreign Ministers issued a statement laying down that the decision to be made in accordance with the wishes of the populations of the territories and other interested governments might comprise one of three provisions: independence, or incorporation in the neighbouring territories, or trusteeship to be exercised by the United Nations or by a member state or by Italy.

The 21-power conference accepted the proposals of the Foreign Ministers.

---

[1] In the House of Commons on June 4, 1946, Labour Foreign Secretary BEVIN, to explain the British government's proposal, made a statement typical of the duplicity of the British Labour Party backing up the policy of British imperialism. Starting from the fact that most of the nomadic tribes of both British and Italian Somaliland grazed their cattle in the Ogaden beyond the frontier for six months of the year, he declared: "In all innocence, therefore, we proposed that British Somaliland and the adjacent part of Ethiopia, if Ethiopia agreed, should be lumped together as a trust territory, so that the nomads should lead their frugal existence with the least possible hindrance, and there might be a real chance of a decent economic life, as understood in that territory. All I want is to give these poor nomads a chance to live; we are paying £1,000,000 a year out of our Budget to help to support them. We do not ask anything; but to have all these constant bothers on the frontier, when one can organize the thing decently — well, after all, it is to nobody's interest to stop these poor people and cattle there getting a decent living. That is all there is to it." Cf. E. SYLVIA PANKHURST, *Ex-Italian Somaliland*, London, 1951, p. 219.

In their next conference in New York during November–December 1946 the Foreign Ministers appointed a four-power commission of investigation to find out public opinion among the populations of the former Italian colonies.

In January–February 1947 the treaty of peace with Italy was signed in London, Washington, Paris and Moscow.

The Commission of Investigation and the Riots of January 11, 1948

The four-power commission met in London in November 1947 and heard the representatives of Ethiopia and Italy, who stated their views on the former Italian colonies. Foreign Minister HAPTE WOLD of Ethiopia explained the danger to Ethiopia of Somaliland being again placed under the administration of the Italian colonialists who for half a century had ruthlessly oppressed and enslaved the Somali people and used the territory for continual encroachments upon Ethiopian territory.

Having closed its talks in London, the four-power commission went to Africa to investigate the situation on the spot and to hear the wishes of the local inhabitants.

The commission arrived in Mogadishu on January 6, 1948. The news of the arrival created excitement in the population. The Italians, to show their popularity before the commission members, organized through three days, from January 6 to 8, noisy processions of buses and lorries packed with their loudly demonstrating employees. They held these demonstrations without requesting permission from the British authorities or even notifying them in advance. The British Chief Administrator, for fear that the demonstration might provoke counteraction from the Somalis and lead to disturbances, suggested that the four-power commission should decide not to view the further processions. But the commission refused on the grounds that the political parties had the right to organize demonstrations. Availing itself of this opportunity, the Somali Youth League requested and received permission to hold a procession on January 11 after first consulting the commission about the time and place of the procession.

Being apprised of the Italians' intention of organizing a procession at the same time, the British administration requested the Italian leaders to hold their demonstration at some other time. The Italians, however, insisted on holding processions every day, so also simultaneously with the Somali Youth League. The British administration, which could act so energetically against the Somalis, condoned even this impudence of the Italians. It could not bring itself either to prohibit the Italian procession or to prevent it by force. It wanted in any case to avoid coming into conflict with the Italians as well as with the commission of investigation.

On what happened on January 11 the British administration issued the same evening a communiqué, which tried to justify the action of the authorities (with reference to repeated warnings addressed to the four-power commission and the Italian leaders), but which also described the events objectively in justification of the British administration:

"On the morning of the 11th it was reported that 25 lorries, mainly Italian-driven, had left Mogadishu to bring in Italian native supporters from the countryside, with a view to breaking up the Somali Youth League procession. At about 8.30 a.m. numerous bands of Italian supporters, many representatives of tribes and clubs known to be in receipt of Italian funds, started to enter the town. They were armed with clubs, bows and arrows and spears. It is said that arrows were fired at women and children outside the Somali Youth League Club building and casualties caused, and at the same time many native supporters of the Italians rushed through the streets throwing stones and attacking Somali Youth League lorries and individuals.

"It is known that the previous day sums of money had been disbursed to these supporters of the Italians. Within a short time the S.Y.L. retaliated and the hooligans of the town, who were obviously awaiting this opportunity, commenced to loot extensively. Violent anti-Italian feeling was immediately aroused, which was fanned by Italians throwing hand grenades and firing shots. Shops and houses, particularly those displaying Italian flags, were looted, and individual Italians were attacked and in many cases killed . . ."[1]

When order was restored, the British administration established a court of inquiry, composed of high British officials, to investigate the cause of the riots and the action of the authorities. The findings of this inquiry were not published on the grounds that the case awaited judicial action. (Namely, the British authorities had arrested and brought to trial five Italians as organizers of the disorders and five Somalis proved to have received money for their participation in the riots). In this way the four-power commission, which demanded from the British administration detailed information on the events, got none. In addition to the above-quoted communiqué, however, the British administration released an official statement on the casualties; according to the records 51 Italians were killed and just as many wounded, the Somali losses amounted to 14 killed and 48 wounded. But it appeared also from the statement that none of the Italian victims had been shot, while 16 Somalis had been shot or injured by arrows, a clear indication that the Somalis had used neither firearms nor bows and arrows, but only knives, sticks and similar primitive weapons while the Italians had been equipped with firearms and their Somali supporters with bows and arrows as well.

From the communiqué and the statement of the British administration it can be inferred beyond doubt that the Italians organized a prearranged pogrom against the Somalis, primarily the Somali Youth League, while the Somalis only responded to violence with violence.

Given these circumstances, one can speak only with indignation about the shameless campaign of protest and slander which the Italian colonialists and their government launched in connection with the riots they themselves had provoked and about the hypocritical opportunism with which the British Labour government supported this manoeuvre of the Italian imperialists.

The Italian government took the occasion to start a large-scale campaign of slander against the Africans and the British administration at the same time. Through diplomatic channels and in official statements it protested against the atrocities suffered by Italians and accused the British military administration of having had a hand in organizing the anti-Italian attacks. And representatives of Italian colonists complained before the four-power commission that several officials of the British administration had personally taken part in the brutalities committed on Italians, shooting, throwing grenades, and looting Italian homes.

The British government in London and the British military administration in Mogadishu officially expressed condolences on account of the Italian dead and wounded, and took care not to reproach Italians for the crimes they had committed. The Italian government asked the British government not to publish the findings of the inquiry "in order to spare the feelings of innocent Italians at home in Italy". The

[1] *Op. cit.*, p. 224.

British government, as we have seen, acceded to the request, and the local administration, under the pretext that "the whole affair was *sub judice*", made no answer to the charges levelled against it.

No less revolting was the fact that the four-power commission heard with sympathy the complaints of the Italians who were primarily responsible for the happenings, as the commission might have known from the warnings and statements issued by the British administration, and it had not a single word to say to refute the evidently mendacious and slanderous charges coming from the Italians.

After the restoration of order the four-power commission began the hearing of Somalis and representatives of the Italian colonists. During its stay in Somaliland it heard representatives of the Somali Youth League and of the organization of Somalis supporting the Italian claims, the *Somalia Conferenza*, as well as Italians living in Somaliland.

The Somali Youth League representative described in detail the horrors which the Somalis had suffered under Italian colonial rule, and pointed out that those who wanted the Italians to come back were "mostly people who have been bribed by the Italians, Chiefs and ex-Italian Government employes who have been promised arrears of pay for the past seven years".[1] He summed up the major demands of the Somalis: constitutional means by which the Somalis might express their wishes; a uniform system of law and administration; the removal of racial restriction; separation of the judicial and executive powers; the interests of the Somali population to be paramount; abolition of the privileges and concessions prejudicial to state ownership of the land or hampering the future political or economic development of the country.

Further on the S.Y.L. representative laid down the claims of the Somali workers (the right to form trade unions, 14 days a year paid holiday, sick-leave in pay for 30 days, compensation for injury at work and death, evening classes for industrial workers, rural schools for agricultural labourers, etc.), and stated the most urgent demands as follows:

"Annulment of all Italian law incompatible with the principles of democracy and the rights of the inhabitants.

"Removal of Italians from the Administration.

"A Commission to investigate the Italian concessions, their contribution to the economic life of the colony, the profits of the shareholders, the exploitation of the Somali workers.

"A court of inquiry to investigate claims against the Italian Government concerning savings bank deposits, arrears of pay to ex-Italian employees and arrears of pay, gratuities, pensions, etc., due to ex-Askaris.

"Promotion of Adult Education.

"The British Military Administration to remove restrictions upon trade with the outside world."[2]

The President of the Somalia Conferenza, ISLAU MAHALLE, presented to the four-power commission a list of 23 points enumerating the demands adopted at a meeting of the Conferenza. This document, which was obviously drawn up at a suggestion of the Italian promoters of the organization, demanded 30-year Italian trusteeship for Somaliland. E. S. PANKHURST writes: "Recognising that this [independence] is not immediately possible, socially, politically or economically, they asked for

[1] *Op. cit.*, p. 234.
[2] *Op. cit.*, p. 235.

374

sincere and disinterested guidance by a European nation, to enable them to govern themselves within 30 years."[1]

The document, to mislead the common Somalis, listed a number of "democratic" rights, too, but it appeared from the wording that those demands were not made in earnest and gave wide scope for arbitrary rule by Italians. For example:

Gradual admission into public administration of Somalis *possessing the necessary qualifications and capacity*, on equal terms with Europeans . . .

Central and local assemblies to be established, at first consultative but exercising increasing powers *until the Central Assembly becomes a true legislative chamber.*

The right to reside anywhere in the territory, *except in any special areas restricted by law.*

All pending claims for payment by Italy's former military and civil employees to be settled and all damages arising from the last war *to be paid by Italy.*

Italy to "*warrant* that no revenge or retaliation will be prepetrated against the Somali people for their behaviour during and after the war up to the cessation of the present administration, and that the territory *will be democratically governed and administered.*"

Security for the realization of the above demands *to be given by Italy.*[2]

A deputation of the Somalia Conferenza, headed by the same ISLAU MAHALLE, was heard by the four-power commission. It took this occasion to vilify the British military administration and to extol the Italian colonialists. Speaking of the British administration, the Conferenza representative said: "There is not any Somali in this territory who had not been looted or killed." (!) And speaking of the Italians: "With Italy there was freedom of work and of agriculture . . . We believe that Italy civilized the world, and we think in a period of thirty years she can give us a government."[3] In reply to the remark that, as stated by other representatives, there had been forced labour during the Italian administration, MAHALLE retorted defiantly: "Those who say that are Somali Youth League, no one else in Mogadishu."[4]

An organization established by Italian settlers in Somaliland still under Italian colonial rule in 1937, the Italian Representative Committee, presented a note to the four-power commission of investigation. While denouncing hypocritically the racial policies of the fascist regime, it praised the "present democratic Italian Government", shamelessly glorified the Italian imperialists for their past colonizing efforts, and welcomed the plain intention of the Italian government to continue those activities in the name of culture and morality.[5] The Representative Committee asserted that 95 per cent of the Somalis wanted the return of the Italians, it charged that the British authorities resorted to bribes and threats to pit the Somalis against the Italians, and that even the riots of January 11 had been organized by the British military administration. It alleged that the British did nothing for the sake of the Somalis, but that the Italians also in the past had done much for the country and its peoples and would make them prosper in the future if allowed to continue their civilizing mission. It demanded that the country be placed under Italian trusteeship adminis-

[1] *Op. cit.*, p. 237.
[2] *Op. cit.*, pp. 237–238.
[3] *Op. cit.*, p. 239.
[4] *Ibid.*
[5] "The Italians are conscious of the civilising work they have performed in this country, with so much love and in a spirit of sacrifice, and they trust, therefore, that they will be able to continue, in harmony with the life of Somalia's population in the new atmosphere of international co-operation, the common work for the prosperity and welfare of everybody." Cf. *op. cit.*, p. 249.

tration, arguing that "the request of Italy to obtain the trusteeship administration must be considered only as a necessity of a large population working within narrow borders".

During their hearing before the commission of investigation, representatives of the settler organization (Baron BERITELLI, Dr. CALZIA and Dr. FALCONE) spoke and behaved so brazenly that no one could doubt that they were still the hardened fascists they had been in the times of MUSSOLINI.

The four-power commission received memorandums also from Somaliland branches of the political parties of Italy.

The Christian Democratic Party had a membership of 65 in the territory. In their memorandum they stressed that the purpose of trusteeship was to promote the development of the Somalis and the improvement of their living standards, that Italy needed the territory as a land where her surplus population might find work. At the same time, however, they betrayed themselves by stating that those who would seek work in Somaliland were not manual workers but "more particularly specialists in labour, clerks, teachers, medical practitioners, persons employed in agriculture, mining technicians and all the staff of the fishing industry". They spoke of the period of the fascist regime as "the old happy stage".[1]

The Left-Wing Bloc of the Socialist, Communist and Azione[2] Parties also presented a memorandum in favour of Italian trusteeship on the grounds that it would be acceptable to the Somalis, too. These parties condemned the racial discrimination introduced by the fascists, but they believed that a difference should exist between the pay of Somali and Italian workers (since among the Somalis there were no qualified turners and mechanics) and proposed a slight increase in the lowest wage categories.

The Question of Somaliland before the United Nations

The four-power commission submitted its report to the Council of Foreign Ministers at their Paris meeting in September 1948. In the meantime the three Western great powers had agreed to place the territory under Italian trusteeship. But the Soviet Union had changed its position and proposed that Somaliland, like all other ex-Italian colonies, should be placed under direct United Nations trusteeship. Since, however, no action could be taken without a unanimous decision of the Council, the stand of the Soviet Union prevented the issue from being decided in favour of Italy. And since the one-year period fixed for the Council of Foreign Ministers to decide had expired, the question was referred for decision to the 3rd session of the UN General Assembly which opened at Paris in September 1948.

The question of the former Italian colonies was not taken up by the General Assembly at its Paris session, but it was considered during the resumed session at Lake Success in the spring of 1959. Meanwhile the great powers had been discussing the question further and managed to agree on a compromise solution by which Somaliland should be placed under Italian trusteeship.

At the time of the Paris session of the General Assembly HAILE SELASSIE made a speech in the Ethiopian Parliament. He announced that the Ethiopian delegation had been instructed to request the United Nations that Somalia and Eritrea, which

[1] *Op. cit.*, pp. 255–256.
[2] The Somaliland branch of the "left-wing" Socialist Party.

Italy had used as military bases, be annexed to Ethiopia, and expressed the hope for "fair and sympathetic consideration of Ethiopia's just claims" by member states of the United Nations.

On November 21, 1948, the British Parliament also dealt with the question of the ex-Italian colonies. An M.P. asked the Secretary of State for Foreign Affairs whether he was aware that it was the desire of the Somali populations of both British and ex-Italian Somaliland that the two territories should be united, and that two large Somali organizations, the Somali National League and the Somali Youth League, had expressed the wish that no part of Somalia should be placed under Italian trust or other administration; he asked further what steps the Foreign Secretary intended to take to meet these demands. The reply stated the opinion that the two aforenamed organizations were not at all as influential as they claimed to be, that the British government was aware of the Somali aspirations and would gladly promote them, as it thought the best solution would be a united Somalia, but other powers opposed it, and that the matter was to be decided by the UN General Assembly, not by the British government.

The Secretary of the Somali Youth League, ABDUL RASHID ALI, replied by an open letter in the *Manchester Guardian*, accusing the British government of bartering Somaliland to Italy. He pointed out that, in exchange for Italy's consent to British trusteeship for Cyrenaica, the British government supported Italy's claim to trusteeship over Somaliland. The open letter stated among other things:

"We Somalis will not acquiesce in Italian rule whether Italy claims to be democratic or not. We have had enough of Italy.

"Your Government has made a farce of the efforts of the Four Power Commission of Investigation when you think of appeasing Italy at the expense of us Somalis.

"You say: 'Our latest information suggests that there is no united hostility to Italy.' Yes, Sir, 5 per cent of the Somalis desire Italian rule and those Somalis are ex-ascaris and other ex-employees, who hope to receive back-pay on Italy's return. These stooges are financed by the local, as well as the official Italians."[1]

Further on the letter stated that the British allegation about the Somali Youth being unrepresentative was a bluff, and pointed out that the League was persecuted and muzzled by the British authorities:

"Some of the League leaders have been already clamped in jail without conviction before a Court of Law and merely on suspicion. Shambas are being taken back from Somali agriculturalists because they are nationalists, and believe in the League's programme.

"... There is frequent parading of British troops and British tanks all over the town. Why all this show of force when you believe that the League 'has lost whatever influence it had'?

"You may misguide the British people, but we Somalis can see through your crooked policy. You are keen on satisfying Italy, and for the purpose you are anxious to barter us and our sons and grandsons."[2]

During the recess between the Paris and Lake Success sessions of the UN General Assembly, Italian political leaders (DE GASPERI, Count SFORZA, PIETRO NENNI and others) widely travelled in European and American states members of the United Nations, to win the support of their governments for the Italian claims. At the same time the great powers continued their negotiations with the view of an agreed position

[1] *Op. cit.*, pp. 262–263.
[2] *Op. cit.*, p. 263.

regarding the future of the former Italian colonies. SFORZA succeeded at last in reaching an agreement with BEVIN, which was then submitted to the United Nations as a British draft resolution. It proposed that ex-Italian Somaliland (and Tripolitania) should remain indefinitely under Italian trusteeship. (In return for this Great Britain was to receive the West of Eritrea and unite it to the Sudan, as well as trusteeship over Cyrenaica; the East of Eritrea would have been annexed to Ethiopia, and Libya would have become a UN trust territory for ten years.)

The Political Committee of the General Assembly heard the Secretary of the Somali Youth League, ABDULLAHI ISSA.[1] Starting from the fact that the treaty of peace with Italy had doubtless ascertained Italy's being unfit to govern her former colonies, ISSA said that the Somalis saw no difference between Italian domination which they had suffered in the past and Italian trusteeship as proposed, because the aim of the Italian policy was "to colonize and to exploit for the benefit of Italians and to keep native peoples in a state of slavery", that the Italians had brought to the country "slavery, misery, suppression and oppression", therefore an Italian come-back would be completely "contrary to the wishes and welfare of our people".

ISSA further pointed out to the Committee that a member of the Italian delegation, ENRICO CERULLI, was the same man who as Governor of Ethiopia during Italian occupation in 1937 had thousands of Ethiopians massacred, and who was well known to the Somali people for his record of "cruelty and tyranny" from the time when he had been a high official of the colonial administration in Somaliland. ISSA requested the United Nations "not to sacrifice people on the altar of political expendiency" and added: "The Somalis prefer death to the return of Italy. Although they lack weapons, they would resist."[2]

The Political Committee, in which the imperialist powers and their satellites constituted the majority, adopted the British resolution, except the provision for the West of Eritrea to be united to the Sudan. But at the plenary meeting of the General Assembly, where a valid decision required a two-thirds majority of the votes, different amendments[3] to the draft failed to obtain the required majority. So no resolution was adopted.[4] The BEVIN–SFORZA scheme was thus defeated, and for the time being Somalia was again saved from an Italian come-back.

[1] ABDULLAHI ISSA was born at Afgoi in 1922. He was educated in Mogadishu, where he went to a Muslim school and later to an Italian school. From 1937 to 1942 he was an employee of the colonial administration. In 1942 the British authorities dismissed him, and from that time on he engaged in business. From 1944 he was an active member of the Somali Youth League, which in 1947 elected him Secretary.

[2] *Op. cit.*, p. 264.

[3] Egypt proposed that Somalia be placed under UN trusteeship, administered jointly by the three Western great powers, Egypt, Ethiopia and Pakistan as well as Italy, which was not a member of the world organization. Liberia suggested that the term of Italian trusteeship over Somalia be limited to fifteen years. Brazil and Peru proposed a period of 25 years for the same purpose.

[4] During the vote by paragraphs only a single provision of the British draft recommended by the Political Committee obtained the two-thirds majority: Eastern Eritrea to be united to Ethiopia; it was passed by 37 votes to 11, but the draft as a whole was finally rejected. Among those who voted in favour of the British proposal were all European and American capitalist states (except Haiti) as well as Australia, New Zealand, Thailand, and South Africa — altogether 35; those voting against it included the socialist countries (U.S.S.R., Ukraine, Byelorussia, Czechoslovakia, Poland, Yugoslavia), Egypt, Ethiopia, Liberia, Iraq, Lebanon, Syria, Yemen, Saudi Arabia, India, Pakistan, Burma, Philippines, Haiti — 19 on the whole.

In the period between the 3rd and 4th sessions of the UN General Assembly, SFORZA worked out a definitive compromise with the three Western great powers in respect of all ex-Italian colonies, covering also Italian trusteeship for Somalia. He also managed to win the consent of the majority of UN members (the NATO countries, Latin American states, some Arab countries and the CHIANG KAI-SHEK clique usurping the seat of People's China).

During the 4th session of the UN General Assembly the question was discussed in detail by the First (Political) Committee of the Assembly. The debate ended in setting up a sub-committee to prepare a draft resolution. This was then debated further, while a number of speakers argued either for or against the sub-committee's draft and several amendments were proposed.

The delegates endorsing the SFORZA compromise were the majority, and they all took a stand in favour of Italian trusteeship, though they advanced different arguments and reasons in support of their view. This applied first of all to the three Western great powers.

The representative of Britain proposed "international trusteeship with Italy as the administering power". France was in support of Italian trusteeship in the spirit of "conciliation and realism". The United States delegate was in favour of Italian trust administration *for an indefinite period* on the ground that the Somalis did not know what they needed to achieve independence by themselves.[19]

On behalf of Latin American countries the delegates from Brazil and Venezuela declared that the question of the former Italian colonies should be decided in co-operation with Italy, and therefore they would not agree to independence for Libya unless Somalia was made an Italian trust territory.

The representative of the CHIANG KAI-SHEK regime proposed acceptance of Italian trusteeship, arguing that the United Nations should not be influenced by the spirit of revenge, accordingly the General Assembly should act in the spirit of conciliation, it was not its business to punish Italy, which had already been punished by the peace treaty.[2]

The Italian representative, Count SFORZA, knowing that the compromise he had agreed upon with the great powers and the majority of UN member states would ensure his success beforehand, devoted his speech to a shameless glorification of

---

[1] Here is an excerpt of the U.S. delegate's statement: "Italian Somaliland is an area with undeveloped political institutions, the organization of whose people is largely tribal and pastoral. We can hardly expect this people to be in a position to determine for themselves what means might best assure their achievement of self-government and independence, and the fulfilment of their national aspirations. It is therefore the view of my Government that the General Assembly has a special responsibility to assure that the solution which we recommend will in reality provide for the best interests of the inhabitants . . .

"During the many months and years which my Government has considered this problem, it has consistently been our view that the Italian Government is the best choice for the responsibility of administering a trusteeship of Italian Somaliland . . .

"The United States has full faith in the determination and ability of the democratic Italian Government and the hard-working Italian people to discharge faithfully this obligation toward the people of Italian Somaliland and toward the General Assembly of the United Nations." Cf. *op. cit.*, p. 304.

[2] The truth is that Italy paid almost nothing of the reparations prescribed by the treaty of peace. Britain and the United States had waived the reparations and gave considerable financial assistance to Italy, which paid little of the reparations due to other states, including Ethiopia which had suffered most from Italian aggression. Moreover, Italy had not even returned the art treasures looted from Ethiopia.

the professed democratism of the actual Italian government, vilified Great Britain (to which, however, he was indebted for his success) as well as the Soviet Union, but spoke flatteringly of the U.S. and French governments which gave unconditional support to the Italian claims, and tried to make them believe that in assuming the obligations of trusteeship Italy was guided solely by the interests of the Somali people:

"Democratic Italy always regarded her colonies, not merely as Italian interests, but as Italian aspects of world interests. It is for this reason that Italy succeeded in contributing to the historical, economic, cultural and moral patrimony of the local populations. . . . The development of Somalia has required a strenuous effort on the part of Italy. That effort could not be interrupted without serious damages and set-backs to the proper development of Somalia; a process still going on, and mainly due to our tenacious faith in the potentialities of the country, and our constant will to associate the Somalis in our Labour and Hopes . . . Italians always lived and worked hand in hand with the local populations, even in the most difficult moments. Neither time nor events, still less extraneous influences, will succeed in obliterating their friendship, based as it is on memories, decades old, of fruitful work carried out together . . . We trust that President Truman's generous plan will soon open the way to solutions and transformations which will never threaten the principles of self-determination."[1]

While Italy, though not being a member of the United Nations yet, could be represented at the meetings of the Political Committee and state the Italian position, the representatives of Somalia, whose future was at stake, were not allowed to speak in the debate, they were only "heard".

ABDULLAHI ISSA, who represented the Somali Youth League, emphasized that the Somali people asked for the immediate independence of the country, but if the General Assembly believed that the territory should be placed temporarily under UN trusteeship, they would not object, provided that Italy would have no part whatsoever in the administration of Somalia. At the same time ISSA unmasked the pro-Italian Somalis as traitors to the Somali people, as ones whom the Italians had given or promised money in case they painted past Italian administration in rosy colours and clamoured for the return of Italy.

This statement by ISSA found confirmation in the hearing by the Committee of two representatives of the Somalia Conferenza (a collector of revenue and an advisor to an Italian judge), who claimed to represent 95 per cent of the Somali population, and who asserted that 30 per cent of the population — thanks to the Italians — were of similar education to that of the members of their delegation Despite the fact that everybody laughed at their absurdities,[2] they were quoted by several supporters of the Italian case to prove that the Somalis were not opposed to the return of Italian rule.

Italian trusteeship for Somaliland was firmly opposed only by the socialist countries and Ethiopia. The Soviet delegate proposed UN trusteeship for five years, the Yugoslav representative was in favour of collective trust administration.

To the majority opinion favouring Italian trusteeship the Ethiopian delegate replied bitterly in these terms:

---

[1] *Op. cit.*, pp. 308, 316–318.
[2] The delegate from Pakistan, for example, wittingly asked why trusteeship, and why not immediate independence, was proposed for Somaliland if the educational level of the population was higher than it had been in India and Pakistan before independence.

"I declare here solemnly, in the name of my country, that the proposal to return Italy to Somaliland, and the refusal to satisfy Ethiopia's claim to Eritrea, take into account neither the desires nor the interests of the population, and abandon the interests of peace and security. They constitute a direct threat to the independence of Ethiopia. If this attempt should succeed, the United Nations Organization would have lent itself to a greater injustice than that which Ethiopia suffered at the hands of the League of Nations. After all the sufferings Ethiopia has gone through, she will not allow herself to be sacrficed on the altar of the United Nations to appease Italy, as was done at the League of Nations. She will abandon all hope in justice from the United Nations, and will take all measures for legitimate self-defence, as provided in the Charter of the United Nations."[1]

Liberia, Burma and some Muslim countries vacillated during the debates. Liberia suggested the establishment of a fact-finding commission to ascertain the opinion of the Somali population. This motion was seconded by Yemen and Burma.

The Yemeni delegate opposed Italian trusteeship and proposed collective UN trusteeship for ten years.

The representatives of Pakistan, Iraq and Saudi Arabia expressed the belief that the majority of the Somali population opposed Italian trusteeship; they declared that they would not vote for it, though they might accept Italy as only one of several administering powers exercising collective trusteeship. Iraq demanded notably that Ethiopia should join Italy as a trust power, and that Italy, once appointed as administering authority, should be forbidden to establish military bases in the territory. (At a later stage Pakistan favoured a ten-year term of Italian trusteeship for the territory which, with the British and French Somali Protectorate and the Ethiopian Ogaden Province, might in the future constitute an independent United Somaliland. In the final vote Yemen, Saudi Arabia, Iraq and Burma supported Italian trusteeship, while Liberia and Pakistan abstained.)

The sub-committee resolved that former Italian Somaliland should be placed under Italian trusteeship for ten years, after which the territory should be granted independence unless the General Assembly should decide otherwise at that time.

The debate over the sub-committee's resolution boiled down to the question of whether or not to fix the period of trusteeship and, if so, for how long; and whether to establish an Advisory Council to assist the administration, and what its composition and functions should be.

The formula devised by the sub-committee for Somalia to win independence after ten years "unless the General Assembly should decide otherwise at that time" gave rise to a heated debate. Even most of SFORZA's Latin American allies thought that this restriction might make the territory's independence precarious, all the more since SFORZA and the U.S. representative clearly proposed that Somaliland should remain under Italian trusteeship "for an indefinite period". Finally, this reservation was rejected by 33 votes to 22, with 4 abstentions.

The delegate of Lebanon supported Italian trusteeship because in his opinion the new Italy was a threat neither to Ethiopia nor to the Somalis, but in view of Ethiopian fears he proposed as a guarantee the appointment of a five-member Advisory Council. The Lebanese proposal was supported by Ecuador and Burma.

This delusive proposal by CHARLES MALIK of Lebanon, one of SFORZA's most faithful allies, was intended unmistakably as a countermove to appease the opponents of Italian trusteeship. MALIK explained that the most proper thing to do would

[1] *Op. cit.*, p. 322.

be to impose collective trusteeship, but since it was opposed by the majority, a compromise solution should be worked out which would satisfy the supporters of Italian trusteeship just as well as those who thought it would be a danger to Somali interests. The Advisory Council he proposed was to be a guarantee to reassure the Somalis. The debate over this proposal, however, brought out that it was only a deceptive manoeuvre.

The debate was centred on the functions and composition of the proposed Advisory Council. The Egyptian delegate suggested the deletion of the word "Advisory", arguing that such a council would be a guarantee only if it was not simply advisory, but if it had an effective say in the trust administration. The representative of the Philippines supported the Egyptian conception and proposed that the members of the Advisory Council should have seats on the Trusteeship Council of the United Nations. The delegation of Poland proposed that the Advisory Council should include three representatives of the Somali population elected by the political organizations, and the Iraqi delegate proposed a representative of Ethiopia as a member of the Advisory Council.

The proponents of Italian trusteeship, including the Lebanese MALIK, were against all these suggestions. MALIK objected that such provisions were needless because Somali interests would be properly protected by the trusteeship agreement between the Trusteeship Council and the administering power, as well as by the proposed Advisory Council which would help Italy and "would be collaborating in the administration": "The peoples of Somaliland could always appeal to the Advisory Council; they could always talk to the members of the council to make sure that no abuse had been exercised by administering authority upon the Somalis."[1] British delegate McNEIL was not satisfied with this hypocritical proposal of MALIK either: he claimed that the Advisory Council must have no share in the administration of the trust territory, that Italy should be the sole administrator. Then MALIK, throwing off the mask, said that it had never been his intention that the Advisory Council should "interfere in the actual administration of the territory".

The great powers and their satellites were opposed also to this weakened version of an Advisory Council (the delegates of France, Belgium, South Africa and others even said so explicitly) and declared their willingness to vote for it only if the Council was to be composed of at most two or three members instead of five. (The Belgian delegate proposed that South Africa should be the fourth!)

Ethiopia was in any case against setting up an Advisory Council, which in her view would provide no guarantee against the Italian colonialists and would not lessen the danger involved in their return, and therefore she refused to accept the seat on the Council proposed by the Iraqi delegation.

The Egyptian proposal for the deletion of the word "Advisory" was rejected by 37 votes to 14, with 8 abstentions, and the Polish proposal for the inclusion of three Somali representatives was rejected by 33 votes to 9, with 17 abstentions. On the other hand, MALIK's amended proposal for the establishment of an Advisory Council composed of three members (Egypt, the Philippines, Colombia) instead of five was adopted by 48 votes to 1 (Ethiopia), with 10 abstentions. Characteristically, the Lebanese resolution was voted also by Egypt, the Philippines and Iraq in spite of the rejection of their own positive proposals. Later, at a plenary meeting of the General Assembly, the representative of the Philippines declared that unless the Advisory Council "had a much higher status than a mere group of observers" its

[1] *Op. cit.*, pp. 341–342.

presence would be either "a luxury or a pretence in which neither the States concerned nor the United Nations could afford to indulge".[1]

The Somali Youth League had requested the Committee to hear its representative before passing a decision, but on a motion from the delegate of Argentina it was decided by 25 votes to 19, with 2 abstentions, that the League might submit its views only in writing.

The sub-committee's amended proposal for ex-Italian Somaliland to be placed under Italian trusteeship for ten years and then be granted independence was adopted in the Political Committee by 48 votes to 7, with 4 abstentions. It was voted against by Ethiopia and the socialist countries, while Liberia, Pakistan, Sweden and New Zealand abstained in the vote.

After adopting the sub-committee's resolution the Political Committee had to decide on two questions:

1. The delegation of India proposed that an annexure containing suggested constitutional principles, to be observed by the Trusteeship Council and Italy as a trust power, should be added to the resolution adopted on Italian trust administration. Since neither the sub-committee nor the Political Committee had examined the text of the proposed annexure, the Committee decided to submit it to the General Assembly without stating any opinion and without taking a vote on it.

2. Since the boundary between Somaliland and Ethiopia was not properly delimited, the Political Committee recommended the General Assembly to instruct its interim committee to study the question of boundaries which were not yet fixed by international agreement, and to report on its findings to the General Assembly at its 5th session.

When the resolution on Italian trusteeship over Somaliland was adopted, the delegation of Argentina proposed that, since the trusteeship agreement would take some time to draw up, negotiate and approve, the United Nations should invite Italy to take over from Britain the "provisional administration" of the territory under UN supervision as soon as possible. Ethiopia, the Soviet Union and other states said that this step was inadmissible, because it would impose Italian rule without safeguards. On a motion by the Chilean delegation the Committee decided (by 38 votes to 8, with 10 abstentions) that Italian administration should not start until after the draft of a trusteeship agreement was negotiated and approved by the General Assembly and the Italian government.

This cautious resolution was needed all the more because already tens of thousands of Italian "volunteers" recruited by the government and equipped with modern weapons were ready in Italy to sail, in violation of the peace treaty, for the ex-colony turned into trust territory, which in the past Italy had used as a basis to build a nice little colonial empire, and not so long before, in the 1930's, even to realize a twice frustrated scheme, the occupation and looting of Ethiopia.

On November 29, 1949, the General Assembly adopted the resolution submitted by the Political Committee without debate. Some amendments were moved by the Polish delegation (for two Somalis to be added to the Advisory Council, the Assembly to invite the Trusteeship Council to draw up the draft trusteeship agreement by itself, without negotiating with the Italian government, and for Somaliland to be granted independence within three years), but the majority of the General Assembly rejected them all.

[1] *Op. cit.*, p. 342.

(The full text of the UN resolution on the ex-Italian colonies and that of the "Declaration of Constitutional Principles" proposed by India are published in the often quoted work by E. S. PANKHURST, *Ex-Italian Somaliland*, pp. 350–354.)

When the news of the many pro-Italian statements in the United Nations reached Somaliland, the Somali Youth League tried, in spite of the ban imposed by the British administration, to hold a procession in Mogadishu on October 5. The police called the people to disperse, but the crowd did not move, and then the police opened fire. A man was shot dead and many were wounded, three of them fatally. Similar demonstrations took place in over twenty towns and villages. The British administration ordered the closing of the offices of all political organizations and the imprisonment or deportation of several Somali sheiks and chiefs. Because of popular resistance in many places these measures were carried out by force. As a result of police intervention two Somalis were killed and several wounded at Dolo, and two were shot at Bardera, where the stone-throwing Somalis hurt a district commissioner and several policemen, too. In Mogadishu four respected chiefs were sentenced to imprisonment for 6, 9 and 12 months respectively. In the United Nations the representative of Liberia, H. F. COOPER, presented a draft resoluting demanding that the British administration should be compelled to permit free expression of Somali opinion. But this motion was defeated by 20 votes to 16, with 9 abstentions.

The Drafting of the Trusteeship Agreement

On December 9, 1949, the Trusteeship Council appointed a special Somaliland Committee to draft the trusteeship agreement. Members of the Committee were representatives of the United Kingdom, the United States, France, Iraq, the Philippines and the Dominican Republic. Italian representatives were invited to take part in the work of the Committee and to state their views on any question. With reference to Article 79 of the UN Charter, Ethiopia demanded to participate with the right to vote, but was allowed only to send observers without the voting right. Egypt and Colombia were also invited to attend, without votes, as members of the Advisory Council (whose third member, the Philippines, had a seat on the Committee as a member of the Trusteeship Council). The Somaliland Committee declared its readiness to hear representatives of the Somali parties and other organizations, but none of them had asked to be heard. (The militant organizations obviously because they firmly opposed the return of Italy, and because to discuss matters concerning Italian trusteeship would have been to abandon their position, to become reconciled to the fact of Italian trusteeship; and the moderate elements because they feared that their action would incur the anger of the future Italian administration.)

The Somaliland Committee met at Geneva on January 9, 1950.

The Italian government prepared a draft of the trusteeship agreement and submitted it to the Secretary-General of the United Nations for consideration by the Somaliland Committee. The Philippine member of the Committee also prepared a draft, while the Dominican and Iraqi representatives proposed changes in some provisions.

The Italian draft teemed with demagogical phrases seemingly vindicating the "honest intentions" of the Italian government, its efforts to protect the interests of the Somalis and promote their advancement towards independence. On the other hand, it revealed the real face and the effective intentions of the Italian imperialists: to retain, under the cloak of trusteeship, all they could of the old colonial positions and privileges, to delay or possibly frustrate for ever the independence of Somaliland.

With the trusteeship agreement Italian imperialism attempted to achieve these aims by inserting in the draft several provisions conflicting with the UN Charter, the UN resolutions and international law.

The Italian government made every effort to prevent a limitation of the period of trusteeship, thereby to prolong indefinitely the date for independence, and therefore its draft made no mention of this aspect of the question.

The wording of the Italian draft would have given Italy a free hand to station armed forces in the territory. The draft claimed for Italy "Power to establish in the Territory whatever military, naval and air installations are necessary for the defence of the Territory, to maintain its own armed forces, and to raise volunteer contingents".[1]

As for the *boundaries* the Italian draft in its Article 1 provided as follows: "The boundaries of the Territory are those resulting from the treaties and conventions concluded between the Italian Government and the adjoining States with effect from January 1, 1935",[2] which would have meant incorporation of the Ogaden, occupied, by the Italian aggressor in 1934, into the Italian trust territory.

As to the *application of Italian law*, the draft of the Italian government provided that the administering authority should have power to apply to Somaliland, temporarily and with the modifications considered necessary, such Italian laws as were appropriate to the conditions and needs of the territory.

In other questions the Italian colonialists endeavoured to attain their goal by resorting to two tricks:

1. In the articles on the political freedoms of the Somalis, they qualified the democratic-sounding provisions by adding certain reservations which made the whole affair entirely illusory.[3]

What was consistent with the development of the inhabitants or with the regulations established by Italian law was of course to be determined by the Italian administration itself, which thus would be given full powers to impose upon the Somalis such measures of racial discrimination as it pleased.

2. In a number of questions, where the interests or rights of the Somali population would have to be guaranteed (for example, in the article on education and in the declaration attached to the draft and describing the civil and political rights),

---

[1] *Op. cit.*, p. 367.

[2] With this manoeuvre, as well as in general, the Italian government, which in words dissociated itself from the fascists, tried to have accepted the repudiation of Italy's obligations undertaken in conventions of the past which the fascist regime had unilaterally declared null and void. Therefore it failed to mention in its draft the question of the validity of international treaties. But the Committee's final draft dealt with the question in a separate provision (Art. 12), which began as follows: "The Administering Authority undertakes to maintain the application of the international agreements and conventions which are at present in force in the Territory..."

[3] Such striking examples:

"The Administering Authority shall guarantee to all inhabitants of the Territory full civil and political rights consistent, as regards the exercise of such rights, with the progressive political, social, economic and educational development of the inhabitants, and with the advancement of traditional institutions towards democratic representative systems.

"...it shall guarantee to them... individual liberty, which may be restricted only in the cases and according to the regulations established by law ... the free exercise of professions, trades and economic activities in accordance with existing local customs and in conformity with such regulations as shall be enacted; ... the right to compete for public employment in conformity with regulations which shall be enacted and which shall determine the particular conditions of eligibility..."

they took care not to use the expression "Somali" or "natives", but they referred to "inhabitants" of the territory or the "indigenous population", by which they understood all inhabitants of the country, including the resident Italians and Arab and other immigrants.

In contrast to the Italian draft agreement, the Philippine draft paid regard to the Somali interests in the first place, and the Philippine delegate, when speaking before the Committee, often objected to the misleading formulations advanced by the Italians. He even proposed their revision to suit the Somali interests, but with little success.

In drafting the final text of the trusteeship agreement the Somaliland Committee unfortunately endorsed almost all Italian proposals.

(a) In some questions it accepted the Italian formulation without any change.

Over and above falling for the Italian trick of mentioning "inhabitants" or "population" instead of "Somalis" or "natives", they even applied this device more widely, for example in Article 14 on land and natural resources, although in its corresponding Article 9 the Italian draft referred to "native populations".

Paragraph 4 on "civil and political rights" in the declaration attached to the Italian draft was recast by the Committee to some extent, but the final text (Article 9 of the Annex) again mentioned "inhabitants of the Territory" in general and included the Italian loopholes like "regulations prescribed by law".

(b) In other cases, while making some changes in the Italian wording, the Committee left the essence of the Italian version unchanged.

Article 3 in the Italian draft concerning the *functions of the Advisory Council* only listed the matters in which the administering authority might request the advice of the Advisory Council without making such advice mandatory for the administration, and the draft allowed the Council no effective voice in any matter.

In the final text of the agreement (Art. 8) the Committee included a different version of the Italian draft's Article 3 but did not change its essence: the administering authority might seek the advice of the Advisory Council and was obliged to inform the Council of the measures taken. But the final text of the agreement, just like the Italian draft, limited the functions of the Advisory Council to giving advice but did not let it have any say in the practice of administration.

In the question of *air, naval, military and police forces* the representative of the Philippines proposed that any plan to recruit troops from outside the territory or to organize such forces in the territory or to establish military facilities in the territory would be made subject to approval by the UN Trusteeship Council. He demanded that "unless authorized by the United Nations, acting through its appropriate organs, the Administering authority shall not establish naval, military and air bases, or erect fortifications in the territory, or station and employ its own armed forces in the territory".[1]

The Iraqi representative proposed that the administering power should be permitted to recruit only volunteer forces in the trust territory. However, the French and Dominican representatives supported the Italian demand for freedom to establish military installations.

Thereupon the Committee adopted a weak formulation providing for consultation with the Advisory Council instead of approval by the United Nations (the advice of the Council, as is known, was not mandatory for the administering authority):

[1] *Op. cit.*, p. 367.

"The Administering Authority may maintain police forces and raise volunteer contingents for the maintenance of peace and good order in the Territory.

"The Administering Authority, after consultation with the Advisory Council, may establish installations and take all measures in the Territory, including the progressive development of Somali defence forces . . ." (Art. 6).

The Philippine delegate, with reference to the relevant paragraph 4 of the Indian annexure already adopted, requested inclusion in the agreement of the following provision:

"In matters relating to defence and foreign affairs, the Administrator shall be responsible to, and carry out the directions of, the United Nations, acting through its appropriate organs."

The Committee could not ignore this position that was already laid down in a UN resolution, but made such a modified version of it which openly gave a free hand to the Italian trust administration to maintain Italian armed forces in the territory and utilize it as a military basis, requiring only that Italy should inform the Trusteeship Council of such steps taken (!). Article 6 of the Annex to the trusteeship agreement provided:

"In matters relating to defence and foreign affairs and in other matters, the Administering Authority shall be accountable to the Trusteeship Council, and shall take into account any recommendations which the Council may see fit to make."

With regard to the question of the *application of Italian law* the Committee included in its final text the above-cited wording of the Italian draft, adding to the qualification of Italian laws this phrase: "and as are not incompatible with the attainment of its independence", while leaving it entirely to the Italian trust administration to decide whether those requirements were met or not.

(c) In a number of questions, including some of the most important ones (the period of trusteeship, the boundary between Ethiopia and Somaliland, the validity of Italy's international treaties, etc.), in view of the resolutions already adopted by the United Nations, as well as of the international conventions in force, and considering the striking contrast between the principles of the UN Charter and the draft provisions proposed by Italy, the Committee was compelled either to reject the Italian formulation or to modify it to a considerable extent.

Regarding the *limitation of the term of trusteeship* the Committee, with reference to a resolution adopted by the General Assembly at it 4th session in November 1949, stated in the preamble of the final text that "The Territory shall be an independent and sovereign State: its independence shall become effective at the end of ten years from the date of approval of the Trusteeship Agreement by the General Assembly."

With regard to the *frontier question*, the Committee felt obliged, considering the UN resolutions in force, to change the Italian draft's wording which attempted to leave out of account previous treaties still in force and to refer instead to the agreements imposed by the Italian fascist aggressor after 1934. The final wording of Article 1 contained the following provision: The boundaries of the territory "shall be those fixed by international agreement and, in so far as they are not already delimited, shall be delimited in accordance with a procedure approved by the General Assembly".

Besides modifying some parts of the Italian draft the Committee gave free scope also to another deceptive manoeuvre of the Italian imperialists in connection with the validity of international treaties. Originally the relevant article of the draft began as follows: "The Administering Authority undertakes to maintain the application of all existing international agreements . . ." and the Italian representative imposed its extension to read ". . . which are at present in force in the Territory".

As to the provisions on the *prohibition of slavery, forced labour, and the control of the traffic in arms, drugs,* etc., the representative of the Philippines proposed the addition of a clause with reference to international treaties in force and binding for Italy. The Italian representative objected, arguing that Italy was already bound by such international engagements and a new reminder would hurt some feelings. The Italian point of view was endorsed also by the British representative, who in turn found this clause to be an affront to the "native population". However, the representative of the International Labour Office, who took part in the deliberations, insisted on the clause proposed by the Philippines, and the Committee finally accepted it.

Entry into Force of the Trusteeship Agreement

The final text of the draft agreement drawn up by the Somaliland Committee was presented to the Trusteeship Council, which on January 27, 1950, accepted it subject to minor changes.[1] The General Assembly adopted a resolution approving the draft trusteeship agreement on December 2, 1950. The only major debated point was that the agreement failed to define the legal status of the Advisory Council as a UN organ and to invest it with full diplomatic privileges and immunities. The Italian representative objected to such provisions being written into the agreement, but after a long debate an arrangement was made by which the Italian government would recognize the Advisory Council as an organ of the United Nations and would conclude an agreement with the Secretary-General of the United Nations concerning its recognition of the Council's status and the privileges and immunities to be accorded at the same time.

The trusteeship agreement on Somaliland is one of those UN documents which were drawn up in the early years of the existence of the world organization, when the vast majority of the states members of the United Nations were politically and economically dependent on the three Western great powers, and which were adopted thanks to this subservient policy toward the great powers at variance with the principles of the UN Charter. The duplicity of the great powers, however, was borne out by the fact that the agreement, besides its deficiencies and provisions contrary to the UN principles, contained a number of democratic provisions as well which were in harmony with the principles of the Charter. This goes especially for the final provision (Art. 25) of the agreement which read as follows:

"The Administering Authority shall submit to the Trusteeship Council at least 18 months before the expiration of the present Agreement a plan for the orderly transfer of all the functions of government to a duly constituted independent Government of the Territory."

The earlier victims of Italian aggression could not acquiesce in the fact that Italy was restored as administrator of a country which she had for nearly a century held under colonial subjection and used as a basis for aggression on Ethiopia. Ethiopia repeatedly and strongly protested against the Italian trusteeship agreement. The vast majority of the Somalis noted with bitterness the conclusion of the agreement,

[1] Before the Trusteeship Council the Italian representative and two delegates who supported him (one from CHIANG KAI-SHEK's "China" and one from Belgium) made an attempt to have a few provisions changed to suit the Italian standpoint, but it was of no avail.

and the Somali Youth League was determined to make use of the possibilities offered by the trusteeship system for continuing the struggle for the rights of the Somalis and the independence of the territory even under Italian administration.

The Italian Come-back

Immediately after the signing of the trusteeship agreement the Italian government entered into negotiations with the British government for the transfer of the territory, and rapidly completed the preparation of its land, naval and air forces for the reoccupation of the former Italian colony. It assigned the post of Administrator of Somaliland to General GUGLIELMO NASI, a notorious war criminal, one of MUSSOLINI's most sanguinary hangmen.

Italian public opinion was not unanimous in appreciating the undertaking of trusteeship. A large part of the Italian people, having learnt from the experiences of over two decades' fascist regime, looked with anxiety on this fresh imperialist adventure of the Italian big bourgeoisie. Opposition was considerable also among members of Parliament and the Senate, too. The left-wing parties, which had for years made propaganda along with the government for the recovery of the colonies, were now agitating vehemently against the undertaking and against the appointment of the fascist hangman General NASI.[1] Even the right-wing M.P.s and senators backing the government, as well as the right-wing press, voiced concern at the considerable cost incurred by the administration of the trust territory. The government was blamed for having assumed trusteeship in an unconstitutional way, without consulting Parliament. Finally, the government was compelled to submit the question for consideration by Parliament.

In the parliamentary debate Prime Minister DE GASPERI, to excuse the government's action, operated with the old demagogical slogan of "Italy's civilizing mission to backward peoples", and claimed that renouncement of the trusteeship of Somaliland after long efforts to obtain it would be a great mistake and "a negation of faith in a better world". As to the delicate problems (the boundary with Ethiopia, General NASI's appointment, the cost of trust administration, etc.), he evaded or dismissed them briefly.[2] On the other hand, he elaborated on what his government considered a question of major importance, the government decision to terminate the Ministry of Italian Africa and to create instead a Trusteeship Administration (a merely formal change, for the personnel of the new Administration was the same as that of the suppressed Ministry).

Being brought to bay by PAJETTA's statements and documents on General NASI, Foreign Minister SFORZA pleaded that the appointment was only temporary and General NASI would be recalled soon (!).

Despite the strong criticism voiced in Parliament the right-wing majority of the government party voted for the acceptance of trusteeship.

[1] Socialist leader P. NENNI accused the government of "the old levity with which the country was in the past pledged to African adventures", and charged that the United Nations derided Italy by entrusting to her the mandate for Somaliland, "which compromises us in the eyes of the African peoples as accomplices of European colonialism". (Cf. *op. cit.*, p. 421.) And G. PAJETTA of the Communist Party submitted to Parliament documents unmasking General NASI as a war criminal.

[2] In speaking of the expenditures, for example, he stated that experts estimated the cost of administration at less than 20 billion lire a year, but in his opinion this could soon be reduced to 16 billion and later possibly to 4 or 5 billion lire.

Already in March 1950 the Italian government, without consulting the Advisory Council (although it should have done so under the trusteeship agreement), and in secrecy (in view of domestic opposition), began shipping large contingents of Italian troops to Somaliland, where it introduced practically a military regime in the guise of trust administration.

The responsible administrative posts were filled with persons actively involved in the atrocities committed during the fascist colonial regime.

The first thing these officials did — and they did it in violation of the trusteeship agreement (Art. 7)—was that they put into force again the fascist laws which had been invalidated under British military administration.

The British-led police force was replaced by Italian *carabinieri*. In a couple of months the number of imprisoned Somalis had trebled. At the time of the Italian take-over, in the Mogadishu prison, for example, there had been 427 inmates, and this figure rose to over 3,000 by May 1950. Leaders, members and supporters of the Somali Youth League—among them chiefs, sheiks and civil servants—were arrested by the hundred and imprisoned for terms ranging from 6 months to 3 years, without trial or hearing, just on the strength of a "penal decree" signed by the arresting officer. In the rare cases when a person was brought to trial he was denied the right to have an attorney. There having been no public prosecutors in the whole of Somalia, except in Mogadishu, such functions were exercised everywhere by the district commissioners or other administrative officials.

As regards the treatment of prisoners, the colonial prisons of the "democratic" Italian Republic were hardly different from the torture chambers installed by the fascist aggressors back in 1941.

The executive and judicial powers were exercised by district commissioners (so-called *Residenti*) who employed the fascist methods of old.

Far from pursuing the policy of Somalization of the civil service started during British occupation, the Italian administration dismissed even many of the functioning Somali officials, especially those in higher positions, already in April 1950 and replaced them with Italians.

The provisions of the trusteeship agreement concerning Somali education were implemented only reluctantly, slowly and incompletely.

In violation of the explicit provisions of the trusteeship agreement the administering power pursued right from the beginning an exclusive economic policy furthering the interests of Italian capitalists.

Exploiting the fact that the frontier between Somalia and Ethiopia (Ogaden) was not yet established, the Italian government made attempts under demagogical pretences to annex Ethiopian territory to the trust territory of Somaliland. (For details about the war crimes of the fascist hangman General NASI and the measures introduced by the Italian trust authority replacing the British military administration, see E. S. PANKHURST, *Ex-Italian Somaliland*, ch. XXIII: "Italian Return to Somaliland", pp. 417–447.)

The Policy of Italian Imperialism in the Trust Territory

The history of trusteeship in Somaliland is in many respects different from the parallel history of other territories under trusteeship.

1. While the other mandates for trusteeship were given to the victors of World War II and imperialist powers which were founders of the United Nations (Britain,

France, Belgium), Italy was one of the defeated powers and was not even a member of the United Nations at the time the trusteeship agreement was concluded.

2. As a consequence the United Nations set up an Advisory Council to supervise the policy of the administering power, and in contrast to other trust territories, this trusteeship agreement solved a major controversial problem: it fixed a date for the independence of the territory.

3. The trusteeship agreement for Somaliland was designed to prepare for independence a country with a large part of its proper area and population being beyond its frontiers, in four different territories, under British and French colonial rule and under the government of feudal Ethiopia (British and French Somaliland, Kenya, the Ethiopian Ogaden). This was why the problem of independence for ex-Italian Somaliland was not only a problem of the Somali people of that country, but also one of the struggle for the unification of all Somali-inhabited areas and the Somali tribes scattered in five countries.

In the nine-year history of Italian trusteeship we have to distinguish two stages; the policy of the Italian imperialists striving to obtain the trusteeship mandate differed from the definitely neocolonialist policy of the victorious colonial powers (Britain, France, Belgium). The Italian imperialists, who had lost their colonies, were guided by a double objective:

1. With the assumption of trusteeship they saw it possible to regain their lost status among the imperialist colonial powers or to maintain their position at least in this form, and were hopeful that in time they would manage, as South Africa did, to evade their obligations and take possession of the trust territory as their own colony.

2. Possession of Somaliland was important to them not only as a still unexploited colony which promised enormous economic benefits for the future, but also as a bridgehead which, strengthened economically and militarily, they might rely upon for starting again the struggle to recover their lost colonies, thus permitting them in a favourable world constellation to renew their often attempted campaigns of aggression for the conquest of new territories.

During the first five years of trusteeship (1950–1955) the policy of the Italian imperialists in this respect was determined by these considerations. They did their best to demonstrate to the outside world that they were genuine democrats who had liquidated the fascist heritage definitively and, acting in the spirit of the United Nations, were faithfully administering the territory entrusted to them. In their annual reports to the United Nations they painted the situation and development of the territory in bright colours, and testified to the fulfilment of their obligations under the trusteeship agreement, to the year-by-year progressive economic and political advancement of the Somali peoples, to the improvement of living standards, and to the fair development of the system of education. The truth was, however, that they violated most of the obligations imposed on the administering authority. They did practically nothing to prepare the territory for independence or to promote the democratization and Africanization of the public administration. The widely advertised "democratic" regime of the Italian trust administration was hardly different from the pre-war oppressive rule of terror of the fascist colonizers. The fascist laws, most of which had been invalidated during British occupation, were again put into force. The positions in the trust administration and the civil service were mostly occupied by Italians, among them a large number of former fascists, besides the few openly pro-Italian elements of the Somali population. One of the most shameful methods of Italian colonial rule, the application of collective punishment, was again widespread. The large differences in the pay of Italian and Somali officials and other employees and workers were maintained. The Somali employees and soldiers dismissed from Italian service during the war still waited in vain for their back pay.

The administering authority concentrated its attention on the problems of economic development. But the economic plans and the related investments were designed, not to improve the miserable living conditions of the Somali masses, but to promote the business interests of Italian and other capitalists. Even the realization of these projects made little progress because the administering authority lacked the necessary financial means.

Under the impact of the post-Bandung events (Sudan, Tanganyika, British Somaliland, Ghana) and the changed international atmosphere the Italian imperialists shifted their policy, since they had to see that the clock of history could not be put back. Still they pursued the aim of controlling the profitable exploitation of the natural resources of Somalia and of using the territory as a military base for their imperialist purposes, but to attain these goals they resorted to new methods, those of neocolonialism. With an eye to the admission of Italy to membership of the United Nations, they introduced certain reforms containing elements of a seemingly democratic system of self-government, but without allowing the Somalis to really have a say in their own affairs.

The Territorial Council established by the trust administration in 1951 was first composed of educated elements, and these were replaced with elected members in 1955. This organ, which only was a consultative body, was transformed into a Legislative Assembly, whose members were directly elected by secret ballot by the adult male population in towns and indirectly by tribal colleges (elected representatives of tribes) in the provinces. At the same time an all-Somali government was set up, composed of a Premier and five (later six) ministers nominated by the Italian Administrator of the territory. Each minister was assisted by an Italian counsellor appointed also by the Administrator. However, the government was answerable to the Administrator, not to the Legislative Assembly, to which though it had to submit its programme for approval. Members of both bodies were free to present bills individually, too, but only with the prior consent of the Administrator. The laws passed by the Legislative Assembly entered into force only after approval by the Administrator, who was empowered to demand modification of such legislation. He had the right in urgent cases also to issue legislative decrees, which had to be submitted later to the legislature for enactment. At the same time the Legislative Assembly might authorize the Administrator to issue edicts in certain specified cases. The Administrator could dissolve the Legislative Assembly if he found it incapable of discharging its functions, or when he thought the normal legislative process was endangered, he could call new elections within 120 days. Foreign affairs, defence and security remained outside the business of the legislature and the government, those matters fell exclusively within the competence of the administering power.

Still in 1955 regional district councils were established, whose members were in part traditional chiefs elected by the tribal councils, in part representatives of political parties and other (economic, cultural or religious) organizations who had been nominated by the administering authority, under the chairmanship of the Italian district commissioners. These councils had powers only to discuss questions of local interest.

In 1955 Somalization was completed in the internal postal services, the radiotelegraphic and customs services, in 1956 in the port authorities, while in 1956 also the Italian district commissioners and regional commissioners were relieved by Somalis.

Up to that time the Italian trust power had persecuted and tried to suppress all political movements of the Somalis, but now it tried to secure their co-operation with the administering authority and to enforce its policy with their help. This scheme was a success to some extent, and the Italians, when they felt they could maintain their influence while helping Somali leaders to power, gradually switched over to the introduction of democratic reforms provided for by the trusteeship agreement.

The first step in preparation for a constitution was taken in September 1957: the task was entrusted to a Political Committee under the Chairman of the Legislative Assembly and the head of the government; other members were ministers, vice-chairmen of the legislature, representatives of the parliamentary parties, and three officials appointed by the Premier. To assist the Political Committee, a Technical Committee was formed which was composed of 11 Italians, 9 Somalis and 2 experts nominated by the Advisory Council.

In December 1958 a law was enacted on the extension of the elective franchise. The right to vote by secret ballot was extended to every male and female inhabitant over 18 years of age, and eligibility was granted to every Somali over 25 years who was able to read and write in Arabic or Italian. In June 1959 the number of ministries was raised to nine, and a post of under-secretary was created in each of the five major ministries, and in November 1959 the government was enlarged to include two ministers without portfolio, one of whom was in charge of the relations with the Legislative Assembly, and the other had the task of preparing the constitutional matters.

At the same time the economic development of the territory was given further momentum, invariably with the slogan of raising the material well-being of the Somali population, but in reality always with the purpose of promoting the interests of the Italian capitalists greedy for colonial profits.

The Italian government's annual reports to the United Nations still exaggerated considerably the results attained in the economic, political and cultural development of the territory and put a better complexion on the situation there, but since some progress was really made towards democracy, as was evidenced in the United Nations by several Somali leading politicians, Italy managed to satisfy even those member states which not so long before had still criticized the Italian administration of Somalia.

The Question of Somaliland in the United Nations

The United Nations, as the second guardian of trust territories, also failed to fulfil its function. Outwardly it complied with all its obligations: in 1950 it set up the standing Advisory Council, every three years (1951, 1954, 1957) it sent a Visiting Mission to supervise the situation in the territory; the Trusteeship Council and the General Assembly, the latter both in its Fourth Committee and in the plenary meetings, took up the question of Somaliland on a number of occasions. This question was included in the agenda of the General Assembly every year from the 7th to the 14th session (1952 to 1959). In reality, however, all these forums proved rather passive and inefficient in respect of Somaliland. None of the imperialist trust powers met with so much forbearance and indulgence on the part of the United Nations as did Italy, who observed least of all her obligations under the trusteeship agreement. This attitude can be accounted for by the fact that the NATO powers, which in those years had wielded the majority in the United Nations, had still been at that time interested in helping imperialist Italy to membership in the world organization, and after 1955 in getting Italy as a UN member to join NATO.

The composition of the Advisory Council and the UN Visiting Missions, as well as of the Trusteeship Council and even the General Assembly, enabled the imperialist NATO powers, especially the United States, to impose their will on all of them.[1] The Advisory Council was satisfied with the passive role which the United Nations, yielding to the Italian proposals, assigned to it in the trusteeship agreement. The Advisory Council did not even try to bring pressure to bear upon the administering authority either by its own actions or indirectly, through the Trusteeship Council, in the interests of the Somalis. In its regular reports to the Trusteeship Council it practically recorded the information, opinion and evaluations supplied by the Italian trust administration.

The administering authority furnished the Advisory Council with a steady flow of written information on the situation of the territory, its political, economic, social and cultural development. It was from the data contained in such one-sided information accepted without reservation that the Advisory Council compiled its annual reports to the UN Trusteeship Council, thereby confirming the parallel reports of the Italian trust power on the fulfilment of its own obligations under the trusteeship agreement. (Cf., for example, the report of the Advisory Council for the period from April 1, 1959, to March 31, 1960. Trusteeship Council doc. T/1516, Apr. 14, 1960.)

The UN Visiting Missions sent to the territory every three years relied first of all upon official information received from the Italian authorities. They routinely heard the representatives of Somali organizations and individual petitioners, but in their reports they hardly ever mentioned the complaints and demands made. Those reports were almost void of any criticism of the trust administration, nor did they formulate any concrete recommendations.[2]

The Trusteeship Council and the Fourth Committee of the General Assembly considered the question of Somalia on numerous occasions, but as regards the essence of the matter (democratic institutions, racial equality, equal pay, self-government, Somalization, preparations for independence), there was no real debate. In their resolutions they confined themselves to expressing their satisfaction with the results attained and voicing the hope that the administering authority would redress the still existing shortcomings. And the plenary meetings of the General Assembly adopted the meaningless resolutions without any serious debate or substantive change.

Both the Trusteeship Council and the General Assembly, as we are going to see, dealt in most cases only with the question of the Italo-Ethiopian boundary. Only once, during the 8th session in 1955, did the Assembly discuss the preparation of the territory for independence, when it recommended the administering power what

---

[1] The members of the Advisory Council were the representatives of Colombia, the Philippines and Egypt, while the UN Visiting Mission in 1951 was composed of representatives of the United States, New Zealand, the Dominican Republic and Thailand, in 1954 those of the United States, New Zealand, El Salvador and India, and in 1957 those of France, Australia, Haiti and Burma.

[2] *United Nations Visiting Mission to Trust Territories in East Africa, 1951: Report on Somaliland under Italian Administration* (Trusteeship Council T/1033), New York, 1952. — *Idem*, 1954 (T/1200), New York, 1955. — *Idem*, 1957 (T/1404), New York, 1958.

necessary steps to take,[1] and during its 9th session it dealt with the financing of the economic development plans of the territory,[2] but apart from this and the frontier dispute with Ethiopia, between 1951 and the end of 1959, it did nothing more than mechanically take note of the reports submitted by the administering authority. After the resolution passed in 1953 the Assembly only returned to a substantive consideration of the question of Somaliland just before the territory's accession to independence, at its 14th session, when in its resolution 1418 (XIV) of December 5, 1959, it congratulated the Italian and Somali governments on the steps taken in preparation of independence, expressing its appreciation for the aid of the Advisory Council and its confidence that the administering authority would implement the UN recommendations before the appointed date of independence (July 1, 1960).

In connection with Somaliland both the United Nations and the trust power, Italy, were preoccupied with two questions: the material assistance to be provided to the territory, and the territorial and frontier dispute. The first point was pressed by the administering power with the slogan of promoting the well-being of the Somali population. Italy pursued a double aim in this respect: to appear before the United Nations as a faithful advocate of Somali interests, and to promote its own interests by making use of the financial and technical assistance granted to Somaliland.

But the most vehement debates were sparked off by the territorial and frontier issue. An old dream of the Somali tribes was to unite all Somali territories (Italian Somaliland, British Somaliland, French Somaliland, the Somali-populated areas of Ethiopia and Kenya) in a single independent state. After the failure of the struggle around the trusteeship agreement and its entry into force it became evident that for the time being it was impossible to expect French Somaliland and the parts concerned of Ethiopia and Kenya to be joined to Somalia. A still more burning question for Somalia, however, was that of the boundary with Ethiopia, the delimitation of which was explicitly provided for by the trusteeship agreement. That this problem, which was important and urgent for both Ethiopia and Somalia, had not been settled either in the eight years of British occupation or in the ten years of Italian trust administration is illustrative of the double-dealing imperialist policies of the British and Italian governments as well as of the irresponsible and unconcerned attitude of the United Nations towards the vital interests of the Ethiopian and the Somali people. The United Nations meant to resolve the controversy of the two interested countries by negotiation between the Ethiopian and Italian governments, that is between the competent representative of the people of one country (Ethiopia) and the representative of another (Italy) whose imperialist interests did not demand the elimination of conflicts between the two parties but worked towards sharpening the conflicts and weakening both Ethiopia and Somalia, in order to make it easier in the future to break the resistance they put up to the imperialist intrigues and manoeuvres of Italy.

The Trusteeship Council, with reference to the provision of the trusteeship agreement for the settlement of the boundary question, had dealt with the problem uninterruptedly from 1953 until the trust territory became independent, and the General Assembly discussed it at each session from 1954 to 1958, adopting resolutions one after another: resolution 854 (IX) of December 14, 1954; resolution 947 (X) of December 15, 1955; resolution 1068 (XI) of February 26, 1957; resolution 1213 (XII)

[1] Cf. General Assembly resolution 755 (VIII) of December 9, 1953.
[2] Cf. General Assembly resolution 855 (IX) of December 14, 1954.

of December 14, 1957; resolution 1345 (XIII) of December 13, 1958. These resolutions achieved nothing, because all they contained was references to previous General Assembly resolutions and to the urgency of a settlement, recognizing the good intentions of the Italian and Ethiopian governments, stating at the same time that no solution had been reached so far, and finally expressing the opinion that the parties should continue negotiating with a view to achieving a final settlement as expeditiously as possible.

Since the negotiations had brought no result, the United Nations decided to invite the King of Norway (!) to nominate an arbitrator. This also was in vain, so that Somalia, when acceding to independence, still carried the heavy burden inherited from the colonial past—the question of the frontier with Ethiopia.

Irrespective of party differences the Somalis, who were denied any substantial voice in the consideration of a problem which was their own, regarded this dispute *de nobis sine nobis* as an assault against their people and country. But the Italians, by posing as defenders of Somali interests in the dispute with Ethiopia, succeeded in making most of the Somalis believe that the failure to settle the issue was due entirely to the stubborn opposition of the Ethiopian government. Thus it was that, in addition to the controversy about the boundary, the Somalis brought with them, as a second burden handed down from trusteeship to independence, distrust and hostility towards the brotherly people of Ethiopia. The definitive settlement of the frontier issue, together with the restoration of confidence and neighbourliness with Ethiopia, was the primary and most urgent task of young independent Somalia.

The Last Chapter of the Somalis' Struggle for Independence

In the early post-war years, as we have seen, the Somali people were divided in two camps by the prospect of the threatening come-back of the Italian imperialists. The vast majority of the Somalis waged a bitter fight to prevent the return of Italy and to achieve the unification of the Somali tribes. At that time the most consistent representative of Somali interests was the Somali Youth League, which came out for the independence of the country, the democratization of government, and the unification of all Somali-inhabited territories. Some of the Somalis clung to their tribal traditions, but in the most important issues—fight against an Italian come-back, independence for Somalia, unification of the Somalis—they also backed the League. An insignificant number of Somalis were led by material interests to wish and support the return of the Italians (ex-colonial officials, as well as former employees and soldiers expecting to receive their back pay). These and their parties rallied in the Somalia Conferenza, which constituted the other, rather vocal though less numerous, camp of the Somali movement, made up of Somalis encouraged and bribed by Italian colonists and officials.

The double nature of the movement (democratic political parties on the one hand, and tribal parties and movements on the other) persisted through the period of trusteeship. Those who stuck to tribal customs, together with their parties, remained hostile to Italian rule but did not engage in organized struggle. As far as they were in a position to do so, they submitted petitions explaining their tribal and individual grievances to various organs of the United Nations.

In the struggle for independence and political and economic rights the tribes still living according to tribal customs, either nomadic or settled, as well as the great number of political and other organizations and their members, in order to voice their complaints and demands, used the means of petitioning the United Nations and its representatives accessible in the country (Advisory Council, Visiting Missions). The Fourth Committee of the UN General Assembly at practically every session received written or oral petitions from a large number of Somali organizations or individuals. Only between December 1951 and July 1952 the Trusteeship Council considered 215 Somali petitions.[1] A similar flood of petitions was dealt with in subsequent years, too. In 1956, for example, the Trusteeship Council considered more than a hundred Somali petitions.[2] These petitions showed world public opinion the real face of the Italian trusteeship regime, confuting the hypocritical and false reports of the administering authority, as well as the reports of the UN Visiting Missions and the Advisory Council, but they produced no concrete results. The Trusteeship Council resolutions concerning the various petitions only expressed the hope that the administering authority would remedy the grievance, or consider the demand, or they recommended the trust power to do so. Further on the petitions heard were mentioned in the Trusteeship Council report to the General Assembly, but the latter simply took note of the report, and everything remained as it was.

The principal standard-bearer of the political struggle for democracy and independence was invariably the Somali Youth League, which refused any kind of co-operation with the Italian administering authority. But Italy had from the outset pursued the aim of winning this largest and most influential organization of the Somali population over to co-operation with the trust administration. The Italians even managed to convince some political leaders step by step that one of the prime conditions of attaining their aims was their willing co-operation with the administration. In 1953 a strife began within the party between proponents and opponents of co-operation and led ultimately to a split of the League, so that the final stage of the Somali independence struggle was encumbered with an ideological struggle among the best sons of the people.

After the end of World War II the Somali Youth League, under the presidency of HAJI MOHAMMED HUSSEIN,[3] came out for the unification of all Somali territories and the liquidation of tribalism, demanded reforms and organized demonstrations against the imposition of Italian trusteeship.

Under HUSSEIN's leadership the League refused to co-operate with the Italian authorities, which therefore banned several branch organizations of the League. In 1953, however, when Secretary ABDULLAHI ISSA took over from HUSSEIN who was on a visit to Cairo, the League established co-operation with the Italian administration. In 1954 HUSSEIN, who had not returned from Cairo and only called by radio for struggle against the Italian, British and French colonialists, was replaced as President of the party by ADEN ABDULLAH OSMAN,[40] and later, early in 1956, by ABDULLAHI ISSA.

[1] Cf. Supplement 4 to the records of the Trusteeship Council during the 7th session of the General Assembly on its activities between December 18, 1951, and July 24, 1952 (A/2150).

[2] Cf. *Yearbook of the United Nations 1956*, pp. 318, 321–323.

[3] HAJI MOHAMMED HUSSEIN, son of a small shopkeeper, was born at Mogadishu in 1913. He went to a local Muslim school but was expelled before completing his studies. During British occupation he took to politics and was one of the founders of the Somali Youth League in 1943.

[4] ADEN ABDULLAH OSMAN was born at Beledwein in 1908. He lived in utter poverty, was not educated in school, but an Italian colonist who employed him taught him to read and write. From 1929 to 1941 he worked in the service of the Italian colonial administration. In 1941 he started business at Beledwein. In 1944 he became an active member of the Somali Youth League. In the party he, along with ISSA, took a stand for co-operation with the Italian authorities.

Under the new constitution general elections were held in 1956. At the elections the Somali Youth League won the absolute majority (43 out of 70 seats), so tha the Italian trust administration appointed ABDULLAHI ISSA to form the government OSMAN was elected Chairman of the Legislative Assembly.

The opposition accused the League of having rigged the elections, pursuing a policy of tribalism and practising corruption. The majority of the League members were also dissatisfied with the compromising policy of the leaders, so the absent HUSSEIN was again elected President of the League. HUSSEIN returned from Cairo and continued conducting propaganda against co-operation with the Italian administration, encouraging the masses to resist. In 1958, however, the right wing gained the upper hand in the League and forced HUSSEIN to resign. OSMAN was again made President of the League, and HUSSEIN, together with the most militant members of the movement, broke definitively with the League and formed a new party called the Great Somali League.

In March 1959 the Legislative Assembly was re-elected. Early in the year antigovernment riots broke out, which provided a pretext for the government to ban the Great Somali League and arrest HUSSEIN on the charge of having organized disturbances. The proscribed party called upon the voters to boycott the elections and submitted a petition to the United Nations, but nothing came either of the boycott call or of the complaint to the United Nations. In the absence of the Great Somali League there was no serious opposition, and the elections ended in a sweeping victory of the Somali Youth League (83 seats of 90), and so the ISSA government continued in power.

After the elections HUSSEIN was set free, but he resumed his propaganda against the Somali Youth League and the government.

On April 16, 1960, delegations from the governments and legislatures of the Italian trust territory and British Somaliland held a joint conference in Mogadishu. After a week of discussion, on April 23, the conference issued a communiqué announcing that ex-Italian Somaliland and the British Somaliland Protectorate, "in accordance with the common will of the Parliaments of the two territories", would unite on July 1, 1960, and the two legislatures would combine to form a single National Assembly. It was announced also that Mogadishu would be the capital city of the country, the seat of government and parliament. It was decided further to build a national army and set up a committee to formulate proposals for the settlement of the administrative, financial and legal questions arising in connection with the union of the two territories.

The scheme got the first response from the United Arab Republic, whose representative to the United Nations, MOHAMMED HASSAN EL-ZAYYAT, announced that his country intended to give the new independent state effective assistance in establishing its national armed forces and in organizing education and public health institutions.

The resolution on the union of the British and Italian Somali territories gave rise to energetic protests on the part of the Emperor of Ethiopia. On May 12 HAILE SELASSIE summoned a number of foreign ambassadors accredited in Addis Ababa, including first of all the diplomatic representatives of Great Britain, France, the United States, the Soviet Union and the United Arab Republic, and stated to them that he regarded the plan for the union of the two former colonial territories as "an ill-concealed plot inspired from abroad to annex Ethiopian territories". He said that the plan for a union of "so-called Somali territories" was but the first step towards the partition of Ethiopia, and therefore he would use every available means to thwart it.

The protest of the Emperor, however, could not change the course of events. Already on May 14, the Italian cabinet confirmed the decision on the granting of independence to the trust territory on July 1, 1960.

Shortly before the day of independence the government repealed the decree banning the Great Somali League, which from that time on could again operate lawfully. This party was in favour of "positive neutrality", and accused the government and the leadership of the Somali Youth League of trying, under the slogan of neutrality, to establish contacts with the Western capitalist powers.

On July 1, 1960, ex-Italian Somaliland became an independent state as the Somali Republic, but the celebration of independence was marred by a bloody incident. The Great Somali League staged an antigovernment demonstration in Mogadishu, and the government sent the police against the demonstrators. The police opened fire, thus killing several people.

BIBLIOGRAPHY

Mark Karp, *The Economics of Trusteeship in Somalia*, Boston, 1960.
А. А. Хазанов, Сомалийская Республика [The Somali Republic], Moscow, 1961.
J. M. Lewis, *A Pastoral Democracy*, London, 1961.
The Somali Peninsula: A New Light on Imperial Motives (Somali Government Publications), London, 1962.
The Somali Republic and African Unity (Somali Government Publications), London, 1962.
Saadia Touval, *Somali Nationalism: International Politics and the Drive for Unity in the Horn of Africa*, Massachusetts, 1963.
John Drysdale, *The Somali Dispute*, London, 1964.
J. M. Lewis, *The Modern History of Somaliland: From Nation to State*, London, 1965.
Robert L. Hess, *Italian Colonialism in Somalia*, Chicago, 1966.
Arthur H. Thrower, *Directory of Somalia*. Diprepu Co., 1969.

ON THE FRONTIER PROBLEMS

D. J. Latham-Brown, "The Ethiopia–Somaliland Frontier Dispute", *The International and Comparative Law Quaterly*, April 1956.
A. A. Castagno, *Somalia* (International Conciliation No. 522), New York, 1959.
The Ethiopia–Somali Frontier Problem, Addis Ababa, 1961.
D. J. Latham-Brown, "Recent Developments in the Ethiopia–Somaliland Dispute", *The International and Comparative Law Quaterly*, January 1961.
Leo Silberman, "Why the Haud Was Ceded", *Cahiers d'Etudes Africaines* (Paris), Vol. 2, 1961.
Ethiopia-Somalia Relations, Addis Ababa, 1962.
The Issue of the Northern Frontier District (White Paper), Mogadishu, 1963.

CHAPTER XXX

FERNANDO PÓO AND RIO MUNI

The Spanish capitalists who had inherited Fernando Póo and Río Muni (called also Spanish Guinea) from their slave-trader ancestors continued the exploitation of these colonies by the old-established methods even after the abolition of slavery, in the 19th century and in the first half of the 20th.

Under Spanish colonial rule the African inhabitants of Fernando Póo (mostly Bubis) and those of Río Muni (mostly Fang) lingered in misery as underprivileged semi-slaves and plantation workers or destitute peasants oppressed by the privileged Spanish settler landlords.

Under General FRANCO's fascist regime servitude in the two colonies remained as it had been for centuries before. Nor did any substantial change take place either in Fernando Póo or in Río Muni during the war years and in the first decade following the war.

The colonial policy which the Spanish imperialists pursued to maintain their rule, the subjection of the African population and the maximum exploitation of those countries had three characteristic features.

1. To increase the number of Spanish settlers and of the Spanish specialists and labourers who undertook to work in the colonies, they created all sorts of privileges for them. In 1962 the number of privileged settlers, officials, employees and workers was more than 3,500.

2. They continued the traditional practice of trading in labour force, "contracting" workers from Cameroon, Nigeria, etc., who were then toiling in conditions reminiscent of slavery. Only one third of the paltry wages was paid to the labourer, the rest was "saved" for him by the employer who would pay it, after deduction of occasional fines and other debts, upon the expiration of contract.

At the end of 1960 Nigerian workers went on strike as a token of protest against the killing of one of their work mates. The organizers of the strike were arrested and tortured. The event raised a general outcry in Nigeria. The Nigerian government interceded and in June 1961 reached an agreement with the Spanish authorities on a pay raise for the Nigerian workers and the improvement of their conditions. But the agreement was not observed. On March 12, 1962, the *West African Pilot* wrote that Nigerian labourers employed in plantations were fined six months' pay for "insult to the supervisor", and others were flung into jail for "laziness", and that two workers were killed. The "contracted" workers from African countries numbered around 30,000 at that time. The governments of Nigeria and Cameroon drew substantial commission on every contracted labourer.

3. To keep the indigenous population in check the Spanish colonizers applied the "divide-and-rule" principle. They "freed" a few thousand of the 200,000 Africans *(emancipados)* or granted them a limited degree of freedom *(emancipación limitada)*. The first category was accorded the same rights as the Spanish settler community, the second enjoyed only some of those rights.

From among the *emancipados* came the African planters and traders, they provided the cadres from which the administration recruited its African officials, employees and policemen, and later they were faithful advocates of the policy of the Spanish imperialists in the colonial General Assembly, the Governing Council, the Provincial Councils and partly even in the ranks of the political parties. Opposed to these two privileged groups (all in all 15,000 people) was a mass of underprivileged Africans. It would be a waste of time to look for detailed information about their living and working conditions either in the statistical publications of the Spanish imperialists or in their reports submitted (from 1960 on) to the United Nations. The Spanish authorities only talked about the amazing economic development of Fernando Póo, whose exports of cocoa, coffee and timber in 1960 amounted to two billion pesetas, and where per capita income ($246 in Fernando Póo, more than in any one of the 19 provinces of metropolitan Spain; and $91 in Río Muni) was higher than in India, Pakistan, Kenya or the Congo. They failed to mention, however, that those huge profits from export, produced by African labour, added to the wealth of Spanish planters and merchants, and that the high average figure was boosted by the income of a few thousand Spaniards whose profits were hundreds and thousands of times the earnings of any one of 200,000 Africans.

It would also be no use seeking information in the newspaper reports and travel accounts, because the Spanish authorities jealously guarded their Guinean paradise and did not let anybody go and look around there: they let in only those who looked at things through the eyes of the Spanish colonialists.

The only authentic data on the living and working conditions of the African masses in Spanish Guinea are to be found in petitions and similar documents which the territory's two large independence organizations, MONALIGE *(Movimiento Nacional de Liberación de la Guinea Ecuatorial)* and I.P.G.E. *(Idea Popular de la Guinea Ecuatorial)* presented to the United Nations General Assembly and various UN Committees. In August 1966 representatives of MONALIGE made a statement to the UN Visiting Mission touring the territory. Here is a portion of that document:

" . . . some 99 per cent of the arable land was under the control of the colonizers. The Spanish settlers were permitted to acquire land freely and without limitation but the indigenous people were limited to four hectares per person . . . it was possible in theory for an indigenous person to acquire additional land under the public auction system. However, not merely were these auctions held only in Madrid, but they were open to all Spanish citizens, corporations and companies, with the result that an indigenous person was clearly at an overwhelming disadvantage. The public auction system had led to the existence of a large number of absentee landlords, and to the establishment of huge plantations . . . Commerce was almost entirely in the hands of the Spanish residents. Prospective African traders enjoyed no protection from the law and were, therefore, in no position to compete in this field . . . the labour structure was pyramidal in structure, with the Spanish residents at the top and the African workers at the base. The wage system was highly discriminatory, and the legislation in force tended to perpetuate this situation . . . The minimum wage set by the law, namely 900 pesetas per month for an eight-hour day, was grossly unsatisfactory ... In contrast, Spanish residents working as agricultural foremen or supervisors received at least 5,100 pesetas per month ..."

Under such circumstances it is understandable why the fascist government did its utmost to hide its colonies from the outside world. It raised difficulties to visits to the territory by foreign observers and refused to comply with the request of the United Nations for annual reports on the colonies to be submitted to the world organization.

Towards the end of the fifties, when after the example of the newly independent countries of the Eastern Sudan, Ghana and French Guinea, independence movements emerged in almost all countries of Black Africa, General FRANCO made one more attempt to shield the Spanish colonies from the wind of change: in 1959 he raised Fernando Póo and Río Muni to the status of Spanish provinces. The representative of Spain to the United Nations stated solemnly that Spain had no colonies, since Fernando Póo and Río Muni were Spanish overseas provinces, and so Spain had nothing to report upon to the United Nations.

But a year later, when independence was granted to almost all West African countries bordering on the Spanish colonies, FRANCO changed his mind.

Franco's Change of Policy

On November 11, 1960, the Spanish government, abandoning its former rigid attitude, announced to the United Nations that it would supply to the UN Secretary-General regular information on its "overseas possessions".

And on December 19 the national legislative body of Spain (the 588-member *Cortes*) was attended for the first time by representatives of Spanish Guinea (three Europeans and three "Negroes"). The event was intended to demonstrate to world public opinion that Spanish Guinea was not a colony but a possession of Spain having equal rights with her provinces in Europe, and that racial equality was assured in the Spanish possessions. The mendaciousness of this propaganda is clearly shown by the fact that over 200,000 Africans of Spanish Guinea could elect just as many representatives as 8,000 European residents did. And how much those three "Negroes" could be considered representative of African interests appeared clearly from a statement which one of them made to the Falangist paper *Arriba*, saying that the participation in the *Cortes* of three Negro and three European representatives of Spanish Guinea "completes the identification of the Equatorial region with the other Spanish provinces".

In January 1961 the FRANCO regime took another step to demonstrate that it was racially unbiassed: it signed a trade agreement for 1961 with France and 13 independent African countries, formerly French colonies.

The Spanish government was prompted to take this step by the economic interests of Spain, on the one hand, and by considerations of its international reputation, on the other. And that it did achieve its aim with the Western capitalist countries, especially its principal protector, the United States, is best illustrated by the fact that the American press published a great many articles in praise of the thriving economy of Spain and the "liberalization" of the FRANCO regime. (In a single week during April 1961, for example, four such articles appeared in *The New York Times*: April 10, 14, 16 and 17.)

But FRANCO's "liberalization" policy was not a serious affair. Compliance with the UN request did not imply acceptance of the spirit of the UN Charter. This was borne out by the numerous statements made by General FRANCO himself and other leaders of the Falangist regime.

In his address to the *Cortes* on June 3, 1961, FRANCO stated: "Our country has never pursued a policy of colonialism . . ." He contradicted his own hypocritical allegation in the same speech, saying: "Independence should be like a ripe fruit which detaches itself without violence or force when its time comes. To call it into being by force, linking it to political caprice, base ambition, rashness and an attempt to impose certain principles and a political and social order which in most cases are contrary to the will and aspirations of these people — to do this is to commit a crime against humanity."

Spanish Admiral CARRERO BLANCO stated at Santa Isabel, the capital of Fernando Póo, on October 8, 1962: " . . . to leave Guinea would be a crime, and Spain will never do that. Even outside pressure will not force us to change our position."

Self-Government for Equatorial Guinea

The United Nations Declaration on decolonization and the subsequent accession to independence of further African countries (Sierra Leone, Tanganyika, Kenya, Zanzibar, Rwanda, Burundi) impelled FRANCO to make new deceptive moves apparently towards the liquidation of the colonial system so as to make it easier to delay the granting of independence to the Spanish colonies.

On August 9, 1963, the Spanish government announced that Fernando Póo and Río Muni would be granted administrative and economic self-government and that negotiations for this purpose would be held in Madrid with invited political leaders of those two provinces. (Political autonomy did not come into question.)

In September 1962 the UN Special Committee on decolonization discussed the question of the Spanish African colonies. Since also the representatives of Morocco and Mauritania, having been invited at their own request, took part in the Special Committee meetings, the debate was first of all about the question of Río de Oro. The Spanish delegate himself spoke in detail also about Río Muni and Fernando Póo and gave an untruthful picture of the situation there. His lies were exposed by the Soviet, Polish and Bulgarian members of the Special Committee who, with reference to the facts disclosed by the petitioners, stated that the Spanish government had not implemented General Assembly resolution 1514 (XV) adopted in 1960, that the fascist regime still stood in the two colonies, and the vast majority of the Africans were denied all rights and suffered from ruthless economic exploitation. They demanded that, pursuant to the 1960 resolution of the United Nations, the Africans should be immediately granted the right of self-determination, and, in accordance with the express wishes of their majority, democratic elections should be held urgently and the territory should accede to independence in the shortest possible time.

The Special Committee decided, "for lack of time", to postpone the detailed discussion of the question till the next session.

On November 29, 1963, the Spanish *Cortes* drew up a bill for a "Basic Law" on granting Spanish Guinea internal self-government by January 1, 1964.

The bill was tabled in the *Cortes* by the Mayor of Santa Isabel. The event took place in the presence of the Emperor HAILE SELASSIE of Ethiopia, who had stopped at Madrid on his way home from the funeral of President KENNEDY of the United States.

Before the bill approved by the *Cortes* was submitted for sanctioning to the chief of the Spanish State, a plebiscite was held in the two provinces on December 15, 1963. All (Spanish and African) permanent residents over 21 years of age were granted the right to vote on the "Basic Law". Of 126,378 registered voters 94,817 took part in the plebiscite: 59,280 voted in favour of self-government, 35,537 voted against it. These figures clearly show that the result of the plebiscite did not tally with the will of the majority of the population. If the votes of the Spanish settlers were left out of consideration, it would appear that only about 20 per cent of the African population voted for self-government, despite the fact that the freedom fighters, who demanded real independence instead of sham autonomy, were prevented by the Spanish authorities from exposing the intended scheme as a fraud. But they did so in their petitions submitted to the United Nations,[1] demanding invalidation of the plebiscite results, but to no avail. And on December 20 the law on "self-government in Equatorial Guinea" was promulgated. However, this self-government was a poor travesty of real autonomy.

Under the "Basic Law" the legislative body of the territory was the General Assembly. Río Muni and Fernando Póo each had a Provincial Council *(Diputación provincial)*, the two bodies constituting the General Assembly. Half the membership of the Provincial Councils was elected by town councils *(Ayuntamientos)* and the other half by corporative bodies; in virtue of a decree of April 7, 1960, half the membership of the town councils was elected by the local corporative entities and the other half by a vote of heads of families. An ordinance of May 24, 1962, had established village councils or local *Juntas* (42 in Fernando Póo and 146 in Río Muni), which were elected by the heads of families and organized according to the principles of corporate representation, but those village councils had no part to play in the election of either the General Assembly or the Provincial Councils.

The executive organ of the country was the Governing Council whose eight members were chosen by the General Assembly (four from among the representatives of Fernando Póo and Río Muni each). One of three candidates proposed by the Governing Council was appointed its President by the plenipotentiary of the Madrid government, the Commissioner-General who had taken the place of the former Governor-General. The Governor-General was the principal guardian of law and order. In this capacity he controlled the armed forces and the police, the postal service , airports, the press and the radio, supervised public meetings, amusement places, etc. He appointed a Civil Governor to Fernando Póo and another to Río Muni, to represent the Governing Council in the two provinces while being answerable for law and order to the Commissioner-General. Finally he was responsible for relations with Spain and any authority external to Equatorial Guinea.

The whole regime of "self-government" was a mere smokescreen. In fact, the Spanish Commissioner-General continued to hold the supreme legislative and executive powers. He directed the work of the Governing Council. In case he thought that some decision of the Council might jeopardize law and order, he could recommend the Spanish government to repeal it; what is more, if in his view the implementation

---

[1] See, e.g., the petition by DANIEL G. MBANDEMEZO, representative of I.P.G.E., of June 15, 1966 (A/6300/Add. 7) and the telegram from LUIS MAHO, a leader of the freedom fighters, addressed to the Special Committee. The latter document, to illustrate the terror introduced by the Spanish authorities to secure the acceptance of the "Basic Law", is about a case in which a group of registered voters, seeing the irregularities during the vote, refused to go to the poll, whereupon the Spanish security forces used firearms against them, killing four people (A/AC. 109/Pet. 255).

of such a decision involved "a serious danger", he could act on his own without waiting for a reply from Madrid. He could propose the replacement of the President or any member of the Governing Council. The legislation passed by the General Assembly had to be submitted to him for assent. If he saw fit, he could send them back for reconsideration. In case of differences of opinion, that is when the General Assembly held to its position, the issue was to be decided by the Madrid government.

Indicative of the powerlessness of the General Assembly and the absolute powers of the Commissioner-General was the following story: On April 29, 1966, the General Assembly resolved to dismiss the Governing Council because, owing to poor work and the wasting of public funds, it was losing face before the people. The issue did not come up for decision, for the Commissioner-General refused to forward the resolution of the General Assembly to the Spanish government.

The budget of the country was to be passed by the General Assembly, but the *Cortes* in Madrid had to approve it as long as the territory received, directly or indirectly, economic assistance from the Spanish State.

It is characteristic that under the Basic Law the Spaniards residing temporarily in the territory enjoyed the same rights as permanent African residents, thus they had the right of voting, which was not accorded to the African (more precisely, Nigerian and Cameroonian) workers contracted for many years.

The preamble of the law referred to the right of peoples to self-determination, stating that the peoples of Equatorial Guinea had the same rights and duties as the people of Spain; accordingly they were entitled to representation in the *Cortes*, to which Fernando Póo and Río Muni each could send three members: the mayor of each provincial capital (Santa Isabel and Bata, respectively), further a member for each Provincial Council and one for the town councils.

The law laid down that self-government would come into force after January 1, 1964, when the General Assembly and the Governing Council were formed following the election of the town and village councils as well as the Provincial Councils.

When the Spanish government in 1960 switched over to a more flexible neo-colonialist policy, the Portuguese fascist government followed with apprehension the measures introduced in the Spanish possessions. It felt especially uncomfortable about the *Cortes* decision of November 29 and the plebiscite held in December as well as the forthcoming elections in Spanish Guinea. In the middle of January President SALAZAR of Portugal sent to Madrid his Foreign Minister, FRANCO NOGUEIRA, in an attempt to induce the Spanish government to go easy with the reforms. But the Spanish dictator, General FRANCO, persisted in going on, because he was aware that his new policy would not in fact lead to the loss of the colonies but would help him to preserve them in a new form and by new methods, and that internationally it would still strengthen his position and chances (ensuring to him the sympathy of the great powers in the first place).

The municipal elections provided for in the Basic Law were held in March, and the Provincial Councils were formed. Each Provincial Council met on May 1 to elect its President, and then the two Councils held a joint sitting to constitute the General Assembly. On May 15, the Governing Council was formed on the basis of a proposal from the General Assembly. On May 27 BONIFACIO ONDO EDÚ was elected President of the Governing Council.

The Basic Law promulgated in December contained only few elements of self-government and authorized the Spanish government to work out the details of the law with the participation of representatives of the Governing Council. The final text of the law was published as decree No. 1885/1964 of the Spanish government on July 3, 1964. Thereupon the Basic Law entered into force on July 16, and the Spanish cabinet on July 24 appointed the two Civil Governors, ADOLFO GOBENA MENDO for Río Muni and SIMON NGOMO NDUMU for Fernando Póo.

The United Nations Special Committee on decolonization again took up the question of the Spanish colonies and, after a debate which lasted from September 30 to October 16, 1964, adopted unanimously a resolution sponsored by 12 Afro-Asian states and Yugoslavia (the United States and Australia abstained in the vote): the Special Committee regretted the delay by the Spanish government in implementing the UN resolution of 1960, and reaffirmed the inalienable right of the peoples of Fernando Póo and Río Muni to self-determination and independence; it urged the Spanish government to take immediate steps to grant independence in pursuance of the resolution adopted by the UN General Assembly at its 15th session in 1960, and requested the Secretary-General to invite the Spanish government to report on the measures taken in the meantime to the UN General Assembly at its next session.

Independence Movements in Equatorial Guinea

In the years following the end of World War II the Africans suffering under the oppressive regime of the Spanish colonialists, after the example of the neighbouring African peoples, expressed more and more often their discontent and their aspirations for independence. Amid the difficult circumstances under the police regime introduced in the colony, however, no organized independence movement could emerge until the late fifties. Under the impact of the events in Ghana and French Guinea, the peoples of Río Muni and Fernando Póo in 1959 took up the fight in an organized manner against the Spanish colonizers.

The first organized political mass party of Equatorial Guinea was the *Idea Popular de la Guinea Ecuatorial* (I.P.G.E.) formed on September 30, 1959. Its chairman was ENRIQUE NKUNA NDONGO, its vice-chairman SALVADOR NSAMIYO ENSEMA. It was followed in 1962 by the transformation into a political party of another mass movement, the *Movimiento Nacional de Liberación de la Guinea Ecuatorial* (MONALIGE).[1] Besides these two large parties there were a number of minor political groups which, having no mass support behind them, existed only in name, played no political role and soon disappeared. But MONALIGE and I.P.G.E. could operate only underground, because the colonial authorities persecuted them relentlessly. A number of activists of both parties were arrested and tortured, many of them killed. Anyway, the two parties courageously fought at home, and some of their representatives asked to be heard as petitioners before the United Nations and stood up for the freedom of their country. They protested at the terror regime of the Spanish authorities and exposed its fraudulence with the plebiscite and "self-government". In 1963, to counteract the freedom fighters' propaganda and to bolster up its own policies, the Spanish administration established, on the model of the Falangists in Spain, a government-supporting party, called the *Movimiento de Unión Nacional de la Guinea Ecuatorial* (M.U.N.G.E.), which it declared to be the only legitimate party in the country, thereby proscribing all other political organizations. Those who were actually (or were believed to be) members of such parties were arrested, imprisoned and deported, tortured and executed. The two large parties, to increase the effective-

[1] MONALIGE is believed to have existed as early as the first post-war years but was organized as a party only in 1962.

ness of their struggle, decided to merge and establish the *Frente Nacional y Popular de Liberación de la Guinea Ecuatorial* (FRENAPO). Thereupon the Spanish administration recognized MONALIGE and admitted its representatives into the Governing Council, but it intensified further the persecution of I.P.G.E. By such and similar means the administration managed to bring some members of both parties to betray their own programmes and to support the policies of the Spanish government. It tried to enlist their help to contain the independence struggle of both parties and paralyze their activities, but it failed in this effort. The masses of the two parties did not stop to fight, and the Spanish authorities continued to persecute the party activists.

The political programmes of MONALIGE and I.P.G.E. were practically the same: amnesty for political prisoners and deportees, free organization of parties, dissolution of the unrepresentative General Assembly, free elections on the basis of universal suffrage, majority government based on the election results, termination of the privileged position of Spanish settlers, equal rights for Africans in every respect, independence for the country in the shortest possible time (by the end of 1966 or early 1967 according to MONALIGE). There was a single point of essential difference between the two party programmes. While the parties were agreed that Fernando Póo and Río Muni should constitute a united independent state, I.P.G.E. came out for federation between independent Equatorial Africa and the Republic of Cameroon.

In word M.U.N.G.E. also stood up for independence, but it was satisfied with Spanish rule dubbed self-government, it held that the country was not yet prepared for independence. It could conceive of independence even in the future only in close relationship with Spain, with Spanish military and economic assistance.

The balance of forces between the parties was hard to assess, because the data available on the numerical strength of the different parties came from the parties themselves, so the figures were neither reliable nor objective.

MONALIGE asserted that its supporters included 90 per cent of the population (!). I.P.G.E. estimated its own membership at about 160,000. M.U.N.G.E. alleged that the number of its supporters, together with the 160,000 I.P.G.E. members (whom it regarded as having joined the ranks of M.U.N.G.E.) amounted to 80 per cent of the population. Considering that the total population of Equatorial Guinea was barely more than 260,000, evidently each of these contradictory figures was in itself absurd. (At most they may have been indicative of the numerical ratio between the three parties as being 90 : 60 : 20.)

The Question of Equatorial Guinea and the United Nations

In its resolution 2067 (XX) adopted on December 16, 1965, the United Nations General Assembly, noting that Río Muni and Fernando Póo had been merged and named Equatorial Guinea, reaffirmed the inalienable right of the peoples of Equatorial Guinea to self-determination and independence, called upon the Spanish government "to set the earliest possible date for independence after consulting the people on the basis of universal suffrage under the supervision of the United Nations ..." At the same time it invited the Special Committee on decolonization "to follow the progress of the implementation of the present resolution and to report to the General Assembly at its twenty-first session".

That the Spanish government did not take the self-determination of Equatorial Guinea seriously is indicated by the fact that early in 1966 in entered into a contract with two American companies (Mobil Oil and Gulf Oil), granting them oil concessions, jointly with Spanish capitalists, in three coastal districts of Río Muni.

In June 1966 the UN Special Committee again discussed the question of Río Muni and Fernando Póo. The representative of Spain made a hypocritical statement painting in rosy colours the situation of the colony allegedly enjoying self-government, and invited the Committee to send some members there to see for themselves the implementation of the UN resolutions. Among the members of the Spanish delegation were ONDO EDÚ and GORI MOLUBELA, these two renegades of the independence movement. The former even took the floor and extolled "self-government", thanked the Spanish government and the United Nations, and repeated the old argument of the imperialists that the country was not prepared for independence and that to demand it was sheer demagoguery for the time being. In the debate over the draft resolution sponsored by 12 Afro-Asian states and Yugoslavia, not only the delegates of the United States, Australia, Chile and Venezuela but also a number of the sponsors of the draft (the representatives of Ethiopia, Sierra Leone, Iraq, Iran and Afghanistan) spoke in terms of appreciation of the recent steps taken by the Spanish colonialists and valued them as a change of their former policy. Only the delegates of the Soviet Union and Tanzania pointed out that the Spanish government still continued to sabotage the UN resolutions. The representative of Tanzania stressed that the Spanish government, if it was really willing to co-operate with the Special Committee, would have to make possible the repatriation of political exiles and refugees, to ensure that the petitioners and political prisoners were not prevented from testifying before the Special Committee delegates during their stay in the country, and to do everything it could to promote the full implementation of the UN recommendations.

The Special Committee passed the resolution unanimously on June 21. Recalling the General Assembly resolutions adopted at its 15th and 20th sessions, it reaffirmed the right of Equatorial Guinea to independence and decided to send to Equatorial Africa, as soon as practicable, a sub-committee to ascertain the conditions in the territory with a view to speeding up the implementation of the General Assembly resolutions.

The Sub-Committee on Equatorial Guinea was composed of representatives of Chile, Denmark, Mali, Poland, Sierra Leone, Syria and Tanzania. The Sub-Committee stopped for two days (August 17–18) in Madrid, where it had conversations with a few senior officials of the Spanish government, and then spent six days (August 19 to 24) in Equatorial Guinea, where it had discussions, in addition to representatives of the colonial authorities (the Spanish Commissioner-General and the two Civil Governors) and of the institutions of the "autonomous regime" (the General Assembly, the Governing Council, the Provincial Councils), also with members of MONALIGE, M.U.N.G.E. and I.P.G.E., as well as a nine-member deputation of the Bubis, and received a memorandum from representatives of the Fang tribe.

During those talks the Commissioner-General did his best to misinform the Sub-Committee. Like the government agencies in Madrid, he also drew an untrue and considerably embellished picture of the situation in the country. Characteristically, in speaking of the parties, he repeated the widely spread lie that I.P.G.E. was handicapped by lack of organization and financial support and had joined the government-backing party, M.U.N.G.E.

The African Civil Governor of Río Muni, NGOMO NDUMU ASUMU, outdid even the Commissioner-General. That renegade of the independence movement boasted of having been associated with all three political groups, MONALIGE, I.P.G.E., and finally M.U.N.G.E., which in his view was representative of all sections of the population, while the first two parties were concerned only with the distribution of official posts. He repeated the Commissioner-General's allegation about the alliance between I.P.G.E. and M.U.N.G.E., and he added that for the time being the alliance was operative only in Río Muni, but that talks were in progress in Fernando Póo, too. In respect of independence he kept repeating the opinion of the Spanish government that the territory should certainly be granted independence, but it was not yet prepared for accepting it.

The Sub-Committee talked with the President of the General Assembly, Gori Molubela (a former member of MONALIGE, who was at the same time President of the Provincial Council of Fernando Póo), whose confused statement made only two things clear: (1) that he could imagine the future of the country after independence only in close relationship with Spain, under the latter's military, economic and technological patronage; and (2) that he, as President of the General Assembly, advocated the separation of Fernando Póo and Río Muni and the transformation of the territory into an independent state. It is characteristic that, in the opinion of the President of the General Assembly, the activity of the political parties had weakened since the introduction of autonomy.

It appeared from the talks with members of the Governing Council that they all shared the opinion of the colonizers that the country was not yet prepared for independence. There was, however, a sharp difference between them on two issues: (1) Some of them (the majority of M.U.N.G.E. members) held the view that for the time being, until the country was adequately prepared, it would be impossible to fix a date for independence; while others (the majority of MONALIGE members) felt that it was possible and even necessary to set a date. As to the exact day these latter could not agree among them: some proposed July 15, 1967 (Macias Nguma), another suggested July 15, 1968 (Rafael Nsue Mchama). (2) Part of the Council members thought that Fernando Póo and Río Muni should be separated, others insisted on safeguarding the unity of the two provinces.

During the talks with the Sub-Committee the members of the Provincial Council of Río Muni, just like the President of the General Assembly, expressed the belief that the peace and security of the country after independence could be conceived only with the economic and military assistance of Spain. They urged negotiations with Spain on the granting of independence and expressed the hope that after independence they might count on assistance from the United Nations and other international organizations, too.

In their discussion with the Sub-Committee and in their written petitions the MONALIGE leaders described in detail the hypocrisy of the Spanish colonizers and the ruthless persecution of the freedom fighters. They explained the programme of their party, asserting that MONALIGE enjoyed the support of the vast majority of the population, and complaining that leaders of the party such as Pastor Torao Sikara and Abileo Bibao, who had polled the highest number of votes in the municipal elections, had been left out of the government.

The M.U.N.G.E. leaders, in their talks with the Sub-Committee, unmasked themselves as agents of Spanish colonialism. They did not tire of repeating how grateful the people were "for the efforts that Spain had made to promote the political, economic, social and cultural development of the territory". Though they did not fail, with reference to promises of the Spanish government, to demand independence by July 1968, yet they found the regime of "self-government" wholly satisfactory,

410

they objected only to the composition of the Governing Council (since four of its nine members were from MONALIGE).

The M.U.N.G.E. leaders claimed that they had agreed with the leaders of I.P.G.E. to merge the two parties, and that the M.U.N.G.E. supporters together with the 160,000 I.P.G.E. members included 80 per cent of the population. On August 22 the talks were joined in by Antonio Eworo and Clemente Ateba, who pretended to be Chairman and Secretary-General of I.P.G.E., respectively, and who confirmed the allegations of the M.U.N.G.E. leaders and added that, since M.U.N.G.E. also was in favour of independence, it could be expected that MONALIGE would join the union of the two parties.

The allegations of the M.U.N.G.E. leaders were convincingly refuted by the statements of I.P.G.E.'s real representatives. I.P.G.E. was prevented by the police terror from setting up a similarly numerous delegation for the talks with the Sub-Committee. Nevertheless, the Sub-Committee had already been in possession of petitions from I.P.G.E. representatives before starting for Africa. Those petitions, which were addressed in part to the UN Special Committee on decolonization and in part to the Sub-Committee itself, described the cruel persecution of I.P.G.E. on the part of the Spanish colonial authorities (arrests, imprisonments, tortures, police terror, etc.) and denounced the system of self-government as a puppet administration. Also before its departure the Sub-Committee had received a statement made by Jesús Mba Ovono, the I.P.G.E. Secretary-General living in exile in Brazzaville, who called attention to the plight of the country under Spanish rule, which could be brought to an end only by complete independence. Finally, he requested the Sub-Committee to insist on talking during its visit not only with the groups authorized and briefed by the police, but with anyone who wished to be heard.

On August 22 a group of I.P.G.E. members also managed to present a communication to the Sub-Committee. This document exposed that the alleged merger of M.U.N.G.E. and I.P.G.E. was a fake and that Eworo and Ateba, who both posed as I.P.G.E. leaders, were not and had never been real members of I.P.G.E. The authors of the communication declared that I.P.G.E. did not associate itself with M.U.N.G.E. which supported the colonizers, but that it sided with MONALIGE which was fighting for independence.

After its return to New York the Sub-Committee received another communication from Oveno, who called attention to the fact that the Spanish government kept 14,000 troops, four warships patrolling the coast, nine jet aircraft and a group of parachutists in the territory, and that Spain meant to introduce there a neocolonialist type of "independence" with the help of those armed forces as well as with the support of the Africans promoting the Spanish interests. He emphasized that the statements made to the Sub-Committee by certain local leaders, namely the Presidents of the Governing Council and the General Assembly, were contrary to the ambitions of the peoples of Equatorial Guinea who wanted complete independence at once.

Finally, he declared that his party welcomed the intention of Spain to grant independence to Equatorial Guinea, but real independence could not come until the Spanish government granted a general and unconditional amnesty to all political prisoners and exiles, dissolved the sham autonomous government, held free elections based on universal adult suffrage under the supervision of the United Nations, called a constitutional conference also under the auspices of the United Nations, to be followed by the formation of a government on the basis of the election results, and withdrew all Spanish armed forces from Equatorial Guinea.

The Sub-Committee, during its stay in Spanish Guinea, talked separately with delegates of the Bubis and the Fang. The Bubi delegates unanimously demanded that Fernando Póo be separated from Río Muni and made an independent state in itself. In support of this demand they argued that the interests of Fernando Póo were consistently disregarded, since the representatives of Río Muni constituted a majority in the General Assembly. The referred, for example, to the fact that Fernando Póo, which contributed 81 per cent of the public revenue of self-governing Equatorial Guinea, received all in all 17 per cent of the funds appropriated for public works and development projects. On the other hand, the representatives of the Fang living in Río Muni (who had emigrated from Fernando Póo) advocated the unification of the two provinces on the assumption that their separation would bring economic disaster to both.

All those talks allowed the Sub-Committee to draw a number of conclusions, the main points of which were the following:

The regime of self-government was unsatisfactory.

The administrative bodies were highly unrepresentative of the will of the people, since they were indirectly elected by a small fraction of the population, although the whole people were in favour of direct elections and universal suffrage.

The political parties were denied official recognition, political activity was curtailed, and the proponents of ideas unwelcome to the administering power were persecuted.

The overwhelming majority of the population, irrespective of party affiliations, wanted complete independence immediately.

As to the date of independence, the opinions differed: some wanted it at once, others proposed the fixing of a date for July 1968 at the latest, by the end of the term of the present Governing Council.

The majority of the population wished the preparations for independence to be made with UN participation.

The African majority of the population was discriminated against with regard to employment and working conditions, the acquisition of land and the pursuit of business, educational facilities and (especially criminal) jurisdiction.

The country was wholly dependent on Spain, since the Spanish government had done nothing either to put an end to economic dependence or to promote the diversification of the country.

The vast majority of the population and all political parties favoured a united independent Equatorial Guinea, separation was advocated only by a minority among the Bubis.

Based on the above conclusions, the Sub-Committee recommended the Spanish government:

to convene a conference with the participation of representatives from all parties of the territory and all sections of the population to work out the details and fix a date for independence which should not be later than July 1968;

to undertake in the meantime the transfer of effective governmental powers to representatives of the people;

to remove all restrictions on political activities of Africans and to establish full democratic freedoms;

to introduce an electoral system based on universal adult suffrage and hold elections on its basis before independence;

to guarantee full equality of rights to Africans (reform the legislation relating to land tenure in accordance with the interests of the African population, improve the labour conditions of Africans and ensure respect for the principle of "equal pay for equal work", permit the formation of representative trade unions, ensure equality before the law without regard to race, etc.);

to render increased material assistance in the economic development of the territory and to promote economic diversification;

to establish institutions of secondary and higher learning and accelerate training programmes for Africans to hold positions of high responsibility in the field of administration;

to continue co-operating with the United Nations by ensuring the participation of UN representatives in the processes leading to independence.

Finally, the Sub-Committee proposed that the UN Special Committee, in consultation with the Spanish government and representatives of Equatorial Guinea, should study the best ways of securing the assistance of the UN specialized agencies especially in economic diversification, education and health.

On September 30 the Sub-Committee met in New York to prepare its report, which was submitted to the UN Special Committee on October 26. The Special Committee discussed the report at its meeting of November 18, 1966. The first speaker in the debate was the representative of the Spanish government. He expressed his disagreement with many findings of the Sub-Committee and wondered why it had stated that there was no freedom of political activity, that the regime of self-government was unsatisfactory and that the Commissioner-General had most of the powers, whereas political parties were active in the territory, the law on self-government had been worked out in agreement with the popular representatives and accepted at a plebiscite in which the entire adult population was qualified to vote.

However, the Special Committee as a whole accepted the conclusions and recommendations of the Sub-Committee and approved its report. The delegate of the United Kingdom, giving as a reason that he had not been in a position to study the report, refrained from stating his views but voted for the report, as did the U.S. representative with a reservation (as to the fixing of a date for independence).

Characteristically, after the adoption of the resolution the Spanish representative again asked for the floor and made another impudent and hypocritical statement. He remarked that it was needless to confirm by resolution the right of the population to self-determination and independence, because the Spanish government had recognized that right long before the relevant recommendation was made by the United Nations, and Equatorial Guinea already had a really autonomous government. And in reply to the delegate of Tanzania he shamelessly asserted that there were no political prisoners in Equatorial Guinea.

Accession to Independence

In September 1967 the UN Special Committee on decolonization adopted a resolution providing that Spanish Guinea should be granted independence before July 1968.

On September 15 the Spanish cabinet decided to convene a conference to Madrid for October 30 to work out the future constitution of Equatorial Guinea. The constitutional conference met on schedule to discuss several drafts for the constitution. It deliberated for weeks but could not arrive at an agreement, so it was closed with a promise to reconvene in the near future. The conference was still going on when, on November 18, ENRIQUE GORI MOLUBELA, President of the Provincial Council of Fernando Póo, had a statement published in the Madrid paper *Ya*, demanding the right of self-determination for Fernando Póo, together with the right to secede from Río Muni which, in his view, should also have the right of self-determination.

The reconvening of the conference was delayed. It was expected that the Spanish government would decide to grant independence to Equatorial Guinea by July 1968, as provided by the UN resolution. The Spanish cabinet was deliberating two weeks at a stretch, but on February 10 it suspended its meeting after deciding to reconvene the constitutional conference.

The conference met at last on April 19. At the opening meeting Foreign Minister CASTIELLA declared that the Spanish government intended to grant independence to Spanish Guinea still during 1968, "at the earliest possible date". Since, however, the differing views of the groups participating in the conference could not be reconciled this time either, it was decided (on July 11, by which date independence should already have been granted pursuant to the UN resolution) that a referendum on independence should be held on August 11, followed by elections in September, and Equatorial Guinea should win independence on October 12.

On July 24 the Spanish *Cortes* passed an act on the granting of independence to Equatorial Guinea by October 12.

The referendum took place on August 16 with the participation of 93.7 per cent of the electorate. The constitution obtained 63.1 per cent of the votes (72,458), while those voting against it made up 35 per cent (41,197).

The elections were held on September 23. The voters elected 35 members to the General Assembly and were expected to choose the future head of state of Equatorial Guinea. But the presidential election brought no result, because none of the four presidential candidates obtained the absolute majority. (The number of valid votes cast was 92,956, of which 36,716 votes went to FRANCISCO MACIAS, the candidate jointly proposed by MONALIGE, FRENAPO and I.P.G.E., and 31,941 votes were cast in favour of BONIFACIO ONDO EDÚ, the candidate of M.U.N.G.E.) The race was decided a week later by a second election round, in which MACIAS emerged victorious. Characteristically, the president-elect of the future "independent" state stressed that the aim of his policy was to maintain close relations with Spain.

Two weeks after the presidential election, on October 12, Spanish Guinea acceded to independence as a unitary state under the name of Equatorial Guinea.

BIBLIOGRAPHY

MANFRED KOSSOK, "Bemerkungen zur iberischen Afrika-Literatur der Gegenwart", in *Geschichte und Geschichtsbild Afrikas*, Leipzig, 1959.
М. М. КОГАН, «Испанские колонии в Африке»
[The Spanish Colonies in Africa], Народы Азии и Африки (Moscow), 4/1961.
"Spanish Colonies in Africa", *Asia and Africa Review*, May 1962.
"Spanish Discreet Decolonization", *Foreign Affairs*, April 1965.

PLATES

1. Tom Mboya

2. Jomo Kenyatta

3. *Mutesa II, the Kabaka of Uganda*

4. *Milton Apollo Obote*

5. *Julius Nyerere*

6. *Sékou Touré*

7. *Félix Roland Moumié*

8. *Sylvanus Olympio*

9. *Félix Houphouët-Boigny*

10. *Léopold Sédar Senghor*

11. Patrice Emery Lumumba